Exchange Rate
MISALIGNMENT
CONCEPTS AND
MEASUREMENT FOR
DEVELOPING COUNTRIES

D0209684

Exchange Rate

MISALIGNMENT

CONCEPTS AND MEASUREMENT FOR DEVELOPING COUNTRIES

Lawrence E. Hinkle
Peter J. Montiel

A WORLD BANK RESEARCH PUBLICATION
Oxford University Press

Oxford University Press

Oxford New York
Athens Auckland Bangkok Bogata Buenos Aires Calcutta
Capetown Chennai Dar es Salaam Delhi Florence Hong Kong Istanbul
Karachi Kuala Lumpur Madrid Melbourne Mexico City Mumbai
Nairobi Paris Sao Paulo Singapore Taipei Tokyo Toronto Warsaw

and associated companies in

Berlin Ibadan

Published by Oxford University Press, Inc.
198 Madison Avenue, New York, New York, 10016

Oxford is a registered trademark of Oxford University Press

Manufactured in the United States of America
First printing June 1999

Library of Congress Cataloging-in-Publication Data

Hinkle, Lawrence E., 1944-
    Exchange rate misalignment : concepts and measurement for developing
countries / Lawrence E. Hinkle and Peter J. Montiel.
        p.   cm.
    Includes bibliographical references and index.
    ISBN 0-19-521126-X
    1. Foreign exchange rates—Developing countries. 2. Foreign exchange
administration—Developing countries.
    I. Montiel, Peter.
    II. Title.
HG3877.H56   1999
332.4'56'091724-DC21   98-52201
                                                                   CIP

Table of Contents

Foreword

John Williamson
Chief Economist, South Asia Region, World Bank

The last week has, I suppose, been a fairly typical one for me. Twice during the week I have encountered distinguished economists analyzing important current problems who asked their audience to accept the new faith that exchange rate policy has been hollowed out by capital mobility, leaving nothing coherent between a fixed exchange rate backed up by a currency board on the one hand, and floating rates on the other. One was Barry Eichengreen, discussing the design of a new international financial architecture at a meeting of the Institute for International Economics. The other was Ernie Preeg, focusing on the outlook for the U.S. economy escaping from its massive current account deficit without a hard landing, in a paper for the Hudson Institute. Interestingly, neither of these analysts ended up by advocating completely freely floating exchange rates without any intervention. Eichengreen took it for granted that floating would be "dirty"; as we all know, "dirty floating" is an emotionally biased term invented by ideological floaters in order to try and discredit exchange rate management. Preeg argued that some "disciplines among the three key currencies on central bank intervention" will be necessary.

If even those who think they have been driven to support floating exchange rates are still taking it for granted that there needs to be some degree of management by the authorities, then two things follow. The first is that there is still a market niche for those of us who try to think about how a system of limited flexibility might best be organized. The other is that there is going to be a continuing need for analysis of where an exchange rate lies in relation to what the authors of this volume call its long-run equilibrium level (the LRER). In the second footnote of the volume the authors gently chastise me for "the somewhat apologetic tone" of my introduction to *Estimating Equilibrium Exchange Rates*, a volume I edited that set itself a fairly similar task, where I seek to defend the value of this exercise. I am delighted that they feel no need for such a qualification. There is indeed a serious job of work to be done, and the authors in this volume set about doing it with determination and a high degree of professional competence. Since it seems I am no longer as intellectually isolated as I have periodically feared since I began drawing analytical distinctions between different concepts of the equilibrium exchange rate back in 1983, and argued that it was important to try and develop empirical estimates of at least one of those concepts (the one that I termed the "fundamental equilibrium exchange rate," which is roughly equivalent to the LRER of this volume), I promise to be less apologetic in future.

Had I been asked to guess ex ante what countries the authors planned to focus most attention on, I cannot imagine that I would have regarded Côte d'Ivoire and Burkina Faso as leading candidates. In fact this choice was driven by operational exigencies in the World Bank in the early 1990s, at a time when people valuing their careers did not talk out loud about the overvaluation of the CFA franc (any more than people with ambitions spoke about the overvaluation of the pound in the British Treasury in 1966). The natural strategy of a conscientious official confronted by a gag order that he believes cannot last long is to quietly initiate a research program that will help to sort out the mess when higher authority is forced to face the facts of life. That is what happened here. We should be profoundly thankful that the Bank had employees who were prepared to take the risk of reacting that way. They have ended up by producing a book that has far wider applicability than to the CFA countries, or indeed than just to developing countries. This book will surely become the standard reference on the estimation of equilibrium exchange rates (or, what amounts to the same thing, on exchange rate misalignments).

I find it difficult to imagine a world in which it would not be important to estimate exchange rate misalignments. Imagine that Argentina really does dollarize, and then an asymmetrical shock leaves it in deep and seemingly permanent depression. Estimating the degree of overvaluation would be important not just as an input into the inevitable national debate on whether to recreate a national currency, but also to estimate how large a general wage cut would be needed to create the desirable real devaluation without using the exchange rate. Or consider the problems that confront the East Asian countries today (early 1999), of knowing whether their now-floating exchange rates have undone a sufficient part of the overshooting of late 1997 to make it sensible policy to start rebuilding reserves in a big way. Or it may even be that there will be a role for this type of analysis one day among the G3, if and when a concern to adjust the U.S. current account deficit re-emerges.

The material in this volume covers all the important approaches to the estimation of the LRER, from the crudest PPP doctrines (currently popularized by *The Economist's* "Big Mac Index") through to the simulations of large macroeconometric models that I have attempted to use and the new approach of using unit-root econometrics to derive estimates from a single equation reduced form. I found it particularly interesting that, as an empirical proposition, relative PPP works for Burkina Faso. The volume also provides an excellent guide to the quite sophisticated literature on different concepts of the real exchange rate, and avoids facile identification of one concept as being "the right one." It warns against all the errors that abound in this field (for example, purporting to explain why devaluation won't work, or claiming that all one needs to do is look at the black-market rate or the Big Mac Index to know what the exchange rate should be).

Some people may believe that crises are an inevitable feature of the capitalist system. Others hold that exchange-rate crises will vanish as more and more countries adopt floating exchange rates. I can understand adherents of both those views dismissing this book as of no interest. But some of us believe that crises can be avoided or at least limited by good economic management, and that having a reasonable idea of where the equilibrium exchange rate lies is an essential requirement for good macro management. Those who share these views will want to see this volume widely used to help policy analysts get a feeling on what can and cannot be said about the equilibrium exchange rate, and so make an important contribution to the improvement of macro management and hence the avoidance of future crises.

About the Authors

Lawrence E. Hinkle is a Lead Economist in a macroeconomic unit of the Technical Department of the World Bank's Africa Region. From 1991 to 1994, he led the Bank's technical preparatory work for the devaluation of the CFA francs. From 1994 to 1997, while much of the research for this book was carried out, he was a visiting fellow in the macroeconomics division of the World Bank's Policy Research Department. His work at the Bank has been primarily in the areas of adjustment policy, exchange rates, trade, monetary, and customs unions.

Peter J. Montiel is Professor of Economics and the James Finney Baxter III Professor of Public Affairs at Williams College. He has recently been the Chair of the Center for Development Economics at Williams College and has worked in the Policy Research Department of the World Bank as well as the Research Department of the International Monetary Fund. His research has been in the area of macroeconomic stabilization in developing countries, and his recent work has focused on capital flows and exchange rate policy.

Acknowledgments

The initial research that eventually led to this book was motivated by one of the major exchange rate crises that punctuated the last decade in the developing world—the devaluation of the CFA francs in 1994. Most of the members of the study team participated in that initial research, although none of us had any idea at the time that our work would ultimately emerge in anything like its current form. Subsequently, as the relevance of our initial research on the misalignment of the CFA francs to other developing countries was highlighted by repeated exchange rate crises elsewhere, analytical techniques used in other countries, and economists experienced with these, were added to the project to complement the initial research and round out the coverage of the study.

As project managers and then editors, we were blessed with a particularly competent team of fellow researchers and co-authors. They both made strong individual contributions and were invaluable sources of comments and guidance on the other papers and the project as a whole. The other members of the study team were:

Theodore O. Ahlers, Country Director, Africa Country Department 13, World Bank;

John Baffes, Economist, Development Prospects Group, World Bank;

Shantayan Devarajan, Research Manager, Development Research Group, World Bank;

Ibrahim A. Elbadawi, Senior Economist, Development Research Group, World Bank;

Nita Ghei, Economist, Consultant, College Park, Md.;

Nadeem Ul Haque, Advisor, IMF Institute, International Monetary Fund.

Steven B. Kamin, Senior Economist, Division of International Finance, Board of Governors of the Federal Reserve System, Washington, D.C.;

Fabien Nsengiyumva, Economist, IMF Institute, International
    Monetary Fund;

Stephen A. O'Connell, Professor of Economics, Swarthmore College,
    Swarthmore, Pa.;

Lant Pritchett, Principal Economist, Resident Mission Indonesia, World
    Bank.

    A special note of thanks is also due to John Williamson. John came to
the project as a reviewer when the manuscript of the book was first taking shape. His insightful and intellectually demanding comments both
shaped the volume and helped motivate us to push the work farther
than we had initially envisaged.

    Ingrid Ivins provided cheerful, careful, and competent research as-
sistance from the first days of the initial work on the CFA francs in 1990
through final completion of this volume in the spring of 1999. Emily
Khine, Camille Darmon, and Jagdish Lal tirelessly processed and repro-
cessed countless versions of the 13 papers that eventually became the
manuscript of this book. The World Bank's Africa Region, Development
Research Group, and Poverty Reduction and Economic Management
Network provided the financial support for the research.

    Finally, we would like to dedicate this book as follows:

> To my father, Lawrence E. Hinkle, M.D., for his lifelong in-
> terest in research and his support.

> To my mother, Maria Montiel, for her unwavering support
> and affection.

LAWRENCE E. HINKLE   PETER J. MONTIEL
WORLD BANK   WILLIAMS COLLEGE

MAY 1999

Acronyms and Abbreviations

ADF	augmented Dickey-Fuller
ADL	autoregressive distributed lag
BN	Beveridge-Nelson
BRER	bilateral real exchange rate
CFA	Communauté Financière Africaine
CGE	computable general equilibrium
CPI	consumer price index
DEER	desired equilibrium exchange rate
DER	dual exchange rate
DF	Dickey-Fuller
DLR	Devarajan, Lewis, and Robinson
DRER	desired equlibrium real exchange rate
EU	European Union
FDI	foreign direct investment
FEER	fundamental equilibrium real exchange rate
G-7	group of seven
GDP	gross domestic product
HBS	Harrod-Balassa-Samuelson
HLM	Haque-Lahiri-Montiel model
ICP	International Comparison Programme
IFS	International Financial Statistics
IIE	Institute of International Economics
IMF	International Monetary Fund
INS	Information Notice System
LIBOR	London interbank offer rate
LIDC	low-income developing country
LRER	long-run equilibrium real exchange rate
NATREX	natural equilibrium real exchange rate
NEER	nominal effective exchange rate
NTB	nontariff barrier
OECD	Organization for Economic Cooperation and Development
OLS	ordinary least squares
PP	Phillips-Perron
PPP	purchasing power parity
REER	real effective exchange rate

RER	real exchange rate
SDR	standard drawing right(s)
SRER	short-run equilibrium real exchange rate
SSA	sub-Saharan Africa
UFC	unit factor cost
ULC	unit labor cost
UNCTAD	United Nations Conference on Trade and Development
UNIDO	United Nations Industrial Development Organization
WPI	wholesale price index

1

Exchange Rate Misalignment: An Overview

Peter J. Montiel and Lawrence E. Hinkle

The collapse of the Smithsonian agreement in March of 1973 marked the end of the Bretton Woods system of fixed exchange rates among the major industrial countries. Initially, many developing countries responded to this event by attempting to sustain their fixed exchange rate parities. Over time, however, the majority of these countries have also moved toward exchange rate arrangements involving more frequent adjustments in nominal exchange rates.[1] Most such arrangements, however, have not left exchange rate determination to the market. Instead, whether in the form of crawling pegs or managed floating, they have invariably featured an important role for the authorities in the setting of nominal exchange rates and thus have led to increased activism in exchange rate management. Consequently, the question of how to choose the appropriate value of the nominal exchange rate has remained a key concern of macroeconomic policy in developing countries. In this context, a broad consensus has emerged in recent years that the overriding objective of exchange rate policy should be to avoid episodes of prolonged and substantial misalignment—meaning situations in which the actual real exchange rate (RER) differs significantly from its long-run equilibrium value.

Unfortunately, following this advice is not as simple as it sounds, even for the most well intentioned policymaker. Leaving aside the substantial difficulties that may arise in setting the actual nominal and real

---

1. For a description of the evolution of developing-country exchange rate regimes since the collapse of the Bretton Woods system, see Agenor and Montiel (1999). See also Caramazza and Aziz (1998) for a review of experiences with fixed and flexible exchange rate regimes in the 1990s.

exchange rates on their intended paths, two fundamental issues have to be confronted. The first is defining exactly what is meant by the long-run equilibrium real exchange rate. The second is estimating what the value of this long-run equilibrium rate is for a given country at any moment in time. Neither issue is trivial. Even though exchange rate misalignment is an important concern for policymakers, the economics profession has yet to reach a consensus on precisely what is meant by the long-run equilibrium real exchange rate. And not surprisingly, therefore, it has provided little systematic guidance on how to measure it.[2]

Despite the absence of consensus, not only do developing-country policymakers continue to confront these issues on a daily basis, but the urgency of getting this key macroeconomic relative price "right" may be increasing over time, as growing financial integration has arguably escalated the costs associated with real exchange rate misalignment. In the developing-country context alone, recent episodes such as the January 1994 devaluation of the CFA francs in West and Central Africa,[3] the Mexican currency crisis at the end of 1994, the Asian crisis that erupted in mid-1997, and the Brazilian devaluation in January 1999 have served as reminders of the macroeconomic disruptions that can be caused by real exchange rate misalignment. The severe macroeconomic dislocations experienced during these episodes suggest that the importance of being able to estimate the degree of misalignment may, if anything, have increased in recent years.

This volume arose from one such episode of misalignment. Most of the papers collected here originated in the course of a practical exercise in measuring real exchange rate misalignment at the World Bank. During the long dialogue over the degree of overvaluation of the CFA francs, World Bank staff were confronted with the problem of estimating the extent of real exchange rate misalignment in a context where it was important to ensure that the estimates were both theoretically defensible and empirically accurate. Hence, the staff did a considerable amount of analytical work on various methodologies for calculating indexes of the actual real exchange rate and for estimating the value of the long-run

---

2. An interesting perspective on the evolution of these issues is provided by John Williamson's introduction to his edited book on the topic, *Estimating Equilibrium Exchange Rates* (1994). The somewhat apologetic tone of that introduction suggests that, in the authors' opinion, the very concept of estimating long-run equilibrium exchange rate needed to be defended within the economics profession.

3. CFA is the abbreviation for Communauté Financière Africaine. The CFA francs are the currencies of the West and Central African Monetary Unions, which together constitute the CFA zone.

equilibrium real exchange rate. This methodological work focused on the types of analysis that could be carried out relatively quickly with (a) the limited amount and periodicity of data usually available in small African countries (for example, a monthly consumer price index (CPI), standard annual national accounts aggregates, annual export and import price indexes, and monthly official and parallel market exchange rates) and (b) the limited staff inputs (for example, one economist and a researcher) that are typically available for work on small developing countries. The staff also directed considerable attention to some empirical problems encountered during this work that are relatively more important in developing than industrial countries, such as unrecorded trade, parallel exchange markets, shifting trade patterns, and large fluctuations in export prices.

This book is intended to preserve and disseminate this work on measuring misalignment because the methodologies that were used are likely to be of practical relevance in many other developing-country applications. The book's objectives are thus to bring this work together, set it in an analytical framework, and complement it with other techniques that—while not employed in the CFA franc context because the operational restrictions described above prevented doing so or because the particular structure of the CFA economies did not make them suitable—might well be applicable in other developing countries. What we hope to achieve is to provide policymakers and their advisers with a compendium of practical techniques for estimating equilibrium real exchange rates, as well as to further the development of this area of research by taking stock of the current state of the art.

The objective of this first chapter is to present an overview of the book and to place the subsequent chapters in context. The remainder of this overview is divided into five sections, corresponding to each of the four parts of the book, plus a concluding section.

Part I of the book considers issues that arise in the definition and measurement of the actual real exchange rate. It is indispensable to treat these first because the choices made in selecting the appropriate actual real exchange rate for a particular application will obviously affect the equilibrium concept relevant to it and also because the reliability of the estimates of the equilibrium exchange rate will clearly depend on how closely empirical proxies can approximate the "true" variable being measured. These definition and measurement issues are reviewed and summarized in the second section of this overview.

Part II turns to the long-run equilibrium real exchange rate (LRER) itself. It contains two chapters that provide overviews of existing literature. The first chapter considers conceptual issues that arise in defining the long-run equilibrium real exchange rate and surveys existing techniques for its empirical estimation. The following chapter sets out an analytical model that synthesizes existing theories about the determinants of the LRER. The basic findings of these two chapters are described in the section below on the determinants of the equilibrium RER.

Part III then analyzes in some detail four methodologies for the empirical estimation of the long-run equilibrium real exchange rate: a PPP-based approach, a recursive trade-equations approach, and two general equilibrium approaches—one based on structural econometric models and the other on a reduced-form methodology utilizing unit-root econometrics. These methodologies are described in the four chapters contained in Part III of the book. They are summarized and evaluated in this overview's section on methodologies for estimating the equilibrium RER.

Part IV of the book, reviewed below in the section on policy and operational considerations, takes up some important related issues. The first chapter in Part IV examines the empirical role of the real exchange rate in promoting external balance, a mechanism that is featured prominently in traditional definitions of the long-run equilibrium real exchange rate but the empirical effectiveness of which has sometimes been questioned. The two remaining chapters in Part IV assess the usefulness of the parallel market premium as an indicator of the LRER and describe operational techniques for estimating the magnitude of nominal exchange rate changes required to correct a given real exchange rate misalignment.

The overview concludes with a final section presenting our assessment of where the enterprise of defining and estimating equilibrium real exchange rates in developing countries currently stands. We find, in brief, that recent developments justify optimism. The three techniques that have traditionally been used for the estimation of equilibrium real exchange rates—based on purchasing power parity, on the trade equations, and on simulations of empirical general equilibrium models—each suffer from particular limitations; but each can be useful under appropriate circumstances. What we have dubbed the reduced-form general-equilibrium approach is a relatively recent technique. Although this method of estimation is not without its own pitfalls, it appears to hold promise of future progress in the empirical estimation of equilibrium real exchange rates for developing countries.

The Real Exchange Rate: Concepts and Measurement

The point of departure for estimating the long-run equilibrium real exchange rate (which we call the LRER) is the measurement of the actual real exchange rate (RER). Unfortunately, this is not a straightforward matter. The difficulties are both conceptual and empirical. Multiple conceptual definitions of the real exchange rate, drawn from different analytical frameworks and suitable for use in different circumstances, have long complicated the analysis of real exchange rate issues. This multiplicity poses the problem of how to choose among alternative definitions of the real exchange rate. In addition, in the empirical measurement of the RER in many developing-country applications one confronts a large number of practical problems that are not often encountered in the case of industrial countries and thus have not been as widely discussed as other more general issues. The first three chapters in Part I of the book take up these definitional and measurement issues in detail.

As discussed subsequently in Part II, the development of LRER theories has followed somewhat different lines in industrial- and developing-country applications. Somewhat surprisingly, the differences have extended to the very definition of the RER itself.

In the context of industrial countries, economists have focused on the "external" RER for both analytical and empirical purposes. When defined in this manner, the RER is measured as the ratio of the foreign to the domestic values of some broad-based price index such as the CPI or the deflator for gross domestic product (GDP), expressed in a common currency by using the nominal exchange rate to convert the price level in one country into the currency of the other. Unfortunately, matters are complicated by the fact that alternative conceptual frameworks imply alternative choices of price indexes. As a result, even within the external real exchange rate category there exist multiple definitions from which to choose. This multiplicity of concepts would be of little consequence if the alternative measures all tended to move together, but they cannot be counted upon to do so—that is, empirically, the choice of price index tends to matter.

In the developing-country context, moreover, the RER tends to be defined in two different ways for analytical purposes: either as the relative price of traded goods in terms of nontraded goods, which is referred to in this book as the two-good internal real exchange rate, or as the relative prices of exportable and importable goods in terms of nontraded goods, which are referred to here as the three-good internal real exchange rates. To complicate matters further, despite the analytical preference for the use of internal RER concepts, the external RER tends to be used for empirical purposes in developing-country applications. This practice raises a number of issues. For example, when is it appropriate to use one definition rather than another? What is the relationship between the definitions? Are there specific pitfalls to which practitioners should be alerted in formulating hypotheses using one RER concept and testing them using another as an empirical proxy? The three chapters in Part I by Hinkle and Nsengiyumva take up these questions, considering each of the three broad definitions of the RER in turn.

The External RER

Chapter 2, the first chapter in Part I, provides a general summary of conceptual and empirical issues that arise in defining and measuring the external real exchange rate. Three alternative definitions, based on different price indexes, are reviewed; and both their theoretical under-pinnings and empirical counterparts are described. Chapter 2 also pro-vides a critical evaluation of the usefulness of external RER measures in developing countries from a conceptual perspective. On a more practi-cal level, issues such as the choice of weighting schemes in the construc-tion of real effective exchange rate (REER) indexes and alternative de-compositions of such indexes for analytical purposes are also discussed. Finally, particular attention is given to measurement problems that arise with special force in developing countires because of parallel exchange rates, unrecorded trade, and rapidly shifting trade patterns.

The three external real exchange rate measures examined are the rela-tive expenditure PPP-based RER, which uses domestic and partner country CPIs; the Mundell-Fleming or aggregate production cost RER, which uses GDP deflators; and the traded-goods RER, which can be constructed using relative unit labor costs in manufacturing, wholesale prices, manufacturing-sector deflators, or export unit values. The CPI-based measure has the important empirical advantage that the domes-tic price data required are widely available on a current basis for most developing countries so that REERs with reasonably comprehensive partner country representation can be computed. The aggregate pro-duction cost RER, in contrast, relies on GDP deflators that are available at much lower frequencies for developing than for industrial countries. This shortcoming also affects some versions of production cost–based RERs for traded goods, such as that based on manufacturing deflators.[4] Both of these cost-based RERs (the aggregate and traded-goods ver-sions) can, in principle, be improved upon as measures of competitive-ness through the use of unit labor cost measures, since these take into account intercountry differences in average labor productivity. How-ever, lack of data on unit labor costs limits the usefulness of such mea-sures in developing countries.

---

4. However, traded-goods RERs computed using wholesale prices, when these are available, do permit the use of higher-frequency data as discussed in Chapter 2.

A more fundamental problem with the cost-based RERs, however, is that they are based on a concept of competitiveness between domestic and foreign goods that are not perfectly substitutable. For countries with a large share of standardized commodities in their exports, the applicability of cost-based RERs may, therefore, be limited. For such countries the relevant concept of competitiveness is not the ability to produce at lower costs and thus sell at lower prices (expressed in a common currency) than other countries producing similar products. Rather, it is the adequacy of domestic incentives to produce goods that are not greatly differentiated from (and thus must sell at similar prices to) those produced by other countries. This difference makes such cost-based concepts seriously misleading in the presence of terms-of-trade changes. An increase in the price of domestic exports—which would increase internal incentives to produce such goods—would, for example, show up as an increase in the GDP deflator or wholesale price index (WPI) and thus inaccurately suggest a deteriorating relative cost performance. Cost-based measures are therefore not usually considered to have particular conceptual advantages over expenditure-based measures in the developing-country context. In view of the data availability advantages of the latter, Chapter 2 concludes that for most developing countries the REER computed using domestic and foreign CPIs is the most useful of the various external RER measures.

However, both expenditure-based and cost-based external RER measures can be very sensitive to the existence of parallel markets and unrecorded trade, as well as to shifting trade shares and weighting schemes. Calculations for Côte d'Ivoire illustrate the significant difference that such factors can make to estimated REERs. Hence, a variety of measures should be calculated and interpreted together to permit cross-checks, rather than relying on a single measure.

Finally, a presentational point noted in Chapter 2, and worth repeating here to avoid subsequent confusion, is that, like nominal exchange rates, all RER measures can be expressed both in foreign-currency terms and inversely in domestic-currency terms. When expressed in foreign-currency terms (that is, in units of foreign currency per unit of domestic currency), an increase in the RER represents an appreciation. However, when the RER is expressed in domestic-currency terms (that is, in units of domestic currency per unit of foreign currency), the inverse is true: an increase in the RER represents a depreciation. Since for some purposes it is useful to express RERs in foreign-currency terms and for others in domestic-currency terms, both versions are widely used in the literature and in this volume. In the interest of clarity, we have noted throughout the text and in the graphs and tables whether the RER is measured in foreign- or domestic-currency terms, but readers should be alert to shifts between the two measures.

The Two-Good Internal RER for Tradables and Nontradables

Chapter 3 turns to the two-good internal real exchange rate, the definition of which is based on the familiar Swan-Salter "dependent economy" model and which is in widest use for analytical purposes in the developing-country context. Although the two-good internal real exchange rate has strong analytical appeal, difficulties with this definition arise in practical applications, stemming from the absence of generally available price indexes for "traded" and "nontraded" goods. Chapter 3 describes and evaluates alternative approaches to the construction of such indexes, which differ according to whether they attempt to measure border prices or domestic prices as well as to whether the relative price indexes are expenditure-based or production-based. These may diverge significantly in developing countries. A familiar proxy for the internal RER, based on partner country WPIs as measures of traded-goods prices and the domestic CPI as an indicator of the price of nontraded goods, may be reasonable as long as the terms of trade and commercial policies are stable. When the terms of trade change, the measure is likely to be a better proxy for the internal RER for importables than for exportables. However, as in the case of the external RER, this measure also proves quite sensitive to parallel exchange rates, unrecorded trade, and changes in trade patterns.

Hinkle and Nsengiyumva also consider the theoretical and empirical relationships between the external RER and two-good internal RER. This is a particularly important problem in the developing-country context since, as indicated above, analysis of RER issues tends to be formulated using the two-good internal RER concept, while for data availability reasons empirical work tends to rely on the external RER. Conceptually, the relationship between the two measures is well known—the home country's internal RER is a function of its external RER as well as of the internal RER of the foreign country and the relative prices of tradable goods in the two countries. Because of the role of the last two factors, a country's internal and external RERs need not move together. Moreover, even if these factors were unchanged, movements in a country's internal RER are likely to be larger than those in its external RER. In Chapter 3, the two measures are compared for a specific country, and the effects on the measured RER of changes in a subset of fundamentals—specifically productivity and trade taxes—are analyzed. The chapter illustrates the familiar result that faster productivity growth in the traded than in the nontraded sector will cause the internal RER to appreciate. Further, it shows that differentially faster productivity growth in the traded-goods sectors of partner countries than in the domestic economy could cause the external RER to depreciate at the same time.

A final important caveat noted by Hinkle and Nsengiyumva concerns the role of the law of one price. The quantitative relationships between the measured internal and external RERs all depend upon the law of one price holding for tradable goods, a supposition that has been strongly challenged by much recent empirical work on large industrial countries. If the law of one price does not hold or holds only loosely as a long-run tendency, then the effect of exchange rate movements on the internal RER will be muted, the internal and external RERs will diverge, and the external RER will not be a reliable indicator of movements in domestic relative prices. The various caveats articulated in Chapter 3 concerning the relationship between the two RER concepts are relevant for the rest of the book, in which some of the empirical work utilizes the external RER.

Chapter 3 thus concludes that, despite its analytical appeal, the two-good internal RER is of limited empirical utility for low-income countries. Data problems make it extremely difficult to measure the two-good internal RER with any accuracy in most countries. In addition, many of these countries experience significant exogenous variations in their terms of trade, which cannot be addressed in a two-good framework.

The Three-Good Internal RERs for Exportables and Importables

The final chapter in Part I, Chapter 4, considers the three-good internal real exchange rate, which disaggregates tradable goods into exportables and importables and produces two real exchange rate measures—corresponding to the relative prices of exportables and importables, respectively, in terms of nontraded goods. Here, the central conceptual issue concerns the choice between a two-good and a three-good framework. Chapter 4 analyzes the conditions under which each of these may be appropriate. The three-good framework is strongly advocated for most cases since fluctuations in the terms of trade and commercial policies are often important in developing countries. These shocks tend to move exportable and importable RERs in opposite directions, making a two-good internal RER essentially meaningless. Hence, in most cases, analysts will want to examine the behavior of both the exportables and importables real exchange rates.[5]

---

5. If for presentational reasons a single RER measure is needed, the price of domestic goods measured in foreign exchange may be used for this purpose as illustrated in Chapter 8.

Overall, the three chapters by Hinkle and Nsengiyumva make the case that for low-income countries, the most useful RER measures are the CPI-based external RERs (or those using unit labor costs if the data are available) and the three-good internal RERs for exportables and importables. The external RER and its components are particularly useful for analyzing the effects of nominal shocks such as nominal exchange rate movements and foreign and domestic inflation. The three-good internal RERs are useful for measuring the effects on domestic relative prices of real shocks such as changes in the terms of trade and commercial policy.

If the law of one price holds for traded goods, it is possible to calculate any of the various internal and external RER measures from given values of the others. However, empirically the law of one price holds at best only loosely for traded goods, and (unknown) measurement errors affect the accuracy of all the empirical RER measures. Since inconsistencies in the data may pose serious analytical problems in some cases, best practice will typically involve constructing and analyzing several RER measures. In the case of the external RER, these would examine alternative assumptions about trade through parallel markets, unrecorded trade, and trade shares. Similarly, different approaches to the estimation of the three-good internal RERs should be compared to the extent possible in each case.

In a number of low-income countries the unavailability of the data required for timely and accurate measurement of the three-good internal and the external RER for traded goods is still a serious analytical constraint. In these cases, improved data collection is a prerequisite for more accurate measurement and analysis of the real exchange rate.

Determinants of the Equilibrium Real Exchange Rate

In Part II, the book turns to the long-run equilibrium real exchange rate (LRER) itself. The two chapters, 5 and 6, in this part, both by Montiel, are overviews: the first of the existing empirical literature devoted to the estimation of the LRER, and the second of theory linking the LRER to its long-run fundamental determinants.

Conceptual Issues and Empirical Research

Chapter 5 actually takes up two separate topics. Since it is the first chapter in the volume that explicitly considers the question of the definition and measurement of the LRER, its first section is devoted to conceptual issues, examining in particular what is meant by the long-run equilibrium real exchange rate, before describing how economists have attempted to estimate it. The purpose of this first section is to sort out some conceptual problems that have arisen in defining and measuring the LRER. These are of various types, two of which are worth mentioning here.

First, some economists question the very notion of distinguishing between the actual RER and its notional equilibrium value, since the actual RER is itself the outcome of the economy's macroeconomic equilibrium. This argument appears to be somewhat confused, however. The distinction between the actual RER and the LRER is not one between disequilibrium and equilibrium, but rather between different types of equilibriums—that is, equilibriums conditioned on different values of macroeconomic variables. The actual RER observed at any moment may be influenced by a variety of factors that may prove to be transitory. These include speculative "bubble" factors, actual values of predetermined variables that differ from their long-run values, and transitory movements in both policy and exogenous variables. When at least some of the variables on which the actual "equilibrium" RER depends are unsustainable, the actual RER will tend to change over time, tracing out an equilibrium path.

It is possible, then, to think of alternative "equilibrium" RERs, for which the notion of equilibrium is defined over different time horizons. For example, we can distinguish conceptually between the actual RER and a "short-run equilibrium" RER (SRER). The latter refers to the value of the RER that would be observed in the absence of speculative (bubble) factors. This value depends on "short-run fundamentals" such as the actual values of predetermined variables as well as actual and expected future values of policy and exogenous variables. Similarly, we can distinguish between this SRER and a long-run equilibrium RER (LRER). In contrast to the SRER, the LRER is a function of the steady-state values of the predetermined variables and the permanent (sustainable) values of policy and exogenous variables, rather than of the actual values of these variables. Finally, we can also distinguish between the LRER and the "desired" LRER (DRER), which is conditioned on optimal values of the policy variables, permanent values of the exogenous variables, and steady-state values of the predetermined variables.

Second, even if one accepts these distinctions and is specifically interested in measuring the LRER, a further complication arises in determining the duration of the "long run" that is relevant for policy purposes. The traditional definition of the LRER based on the simultaneous attainment of internal and external balance, established by Nurkse (1945), suggests that the long run should be long enough for cyclical effects to have worked themselves out. However, in specifying "external balance" as a situation in which the current account is financed by sustainable net capital inflows, this definition leaves open the question of whether the long run implies that the economy has reached a steady-state international net creditor position. Alternative definitions of external balance, built on different assumptions about the economy's net external creditor position, are examined in Chapter 5.

The second part of Chapter 5 surveys existing methods of estimating the LRER (based on various definitions of "external balance") in both industrial and developing countries. After reviewing evidence on the validity of purchasing power parity (PPP) as a theory of the LRER, applications of three alternative approaches to empirical estimation of the LRER are surveyed: (a) a recursive partial-equilibrium trade-equations approach, (b) an approach based on the simulation of macroeconometric models, and (c) two varieties of reduced-form estimation, a traditional one and one based on unit-root econometrics. Each of these techniques is subsequently described, analyzed, and illustrated in detail in Part III of this book. Thus, the role of this survey is to provide background for the individual estimation techniques to be described later, as well as to explore the relationships among them.

An Analytical Model

Chapter 6 then presents a theoretical model of the determination of the LRER that is intended to synthesize previous literature on the determinants of the LRER. The role of this chapter is to identify the set of variables that may potentially act as long-run fundamentals and to determine the qualitative nature of their influence on the LRER. The variables identified there are domestic supply-side factors, fiscal policy, changes in the international economic environment, and commercial policy. Each of these is discussed in turn below.

Domestic supply-side factors. These essentially refer to differences in sectoral productivity growth rates—particularly, the Balassa-Samuelson effect. Traditionally, this effect has been interpreted as arising from faster productivity growth in the traded-goods sector than in the nontraded-goods sector. Differential productivity growth of this type requires an appreciation of the long-run equilibrium value of the internal RER.

Fiscal policy. Permanent changes in the distribution of government spending between traded and nontraded goods affect the LRER in different ways. Additional tax-financed spending on nontraded goods, for example, creates incipient excess demand in that market, requiring a real appreciation to restore equilibrium. By contrast, tax-financed increases in spending on traded goods put downward pressure on the trade balance and require a real depreciation to sustain external balance.

Changes in the international economic environment. Changes in an economy's external terms of trade, the flows of external transfers, the world inflation rate, and the level of world real interest rates, all may potentially influence the LRER. Improvements in the terms of trade tend to appreciate the equilibrium real exchange rate for importables by improving the trade balance and creating excess demand for nontraded goods. Whether the long-run real exchange rate for *exportables* depreciates or appreciates is ambiguous in the theoretical model. Empirically, however, the exportables RER almost always depreciates when the terms of trade improve because the price of exports tends to rise much more than the price of nontraded goods. Increases in the flow of external transfers received also appreciate the equilibrium RER through positive effects on the sustainable current account balance.

In the model analyzed in Chapter 6, changes in world inflation affect the equilibrium real exchange rate through effects on transactions costs associated with changes in real money balances. The direction of these effects on the LRER depends on whether such costs are incurred primarily in the form of traded or nontraded goods. The absorption of either type of goods by transactions costs effectively reduces their supply. Hence, when transactions costs are incurred in the form of traded goods, an equilibrium real depreciation is required to maintain external balance; but when they are incurred in the form of nontraded goods, an equilibrium real appreciation is required to maintain internal balance.

The effects on the LRER of changes in world real interest rates depend on the nature of the domestic economy's financial links with the rest of the world. In the analytical model described in this chapter, although the domestic economy is financially open, its real interest rate is independent of the world rate in the long run, being determined instead by the domestic rate of time preference. In this model, reductions in world real interest rates cause the long-run equilibrium real exchange rate to depreciate. The reason is that lower world interest rates induce capital inflows that reduce the country's net creditor position over time, and the long-run loss of net interest receipts requires a real depreciation to maintain external balance. The opposite result is, however, possible with alternative assumptions about the determination of domestic interest rates as explained in footnote 12 below.

Commercial policy. Finally, trade liberalization is associated with a long-run depreciation of the equilibrium RER. The effect of liberalization is to switch resources into the nontraded (or non-import-competing) sector. The emergence of incipient excess supply in the nontraded-goods market requires a depreciation of the real exchange rate.

The challenge in estimating the LRER, of course, is assessing the quantitative influence on the LRER—if any—of changes in each of the above variables. Alternative methods of doing so are described in Part III of the book.

Methodologies for Estimating the Equilibrium RER: Empirical Applications

The heart of the book is Part III, in which alternative techniques for estimating the LRER are presented. Four such techniques—all of them briefly reviewed earlier in the empirical survey—are analyzed individually and illustrated with specific empirical applications in the four chapters, 7 to 10, that make up this part of the book. Chapter 7 focuses on the two estimation techniques that are in widest operational use: the purchasing-power-parity (PPP)-based approach and a recursive partial-equilibrium approach based on adjustments in the economy's external resource balance, which we have dubbed the trade-equations approach. There are two versions of the trade-equations approach in wide use. The first one is a Mundell-Fleming version that takes export volumes to be determined on the demand side of the market; export supply is taken to be perfectly elastic. The second one is a three-good version that takes export demand to be perfectly elastic; export volumes are correspondingly determined on the supply side of the market. Empirical application of the trade-equations approach also involves two analytical tasks—measurement of the underlying (or structural) resource balance and determination of a target long-run resource balance—that are common to most other methodologies for estimating the LRER empirically.[6] Chapter 7 provides a general overview of the trade-equations approach with an illustration for Côte d'Ivoire. Chapter 8 presents an application of the three-good trade-equations approach, which focuses on the role of one specific "fundamental" (the terms of trade), and applies the technique to a larger group of 12 CFA countries. The last two chapters in Part III analyze the two more explicitly general-equilibrium approaches. Chapter 9 describes how simulations of fairly traditional empirical macroeconomic models can be used to estimate the LRER in developing countries. Chapter 10 provides a detailed description and two applications of a relatively new approach based on single-equation reduced-form estimation using unit-root econometrics. The following section summarizes the findings of each of these four chapters.

The Relative PPP-Based Approach

The simplest and most venerable technique for estimating the LRER in developing countries, no less so than in industrial countries, is the PPP

---

6. The term "resource balance" is used throughout this volume to refer to the difference between exports and imports of goods and nonfactor services. It is equal to gross domestic savings less gross investment.

approach. Chapter 7 of Part III, by Ahlers and Hinkle, describes the PPP-based method, as well as the trade-equations method discussed below. The Ahlers and Hinkle exposition is based on an illustration of how the simple PPP method could have been used to estimate the degree of misalignment that characterized Côte d'Ivoire prior to the devaluation of the CFA franc.

Relative PPP may be applied either broadly to the external RER for all goods or more narrowly to just the RER for traded goods. The rationale for applying relative PPP to traded goods, as an application of the law of one price, is stronger; and this is the standard practice in industrial countries. However, lack of data on the RER for traded goods, as in the Côte d'Ivoire example considered in Chapter 7, usually limits one to the use of RER for all goods in developing countries.

The use of the relative PPP-based method can be justified in one of two ways. On the one hand, the analyst may simply adopt ex ante the traditional relative-PPP view on the determination of the long-run equilibrium real exchange rate, which essentially takes the LRER to be a constant.[7] On the other hand, the LRER may be considered by the analyst to be determined by a broad set of fundamentals, which may turn out ex post to be stationary in a time-series sense for the specific application at hand. In the first case, the decision to apply the PPP approach would be made before looking at the data. In the second case, the PPP approach would be adopted only after the RER in the country under review passes a test of stationarity.

When relative PPP is assumed to hold ex ante, measuring the equilibrium real exchange rate essentially involves removing the effects of nonsystematic transitory shocks. In practice these are eliminated by identifying a base period in which such shocks are believed, on the basis of independent evidence, to have been negligible—a procedure that ensures that the actual real exchange rate coincided with its equilibrium (PPP) value during that period. Thus the actual real exchange rate in the base period represents the estimate of the equilibrium rate. The nominal exchange rate consistent with the LRER from that moment on can then be calculated by simply adjusting the nominal exchange rate for the cumulative difference between domestic and foreign inflation.

The alternative case is that the LRER is interpreted as subject to change in response to changes in underlying fundamentals but turns out empirically to be stationary for a particular country. In this case, the stationarity of the RER forces the analyst to take the position that its

---

7. This is in contrast to the *absolute* version of PPP, which takes the LRER to be unity.

fundamental determinants are either individually stationary—that is, that the "permanent" values of the fundamentals have not changed during the sample period, though the fundamentals may have been subject to transitory fluctuations—or that any nonstationary fundamentals must be cointegrated among themselves. In either situation, the LRER can still be measured using a base-year value, though the identification of a suitable base year is more complicated under this interpretation, as explained below. Ahlers and Hinkle refer to the PPP-based method that estimates the LRER using the value of the RER during some base year as the "PPP base-year" approach. It calculates misalignment by simply plotting the real exchange rate over time and comparing its value during the period of interest to the corresponding value in the base year in which the real exchange rate was judged to be at its long-run equilibrium value.

The empirically oriented exposition of the PPP base-year approach by Ahlers and Hinkle is particularly appropriate because in this methodology everything depends on the identification of a suitable base year. As mentioned above, how the base year is chosen depends on whether the rationale underlying the procedure is a simple ex ante relative PPP-based one or a more sophisticated one in which the real exchange rate is driven by stationary fundamentals. In the simple PPP case, the "independent evidence" of equilibrium referred to previously is likely to concern the behavior of a particular outcome variable, such as the resource balance. In contrast, from the "stationary fundamentals" perspective, the base year chosen should be a recent year in which the actual exchange rate is believed to have been close to its equilibrium value because all the fundamentals were close to their sustainable values. This requirement makes the application of the PPP methodology more complicated in the latter case.

As explained in the survey of empirical estimation in Chapter 5, the set of fundamentals to be considered in choosing a base year may include both exogenous and policy variables. In assessing the behavior of the exogenous variables, the analyst may look, for example, for terms of trade that are reasonably close to their likely long-run trend levels and for capital flows that are consistent—in amount and terms—both with the likely long-term availability of capital and the country's debt-servicing capacity. For assessing the permanence of the policy stance, the relevant criteria may involve the attainment of growth, investment, and inflation targets during various years over the sample period.

A common problem in selecting appropriate base years is that, because of policy shortcomings and external constraints, years in which exogenous variables were at sustainable levels are not always years in which policy variables were at desirable levels. Thus, the choice of a base year tends to call for subjective judgments in determining when the real exchange rate was near its long-run equilibrium value. For example, historically, desirable growth and investment levels have sometimes been attained only when the terms of trade were temporarily inflated or when capital flows were unsustainable. Conversely, sustainable terms of trade and capital flows have often been associated with undesirable growth and investment outcomes. Hence, in applying the PPP base-year approach under the "stationary fundamentals" interpretation, the analyst is often forced to make tradeoffs between the sustainability of exogenous variables and that of policy variables.

One way to deal with this problem is to estimate the sustainable values of the fundamentals on the basis of their sample means or, in the trend-stationary case, as their trend values within the sample. In effect, this procedure amounts to estimating the LRER as the sample mean or the trend value of the RER within the sample, rather than as the particular value of the RER in a specified base year. This procedure can be referred to as the PPP average or trend approach. Ahlers and Hinkle also illustrate this alternative method of estimating the LRER in applications of the PPP-based method. Empirically, a large appreciation of the RER relative to its trend value in a short period of time is one of the most reliable statistical indicators of misalignment and a potential exchange rate crisis.

The relative PPP-based approach, however, has one severe limitation: if the RER is nonstationary, its equilibrium value will be affected by changes in the fundamental variables that determine it. If these fundamentals are subject to permanent changes, and the evidence suggests that they usually are, then techniques for estimating the long-term value of the equilibrium exchange rate must take these changes into account. In other words, estimates of the LRER must depend on the estimated permanent changes in the fundamentals.

The Trade-Equations Approach

The PPP-based approach described above was originally motivated by the relative-PPP theory of exchange rate determination. Similarly, the trade-equations methodology is also based on a venerable analytical tool in open-economy macroeconomics—in this case, the partial-equilibrium "elasticities" approach to exchange rate determination. This methodology is based on the notion that the primary macroeconomic role of the real exchange rate is to influence the resource balance through expenditure-switching mechanisms. It is more sophisticated than the simplest interpretation of the empirical PPP approach in that it acknowledges that the equilibrium real exchange rate is not necessarily constant.

Ahlers and Hinkle describe and illustrate the trade-equations approach as well as the relative-PPP approach. As mentioned previously, there are two standard versions of the trade-equations approach. The version most commonly used in industrial countries is based on the Mundell-Fleming production structure. In this framework, complete specialization in the production of one good by both the domestic and foreign countries (each country's own GDP) makes export supply functions perfectly elastic, while the domestic and foreign goods are taken to be imperfect substitutes in demand. Export and import quantities are consequently both demand-determined, and the real exchange rate exerts its effect on the trade balance through its influence on the domestic demand for imports and on the external demand for the country's exports. This perspective is typically adopted for industrial countries, as well as for some developing countries whose exports are dominated by differentiated manufactured goods. The alternative version is usually applied to developing countries in which exports are instead dominated by undifferentiated primary products. In this case, it is more appropriate to consider export demand as being infinitely price-elastic and to recognize a finite export supply elasticity.[8] The quantity of exports is thus determined by the elasticity of export supply.

In both versions of the trade-equations approach, the resource balance will in general depend on the real exchange rate as well as other variables. For given values of the latter, the "equilibrium" value of the real exchange rate must be that which generates the "equilibrium" value of the resource balance—that is, that value of the resource balance that is consistent with balance of payments equilibrium. Given a target for external reserves and an exogenously determined volume of net resource flows (net capital inflows plus net interest receipts plus net transfers), the equilibrium value of the resource balance is determined. Alternatively, for fully creditworthy countries in which capital markets can be assumed to provide the financing required to cover a resource deficit, a sustainable or trend saving-investment balance can be projected separately and assumed to determine the equilibrium resource balance. In either case, the equilibrium value of the real exchange rate can then be calculated from the required change in the initial resource balance for given initial values of exports and imports if the relevant import and export demand or supply elasticities are known.

The three key empirical requirements for implementing the trade-equations approach are: (a) estimates of the elasticity of exports and imports with respect to the real exchange rate; (b) methods for determining a target resource balance to be used in the analysis; and (c) techniques for estimating the effects on the initial resource balance of

---

8. Conceptually, this approach implies supposing that the home country produces at least one other type of good besides the exportable good.

variables that affect it, other than the real exchange rate. Empirical estimates of the relevant elasticities needed for step (a) are given in Chapter 11 on trade flows and the RER. Steps (b) and (c), which are also required in many applications of the other methodologies discussed subsequently, are analyzed in detail by Ahlers and Hinkle.

The specification of the target resource balance, step (b), is often one of the most problematic steps in the empirical estimation of the LRER. A particularly useful contribution of the Ahlers-Hinkle chapter, therefore, is its inclusion of a comprehensive discussion of practical methods for specifying the volume of net capital inflows and reserve accumulation required to derive the target resource balance. The authors describe two polar ways of establishing sustainable capital flows and a target resource balance: one for noncreditworthy countries that must rely entirely on aid flows and the other for creditworthy countries that have full access to credit markets. In the case of noncreditworthy countries—that is, countries that absorb external resources primarily in the form of aid flows— resource balance targets are essentially based on projections of aid availability. Such projections can be derived from independent information (for example, from donor sources) or can be projected on the basis of past history. For countries that are judged creditworthy by international financial markets, a variety of means is available to project sustainable capital flows. These can be based on demand-side or supply-side determinants. The former refer to domestic saving-investment balances that are deemed desirable or are otherwise judged sustainable. The latter may be based on debt stocks that are judged compatible with a country's intertemporal budget constraint or on credit allocation rules of thumb used by international lenders. However calculated, an increased inflow of capital permits the accommodation of a larger "equilibrium" resource balance deficit and is thus consistent with a more appreciated value of the equilibrium real exchange rate.[9]

As noted above, the resource balance may depend on variables other than the real exchange rate, such as the level and composition of aggregate demand, the external terms of trade, and commercial policy. Hence, it is usually necessary to determine the underlying or structural resource balance corresponding to a particular value of the RER by adjusting the actual resource balance in the given year for cyclical, exogenous, and policy changes that affect it.

The simplest solution to this problem is to identify a base year, similar to that used in the relative PPP-based approach, in which the actual

---

9. For a description of the application of this methodology in the context of financial programming exercises, see Khan, Haque, and Montiel (1990).

RER and its fundamental determinants are believed to have been close to their equilibrium levels. This technique is sometimes employed in empirical applications of all of the methodologies for estimating the LRER as explained in Chapters 8 to 10.

However, for the reasons explained on pages 16 and 17 above, a suitable base year may not be available in many cases. Ahlers and Hinkle demonstrate an alternative two-step procedure for taking into account the effects of changes in variables other than the RER that influence the resource balance such as the terms of trade, taxes on international trade, and underutilized productive capacity. First, the initial resource balance is adjusted to reflect the impact of changes in these variables, resulting in an "adjusted" resource balance.[10] Second, the required change in the real exchange rate is calculated as that which would cause a change in the resource balance equal to the difference between its adjusted and target values. For example, for a given target resource balance, the achievement of a higher long-run growth target for the economy may require a shift in the composition of aggregate demand from consumption to investment. If the import intensity of investment spending exceeds that of consumption, an increase in the share of investment in aggregate demand would increase the resource balance deficit associated with any given real exchange rate. Thus, such a change in the composition of demand would result in a larger adjusted resource balance deficit. To reconcile the larger projected resource balance deficit with the unchanged projected long-run equilibrium value of capital inflows, a larger real depreciation would be required. Hence, the adoption of a more ambitious long-run growth target would imply a more depreciated long-run equilibrium real exchange rate.

The second chapter in Part III, Chapter 8 by Devarajan, links the partial-equilibrium trade-equations approach with general equilibrium models. Devarajan shows how the trade-equations approach can be extracted from a restricted form of a computable general equilibrium (CGE) model. The particular model on which the Devarajan chapter is based (taken from Devarajan, Lewis, and Robinson (DLR, 1993)) utilizes a three-good framework, with exports, imports, and domestic goods. As indicated above, the extension to three goods has important advantages in

_____

10. To the extent that the composition of aggregate demand (for example, between consumption and investment, between private or public expenditure, or between different categories of government spending) affects the resource balance, the change in the real exchange rate required to achieve the target resource balance target will depend on how the target resource balance is attained. The adjustment procedure suggested by Ahlers and Hinkle also permits taking into account such effects.

developing-country applications. Because of its two-good production structure, the Mundell-Fleming approach cannot distinguish between the terms of trade and the real exchange rate. Thus, it cannot be used to analyze the impact of changes in fundamentals that involve changes in the domestic relative price of exportables and importables, such as the terms of trade and commercial policy. A three-good framework is necessary to analyze how the LRER is affected by changes in the relative prices of imports and exports. The particular concern of the Devarajan chapter is to demonstrate how the effects on the LRER of changes in such fundamentals can be handled in this expanded framework.[11]

The DLR method is based on three equations: (a) a "transformation function" linking the exports-GDP ratio to the relative price of exports in terms of domestic goods, (b) a "substitution function" relating the imports-GDP ratio to the relative price of imports in terms of domestic goods, and (c) an identity deriving the resource balance–GDP ratio from the export and import ratios. Given a target value for the resource balance, as well as exogenously determined export and import prices, the system can be solved for the equilibrium value of the price of domestic goods and, therefore, for the real exchange rates for exportables and importables. Devarajan's chapter thus illustrates how a general-equilibrium "fundamentals" approach to the determination of the LRER can be simplified and tailored to a specific application. An attractive feature of this method relative to the more explicitly general equilibrium approaches described below is that it benefits from the primary operational advantage of partial-equilibrium approaches: it requires minimal data and is easy to implement.

To illustrate the relative ease with which this methodology can be implemented empirically, the DLR model was applied to the estimation of misalignment in 12 of the 13 countries in the CFA zone on the eve of the devaluation of the CFA franc. Since the CFA countries are specialized primary exporters, changes in the terms of trade proved to be the dominant influence on the LRER in this case, justifying the focus on this variable. The results indicated a substantial degree of misalignment, averaging 31 percent but varying substantially among the CFA countries, with middle-income countries and oil producers exhibiting the most pronounced degree of misalignment. As we shall see below, these estimates are consistent with those obtained in the subsequent chapter by Baffes, Elbadawi, and O'Connell for Côte d'Ivoire and Burkina Faso, using a single-equation methodology. Both Devarajan and Baffes,

---

11. Devarajan also shows how the DLR methodology can be applied to examine the effects of changes in other fundamentals conventionally considered in the trade-equations approach in industrial countries such as capital flows.

Elbadawi, and O'Connell find a substantial degree of overvaluation in Côte d'Ivoire by 1993. In contrast, the real exchange rate for Burkina Faso is found to be quite close to the LRER estimated under both methodologies.

The two operational estimation techniques described in Chapters 7 and 8 impose minimal data requirements, appear to make few demands on empirical knowledge about the structure of the relevant economy, and are computationally straightforward. Thus, they have been the techniques of choice for estimating the LRER when research resources are limited or when the context in which estimates of the LRER are needed does not allow time for further research. They remain extremely useful under both sets of circumstances.

The Structural General-Equilibrium Approach

A key shortcoming of the trade-equations approach, however, is that it may not do enough justice to the general-equilibrium nature of the proccess by which the equilibrium RER is determined. While the demand for imports and exports undoubtedly depends on their relative prices in terms of other goods, it also depends on the level and composition of domestic spending (as the "absorption" approach of Alexander (1951) emphasized), as well as on the costs of production of exportables and importables. The problem is that variables such as these and the capital flows that determine the "equilibrium" value of the resource balance are themselves endogenous and thus are determined by the ultimate fundamentals identified in the discussion above of the long-run equilibrium RER. Consequently, the real exchange rate is deeply embedded in the economy's short-run macroeconomic equilibrium. The trade-equations approach, however, employs a recursive partial-equilibrium methodology. Given required changes in an economy's resource balance, it determines new equilibrium values for the RER, imports, and exports but not for other important macroeconomic variables such as government revenue, saving, and investment. Nor does it explicitly allow for feedback from the RER to the variables determining the target resource balance (capital flows or the saving-investment balance). While rough adjustments can be made for some of the more important income and feedback effects, one would be more confident of the results if they were determined in a complete general-equilibrium framework that takes into account all important macroeconomic interactions in a fully consistent manner.

Chapters 9 and 10, the two remaining chapters in Part III, implement general-equilibrium methods for detecting empirically the influence of changes in some fundamentals on the LRER. By and large, these chapters take a practical approach. Their objective is to estimate the value to which a country's RER would tend to converge over time, given sustained values of certain "fundamentals," including both policy variables and variables that are exogenous to the economy. It is important to emphasize that these chapters set a limited task for themselves. They are concerned neither with deriving *optimal* values of the policy variables, which have been considered necessary for some definitions of the LRER, nor with detailed exploration of the time-series properties of the truly exogenous variables. These restrictions greatly simplify both the conceptual and empirical issues and are logically defensible. Both the optimal setting of the broad range of policy instruments that may influence the long-run equilibrium real exchange rate and the specification of appropriate techniques for decomposing movements in exogenous variables into permanent and transitory components are logically separate from the issue of how particular values of the policy and exogenous variables affect the long-run equilibrium real exchange rate. Thus, Chapters 9 and 10 focus on the task of assessing how the value of the LRER is empirically affected by once-and-for-all changes in the values of whatever subset of these variables is relevant for the particular technique being used.

Chapter 9, by Haque and Montiel, adopts a structural general-equilibrium modeling approach. The model employed, taken from Haque, Lahiri, and Montiel (HLM, 1993), is based on a Mundell-Fleming production structure and assumes a high degree of integration of the domestic economy with international financial markets. In that sense, the HLM model is best suited for applications to middle-income developing countries with diversified manufactured exports and an open capital account. The model was estimated with panel data from a large sample of developing countries. Consequently, the simulations produced with the HLM model are intended to be representative of such economies, illustrating the outcomes in a model economy, rather than generating an estimate of the LRER for a specific country.

In estimating changes in the LRER using simulations from an empirical macroeconomic model, the Haque-Montiel chapter is closely related to the work of Williamson (1994) and others on the estimation of the LRER for industrial countries. However, in addition to being based on a "representative" economy, the simulation exercises in Chapter 9 differ from those conducted by Williamson in two other ways. First, in contrast to the Williamson approach, Haque and Montiel make no attempt to identify "desirable" values of the policy fundamentals. Second, they report "analytic" simulations, consisting of tracing the dynamic responses of the model economy to permanent shocks administered to individual fundamental variables, with a view to exploring how such shocks would affect the equilibrium real exchange rate that characterizes the new postshock steady state. In such simulations, policy and external variables are exogenous, and the sustainable trade balance is endogenously determined simultaneously with the LRER. By contrast, the simulations in Williamson (1994) are "real-time" simulations, which solve for the value of the RER associated with the achievement of internal and external balance targets within a specified policy-relevant period of time. Since the external balance target is specified exogenously and the time frame allowed to attain it will in general be shorter than that required for the model to approach its steady-state configuration, the attainment of such targets in general requires endogenous adjustment of policy variables.

The simulations in Chapter 9 confirm that nominal variables—namely, the nominal exchange rate and monetary policy—have no effect on the LRER, which is a real variable. This result is a consequence of the model's long-run neutrality to monetary shocks. In contrast, permanent changes in "real" fundamentals do affect the LRER. To complement the exercises conducted in the preceding chapters, the simulations of real shocks by Haque and Montiel analyze the effects of changes in some fundamentals not considered there. These are the effects of a permanent change in the world real interest rate and in external demand, considered separately, as well as a shift in the composition of government spending from foreign to domestic goods. A permanent increase in the world real interest rate depreciates the LRER in the HLM model, while increases in both external demand and in government spending on domestic goods cause the LRER to appreciate.[12]

The Haque-Montiel simulations are used to estimate the elasticity of response of the LRER to permanent changes in the set of fundamentals considered. These results can be used in a number of ways:

a. The elasticities themselves can be used directly to estimate changes in the LRER in specific applications when one of the fundamentals has changed in a known way,

b. The structural parameter estimates of the model can be imposed in a structural model of an actual economy for which the LRER is

---

12. The qualitative result for the external real interest rate here is the opposite of that derived in the theoretical model in Chapter 6. The reason is that the way that imperfect capital mobility is modeled in the theoretical paper causes the domestic real interest rate to remain unchanged in response to increases in the external rate (since it is determined by the exogenous domestic rate of time preference). The Haque-Montiel model, in contrast, assumes that the domestic interest rate is determined by the world interest rate so that the domestic real interest rate rises one-for-one with increases in the world rate. The negative effect of the higher domestic interest rate on the demand for domestic goods causes the LRER to depreciate in the Haque-Montiel model.

to be estimated, and then simulations similar to those of Haque and Montiel can be run using data for that economy

c. The model's specification can be used as guidance for actual estimation of a similar structural model for the economy in question, and the required simulations can be based on the estimated model.

Haque and Montiel illustrate the second of the above possibilities in an application to Thailand. Retaining the estimated representative parameters but using Thai macroeconomic data, they estimate the LRER for Thailand in 1995 on the assumption that the actual and equilibrium real exchange rates coincided in 1991. They find that between 1991 and 1995 the Thai LRER depreciated by 17 percent. Since the actual real exchange rate depreciated by only about 4 percent over the same time, Haque and Montiel estimate that the baht was overvalued by about 13 percent in 1995.

In principle, the general-equilibrium modeling approach illustrated in Chapter 9 is the most attractive method for estimating the LRER. It permits the incorporation of the full range of macroeconomic influences that may potentially affect the LRER and imposes a minimum of restrictive and possibly erroneous assumptions about the structure of the economy. Two traits argue strongly in favor of this methodology: the richness of the macroeconomic interactions that can be taken into account in estimating the LRER by simulating a fully dynamic aggregate macroeconomic model and the flexibility that this method offers in defining alternative versions of the LRER over different time horizons. Morcover, an important feature of this approach for policy purposes is that its structural nature makes transparent the mechanism through which the LRER is determined, at least in principle.

This structural general-equilibrium approach, however, is subject to a variety of limitations. Some of these are shared with other approaches. For example, when implemented in "real-time" simulations—which are its most operationally relevant form—the structural general-equilibrium approach relies, like the trade-equations approach, on an exogenous specification of the equilibrium resource balance. More important, the estimation of general-equilibrium macroeconomic models places very strong demands on economic theory, on the power of statistical techniques, and on the availability and quality of data. Even in industrial countries, where off-the-shelf models with known track records are often available, doubts about model specification, empirical estimation, and parameter stability have eroded confidence in these models during recent years. With no previous track record, made-to-suit models for individual developing countries with limited data and more frequently changing economic structures and policy regimes confront a higher hurdle of credibility. Furthermore, the modeling approach has serious operational limitations. In the absence of a previously existing model, it is likely to be very time consuming and expensive to implement. It may thus be more suited to large research projects in countries with long time-series data than to operational applications in most low-income developing countries. For the near future, estimates of the LRER derived from simulations of dynamic macroeconomic models should be treated as indicative in developing-country applications and used to supplement and inform other approaches to estimation.

The Reduced-Form General-Equilibrium Approach

The final chapter in Part III—Chapter 10, by Baffes, Elbadawi, and O'Connell—abandons the specification of structural models, adopting a single-equation reduced-form methodology. It relies on unit-root econometrics to measure the effect that potential fundamentals have on the LRER in two CFA franc countries, Côte d'Ivoire and Burkina Faso.[13] The attraction of this method is that, like the structural general-equilibrium approach, it incorporates the full general-equilibrium interaction of the fundamentals in a dynamic structure that generates a time series, rather than just a point estimate, for the LRER. Yet, relative to the structural general-equilibrium approach, it places fewer demands on both theory and data. From the perspective of theory, the method requires an appropriate specification of long-run relationships, but the dynamic structure of the economy does not need to be imposed ex ante. Instead, it is determined entirely by the data. The data required, in turn, are only those that would enter the reduced-form equation for the real exchange rate in a short-run macroeconomic equilibrium model. Structural equations for the economy do not have to be estimated, and data on other short-run endogenous macroeconomic variables are not required.

The fundamentals considered by Baffes, Elbadawi, and O'Connell for the two countries in their study include many of those examined in the previous chapters: the terms of trade, trade openness (as a proxy for commercial policy), capital flows, and the composition of domestic absorption (the share of investment in GDP). Interestingly, these variables prove to be nonstationary and cointegrated with the real exchange rate in Côte d'Ivoire but stationary in Burkina Faso. In the case of Burkina Faso, all but the composition of absorption prove to be statistically significant determinants of the (stationary) real exchange rate. Thus, Burkina Faso provides an illustration of how in certain cases PPP can continue

---

13. Previous applications of this methodology to developing countries include Elbadawi (1994), as well as Elbadawi and Soto (1994, 1995).

to provide an adequate representation of the behavior of the LRER, despite the role of "fundamentals" in influencing the LRER. As mentioned previously, the key ingredient in reconciling PPP with a fundamentals-driven theory of the LRER is stationarity of the fundamentals, as in Burkina Faso.

Baffes, Elbadawi, and O'Connell show how their estimated cointegrating equations can be used to construct estimates of the LRER. Given the estimated cointegrating equation, they utilize a variety of statistical techniques to estimate the permanent values of the fundamentals (including employing the actual values, calculating moving averages, and computing Beveridge-Nelson decompositions). In addition, Baffes, Elbadawi, and O'Connell employ counterfactual simulations of the fundamentals, an innovation that can allow these variables to take on out-of-sample values and permits measuring normative as well as positive misalignment. Substituting their estimates of the permanent or sustainable values of the fundamentals into the cointegrating regressions, they derive for both countries LRER estimates that can be compared with the actual RER to provide measures of misalignment. The results suggest that overvaluation was severe in Côte d'Ivoire in 1993 (approximately 34 percent in domestic-currency terms), just prior to the devaluation of the CFA franc, but that Burkina Faso escaped major episodes of overvaluation during the sample period.[14] This finding is consistent with the widely held view that overvaluation was a more serious problem among the middle-income CFA countries than for the low-income countries.

As already indicated, the reduced-form methodology has significant advantages over both the traditional PPP and trade-equations approaches, on the one hand, and simulations of general-equilibrium models, on the other. Accordingly, it has begun to receive a substantial amount of attention from researchers as a technique for estimating the LRER in both industrial- and developing-country contexts.[15] Because of these advantages, it is a promising avenue for further research. Nevertheless, the methodology is not without its own shortcomings. Chief among these are that the statistical tests involved have low power in small samples and that the dynamic specifications required in some of the statistical techniques employed absorb a large number of degrees of freedom, particularly when a priori exclusion restrictions cannot be imposed on the set of included fundamentals. As a result, estimates of the LRER derived using this technique may be fragile. In particular, they may not

---

14. Devarajan also found only a mild misalignment in Burkina Faso.
15. See the survey of empirical research in Chapter 5.

prove to be robust with respect to the set of included fundamentals or to procedures for selecting the "best" model in circumstances in which the set of potential fundamentals is large and time series are short, as is typically the case in developing countries. Operationally, like the trade-equations and structural general-equilibrium approaches, the procedure usually requires an exogenous specification of the equilibrium resource balance. In addition, use of the reduced-form methodology may be hindered not only by inadequate time-series data in low-income countries but also, in crisis situations, by the time-consuming nature of the fairly sophisticated econometric analysis that is involved in implementing it.

Policy and Operational Considerations

The last part of the book, Chapters 11 to 13, rounds out the analysis of techniques for estimating the LRER by discussing three operational considerations. The first has to do with the applicability of the analysis in this book to small low-income countries. All of the approaches to estimating the LRER described here rely on the key macroeconomic role of the real exchange rate in influencing the trade balance by allocating demand and supply between traded and nontraded (or foreign and domestic) goods. Many observers, however, question the empirical strength of this influence, particularly for small low-income countries, on the basis of various types of elasticity pessimism. This issue is taken up in Chapter 11, the first chapter in Part IV. The second consideration has to do with countries having dual exchange markets. The question in this case is how much information the parallel exchange rate—which can be observed directly—contains about the LRER that would prevail if the exchange markets were unified. In an extreme case, if the parallel rate is simply taken as revealing the value of the "true" long-run equilibrium real exchange rate, one would circumvent the need to implement any of the techniques described in this book for measuring the LRER in countries with dual exchange markets. The validity of this approach is considered in Chapter 12. The final issue taken up in Part IV is not directly related to the estimation of the LRER but is likely to be of interest in operational attempts to correct misalignment. It concerns how to estimate, in operational applications, the nominal exchange rate movement required to eliminate any misalignment identified using one of the previously described techniques for measuring the LRER.

Empirical Estimates of Trade Elasticities

Chapter 11 by Ghei and Pritchett analyzes a topic that is central to the macroeconomic role of the real exchange rate and therefore that must be addressed in the definition and estimation of the LRER: what effect does the real exchange rate have empirically on trade flows and external adjustment in developing countries? While the role of relative prices in adjusting trade balances has long been a central tenet of open-economy macroeconomics, this tenet has been questioned by "elasticity pessimists" as well as by advocates of "global monetarism." More recently, the effects of real exchange rate changes on the trade balance have also been called into question by sophisticated empirical analysis (see Rose 1990). Since most definitions of the LRER emphasize the role that the RER plays in the simultaneous achievement of internal and external balance, this issue is an important one for this book.

Ghei and Pritchett ask whether the empirical effectiveness of the real exchange rate in adjusting the trade balance is sufficiently strong to link "external balance" outcomes to the path of the RER, particularly in small low-income countries, for which "elasticity pessimism" has been most widespread. They further ask how, if the RER does significantly affect trade flows, useful estimates of the relevant elasticities can be obtained even for countries in which notional import demand cannot be observed in the historical data because of the prevalence of foreign exchange rationing. Ghei and Pritchett group reasons for doubting elastic import and export responses under three types of elasticity pessimism regarding the elasticity of import demand and export supply in the developing country itself as well as the elasticity of demand for the country's exports in world markets. They find that none of the three pessimisms is justified, even for small low-income countries for which such concerns are most often articulated. Along the way, they provide representative values of the relevant elasticities for small low-income countries. These values can be used by practitioners in empirical applications of the trade-equations approach for countries where the accurate estimation of such elasticities proves to be impractical. Ghei and Pritchett conclude that a reasonable range for the aggregate price elasticity of demand for imports is -0.7 to -0.9, even for low-income countries, and that elasticities of export supply tend to be in the range of 1.0 to 2.0. Consequently, given the typically high world price elasticity of demand for exports from individual countries, RER movements should generally be expected to have significant effects on trade balances.

Using the Parallel Market Premium as an Indicator of Misalignment

The frequent use of quantitative restrictions on the availability of foreign exchange under managed exchange rate systems in many developing countries has in the past given rise to parallel exchange rates as excess demand for foreign exchange spills over into the unofficial market. Since private traders buy and sell foreign exchange at a price that is freely determined in the parallel market, it is natural to interpret the freely determined exchange rate in the unofficial market as a "shadow" exchange rate—that is, as an indicator of the value that the official exchange rate would reach if left to market forces and thus as an estimate of the LRER. Chapter 12, by Ghei and Kamin, on the use of the parallel market premium as an indicator of misalignment, emphasizes that there are at least two reasons why this interpretation is not appropriate.

First, even if the parallel rate accurately represented the value that a freely floating rate would reach if a unified floating system were in effect, that floating rate would not necessarily equal the LRER at any given moment. The reason is that, as an asset price, the spot value of the floating rate would in part depend on its expected future value as well as on the current stock of foreign exchange in residents' hands, both of which are dynamic variables that need not be at their steady-state values for any arbitrarily chosen initial configuration of the economy.[16] When macroeconomic conditions and policies are volatile, as frequently is the case in developing countries with parallel exchange markets, adverse expectations may drive the parallel exchange rate to levels much more depreciated than the LRER.

Second, even when financial markets are tranquil and macroeconomic conditions are close to their average levels, the parallel market exchange rate may still provide a poor approximation of the rate that would prevail under a unified float and hence of the LRER as well. As Ghei and Kamin show, the very conditions that may give rise to a parallel market in the first place—an overvalued official exchange rate, combined with foreign exchange rationing to conserve international reserves—may lead to scarcities of and excess demand for foreign exchange in the parallel market. Unless these demands are restrained by other barriers to imports, therefore, the parallel market exchange rate is likely to be more depreciated than the equilibrium unified rate and would be even more so under unstable macroeconomic conditions.[17]

Ghei and Kamin conduct some empirical exercises to evaluate this conclusion. They compare the parallel market exchange rate with estimates of the equilibrium unified rate computed using averages of the official rate over long periods in which the exchange market was uni-

---

16. This point is simply the familiar one that in flexible exchange rate models shocks typically trigger exchange-rate dynamics as in Dornbusch (1976). Note that if under a floating exchange rate regime the market-determined exchange rate were always equal to the LRER, there would be no need to estimate the LRER for major industrial countries during clean floats as in the research on these countries described in the empirical survey in Chapter 5.

17. Montiel and Ostry (1994) reached a similar conclusion.

fied. They find that, consistent with their theoretical analysis, for Latin American countries the parallel rate tended to be substantially more depreciated than their estimate of the equilibrium unified rate. For countries in Africa and South Asia, in contrast, the parallel rate was not significantly more depreciated than the estimated equilibrium unified rate. However, Ghei and Kamin attribute this outcome to special circumstances prevailing in these countries—namely, poorly enforced exchange controls in African countries and extremely well-enforced import controls in Asian countries. Overall, they conclude that under general conditions the parallel premium is a biased and volatile indicator of misalignment between the official rate and a unified long-run equilibrium exchange rate.

Setting the Nominal Exchange Rate

The primary purpose of estimating the degree of misalignment, of course, is to move the nominal exchange rate in the direction of equilibrium. As mentioned at the outset, moving the nominal exchange rate to attain a desired path of the actual RER is not a straightforward task. The degree to which a domestic price level response will erode any gains in competitiveness achieved through a nominal devaluation, for example, is likely to depend on structural characteristics of the economy such as the nature of the wage-price mechanism, as well as on the nature of the accompanying macroeconomic policies and the initial degree of misalignment. Without a complete and reliable structural model of the economy with endogenous *nominal* variables, ex ante estimates of the real exchange rate change that will accompany a given change in the path of the nominal exchange rate in any given application can only be crude approximations.

Nevertheless, such approximations must inevitably be made in the course of exchange rate management since most policy variables are set in nominal terms. In the absence of a macroeconomic model that determines nominal as well as relative prices, two sources of guidance are available on the relative sizes of the nominal and real changes that are likely to follow a devaluation: the experience of other countries that have successfully devalued and the accounting relationships between the nominal and real changes. The last chapter in this book, by Ghei and Hinkle, examines the usefulness of these two sources of information for estimating the change required in the nominal exchange rate when one has already made an estimate of the real change required using one or more of the methodologies discussed above.

Both theoretically and empirically any combination of RER realignment and inflation is possible after a devaluation—a depreciation, an appreciation, or no change in the RER, accompanied by an acceleration of the trend inflation rate or a return to predevaluation price trends. The key to a successful devaluation is monetary discipline and appropriate demand management policies. Successful devaluations (that is, those accompanied by appropriate macroeconomic policies) in open developing economies have typically led to a depreciation of the external RER of 30–65 percent of the nominal devaluation in domestic-currency terms. The RER typically depreciates on impact by the full amount of the devaluation and then gradually appreciates as the domestic price level shifts upward. In successful devaluations, the aggregate price level has generally shifted upwards by 20–55 percent of the nominal devaluation expressed in percentage terms in domestic currency with no increase in the long-term trend inflation rate.

Chapter 13 by Ghei and Hinkle describes a simple method for preparing "first-pass" estimates of the effects of nominal exchange rate changes on actual RERs in developing countries. The chapter sets out a consistent accounting framework in the form of an eight-equation structure, which can easily be incorporated into a spreadsheet format. This framework can be used to calculate the nominal exchange rate required to achieve a given real exchange rate target, conditional on an assumption about the response of domestic nominal wages to the nominal devaluation or to the change in domestic prices. Alternatively, the framework can be used to calculate the real exchange rate adjustment that a given nominal exchange rate would produce, on the basis of assumptions about the behavior of nominal wages or the degree of pass-through. Although the methodology, not being based on a general-equilibrium model, can provide only first-pass approximations to the nominal changes, it can be a useful tool in the hands of informed analysts. As an illustration of its usefulness, the authors analyze various policy scenarios used to determine the effectiveness of the nominal CFA franc devaluation in altering the real exchange rate and compare these with the actual outcome.

In short, the accounting framework described in this last chapter describes a simple yet reasonably accurate method for translating a desired real exchange rate movement into a required adjustment in the instrument actually controlled by the authorities—the nominal exchange rate. It thus complements the methodologies for measuring real exchange rate misalignment that came before.

Conclusions

Developing countries that avoid extreme exchange rate arrangements—currency boards and floating rates with purely domestic objectives for monetary policy—need to manage the nominal exchange rate. In doing so, they have long been enjoined to avoid misalignment—that is, the emergence of large gaps between the actual real exchange rate and some notion of a sustainable "equilibrium" real exchange rate. Defining and measuring this sustainable equilibrium real exchange rate, however, has not proven to be an easy task, either for practitioners or for researchers. Unfortunately, the urgency of doing so has not gone away and may even have increased in recent years as the result of increasing financial integration.

This book provides a unified overview of the conceptual and empirical problems that arise in defining and measuring the real exchange rate in specific applications. It then explores and illustrates alternative empirical methods for measuring the long-run equilibrium real exchange rate. Four distinct approaches to doing so are considered. Although all of these approaches have shortcomings, there are circumstances under which the use of each may be appropriate. Hence, to conclude this overview, we briefly summarize the main advantages and disadvantages of each approach and describe the situations for which each is best suited.

The relative PPP-based approach can be justified as a method of estimating the LRER when the RER is shown to be stationary in a time-series sense. In this case, estimation of the LRER boils down to choosing an appropriate base period consisting of one or more years during which the RER was close to its equilibrium value (the PPP base-year approach) or taking a sample average of the actual RER (the PPP-average or trend approach). However, the applicability of these relatively simple methods is restricted by the empirical observation that real exchange rates in developing countries often prove to be nonstationary. Nevertheless, because of the simplicity of its application and the complexity of alternative methodologies, the PPP approach is likely to continue to be the only feasible approach for the estimation of misalignment in large multicountry research studies and hence to remain the method of choice for such studies. It is also useful for initial detection of misalignment, particularly in high-inflation countries, and for identification of hypotheses for subsequent analysis using more sophisticated techniques.

When the RER is nonstationary, this nonstationarity must be the result of nonstationarity in some subset of its fundamental determinants. Estimating the LRER then consists of three steps: identifying the relevant set of nonstationary fundamentals, determining their "long-run equilibrium" (sustainable) values, and determining how these fundamentals are empirically linked to the LRER. The remaining three methods of estimation described in the following paragraphs permit the incorporation of permanent changes in the fundamentals into the analysis.

The *trade-equations approach* is a well-established estimation technique that allows the estimated LRER to depend on the values taken by fundamentals. This approach is structural so the determination of the LRER can be understood. It makes use of a small set of behavioral parameters that are widely estimated and thus readily available, and it is relatively simple to apply. Hence, the trade-equations approach has been the work-horse of empirical analysis and is still widely used by the IMF and others for industrial as well as developing countries.[18] However, it relies on an ad hoc specification of the trade balance, and its recursive partial-equilibrium framework may ignore potentially important macroeconomic interactions. Furthermore, like other methodologies, the trade-equations approach requires often problematic estimates of the under-lying and target resource balances and forecasts of the "permanent" values of potentially volatile fundamental variables such as the terms of trade and private capital flows. Nevertheless, in country applications in which data limitations or time constraints do not permit the implemen-tation of the more sophisticated approaches described below, the trade-equations approach may be the only feasible way of taking into account changes in the fundamentals. Under these circumstances the trade-equations approach, despite its limitations, may be the method of choice.

In principle, *simulation of empirical general-equilibrium models* should dominate other estimation methods. This approach allows the estimated LRER to reflect the full range of known macroeconomic interactions in the economy. Since the entire dynamic path of the RER from its current value to the steady-state (or semisteady-state, if conditioned on some slowly adjusting variable) LRER can be simulated, the approach also provides complete information about the dynamics. The model-based general-equilibrium method, however, suffers from a variety of short-comings. When implemented in the form of "real-time" simulations, it remains dependent, like the trade-equations approach, on an exogenous specification of the equilibrium resource balance and on forecasts of sometimes volatile exogenous variables. Moreover, it places relatively strong demands on economic theory, on the power of statistical tech-niques, and on the availability and quality of data. Made-to-suit models for individual developing countries with limited data and possibly un-stable economic structures are vulnerable to doubts about model speci-fication and parameter stability. Estimates derived from such models may thus fail to command much credibility, particularly when the mod-els on which they are based have no previous track record. For the near future, it is likely that estimates of the LRER derived from simulations of macroeconomic models should be treated as indicative and used to supplement and inform other approaches to estimation. Model simula-tions may be most attractive in applications in which an existing model

---

18. See, for example, Isard and Faruqee (1998) and Wren-Lewis and Driver (1998).

has demonstrated its usefulness through an established record of tracking the macroeconomic performance of a particular economy.

Recent developments in unit-root econometrics seem to hold special promise for the estimation of long-run equilibrium real exchange rates. Estimates of the LRER based on cointegrating equations are derived from a *single-equation reduced-form approach*. This approach follows naturally from the time-series tests for stationarity required to assess the applicability of the simple PPP-based approach. Relative to the general-equilibrium models, it places fewer demands on economic theory since the theory required is about long-run relationships, not short-run macroeconomic dynamics. Moreover, fewer data (time series) are required since the researcher needs time-series data only for the variables that can be expected to appear in the reduced-form equation for the real exchange rate in short-run macroeconomic equilibrium. For these reasons, the reduced-form methodology has the potential to significantly advance our ability to generate credible empirical estimates of the LRER in specific country cases.

Despite these advantages, it would be premature to suggest that cointegration-based estimation of the LRER should dominate the other techniques under all circumstances. The method shares some of the other approaches' limitations and is subject to others that are specific to it. When net capital inflows are treated as a fundamental, for example, the problematic estimation of a target resource balance is a required input for this approach, just as it is for several others. Even when they are not, an independent method for estimating the "permanent" values of the fundamentals such as the terms of trade is indispensable for the implementation of the reduced-form single-equation approach. Determining the permanent value of these may prove to be as problematic as the estimation of a target resource balance. Moreover, as indicated above, the statistical tests associated with this approach tend to have low power in small samples. They are particularly vulnerable to low degrees of freedom when a priori exclusion restrictions cannot be imposed on the fundamentals or when the time-series data of the country under study is characterized by structural breaks. Thus, while the method may require fewer time-series than general equilibrium models, achieving results of reasonable confidence may only be possible with time series of greater length than may be available in many developing countries. Estimates of the LRER derived using the reduced-form technique may thus prove to be too fragile to dominate those from the more transparent structural approaches, particularly in policy applications.

Nonetheless, the results achieved with the reduced-form method to date, both in the previous research surveyed in Part II of the book as well as in Chapter 10 in Part III, provide justification for additional work using this approach. More research is also needed comparing the results from the reduced-form methodology with those obtainable from the other approaches set out here. Our hope is that this book will contribute to motivating such research.

Where, then, do we currently stand in our ability to estimate the LRER in developing countries, and what are the policy implications of the current state of the art? The "true" value of the LRER, of course, is unobservable, even ex post. Thus, we cannot evaluate the various methodologies examined in this book in the same manner that theories of nominal exchange rate determination under floating exchange rates are evaluated empirically—that is, by their ability to track the variable being explained in sample or to predict it out of sample. However, other methods of evaluating these techniques are available. Two such methods are described in the survey of empirical work in Chapter 5. First, empirical estimates of the LRER for particular countries can be judged by how well measures of misalignment derived from such estimates are able to replicate historical episodes for which RER misalignment has emerged as the consensus diagnosis ex post. Second, if the notion of the LRER has any meaning, then a current gap between the actual RER and the estimated LRER should have predictive value for (that is, should Granger-cause) the future *actual* RER. Both of these tests have been met by available techniques for estimating the LRER. Moreover, error-correction equations based on lagged estimates of misalignment from the reduced-form general-equilibrium methodology, as well as on *lagged* changes in fundamentals, have proved able to explain a substantial part of the variance of the *change* in the actual RER (a stationary variable) in several applications.

Although much has been learned about the estimation of the LRER in recent years, much still remains to be learned. Accurately establishing precise targets for a managed exchange rate—for example, for a new pegged rate after a devaluation—is currently beyond the state of the art. Furthermore, if some of the fundamental variables determining the LRER such as the terms of trade or capital flows are completely unpredictable or subject to repeated shock to their "permanent" values, the LRER will also be unpredictable or volatile. More research is also needed on how the results from different methodologies for estimating the LRER are likely to be related to each other in different country cases.

Yet, while we may not at present know enough to calculate the LRER in specific applications with great precision, we do know enough to sound warning signals of serious misalignment.[19] The implication for

---

19. For a discussion of the interpretation of apparent misalignments, see Isard and Faruqee (1998), pp. 1–3 and 16–17.

nominal exchange rate policy is this: except perhaps for periods of large economic dislocations, ignorance about the empirical value of the LRER cannot be used to underpin arguments for extreme exchange rate arrangements—for example, currency boards or completely clean floats with only monetary targets—that imply abandoning the management of nominal exchange rates. We hope that the cautiously optimistic tone of this conclusion can be put to the test in future work motivated by the contents of this book.

Part I

The Real Exchange Rate: Concepts and Measurement

2

External Real Exchange Rates: Purchasing Power Parity, the Mundell-Fleming Model, and Competitiveness in Traded Goods

Lawrence E. Hinkle and Fabien Nsengiyumva*

The real exchange rate is generally defined in the economic literature in two principal ways: either (a) in *external* terms as the nominal exchange rate adjusted for price level differences *between countries* (that is, as the ratio of the aggregate foreign price level or cost level to the home country's aggregate price level or cost level measured in a common currency) or (b) in *internal* terms as the ratio of the domestic price of tradable to nontradable goods *within a single country*. The first of these concepts of the RER derives originally from the purchasing power parity (PPP) theory. It compares the relative value of currencies by measuring the relative prices of foreign and domestic consumption or production baskets. Following the terminology adopted by De Gregorio and Wolf (1994), this chapter refers to this RER concept as the *external* real exchange rate because it compares the relative prices of baskets of goods produced (or consumed) in different countries. The second concept, the internal RER, captures the internal relative price incentive in a particular economy for producing or consuming tradable as opposed to nontradable goods. The real exchange rate in this case is an indicator of domestic resource allocation incentives in the home economy. To

* Ms. Ingrid Ivins provided research assistance in the preparation of this chapter. Ted Ahlers developed the original computer spread sheet used for calculating multilateral RER indexes. The authors are grateful to Amparo Ballivian, Shanta Devarajan, Peter Montiel, and three anonymous readers for helpful suggestions and comments on earlier drafts.

distinguish this second concept from the first, this real exchange rate is referred to here as the *internal* RER.

Within each of these two broad RER concepts, there are several alternative formulations derived from different analytical approaches. There are three primary versions of the external RER. These are based alternatively on purchasing power parity theory, on the Mundell-Fleming one composite good model, and on the law of one price and competitiveness in the pricing of internationally traded goods. Similarly, there are several different definitions of the internal RER based on two-, three-, or multi-good models. The existence of multiple concepts and alternative measures of the RER raises questions concerning the theoretical and empirical relationship among these, the interpretation of differences in their behavior, and the appropriate measure to use in given circumstances.

The three chapters in Part I of this book discuss the different theoretical concepts of the RER, their empirical measurement, and the relationships among them. This chapter reviews indexes for measuring the *external* RER in developing countries. Measurement of the internal RER and the relationship between the internal and external RERs are discussed in the following two chapters on the two-good and three-good internal RERs.

Several different types of problems are encountered in the measurement of the external RER. At a conceptual level, one set of problems arises from the multiplicity of theories underlying the external RER. The various theories that have motivated the different definitions of the external RER imply the use of different empirical price and cost indexes in computing the external RER. Some theories are also ambiguous as to exactly what baskets and weightings of domestic and foreign goods should be used empirically. These conceptual problems are common to both industrial- and developing-country applications.

A second set of problems is practical and empirical. These problems tend to be particularly acute in developing-country applications. Parallel foreign exchange markets, substantial smuggling and unrecorded trade, and large shifts in the terms of trade, trade policy, and trade patterns create complexities not commonly encountered in measuring the external RER in industrial countries. Moreover, even after one has sorted through the conceptual issues involved in the use of alternative price or cost indexes, it is often difficult to find reasonably exact empirical measures of the desired indexes in developing countries. For many developing countries only the consumer price index (CPI) and the gross domestic product (GDP) deflator are available. Hence, the analyst's choice is often limited to these.

In light of the above problems, this chapter attempts to describe best practice in the calculation of external RER indexes for developing countries. It has three objectives:

a. To review and operationalize the definitions of the three principal theoretical concepts of the external RER as a starting point for the subsequent discussion of their empirical measurement;
b. To examine important empirical problems that often complicate the measurement of the external RER in developing countries; and
c. To clarify the interrelationships among the different external RERs.

This chapter and the following two are intended as user's guides. They therefore give enough details of the methodologies and calculations that readers who wish to use these indexes can replicate the calculations. Data from Côte d'Ivoire prior to the devaluation of the CFA francs in January 1994 are used to illustrate the calculations.

The rest of this chapter is divided into four sections and two appendixes. Certain features are common to all external RER indexes, but others depend upon the particular concept being measured. The next section discusses those features that are common to all external RER indexes. The following section on the measurement of different RER concepts then reviews the three principal external RER concepts and examines the methodological issues that are specific to measuring each of these. This is followed by a section comparing the effects of changes in the terms of trade on the three external RERs and their implications for competitiveness. The final section summarizes and concludes. Appendix A briefly reviews the International Comparison Programme and the purchasing power parity exchange rates derived from it. Appendix B sets out in more detail the relationship between competitiveness and the different external RERs.

Common Features of All External Real Exchange Rate Indexes

The concept of the external real exchange rate derives originally from expenditure or purchasing power parity (PPP) theory. Over time, two additional concepts of the external RER developed based on the law of one price and competitiveness in production of traded goods and on the Mundell-Fleming one composite good model or competitiveness in aggregate production costs of all goods. Relative labor costs expressed in foreign currency are a fourth, although somewhat less common, measure of the external RER.

To empirically calculate these external RER indexes, four elements are needed: (1) the operational mathematical formulas to be used, (2) appropriate measures of the nominal exchange rate, (3) country weights and the averaging method to be used in computing the multilateral RER, and (4) empirical counterparts of the price or cost indexes desired theoretically. The first three elements—the operational formulas, the nominal exchange rate, and the country weights—are common to the various different versions of the external RER. The fourth element, the appropriate price or cost index, varies with the version of the external RER being constructed. This section reviews the elements that are common to all external RER indexes.

Computation of External RERs: Common Formula and Conventions

Similar conventions and formulas are used for calculating all of the basic versions of the external RER. The following subsection sets out these conventions, which are used in the remainder of the volume. Readers already familiar with these conventions may wish to skim this subsection.

Domestic Versus Foreign Currency Terms

Nominal exchange rates and external RER indexes can be measured in domestic-currency terms (units of domestic currency per unit of foreign exchange, E_{dc}) or in foreign-currency terms (units of foreign exchange per unit of domestic currency, E_{fc}). The domestic- and foreign-currency measures are the inverses of each other, as shown in equation 2.1:

$$(2.1) \qquad E_{dc} = \frac{1}{E_{fc}}.$$

The term appreciation (depreciation) is used to refer to an increase (decrease) in the value of the home currency relative to foreign currencies. An appreciation corresponds to an *increase* (or an upward movement graphically) in the RER indexes in foreign-currency terms but to a *decrease* (or a downward movement) in an index in domestic-currency terms since this is the inverse of the index in foreign-currency terms. For some purposes, it is useful to express RER indexes in domestic-currency terms and for others in foreign-currency terms. Both versions are widely used in the literature and are used in this volume. For ease of exposition, most of the equations in this chapter are expressed in domestic-currency terms; but, unless otherwise noted, all graphs are in foreign-currency terms so that an upward movement indicates an appreciation.[1]

---

1. Appendix C of Chapter 7 on operational approaches to estimating equilibrium RERs gives formulas for converting appreciations and depreciations in foreign-currency terms to domestic currency and vice versa.

The Bilateral RER

Irrespective of the price or cost concept employed, the external RER for the home economy can be defined either in relation to one trading partner or to an average for all of its main trading partners or competitor countries. In the first case of a pair of countries, it is called a *bilateral* real exchange rate (BRER). In the second multicountry case, it is called a *multilateral* real exchange rate, which is also known as a real *effective* exchange rate (REER), and is calculated as a weighted average.

The bilateral RER is the simplest and easiest to calculate of the external RER indexes. It compares the price of a representative consumption or production basket in the home country with the price of a representative basket in a foreign country measured in the same currency, either domestic or foreign, and indicates the relative value of the domestic and foreign currencies. The bilateral RER is useful both as a bilateral and as a more general indicator of the external RER in cases in which a country belongs to a currency bloc, such as the dollar or the franc zones, or has one dominant trading partner. For these reasons, the bilateral RER has been widely used in empirical work, particularly before the increased availability of high-powered personal computers facilitated the calculation of multilateral RERs.

The external bilateral RER index in domestic-currency terms ($BRER_{dc}$) between the domestic economy (d) and a foreign country (f) is given by equation 2.2:

(2.2)
$$BRER_{dc} = \frac{E_{dc} \cdot P_{Gf}}{P_{Gd}}$$

where E_{dc} is the index of the nominal exchange rate, defined as units of domestic currency per one unit of foreign currency. P_{Gf} and P_{Gd} are the foreign and the domestic general or aggregate price indexes, respectively.[2] The subscript *dc* indicates that the RER is defined in domestic-currency terms. A decline in the $BRER_{dc}$ index (which corresponds to a real exchange rate appreciation) reflects an increase in the price or cost of domestic goods and services relative to foreign goods and services. The equivalent definition of the external bilateral real exchange rate index in foreign-currency terms is shown in equation 2.3:

(2.3)
$$BRER_{fc} = \frac{E_{fc} \cdot P_{Gd}}{P_{Gf}} = \frac{1}{BRER_{dc}}.$$

---

2. To simplify the notation in this chapter, the bases for all indexes are set at 1.00 in the reference period rather than at 100.

Bilateral RERs in relation to the dollar, the two other major currency blocks (the yen, and the DM or the euro), the currency in terms of which a country pegs or manages its exchange rate, and the currency of a country's principal trading partner are often particularly useful for analytical purposes. These bilateral RERs are both as simple to calculate and more broadly representative than the bilateral RERs with smaller trading partners.

Table 2.1 illustrates how radically bilateral RERs of developing countries can diverge as a result of movements in the major currencies and the policies of individual countries. It shows the bilateral RERs between Côte d'Ivoire and its competitors, along with weighted averages for country groupings. While Côte d'Ivoire's RER appreciated moderately (by 8–9 percent) from 1985 to 1993 relative to France and European countries as a group and depreciated relative to Japan (by 12 percent), it appreciated by 60 percent relative to the dollar, by almost 100 percent relative to the currencies of its non-African developing-country competitors, and by more than 400 percent relative to its African competitors. Similarly, figure 2.1 shows the movement of the bilateral RERs between

Figure 2.1 *The Bilateral RERs Between Côte d'Ivoire and France, Germany, Japan, and the United States, 1980–96 (1985=100)*

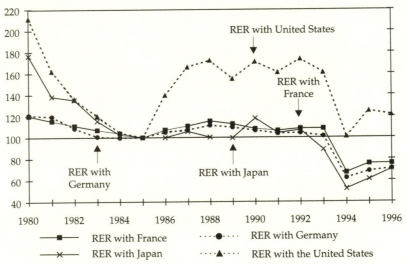

Note: The RERs were calculated using CPIs and official exchange rates. An upward movement represents an appreciation of the RER for Côte d'Ivoire.
Source: Computed from World Bank data.

Table 2.1 Bilateral Real Exchange Rate Indexes for Côte d'Ivoire Computed Using CPIs and Official Exchange Rates, 1980–96 (1985=100)

Country	Adjusted IFS country weights %	1980	1981	1982	1983	1984	1985	1986	1987	1988	1989	1990	1991	1992	1993	1994	1995	1996
European Countries[a]	53.9	122.1	116.7	110.1	105.5	102.6	100.0	107.9	111.0	114.4	111.1	107.0	103.9	106.5	109.1	67.6	76.6	76.7
France	25.9	120.2	115.3	111.0	106.9	103.8	100.0	107.0	110.7	115.3	112.6	108.0	106.4	108.4	108.4	67.2	75.5	75.8
Netherlands	5.5	118.9	118.3	106.3	100.7	99.7	100.0	104.9	107.6	112.5	112.6	109.7	106.4	107.2	106.3	65.4	72.0	74.0
Italy	4.4	140.2	131.7	119.7	106.7	101.4	100.0	104.9	107.3	110.7	103.6	98.8	94.5	99.2	115.7	73.4	89.5	81.6
Germany	7.2	120.9	119.6	108.6	100.7	99.7	100.0	105.1	106.9	111.3	109.4	106.4	103.7	104.1	101.2	62.0	68.4	70.8
United Kingdom	6.4	127.6	110.7	105.0	105.6	103.8	100.0	121.6	124.6	121.8	115.9	113.0	105.6	113.4	125.4	77.1	92.0	90.7
Spain	1.9	121.5	115.5	106.9	113.3	103.8	100.0	107.7	111.2	108.0	96.9	90.9	85.9	88.8	100.7	65.1	73.6	72.2
Belgium-Luxembourg	2.7	112.0	111.8	112.5	106.5	103.0	100.0	105.7	107.1	112.5	110.4	105.2	102.2	104.4	104.4	63.4	70.0	72.0
Other Industrial Countries[a]	20.1	191.9	148.3	131.7	115.1	101.7	100.0	124.1	139.9	138.3	127.9	144.4	132.8	142.5	128.9	79.1	95.9	98.5
United States	9.8	211.3	162.1	135.8	119.9	104.5	100.0	139.6	165.9	172.1	154.9	170.9	160.8	173.4	160.8	100.9	124.7	121.2
Japan	7.0	176.5	138.2	135.2	115.4	102.6	100.0	99.9	105.6	100.2	99.5	117.8	104.1	106.9	88.6	52.0	60.9	70.3
Canada	1.8	198.3	153.0	126.4	108.6	99.5	100.0	139.0	156.6	150.8	130.4	142.5	130.0	150.1	150.3	102.1	127.6	124.9
Australia	1.6	148.3	113.4	102.5	95.6	85.8	100.0	136.3	148.1	133.2	115.6	127.1	121.2	141.3	143.3	84.0	100.7	93.0

(Table continues on next page)

47

(Table 2.1 continued)

Country	Adjusted IFS country weights %	1980	1981	1982	1983	1984	1985	1986	1987	1988	1989	1990	1991	1992	1993	1994	1995	1996
CFA Countries[a]	2.0	134.6	132.2	125.6	113.8	106.5	100.0	101.8	96.2	101.2	104.0	102.0	103.7	108.1	114.1	106.4	106.8	104.9
Cameroon	2.0	134.6	132.2	125.6	113.8	106.5	100.0	101.8	96.2	101.2	104.0	102.0	103.7	108.1	114.1	106.4	106.8	104.9
African Countries (non-CFA)[a]	12.9	133.1	74.0	59.9	61.2	82.8	100.0	222.3	436.4	403.1	408.1	448.7	449.5	570.1	547.1	297.6	243.6	222.5
Nigeria	6.4	238.0	188.3	169.6	134.9	93.0	100.0	263.8	669.2	527.9	538.2	635.9	680.7	913.1	740.8	288.8	211.5	172.2
Ghana	6.4	74.4	29.1	21.2	27.8	73.7	100.0	187.4	284.6	307.7	309.4	316.7	296.8	355.9	404.0	306.6	280.5	287.6
Developing Countries (excluding Africa)[a]	11.1	148.8	120.7	104.6	99.4	93.6	100.0	153.6	194.8	200.8	185.6	220.4	212.9	219.5	197.4	123.9	142.4	136.4
Malaysia	4.4	178.1	145.4	123.9	108.2	95.6	100.0	146.9	176.2	192.6	182.8	206.8	197.6	194.8	181.0	113.9	131.8	128.5
Indonesia	2.7	145.3	110.3	93.9	105.2	97.6	100.0	155.2	224.5	230.5	214.5	240.9	228.7	245.8	220.2	135.1	163.3	158.2
Colombia	2.2	147.3	112.8	94.6	88.6	88.7	100.0	163.4	203.9	211.8	203.1	240.0	227.6	238.8	211.4	106.7	122.0	115.2
China	1.8	101.3	95.1	92.1	85.8	89.2	100.0	156.4	190.9	170.7	140.1	203.9	212.0	224.6	191.5	159.9	168.5	154.9
Total[a]	100.0	138.5	116.2	105.2	99.6	98.7	100.0	126.5	147.2	148.5	142.9	148.0	142.8	152.0	148.5	91.1	100.3	99.2

Note: a. The REERs for the regional groupings have been computed as geometric averages of the bilateral RERs in their constituent countries.
Source: Computed from World Bank data.

48

the CFA franc, French franc, and the major currency blocks. France, the United States, Germany, and Japan are also Côte d'Ivoire's four largest trading partners and account for one half of the weights in table 2.1.

The Multilateral or Effective RER (REER)

The multilateral or real *effective* exchange rate index (REER) is used when multiple trading partners are considered.[3] It is a weighted external real exchange rate index. The REER is defined in domestic-currency terms as shown in equation 2.4:

$$(2.4) \qquad REER_{dc} = \prod_{i=1}^{m} \left[E_{dc_1} P_{Gi} \right]^{\omega_{id}} \cdot \frac{1}{P_{Gd}}$$

where m is the number of trading partners or competitors of the home country and $\prod$ denotes the product of the bracketed terms over the m countries. The geometric averaging method is used where ω_{id} is the appropriate weight for each foreign country i ($i = 1, ...m$) and the sum of weights must equal one, as shown in equation 2.5:

$$(2.5) \qquad \sum_{i=1}^{m} \omega_{id} = 1 .$$

The equivalent definition of the REER in foreign-currency terms is expressed by equation 2.6 as follows:

$$(2.6) \qquad REER_{fc} = \prod_{i=1}^{m} \left[\frac{E_{fc_i}}{P_{Gi}} \right]^{\omega_{id}} \cdot P_{Gd} = \frac{1}{REER_{dc}}.$$

The REER can also be defined as an arithmetic average. Although the arithmetic average is easier to calculate, the geometric averaging technique is used in the above formulations because a geometric index has certain properties of symmetry and consistency that an arithmetic index

---

3. The term "effective" has two common but different meanings when used to describe exchange rates in the economic literature. Its first meaning is "weighted average," and this is the sense in which the term effective is used here. The second common meaning of an effective exchange rate is one that includes the effects of tariffs, subsidies, and other charges on the domestic costs of imports and domestic prices of exports. Such exchange rates are referred to in this book as including taxes. The terms bilateral, multilateral, and effective indicate the number of external trading partners to which an RER applies and, therefore, do not apply to the internal RER, which is an indicator of relative internal domestic prices in a particular country.

does not. In analyzing RER indexes, one is often interested in determining not only the level of the index at a particular point in time but also the *rate* at which the RER is appreciating or depreciating over time. In an arithmetic index, the percentage changes between any two dates depends upon the reference date used for the index so that rescaling (or rebasing) the index from the original base year equal 100 to a different reference year equal 100 affects the percentage changes in the index. A geometric index, in contrast, gives RER levels for which the percentage change between two dates is not influenced by the choice of the base period and may, therefore, be readily rescaled to have a different reference year equal 100. In addition, an arithmetic index, in effect, gives larger weights to currencies that have appreciated or depreciated to a significant extent relative to the home currency. A geometric average treats depreciating and appreciating currencies in an entirely symmetric manner.[4]

There are two equivalent ways of calculating the real effective exchange rate. These two methods decompose the components of the REER index differently and provide supplementary empirical information useful in analyzing the evolution of the effective exchange rate indexes.[5] The first method calculates the REER as a geometric weighted average of the bilateral RERs of the home country with each of its main trading partners or competitors. The real effective exchange rate in domestic-currency terms is then given by equation 2.7:

(2.7) $$RER_{dc} = \prod_{i=1}^{m} BRER_{dc_i}^{\omega_{id}}$$

where $BRER_{dc}$ is the bilateral real exchange rate in domestic currency as defined by equation 2.2.

The second method calculates the REER as the product of the nominal effective exchange rate and the effective relative price index. Equation 2.4 is then rewritten as equation 2.8:

(2.8) $$REER_{dc} = \frac{NEER_{dc} \cdot EP_{Gf}}{P_{Gd}}$$

in which:

---

4. The properties of the geometric averages are discussed further in Brodsky (1982) and Maciejewski (1983).

5. These two methods are shown here only for the real effective exchange rate defined in domestic-currency terms (equation 2.4). They are equally applicable to the REER defined in foreign-currency terms.

(2.9)
$$NEER_{dc} = \prod_{i=1}^{m} E_{dc_i}^{\omega_{id}}$$

(2.10)
$$EP_{Gf} = \prod_{i=1}^{m} P_{Gi}^{\omega_{id}} \ .$$

$NEER_{dc}$ is the nominal effective exchange rate in domestic-currency terms between the home economy and its trading partners or competitors. EP_{Gf} is the geometric weighted average (or effective) foreign aggregate price index for the home country's trading partners.

The real effective exchange rate indexes obtained from equations 2.7 and 2.8 are exactly the same, as the two equations are mathematically equivalent. However, the two alternative calculations generate different statistical information as by-products.

Computing the REER as the weighted average of bilateral RERs can provide calculations of bilateral RER indexes for individual countries or subsets of countries. In cases in which a country pegs its exchange rate to or targets it on that of another country, it is often useful to analyze the home country's REER in terms of (a) changes in the home country's bilateral RER with the peg currency caused by differences in inflation rates in the home and peg countries and (b) changes in the home country's REER relative to the bilateral RER with the peg currency caused by inflation and exchange rate movements in third-country currencies. This relationship is given in equation 2.11:

(2.11)
$$REER_{dc} = BRER_{dc_b} \cdot \frac{REER_{dc}}{BRER_{dc_b}}$$

where $BRER_{dc_b}$ is the bilateral RER with the base or target currency.

Calculating the REER as the product of the nominal effective exchange rate and the effective relative price index, by contrast, makes possible a separate analysis of the effects of movements in nominal exchange rates and foreign prices as shown in equation 2.8 above.[6] It also permits a further decomposition of the NEER to express movements in it in terms of changes in the exchange rate between the home currency and its peg currency and in the NEER relative to the peg currency. This decomposition is shown in equation 2.12:

(2.12)
$$NEER_{dc} = E_{dc_b} \cdot \frac{NEER_{dc}}{E_{dc_b}}$$

---

6. NEERs for selected developing countries are reported in IFS.

where E_{dc_b} is the nominal exchange rate with the base or target currency. Such a decomposition is often useful because the pegged rate in equation 2.12 is typically a policy variable or target while the NEER relative to the peg currency is exogenous for the pegging country.

The usefulness of these alternative REER decompositions can be illustrated with data from Côte d'Ivoire. Figure 2.2, for example, decomposes its REER into its NEER and effective relative price indexes. It indicates that Côte d'Ivoire's relative price performance was actually quite good in the period 1985–93, with its prices falling by 20 percent relative to its trading partners. However, its REER, nevertheless, appreciated by almost 50 percent as a result of the 85 percent appreciation in its NEER.

When the home country's currency is pegged, like Côte d'Ivoire's, to another currency, it may be also useful to use equation 2.12 to express the NEER in terms of the bilateral exchange rate relative to the peg currency and the NEER relative to the peg currency. This procedure separates the effects of changes in the peg, a policy variable, from the other exogenous changes in the NEER. For the CFA countries, however, such

Figure 2.2 *The Nominal Effective Exchange Rate (NEER), Relative Consumer Prices, and REER for Côte d'Ivoire, 1980–93 (1985=100)*

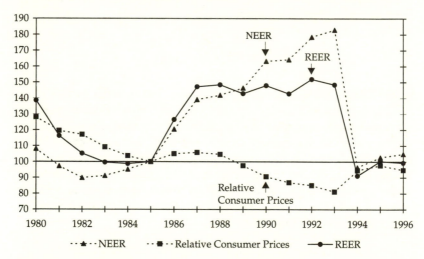

Note: The NEER and REER were calculated using official exchange rates and adjusted IFS country weights. The relative consumer price index is the CPI for Côte d'Ivoire divided by the weighted average of the CPIs for its foreign competitors. An upward movement represents an appreciation of the NEER, REER, or relative consumer prices.
Source: Computed from World Bank data.

a decomposition is not necessary as the pegged rate to the French franc remained at 50:1 for the entire period from 1948 through 1993. Hence, all of the variation in Côte d'Ivoire's NEER during this period was due to exogenous changes in the exchange rate between the French franc and other currencies.

It is worth noting, however, that because of different trading patterns, and hence country weights, the NEER for the home currency and that for the peg currency may behave quite differently. Figure 2.3 shows that, while the NEER for France appreciated by about 15 percent in the period 1985–93, the NEER for Côte d'Ivoire appreciated by 320 percent because of its different trading partners. Hence, Côte d'Ivoire experienced a huge nominal appreciation as a result of its peg to the French franc, even though the NEER for the franc itself only appreciated moderately. Such divergences can have significant implications for decisions about the appropriateness of maintaining a given peg.

Figure 2.3 *The Nominal Effective Exchange Rates (NEER) for Côte d'Ivoire and France at Official Exchange Rates, 1980–96 (1985=100)*

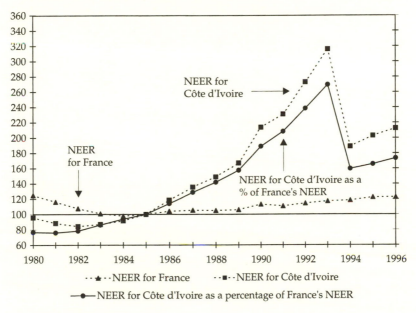

Note: The NEERs have been calculated using IFS country weights. An upward movement represents an appreciation of the NEER.
Source: Computed from World Bank data.

Similarly, figure 2.4 uses equation 2.11 to express Côte d'Ivoire's REER in terms of its RER relative to the French franc, the peg currency, and the REER between the French franc and the currencies of Côte d'Ivoire's other trading partners. It shows that while Côte d'Ivoire's bilateral RER appreciated by about 10 percent relative to the French franc, Côte d'Ivoire's REER appreciated by an additional 20 percent relative to France's RER because of larger real depreciations by Côte d'Ivoire's trading partners.

Determining the Appropriate Nominal Exchange Rate

Industrial countries typically have unified exchange rates and currencies that are freely convertible for current and most capital transactions. In these circumstances, the single nominal exchange rate truly represents the market price of foreign exchange.

In developing countries, however, the situation may be more complicated. Although convertible currencies and unified exchange rates are becoming more common, many developing-country currencies are still

Figure 2.4 *The Bilateral RER with France and the REER for Côte d'Ivoire, 1980–96 (1985=100)*

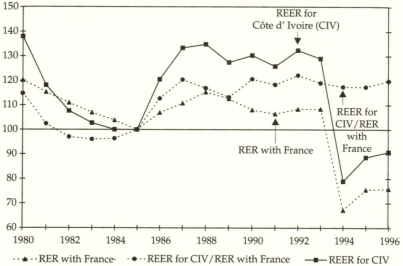

Note: CIV=Côte d' Ivoire. The RER and REER were calculated using CPIs official exchange rates and IFS country weights. An upward movement represents an appreciation of the RER and REER for Côte d'Ivoire.
Source: Computed from World Bank data.

not readily convertible for capital transactions. Sometimes current trans-actions are also subject to exchange controls; and smuggling, unrecorded, and misrecorded trade may be common. Hence, at different points in time there may be a quite significant parallel (or black) market for for-eign exchange in the home country, in some of its major trading part-ners, or both. The coverage and importance of these parallel markets may vary from country to country and from period to period. Under such circumstances, an RER computed using only official nominal ex-change rates could be quite misleading as an economic indicator.

When a parallel market exists, a country has, in effect, *two* external real exchange rates, one for transactions at the official nominal rate and one for transactions at the parallel rate. These two rates may create quite different incentives for different types of activities. Which of the two RERs is the more relevant analytically will depend upon the situation in the country concerned. It may in some cases be desirable to use both these RERs for analytical purposes rather than trying to arrive at a single unique measure of the external RER.

Jorgensen and Paldam (1986) argue, however, that an average of the parallel and official rates is usually much more stable and representa-tive than either of the two rates separately. Misalignments in the paral-lel and official rates tend to be in opposite directions (the parallel rate being undervalued when the official rate is overvalued) and policy shocks such as large devaluations often move the two rates in opposite direc-tions. Hence, when a parallel market exists in the home country or its trading partner(s), one possibility for calculating a single representative bilateral RER is to use a weighted average of the official and parallel market nominal exchange rates. The weights should reflect the share of transactions at each rate and corrections should be applied to the paral-lel rate for the extra risks and other costs of transactions in the informal market. In practice, however, it is likely to be quite difficult to obtain the data required to arrive at anything more than reasonable assumptions about the shares of transactions taking place in the official and parallel markets and about the extra costs of transactions at the parallel rate.

Parallel foreign exchange markets may exist for the home country or for one or more of its trading partners. When it is the home country that has a parallel market, potentially all of its trade and capital flows with all of its trading partners could be affected by the parallel rate. When it is a major trading partner (or partners) that has a parallel market, the overall analytical problem is less serious; but bilateral trade and capital flows with these countries may still be significantly affected by the par-allel rate. For any given developing country, the effect of parallel rates on the multilateral RER will depend upon both the size of the black market premiums and the weights assigned to countries having parallel rates. Box 2.1 illustrates the effects of other countries' parallel market rates on the bilateral and multilateral RERs of Côte d'Ivoire, which itself had a unified exchange rate.[7]

Box 2.1 *The Effects of Parallel Markets on Côte d'Ivoire's Bilateral and Multilateral RERs*

In the case of Côte d'Ivoire, the home currency, the CFA franc, was itself actually freely convertible in the 1980–93 period. However, Nigeria, which was Côte d'Ivoire's second largest trading partner after France in 1993 (accounting for 11 percent of total trade) had an important parallel market that had significant effects on Côte d'Ivoire's bilateral and multilateral RERs.

The Bilateral RER. Figure 2.B.1 shows how the official and parallel exchange rates for the naira and the parallel market premium have varied over time. Figures 2.B.2 and 2.B.3 illustrate the effects of the divergence between the parallel and official exchange rates on the bilateral RER between Côte d'Ivoire and Nigeria. Figure 2.B.2 shows the bilateral RERs calculated using CPIs and the parallel and official exchange rates. The trends in the official and parallel RERs are quite different in the period 1981–85 when Côte d'Ivoire's official RER depreciated 130 percent while its parallel RER fluctuated moderately but changed little over the period as a whole. The large devaluations of the naira during 1986–87, which substantially reduced the parallel market premium on the naira as shown in figure 2.B.1, then caused Côte d'Ivoire's official RER to appreciate much more strongly than its parallel RER. Variations in the official RER have also been much more pronounced than those in the parallel RER, although the changes in both have been substantial. Thus, transactions taking place in the official and parallel markets have been subject to quite different incentives; and the conclusions at which one arrives may depend upon which of the two RERs is used.

(Box continues on page 54)

---

7. For a further discussion of parallel markets and the use of the parallel rate as a guide for setting the official exchange rate, see Chapter 12 by Ghei and Kamin in Part IV of this volume.

Figure 2.B.1 *The Official and Parallel Naira/US$ Exchange Rates and the Parallel Market Premium, 1980–96*

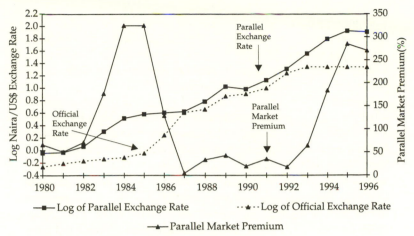

—■—Log of Parallel Exchange Rate   ···▲··· Log of Official Exchange Rate

—▲— Parallel Market Premium

Note: An upward movement represents a depreciation of the naira.
Source: PIC's *Currency Year Book.*

Figure 2.B.2 *The Bilateral RER Between Côte d'Ivoire and Nigeria Computed Using CPIs at Official, Parallel, and Weighted Average Exchange Rates, 1980–96 (1985=100)*

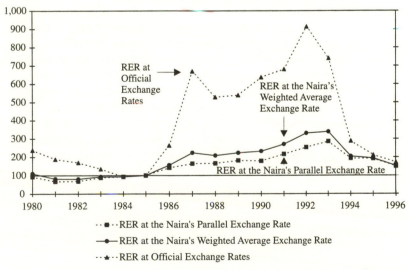

···■··· RER at the Naira's Parallel Exchange Rate

—●— RER at the Naira's Weighted Average Exchange Rate

···▲··· RER at Official Exchange Rates

Note: The weighted average is calculated using 36 percent for the official rate and 64 percent for the parallel rate based on the adjusted IFS country weights in table 2.3. An upward movement represents an appreciation of the RER for Côte d'Ivoire.
Source: Computed from figure 2.B.1 and World Bank data.

(Box 2.1 continued)

Figure 2.B.2 also gives a weighted average bilateral RER that was computed using a weight of 0.36 for the official rate and 0.64 for the parallel rate. These weights were based on World Bank staff estimates of the shares of trade taking place at the official and parallel rates.* Because of the shortage of data, these estimated weights are little more than educated guesses that give an idea of what the average bilateral RER might have been. The official, parallel, and average bilateral RERs give quite different impressions of the magnitude and timing of the appreciation in the measured RER. Which of them is the more representative indicator for transactions between Côte d'Ivoire and Nigeria is an empirical question that depends upon one's assumptions about the relative importance of trade at the official and parallel rates. Hence, detailed knowledge of the functioning of any parallel markets is critical for measuring the actual bilateral RER accurately. In cases where both the home country itself *and* its trading partner have parallel markets, computing a representative bilateral RER may be further complicated; and an understanding of parallel markets becomes even more critical.

The Multilateral RER. In addition to Nigeria, five of Côte d'Ivoire's other developing-country competitors appearing in the official weights used in IFS had parallel markets during 1980–93. (These countries were China, Colombia, Ghana, Indonesia, and Malaysia.) Together these six countries accounted for 14.8 percent of the country weights used for Côte d'Ivoire in IFS. Figure 2.B.3 illustrates the effect of taking into account parallel markets when measuring real effective exchange rate (REER) and the potential sensitivity of the REER to assumptions about parallel exchange rates. It shows the REER for Côte d'Ivoire calculated using both the official and parallel rates for the countries having parallel exchange rates. Figure 2.B.3 also gives a weighted average of the

---

* Because of lack of data on the extra costs and risks of transactions in the parallel market, no adjustment for these was made to the parallel rate.

(Box continues on next page)

Figure 2.B.3 *The REER for Côte d'Ivoire Computed at Official, Parallel, and Weighted Average Exchange Rates, 1980–95 (1985=100)*

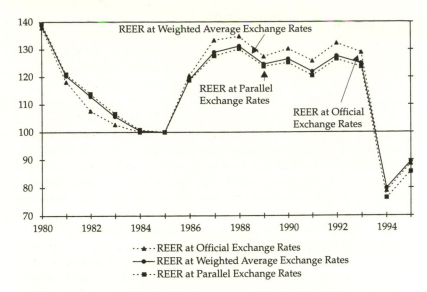

Note: The REER was calculated using CPIs and IFS country weights. An upward movement represents an appreciation of the REER for Côte d'Ivoire.
Source: Computed from PIC's *Currency Year Book* and World Bank data.

(Box 2.1 continued)

parallel and official REERs, using weights equal to the estimated shares of recorded and unrecorded trade for Ghana and Nigeria and equal weights for the parallel and official rates for the other countries having parallel markets. While the differences in Côte d'Ivoire's REER are not as pronounced as in the bilateral RER between Côte d'Ivoire and Nigeria (because the six countries with parallel markets account for only 14.8 percent of the total weights in the REER and the parallel market premium was not as large for the other countries as for Nigeria), the use of parallel rates still affects the overall index by as much as 10 percent in a given year.

Multilateral or Effective RERs (REERs): Weighting Schemes, Unrecorded Trade, and Hyperinflation

The calculation of multilateral RERs or real *effective* exchange rates (REERs) presents a number of additional empirical problems beyond those involved in computing bilateral RERs—namely, the choice of a weighting scheme appropriate for a particular country, adjustments for unrecorded trade, and the effects of hyperinflation.

Weighting Schemes

Unfortunately, the determination of appropriate country weights for use in calculating REERs sometimes poses difficult conceptual and empirical problems, particularly in developing countries. For countries without parallel exchange markets and substantial unrecorded or misrecorded trade, actual trade weights can usually be calculated without too much difficulty. However, when the intercountry pattern of trade is significantly different for imports and exports, it may be preferable for some analytical purposes to calculate separate REERs for imports and exports rather than, in effect, just averaging these together in a single REER for all trade. In addition, if (a) the home country experiences significant competition in its export markets from third countries with which it does not trade much directly or (b) its pattern of intercountry trade is at the margin significantly different from the average (for example, nontraditional exports are sold in different markets from traditional commodity exports), the problem of determining appropriate weights is further complicated. For countries that have, or whose major trading partners have, parallel exchange markets, or significant unrecorded or misrecorded trade, determination of even actual trade weights can be problematic. Furthermore, trade is sometimes denominated in a major currency rather than in the trading partners' currencies (for example, many commodities are priced in U.S. dollars) so that country weights may need to be adjusted to reflect the currency composition of trade rather than its geographic origin and destination.

Moreover, patterns of trade are not independent of the bilateral RERs but, rather, are influenced by them. Fixed weight averages become less representative as bilateral RERs and trading patterns change over time, and it is necessary to update country weights periodically. Hence, for calculating REERs, it is desirable to have country weights that reflect reasonably well the structure of trade in the period being analyzed. Fairly recent weights should be used for current policy analysis and representative ones from the past for historical or econometric analysis of time-series data. Using current weighting schemes or Fisher indexes also mitigates the problem of changing trade structure but increases the complexity of the calculations required.[8]

Ideally, it is desirable that, for a given country, the reference period for the weighting scheme for calculating the multilateral RER and the base (or equilibrium) year be the same so that the weights reflect the equilibrium RER. This approach, however, may require different base years for different countries and complicates the computation of a consistent set of REER indexes for a group of countries. Hence, when consistent REER indexes are needed for groups of countries, it is standard practice to calculate all of them using country weights for the same year. However, it is unlikely that the real exchange rates of all developing countries will be in equilibrium at the same time. Hence, for interpreting real exchange rate movements for an individual country, its REER is usually "rebased" or rescaled so that it equals 100 in a representative "equilibrium year" for that country. As long as the reference year for the trade weights and the equilibrium year to which the REER index is rebased are reasonably close in time and the trade pattern has not changed significantly in the interim, this practice is satisfactory for most empirical purposes. It does, however, reinforce the desirability of using geometric rather than arithmetic averaging as discussed earlier.[9]

Shares of Direct Trade

Several different country weighting schemes are employed in the literature for calculating REERs. The simplest and most transparent way to determine country weightings is to use shares of total direct trade (imports and exports) as calculated—for example, from the statistics published in the IMF's *Direction of Trade*. This procedure is simple enough to give the analyst many options for the choice of base year and also permits calculation of relatively up-to-date trade weights. The IMF, in fact, uses such a simplified procedure of calculating competitiveness weights on the basis of bilateral trade flows for new member countries in which data deficiencies and unstable trade patterns preclude utilization of the more sophisticated weighting methodology discussed below (see Zanello and Desruelle 1997).

Since trade patterns can change considerably as a result of changes in bilateral RERs and other factors, the first step in devising a weighting

---

8. A Fisher index is a geometric average of the indexes calculated using weights of the initial year and of the most recent year.

9. The problem of choosing an appropriate base year for analytical purposes is discussed further in Chapter 7 on operational methodologies for estimating the equilibrium RER.

scheme is to establish an appropriate, up-to-date base year for the country concerned. Table 2.2 illustrates this problem for Côte d'Ivoire. It gives country shares for Côte d'Ivoire's imports, exports, and total trade for 1985, the last reasonable base year before the impact of the shocks of the mid-1980s, and for 1993, the year before the devaluation. A comparison of the movements in the bilateral RERs in table 2.1 and the changes in the trade shares in table 2.2 illustrates how trade shares can change with movements in RERs. In 1985 the dollar peaked relative to the French and CFA francs, after appreciating sharply in the early 1980s, and then began to depreciate. In 1985, Côte d'Ivoire was also hit by a large decline in its terms of trade. The trade share figures for 1993 show the considerably different trade pattern that existed by the time of the devaluation of the CFA franc in January 1994, as the share of Côte d'Ivoire's total trade with other African countries had increased by 16 percentage points in the intervening years while that with industrial countries had fallen correspondingly.

Figure 2.5 shows how the REER differs when computed using the different trade weights for 1985 and 1993. At 1985 weights, the REER

Figure 2.5 *The REER for Côte d'Ivoire Calculated Using 1985, Average 1980–82, and 1993 Total Trade Weights and Old IFS Country Weights, 1980–93 (1985=100)*

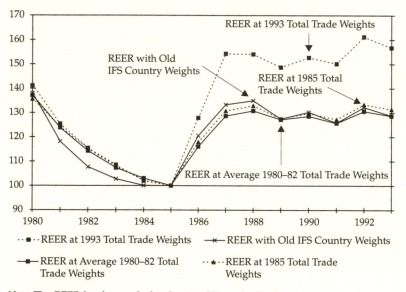

Note: The REER has been calculated using CPIs and official exchange rates. An upward movement represents an appreciation of the REER for Côte d'Ivoire.
Source: Computed from World Bank data.

Table 2.2 Shares in Percent of Côte d'Ivoire's Exports, Imports, and Total Trade by Country, in 1985 and 1993

Country	Exports (%)		Imports (%)		Total trade (%)	
	1985	1993	1985	1993	1985	1993
European countries	*65.0*	*54.9*	*59.7*	*50.5*	*63.0*	*53.0*
France	16.6	16.7	34.3	30.5	22.9	22.4
Other EU	47.3	35.2	22.9	17.5	38.1	27.8
Other European countries	1.2	3.2	2.5	2.5	2.0	2.8
Other industrial countries	*13.2*	*6.8*	*13.7*	*7.2*	*13.4*	*7.1*
United States	11.7	5.8	7.3	4.4	10.2	5.2
Japan	1.0	0.5	5.3	2.7	2.6	1.5
Other	0.5	0.5	1.1	0.1	0.6	0.4
CFA countries	*10.4*	*18.4*	*7.3*	*1.3*	*9.3*	*11.3*
Other UMOA	9.5	14.1	2.6	0.7	7.0	8.5
UDEAC	1.0	4.3	4.8	0.6	2.3	2.7
Non-CFA African countries	*2.3*	*11.2*	*12.7*	*32.4*	*6.0*	*20.2*
Nigeria	0.6	1.3	11.9	24.4	4.6	11.0
Other African countries	1.7	9.8	0.8	8.0	1.4	9.2
Non-African developing countries	*9.1*	*8.3*	*6.4*	*8.3*	*8.1*	*8.2*
Total developing countries	*21.9*	*37.9*	*26.4*	*42.0*	*23.4*	*39.7*

Source: IMF, *Direction of Trade.*

appreciated by 32 percent between 1985 and 1993, whereas at 1993 weights it appreciated by 57 percent. The REER using the 1985 base-year weights is appropriate for assessing the misalignment of the RER over the period 1980–93. The 1993 weights, which reflected the then current structure of trade, should be used to assess the immediate impact of the January 1994 devaluation, however.

A developing country may import from and export to different sets of countries. Hence, its export- and import-competing industries may be affected by the bilateral RERs with sets of quite different countries. Figure 2.6 compares the multilateral RERs for Côte d'Ivoire's import and export markets computed using the 1985 trade shares for imports and exports given in table 2.2. It shows that the REER with the countries from which Côte d'Ivoire imports appreciated considerably more (44 percent) than the REER with the countries to which it exports (25 percent).

In some cases, it may also be desirable to disaggregate the REERs for imports and exports. For example, an oil exporter may sell its oil and nonoil exports in different markets under different competitive conditions. In this case it may be desirable to calculate separate REERs for oil

Figure 2.6 *The REERs for Côte d'Ivoire's Export and Import Markets Calculated Using 1985 Export and Import Weights, 1980–93 (1985=100)*

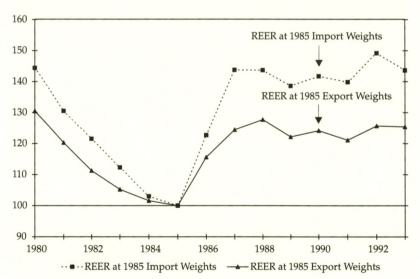

Note: The REER has been calculated using CPIs and official exchange rates. An upward movement represents an appreciation of the REER for Côte d'Ivoire.
Source: Computed from World Bank data.

and nonoil exports. Similarly, a particular country may export nontraditional products to markets that are significantly different from those in which it sells its traditional export commodities; or a country's traditional and nontraditional exports may experience quite different movements in their terms of trade. In such cases, it may be desirable to compute separate REERs for traditional and nontraditional exports in order to give a clearer picture of the incentives for export expansion and diversification.

Third-Country Competition

Exports of the home country compete both with domestic production of the same product in its trading partner i and with exports from other countries, which may not trade at all with the home country, selling in the same market in country i. Ideally, competitiveness weights should take into account not only the aggregate trade flows between the home country and its trading main partners but also the effects on these trade flows of competition in export markets from third countries, which are not important direct trading partners of the home country. For example, although Côte d'Ivoire has only a small amount of direct trade with Malaysia, both countries export very similar primary products to the United States, which is one of Côte d'Ivoire's major trading partners. Hence, a change in the bilateral RER between the ringitt (Malaysia's currency) and the U.S. dollar is likely to have an impact on Côte d'Ivoire's exports to the United States.

Empirically, taking into account competition from third countries is much more difficult than simply allowing for direct trade—as it requires a model of competition in international markets that is not available to most analysts. The only weights incorporating such third-country competition available for calculating REERs are those from the IMF's Information Notice System (INS) used in International Financial Statistics. Table 2.3 shows the original IFS competitiveness weights for Côte d'Ivoire, which were in use at the time the CFA franc was devalued in 1994. These weights were based on data for the period 1980–82. They reflected both the relative importance of Côte d'Ivoire's trading partners in direct bilateral trade and competition from third countries.[10]

Figure 2.5 compares the REERs for Côte d'Ivoire computed using the original IFS weights and actual trade shares both for the 1980–82 base period used in computing these weights and for 1985. The main differences between the original IFS weights and the actual trade shares are that the IFS gave significantly higher weights to third-country competitors

---

10. See Wickham (1987) and McGuirk (1987) for a discussion of the original weighting scheme employed by the IMF at that time.

Table 2.3 *Côte d'Ivoire: Average 1980–82 Total Trade Weights, Official and Adjusted IFS Country Weights, and 1993 Total Trade Weights*

	Average 1980–82 total trade weights (%)	Old IFS country weights (%)	Adjusted old IFS country weights (%)	New IFS country weights (%)	1993 total trade weights (%)
European countries	*62.3*	*56.5*	*53.9*	*62.8*	*53.0*
France	30.1	27.2	25.9	21.6	22.4
Netherlands	9.4	5.8	5.5	6.3	5.8
Italy	7.5	4.6	4.4	6.5	5.8
Germany	6.1	7.5	7.2	10.6	6.1
United Kingdom	3.3	6.7	6.4	5.9	2.8
Spain	2.9	2.0	1.9	2.9	3.3
Belgium-Luxembourg	2.2	2.8	2.7	5.8	4.0
Portugal	0.8	n.a.	n.a.	n.a.	n.a.
Switzerland	n.a.	n.a.	n.a.	1.8	n.a.
Sweden	n.a.	n.a.	n.a.	1.4	n.a.
Other European Countries	n.a.	n.a.	n.a.	n.a.	2.8
Other industrial countries	*12.9*	*21.1*	*20.1*	*23.5*	*7.1*
United States	8.6	10.3	9.8	11.7	5.2
Japan	3.7	7.3	7.0	7.2	1.5
Canada	0.4	1.8	1.8	3.1	0.3
Australia	0.2	1.7	1.6	1.4	0.1
CFA countries	*7.8*	*1.6*	*2.0*	*0.0*	*11.1*
Burkina Faso	2.3	n.a.	n.a.	n.a.	2.9
Mali	2.3	n.a.	n.a.	n.a.	3.5
Senegal	1.8	n.a.	n.a.	n.a.	n.a.
Togo	0.7	n.a.	n.a.	n.a.	1.0
Niger	0.7	n.a.	n.a.	n.a.	0.9
Cameroon	n.a.	1.6	2.0	n.a.	n.a.
Gabon	n.a.	n.a.	n.a.	n.a.	2.1
Other CFA Countries	n.a.	n.a.	n.a.	n.a.	0.7

(Ghana, Brazil, China, Indonesia, Malaysia, Colombia, and Cameroon) and non-European industrial countries (the United States, Japan, Canada, and Australia) and significantly lower weights to the European and other CFA countries than their shares of total trade. Despite these differences in the country weights, the REERs for Côte d'Ivoire calculated using the original IFS weights, average 1980–82 trade shares, and 1985 trade shares actually tracked each other fairly closely.

The original IFS competitiveness weights were subsequently updated during 1994–96 for 146 countries using disaggregated world trade data for 1988–90. These new weights are based on separate models of world trade and competition in the markets for nonoil primary products, manu-

	Average 1980–82 total trade weights (%)	Old IFS country weights (%)	Adjusted old IFS country weights (%)	New IFS country weights (%)	1993 total trade weights (%)
Non-CFA African countries	**3.4**	**5.7**	**12.9**	**0.0**	**20.2**
Nigeria	2.4	2.3	6.4	n.a.	11.0
Morocco	0.6	n.a.	n.a.	n.a.	0.6
Mauritania	0.2	n.a.	n.a.	n.a.	0.6
Ghana	0.2	3.4	6.4	n.a.	2.1
Guinea	n.a.	n.a.	n.a.	n.a.	2.0
South Africa	n.a.	n.a.	n.a.	n.a.	1.0
Zaire	n.a.	n.a.	n.a.	n.a.	0.6
Sierra Leone	n.a.	n.a.	n.a.	n.a.	0.5
Mozambique	n.a.	n.a.	n.a.	n.a.	0.5
Other African countries	n.a.	n.a.	n.a.	n.a.	1.3
Non-African developing countries	**13.7**	**15.1**	**11.1**	**13.7**	**8.2**
Algeria	2.1	n.a.	n.a.	n.a.	n.a.
Taiwan (China)	1.6	1.3	0.0	1.3	1.2
Venezuela	4.4	n.a.	n.a.	n.a.	n.a.
Saudi Arabia	1.4	n.a.	n.a.	n.a.	n.a.
Pakistan	1.0	n.a.	n.a.	n.a.	n.a.
Thailand	0.6	n.a.	n.a.	n.a.	1.3
Brazil	1.4	4.8	0.0	4.2	0.9
China	0.9	1.5	1.8	2.0	1.1
Indonesia	0.3	2.2	2.7	1.3	0.3
Malaysia	n.a.	3.6	4.4	1.9	0.4
Colombia	n.a.	1.8	2.2	1.7	n.a.
Korea	n.a.	n.a.	n.a.	1.4	n.a.
Poland	n.a.	n.a.	n.a.	n.a.	0.7
Tunisia	n.a.	n.a.	n.a.	n.a.	0.5
Other developing countries	n.a.	n.a.	n.a.	n.a.	1.8
Total developing countries	**24.9**	**22.4**	**26.0**	**13.7**	**39.5**

Source: IMF.

factures, and, where significant, tourism. The choice of the 1988–90 base period was a compromise between the use of up-to-date information, on the one hand, and comprehensive coverage, on the other. The methodology and data used to compute the new weights are described in Zanello and Desruelle (1997).[11] Even the new competitiveness weights

---

11. As explained in Zanello and Desruelle (1997), in the updating, a somewhat different weighting system—based on data for 1989–91—was employed for calculating the REERs using unit labor costs in manufacturing for 17 industrial countries rather than the system for calculating weights for computing REERs using CPIs for all countries, which is discussed above.

are, unfortunately, not readily available to all analysts; may be out of date for some countries; and are difficult for others to update or adjust for such factors as unrecorded trade and shifting trade patterns.

The updating of the IMF's competitiveness weights was finalized after most of the REER calculations and analysis reported in this chapter had been completed, and the new weights were not used in the REER indexes shown in most of the graphs and tables. For illustrative purposes, figure 2.7 compares the REERs computed with the original IFS weights, the new IFS weights, and 1993 trade shares. If the new IFS weights were actually the correct ones to use, then the measure of the REER actually used at the time of the devaluation was off by 20 percent because of incorrect weights; and the adjustments made by Bank and Fund staff for unrecorded trade (see below) only made matters worse, increasing the error by another 20 percent. However, the new weights themselves raise some puzzling questions, for example: should neighboring African countries really have been given a zero competitiveness

Figure 2.7 *The REER for Côte d'Ivoire Computed with New and Old IFS Country Weights, Adjusted IFS Country Weights, and 1993 Total Trade Weights, 1980–93 (1985=100)*

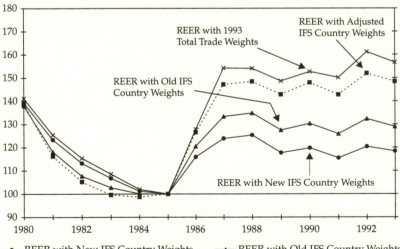

Note: The REER has been calculated using CPIs and official exchange rates. An upward movement represents an appreciation of the REER for Côte d'Ivoire.
Source: Computed from World Bank data.

weight despite a trade share of 31 percent in 1993 (table 2.3)? Was the REER fully 40 percent less appreciated than 1993 trade shares indicated?

Unrecorded Trade

Another practical complication that may be important for some SSA and other low-income countries is the existence of a significant amount of unrecorded trade through parallel markets. Such unrecorded trade is likely to be greater the higher are tariffs and nontariff barriers to official trade and the greater is the parallel market premium. In such cases, some adjustments may be required to all weighting schemes that are based on the official direction of trade statistics. Any adjustments for unrecorded trade should be consistent with the treatment of parallel market exchange rates discussed previously.

For example, in calculating adjusted REER indexes for the CFA countries, the original IFS weights for Ghana and Nigeria were revised upward for some countries to take into account the high level of unrecorded trade with these two countries that is not reflected in the official trade statistics. Thus, as shown in table 2.3, for Côte d'Ivoire the weight for Ghana was increased from 0.034 to 0.064 and that for Nigeria from 0.023 to 0.064 to allow for unrecorded trade. Figure 2.8 illustrates the possible effects of an adjustment for unrecorded trade on the REER. It shows that the REER appreciated by almost twice as much between 1985 and 1993 with the adjusted weights (50 percent) as with the unadjusted ones (28 percent). Use of the parallel exchange rates for the unrecorded trade reduces the difference to 10 percent, however.

Hyperinflation

Once the country weights have been determined, the calculation of the REER as a geometric weighted average of the bilateral RERs (shown in equation 2.7 above) is straightforward. However, a possible additional complication may arise in calculating separate NEER and effective price indexes as components of the REER (as in equation 2.8 above). If any of the trading partners—even those with small country weightings in the home country's index—are experiencing hyperinflation, including these countries in the calculation may distort the separate NEER and effective relative price indexes. The only practical way to get around this problem and arrive at analytically useful NEER and relative price indexes is to delete the hyperinflation countries and adjust the weights for the remaining countries accordingly. The REER index itself, in contrast, will not be distorted because hyperinflations are usually accompanied by offsetting hyperdevaluations. Hence, the REER indexes calculated including and excluding countries experiencing hyperinflation can be com-

Figure 2.8 *The REER for Côte d'Ivoire Computed Using IFS Country Weights and Adjusted IFS Country Weights, and Official and Weighted Average Exchange Rates, 1980–93 (1985=100)*

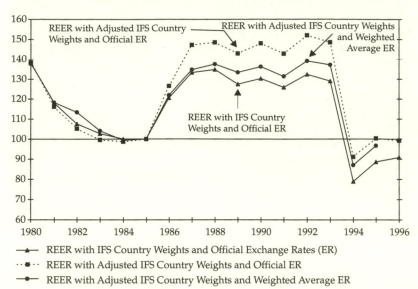

—▲— REER with IFS Country Weights and Official Exchange Rates (ER)
··■·· REER with Adjusted IFS Country Weights and Official ER
—●— REER with Adjusted IFS Country Weights and Weighted Average ER

Note: An upward movement represents an appreciation of the REER for Côte d'Ivoire.
Source: Computed from World Bank data.

pared to see if the adjustments to the country weights necessary to calculate separate NEER and relative price indexes are reasonable.

For example, Brazil, which experienced hyperinflation in the 1980s, was assigned a weight of .048 in the old IFS competitiveness weights for Côte d'Ivoire. Figure 2.9, which compares the NEER and relative price indexes for Côte d'Ivoire computed with and without Brazil, shows how even one such hyperinflation country can distort these indexes. Côte d'Ivoire's NEER including Brazil appreciated by 220 percent between 1985 and 1993, whereas without Brazil it appreciated by only 45 percent. Similarly, Côte d'Ivoire's price level relative to its competitors declined by 60 percent if Brazil is included but by only 10 percent if it is excluded. The behavior of Côte d'Ivoire's REER index, on the other hand, was relatively little affected by the inclusion or exclusion of Brazil.

The Choice of Appropriate Country Weights

Hence, in addition to actual recorded trade flows, the choice of appropriate country weights may be affected by a number of additional factors, including parallel foreign exchange markets, unrecorded trade, and changing patterns of trade. Other relevant factors may include third-country competition in export markets, the pricing of trade in major currencies rather than in the trading partners' currencies, and hyperinflations–hyperdevaluations in competing countries. In addition, in some cases, it may be useful analytically to calculate separate REERs for imports and exports when the factors affecting these differ significantly. Given the analytical complexity of making systematic adjustments for all of the above factors and the shortage of empirical data needed for doing so, the choice of appropriate country weights may in some cases be as much art as science. Different (reasonable) weighting systems can affect measurement of the REER by as much as 25 percent in a particular year. Hence, the choice of weights may call on the analyst for substantial judgment as empirical accuracy may be a matter of knowing which factors are important (and which are not) in a specific case and making the most reasonable adjustments for the important factors with

Figure 2.9 *The NEER, Relative Prices, and Expenditure-PPP REER at Old IFS Country Weights for Côte d'Ivoire with and without Brazil, 1980–96 (1985=100)*

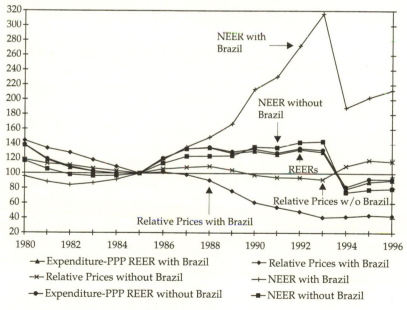

Note: An upward movement is an appreciation.
Source: Computed from World Bank data.

the limited empirical information available. It is also important to check the sensitivity of the REER index to alternative weighting schemes. While the task of determining appropriate weights may seem daunting, arriving at reasonably accurate and up-to-date weights for one small country is inherently simpler than determining a consistent set of general-equilibrium weights for all countries.

Measurement of the Different RER Concepts: Choosing Appropriate Price or Cost Indexes

All three of the primary versions of the external RER are widely used in empirical applications. The computational formulas and conventions, nominal exchange rates, and country weighting schemes discussed above are common to all of these. The differences among the measures result primarily from using different foreign and domestic price indexes in their calculations.[12] Since the different versions of the external RER are based on different types of price indexes, empirical measures of them will be similar only if the price indexes are. If these price indexes always moved in parallel, the choice between the indexes might make little practical difference in determining the change in the external RER. However, as discussed below, for a given country the different types of price indexes, and the corresponding measures of the external RER, may differ significantly because of changes in the terms of trade, trade policy, or productivity. Unfortunately, changes in these factors, particularly the terms of trade and trade policy, tend to be much larger in developing countries than in industrial ones, magnifying the differences between different external RER measures.

In constructing external RER indexes, similar types of price indexes should be used for both the home country and its foreign competitors, with the type of index depending upon the theoretical concept being used. Thus, it is not conceptually consistent, in calculating an external RER, to use a consumption price index for the home country and a production price index for its competitors because the resulting ratio would be based neither on expenditure price nor on production cost parity. Similarly, it would be inconsistent to compare a value-added deflator for one country with a final product price index for another.

This section discusses the choice of appropriate price or cost indexes for measuring each of the three primary versions of the external RER.

---

12. The statistical problems involved in the construction of price indexes are not discussed in this chapter. See Maciejewski (1983) for an extensive discussion of statistical issues.

The following three subsections take up, in turn, the empirical indexes needed for measuring the expenditure-PPP, Mundell-Fleming, and traded-goods versions of the RER.

The Expenditure-PPP External RER

Purchasing power parity, the oldest theory of the equilibrium exchange rate, may be applied to the prices of all goods, as discussed here, or only to the prices of traded goods, as discussed below in the subsection on the external RER for traded goods. There are two versions of PPP: absolute and relative. Since both versions are concerned with purchasing power, they employ expenditure price rather than production cost indexes. However, the two versions use different baskets of goods; absolute PPP requires standardized baskets whereas relative PPP requires representative ones.

Absolute PPP

The original absolute form of PPP theory holds that the equilibrium nominal exchange rate between two currencies is equal to the ratio of the actual domestic and foreign prices of an *identical* standardized basket of goods in the home and foreign countries as shown in equation 2.13:

$$(2.13) \qquad E_{dc} = \frac{P_{Ad}}{P_{Af}}$$

where P_{Ad} and P_{Af} are the actual domestic- and foreign-currency prices of the standardized basket of goods.[13] Note that absolute PPP both determines an equilibrium *nominal* exchange rate and implies that the real exchange rate in equation (2) equals one.

Because, among other things, of the shortage of data on the actual costs of standardized baskets of goods in different countries, absolute PPP has not been much used empirically.[14] Recently, however, in order

---

13. See Rogoff (1996). If the baskets of goods are not identical in two countries, the nominal exchange rate cannot be uniquely determined as the ratio of the cost of the baskets in the two currencies because the cost of the baskets will in general depend upon their composition. Absolute PPP is theoretically unattractive in that a standardized basket of goods will not be representative of the expenditure patterns in two countries unless they have identical consumption patterns. (See Officer 1982). Absolute PPP is also sometimes referred to as "strong PPP."

14. *The Economist's* "Big Mac Index" is, as noted in appendix A, a simple one-good absolute PPP nominal exchange rate and is the most commonly encountered example of the empirical use of absolute PPP.

to make possible more accurate comparisons of income and consumption levels across countries, a large research effort known as the International Comparison Programme (ICP) was carried out to price standardized baskets of goods in different countries. From the comparative purchasing power parity indexes derived under the ICP, implicit nominal PPP exchange rates can be calculated as the relative cost of the standardized basket of goods in the countries being compared. These ICP exchange rates have been used in a few multicountry studies as estimates of the equilibrium nominal exchange rate and are discussed further in appendix A.

Relative PPP

In its relative form, PPP holds that the nominal exchange rate is proportional to the ratio of the domestic and foreign price levels as expressed by equation 2.14:

$$(2.14) \qquad\qquad E_{dc} = \left(\frac{P_{Gd}}{P_{Gf}} \right) \cdot k$$

where k is a constant.[15] Relative PPP in equation 2.14 implies that the real exchange rate in equation 2.2 is a constant.

Conceptually, for the expenditure version of relative-PPP external RER price indexes should be comprehensive, *representative* expenditure-based indexes including both traded and nontraded goods.[16] Because of the ready availability of consumer price indexes for representative baskets of goods for most countries, the relative expenditure-PPP version of the external RER has been extensively used empirically. Unless other-

---

15. Because k is an arbitrary constant, rather than a specific number, the "prices" in equations 2.2 and 2.14 may be either actual prices or indexes. The value of k will depend upon which of these is used but will still be constant. Relative PPP is also sometimes referred to as "weak PPP," and some formulations of it allow k to follow a time trend.

16. The representative baskets should include both traded and nontraded goods in whatever proportions they are actually purchased in the domestic and foreign economies. Use of a standardized but arbitrary basket in calculating the relative-PPP version of the RER would require an improbable behavioral assumption—that households and firms in both countries know the composition of this standardized basket and value currencies accordingly rather than in terms of their actual expenditure patterns. Even the use of representative baskets of goods in measuring expenditure PPP could, however, be problematic if the composition of these baskets tends to change systematically over time because of the demand and supply factors discussed in Chapter 5.

wise specified in this volume, the term PPP always refers to relative expenditure PPP. References to absolute PPP are explicitly identified as such.

The consumer price index (CPI) is usually broadly representative of both traded and nontraded goods. It is the most commonly used index in the calculation of the expenditure-PPP version of the external RER. The CPI is available monthly in most developing countries so that the movements in the RER computed from it can also be tracked on a monthly basis.[17] The IMF publishes in International Financial Statistics (IFS) external RER indexes based on consumer price indexes for most industrial and developing countries. IFS treats the expenditure-PPP version of the external REER as "the REER" for developing countries, although, as discussed below, it gives primacy to the REER for traded goods computed using unit labor cost in manufacturing for 17 industrial countries for which the required data are available.

Two main caveats concerning expenditure-PPP external RER indexes are worth noting. First, CPIs are subject to the influence of price controls, subsidies, and indirect taxes; and CPI levels and movements may be affected by these. Hence, in interpreting RERs based on CPIs it is necessary to distinguish between the effects of changes in indirect taxes, subsidies, and price controls and movements in the general price level.[18] Second, CPIs for different countries are not based on the same baskets of goods (or even ones that are necessarily fairly comparable), and their weightings often reflect patterns of consumer spending that may differ in the home country from those in its foreign competitors. These differences in expenditure patterns do not pose a conceptual problem from the point of view of relative-PPP theory, which applies to representative domestic and foreign baskets that may differ in composition, but do limit the usefulness of RERs based on CPIs for comparing standards of living.

Compared with the CPI, the wholesale price index (WPI) is usually more heavily weighted with traded goods and underweighted with

---

17. For example, monthly CPIs were available for the period 1980–93 for all of the CFA countries except Benin and Mali.

18. CPIs are also subject to seasonal variations. Although seasonal variations do not pose any particular problems for analysis of annual data, such as those reported in this chapter, they may cause seasonal fluctuations in RER indexes calculated using quarterly or monthly data. The IMF thus adjusts for seasonal variations in computing REERs as explained in Zanello and Desruelle (1997). Although it may be possible for other analysts to adjust home country data for seasonal variations, it may be too time consuming to do so for competing countries unless seasonally adjusted CPI data can be obtained from other sources.

nontraded goods. Thus, the WPI is not an appropriate candidate for calculation of the expenditure-PPP version of the external RER, although the WPI may be used for the traded-goods version of the external RER as noted below. Two plausible alternatives to the CPI for expenditure PPP are the absorption deflator and the overall consumption deflators from the national accounts. However, neither of these is commonly used in the computation of the expenditure-PPP version of the RER. National account data are typically available only annually for low-income developing countries whereas the CPI is usually available monthly. In addition, both the absorption and the total consumption deflators include public consumption, the price of which often is not determined by market forces. Absorption also includes investment, which makes it a broader measure of the expenditure price level than the CPI but which some analysts prefer to consider as an "intermediate" product for producing final consumption.[19]

Although for the foregoing reasons the absorption and consumption deflators are not often used, in specific circumstances they may be worth considering. For example, CPIs were not available for Benin and Mali for the period for which the overvaluation of the CFA franc was being analyzed. Since the private consumption deflator from the national accounts was the most comparable of the price indexes actually available, it was used as a proxy for the CPI for estimating the expenditure-PPP version of the RER for these two countries. Bilateral RERs can also be readily constructed using absorption and consumption deflators for those competitors for which comparable data are available, but construction of similar multilateral RERs may be more problematic because of problems with timely data availability and comparability for some developing-country competitors.

The Mundell-Fleming or Aggregate Production Cost Version of the External RER

The second principal external RER concept is based on the standard Mundell-Fleming open economy macroeconomic model used for industrial countries. In this model, each country is assumed to produce a single unique aggregate good (that is, its GDP), which it both consumes and exports. This composite good is in imperfect competition with the unique composite goods produced and exported by other countries and faces less than perfectly price-elastic foreign and domestic demand. The price of each country's good is determined by its cost of production. Hence, in the Mundell-Fleming model, the price index in the definition of the

---

19. See, for example, Jorgenson and Paldam (1986).

external RER (given in equation 2.2) is an output price index or production cost index for the economy, which is composed of *exports* and goods produced and sold domestically by a country, rather than an expenditure price index as in the PPP theory, which is composed of *imports* plus goods produced and sold domestically. The Mundell-Fleming version of the external RER can also be viewed as measuring competitiveness in the aggregate production of all goods, both traded and nontraded.[20] In this formulation, the home and foreign GDP (value-added) deflators are clearly the appropriate price indexes to use in computing the external RER. Thus, in foreign-currency terms, the Mundell-Fleming RER ($MFRER_{fc}$) is computed as shown in equation 2.15:

(2.15)
$$MFRER_{fc} = \frac{E_{fc} \cdot P_{GDPd}}{P_{GDPf}}$$

where P_{GDPd} and P_{GDPf} are, respectively, the domestic and foreign GDP deflators.

The Mundell-Fleming model assumes that the home country's GDP and exports are a single composite good whose prices move in parallel. Similarly, the foreign-currency price of imports is assumed to move in parallel with the foreign country's GDP deflator. Hence, the foreign-currency prices of exports and imports are determined as indicated in equations 2.16 and 2.17:

(2.16)
$$E_{fc} \cdot P_{GDPd} = E_{fc} \cdot P_{Xdc} = P_{Xfc}$$

---

20. Some authors interpret the Mundell-Fleming RER as a way of stating purchasing power parity theory in terms of aggregate production costs of all goods, both traded and nontraded. Since the competitiveness of the traded-goods sector depends, among other things, upon cost of inputs produced by the nontraded sector and the opportunity cost of the factors employed in it, these authors view aggregate "cost structure parity" as preferable to the version of the external RER that only takes into account competitiveness in producing traded goods. (See Officer 1982, Chapter 8, for the arguments favoring production cost over expenditure price parity theories.) This aggregate producer *cost* parity theory is also sometimes interpreted as producer *price* parity theory. Perfect competition in domestic and foreign markets would force the domestic price of any commodity (and thus the general price level) to equal its cost of production, including labor, capital, and intermediate inputs. Hence, some authors replace the production cost index by the general producer price level in the formulas defining the Mundell-Fleming RER and arrive at a formulation quite similar to that for expenditure PPP. However, the price index used in cost parity theory should, in principle, be a production cost (or price) index whereas that used in expenditure-PPP theory is an expenditure or cost of living related index.

$$(2.17) \qquad\qquad\qquad P_{GDPf} = P_{Mfc}$$

where P_{Xdc} is the home country's export price deflator measured in domestic currency, P_{Xfc} is its export price deflator measured in foreign currency, and P_{Mfc} is the home country's import price deflator measured in foreign currency. Substituting the right hand sides of equations 2.16 and 2.17 into equation 2.15 yields equation 2.18:

$$(2.18) \qquad\qquad MFRER_{fc} = \frac{P_{Xfc}}{P_{Mfc}} = TOT$$

where TOT is the home country's terms of trade. Thus, the Mundell-Fleming formulation makes no distinction between the terms of trade and the RER. Since the export price deflator is assumed to equal the home country's GDP deflator and the import price deflator is assumed to equal the foreign country's GDP deflator, the RER and the terms of trade are the same; and both are endogenous in Mundell-Fleming models.

The Mundell-Fleming model is appropriate for many industrial countries because their trade is dominated by differentiated manufactured products, their terms of trade often do not vary substantially, and their CPIs and GDP deflators move largely in parallel. In these circumstances, an external RER computed using GDP deflators provides a good indicator of changes in the degree of competitiveness in aggregate production of both traded and nontraded goods and takes into account the interaction between these two sectors as discussed in the section below on the comparison of alternative external RER measures.[21] It is a broader production cost measure than the unit labor cost as it includes in principle the cost of all factors of production per unit of value added.

While the above assumptions may be reasonable for industrial countries producing diversified manufactured exports, they are less so for small developing countries that rely heavily on exports of a few primary products and whose terms of trade are exogenously determined. In these countries, export prices often move much more sharply than the GDP deflator, and it is often desirable analytically to distinguish between the terms of trade and the RER. Production cost and price indexes (such as the GDP deflator) include export prices but exclude the prices of imports of final goods,[22] whereas an expenditure price index (such as the CPI) does the opposite, including the prices of imports of

---

21. See for example Edwards (1990, p. 74), Lipschitz and McDonald (1991), Williamson (1994), and Stein, Allen, and Associates (1995).

22. The prices of imported inputs may be reflected in some production cost indexes.

final goods and excluding the prices of exports. When the terms of trade (the relative prices of imports and exports) change, the movements in production and expenditure price indexes may differ significantly. In these circumstances, the GDP deflator and the Mundell-Fleming RER may be heavily influenced by swings in the volatile prices of commodity exports and will tend to diverge from the CPI and the expenditure-PPP RER.

Another limitation in using the Mundell-Fleming RER for developing countries is that the GDP deflator is available only on a yearly basis for most developing countries, whereas it is often available quarterly for industrial countries. In addition, the GDP deflator may not always be ideal for international comparisons among developing countries because nonstandardized methods are used for its computation in some low-income countries.

The External RER for Traded Goods

The external RER for traded goods is defined as the relative cost of producing traded goods, measured in a common currency, in the home and foreign country. This third version of the external RER uses output price, production cost, or factor cost indexes for *traded* goods in the home and foreign country in equation 2.2 rather than price or cost indexes for *all* goods as in the expenditure-PPP and Mundell-Fleming RERs. The external RER for traded goods measures competitiveness only among the subsets of goods, produced in the home and foreign countries, that are internationally traded. It, in effect, adjusts the nominal exchange rate to reflect relative prices, costs, or unit costs in the traded-goods sectors at home and abroad.

The law of one price and purchasing power parity theory may be applied either broadly to the external RER for *all* goods or more narrowly to the external RER for *traded* goods. The law of one price holds that, because of competition among sellers and arbitrage in goods markets, the prices of identical goods sold in different countries will be the same after adjustment for transactions costs such as transportation and tariffs. Algebraically, the law of one price may be written for goods i as in equation 2.19:

$$(2.19) \qquad\qquad P_{i,dc} = E_{dc} \cdot (1 + t_i) \cdot P_{i,fc}$$

where t_i is a broad measure of transportation, tariffs, and other transactions costs.

If the prices of individual goods tend to be equalized by the law of one price, so will the prices of baskets of these goods. If the law of one price held for all goods, both traded and nontraded, and transactions costs were negligible, absolute PPP would also hold for *all* goods since the price of a standard basket of these would be equalized. If transactions costs were non-negligible but constant and the law of one price held for all goods, then relative PPP would hold for all goods since the ratio of the prices of a basket of goods in two competing countries would be constant.

However, there is little reason to suppose that international competition will tend to equalize the prices of goods that are not traded. Hence, the law of one price is more logically applied only to *traded* goods. In this case, if transactions were negligible, absolute PPP would hold for homogeneous traded goods. If transactions costs were non-negligible but constant and the law of one price held for traded goods but not for nontraded goods, relative PPP would hold for traded goods. Hence, for those traded goods to which the law of one price applies, the external RER should be a constant.[23]

Internationally traded goods are of two basic types: homogeneous, standardized commodities, and more diversified products, usually manufactured. Developing countries typically export combinations of these two types of products, which may range from almost 100 percent standardized commodities to almost 100 percent manufactures depending upon the country. The law of one price is most applicable to homogeneous commodities and would suggest full price equalization after allowance for transportation, tariffs, and other transactions costs. Diversified manufactures are, in contrast, usually imperfect substitutes. However, international markets for traded goods are large, with many potential sources of supply, and tend to be highly competitive. Hence, even if manufactured products are not perfect substitutes, the cross-elasticities between them are significant; and their prices and costs of production must be reasonably competitive.

Theoretically, how much prices will be equalized by international trade depends critically upon whether traded goods are homogeneous perfect substitutes or differentiated imperfect substitutes. For standard-

---

23. This relationship should, in theory, hold for both bilateral and multilateral RERs. However, the assumptions underlying the theoretical argument that the relative cost of a basket of internationally traded goods should be stable can be questioned on the following grounds: (a) the composition of tradable goods can change with the passage of time; (b) if the weightings of different categories of goods are different in different countries, a change in the relative prices of some tradables can cause the relative prices of different baskets including these to vary; and (c) changes in trade policy or transactions costs can alter the price differentials between countries. See Goldberg and Knetter (1997) and Isard and Faruqee (1998) for a fuller discussion of this point.

ized commodities, theoretically, complete price equalization should take place; and the empirical evidence is that it does. Although the tendency for the prices of differentiated manufactured goods to be equalized is less strong, a rise in their costs or prices, expressed in foreign currency, still usually leads to a loss of competitiveness and market share. (The empirical evidence on the validity of the law of one price is further discussed in Chapter 3, pages 129 through 131). Hence, the RER for traded goods is often used as an indicator of the competitiveness of industrial countries' external sectors and is often employed as the relative price variable in trade equations for these countries. Since this RER focuses exclusively on the traded-goods sector, it has the important advantage of minimizing the effect of productivity bias resulting from more rapid growth of productivity in the traded-goods sector than in the nontraded-goods sector.[24]

However, the usefulness of the RER for traded goods for a particular developing country will depend upon the mixture of homogeneous and diversified traded goods that it produces, as will the degree of price equalization to be expected. At the limit, countries that produced only homogeneous commodities would be price takers and face perfectly elastic foreign demand. In this case, international demand rather than home country costs would determine prices; and there would be full equalization of domestic and foreign prices. If transactions costs are negligible (as is the case for gold, for example) the traded-goods version of the external RER must equal one.[25] If transaction costs are non-negligible but constant, which is the more common case, the external RER for homogeneous goods will also tend to be constant. However, many developing countries produce a mix of homogeneous and differentiated goods so that their overall external RER for traded goods may vary with their competitiveness.

While the choice of empirical price indexes for the expenditure-PPP and Mundell-Fleming versions of the external RER is reasonably straightforward, finding empirical measures of competitiveness in producing traded goods is more problematic because lack of data is a serious constraint for most developing countries. Four alternative price indexes have been suggested in the economic literature as possible candidates for measuring competitiveness in producing traded goods: unit labor costs for traded goods or manufacturing, the wholesale price index (WPI),

24. See the discussion of the Balassa-Samuelson effect in Chapters 3, 5, and 6 and Wren-Lewis and Driver (1998), Chapter 3.

25. See Rogoff (1996) for data showing that the law of one price holds for gold prices in different countries.

value-added deflators for manufacturing and other sectors producing traded goods, and export unit values.[26] IFS reports external RER indexes for 17 industrial countries computed using these four price indexes for traded goods. The advantages and drawbacks of using each of these four indexes are reviewed briefly below, and the relationship among profitability, competitiveness, and the different external RERs is discussed in appendix B.

Unit Labor Costs in Manufacturing

The IMF regards relative unit labor costs in manufacturing, measured in a common currency, as the single most useful measure of competitiveness in producing traded goods in industrial countries. Zanello and Desruelle (1997) argue that unit labor costs in manufacturing "capture cost developments in an important sector exposed to international competition. They offer a reliable gauge of the relative profitability. And, they bring into focus the largest component of nontraded costs and of value added, thus proxying for significant developments in total variable costs." For 17 industrial countries, IFS, in fact, reports the REER computed using unit labor costs in manufacturing most prominently as "the REER," rather than the expenditure-PPP REER computed using CPIs, which is reported for developing countries.[27]

Because of the difficulty of obtaining data on unit labor cost in most developing countries, the REER computed with unit labor costs is of much less use for them.[28] Unit labor cost may be calculated either directly as total labor costs divided by the total value of output or indirectly as the average wage rate divided by labor productivity. Unfortunately, many developing countries, including Côte d'Ivoire and the majority of low-income countries, lack the data necessary to calculate unit labor costs by either method. The REER computed using unit labor costs has been included in this chapter for use in more advanced developing countries for which the necessary data are available. However, it is not

---

26. See Mills and Nallari (1992).

27. A set of competitiveness weights (reflecting only trade in manufactured products) that is different from the one used for calculating REERs (which use CPIs) is used for calculating REERs that are based on unit labor costs. In addition, unit labor costs may be highly sensitive to cyclical changes in productivity, caused by labor hoarding. IFS reports both an unadjusted and a "normalized" unit labor cost index that adjusts for cyclical changes in productivity. RERs based on relative unit labor costs are discussed further in this chapter's section on the comparison of alternative external RER measures and in Zanello and Desruelle (1997).

28. Even for some industrial countries, the IMF has to interpolate from quarterly data to obtain a monthly series on unit labor costs in manufacturing.

likely to be a practical empirical option for many low-income develop-ing countries with limited data.[29]

Consequently, some authors have simplified the relative unit labor cost version of the external RER for developing countries by assuming that productivity differentials are constant and restating this version of the RER as the relative nominal wage rate expressed in foreign exchange terms or relative to per capita GDP. Wage data also have important em-pirical advantages: levels as well as changes are meaningful, and wage data can be easily compared with other indicators such as GDP per capita. Relative wage indicators may be used either narrowly for the traded-goods sector or more broadly for the aggregate production of all goods. Although these simplified indicators may be biased when productivity changes at different rates in the countries being compared or labor force participation rates differ significantly (if per capita GDP is used), data are at least available for calculating such relative labor cost indicators for some developing countries. These indicators also provide useful in-formation about competitiveness that is readily comprehensible by non-technical audiences.[30]

However, even the simplified approach of measuring the external RER as relative labor costs expressed in a common currency could not be used for the CFA countries as adequate time-series data on nominal wages were not available. The best that could be done with the frag-mentary wage data available was, as illustrated in figure 2.10, to ana-lyze the relationship of wages to GNP per capita. This relatively simple presentation does, however, give a striking impression of how inflated relative labor costs in the formal sector were in the CFA countries prior to the January 1994 devaluation.

Wholesale Price Indexes

WPIs are relatively heavily weighted with traded goods and are, there-fore, generally more representative of traded-goods prices than are other aggregate indexes of traded and nontraded goods. RERs for traded goods, computed with WPIs, are thus often used in import and export equations for industrial countries.[31]

Unfortunately, WPIs, like measures of unit labor costs, are not avail-able for many developing countries (including Côte d'Ivoire). Hence,

---

29. See Guerguil and Kaufman (1998) for an example, for Chile, of the type of analysis that can be done when data on unit labor costs are available.

30. See Halpern and Wyplosz (1997) and Krajnyák and Zettelmeyer (1997) for examples of analyses using wage rates in foreign currencies to measure the RER.

31. See Wren-Lewis and Driver (1998). For an example of the use of WPIs for some developing countries, see Fleissig and Grennes (1994).

Figure 2.10 *Annual Labor Compensation in the Largest CFA Economies, 1986–88, as a Multiple of GNP per Capita*

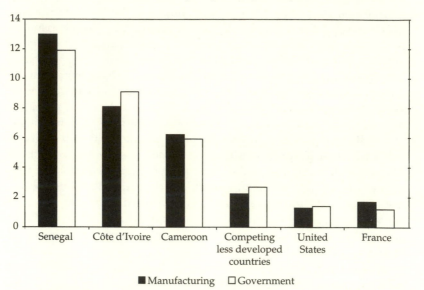

■ Manufacturing   □ Government

Note: "Competing less developed countries" is the average for six adjusting developing countries—Morocco, Ghana, Tunisia, Indonesia, Mauritius, and Malaysia.
Source: Computed from World Bank data.

the home country's cost of aggregate production is sometimes measured by its CPI or GDP deflator, with the WPI being used to measure the price of traded goods of foreign competitors.[32] However, this ratio gives a mixed indicator of competitiveness because the foreign prices of *traded* goods (as measured by foreign WPIs) are compared with the domestic price or production costs of *all* goods (as measured by the GDP deflator or CPI). This indicator may be biased by differential changes in productivity in the traded and nontraded sectors as discussed in the following chapter on the two-good internal RER.[33]

Value-Added Deflators for Manufacturing

For the industrial countries, IFS reports external RER indexes based on value-added deflators for the manufacturing sector as a measure of competitiveness in producing traded goods. These deflators are calculated as the quotient of the current and constant price estimates of value added

32. See, for example, Stein, Allen, and Associates (1995), Chapter 5.
33. This indicator is sometimes also used as a proxy for the internal RER as noted in Chapter 3.

in the manufacturing sector, adjusted for changes in indirect taxes. There is, unfortunately, an important conceptual problem with using this indicator as a *single* RER for most developing countries. Although the manufacturing sector may be broadly representative of tradable goods production for industrial countries, it is much less so for developing countries in which many of the actual and potential exports and import substitutes are agricultural products. Nevertheless, relative manufacturing sector deflators, when available, may still be a useful partial indicator of competitiveness trends in *manufacturing*.[34] Unfortunately, as is the case with unit labor costs and WPIs, the data required for calculating an index of relative manufacturing sector deflators are not available for many developing countries.

The only CFA country for which the value-added deflator for the manufacturing sector was available is Côte d'Ivoire. Even for it, this deflator was only available for the period 1985–93, and the data required for making adjustments for indirect taxes were lacking. Although it is possible to construct bilateral RERs using manufacturing deflators for Côte d'Ivoire's industrial-country trading partners, a representative multilateral RER cannot be constructed because of lack of data on manufacturing deflators for Côte d'Ivoire's developing-country trading partners. This problem is a general one. Lack of data on unit labor costs, WPIs, and manufacturing-sector deflators for many developing countries generally prevents computation of REERs based on these indicators even when the required data are available for the home country.

Export Unit Values

A fourth indicator used to assess competitiveness in traded-goods production in industrial countries is the external RER based on relative export unit values in manufacturing. International Financial Statistics reports this indicator for 17 industrial countries. In this indicator, the unit values serve as proxies for export costs or prices. If the price of the home country's manufactured exports fall relative to its competitors', its exports should become more competitive.

This RER concept is useful only for countries exporting a group of diversified heterogeneous manufactured products that are in imperfect competition with those of their trading partners.[35] Export unit values

---

34. See Chapter 3 for a discussion of using sectoral value-added deflators for calculating the *internal* RER.

35. Even for countries exporting differentiated products, the use of export deflators or unit value indexes may bias measures of the external RER since these indexes include only products exportable at the current exchange rate and do not cover those potentially exportable at a more depreciated exchange rate. See Clark and others (1994).

are less useful in cases in which the home country exports significant amounts of homogeneous primary products (such as cocoa, coffee, and cotton in the Côte d'Ivoire example). In this case, competition in international commodity markets will tend to equalize export prices (and unit values that are proxies for them) expressed in a common currency, and the countries concerned will be price takers facing perfectly elastic foreign demand as discussed earlier. This external RER measure will also be biased if the unit value of a developing country's exports increases over time as a result of structural increases in value added in the export sector—for example, through greater processing of primary products or diversification into higher-value products. Hence, the external RER based on export unit values is often of less help than in industrial countries in assessing the competitiveness of developing countries in producing traded goods (unless disaggregated data are available for the manufacturing exports separately) and was not computed for Côte d'Ivoire.

Comparison of Alternative External RER Measures: Competitiveness and the Terms of Trade

The preceding sections have discussed the three basic versions of the external RER: the expenditure-PPP, the Mundell-Fleming or aggregate production cost, and the traded-goods RERs. Although these three RER measures are all used to draw inferences about a country's competitiveness, fluctuations in the terms of trade can cause them to diverge significantly. The following two subsections consider first the relationship between competitiveness and the different external RERs and then the effects of fluctuations in the terms of trade on them.

Competitiveness and the External RER

To more firmly link the different concepts of external competitiveness to internal price incentives, the IMF has done a considerable amount of work on the relationship between the various measures of the external RER and the profitability of production and investment, both in the traded-goods sector and in aggregate domestic production. In this work, an improvement in the competitiveness of an economy is defined as an increase in the relative share of profits in value added and is expected to lead to an expansion of output and investment. To take into account both the cost of inputs produced in the nontraded-goods sector and the opportunity cost of the factors employed by it, this interpretation of competitiveness has been applied to aggregate domestic production of both traded and nontraded goods as well as to traded goods separately. The IMF's analytical work on the relationship between profitability, competitiveness, and the different external RERs is reviewed in appendix B, on which the following discussion is based.

To take into account total factor productivity in assessing competitiveness in producing traded goods, one formulation of the external RER for traded goods suggests using total unit factor cost (UFC) of producing traded goods, including wages, interest, rents, and profits, adjusted for total productivity and measured in foreign exchange. A simplification of this approach discussed in the preceding section incorporates the idea of competitiveness, implying an increase in profitability. It uses unit *labor* costs of producing traded goods, rather than *total* unit factor costs, measured in foreign exchange terms.

The rationale behind using unit labor is that the cost of labor usually represents the largest share in the total cost of production and that the shares of different factors change slowly over time. Labor is usually the least mobile factor of production internationally, whereas capital goods are internationally traded and financial market integration tends to equalize long-term real interest rates in liberalized economies. Unit labor costs are in a certain sense the most fundamental measure of a country's productivity, domestic production costs, and real factor incomes. Relative labor costs can also be directly related both to the internal RER and to other measures of the external RER; and real exchange rates and real wages tend to be closely linked, both theoretically and empirically. Hence, relative unit labor costs are widely used to assess external competitiveness in producing traded goods, as discussed earlier.

Marsh and Tokarick (1994) see three advantages in using unit labor cost for assessing competitiveness in industrial countries. First, data on labor costs are generally available on a comparable basis for these countries. Second, unit labor costs are an important component of overall production costs. And, third, the containment of wage costs is often an important component of policies designed to achieve macroeconomic stability and competitiveness in industrial countries. Because of these advantages, the IMF reports the RER computed using unit labor costs in manufacturing as the primary measure of competitiveness in industrial countries.

The main limitation of external RER indexes based on unit labor costs is, of course, that they take into account only one factor of production. As explained in Lipschitz and McDonald (1991) and Marsh and Tokarick (1994), relative unit labor costs accurately measure the relative profitability of producing traded goods only under certain conditions: that is, if prices of traded goods are determined by international competition, if the capital stock is fixed, if all countries have the same technology, and if no imported inputs are used. Under these conditions, increases in relative unit labor costs in the home country will reduce the share of profits in the traded-goods sector and lead to a deterioration in the country's competitiveness and external trade position. If the foregoing conditions are not met, however, movements in relative unit labor costs can sometimes give misleading signals about profitability. As the capital-labor ratio differs across countries, this difference may introduce a bias into such indexes.[36] Moreover, production activities typically use intermediate inputs, which are not included in factor costs. Imported and domestic inputs may be used in differing proportions in the home and foreign countries and may have different shares in total cost. Their prices may also vary significantly across countries. For instance, if petroleum and other forms of energy are important intermediate inputs and their relative prices change significantly, competitiveness may improve or deteriorate without any corresponding change in unit labor costs. Hence, some economists prefer to use broader measures of competitiveness than relative unit labor costs.

The RER measured in terms of the *aggregate* cost or price level is partially a function of unit labor costs in the traded and nontraded sectors but encompasses more information. It takes into account changes in the prices of imported intermediate inputs and developments in the nontraded-goods sector. As noted earlier, external competitiveness in producing traded goods should, ideally, take into account both the cost of inputs produced in the nontraded-goods sector and the opportunity cost of the factors employed by it. Hence, cost competitiveness theory has been applied by some authors to *aggregate production* of all goods, both traded and nontraded.[37] These authors prefer to use the GDP deflator or the CPI to calculate the external RER as a measure of competitiveness in the aggregate production of all goods. For them, the Mundell-Fleming and expenditure-PPP versions of the RER, rather than the external RER for traded goods, are the preferred measures of competitiveness.

Effects of Fluctuations in the Terms of Trade

The three principal versions of the external RER are thus all used as measures of a country's external competitiveness. These external RER indexes all contain the nominal exchange rate. Movements in nominal exchange rates tend to be much larger than those in the various measures of relative domestic and foreign prices because floating exchange

---

36. See Edwards (1990).
37. See, for example, Officer (1982).

rates are quite flexible and respond quickly to monetary as well as real shocks. Since changes in nominal exchange rates often swamp those in relative prices, the nominal exchange rate and the different measures of the external RER usually show a pronounced tendency to move together statistically, particularly in the short term in industrial countries.[38]

Over the longer term, changes in three variables—productivity, tariffs, and the terms of trade—can, nevertheless, cause the different measures of the external RER to diverge significantly. Changes in productivity and tariffs, although important in some cases, tend to be less dramatic than those in the terms of trade. These are most conveniently analyzed using the two- and three-good internal RERs discussed in the next two chapters. However, when a country's terms of trade change significantly, the effects of such a change tend to be evident even in aggregate external RERs. Hence, this subsection examines the effects of fluctuations in the terms of trade on the three principal external RERs in a typical developing country.[39]

When the external terms of trade change significantly, movements in the CPI (which reflects the cost of imported goods) and in the GDP deflator (which reflects the cost of exports) may diverge. Typically, when the terms of trade improve, the GDP deflator will rise faster than the CPI. But, when the terms of trade deteriorate, the opposite will happen—the CPI will rise faster than the GDP deflator. Hence, the expenditure-PPP and Mundell-Fleming RERs computed using these price indexes will diverge.

Figure 2.11 compares the behavior of the GDP deflator, the CPI, the private consumption deflator, and the price deflator for manufacturing for Côte d'Ivoire (the only available indicator of the behavior of the prices of differentiated traded goods as noted in the section on the external RER for traded goods). It shows how in the period 1985–93 the CPI and the private consumption deflator both rose while the GDP deflator fell by 11 percent as a result of the sharp drop in commodity export prices.[40]

---

38. For a further discussion of the empirical relationship between the nominal and real exchange rates, see the paragraphs on the law of one price in Chapter 11, footnote 7 in Chapter 13, and Clark and others (1994).

39. For a further discussion of other factors that can cause the external RER for traded goods and the RER for all goods to diverge, see MacDonald (1997), pages 6-11.

40. Until 1987 the CPI and private consumption deflators tracked each other fairly closely. However, in 1992–93 the CPI series was revised from 1987 onward. Since then the two series have increasingly diverged as shown in figure 2.11.

Figure 2.11 *Price Deflators and the Terms of Trade for Côte d'Ivoire, 1980–93 (1985=100)*

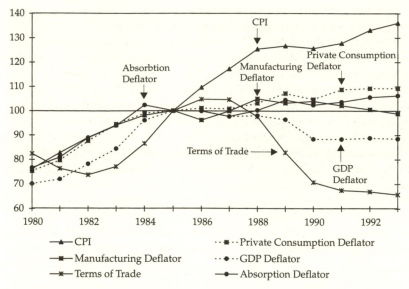

Note: The manufacturing deflator for Côte d'Ivoire is available only from 1985 onward.
Source: Computed from World Bank data.

Figure 2.12 shows the effects of the different behavior of the CPI and GDP deflators during 1980–93 on the expenditure-PPP and Mundell-Fleming versions of the REER. It shows that, when Côte d'Ivoire's terms of trade dropped by 35 percent between 1985 and 1993, the expenditure-PPP version of its REER appreciated by 45 percent whereas the Mundell-Fleming REER appreciated by only 10 percent as a result of falling export prices. This figure is a good example of the differences between aggregate expenditure and production cost external RERs that can be caused by changes in the external terms of trade.

In addition, the relative prices of traded and nontraded goods will not necessarily behave in the same fashion both at home and abroad. Hence, it is possible for the aggregate and traded-goods production costs RERs to give quite different signals from time to time. As traded goods contain both imports and exports, the net effect of fluctuations in the terms of trade on external RERs measuring competitiveness in producing traded goods is theoretically ambiguous. Rising import and rising exports prices will *both* tend to appreciate external RERs for traded goods, and declines in both import and export prices will tend to depreciate both these RERs. The net effect of a change in the terms of trade will depend upon the relative size of the changes in export and import prices and on the sizes of the export and import competing sectors. Thus, the direction of the net effect cannot be determined a priori.

The very limited data on the traded-goods external RER measures that are available for developing countries also make it difficult to make empirical comparisons of the movements in the RERs for traded goods with those in the expenditure-PPP and Mundell-Fleming RERs. Nevertheless, in practice, for developing countries exporting primary commodities, a deterioration in the terms of trade caused by declining commodity prices will be reflected much less strongly, if at all, in standard IFS measures of the external RER for traded goods computed using the prices of diversified manufactured goods, than in the Mundell-Fleming REER.

As figure 2.11 shows, the prices of manufactured goods fell by 2 percent in Côte d'Ivoire in the early 1990s, while the private consumption deflator rose by 10 percent. Thus, domestic prices of traded goods may have been falling relative to domestic prices of nontraded goods,

Figure 2.12 *The REER for Côte d'Ivoire Computed Using CPIs, GDP Deflators, and Domestic CPI–Foreign WPIs, and the Terms of Trade, 1980–95 (1985=100)*

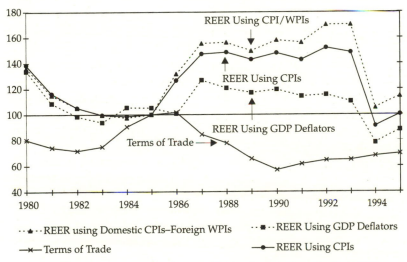

· · ▲ · · REER using Domestic CPIs–Foreign WPIs   · · ■ · · REER Using GDP Deflators

——✕—— Terms of Trade   ——●—— REER Using CPIs

Note: The REERs have been calcualted using official exchange rates and adjusted IFS country weights. An upward movement represents an appreciation of the REER for Côte d'Ivoire.
Source: Computed from World Bank data.

causing the *internal* RER to appreciate and *internal* competitiveness to deteriorate as shown in figures 3.1 and 3.2 of Chapter 3 on the two-good internal RER. Similar divergences in the prices of traded and nontraded goods can also occur in foreign countries. Figure 2.13 compares the bilateral RERs for Côte d'Ivoire with France and the United States calculated using manufacturing deflators with the same RERs calculated using the CPIs and GDP deflators. It suggests that after 1985 external competitiveness in producing manufactured goods compared with both France and the United States was significantly better than the changes in the nominal exchange rates and relative CPIs would indicate.[41] Thus, indicators of external competitiveness in traded goods and in aggregate production can sometimes give different pictures, and one needs to exercise some care in interpreting them empirically.[42]

The significance of RERs for traded goods for a developing country will also depend upon the relative importance of homogeneous commodities, subject to the law of one price, and differentiated nonstandardized products in its trade. For example, manufactures accounted for only 16 percent of Côte d'Ivoire's exports in 1993, with standardized primary commodities accounting for nearly all of the remainder. Hence, the macroeconomic effect of better price performance in manufactures was quite limited. For countries exporting primary products, the external RER for aggregate production is a broader indicator than the RER for traded goods. However, as noted above, when the terms of trade change significantly aggregate cost-price indicators giving larger weights to imports (such as the CPI) may diverge quite significantly from those giving larger weights to exports (such as the GDP deflator). In this case, it is usually more informative to calculate separate RER indexes for imports and exports as discussed in Chapter 4 on the three-good internal RER.

Summary and Conclusions

This concluding section first summarizes the different measures of the external RER. It then briefly reviews the major factors causing the behavior of these RER measures in developing countries to differ from that in industrial countries.

---

41. The bilateral Mundell-Fleming RERs are not reliable indicators in this case as they are distorted by the effects of the falling prices of commodity exports on Côte d'Ivoire's GDP deflator.

42. Neither bilateral RERs for trade in manufactured products with most developing countries nor REERs for manufactured goods can be calculated for Côte d'Ivoire because of lack of comparable data for Côte d'Ivoire's developing-country competitors.

Figure 2.13 *The Bilateral RERs Between Côte d'Ivoire and the United States and France Calculated Using CPIs, GDP Deflators, and Value-Added Deflators for Manufacturing, 1988–93 (1985=100)*

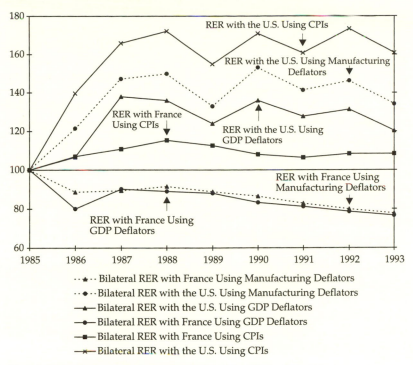

Note: An upward movement is an appreciation of the RER for Côte d' Ivoire.
Source: Computed from World Bank data.

Measurement of the External RER: A Summary

The four primary versions of the external RER—the expenditure-PPP, Mundell-Fleming or aggregate cost, competitiveness in traded goods, and relative labor cost concepts—are summarized in table 2.4. These alternative RER indexes provide different but related information.

Empirically, the use of *CPIs* in measuring *relative expenditure PPP* is well established. CPIs are widely available on a fairly current basis for most developing countries and permit the reasonably easy computation of the expenditure-PPP version of the external RER. This is a useful, internationally comparable measure that provides a good indicator of movements in relative price levels between countries and of nominal shocks to exchange rates and price levels. However, it, like all external RERs, can be quite sensitive to assumptions about parallel exchange markets, unrecorded trade, and shifting trade shares as discussed below.

Table 2.4 Summary of External RER Measures

RER Measure	Price-Cost Index Used in Computation	Availability of Developing Country Data	Comments
1. Purchasing Power Parity			
a. Expenditure PPP—Relative	CPIs	Monthly in most countries	Most widely used measure in developing countries.
b. ICP Exchange Rates—Absolute	ICP Price Data	Selected years for participating countries	Data are available only with a long time lag. These are nominal rather than real exchange rates.
2. Mundell-Fleming Aggregate Production Cost RER	GDP Deflators	Annually, most countries	GDP deflators may be heavily influenced by volatile commodity prices.
3. RERs for Traded Goods			
a. Relative Unit Labor Cost in Manufacturing	Manufacturing Unit Labor Costs	Annually, a few countries	Useful partial indicator for manufacturing sector when available.
b. Relative Manufacturing Sector Deflators	Manufacturing Sector Deflators	Annually, some countries	Useful partial indicator for manufacturing sector when available.
c. Relative Wholesale Prices	WPIs	Monthly, a few countries	Not suitable for most developing countries because of predominance of primary commodities.
d. Relative Export Unit Values	Export Unit Value Indexes	Annually, some countries	Not suitable for most developing countries because of predominance of primary commodities.
4. Relative Labor Cost in Production of All Goods			
a. Relative Wages	Average Wage Rates	Annually, some countries	Useful when available but may be biased by productivity changes.
b. Relative Average Unit Labor Cost	Average Unit Labor Costs	Annually, very few countries	Useful when available, but very few countries have necessary data.

Similarly, *GDP deflators* are commonly used to measure the *Mundell-Fleming or aggregate production cost* RER. This measure is widely used in empirical analysis of industrial countries, to which the Mundell-Fleming model of trade in differentiated manufactured products is well suited. This model is, however, much less appropriate for developing countries that export significant quantities of primary commodities and whose terms of trade fluctuate considerably. Volatility in the export prices of primary commodities can cause the Mundell-Fleming RER to diverge significantly from the expenditure-PPP version of the RER and limit the utility of the former to those developing countries that export diversified manufactured products. In addition, although the GDP deflator is usually available quarterly in industrial countries for computing the Mundell-Fleming RER, it is often available only annually in developing countries, making it hard to monitor the Mundell-Fleming RER on a current basis.

The *traded-goods* version of the RER is widely used for the OECD countries. The IMF regularly publishes data on four of these RERs—relative unit labor costs in manufacturing, relative wholesale prices, relative manufacturing sector deflators, and relative export unit values—for 17 industrial countries. The IMF, in fact, treats the external REER for traded goods computed using unit labor costs in manufacturing as "the REER" for 17 industrial countries rather than the REER computed using CPIs, which is used for developing countries. However, the limited availability of data on unit labor costs, productivity, and wholesale prices makes computation of these four measures of the external RER for traded goods problematic for most low-income developing countries. In addition, the usefulness of relative export unit values and wholesale prices in developing countries is limited by the prevalence of standardized commodities in their exports, for which they are price takers.

In those developing countries in which the required data are available, relative unit labor costs and manufacturing sector deflators can be useful partial indicators of competitiveness in producing manufactured goods and differentiated nontraditional exports. Such indexes can be used for making comparisons to industrial countries, although lack of data for competing developing countries will generally prevent the calculation of multilateral REERs that include them. However, these RER measures will be representative neither of the incentives facing primary commodity exports nor of the export sector as a whole. The macroeconomic significance of these measures will depend upon the relative sizes of a country's manufacturing and commodity-producing sectors.

Although, when the required data are available, it is preferable to use unit labor costs to take into account the effects of productivity changes, relative labor costs expressed in foreign exchange can also be useful indicators for developing countries where unit labor cost data are not available. Labor is usually the least mobile factor of production internationally. Hence, aggregate unit labor costs in the production of all goods are, in a certain sense, the most fundamental measure of a country's productivity, domestic production costs, and real factor incomes. Relative labor costs can also be directly related both to other measures of the external RER and to the internal RER. Unfortunately, as is the case with the measures of competitiveness in traded goods, the use of relative labor costs in developing countries is often limited by data availability. While ad hoc comparison of labor costs among representative developing and industrial countries is common and quite useful, systematic multilateral comparisons of these are not usually possible. External RERs based on labor costs may also diverge from those based on CPIs because of gains and losses in income caused by movements in the terms of trade.

The only other empirical index generally available for measuring the traded-goods version of the RER is the mixed one, which uses foreign country WPIs to represent traded-goods prices together with home country GDP deflators or CPIs to represent aggregate domestic production costs. Unfortunately, this indicator is significantly affected by productivity bias as explained in the following chapters on the internal RER. As noted there, it is best used only as a proxy for the RER for imports when more accurate measures are not available.

Factors Affecting the Behavior of External RERs in Developing Countries

The two most important factors that complicate the interpretation of standard industrial-country RER measures in developing countries are the volatility of commodity export prices and major changes in trade policy. Both of these can cause the expenditure-PPP, Mundell-Fleming, and traded-goods versions of the RER to diverge significantly and limit the representativeness of any single measure of the external RER. The Mundell-Fleming RER is particularly sensitive to the terms of trade because it uses the GDP deflator, which includes volatile commodity export prices. When the terms of trade fluctuate significantly or when productivity grows at different rates in different sectors at home and abroad, it is often desirable to look at separate RERs for imports and exports, a subject that the following chapters on the internal RERs discuss at length.

The expenditure-PPP version of the RER, particularly if computed using import weights, gives a good indication both of the relative general price level and of the competitive environment faced by import-substituting industries and manufactured exports. Available measures

of the RER for differentiated traded goods (for example, relative manufacturing deflators, unit labor costs, or wages) can give additional information about the manufacturing sector and should be weighted by trade
shares that exclude primary commodities.

The measurement of relative price incentives for primary commodity exports is, however, a different problem. Since the price elasticity of
demand for commodity exports is effectively infinite for small producers, the problem in small countries is basically one of the internal incentives for producing these commodities—that is, of the internal RER for
commodity exports, which the next two chapters treat in detail.

In addition to the general problems posed by volatile terms of trade
and changes in trade policy, the measurement of the external RER in
developing countries can be complicated by parallel markets, unrecorded
trade, and quickly shifting trade patterns. Parallel exchange rates can
diverge significantly from official exchange rates, causing similar divergences in parallel and official RERs. As figure 2.B.3 illustrated, because
of parallel markets in competing countries, the parallel REER differed
from the official REER for Côte d'Ivoire by 5 percent to 10 percent during 1980–93, even though Côte d'Ivoire itself had a unified exchange
rate. The decisions on which of these REERs is the most representative
or whether both the parallel and official REERs should be used may be
important for the subsequent analysis. Unrecorded trade can similarly
affect the results (by 20 percent in the case of Côte d'Ivoire in 1993 as
shown in figure 2.7). Adjustments for unrecorded trade usually tend to
increase the weights assigned to countries with parallel exchange markets as unrecorded trade tends to take place through informal market
channels at parallel rates.

Fixed weight averages become less representative for computing
REERs as bilateral RERs and trading patterns change over time, and it is
necessary to update country weights periodically. Shifting trade patterns can outdate standard base-year country weights fairly quickly and
give a misleading impression of current relative prices. As figure 2.5
shows, in 1993 the REER for Côte d'Ivoire was 25 percent more appreciated at current year (1993) weights than at base-year (1985) weights.
While the new IFS country weights may be useful for intercountry analysis, they may be out of date or otherwise unrepresentative for some developing countries. Alternative (reasonable) weighting systems can affect the measurement of the REER by as much as 25 percent in some
circumstances. Hence, some attention should be devoted to carefully
choosing the weights for calculating the REER for a particular developing country; and the sensitivity of the REER index to alternative weighting systems should be checked. For calculating REERs, it is desirable to
have country weights that reflect reasonably well the structure of trade

in the period being analyzed: that is, fairly recent weights for current and forward-looking policy analysis and representative weights from the past for historical or time-series analysis.[43]

When a country experiences significant changes in its terms of trade or trade policy, the different external RER measures may diverge significantly. Computation of the RERs themselves may also be sensitive to assumptions about parallel markets, unrecorded trade, and trade patterns. Hence, to the extent data availability permits, one should calculate and interpret the relevant measures together rather than concentrate exclusively on a single external RER measure. Analyzing the relevant measures together helps to give a fuller picture of what may be happening empirically and to avoid potentially misleading signals that might be given by any one measure taken in isolation.[44] Divergent movements in different measures can sometimes be consistently interpreted, but the analyst needs to pay some attention both to the theoretical relationship among the various concepts and to data problems involved in their empirical measurement.

---

43. For example, an appropriate base year or a Fisher average of indexes using beginning- and end-year weights.

44. See Clark and others (1994) for a further discussion of this point.

Appendix A

International Comparison Programme Exchange Rates

Intercountry comparisons of nominal national incomes (or GDPs) measured in different currencies require their conversion into a common numeraire such as the U.S. dollar or the IMF's standard drawing right (SDR). The market (or official) nominal exchange rate is the only readily available exchange rate that can be used for this purpose. However, the use of market exchange rates for making intercountry comparisons of income levels is problematic for two reasons. First, market exchange rates can fluctuate significantly even in the short term and may diverge from their equilibrium levels for temporary or even protracted periods. Second, even equilibrium rates at best reflect only price parity for traded goods. As discussed in Chapter 5 on the determinants of the equilibrium RER, market-determined rates do not usually reflect parity in the prices of nontraded goods, except perhaps among selected industrial countries in the ultra-long term because of the Balassa-Samuelson effect.

Hence, conversions using market exchange rates may be distorted by both exchange rate fluctuations and differences in price levels; and relative price levels may bear little relationship to intercountry differences in real incomes. Conceptually, for making intercountry comparisons it is desirable to have nominal exchange rates based on a standardized basket of goods and relative prices that reflect purchasing power parity more accurately than do market rates. This appendix briefly discusses the problem of estimating such "purchasing power parity" exchange rates and the International Comparison Programme (ICP) that has been undertaken for this purpose. In order to distinguish these nominal exchange rates from the relative-PPP version of the real exchange rate discussed in the text, these rates are referred to here as ICP exchange rates.

The Meaning of "Purchasing Power Parity"

Intercountry comparisons and aggregations of GDPs are more meaningful economically if the nominal conversion factors used reflect a standardized basket of goods and set of relative prices rather than each
country's own particular basket of goods and relative prices. The conversion factor would then give each currency's purchasing power relative to the numeraire currency. Converting GDPs measured in terms of
current domestic prices and national currencies by such "purchasing
power parity" or ICP exchange rates into a common numeraire currency
would then yield GDP data valued in the numeraire currency and comparable across countries.

The One Good Case

At a disaggregated one-good level, the ICP exchange rate (*ICPER*) between a given home country *j* and foreign country *k* is defined as the
ratio of nominal prices for a single specific good *i*, as shown in equation
2.A.1:

$$(2.A.1) \qquad\qquad ICPER_{ijk} = \frac{P_{ij}}{P_{ik}}.$$

The ICP exchange rate is the number of units of domestic currency per
unit of foreign currency required for the purchase of good *i*. *The
Economist's* "Big Mac Index" is an example of a one good ICP exchange
rate. It is simply the ratio of the domestic-currency price of a Big Mac in
the home country to its price in the numeraire country.[45]

The nominal domestic price of a given good in any country, when
converted to the currency of the numeraire country by its ICP exchange
rate, is equal to its price in the numeraire country and, therefore, is the
same in all countries.[46] Hence, meaningful real quantity comparisons
are possible across countries when ICP exchange rates are used. The
expenditures on final output of good *i* in country *j* can also be priced in
the currency of the numeraire country (in most cases, the United States)
by dividing nominal national currency expenditures on good *i*, $P_{ij} Q_{ij}$, by
its corresponding ICP exchange rate $[(P_{ij} Q_{ij})/(P_{ij}/P_{i,US})]$. This procedure
is equivalent to valuing the quantity in country *j* at the numeraire country price $(P_{i,US} Q_{ij})$ for good *i*.

The ICP exchange rate is different from the external real exchange
rate between countries *j* and *k*. The external RER in the one good case is
given by equation 2.A.2:

---

45. See *The Economist* (1995, August 26 and 1996, April 27).
46. For any country *j*, equation 2.A.1 gives that $P_{ij}/ICPER_{i,jk} = P_{ik}$.

(2.A.2)
$$RER_{ij} = \frac{E_{dc} \cdot P_{ij}}{P_{ij}} = E_{dc} \left(\frac{1}{ICPER_{i,jk}} \right),$$

and, conversely, as equation 2.A.3 shows,

(2.A.3)
$$ICPER_{ijk} = \frac{E_{dc}}{RER_{jk}}.$$

The ICP exchange rate is the ratio of two nominal prices in different currencies and is itself a *nominal* exchange rate.

As equation 2.A.3 indicates, the ICP exchange rate will equal the nominal exchange rate only in the special case when the external RER is equal to one, that is, when absolute PPP holds (see page 73). In general, if the external RER is greater than one, then the ICP exchange rate will be lower than the nominal exchange rate in domestic-currency terms.

The Multi-Good Case

In order to determine the overall purchasing power of home country j's currency relative to that of a foreign country k in the standard multi-good case, a large number of prices for individual items have to be averaged in some way to yield a ratio of weighted averages of prices. The overall or aggregate ICP exchange rate for GDP is thus conceptually a function of the sets of domestic and foreign prices (P_j, P_k) and their respective weights (W_j, W_k), as expressed in equation 2.A.4:

(2.A.4)
$$ICPER_{jk} = f(P_j, P_k, W_j, W_k).$$

The core problem in constructing multi-good ICP exchange rates for converting aggregate national accounts is to choose the appropriate sets of prices and weights and to determine the precise form of the function f in equation 2.A.4. Note that the resulting ICP rates are *absolute* PPP exchange rates calculated with a particular standardized basket of goods.

The International Comparison Programme

The International Comparison Programme, set up by the United Nations and the University of Pennsylvania with the support of the World Bank, has generated substantial data on ICP exchange rates and on ICP-based real GDP and its components. The ICP has concentrated on the expenditure side of GDP rather than the production side because more accurate data are available for market prices than for factor cost, and for expenditures than for sectoral output. The exchange rates estimated by the ICP are based on extensive price surveys, which were conducted in

participating countries in phases every three to five years. Six phases
have been completed, beginning in 1970. A total of 90 countries have
now participated at some point in ICP surveys.

During the ICP surveys, data on final product prices (which include
taxes and subsidies) and quantities are collected for more than 400 types
of goods and services in each of the countries surveyed. These price
data are then aggregated into approximately 150 basic categories of goods
and services. All of each country's individual final output items are assigned to one or another of the 150 categories.

The averaging procedure used in the ICP involves a specialized
method designed to allow for the fact that every item is not priced in
every country.[47] The averaging procedure most widely employed in the
international comparisons is known as the Geary-Khamis method. It is
summarized in the following sets of equations, 2.A.5 and 2.A.6:

$$(2.A.5) \qquad ICPER_j = \frac{\sum_{i=1}^{m} P_{ij}\, q_{ij}}{\sum_{i=1}^{m} \Pi_i\, q_{ij}} \qquad j = 1,......, n (\text{countries})$$

$$(2.A.6) \qquad \Pi_i = \sum_{j=1}^{n} \frac{P_{ij}}{ICPER_j} \left[\frac{q_{ij}}{\sum_{j=1}^{n} q_{ij}} \right] \qquad i = 1, ..., m (\text{goods}) ,$$

where

n	= number of countries
m	= number of categories of goods
P_{ij}	= price of good i in country j
q_{ij}	= quantity of good i in country j
Π_i	= international price of good i
$ICPER_j$	= aggregate ICP exchange rate between country j and the numeraire currency.

The Geary-Khamis method yields a vector of international relative
prices for the m goods and a vector of aggregate ICP exchange rates for
the n countries such that the international price for an individual good
is a quantity-weighted average of the relative prices in individual coun-

---

47. See Summers and Heston (1991).

tries. With this method, the aggregate ICP exchange rate for a given country j is calculated (in equation 2.A.5) as the ratio of total expenditures on GDP valued at the country j's own prices (P_{ij}) to total expenditures on its GDP valued at international prices $(\tilde{O}_i)$. Data on domestic expenditures on the basic categories of goods for a country are divided by their domestic prices to obtain quantities. These quantities are multiplied by their international prices and aggregated to obtain GDP and its components in international prices for the country.

International prices are calculated simultaneously (in equation 2.A.6) as the quantity-weighted average of domestic prices of the countries being compared, with the domestic prices converted into a common currency using the country's aggregate ICP exchange rate. The price in each country is weighted by that country's share of each of the basic product categories in the total output of the participating countries. The ICP exchange rates and the international prices are generated simultaneously from the above system of $m + n$ linear equations, using prices and quantities in individual countries as inputs. Only $m + n - 1$ equations of the system described by 2.A.5 and 2.A.6 are independent, and in the calculations the ICP exchange rate for the numeraire country is set equal to one so that international prices are expressed in the numeraire currency.

Empirical Uses of ICP Data

The ICP data have been used for comparing per capita income levels and aggregating GDP across countries.[48] They have also been used in studies of various macroeconomic subjects such as cross-country differences in long-run economic growth and the relationship between prices, income levels, and real quantities.[49]

In comparing nominal GDPs converted at market exchange rates with ICP-based GDPs, three conclusions are generally reached.[50] The first is that ICP-based GDPs dramatically alter the rankings of the world's largest economies. For example, using market exchange rates in 1992, the five largest economies ranked by GDP were the United States, Japan, Germany, France, and Italy. However, using the 1990 ICP-based GDPs yields the following ranking: the United States, China, Japan, Germany, and India. The second conclusion is that ICP exchange rates for developing countries are generally lower than nominal market exchange rates with the U.S. dollar (in domestic-currency terms), as one would expect, because of the Balassa-Samuelson effect discussed in the chapter on the two-good internal RER. Figure 7 in Chapter 7, which

48. See, for example, Kravis, Heston, and Summers (1982).
49. See, for example, the World Bank (1993).
50. See Wagner (1995).

compares the aggregate ICP dollar exchange rate for Côte d'Ivoire with the market rate, illustrates this point. Third, the difference between aggregate ICP exchange rates for GDP and market exchange rates tends to vary inversely with per capita income. As a result, valuation of GDP in terms of ICP exchange rates yields generally higher income for poorer countries than valuation at nominal exchange rates.[51]

---

51. See, for example, Rogoff (1996) for data and regressions documenting these findings.

Appendix B

The Relationship between Profitability, Competitiveness, and the Different External RERs

To more firmly link the different concepts of external competitiveness to internal price incentives, the IMF has done a considerable amount of work on the relationship between measures of the external RER and the profitability of production and investment, both in the traded-goods sector and in aggregate domestic production. In this work, an improvement in the competitiveness of an economy is defined as an increase in the relative share of profits in value added and is expected to lead to an expansion of output and investment. To take into account both the cost of inputs produced in the nontraded-goods sector and the opportunity cost of the factors employed by it, this interpretation has been applied to aggregate domestic production of both traded and nontraded goods as well as to traded goods separately.

The rest of this appendix discusses the relationship between profitability, competitiveness, and the external RERs for both traded goods and aggregate production. The analytical approach employed below follows that used by IMF staff in Lipschitz and McDonald (1991) and in Marsh and Tokarick (1994). The following subsections start by setting out the analytical framework and then discuss profitability first in terms of the cost of producing *traded* goods and subsequently in terms of *aggregate* production costs.

Analytical Framework

To provide a common framework for discussing indicators of profitability (defined as the share of profits in value added), it is useful to start with a basic analytical structure that describes the supply side of the

home economy. Consider the case of a small open economy that produces both tradable (T) and nontradable (N) goods. Assume that each
category of goods is produced by a two-tier production function, combining value added and imported and nontraded intermediate inputs,
as shown in equation 2.B.1:

$$(2.B.1) \qquad Q_i = F_i\big[V_i(L_i,K_i),I_{Ni},I_{Mi}\big] \qquad i=T,N \ ,$$

where Q_i denotes domestic output of good i and V_i, K_i, L_i, I_{Ni}, and I_{Mi} are,
respectively, value added and inputs of capital, labor, nontradable and
imported intermediate goods. To simplify the presentation, we will assume that the value-added function is based on a constant returns-to-
scale Cobb-Douglas technology and that both imported and nontradable
intermediate inputs are fixed proportions of domestic output, as shown
in equations 2.B.2 through 2.B.4:

$$(2.B.2) \qquad\qquad V_i = A_i L_i^{\theta_i} K_i^{1-\theta_i}$$

$$(2.B.3) \qquad\qquad I_{Ni} = \varphi_{Ni} Q_i$$

$$(2.B.4) \qquad\qquad I_{Mi} = \varphi_{Mi} Q_i \ ,$$

where A_i is a scale technological factor that also measures the total productivity of labor and capital in sector i, θ is the share of labor in value
added, and φ_{Ni} and φ_{Mi} are technical input-output coefficients.

Assuming perfect competition, with constant returns to scale in both
sectors, profit maximization implies that the average factor product is
equal to the marginal factor product and that total nominal value added
in each sector is fully distributed among the two factors of production.
Thus, we end up with equation 2.B.5:

$$(2.B.5) \qquad\qquad P_{Vi}V_i = w_iL_i + r_iK_i \ ,$$

where P_V is the value-added deflator, w is the nominal wage rate, and r
is the nominal rate of return on capital. Dividing both sides of the above
equation by V_i, we obtain equation 2.B.6:

$$(2.B.6) \qquad\qquad P_{Vi} = \frac{w_i \cdot L_i}{V_i} + \frac{r_i \cdot K_i}{V_i} = a_{Li} \cdot w_i + a_{Ki} \cdot r_i \ ,$$

where a_{Li} and a_{Ki} are, respectively, the labor and capital employed per
unit of value added in sector .

The first term on the right-hand side of equation 2.B.6 is labor costs
per unit of value added, or unit labor cost (ULC), and the second term

gives capital income per unit of value added, or the unit profit rate (UP).[52] We can then write equation 2.B.7:

(2.B.7) $$P_{Vi} = ULC_i + UP_i.$$

Perfect competition in the tradable and nontradable sectors and profit maximization also imply that final output prices in each sector equal the sum of value added and the cost of intermediate inputs as shown in equations 2.B.8 and 2.B.9:

(2.B.8) $$P_T \cdot Q_T = P_{VT} \cdot V_T + P_N \cdot I_{NT} + P_M \cdot I_{MT}$$

(2.B.9) $$P_N \cdot Q_N = P_{VN} \cdot V_N + P_N \cdot I_{NN} + P_M \cdot I_{MN} ,$$

where P_T is the final product or output price of traded goods, P_N is the final product price of nontraded goods, and P_M is the price of imported goods. Dividing both sides of equation 2.B.8 by Q_T and both sides of equation 2.B.9 by Q_N and substituting from equations 2.B.3 and 2.B.4, we obtain the following equations, 2.B.10 and 2.B.11, for the prices of tradable and nontradable goods,:

(2.B.10) $$P_T = \varphi_{VT} \cdot P_{VT} + \varphi_{NT} \cdot P_N + \varphi_{MT} \cdot P_M$$

(2.B.11) $$P_N = \varphi_{VN} \cdot P_{VN} + \varphi_{NN} \cdot P_N + \varphi_{MN} \cdot P_M ,$$

where for $i = T, N$:

$$\varphi_{Vi} = \frac{V_i}{Q_i} = \text{the share of value added in the output of the I}^{th} \text{ final good.}$$

Relative Unit Labor Costs in Producing Traded Goods

Another formulation of the external RER—which takes into account productivity changes in assessing competitiveness—for traded goods suggests

---

52. The relative shares of profits may, however, not be a good indicator of external competitiveness if there are significant differences in technology (reflected, for example, in the degree of factor substitutability) between the home country and its competitors. An alternative indicator of competitiveness, which takes into account differences in technology among countries, is the rate of return on capital (see Lipschitz and McDonald 1991). However, if capital is highly mobile across countries, differences in the rate of return on capital will tend to be equalized over time. Furthermore, even with differences in technology between countries an *increase* in the relative share of profits in a country will imply an increase in relative profitability.

using total unit factor cost (UFC) of producing traded goods. This cost measure includes wages, interest, rents, and profits, adjusted for total productivity and measured in foreign exchange.[53] A simplification of this approach incorporates the idea of competitiveness implying an increase in profitability. It uses unit *labor* costs of producing traded goods, rather than *total* unit factor costs, measured in foreign exchange terms.

The rationale behind using unit labor is that the cost of labor usually represents the largest share in the total cost of production and that the shares of different factors change slowly over time. Labor is usually the least mobile factor of production internationally, whereas capital goods are internationally traded and financial market integration tends to equalize long-term real interest rates in liberalized economies. Hence, unit labor costs are in a certain sense the most fundamental measure of a country's productivity, domestic production costs, and real factor incomes. Relative labor costs can also be directly related both to the internal RER and to other measures of the external RER; and real exchange rates and real wages tend to be closely linked, both theoretically and empirically.[54]

Thus, the following external RER index based on unit labor cost in foreign-currency terms in the traded-goods sector ($BRERT_{ULC}$) is often calculated, as shown in equation 2.B.12:

$$(2.B.12) \qquad BRERT_{ULC} = \frac{E_{fc} \cdot ULC_{Td}}{ULC_{Tf}}$$

with:

$$(2.B.13) \qquad ULC_T = \frac{w_T \cdot L_T}{V_T} = a_{LT} \cdot w_T$$

from equation 2.B.6.

---

53. Attainment of strict cost parity in unit factor costs requires the assumptions that traded goods are homogeneous and that their prices are determined by international competition, that technology is homogeneous in the home country and its competitors, that the countries use the same relative amounts of imported inputs, and that they pay the same prices for them, and that the capital stock is fixed. When technologies differ or the home country and some of its competitors face different price movements for imported inputs, unit factor costs may vary. They may also be affected by differences in productivity in the production of nontraded goods as discussed below.

54. See, for example, Dornbusch and Helmers (1988), Chapter 5, and De Gregorio and Wolf (1994). For a discussion of the quantitative relationship between labor costs and internal and external exchange rates, see Chapter 13.

A variant of the above approach measures relative profitability in producing differentiated traded goods. This RER adjusts relative unit labor costs by the value-added deflators in the traded-goods sectors in the home country and its competitors and establishes conditions for the share of profits in GDP to increase.[55] As Lipschitz and McDonald (1991) show, relative unit labor costs can also be used to determine the relative shares of profits in traded-goods production. From equation 2.B.7, the sum of unit labor costs and unit profits in the traded-goods sector is equal to the value-added deflator, as shown in equation 2.B.14:

(2.B.14) $$P_{VT} = ULC_T + UP_T.$$

Dividing by P_{VT} yields equation 2.B.15:

(2.B.15) $$\frac{ULC_T}{P_{VT}} + \frac{UP_T}{P_{VT}} = 1.$$

In the case of a Cobb-Douglas production function with constant returns to scale, the terms ULC_T/P_{VT} and UP_T/P_{VT} are, respectively, labor's and capital's shares in a unit of value added. Hence, Lipschitz and McDonald (1991) suggest the following measure of relative profitability (or competitiveness) in producing traded goods in the home and foreign countries, as shown by equation 2.B.16:

(2.B.16) $$BRERT_{PRF} = \frac{ULC_{TD}/P_{VTd}}{ULC_{Tf}/P_{VTf}}.$$

$BRERT_{PRF}$ is the ratio of labor's share in value added in the traded-goods sector in the foreign country to that in the home country.

If traded goods are homogeneous across countries and no intermediate inputs are used in producing them, the law of one price will equate the value-added deflators (the price of traded goods in this case) when expressed in a common currency; and $BRERT_{PRF}$ will be identical to $BRERT_{ULC}$. When traded goods are not homogeneous, $BRERT_{PRF}$ will provide additional information about relative profit margins in the foreign and domestic traded-goods sectors.

Relative unit labor costs, $BRERT_{ULC}$, are widely used to assess external competitiveness in producing traded goods as noted above. Marsh and Tokarick (1994) see three advantages in using unit labor cost for assessing competitiveness in industrial countries. First, data on labor costs are generally available on a comparable basis for these countries.

---

55. See Lipschitz and McDonald (1991) and Marsh and Tokarick (1994).

Second, unit labor costs are an important component of overall production costs. And, third, the containment of wage costs is often an important component of policies designed to achieve macroeconomic stability and competitiveness in industrial countries. Because of these advantages, the IMF reports the RER computed using unit labor costs in manufacturing as the primary measure of competitiveness in industrial countries.

The main limitation of external RER indexes based on unit labor costs is, of course, that they take into account only one factor of production. As explained in Lipschitz and McDonald (1991) and Marsh and Tokarick (1994), $BRERT_{ULC}$ accurately measures the relative profitability of producing traded goods only under certain conditions: that is, if prices of traded goods are determined by international competition, if the capital stock is fixed, if all countries have the same technology, and if no imported inputs are used. Under these conditions, increases in relative unit labor costs in the home country will reduce the share of profits in the traded-goods sector and lead to a deterioration in its competitiveness and external trade position. If the foregoing conditions are not met, however, movements in relative unit labor costs can sometimes give misleading signals about profitability. As the capital-labor ratio differs across countries, this difference may introduce a bias into such indexes.[56] Moreover, production activities typically use intermediate inputs, which are not included in factor costs. Imported and domestic inputs may be used in differing proportions in the home and foreign countries and may have different shares in total cost. Their prices may also vary significantly across countries. For instance, if petroleum and other forms of energy are important intermediate inputs and their relative prices change significantly, competitiveness may improve or deteriorate without any corresponding change in unit labor costs. Hence, some economists prefer to use broader measures of competitiveness than relative unit labor costs.

Measures of External Competitiveness Based on Relative Aggregate Production Cost and Price Indexes

$BRERT_{ULC}$ focuses on relative profitability conditions in the traded-goods sector of the home country compared with the traded sector in foreign countries. It does not take into account developments in the nontraded-goods sector. These may have important implications for the performance of the traded-goods sector, for example, through the cost of nontraded intermediate inputs and the opportunity cost of production factors that are mobile across sectors. As developments in the nontraded-goods sec-

---

56. See Edwards (1990).

tor will influence overall internal resource allocation and productivity in an economy, it is also desirable to have profitability indicators based on aggregate production costs or prices including both traded and nontraded-goods prices.

Assuming that the domestic and foreign aggregate output price indexes are geometric weighted averages of traded and nontraded prices, with weights α and δ, we have the following equations (2.B.17 and 2.B.18) for the domestic and foreign price levels:

(2.B.17) $$P_{Gd} = P_{Nd^{\alpha}} \cdot P_{Td^{1-\alpha}} \quad \text{with} \quad 0 \prec \alpha \prec 1$$

(2.B.18) $$P_{Gf} = P_{Nf^{\delta}} \cdot P_{Tf^{1-\delta}} \quad \text{with} \quad 0 \prec \delta \prec 1 ,$$

where the subscript d refers to the home country and f to the rest of the world. Substituting these into the definition of the external RER expressed in foreign-currency terms—equation 2.3 in the text—yields equation 2.B.19:

(2.B.19) $$BRER_{fc} = \frac{E_{fc} \cdot P_{Td}^{1-\alpha} \cdot P_{Nd}^{\alpha}}{P_{Tf}^{1-\delta} \cdot P_{Nf}^{\delta}}.$$

With P_V determined by equation 2.B.7, equations 2.B.10 and 2.B.11 for P_T and P_N may be written as shown in the set of equations, 2.B.20:

(2.B.20) $$P_{Td} = \varphi_{VTd}(ULC_{TD} + UP_{TD}) + \varphi_{NTd} P_{Nd} + \varphi_{MTd} P_{Md}$$

$$P_{Nd} = \varphi_{VNd}(ULC_{Nd} + UP_{Nd}) + \varphi_{NNd} P_{Nd} + \varphi_{MNd} P_{Md}$$

$$P_{Tf} = \varphi_{VTf}(ULC_{Tf} + UP_{Tf}) + \varphi_{NTf} P_{Nf} + \varphi_{MTf} P_{Mf}$$

$$P_{Nf} = \varphi_{VNf}(ULC_{Nf} + UP_{Nf}) + \varphi_{NNf} P_{Nf} + \varphi_{MNf} P_{Mf}.$$

Equations 2.B.19 and 2.B.20 show that the RER measured in terms of the *aggregate* cost or price level, $BRER_{fc}$, is partially a function of unit labor costs in the traded and nontraded sectors but encompasses more information. It takes into account changes in the prices of imported intermediate inputs and developments in the nontraded-goods sector. As noted earlier, external competitiveness in producing traded goods should, ideally, take into account both the cost of inputs produced in the nontraded-goods sector and the opportunity cost of the factors employed by it. Hence, some authors have applied cost-competitiveness theory to *aggregate production* of all goods, both traded and nontraded.[57] These authors prefer to use the GDP deflator or the CPI to calculate the external RER as a measure of competitiveness in the aggregate production of all goods, and for them the Mundell-Fleming and expenditure-PPP versions of the RER are the preferred measures of competitiveness.

---

57. See, for example, Officer (1982).

3

The Two-Good Internal RER for Tradables and Nontradables

*Lawrence E. Hinkle and Fabien Nsengiyumva**

The external RER, discussed in the preceding chapter, measures the relative domestic and foreign price levels expressed in a common currency. By contrast, the internal RER, which is the subject of this chapter, measures a relative price between two different categories of *domestic* goods: tradables and nontradables. Most economists working on industrial countries focus on external RERs in their models and analyses.[1] Economists working on developing countries, however, often prefer to work with theoretical models that use internal RERs,[2] although much of the empirical work on developing countries has in fact used external RER measures because these have been more readily available.

Internal RERs may be based on two-, three-, or multi-good macroeconomic models. The first internal RER concept to be developed was based on models that incorporated two types of goods, tradables and nontradables. These two-good models necessarily assume, explicitly or implicitly, that the terms of trade between exportables and importables are fixed so that these can be aggregated into a single composite trad-

* Ms. Ingrid Ivins provided research assistance in the preparation of this chapter. The authors are grateful to Amparo Ballivian, Shanta Devarajan, Peter Montiel, Stephen O'Connell, and three anonymous reviewers for very helpful comments on earlier drafts.

1. For some recent examples, see Clark and others (1994); Williamson (1994); Stein, Allen, and Associates (1995); and Wren-Lewis and Driver (1998).

2. See, for example, Devarajan, Lewis, and Robinson (1993); Edwards (1989 and 1994); and Elbadawi (1994).

able good. Consequently, these models are not very useful for analyzing the effects of changes in the external terms of trade, which are often important determinants of exchange rate movements in developing countries.

To incorporate variations in the terms of trade in the analysis, one needs to distinguish analytically between at least three goods—importables, exportables, and nontradables—and two real exchange rates: one for importables and one for exportables. There is, then, no longer a single unique measure of the internal real exchange rate; and the analyst must determine whether to use multiple RER measures or to derive some kind of representative average of them. The more recent use of three-good models permits explicit treatment of movements in the terms of trade, albeit at the price of complicating the analysis of the internal RER.

Although the theory of the internal RER is well developed, the actual computation of the different versions of the internal RER, nevertheless, poses both conceptual and empirical problems. In theory, the internal RER should be measured by using appropriate domestic price indexes of tradables and nontradables. However, the composition of these two categories of goods depends itself upon the level of the real exchange rate. In practice, moreover, price data are usually available only for exports, imports, and domestically produced goods, not for tradable and nontradable goods. In addition, relatively little empirical work has been done on how to compute internal RERs directly, and procedures for doing so are not well documented in the literature.

External RER measures, although developed primarily for industrial countries, can be utilized as well for developing countries and are reported for them in *International Financial Statistics*. Because of the above conceptual and empirical difficulties in measuring the internal RER, external RER measures have often been used as proxies for the internal RER. Sometimes, unfortunately, analysts have substituted an external RER for the internal RER without paying much attention to the empirical relationship between their external RER measures and the internal RERs for which they are used as proxies. Because of the lack of the data needed for computing the internal RER directly, other analysts have calculated rough estimates of them from price or national accounts data. The effects of parallel markets, smuggling, large fluctuations in the terms of trade, and other empirical complexities encountered in developing countries have often been ignored. An additional source of confusion in the literature is that different authors sometimes use the same empirical price indexes to measure both the external and internal real exchange rates so that it is impossible in some cases to know which concept of RER is actually being analyzed.

For analytical purposes, it is, therefore, useful to know how the movements in the internal and external RERs are related. When will the measures tend to move together, and when are they likely to diverge? In light of these differences, what is the best RER measure to use in particular developing countries?

Internal and external RERs are related to each other. The value of one can, in principle, be calculated from the data used for computing the other. The general *theoretical* relationship between the two-good (tradables and nontradables) internal RER and the external RER has been known at least since the original work on productivity bias in the 1960s by Balassa and Samuelson.[3] It has been well documented in the literature.[4] However, little has been published about the relationship of the three-good (importables, exportables, and nontradables) internal RER to the external RER. There has also been little analysis of the *empirical* relationship among the different RERs, in part because few analysts have made the direct calculations of the internal RER necessary for such an analysis.

This chapter on the two-good internal RER and the next one (Chapter 4) on the three-good internal RER are intended to help readers deal with the above problems of multiplicity and empirical ambiguity of concepts, limited data and other measurement constraints in developing countries, and the relationship between different internal and external RER measures. These chapters have three objectives:

a. To review and operationalize the various definitions of the internal RER as a starting point for the empirical measurement of these concepts;
b. To relate these theoretical definitions to actual price and national accounts data available for developing countries, to set down a methodology for directly estimating the internal RER from standard national accounts that is not well documented in the empirical literature, and to examine empirical problems typically encountered in constructing internal RER indexes; and
c. To clarify the theoretical and empirical interrelationships between the different measures of, and proxies for, the internal and external RERs and the conditions under which these are likely to move in parallel or diverge.

The remainder of this chapter is divided into four sections and one appendix. The next section reviews the theoretical definition and empirical measurement of the two-good internal RER for tradables and nontradables. The following section sets out the relationship between the two-good internal RER and the external RER. The subsequent section then discusses the use of external RERs as empirical proxies for the internal RER. The final section summarizes and concludes. The final

---

3. Balassa (1964) and Samuelson (1964).
4. For examples, see Edwards (1988 and 1989) and Guillaumont Jeanneney (1993).

section of the next chapter on the three-good internal RER compares the two- and three-good RERs and discusses the accuracy and interpretation of the various internal RER measures. This chapter also contains an appendix, which sets out in detail a methodology for directly estimating the internal RER from standard national accounts data.

The Two-Good Internal RER for Tradables and Nontradables: Concepts and Measurement

This section discusses the internal RER in a standard two-sector framework of a small open economy with one sector producing tradable goods and a second producing nontradables. It first reviews the theoretical definition of the internal RER in the two-good framework and then examines a number of conceptual and empirical problems involved in its measurement.

Theoretical Definition of the Internal RER in a Two-Good Framework

In the two-sector framework of Salter and Swan, the "domestic currency" internal RER ($IRERT_N$) for the home economy is commonly defined as the relative price of tradable to nontradable goods[5] as shown in equation 3.1.a:

$$(3.1.a) \qquad IRERT_N = \frac{P_{Td}}{P_{Nd}} \, ,$$

where P_{Td} and P_{Nd} are the domestic-currency price indexes of tradable and nontradable goods, respectively.[6] An increase in $IRERT_N$ is a depreciation. As with external RERs, the internal RER may also be expressed in foreign-currency terms. The equivalent definition of the internal RER in foreign-currency terms ($IRERN_T$) is simply the inverse of $IRERT_N$ shown in equation 3.1.b:

$$(3.1.b) \qquad IRERN_T = \frac{P_{Nd}}{P_{Td}} = \frac{1}{IRERT_N}.$$

In this case an increase in $IRERN_T$ is an appreciation. Although the idea of referring to an internal RER in "foreign-currency terms" may seem

---

5. See, for example, Salter (1959) and Bruno (1976).
6. To simplify the notation in this chapter, the bases for all indexes are set at 1.00 in the reference period rather than at 100.

strange, this terminology preserves comparability in the discussion of appreciations and depreciations of internal and external RERs. For ease of exposition, most of the equations in this chapter are expressed in domestic-currency terms; but, unless otherwise noted, all figures are in foreign-currency terms so that they are comparable to those in the preceding chapter on the external RER, with an upward movement being an appreciation.

Another potentially confusing aspect of the standard terminology is that the nominal exchange rate does not explicitly appear in the basic definition of the internal RER. However, the nominal exchange rate does enter implicitly as a determinant of the domestic-currency price of tradable goods. If the law of one price (equation 2.19) applies to tradables, the domestic-currency price of tradables is given by:

$$(3.2) \qquad\qquad P_{Td} = E_{dc} \cdot P_{Tf} \cdot (1+t)$$

where P_{Tf} is the foreign-currency border price (including transportation costs but excluding trade taxes and other domestic trade restraints, which are included in t) of tradables and t is the average ad valorem net trade tax rate on tradables.[7] Substituting equation 3.2 into equation 3.1.a then gives equation 3.3 for the internal real exchange rate:

$$(3.3) \qquad\qquad IRERT_N = \frac{E_{dc} \cdot P_{Tf}(1+t)}{P_{Nd}}.$$

In contrast to the basic definition of the internal RER in equations 3.1.a and 3.1.b, equation 3.3 now includes the nominal exchange rate as a result of the assumption that the law of one price holds for tradable goods. In effect, the law of one price defines tradable goods as those goods whose prices are determined entirely by international border prices and the nominal exchange rate. In this formulation, all other goods are implicitly nontraded in the sense that their prices are determined by other factors besides international prices. An important caveat about the internal RER, discussed in subsequent sections, is worth an advanced mention here. If the law of one price (equation 3.2) does not hold or holds only loosely in the long term because of strategic pricing of non-homogeneous traded goods, then it will be hard to relate the internal RER firmly to either the nominal exchange rate (as equation 3.3 does) or to the external RER.

---

7. Administered price schemes may also act as taxes or subsidies on imports or exports. However, if a good is subject to a prohibitive tariff or a binding import or export quota, then at the margin it is nontradable and should be treated this way in empirical analysis.

Since the purpose of the internal RER is to capture the relative domestic incentives for both producing and consuming tradable and nontradable goods, in principle one should include the effect of taxes, subsidies, and trade restraints in its calculation. A comparison of the internal RERs inclusive and exclusive of taxes gives a measure of the extent to which the home country's trade and price policies cause relative domestic prices to diverge from relative border prices.[8] When countries are experiencing a period of "import compression" characterized by high tariffs, widespread exchange controls, and other quantitative restrictions on imports, RERs including and excluding taxes may differ considerably.

The relative domestic price of tradable and nontradable goods is an indicator of the incentives for both producing and consuming the two categories of goods. It is a key relative price in determining an open economy's external current account position. A rise in price makes the production of tradables relatively more profitable, inducing resources to move out of the nontradables sector into the tradables sector. It also simultaneously creates an incentive for consumers to reduce consumption of tradable goods by substituting nontradables for them. Switching domestic resources from the production of nontradable to tradable goods and switching domestic expenditures from tradables to nontradables both improve the home economy's external current account position.

Empirical Measurement of the Two-Good Internal RER

Although the theoretical concepts of the internal real exchange rate set out above are reasonably straightforward, their empirical measurement raises difficult practical problems particularly in finding operational counterparts for the required price indexes of tradable and nontradable goods. This subsection discusses conceptual and practical issues involved in directly calculating such price indexes.

Difficulties in Empirically Measuring the Prices of Tradables and Nontradables

The theoretical definition of the internal real exchange rate relies upon a neat division of goods into "tradables" and "nontradables." However, in constructing the price indexes required for calculating the internal RER, a major conceptual issue is how to actually classify goods (or sectors) as tradable and nontradable. In principle, tradables consist of all

---

8. For the same reason external proxies for the internal RER are, as discussed below, likely to track the internal RER excluding taxes more closely than the internal RER including taxes (see also Edwards 1994).

goods that do or *could* enter into international trade as exports or imports. The prices of potentially tradable goods should be closely linked to those of traded goods. Tradables do not actually have to be traded but only be capable of being exported or imported. Tradability is, thus, a quality that can be possessed by many goods to varying degrees. Furthermore, the nature and degree of their tradability depends upon the real exchange rate—as the RER depreciates, more goods will become exportable but fewer goods will be imported. Only a few real-world goods and services are totally nontradable irrespective of the real exchange rate, and it is not clear how useful empirically an index based solely on these few goods would be. Hence, it is difficult to state an operational definition of tradability that does not require one to also specify the level of the RER to be assumed in determining tradability.

In addition to the conceptual problem of arriving at an operational definition of tradability, the data required for calculating the internal RER are often not directly available. In theory, the internal RER should be measured by using appropriate domestic price indexes of tradables and nontradables. In reality, however, the price statistics available for most countries do not normally distinguish explicitly between tradable and nontradable goods or even between traded and nontraded goods. Data are usually available only for exports and imports. If exported products are also consumed domestically and the home country produces close substitutes for some imports, exports and imports may constitute only a part of the total production and consumption of goods traded at the current exchange rate. They may be an even smaller part of tradable goods, which include potentially exportable and importable goods that are not actually traded at the current exchange rate.[9] Regardless of what data may be desirable for conceptual reasons, in practice one is usually limited to a choice among a few imperfect data series that separate goods into imports, exports, and other domestic goods rather than into tradable-nontradable or traded-nontraded goods.[10] Use of data for the narrower concepts of exports and imports tends to understate the relative importance of the tradable sector.

---

9. However, if some imports are restricted by prohibitive tariffs, quotas, or other binding nontariff barriers, these may effectively be nontradable goods.

10. An additional source of confusion is that in practice, the meaning of the term "traded goods" is often ambiguous. Sometimes it refers to the total production of export goods, whether exported or sold domestically, plus the total of imports and close import substitutes produced domestically. And sometimes it refers to the total trade of a country—that is, to the sum of exports and imports. In this chapter the term "traded goods" is used to refer to the first concept. The total of imports and exports is referred to as "total trade," with the other goods that are produced and consumed internally within the home economy referred to as "domestic goods."

However, only domestic prices are needed to measure the internal RER. Hence, parallel exchange rates, unrecorded trade, and shifts in trade patterns, which can complicate measurement of the external RER, do not pose any problems for measuring the internal RER unless they lead to distortions in domestic price statistics. The considerations involved in choosing an appropriate equilibrium year or representative average as a base for computing internal RER indexes are also similar to those for the external RER as discussed in Chapter 7 on operational methodologies for estimating the equilibrium RER.

Because of the difficulty of actually obtaining price data for tradable-nontradable and traded-nontraded goods, most empirical studies either adopt simplifying assumptions for calculating the internal RER directly or use indirect proxies for it. The following subsections discuss two methods for directly calculating the internal RER. Because of various statistical problems sometimes encountered with the two direct methods, an alternative indirect approach, which uses an external RER as a proxy for the internal RER, has also been widely followed in empirical work. This indirect approach is discussed below in the section on the relationship between the internal and external RERs.

Direct Methods for Estimating the Internal RER in a Two-Good Framework

Two methods have been used in the literature for calculating the internal RER directly. The first direct method uses expenditure data from the national accounts to measure the internal RER as the ratio between the domestic prices of goods actually exported and imported and the price of domestically produced and consumed goods—rather than as the ratio between the prices of tradables and nontradables or between traded and nontraded goods. The second direct method attempts to split sectors of production into tradable and nontradable categories. Value-added in current and constant prices in the tradable and nontradable sectors are then used to compute implicit price deflators for them.

One conceptual problem common to both the foregoing procedures for directly calculating the ratio P_{Td}/P_{Nd}, the internal RER in the two-good framework, is conceptual. The two-good framework aggregates exports and imports into one composite tradable good. Since this framework implicitly assumes that the relative prices of imports and exports are fixed, theoretically the price of tradables could be measured as the price of either exports or imports. In practice, however, imports and exports will usually be different baskets of goods whose prices also move differently whenever the home country's terms of trade fluctuate. The standard solution to this problem is to simply ignore the variations in the terms of trade and aggregate imports and exports into one composite traded good. A price index for total trade is then computed as an average of the prices of exports and imports weighted by their shares in total trade.

However, the price index for total trade that the above procedure yields is not directly related to standard national accounts price indexes for either production or expenditure. In the national accounts, traded goods are imports on the demand (or expenditure) side of the economy, whereas on the supply (production or value-added) side traded goods are exports. The price index for total trade described in the preceding paragraph, and the estimated internal RER based on it, is an average that is not fully consistent with relative prices from either the value-added or the expenditure accounts.[11] This inconsistency is inherent in the two-good framework. There is no remedy for it other than to shift to a three-good framework, which allows for separate price indexes for imports and exports and variations in the terms of trade.[12]

Direct Expenditure-Based Estimates of the Internal RER for Tradable Goods

While the above simplification allows one to use existing or easily calculated price indexes to represent the prices of tradables and nontradables, it underestimates the share of tradables in total production for two reasons. First, tradables are those goods that are exportable or importable. To the extent that some products that are exported are also consumed domestically, the production of exportables will exceed exports. Similarly, if some domestically produced products are very close substitutes for imported products, the consumption of importables will exceed imports. Hence, even for a given RER, the sum of exports and imports will be an underestimate of the sum of exportables and importables and, therefore, of tradables. In cases where significant quantities of major products such as staple foods (such as rice) are both produced and consumed domestically and also imported or exported, the relative importance of traded goods in the economy could be significantly underestimated.[13] Second, goods potentially tradable at a more

---

11. Since nontraded goods are both produced and absorbed entirely within the domestic economy, P_{Nd} is the same whether it is measured by an expenditure or production price index.

12. See the appendix for a further discussion of this point.

13. If the necessary data on domestic consumption of export products and production of close import substitutes (goods whose prices are effectively determined by competing imports through the law of one price) are available, then in principle one could actually calculate the prices of traded and nontraded goods rather than just those of total trade and other domestic goods. Unfortunately, the required data are not available for most developing countries.

depreciated RER, but not actually traded at the current RER, are counted as nontraded. As a result, the size of the tradable sector may be further underestimated.

A method of directly calculating the internal RER was suggested by the work of Devarajan, Lewis, and Robinson (1993). This methodology is explained in detail in the appendix since it is not well documented elsewhere in the empirical literature. To deal with the problem of tradability depending upon the level of the RER, Devarajan, Lewis, and Robinson (1993) redefine the nontraded category as "semitraded" and provide for substitution between exports and semitraded goods in production and between imports and semitraded goods in consumption in determining the equilibrium RER. A price index for total trade is calculated as a (geometric) weighted average of the domestic-currency price deflators for exports and imports from standard national accounts statistics. A deflator for domestic goods, which are both produced and absorbed internally in the home economy, is derived as a residual by subtracting exports from GDP or by subtracting imports from absorption.[14] As explained in the appendix, depending upon the approach followed, one may derive in this way either a final product price index or a value-added price index for domestic goods. The internal RER is then simply calculated as the ratio between the estimated price indexes for total trade (exports plus imports) and domestic goods.[15]

Figure 3.1 shows the price deflators for total trade and domestic goods computed using the above procedure and the resulting estimated internal RER for Côte d'Ivoire for the period prior to the devaluation of the CFA franc. The internal RER is shown in foreign-currency terms (P_{Nd}/P_{Td}, see equation 3.1.b) in the figure so that an upward movement is an appreciation. The internal RER may also be computed as the weighted average of the RERs for imports and exports as explained below.[16]

For most low-income countries, national accounts data, and hence direct estimates of the internal RER based on them, are available only on an annual basis. For countries where the required data are available, it is possible to estimate a monthly series for the internal RER by disag-

---

14. For another example of deriving the price of nontraded goods by substraction, see Sjaastad (1998).

15. See the appendix, figure 3.A.8.

16. A fixed base year, current weighting scheme, or Fisher index may be employed in computing the price indexes and the RER depending upon how the resulting RER indexes will be used. The indexes reported here have been calculated using a current weighting scheme so that the indexes would reflect the changes in the production structure.

Figure 3.1 Expenditure-*Based Price Deflators for Total Trade and Domestic Goods and the Estimated Two-Good Internal RER for Côte d'Ivoire, 1980–93 (1985=100)*

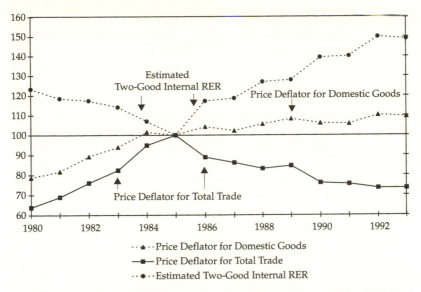

Note: The final product price deflator for domestic goods has been calcualted as the ratio of expenditures on domestically produced consumption and investment goods in current prices to that in constant prices as explained in the appendix. The final product price deflator for total trade has been calculated as total trade (export plus imports of goods and nonfactor services) in current prices divided by total trade in constant prices. The two-good internal RER is expressed here as P_{Nd}/P_{Td} so that an upward movement of it represents an appreciation. *Source:* Computed from World Bank data.

gregating the CPI into importables, exportables, and nontradables. However, for many countries the share of exportables in the CPI may be low or nil so that, when estimated in this way, the price of tradables will usually represent only importables.

Direct Production-*Based Estimates of the Internal RER for Tradable Goods*

The second method of directly estimating the internal RER in a two-good framework divides domestic sectors of production into those producing tradable and nontradable goods. Value added in producing tradable (nontradable) goods is then derived in both current and constant prices by summing value added produced in those sectors classified as tradable (nontradable). The implicit price deflators for tradables (P_{Td}) and nontradables (P_{Nd}) are calculated by dividing value added in current prices by value added in constant prices. The resulting price indexes for tradables and nontradables are current weighted value-added deflators. The internal RER for traded goods is then simply calculated as the ratio of P_{Td} and P_{Nd}.

This method of calculating the internal RER has, however, two major shortcomings. The first results from the conceptual difficulty of neatly classifying the different sectors of production as tradable and nontradable sectors. The second comes from the high level of aggregation of the data on GDP by sector of origin that is actually available in many developing countries.

The production-based methodology requires some operational allocation criteria for dividing the different sectors of domestic production between tradables and nontradables. One criterion suggested by the economic theory would classify a sector as producing a traded good if its pricing behavior follows the law of one price. In a strict sense, this law requires that the change in domestic price for a good i be equal to the change in the foreign price of the same good adjusted for the change in the exchange rate (see equation 3.2). In a broader sense, the law simply requires that perfect substitutability and commodity arbitrage exist between the same domestic and the foreign goods (taking into account tariffs, transports, insurance, and so forth). Several studies have shown, however, that if this criterion is used, few sectors of production would qualify as tradables, even at relatively fine levels of disaggregation.[17]

Another allocation criterion often used in the literature is the degree of participation in foreign trade. For example, De Gregorio, Giovannini, and Wolf (1994) in a study of 14 industrial countries belonging to the Organization for Economic Cooperation and Development (OECD) define a sector as "tradable" if an average of 10 percent or more of its total production in the 14 countries is exported, a definition that is still in use by researchers for industrial countries.[18] On this criterion, the agriculture, mining, manufacturing, and transportation sectors are classified as tradable and all other sectors as nontradable, a sectoral classification that De Gregorio, Giovannini, and Wolf find is fairly robust to moderate variations in the 10 percent threshold percentage. Other authors do not establish an explicit quantitative criterion for defining "tradable." They simply make a qualitative judgment about which production sectors should be classified as tradables based on the extent of actual or potential participation in foreign trade—and treat the rest of the sectors as

---

17. See Goldstein and Officer (1979) for a discussion of these studies.
18. See, for example, Chinn and Johnston (1997).

producing nontradables. Goldstein and Officer (1979), for example, assign to the tradable sector the following sectors in the case of industrial countries: agriculture and related activities, mining and quarrying, and manufacturing. Similarly, in calculating the internal RER for two developing countries, Colombia and Kenya, Wickham (1993) defines the tradables sector as encompassing agriculture, mining, and manufacturing; and Canzoneri, Cumby, and Diba (1996) define the tradable sector as manufacturing, agriculture, forestry, and fishing in a study of 13 OECD countries.

There is, however, no general consensus on the appropriate qualitative dividing line to use in classifying sectors as tradable and nontradable. In practice, sectors for which the exports to domestically produced output ratio and the imports to domestically produced output ratio are both zero are generally classified as nontradables. (These sectors are mainly public services and construction.) For those sectors for which at least one of these ratios is not zero, however, it is desirable to specify quantitative criteria for deciding which sectors are tradable or nontradable, or to determine what percentage of the output of each is tradable or nontradable. The various criteria used in the empirical literature still remain arbitrary and are not necessarily appropriate for all countries.

To be able to empirically separate sectors of production into tradable and nontradable, one needs sectoral output in current and constant prices at a reasonable level of disaggregation. Such data are sometimes not available in low-income developing countries or, if available, are aggregated into a few very large sectors. Because of the high level of aggregation of the available data on GDP by sector of origin, some sectors classified as producing tradable goods will undoubtedly include substantial nontradable output and vice versa. Thus, it is often not possible to separate tradable sectors from nontradable ones in a meaningful way.

For example, for the thirteen CFA countries, reasonably disaggregated data in current and constant prices for GDP by sector of origin are available only for Côte d'Ivoire and a few other countries. For Côte d'Ivoire, the following sectors were qualitatively classified as tradable sectors on the basis of what Bank staff knew about the structure of trade and production at the existing exchange rate: export agriculture, foodcrop agriculture, forestry, petroleum and mining, agro-industries, other industries, and export trade. All other sectors of production—energy, construction, transportation, internal trade, services, and public administration—were classified as nontradable. In contrast to the expenditure-based estimate of the internal RER for which the required data are available starting in 1960, a production-based RER measure could be computed only for the period since 1985, when disaggregated data on value added by sector became available.

Figure 3.2 Production-*Based Estimates of Value-Added Deflators for Tradable Goods and Nontradable Goods and the Two-Good Internal RER for Côte d'Ivoire, 1985–93 (1985=100)*

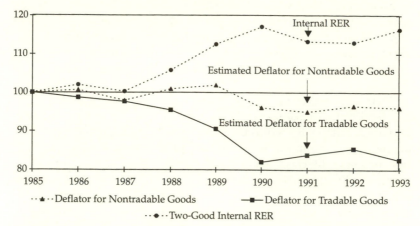

Note: The tradable sectors include export agriculture, foodcrop agriculture, forestry, petroleum and mining, agro-industries, other industries, and export trade. In the Côte d'Ivoire national accounts, part of the manufacutring sector is included in agro-industries and part in other countries. The nontradable sectors are energy, construction, transportation, services, internal trade, and public administration. The two-good internal RER is expressed here as P_{Nd}/P_{Td} so that an upward movement of it represents an appreciation.
Source: Computed from World Bank data.

Figure 3.2 shows the production-based (value-added) estimates of deflators for tradable and nontradable goods and the corresponding internal RER for tradable goods for Côte d'Ivoire for 1985–93. Figures 3.3a, 3.3b, and 3.3c then compare the production-based (value-added) estimate of the two-good internal RER and its components with the expenditure-based estimate for Côte d'Ivoire.[19] Because of the conceptual and empirical limitations of the production-based methodology, the resulting production-based estimate of the internal RER diverges from the expenditure-based estimate by 30 percent over an eight-year period (see figure 3.3c). The estimated price deflators for total trade and tradable goods (figure 3.3b) are at least roughly consistent, both falling but diverging by 14 percent over eight years. However, the estimated expenditure deflator for domestic goods and the value-added deflator for

---

19. The expenditure-based estimate has been expressed in value-added terms to make it more directly comparable to the production-based estimate. See the appendix for an explanation of the relationship between value-added and final product price deflators.

Figure 3.3a *Comparison of the Value-Added Deflators for* **Nontradable** *and* **Domestic** *Goods for Côte d'Ivoire, 1985–93 (1985=100)*

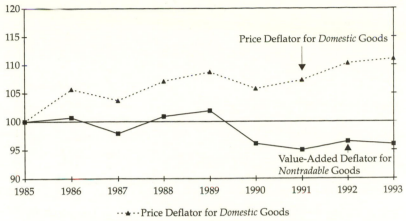

··▲·· Price Deflator for *Domestic* Goods

—■— Value-Added Deflator for *Nontradable* Goods

Note: The expenditure-based price deflator for domestic goods has been calculated as the ratio of domestic consumption and investment goods in current prices to that in constant prices as explained in the appendix. The production-based value-added deflator for nontradable goods has been calculated as explained in the note to figure 3.2.
Source: Computed from World Bank data.

Figure 3.3b *Comparison of the* **Production-***Based Value-Added Deflator for* **Tradable** *Goods and the* **Expenditure-***Based Deflator for* **Total Trade** *for Côte d'Ivoire, 1985–93 (1985=100)*

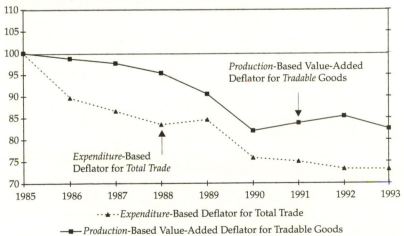

··▲·· *Expenditure*-Based Deflator for Total Trade

—■— *Production*-Based Value-Added Deflator for Tradable Goods

Note: The expenditure-based deflator for total trade has been calculated as the weighted average of the deflators for exports and imports as explained in the appendix. The production-based value-added deflator for tradable goods has been calculated as explained in the note to figure 3.2.
Source: Computed from World Bank data.

Figure 3.3c *Comparison of Expenditure- and Production-Based Estimates of the Two-Good Internal RER for Côte d'Ivoire, 1985–93 (1985=100)*

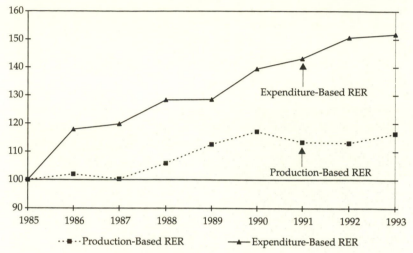

Note: The expediture-based estimate of the two-good RER for total trade has been calculated here using the deflators for domestic goods and total trade. It differs slightly from the two-good internal RER for total trade calculated using final product prices shown in figure 3.1 (see the appendix, figure 3.A.8). The production-based estimate of the two-good internal RER is calculated as in figure 3.2. The two-good internal RER is expressed here as P_{Nd}/P_{Td} so that an upward movement of it represents an appreciation.
Source: Computed from World Bank data.

nontradables (figure 3.3a) follow different trends, with the former rising by 11 percent and the latter dropping by 4 percent. The changes in the production-based estimate of the internal RER are more damped than those in the expenditure-based estimates, as one would expect because of the production-based methodology's imperfect separation of tradable and nontradable sectors.

The magnitude of the above divergences suggests that considerable care is needed in trying to estimate the internal RER using the two procedures described above. For those countries in which the required data on GDP disaggregated by sector of origin are available, the production-based estimate of the two-good RER is worth calculating as a cross check on the expenditure-based estimate. However, the two resulting estimates may differ substantially, as in the Côte d'Ivoire case. The analyst will need to look at other data, such as the WPI-CPI proxy discussed in the next section, in order to determine which is giving the more reliable signal. Moreover, when there are large movements in the terms of trade, as in Côte d'Ivoire, any measure of the two-good internal RER will average together radically different changes in the internal RERs for imports and exports and consequently may convey very little useful information. (See the section titled "The Three-Good Internal RERs for Imports and Exports: Concepts and Measurements" in Chapter 4 for a further discussion of this point.)

The Relationship between the External RER and the Two-Good Internal RER

This section reviews the theoretical and empirical relationship between the two-good internal RER for tradables and the external RER, following the standard presentation. The first subsection discusses the relationship between internal and external competitiveness and the law of one price. The second subsection looks at the theoretical relationship between the internal and external RERs in the absence of trade taxes and administered prices. The third considers an empirical example. And the fourth subsection then examines the effects of introducing trade taxes and administered prices.

The Law of One Price and Internal vs. External Competitiveness

Internal and external RERs are often used to draw inferences about a country's competitiveness, and there has been much popular debate over the relationships between competitiveness, productivity, and exchange rates.[20] Hence, at this point it is natural to ask: what is the relationship between the internal and external RERs and competitiveness?

What constitutes a "competitive" price and how much prices will be equalized by international trade depends critically upon whether traded goods are homogeneous perfect substitutes (for example, primary commodities) or differentiated imperfect substitutes (for example, most manufactures). There are two basic concepts of competitiveness—internal and external—and their relevance in a given situation depends upon the nature of the goods being traded.

Homogeneous Goods and the Law of One Price

For homogeneous goods, external competitiveness is a "yes" or "no" question. Prices are set by international markets and the law of one price. Theoretically, there should be only one price after allowance for transportation,

---

20. For an example, see Krugman (1994).

tariffs, trade restrictions, and other transactions costs. Homogenous goods are either sold at the internationally determined price, or they are not sold at all. Complete price equalization should take place; and the empirical evidence is that it does.[21] Because homogeneous commodities are typically a much larger percentage of developing-country exports than of their imports, the law of one price is more likely to apply to their exports than to their imports.

For homogeneous goods, whatever a small country produces can be sold at the international market price. Therefore, the question of market share becomes one of internal competitiveness—that is, of what quantity can profitably be produced in the home country—and hence is a question of domestic price incentives and profitability in the production of tradables. Such *internal* competitiveness is the internal profitability *in the home country* of producing tradable goods relative to producing nontradables. Internal competitiveness is what the internal RER is designed to measure.

Differentiated Goods and Imperfect Competition

For differentiated goods that are imperfect substitutes, some differences in price should persist depending upon the degree of substitutability and the cross-price elasticities of demand among close substitutes. After reviewing the empirical evidence concerning the large industrial economies, Rogoff (1996) concludes that "outside a fairly small range of various homogeneous goods, short-run international arbitrage has only a limited effect on equating international goods market prices." Similarly, Isard (1997) writes that "in reality the law of one price is flagrantly and systematically violated by the empirical data." There is a large literature that analyzes the extensive and protracted divergences of markets for differentiated goods from the law of one price in large industrial countries.[22] However, although the empirical evidence is limited, the law of one price appears to be less problematic in small developing economies, in which the tendency is to automatically pass through the effects of exchange rate movements to the domestic prices of traded goods as discussed in Chapter 11 on the RER and trade flows.

External competitiveness for differentiated goods is a matter of degree rather than a "yes" or "no" question. For these imperfect substitutes, external demand is less than perfectly elastic. More can be sold, but only at a lower price. A key indicator of competitiveness in the pricing of imperfect substitutes is changes in their market shares. Competitive pricing will lead to a stable or increasing market share, whereas

---

21. See Clark and others (1994).
22. For a recent summary of this literature, see Goldberg and Knetter (1997).

uncompetitive pricing will be reflected in a falling market share. For differentiated traded goods, pricing to market and incomplete pass-through of changes in exchange rates to domestic prices may be common. Hence, *external* competitiveness is a question of the relative price *compared with those of competitor countries* at which the home country's *traded* goods are sold—that is, of the external RER for traded goods. Since the home country still needs internal incentives for producing an adequate volume of traded goods, in this situation measures of both internal and external competitiveness are usually relevant.

Internal Competitiveness

The internal RER has developed as the primary indicator of internal competitiveness, and theories about it have addressed the question of what level of the internal RER is necessary to achieve macroeconomic balance. Thus, analysis of internal competitiveness has been fully integrated with that of macroeconomic balance. Furthermore, since the theories of the internal RER typically assume that a country produces homogenous traded goods to which the law of one price applies, internal competitiveness automatically implies external competitiveness under these theories.

External Competitiveness

In contrast, external competitiveness has often been defined in two somewhat different ways, either in terms of (a) macroeconomic balance or (b) differentiated products and market shares for traded goods.[23] The macroeconomic balance approach to external competitiveness has focused on the external RER for all goods. In the macroeconomic balance interpretation, a competitive external RER is synonymous with an equilibrium RER—it is an RER that achieves a sustainable internal and external balance for the home country. Depending upon the model being used, either the expenditure-PPP or Mundell-Fleming RER may be used in analyzing macroeconomic balance. In this usage, a depreciation in the RER and an increase in competitiveness are equivalent. Note that in this interpretation a country can become "too competitive" when its RER depreciates excessively and becomes undervalued. Economists following this macroeconomic balance approach generally set out the model that they consider relevant for determining macroeconomic balance in a given country and then try to find the closest empirical counterpart of the theoretical measure of the RER required by their model.

The second common way of viewing external competitiveness is in terms of market shares of international trade in differentiated products.

---

23. See Clark and others (1994).

Economists adopting this approach typically define competitiveness as the relative cost in foreign exchange terms of producing traded goods. They then try to find the most accurate empirical measure of it. This interpretation of competitiveness is closer to microeconomic concepts—such as domestic resource cost—that establish measures of competitiveness for specific firms or industries. Macroeconomic RER indexes can provide useful indicators of price competitiveness in this sense, although many microeconomic factors such as quality, reliability, after-sale service, delivery times, financing arrangements, and so forth do not lend themselves to quantification in a macroeconomic index.[24]

A rise in costs or prices, expressed in foreign currency, in the traded sector of the home country, relative to costs or prices of its competitors, will lead to a loss of competitiveness and market share and, thus, to a deterioration in the home country's trade balance. Relative PPP may be assumed to hold for the external RER for traded goods, or it may be used as the relative price in empirical trade equations for import and export demand in industrial countries.[25] How large a change in the external RER for traded goods is required to produce a given improvement in a country's market shares and the trade balance is, in the latter case, an empirical question of the size of the price elasticities of demand for its imports and exports.[26]

The Theoretical Relationship between the Two-Good Internal RER and the External RER

In order to determine the relationship between the external RER and the internal RER for tradables, let us assume for convenience that there are only two countries, the home country and the rest of the world (or the foreign country). If both the domestic and the world aggregate price indexes are geometric weighted averages of tradable and nontradable prices, with weights α and a for nontradables, then, as shown in equations 3.4 and 3.5:

(3.4) $$P_{Gd} = P_{Nd}^{\alpha} \cdot P_{Td}^{1-\alpha} \text{ with } 0 < \alpha < 1$$

(3.5) $$P_{Gf} = P_{Nf}^{a} \cdot P_{Tf}^{1-a} \text{ with } 0 < a < 1.$$

24. For a discussion of some of the issues involved in assessing the microeconomic competitiveness of firms and industries see Fane (1995).

25. See for example Wren-Lewis and Driver (1998).

26. This approach also usually requires balance of payments targets from another source to determine how large a change in the RER is required, as discussed in Chapter 7.

Empirically the domestic and foreign price levels, P_{Gd} and P_{Gf}, and the prices of tradables and nontradables may be measured by either expenditure or production price indexes. The values of α and a will generally depend upon which of these types of price indexes is used.

The bilateral external RER between the home and foreign countries is defined in foreign-currency terms in equation 2.3 in Chapter 2 as in equation 3.6:

$$(3.6) \qquad BRER_{fc} = \frac{E_{fc} \cdot P_{Gd}}{P_{Gf}}.$$

The type of external RER yielded by equation 3.6 will depend upon the type of price indexes used in equations 3.4 and 3.5. If expenditure price indexes are used to measure the prices of tradables and nontradables and to compute the internal RER, equation 3.6 will yield the expenditure-PPP external RER. If production price indexes are used, equation 3.6 will yield the Mundell-Fleming external RER.

Replacing P_{Gd} and P_{Gf} in equation 3.6 by their respective definitions in equation 3.4 and 3.5 and rearranging the terms, we obtain equation 3.7:

$$(3.7) \qquad BRER_{fc} = \frac{(P_{Nd}/P_{Td})^{\alpha}}{(P_{Nf}/P_{Tf})^{\alpha}} \frac{E_{fc} \cdot P_{Td}}{P_{Tf}}.$$

The ratio P_{Nd}/P_{Td} is the internal RER for the home country, and the ratio P_{Nf}/P_{Tf} is the internal RER of the foreign country, defined in both cases as the relative price of nontradable goods to tradable goods ($IRERN_T$). Equation 3.7 can then be rewritten as equation 3.8:

$$(3.8) \qquad BRER_{fc} = \frac{IRERN_{Td}^{\alpha}}{IRERN_{Tf}^{a}} \cdot \frac{E_{fc} \cdot P_{Td}}{P_{Tf}}$$

where $RERN_{Td}$ and $RERN_{Tf}$ are the internal RERs for the home and the foreign countries, respectively, in foreign-currency terms. Note that the second term on the right-hand side of equation 3.8, $E_{fc} \cdot P_{Td}/P_{Tf}$, is the *bilateral external RER for traded goods*.

In a simplified case in which the law of one price applies to tradables, there are no trade taxes, and other transaction costs are included in their border price (P_{Tf}), the domestic price of tradables is equal to the foreign price of tradables multiplied by the nominal exchange rate in domestic-currency terms ($E_{dc} = 1/E_{fc}$). Hence, the term $E_{fc} \cdot P_{Td}/P_{Tf}$ in equation 3.8, the external RER for traded goods, is equal to one. We then obtain the following relationship (equation 3.9) between the external RER of the home country and the ratio of the internal RER of the home country to that of the foreign country:[27]

(3.9)
$$BRER_{fc} = \frac{IRERN_{Td}^{\alpha}}{IRERN_{Tf}^{\alpha}}.$$

Taking the logarithms of both sides and then differentiating equation 3.9 gives, for small changes, equation 3.10:

(3.10)
$$\widehat{BRER}_{fc} = \alpha \cdot \widehat{IRERN}_{Td} - a \cdot \widehat{IRERN}_{Tf}$$

with the "hat operator" ($\wedge$) on a variable X defined in the standard fashion as $\Delta X/X$. Conversely, solving equation 3.10 for the home country's internal RER yields equation 3.11:

(3.11)
$$\widehat{IRERN}_{Td} = \frac{1}{\alpha} \cdot \widehat{BRER}_{fc} + \frac{a}{\alpha} \cdot \widehat{IRERN}_{Tf} .$$

As shown by equations 3.10 and 3.11, the internal and external RERs for the home country will differ and will not necessarily always move in the same direction. It is easiest to see the relationship between the home country's internal and external RERs in equation 3.10. First, if there is no change in the foreign country's internal RER, the second term on the right side of equation 3.10 will equal zero; and the change in the home country's external RER will be proportional to the change in its internal RER, as shown in equation 3.10.a:

(3.10.a)
$$\widehat{BRER}_{fc} = \alpha \cdot \widehat{IRERN}_{Td} .$$

Since α, the share of the nontradable sector in the home economy, is positive but less than one, the change in the home country's external RER will always be smaller than the change in its internal RER. The larger α is, the greater the size of the change in the external RER will be. Conversely, the change in the internal RER will always be larger than

---

27. In the two-country framework assumed here, P_{Tf} and P_{Td} represent the same baskets of goods because the home country's exports are necessarily the foreign country's imports and vice versa. In a multicountry case, the foreign countries may trade among themselves as well as with the home country, and their basket of tradable goods is not likely to be identical to the home country's. Hence, $E_{fc} \cdot P_{Td}$ can be equated to P_{Tf} only if P_{Tf} is the foreign price index of the *home* country's basket of traded goods. If such an index is not available empirically and some other empirical price index is used, $E_{fc} \cdot P_{Td}/P_{Tf}$ will not be equal to one. In this case, there will be an additional term in the actual empirical multilateral formulation of equation 3.9.

the corresponding change in its external RER. If, for example, the external RER depreciates because of foreign inflation or a devaluation, the internal RER will depreciate by more through the effect of the law of one price on the prices of traded goods, which change by the full amount of the devaluation or foreign price increase.

Second, since $0 < a < 1$, $-a$ will be negative, and changes in the home country's external RER will be negatively related to changes in the foreign country's internal RER. If, for example, the foreign country's internal RER appreciates as a result of faster productivity growth in its tradable than in its nontradable sector (the Balassa-Samuelson effect), this appreciation will tend to depreciate the home country's external RER.[28] It is even possible in some circumstances for the home country's internal and external RERs to move in opposite directions. Such a situation will occur when the following equation, 3.12, holds:

$$(3.12) \qquad \left| \alpha \cdot \widehat{IRERN}_{Td} \right| < \left| a \cdot \widehat{IRERN}_{Tf} \right|.$$

For example, if the nontradable sector is of the same relative size in the home and foreign countries (that is, $\alpha = a$) and the foreign country's internal RER appreciates more than the home country's internal RER (caused, for example, by faster productivity increases), then the home country's external RER will depreciate even though its internal RER has appreciated. The likelihood of such contrary movements in a country's internal and external RERs will be greater if (a) the change in the foreign country's internal RER is larger or (b) the share of nontradables in the foreign economy, a, is larger relative to the share of nontradables in the home economy, α (or, equivalently, if the foreign economy is less open relative to the home economy).

Third, different rates of productivity growth in the tradable and nontradable sectors are one of the most important empirical factors affecting the relationship between the internal and external RERs. As discussed in Chapters 5 and 6 on the determinants of the equilibrium RER, Balassa (1964) and Samuelson (1964) postulated that faster productivity growth in the tradable than in the nontradable sector would lead to a declining relative price of tradables. Hence, in all countries experiencing faster productivity growth in the tradables than in the nontradables would, other things being equal, have *internal RERs that appreciate over time*.[29] Furthermore, Balassa and Samuelson showed that, if productivity

---

28. Similarly, if shifts in internal demand change the internal RER (for example, through greater government spending on nontradables), these can also cause movements in the external RER.

29. Highly income-elastic demand for nontradables can also cause an appreciation of the internal RER as discussed in Chapter 5.

in the tradable sector relative to productivity in the nontradable sector grew faster in a country than it did in its trading partners, the country's *external* RER would also appreciate, although less rapidly than its internal RER. This appreciation in the external RER occurs because the relatively more rapid productivity growth in the tradable than the nontradable sector in the home country causes it to experience a larger increase in the relative price of nontradables than its trading partners. At the same time, the law of one price equalizes the domestic and foreign prices of tradable goods, causing the external RER for traded goods to remain constant.

Finally, the above relationships all assume that the law of one price holds for tradable goods. However, as noted earlier in the discussion of competitiveness, there is considerable empirical evidence, except for a few homogeneous commodities, of extensive and protracted divergences of the prices of traded goods from the law of one price. If the law of one price does not hold, the external RER for traded goods will no longer be a constant; and the relationship between the internal and external RERs will be affected by pricing-to-market and other strategic pricing behavior of firms as well as by the other variables shown in equation 3.10. In particular, if the pass-through to traded-goods prices of exchange rate movements affecting the external RER is only partial, the effect of exchange rate movements on the internal RER will be smaller than implied by equation 3.11.[30]

An Empirical Example

Empirically, the *different price indexes* used in computing internal and external RERs can at times cause them to behave quite differently. As noted in equations 3.6 and 3.7, the external RER is expressed in terms of relative aggregate price levels, whereas the internal RER is expressed in terms of relative domestic prices of traded and nontraded goods. The prices of traded goods, particularly exports in commodity-producing developing countries, tend to be more volatile than the prices of nontraded goods. The aggregate price level, which includes both traded and nontraded goods, will also tend to be somewhat more volatile than the price of nontraded goods alone. Hence, a country's internal RER will tend to be more volatile than its external RER because its numerator (the price of traded goods) is more volatile and its denominator (the price of nontraded goods) is less volatile than its aggregate price level.

---

30. See Gordon (1994) for a further discussion of this point.

Figure 3.4 *The External RER (REER) at* **Official** *and* **Weighted** *Average Official and Parallel Exchange Rates and the Internal RER for Total Trade at Domestic Prices,* **Including** *Taxes,* **Computed** *Relative to the Price of Domestic Goods, and the Aggregate Price Level for Côte d'Ivoire, 1980–93 (1985=100)*

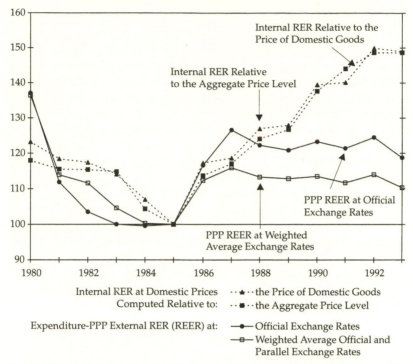

Note: The internal RER at domestic prices expressed relative to the price deflator for domestic goods is calculated as the final product price deflator for domestic goods divided by the deflator for total trade as explained in the appendix. The internal RER at domestic prices expressed relative to the aggregate price level is calculated as the private consumption deflator divided by the deflator for total trade. The private consumption deflator has been used here and in the following graphs so that the inconsistency between the CPI and the private consumption deflator time series noted in footnote 40, Chapter 2, would not distort the comparisons between the internal and external RERs. The real effective exchange rate has been computed using CPIs for all countries other than Côte d'Ivoire, the private consumption deflator for Côte d'Ivoire, and adjusted IFS country weights. An upward movement is an appreciation.
Source: Computed from World Bank data.

Figure 3.4 illustrates the above point. It compares the internal RER for traded goods for Côte d'Ivoire, expressed relative to both the price of domestic goods and to its aggregate price level, to the expenditure-PPP external RER.[31] The primary difference between the internal and external RERs is due to the volatility in the price of traded goods, which causes both measures of the internal RER to fluctuate more than the external RER. In contrast, the differences in the movements of the prices of domestic goods and in the aggregate price level cause only minor divergences in the measures of the internal RER.

Productivity growth and changes in the internal RER in foreign countries can also affect the relationship between the internal and external RERs. The Balassa-Samuelson effect has been well documented for industrial countries as discussed in the survey of empirical research in Chapter 5. The stereotypical pattern seen in RER data for industrial countries experiencing rapid productivity growth is a strong appreciation in the internal RER, a significant but more modest appreciation in the external RER, and stability or depreciation in the external RER for traded goods.

Unfortunately, many low-income developing countries do not have data for any measure of productivity. This lack of data has inhibited empirical research on effects of productivity growth on RERs in these countries.[32] The growth rate of per capita GDP is the only general indicator of long-term productivity growth available for many developing countries. It is thus often used as a proxy for productivity in regression analysis of exchange rates.

As figure 3.4 shows, Côte d'Ivoire's external and internal RERs both depreciated during 1980–85 and then appreciated during 1985–93. Côte d'Ivoire's OECD trading partners, which account for 78 percent of the country weightings in its REER, probably experienced some appreciation of their internal RERs as a result of productivity changes. Hence, one would expect that, as indicated by equation 3.11, Côte d'Ivoire's internal RER should have appreciated more than its external RER. Figure 3.4 shows that, even after adjusting for the different numeraire used in internal and external RERs, the internal RER, as expected, appreciated by about 40 percent more over the period 1985–93 than the external RER at weighted average exchange rates. Part of this apparent excess

---

31. As discussed in Chapter 2, a potentially serious practical problem in measuring external RERs in developing countries is the existence of parallel exchange markets. To illustrate this complication, figure 3.4 also shows the external RER for Côte d'Ivoire computed at weighted average parallel and official exchange rates. The internal and external RERs have both been computed using expenditure price indexes.

32. To date, the only developing countries for which the Balassa-Samuelson effect has been empirically documented are Korea and Taiwan (Caramazza and Aziz 1998).

appreciation was undoubtedly due to the sharp decline—for which the two-good framework does not explicitly allow—in Côte d'Ivoire's export prices as explained in the next chapter's section on the terms of trade.

As in most developing countries, no data on sectoral productivity or even on overall productivity are available for Côte d'Ivoire to illustrate the Balassa-Samuelson effect. In the absence of such data, it is not possible to give an example of the effects of differential productivity growth on the relationship between Côte d'Ivoire's internal and external RERs. Similarly, because of lack of data it is difficult to estimate how much of the observed appreciation in Côte d'Ivoire's internal and external RERs was caused by productivity growth and how much by other real shocks (such as the decline in real export prices). The behavior of real GDP per capita does, however, give a broad indication of trends in aggregate productivity. Real GDP per capita in Côte d'Ivoire fell at an average rate of 4.2 percent per year during 1985–93. This substantial decline would suggest that aggregate productivity must also have fallen and that the observed appreciation of the internal and external RERs was probably caused by factors other than productivity growth.

The Effect of Trade Taxes and Administered Prices

The simplified formulation above does not allow for the effects of taxes on international trade or of administered internal prices, which may cause domestic prices to diverge from border prices. When such tax or administered price effects are significant, they will affect the relationship between the internal and external RERs. The above equations then need to be modified to allow for them.[33]

As $E_{dc} = 1/E_{fc}$, the terms in equation 3.2 for the law of one price may be rearranged to give equations 3.13 and 3.14:

(3.13)
$$E_{fc} \cdot P_{Td} = P_{Tf}(1+t)$$

(3.14)
$$\frac{E_{fc} \cdot P_{Td}}{P_{Tf}} = 1+t \quad \cdot$$

Thus, in equation 3.8 the term $E_{fc} \cdot P_{Td}/P_{Tf}$ is equal to $1+t$ rather than to 1. Equation 3.10 now becomes equation 3.15:

---

33. The discussion here concerns the effects of trade taxes on the observed or measured RER. Their effects on the equilibrium RER are discussed in Chapter 6.

$$(3.15) \qquad BRER_{fc} = \frac{IRERN_{Td}^{\alpha}}{IRERN_{Tf}^{\alpha}} \cdot (1+t).$$

And equations 3.10 and 3.11 now become 3.16.a and 3.16.b:

$$(3.16.a) \qquad \widehat{BRER}_{fc} = \alpha \cdot \widehat{RERN}_{Td} - a \cdot \widehat{IRERN}_{Tf} + \widehat{(1+t)}$$

$$(3.16.b) \qquad \widehat{RERN}_{Td} = \frac{1}{\alpha} \cdot \widehat{BRER}_{fc} + \frac{a}{\alpha} \widehat{IRERN}_{Tf} - \frac{1}{\alpha} \cdot \widehat{(1+t)}.$$

The effect of trade taxes is thus to create a further divergence between the internal and external RERs of the home country. In other words, changes in trade taxes, as well as in the foreign country's internal RER, can cause the home country's external RER to behave differently from its internal RER. For countries experiencing "import compression," t may increase significantly, and the divergence between the internal and external RERs may be quite substantial. An increase in protection (that is, an increase in $1 + t$), other things being equal, will depreciate the internal RER by raising the domestic price of tradables (equation 3.16.b) and hence may (partially) offset an appreciation of the external RER. Conversely, trade liberalization or a reduction in trade taxes will tend to appreciate the internal RER and tend to offset a depreciation in the external RER because, for example, of a devaluation.

Figure 3.5 illustrates the effects of trade taxes on the relationship between the internal and external RERs. It compares Côte d'Ivoire's internal RER measured at domestic prices (which include taxes) and at border prices (which exclude taxes) to the external RER.[34] As figure 3.5 shows, there were significant differences in the behavior of the internal RERs measured at border and domestic prices. The apparent effect of changes in trade taxes and administered prices was to moderate the decline in the relative domestic prices of traded goods in 1985–93 and hence to reduce the appreciation in the internal RER at domestic prices (including taxes) relative to that in the internal RER at border prices (excluding taxes).

However, part of the difference between the two internal RERs may be attributable to statistical discrepancies between the domestic price and border price data. Ideally, it would be desirable to have independent measures of border prices, trade taxes, and domestic prices in order to check for statistical discrepancies. Unfortunately, such data were not available for Côte d'Ivoire and are not available in many other low-income countries.

---

34. Again, the REER is shown at both official and weighted average parallel and official exchange rates.

Figure 3.5 *The External RER (REER) at Official and Weighted Average Official and Parallel Exchange Rates, and the Internal RER for Total Trade Including and Excluding Taxes Relative to the Price of Domestic Goods, 1980–93 (1985=100)*

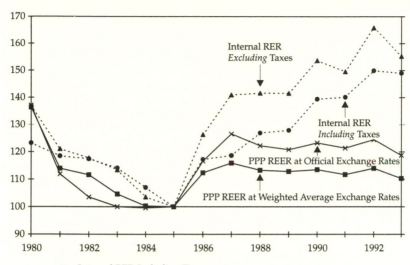

--•--Internal RER Including Taxes
--▲--Internal RER Excluding Taxes
—✕—Expenditure-PPP External REER at Official Exchange Rates
—■—Expenditure-PPP External REER at Weighted Average Official and
　　Parallel Exchange Rates

Note: The external RER has been calculated using effective foreign CPIs and adjusted IFS country weights. The private consumption deflator has been used in lieu of the the CPI for Côte d'Ivoire for reasons explained in the note to figure 3.4. The internal RERs for total trade including and excluding taxes have been calculated as explained in the appendix. An upward movement represents an appreciation of the internal and external RERs.
Source: Computed from World Bank data.

Furthermore, the above two-good framework implicitly assumes that taxes and subsidies on imports and exports are symmetric. Since imports and exports are nearly always taxed differently, the effects of trade taxes on the internal RER are best analyzed in the next chapter's three-good framework, which allows for such differential taxation.

External RERs as Proxies for the Two-Good Internal RER

Because of the timely availability of consumer and wholesale price indexes, the relative ease of calculating external RER indexes, and the limited empirical work that has been done on the direct estimation of internal RER indexes, many empirical studies have used external RERs as *proxies* for the internal RER. This indirect approach involves two significant modifications in the computation of the internal RER: (a) the use of a general domestic price index for the home country instead of the price of nontradable goods, and (b) the use of an aggregate foreign price index, usually the WPI, multiplied by the nominal exchange rate as a proxy for the domestic price of traded goods in the home country. In the empirical literature such proxies have generally only been used in a two-good framework, although the approach could in principle be modified for use with three goods.

Use of an Aggregate Domestic Price Index for the Home Country

The indirect approach measures the internal RER by using a representative *aggregate* domestic price index for the home country that includes both tradable and nontradable goods instead of a price index for just nontradable goods. The aggregate domestic price indexes (P_{Gd}) typically used for the home country give *representative* weightings to tradables and nontradables that reflect their relative importance in the home economy. In this approach, the aggregate price index is not intended to represent P_{Nd}.[35] Rather, one can draw inferences about the ratio P_{Td}/P_{Nd} (that is, $IRERT_N$) from the ratio P_{Td}/P_{Gd} (which we will label as $IRERT_G$) because P_{Gd} is an aggregation of tradable and nontradable price indexes. This approach is commonly used because at least one domestic aggregate price index, the CPI, is available on a timely basis for most developing countries. In addition, much related empirical work (for example, that on price elasticities of imports and exports) uses the general domestic price level as the numeraire in calculating relative prices and is more directly comparable with the internal RER expressed relative to the general price level ($IRERT_G$) than to the one expressed relative to the price of nontraded goods ($IRERT_N$).

The indirect approach thus, in effect, redefines the internal RER as shown in equation 3.17:

35. An alternative approach, which has been followed by a number of authors, uses an aggregate price index as a proxy for the price of nontraded goods in the home country. (See, for example, Devereux and Connolly 1996, who use the CPI as a proxy for the price of nontraded goods.) In this case, the aggregate price index with the heaviest weighting of nontraded goods should be used. Note, however, that if a price index for traded goods (such as the WPI) is used for the home country as well as for the foreign country, the external RER for traded goods is being measured rather than a proxy for the internal RER.

(3.17)
$$IRERT_G = \frac{P_{Td}}{P_{Gd}} = \frac{E_{dc} \cdot P_{Tf}(1+t)}{P_{Gd}}.$$

The rationale for this approach is that an aggregate price index is a weighted average of the prices of traded and nontraded goods as defined in equation 3.4. By substituting for P_{Gd} from the equation used in the definition of $IRERT_G$ (equation 3.17) and rearranging the terms, we can obtain the following direct relationship, equation 3.18, between $IRERT_N$ (as defined in equation 3.1) and $IRERT_N$:

(3.18)
$$IRERT_N = IRERT_G^{\frac{1}{\alpha}}$$

where α is the weight of nontradable goods in the aggregate index, P_{Gd}.[36] Equation 3.18 indicates that the value of $IRERT_N$ can be deduced from the value of $IRERT_G$ and α. In other words, if we know the value $IRERT_G$ and the value of the parameter α, we can automatically calculate the value of $IRERT_N$.

However, if α is not known, a price index for only domestic goods cannot be calculated. Since the value of α is often not readily available, many authors use internal RER indexes expressed relative to the aggregate price level ($IRERT_G$) and implicitly utilize equation 3.18 to draw inferences about the relative price of traded to nontraded goods ($IRERT_N$). Care needs to be taken in interpreting such internal RER indexes expressed relative to the aggregate price level for three reasons. First, in general, the greater the weight of traded goods in the general price index is (that is, the smaller the value of α), the greater the divergence between P_{Gd} and P_{Nd} (and hence between and $IRERT_N$ and $IRERT_G$) will be and the more damped the movements in $IRERT_N$ will be relative to those in $IRERT_N$.[37] Second, the value of the parameter α can change over time (for example, as the result of a devaluation), making the relation between $IRERT_N$ and $IRERT_G$ less stable. Third, even with a constant value of α, the relation between $IRERT_N$ and $IRERT_G$ is not linear, implying that a trend in $IRERT_G$ will not necessarily be precisely the same as a trend in $IRERT_N$.

---

36. Note that $1 - \alpha$ may have a different value depending upon whether one uses a production or expenditure price index. For a production index, $1 - \alpha$ will be the share of exports in total output. For an expenditure index, $1 - \alpha$ will be the share of imports in total expenditure. See the appendix for further discussion of this point.

37. To reduce this divergence, the alternative methodology noted in footnote 33 uses the aggregate domestic price index with the highest weighting of nontraded goods (that is, the highest value of α).

In calculating proxies for the two-good internal RER, the domestic CPI is commonly used as the aggregate domestic price index for the home country.[38] Two related arguments are generally cited for using this index. First, the CPI usually contains a representative proportion of nontraded goods. Second, it is readily available in most developing countries, generally on a monthly basis. Hence, the CPI is usually preferred to other aggregate price indexes based on the national accounts because these are usually available only on a yearly basis, often only after a significant delay.

Sometimes the GDP deflator has been used when the CPI was not available.[39] However, a production deflator (which includes exports) and an expenditure deflator (which includes imports) may behave quite differently when the terms of trade change.[40] In addition, it is inconsistent to use a final product price in the numerator of an RER (the foreign WPI) and a value-added price (the domestic GDP deflator) in the denominator. In order to preserve comparability across countries, we suggest using the domestic private consumption deflator instead of the GDP deflator when the CPI is not available. It is also possible to use the absorption deflator if a broader measure of the aggregate price level is desired for a particular country and comparability with the published REERs of other countries is not necessary.

Figure 3.4 above illustrates the relationship between the two-good internal RER expressed relative to nontraded goods, $IRERT_N$, and the internal RER expressed relative to the aggregate price level, $IRERT_G$, for Côte d'Ivoire.[41] In this case, $IRERT_G$ actually tracks $IRERT_N$ quite closely.

The Use of External Proxies for the Price of Traded Goods

A common proxy for the internal RER uses the foreign WPI together with the domestic CPI for the home country. The use of a foreign price index as a proxy for the price of the home country's traded goods is based on the assumption that the prices of the home country's exports and imports are determined by the law of one price. Thus, the domestic price index for tradables (P_{Td}) can be estimated by multiplying an

---

38. See, for example, Edwards (1990).

39. See, for example, Cottani, Cavallo, and Khan (1990).

40. Figure 2.4 in Chapter 2 illustrates the divergences among the CPI, GDP, and absorption deflators that a change in the terms of trade can cause.

41. Figure 3.4 shows the reciprocals of these two RERs so that an upward movement of the indexes is an appreciation. Expenditure price indexes were used for computing both RERs.

appropriate measure of the foreign price of tradables (P_{Tf}) by the nominal exchange rate. The problem is then to find the best measure for P_{Tf}. The foreign wholesale price index (WPI_f), rather than foreign CPIs and GDP deflators, has usually been selected for this purpose in empirical studies because it is relatively heavily weighted with traded goods and has a smaller nontraded component than other available foreign price indexes.[42]

However, as a number of authors have noted, the foreign WPI has various shortcomings as a proxy for the price of the home country's traded goods. The primary problem is that the foreign WPIs may not track very closely the foreign prices of traded goods actually faced by producers or consumers in a given developing country because of large differences in commodity composition.[43] Another uncertainty in using the WPI is that it measures the prices of commodities at varying stages of production. Inclusion of intermediate goods in the WPI opens the possibility of double counting but also makes the index more relevant for countries that import intermediate products.[44]

Although the foreign WPI may be reasonably representative of the prices of a developing country's imports and nontraditional exports, it is less likely to adequately reflect the fluctuations in the volatile prices of primary commodity exports. In principle, this tracking problem could be solved by using the foreign WPI as a proxy for import prices and calculating a separate foreign price index for the home country's exports as a weighted average of the relevant commodity prices and the foreign WPI for nontraditional exports. Such calculations could, however, be fairly time consuming; and we do not know of an empirical study that has actually computed such a price index.

In addition, even when multiplied by the nominal exchange rate to convert it to domestic currency, the foreign WPI does not allow for the effects of changes in tariffs and other home country trade policies on the internal RER. Thus, the use of the foreign WPI results implicitly in a proxy for the border price of traded goods that *excludes* taxes.[45]

Figures 3.6, 3.7, and 3.8 compare the effective[46] foreign wholesale price index expressed in CFA terms with the border and internal price indexes

---

42. See for example Balassa (1990), Edwards (1988, 1989, 1990), Cottani, Cavallo, and Khan (1990), Grobar (1993), and Goldfajn and Valdes (1996).

43. See Wickham (1993).

44. See Goldstein and Officer (1979).

45. The direct calculations of the internal RER discussed above can yield estimates both including and excluding the effects of trade taxes by using import and export price indexes including and excluding taxes.

46. The term "effective" is used here in the same sense as in the preceding chapter on the external RER to mean a weighted average.

Figure 3.6 *The Export Price Deflator from the National Accounts, UNCTAD Export Unit Value Index in CFA Terms, and the Effective Foreign Wholesale Price Index in CFA Terms at Official Exchange Rates for Côte d'Ivoire, 1980–93 (1985=100)*

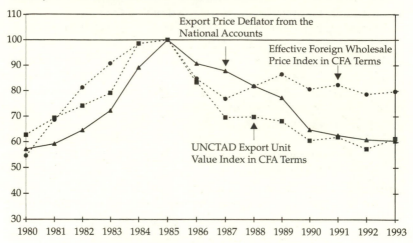

··■·· UNCTAD Export Unit Value Index in CFA Terms
——▲—— Export Price Deflator from the National Accounts
··◆·· Effective Foreign Wholesale Price Index in CFA Terms

Note: The UNCTAD export unit value index in U.S. dollar terms was converted to CFA terms by multiplying it by an index of the CFA/US$ exchange rate. The effective foreign WPI was converted to CFA terms by dividing it by the nominal effective exchange rate in foreign currency terms.
Source: Computed from World Bank data.

for Côte d'Ivoire's exports, imports, and total trade. Figure 3.6 shows that over the eight-year period from 1985–93, the effective foreign WPI diverged by 20 percent from the border price index for Côte d'Ivoire's exports, which are largely primary products. In contrast, as shown in figure 3.7, the effective foreign WPI is a much better proxy for the border price of Côte d'Ivoire's imports, which it tracks quite closely. Not surprisingly, the performance of the effective WPI as a proxy for Côte d'Ivoire's border price index for total trade (figure 3.8) falls in between the two extremes as the total trade index is a weighted average of the border prices of imports and exports. Figures 3.6, 3.7, and 3.8 also show that the effective foreign WPI in CFA terms tracks movements in border prices—as represented by the import unit value indexes computed by the United Nations Conference on Trade and Development (UNCTAD)—much more closely than in internal prices because of the effects of trade

Figure 3.7 *The Import Price Deflator from the National Accounts, the UNCTAD Import Unit Value Index in CFA Terms, and the Effective Foreign Wholesale Price Index in CFA Terms at Official Exchange Rates for Côte d'Ivoire, 1980–93 (1985=100)*

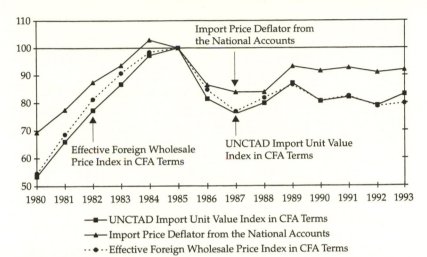

Note: The UNCTAD import unit value index in U.S. dollar terms was converted to CFA terms by multiplying it by an index of the CFA/US$ exchange rate. The effective foreign WPI was converted to CFA terms by dividing it by the nominal effective exchange rate in foreign currency terms.
Source: Computed from World Bank data.

taxes, nontariff barriers, and domestic pricing interventions on internal prices.

The WPI-CPI Proxy for the Internal RER

In computing an external proxy for the internal RER based on the foreign WPIs and the home country's CPI, both the foreign wholesale price and the nominal exchange rate indexes should be trade weighted. The proxy for the internal RER (*REERW*) is then calculated as in the following equation, 3.19:

$$(3.19) \qquad REERW = \frac{NEER_{dc} \cdot EWPI_f}{CPI_d}$$

where $NEER_{dc}$ is the nominal effective exchange rate in domestic-currency terms between the home economy and its main trading partners

Figure 3.8 *The Estimated Total Trade Deflators from the National Accounts and from UNCTAD Import and Export Unit Value Indexes and the Effective Foreign Wholesale Price Index in CFA Terms at Official Exchange Rates for Côte d'Ivoire, 1980–93 (1985=100)*

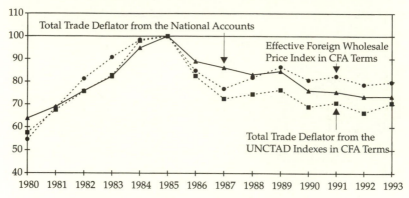

——▲—— Total Trade Deflator from the National Accounts
··■·· Total Trade Deflator from the UNCTAD Indexes in CFA Terms
··◆·· Effective Foreign Wholesale Price Index in CFA Terms

Note: The UNCTAD unit value indexes in U.S. dollar terms were converted to CFA terms by multiplying them by an index of the CFA/US$ exchange rate. The effective foreign WPI was converted to CFA terms by dividing it by the nominal effective exchange rate in foreign currency terms.
Source: Computed from World Bank data.

or competitors, $EWPI_f$ is the effective foreign wholesale price index for the same countries, and CPI_d is the domestic consumer price index for the home country.[47]

As noted above, the effective foreign WPI is a more logical proxy for border prices than for internal prices of traded goods since it does not take into account trade taxes, nontariff barriers, and other home country pricing policies. Thus figure 3.9 compares the WPI-CPI proxy for the internal RER with the two-good internal RER measured at border prices, that is, *excluding* trade taxes. Figure 3.10 shows a similar comparison between the WPI-CPI proxy and the internal RER measured at domestic prices, that is, including taxes, although these two measures are not

---

47. In a recent refinement of this approach, Clark and MacDonald (1998) use the ratio of the domestic CPI to the domestic WPI (or PPI) relative to the equivalent foreign effective (trade-weighted) ratio as a proxy for the two-good internal RER.

Figure 3.9 *Comparison between the Internal RER for Total Trade at Border Prices, Excluding Taxes, and the WPI-CPI Proxy at Official and Weighted Average Exchange Rates for Côte d'Ivoire, 1980–93 (1985=100)*

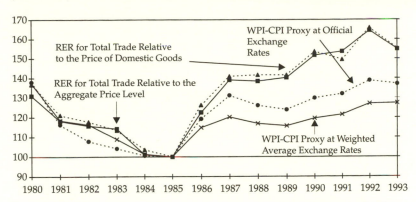

··▲·· RER for Total Trade at Border Prices Relative to the Price of Domestic Goods
—■— RER for Total Trade at Border Prices Relative to the Aggregate Price Level
··●·· WPI-CPI Proxy at Official Exchange Rates
—×— WPI-CPI Proxy at Weighted Average Official and Parallel Exchange Rates

Note: The internal RER for total trade at border prices, excluding taxes, is shown relative both to the price of domestic goods and to the aggregate price level. The WPI-CPI proxy has been calculated using adjusted IFS country weights. The private consumption deflator has been used as the aggregate price level (see the note to figure 3.4). An upward movement represents an appreciation of both the internal RERs and the WPI-CPI proxy.
Source: Computed from World Bank data.

directly comparable. To permit direct comparison between the WPI-CPI proxy—which uses an aggregate price index for the home country— and the internal RER, in both figures the two-good internal RERs are shown as the ratios of the price of total trade relative to the aggregate price level rather than relative to the price of domestic goods. Figure 3.10 shows that, because of underweighting of volatile export prices, the WPI-CPI proxy does not track the internal RER at border prices very well, diverging from it in a number of years by 15 percent to 18 percent. The proxy (figure 3.10) does track the internal RER including taxes some- what better. However, this RER measure is not an appropriate standard for judging the WPI-CPI proxy as there is no justification for including trade tax effects in the comparison; and the improvement in fit is prob- ably a random coincidence. Since the WPI-CPI proxy may not track the two-good internal RER at border prices very well and alternative RER measures can be directly computed, it should not be used as a proxy for the internal RER unless variations in the terms of trade and trade taxes are small.

The WPI-CPI proxy for the internal RER is similar to other multilateral external RERs and can be very sensitive to assumptions about unrecorded trade, parallel exchange markets, and country weights as discussed in Chapter 2. In addition, because, among other things, productivity worldwide has tended to rise faster in the traded-goods sector than in the nontraded sector, WPIs—which give a relatively heavier weight to traded goods—have tended to rise less rapidly than CPIs. Hence, the WPI-CPI proxy will show a trend of real appreciation even if

Figure 3.10 *Comparison between the Internal RER for Total Trade at* **Domestic** *Prices, Including Taxes, and the WPI-CPI Proxy at Official and Weighted Average Exchange Rates for Côte d'Ivoire, 1980–93 (1985=100)*

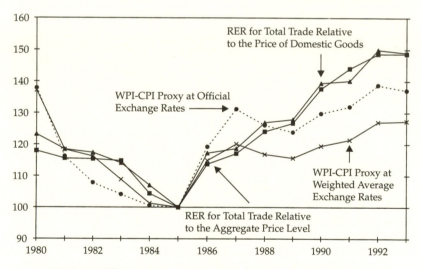

—▲—RER for Total Trade at Domestic Prices Relative to the Price of Domestic Goods
—■—RER for Total Trade at Domestic Prices Relative to the Aggregate Price Level
··●··WPI-CPI Proxy at Official Exchange Rates
—✕—WPI-CPI Proxy at Weighted Average Official and Parallel Exchange Rates

Note: The internal RER for total trade at domestic prices has been calculated relative to the price of domestic goods and to the aggregate price level. The WPI-CPI proxy has been calculated using adjusted IFS country weights. The private consumption deflator has been used as the aggregate price level (see the note to figure 3.4). An upward movement represents an appreciation of both the internal RERs and the WPI-CPI proxy.
Source: Computed from World Bank data.

Figure 3.11 *Effective Foreign CPI and WPI and Real Effective Exchange Rates Computed Using Foreign CPIs, Foreign WPIs, and the Domestic CPI for Côte d'Ivoire, 1980–93 (1985=100)*

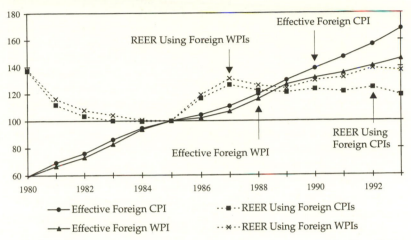

Note: The private consumption deflator has been used in lieu of the CPI for Côte d'Ivoire and was used in computing both of the REERs shown here (see the note to figure 3.4). An upward movement represents an appreciation of the RER for Côte d'Ivoire.
Source: Computed from World Bank data.

the CPI and WPI are rising at the same rate at home and abroad but the CPI is rising faster than the WPI in both.[48] Figure 3.11 shows that the effective foreign CPI for Côte d'Ivoire's trading partners rose by about 25 percent more than the effective foreign WPI between 1985 and 1993 as a result, in part, of differential productivity growth. For the same reason, Côte d'Ivoire's external REER computed using foreign WPIs appreciated almost twice as much (40 percent) between 1985 and 1993 as its REER computed using foreign CPIs (20 percent).[49]

---

48. The internal RER itself will also show an appreciating trend if productivity in the home country is rising faster in the tradable than in the nontradable sector. See the discussion of the Balassa-Samuelson effect in Chapters 5 and 6.

49. The above paragraph discusses the differences between using foreign WPIs and foreign CPIs in measuring the REER. Jorgensen and Paldam (1986) examine the differences between the movements in the domestic CPIs and the domestic WPIs for eight Latin American countries for which WPI data are available for 1946–85. They find that the domestic WPIs and domestic CPIs followed the same trend for these countries so that empirically for these countries it does not matter whether the domestic WPI or CPI is used. By contrast, Sjaastad (1998)

Summary

This chapter's findings may be summarized under two rubrics concerning, first, the measurement of the two-good internal RER and, second, the relationship between the internal and external RERs.

Measurement of the Two-Good Internal RER

Although the two-good internal RER can be precisely defined theoretically, in practice measuring it accurately in developing countries is quite difficult. The data required for computing expenditure-based measures of the two-good RER are available on an annual basis in most countries, but the disaggregated GDP data on value added by sector of origin required for calculating accurate production-based measures are hard to come by. Production- and expenditure-based measures of the two-good RER may, in any case, diverge significantly in developing countries. For those countries for which the required data on GDP by sector of origin are available, the production-based measure is worth calculating as a cross-check on the expenditure-based one. If the two measures differ substantially, the analyst will need to look at other data in order to determine which is the more reliable.

The REER computed using foreign WPIs and the domestic CPI—which is a common proxy for the internal RER—may or may not provide useful additional information. Only in cases in which the terms of trade are relatively stable is this measure likely to be a reasonable proxy for the internal RER for tradables. When the terms of trade do change, the REER using WPI_f / CPI_d may perform better as a proxy for the internal RER for imports than for the two-good RER as discussed in the next chapter. However, as with other external RERs, measurement of the WPI_f / CPI_d proxy can be very sensitive to parallel exchange rates, unrecorded trade, weighting schemes, and rapid shifts in trade patterns.

Finally, when there are significant movements in the terms of trade, *any* measure of the two-good internal RER will average together quite different changes in the internal RERs for imports and exports and consequently may convey very little useful information.

The Relationship between the Internal and External RERs

There is a fixed mathematical relationship between the two-good internal RER and the external RER, which is set out in equations 3.8 through

---

finds, in a study of seven small open industrial economies, that the RER computed using foreign and domestic CPIs is a very poor proxy for the internal RER for tradables with an extremely high average error component.

3.10 above. If the law of one price holds for a particular country, the key features of this relationship are the following:

a. A change in a country's internal RER will, other things being equal, always be larger than the corresponding change in its external RER.
b. A change in a home country's external RER will be negatively related to changes in a foreign country's internal RER; and, if the change in the foreign country's internal RER is large enough, the home country's internal and external RERs may move in opposite directions.
c. Changes in trade taxes create a further divergence between a country's internal and external RERs. These are best analyzed in a three-good framework, which allows for different behavior of the RERs for imports and exports.

One of the primary advantages of the two-good framework is that it permits a straightforward analysis of the effects of changes in productivity on the RER. In particular, other things being equal:

a. If productivity rises faster in a country's tradable sector than in its nontradable sector, its internal RER will appreciate.
b. If productivity also grows relatively faster in the home country's tradable sector than in the foreign country's, its external RER will also appreciate.
c. If the law of one price holds for tradable goods, the external RER for tradable goods will be a constant.

The stereotypical pattern seen in the RER data for industrial countries experiencing rapid productivity growth is a strong appreciation in the internal RER, a significant but more modest appreciation in the external RER, and stability or depreciation in the the external RER for traded goods.

The above relationships all depend upon the law of one price holding for tradable goods. However, there is considerable empirical evidence, except for a narrow range of homogeneous commodities, of extensive and protracted divergences of the prices of tradable goods from the law of one price in industrial countries, although the law appears less problematic in small developing economies. If the law of one price does not hold or holds only loosely as a long-run tendency, the external RER for traded goods will no longer be a constant; and the relationship between the internal and external RERs will be affected by pricing-to-market and other strategic pricing behavior of firms. In particular, if the pass-through to the domestic prices of traded goods of exchange rate movements affecting the external RER is only partial, the effect of exchange rate movements on the internal RER will be muted, the internal and external RERs may diverge, and considerable care will be needed in analyzing the effects of exchange rate movements on reductive domestic prices.

Appendix

Direct Estimation of the Internal RER from National Accounts Data

Price indexes for traded and nontraded goods that are suitable for directly computing the internal RER are not immediately available in most developing countries. However, with some simplifying assumptions, it is possible to derive reasonable estimates of these indexes from standard national accounts statistics.

The primary empirical problem encountered in doing so is that exports, imports, and domestic goods usually incorporate imported inputs. Price deflators for imports and exports are contained in the national accounts. A price deflator for nontraded goods can also be readily computed for domestically produced goods sold on the domestic market. However, both exports and domestic goods typically include some imported inputs used in their production. Hence, to be able to derive value-added price deflators for exports and domestic goods, one needs either data on imports used as intermediate inputs in producing these goods or some reasonable simplifying assumption for netting out these imports.

This appendix, following an approach suggested by the work of Devarajan, Lewis, and Robinson (1993), addresses the problem of how, on the basis of national accounts data normally available in low-income developing countries, to allow for imported inputs and derive reasonable estimates of the price indexes of exports, imports, and domestic goods required for direct calculation of the internal RER. Since the national accounts price indexes normally include taxes, the resulting internal RER estimate also *includes* taxes.

The first section of this appendix states the standard national accounts identities and specifies the assumptions about imported intermediate goods required for computing price indexes of exports, imports, and domestic goods from the identities. The second section shows how final output and value-added price indexes can be calculated for traded and domestic goods. The third section discusses two alternative methodologies for handling the problem of imported inputs that have been suggested by other authors and compares the estimates produced by the alternative methodologies. The fourth and final section illustrates the calculation of the internal RER computed using these price indexes for Côte d'Ivoire.[50]

National Accounts Identities and Imported Intermediate Goods

Depending on the information the internal RER is intended to convey, the price indexes used in computing it may be either final product price indexes or value-added price indexes. The presentation below derives both types of indexes. Since the price indexes are normally at market prices rather than factor costs, both the value-added and final product price indexes will *include* taxes.

The n goods and services produced or absorbed by an economy are classified into three categories: exported goods, imported goods, and "domestic, or not traded, goods." The latter are goods entirely produced and absorbed in the domestic economy, although they may incorporate imported inputs. The advantage of using this classification as a starting point is that data on these three categories of goods can be readily obtained from standard national accounts statistics.

The basic national accounting identity in an open economy equates gross domestic product at market prices (*GDP*) with the sum of total consumption (*C*), total investment (*I*), and net exports (*X – M*), as shown in equation 3.A.1:[51]

---

50. The methodology presented below requires reasonably accurate domestic price and national accounts statistics. The effects of parallel markets and unrecorded trade may, however, distort these statistics in some countries. When the official exchange rate is overvalued, imports may be overstated as to price, quantity, or both, in order to finance capital flight. (However, high tariffs work in the opposite direction, encouraging understatement of imports.) Exports, in contrast, may be understated or unrecorded because of the desire to retain foreign exchange earnings abroad. Official estimates of net exports will then be too low, as will expenditure estimates of GDP. (Value-added estimates of GDP may be more accurate depending upon how they are derived, with the result that there may be a large statistical discrepancy between the expenditure and value-added estimates.) Import prices and the RER for imports may thus be overstated; and export prices and the RER for exports understated.

51. All national accounts identities discussed in this appendix are valid in both constant and current prices.

(3.A.1)
$$GDP = C + I + X - M.$$

The left side of this identity is total domestic value added in the economy. It does not include intermediate inputs, either locally produced or imported. On the right side, the sum of the first two variables (C and I) is total spending or absorption (A) of domestic residents on domestic and imported final goods. Exports are domestically produced but may include imported inputs or re-exported imports. Imports may be final or intermediate goods or re-exports.

By rewriting the right side of the above identity, we can reformulate it to separate out imported inputs. Imports may be used for final consumption (M_C), for investment (M_I), or as intermediate inputs (M_V). It is also possible that some imports are re-exported. To simplify the presentation, we will assume here that there are no re-exported imports, although these can be readily allowed for in cases in which they are important. The following identity, equation 3.A.2, gives total imports as the sum of its components:

(3.A.2)
$$M = M_C + M_I + M_V.$$

Imported intermediate goods (M_V) are used either in producing domestic goods (M_{VD}) or exported goods (M_{VX}) as indicated by equation 3.A.3:

(3.A.3)
$$M_V = M_{VD} + M_{VX}.$$

Equation 3.A.2 can then be rewritten as 3.A.4:

(3.A.4)
$$M = M_C + M_I + M_{VD} + M_{VX}.$$

Total consumption and total investment are both composed of domestic and imported goods as shown in equations 3.A.5 and 3.A.6:

(3.A.5)
$$C = C_D + M_C$$

(3.A.6)
$$I = I_D + M_I.$$

C_D and I_D are domestically produced and absorbed final goods used for consumption and investment purposes, respectively. Both C_D and I_D may include imported inputs. C_D plus I_D equals total nontraded goods.

Substituting 3.A.4, 3.A.5, and 3.A.6 into 3.A.1 and rearranging the terms gives 3.A.7:

(3.A.7)
$$GDP + M_V = C_D + I_D + X$$

or, using equation 3.A.3, we end up with equation 3.A.8:

$$(3.A.8) \qquad GDP = (C_D + I_D - M_{VD}) + (X - M_{VX}).$$

In equation 3.A.7 total intermediate imported goods are added to total domestic value added (GDP) to give domestic aggregate output of final goods. Part of this final output is absorbed domestically and another part is exported. The price indexes for total domestic goods, $C_D + I_D$, and exports, X, in equation 3.A.7 are final product prices. The price index for total final output of domestically absorbed products, C_D plus I_D, is labeled P_{Nd1} here. It can be derived from national accounts statistics if data are available in current and constant prices for the three categories of imports specified in equation 3.A.2.[52] The price deflator for exports, which is labeled P_{X1}, can also be directly derived from national accounts using exports in current and in constant prices.

In equation 3.A.8, intermediate imported goods are subtracted from each term on the right-hand side to express total domestic value added in terms of its uses. The first term on the right side is domestic value added that is locally absorbed. The second term is domestic value added in exporting. The price index for $C_D + I_D - M_{VD}$ is a value-added deflator. It is labeled P_{Nd2} here. Similarly, the price deflator for value added in exporting, $X - M_{VX}$, is labeled P_{X2}.

The value-added price indexes for exports and domestic goods, however, cannot be directly calculated by using only standard national accounts statistics. The disaggregation of M_V into intermediate imports used in producing domestic goods (M_{VD}) and those used in producing exported goods (M_{VX}) is not normally made in published national accounts statistics, and data for these two variables are generally not readily available. Hence, to be able to derive P_{Nd2} and P_{X2}, we will make an assumption that the share of imported inputs in producing domestically absorbed goods (m_{vd}) and the share of imported inputs in producing exported goods (m_{vx}) are equal, as shown in equation 3.A.9:

$$(3.A.9) \qquad m_{vd} = \frac{M_{VD}}{C_D + I_D} = m_{vx} = \frac{M_{VX}}{X}.$$

The foregoing assumption permits the calculation of imports used in producing domestic goods, M_{VD}, and in producing exports, M_{VX}, if data on total imported intermediate inputs (M_V) are available. It implies that

---

52. Such data are available, mainly in current prices, for some countries in the IMF's "Recent Economic Development" reports. They may also be available in the background statistics used to prepare the national accounts.

m_{vd} and m_{vx} are both also equal to the ratio of imported intermediate inputs to aggregate output of final goods, as shown by equation 3.A.10:[53]

(3.A.10)
$$m_{vd} = m_{vx} = \frac{M_V}{GDP + M_V}.$$

This ratio can generally be calculated from the national accounts whenever the disaggregation of total imports between final and intermediate uses is available or can be estimated.[54]

Calculation of Price Deflators for Exports, Imports, and Domestic Goods

Price deflators can be computed from national accounts statistics for a given variable by dividing its value in current prices by its value in constant prices. This section shows how final output and value-added price deflators can be calculated for the different variables in the national accounts identities in equations 3.A.7 and 3.A.8.

---

53. From identities 3.A.3 and 3.A.7, we have that

$$\frac{M_V}{GDP + M_V} = \frac{M_{VD} + M_{VX}}{C_D + I_D + X}.$$

Dividing and multiplying each member of the right-side quotient by the same numbers, we obtain that:

$$\frac{M_V}{GDP + M_V} = \frac{M_{VD}}{C_D + I_D} \cdot \frac{C_D + I_D}{C_D + I_D + X} + \frac{M_{VX}}{X} \cdot \frac{X}{C_D + I_D + X}.$$

Given the definition of m_{vd} and m_{vx} as specified by equation 3.A.9,

$$\frac{M_V}{GDP + M_V} = m_{vd} \cdot \frac{C_D + I_D}{C_D + I_D + X} + m_{vx} \cdot \frac{X}{C_D + I_D + X}.$$

As m_{vd} is assumed to be equal to m_{vx}, then

$$\frac{M_V}{GDP + M_V} = m_{vd} = m_{vx}.$$

54. Note that the values of m_{vd} and m_{vx} in current prices may be different from their values in constant prices. If disaggregated import data are only available in current prices, it is necessary to make an additional assumption in order to calculate M_v in constant prices. We assumed that the shares of intermediate products in total imports are the same in current and constant prices so that:

$$\frac{M_v \text{ current}}{M \text{ current}} = \frac{M_v \text{ constant}}{M \text{ constant}}.$$

Export Deflators

In the above national accounts identities there are two measures of exports. The first one is total exported output (X). The second is total value added ($X - M_{VX}$) in exporting.[55] An export price deflator can be computed for each of these measures by using national accounts data in current and in constant prices. The export price index for total exported output is given by equation 3.A.11:

$$(3.A.11) \qquad P_{X1} = \frac{X \text{ in current prices}}{X \text{ in constant prices}}.$$

The export price index for value added in exporting is given by

$$P_{X2} = \frac{[X - M_{VX}] \text{ in current prices}}{[X - M_{VX}] \text{ in constant prices}}.$$

P_{X2} can be calculated as shown in equation 3.A.12:

$$(3.A.12) \qquad P_{X2} = \frac{[(1 - m_{vx})X] \text{ in current prices}}{[(1 - m_{vx})X] \text{ in constant prices}}$$

with $m_{vx} = M_V / (GDP + M_V)$ from equation 3.A.10. Figure 3.A.1 shows that these two export deflators for Côte d'Ivoire were actually quite close in value, differing by 1 percent or less.

Import Deflators

Similarly, there are two alternate definitions of the import deflator. The standard one can be estimated by dividing total imports in current prices by total imports in constant prices as shown in equation 3.A.13:

$$(3.A.13) \qquad P_{M1} = \frac{M \text{ in current prices}}{M \text{ in constant prices}}.$$

The second definition only includes imports of final goods. It excludes imports used as intermediate inputs in producing exports and nontraded goods. This import deflator can be calculated as follows:[56]

---

55. We assumed earlier that there are no re-exported imports. If there are re-exports, one should distinguish between total exports, which include re-exports, and total exported domestic output.

56. Note that P_{M2} is a price index related to the expenditure side. It is *not* a value-added price index like P_{Nd2} and P_{X2}. It is simply a price index for imports of final products.

Figure 3.A.1 *Final Product Price and Value-Added Deflators for Exports for Côte d'Ivoire, 1980–93 (1985=100)*

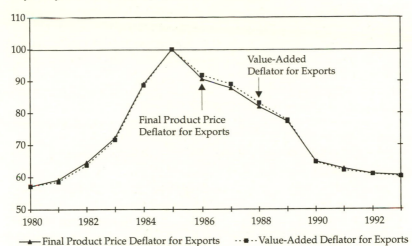

—▲—Final Product Price Deflator for Exports   ··■··Value-Added Deflator for Exports

Note: The final product price deflator for exports is the export price deflator. The value-added deflator for exports is calculated as $(1 - M_{vx})X$ in current prices divided by the same expression in constant prices, where $M_{vx} = M_v / (GDP + M_v)$ and M_v is the intermediate goods component of imports. The share of imports of intermediate goods in total imports is assumed to be the same in current and constant prices.
Source: Computed from World Bank data.

$$P_{M2} = \frac{[M - M_V] \text{ in current prices}}{[M - M_V] \text{ in constant prices}}.$$

Or, equivalently, using identity 3.A.2, we get 3.A.14:

(3.A.14) $$P_{M2} = \frac{[M_C + M_I] \text{ in current prices}}{[M_C + M_I] \text{ in constant prices}}.$$

Since disaggregated import data are available for Côte d'Ivoire only in current prices, the shares of intermediate goods in total imports were assumed to be the same in current and constant prices. As a result of this assumption, P_{M2} equals P_{M1} for Côte d'Ivoire.

Aggregate Price Indexes

Three aggregate price indexes can be calculated from national accounts data in current and constant prices. The first, the most common, is the GDP deflator (P_{GDP}). This index is calculated as the ratio of GDP in current prices to the GDP in constant prices. The second is an aggregate output price index (P_Q). The aggregate output of an economy, Q, is the sum of total value-added (GDP) and intermediate inputs.[57] P_Q is computed as follows:

$$P_Q = \frac{[GDP + M_V] \text{ in current prices}}{[GDP + M_V] \text{ in constant prices}}.$$

The third aggregate price index is the absorption deflator (P_A). It is calculated as the ratio of total absorption (consumption plus investment) in current prices divided by total absorption in constant prices.

Price Indexes for Domestic Goods

Because domestic goods are both domestically produced and absorbed, the price index for them can be derived from either the supply or the demand side of an economy. If the national accounts are consistent, that is, if the national accounts identity holds both in current and in constant prices, the price index for domestic goods will be the same whether computed from the supply or the demand side. The following two subsections show how the final output deflator for domestic goods, P_{Nd1}, and value-added deflator for domestic goods, P_{Nd2}, can be derived from the supply and demand sides.

Calculation from the Supply Side

As indicated above, P_{Nd1} relates to $C_D + I_D$, which is total final output of domestic goods, and P_{Nd2} relates to $C_D + I_D - M_{VD}$, which is value added in producing domestic goods. From identities 3.A.7 and 3.A.8 and the assumption in 3.A.9, the following expressions (3.A.15 and 3.A.16) for these two aggregates can be obtained:

(3.A.15) $C_D + I_D = GDP + M_V - X$

(3.A.16) $C_D + I_D - M_{VD} = GDP - (X - M_{VX}) = GDP - (1 - m_{vx})X.$

As these expressions are valid both in current and constant prices, P_{Nd1} and P_{Nd2} can be obtained from them by dividing the values in current

---

57. Note that domestically produced intermediate inputs are not separately added in to Q in order to avoid double counting. These domestic inputs are produced and consumed by different producers in the economy and are already included in value added. Sectoral aggregate domestic output of a good (or a service) J ($J = 1, ..., n$) includes all intermediate (domestic or imported) inputs used in its production, but the total aggregate domestic output of an economy is the sum of all sectoral aggregate domestic outputs minus all locally produced intermediate inputs.

prices by the values in constant prices. We then have equations 3.A.17 and 3.A.18:

(3.A.17) $$P_{Nd1} = \frac{[GDP + M_V - X] \text{ in current prices}}{[GDP + M_V - X] \text{ in constant prices}}$$

(3.A.18) $$P_{Nd2} = \frac{[GDP - (1 - m_{vx})X] \text{ in current prices}}{[GDP - (1 - m_{vx})X] \text{ in constant prices}}$$

with $$m_{vx} = \frac{M_V}{GDP + M_V}.$$

P_{Nd1} can be computed using equation 3.A.17 and P_{Nd2} using equation 3.A.18 whenever imports of intermediate goods in current and constant prices are available or can be estimated.[58]

Calculation from the Demand Side

The domestic goods price deflator on the demand side is derived from total absorption, which is equal to total consumption plus total investment, as shown in equation 3.A.21:

(3.A.21) $$A = C + 1 = C_D + I_D + M_C + M_I$$

or, adding and subtracting M_{VD} on the right side, yields equation 3.A.22:

---

58. We also can define P_{Nd1} and P_{Nd2} in terms of prices related to the component variables of the right-hand side of equations 3.A.15 and 3.A.16. For instance, the price equation derived from 3.A.16 is

$$P_{GDP} = \tau_Q \cdot P_{X2} + (1 - \tau_Q)P_{Nd2}$$

with

$$\tau_Q = \frac{[(1 - m_{vx})X] \text{ in constant prices}}{GDP \text{ in constant prices}}$$

and P_{GDP} being the GDP deflator. The value-added price index of nontraded goods is then:

$$P_{Nd2} = \frac{P_{GDP} - \tau_Q \cdot P_{X2}}{1 - \tau_Q}.$$

(3.A.22)
$$A = C + I$$
$$= (C_D + I_D - M_{VD}) + (M_C + M_I + M_{VD}).$$

Substituting equations 3.A.4 and 3.A.9 in 3.A.22 yields equation 3.A.23:

(3.A.23) $A = C + I = (C_D + I_D + M_{VD}) + (M - m_{vx} \cdot X).$

The aggregate domestic goods for which P_{Nd1} and P_{Nd2} are defined are, then, given by equations 3.A.24 and 3.A.25:

(3.A.24) $$C_D + I_D = C + I - M_C - M_I$$

(3.A.25) $$C_D + I_D - M_{VD} = C + 1 - (M = m_{VX} \cdot X) \ .$$

As equations 3.A.24 and 3.A.25 are valid both in current and constant prices, P_{Nd1} and P_{Nd2} can be calculated from equations 3.A.26 and 3.A.27:[59]

(3.A.26) $$P_{Nd1} = \frac{[C + I - M_C - M_I] \text{ in current prices}}{[C + I - M_C - M_I] \text{ in constant prices}}$$

(3.A.27) $$P_{Nd2} = \frac{[C + I - (M - m_{vx} \cdot X)] \text{ in current prices}}{[C + I - (M - m_{vx} \cdot X)] \text{ in constant prices}}$$

with $m_{vx} = \dfrac{M_V}{GDP + M_V}$ as defined above.

Figure 3.A.2 shows P_{Nd1} and P_{Nd2} calculated in this way for Côte d'Ivoire. As is the case with the export deflators, the two estimated deflators for domestic goods are quite close, differing by 1 to 2 percent or less.

---

59. P_{Nd1} and P_{Nd2} can also be expressed in terms of the absorption and import deflators. For instance, the following definition for the absorption deflator P_A can easily be derived from equation 3.A.21:

$$P_A = \tau_A \cdot P_{M2} + (1 - \tau_A) P_{Nd1}$$

with $$\tau_A = \frac{[M_C + M_I] \text{ in constant prices}}{[C + I] \text{ in constant prices}}.$$

The domestic goods price deflator is then given by:

$$P_{Nd1} = \frac{P_A - \tau_A \cdot P_{M2}}{1 - \tau_A}.$$

Figure 3.A.2 *Final Product Price and Value-Added Deflators for Domestic Goods for Côte d'Ivoire, 1980–93 (1985=100)*

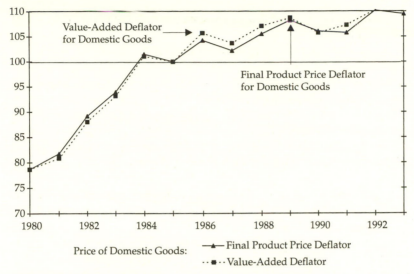

Price of Domestic Goods: ──▲── Final Product Price Deflator
··■·· Value-Added Deflator

Note: The final product price deflator for domestic goods has been calculated as the ratio of expenditures on domestically produced consumption and investment goods in current prices to that in constant prices. The value-added deflator for domestic goods has been calculated as $(GDP - (1 - M_{vx})X)$ in current prices divided by the same expression in constant prices, where $M_{vx} = M_v/(GDP + M_v)$ and M_v is the intermediate goods component of imports. The share of imports of intermediate goods in total imports is assumed to be the same in current and constant prices.
Source: Computed from World Bank data.

Alternative Assumptions about Imported Inputs

The foregoing methodology requires import data that can be disaggregated into imports for final consumption (M_C), imports for investment (M_I), and imports of intermediate inputs (M_V). Unfortunately, such disaggregated data are not available in a number of low-income countries. Hence, we considered two alternative assumptions for calculating the price indexes for exports, imports, and domestic goods, which make it possible to compute the price deflator for domestic goods *without* disaggregated data for imports that the above procedure requires. The two alternatives are to assume (a) that imported inputs are either negligible or do not significantly affect the price indexes or (b) that the import content of absorption and the import content of exports are equal. The price indexes for Côte d'Ivoire were calculated on both these assumptions, and the results were compared to those from using disaggregated import data to see how the price indexes were affected empirically.

The assumption of negligible imported inputs appears at first view fairly extreme. In general, imports of intermediate goods constitute a reasonably large share of total imports in most developing countries. They represented, for example, 36 percent of total imports for Côte d'Ivoire in 1992.

The assumption that imported intermediate inputs are negligible implies that the import content of domestic goods, M_{VD}, and the import content of exports, M_{VX}, are both equal to zero. Since there are no imported inputs, the distinction between GDP and the total value of final output, GDP plus M_V, disappears. Similarly, the deflators for final output of domestic goods, P_{Nd1}, and value added in producing domestic goods, P_{Nd2}, are equal. The deflators for domestic goods, calculated from the production accounts, are then given by equation 3.A.28:

$$(3.A.28) \qquad P_{Nd1} = P_{Nd2} = \frac{[GDP - X] \text{ in current prices}}{[GDP - X] \text{ in constant prices}}.$$

Since there are no imported inputs, the deflators for value added in exporting, P_{X2}, and the value of exports, P_{X1}, are also the same. To calculate P_{Nd1} and P_{Nd2} from the expenditure accounts, the term $[GDP - X]$ in equation 3.A.28 is replaced by $C + I - M$.

The assumption that the import content of absorption (labeled m_a) and the import content of exports (m_{vx}) are equal seems more reasonable for cases in which disaggregated import data are not available. As explained in footnote 56, this assumption implies that each of these two shares is equal to the overall import content of total resources (that is, to GDP plus imports) as shown by equation 3.A.29:

$$(3.A.29) \qquad m_{vx} = m_a = \frac{M}{GDP + M}.$$

Unless one makes additional assumptions, this approach makes possible only the calculation of the value-added deflator for domestic goods, P_{Nd2}, because it does not distinguish between imports of final goods and imported inputs used in producing domestic goods. This deflator is still given by equations 3.A.18 and 3.A.27 but with m_{vx} defined by 3.A.29. In this approach, P_{X2} is also given by equation 3.A.12 but with m_{vx} again given by 3.A.29.[60]

---

60. This assumption was suggested by Philippe Callier during the analytical work on the devaluation of the CFA franc. See Callier (1992). He assumed that import content of absorption (labeled m_a) and import content of exports (which is m_{vx}) were equal. Following our disaggregation of imports, Callier's assumption is equivalent to having:

Figure 3.A.3 compares the final output price deflator for domestic goods, P_{Nd1}, calculated using the negligible imported inputs assumption and this attachment's import disaggregation methodologies (equations 3.A.17 and 3.A.26). It shows that the alternative estimates can differ by 3 to 5 percent. Similarly, figure 3.A.4 compares the value-added deflator for domestic goods, P_{Nd2}, calculated using the three different methodologies.[61] Here the difference between the highest and lowest estimates is 6 to 7 percent. Figure 3.A.5 makes the same comparison for the value-added deflator for exports. Taken together, the figures show that, although the errors from assuming that imported inputs are not large, it is still

$$m_a = \frac{M_C + M_I + M_{VD}}{C + I} = m_{vx} = \frac{M_{VX}}{X}.$$

From equations 3.A.5, 3.A.6 and 3.A.8, such an assumption makes GDP equal to:

$$GDP = (1 - m_a)(C + I) + (1 - m_{vx})X$$

or, using equation 3.A.1,

$$GDP = (1 - m_a)(GDP - X + M) + (1 - m_{vx})X$$

as m_u is assumed to be equal to m_{vx}, then,

$$GDP = (1 - m_{vx})(GDP + M)$$

which gives that

$$m_a = m_{vx} = \frac{M}{GDP + M}.$$

61. The three methodologies are based, respectively, on the following equations:

1. Equation 3.A.18 or 3.A.27 with

$$m_{vx} = \frac{Mv}{GDP + M_v};$$

2. Equation 3.A.28; and
3. Equation 3.A.18 or 3.A.27 with

$$m_{vx} = \frac{M}{GDP + M}.$$

Figure 3.A.3 *Estimated Final Product Price Deflator for Domestic Goods Calculated Using the Import Disaggregation and Negligible Imported Inputs Methodologies for Côte d'Ivoire, 1980–93 (1985 = 100)*

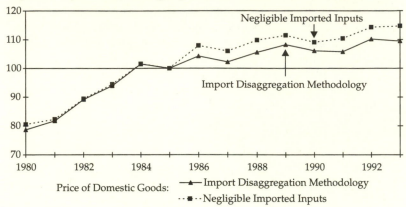

Price of Domestic Goods: —▲— Import Disaggregation Methodology
                          ··■·· Negligible Imported Inputs

Note: The import disaggregation methodology for computing the final product price deflator for domestic goods is explained in the note to figure 3.A.2. The negligible imported inputs methodology assumes that there are no imports of intermediate goods and computes the final product price deflator for domestic goods as $(GDP - X)$ in current prices divided by the same expression in constant prices.
Source: Computed from World Bank data.

Figure 3.A.4 *Estimated Value-Added Deflators for Domestic Goods Calculated Using the Import Disaggregation, Negligible Imported Inputs, and Equal Import Content Methodologies for Côte d'Ivoire, 1980–93 (1985=100)*

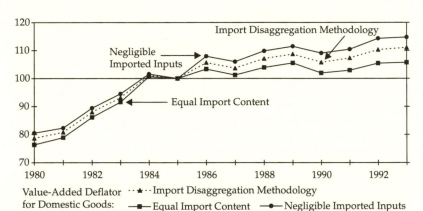

Value-Added Deflator   ··▲·· Import Disaggregation Methodology
for Domestic Goods: —■— Equal Import Content   —●— Negligible Imported Inputs

Note: The import disaggregation methodology for calculating the value-added deflator of domestic goods is explained in the note to figure 3.A.2. The equal import content methodology calculates the value-added deflator of domestic goods as $(GDP - (1 - M_{vx})X)$ in current prices divided by the same expression in constant prices, where $M_{vx} = M/(GDP + M)$. For the negligible imported inputs methodology, see the note to figure 3.A.3.
Source: Computed from World Bank data.

Figure 3.A.5 *Estimated Value-Added Deflator for Exports Calculated Using the Import Disaggregation, Negligible Imported Inputs, and Equal Import Content Methodologies for Côte d'Ivoire, 1980–93 (1985=100)*

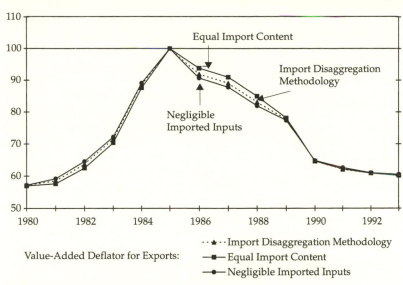

Value-Added Deflator for Exports:
- ··▲·· Import Disaggregation Methodology
- ─■─ Equal Import Content
- ─●─ Negligible Imported Inputs

Note: The import disaggregation methodology for calculating the value-added deflator for exports is calculated is explained in the note to figure 3.A1. The equal import content methodology calculates the value-added deflator for exports as $(1 - M_{vx})X$ in current prices divided by the same expression in constant prices, where $M_{vx} = M/(GDP + M)$ in both current and constant prices. The negligible imported inputs methodogy assumes that there are no imports of intermediate goods. Therefore, the value-added deflator and final product price deflator for exports are equal.
Source: Computed from World Bank data.

worth the effort to allow for the effects of imported inputs on the price deflators. Hence, when disaggregated data are available for imports, these should be used as suggested in this appendix to make adjustments for imported inputs. When such data are not available, it is better to assume that the import content of absorption and exports are equal—an assumption that implies that they are also equal to the ratio of imports to total resources (GDP plus imports)—than that imported inputs are negligible.

Direct Calculation of the Internal RER in a Three-Good Framework

The price deflators for exports, imports, and domestic goods computed as explained above may be used to directly calculate the internal RERs for exports and imports.

The RER for Exports

The real exchange rate for exports is measured by the ratio of export price index to the domestic goods price index. For the price index of exports, there are two choices: the final product price of exported goods (P_{X1}) and the value-added deflator for exports (P_{X2}). Similarly, for the price index of domestic goods, the final output price, P_{Nd1}, or the value-added deflator, P_{Nd2}, can be used. To produce a consistent unbiased estimate, the same type of price index should be used for exports and domestic goods. For example, if the value-added deflator is used for domestic goods, it should also be used for exports.

Combining the two candidates for the export price index with the two similar candidates for nontraded goods, the following two measures (equations 3.A.31 and 3.A.32) of the RER for exports can be computed:

$$(3.A.31) \qquad RERX1_N = \frac{P_{X1}}{P_{Nd1}},$$

where $RERX1_N$ is in terms of final output deflators, and

$$(3.A.32) \qquad RERX2_N = \frac{P_{X2}}{P_{Nd2}}$$

where $RERX2_N$ is in terms of value-added deflators. Figure 3.A.6 compares these two alternative measures of the RER for exports. It shows that their values are very close for Côte d'Ivoire and that in this case either measure can be used.

The RER for Imports

The RER for imports is measured as the ratio of the domestic price index for imports to the price index for domestic goods. The price index of imports could be represented by the price index for all imports, P_{M1}, or by that for just final goods, P_{M2}. The common approach—and the one adopted here—is to use the price index for all imports. As P_{M1} is a final output price, if feasible, it is better to use the final output price for domestic goods, P_{Nd1}, rather than the value-added deflator, P_{Nd2}. We thus have the following two possible measures—equations 3.A.33 and 3.A.34—of the RER for imports.

$$(3.A.33) \qquad RERM1_N = \frac{P_{M1}}{P_{Nd1}}$$

$$(3.A.34) \qquad RERM2_N = \frac{P_{M1}}{P_{Nd2}}.$$

Figure 3.A.6 *Internal RER for Exports Calculated Using Final Product Price Deflators and Value-Added Deflators for Côte d'Ivoire, 1980–93 (1985=100)*

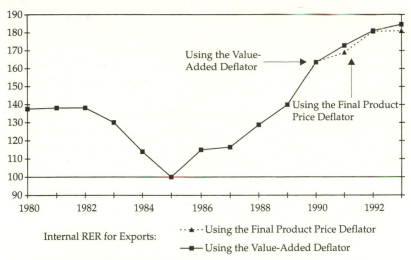

Internal RER for Exports: ···▲···Using the Final Product Price Deflator
—■—Using the Value-Added Deflator

Note: The internal RER for exports using the final product price deflator is calculated as the final product price deflator for domestic goods divided by the final product price for exports. The internal RER for exports using the value-added deflator is calculated as the value-added deflator for domestic goods divided by the value-added deflator for exports. An upward movement is an appreciation.
Source: Computed from World Bank data.

Figure 3.A.7 compares these two measures. The preferred version, $RERM1_N$, uses P_{Nd1}. The alternative version, $RERM2_N$, uses P_{Nd2} where P_{Nd1} is not available. The alternative version of the RER for imports tracks the preferred version as well as P_{Nd2} tracks P_{Nd1} in figure 3.A.2, differing from it by 1–2 percent or less.

Direct Computation of the Internal RER in the Two-Good Framework

The internal RER in the two-good framework can be calculated directly as a weighted average of the RER for exports and the RER for imports. Conceptually, the only RERs for exports and for imports that should be combined are $RERN_{X1}$ and $RERN_{M1}$ as they are the only ones calculated using import and export price indexes of the same type (that is, final output prices) with the same measure of domestic goods prices (P_{Nd1}). However, when the data on imports of intermediate goods are not available, one has no choice but to work with the value-added deflator P_{Nd2} and use $RERX2_N$ and $RERM2_N$.

Figure 3.A.7 *Internal RER for Imports Calculated Using Final Product Price and Value-Added Deflators for Côte d'Ivoire, 1980–93 (1985=100)*

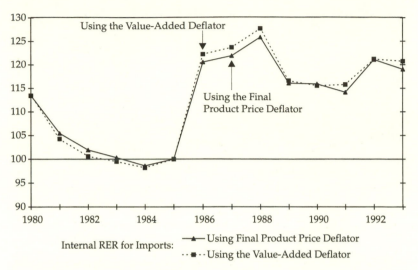

Internal RER for Imports: ——▲—Using Final Product Price Deflator
·· ■ ··Using the Value-Added Deflator

Note: The internal RER for imports using the final product price deflator is calculated as the final product price deflator for domestic goods divided by the final product price deflator for imports. The internal RER for imports using the value-added deflator is calculated as the value-added deflator for domestic goods divided by the value-added deflator for imports. An upward movement is an appreciation.
Source: Computed from World Bank data.

With a geometric averaging method in which the weights are the shares of imports and exports in total trade,[62] the internal RER in the two-good framework is calculated as shown in equation 3.A.35:

$$(3.A.35) \qquad RERT_N = RERM_N^\alpha \cdot RERX_N^{1-\alpha}.$$

The implicit domestic price deflator for traded goods associated with $RERT_N$ is similarly the weighted average of the price index of exports and the price index of imports, as shown in equation 3.A.36:

$$(3.A.36) \qquad P_{Td} = P_{Md1}^\alpha \cdot P_{Xd1}^{1-\alpha}.$$

---

62. Base-year (constant) weights or current-year weights may be used in the averaging process. Base-year weights are useful if the base year represents an equilibrium to which the economy is expected to return. If, however, there have been significant structural changes since the base year, current-year weights will reflect more accurately the relative importance of the import and export sectors.

Figure 3.A.8 *Internal RER for Total Trade Calculated Using Final Product Price and Value-Added Deflators for Côte d'Ivoire, 1980–93 (1985=100)*

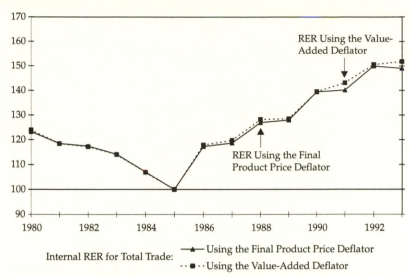

Internal RER for Total Trade:
— ▲ — Using the Final Product Price Deflator
· · ■ · · Using the Value-Added Deflator

Note: The internal RER for total trade using the final product price deflator is calculated as the final product price deflator for domestic goods divided by the final product price deflator for total trade. The internal RER for total trade using the value-added deflator is calculated as the value-added deflator for domestic goods divided by the value-added deflator for total trade. An upward movement is an appreciation.
Source: Computed from World Bank data.

And the alternative equivalent calculation of $RERT_N$ is given by equation 3.A.37:

$$(3.A.37) \qquad RERT_N = \frac{P_{Td}}{P_{Nd1}} = \frac{P_{Md1}^{\alpha} \cdot P_{Xd1}^{1-\alpha}}{P_{Nd1}}.$$

Figure 3.A.8 shows the two-good RER for total trade calculated using both the final product price and value-added deflators. As in the case of the RERs for exports (figure 3.A.6) and for imports (figure 3.A.7), the two measures track each other very closely.

4

The Three-Good Internal RER for Exports, Imports, and Domestic Goods

Lawrence E. Hinkle and Fabien Nsengiyumva*

The analysis in the preceding chapter was based on the two-good version (tradables and nontradables) of the internal RER. Even though tradables themselves are composed of two kinds of goods—exportables and importables—the two-sector framework assumes that the distinction between the two is immaterial for most questions.[1] In two-good models, the relative price of exportables and importables (the terms of trade) are implicitly held constant so that the two goods may be meaningfully aggregated into a single homogeneous tradable good.

However, there are pronounced differences in the kinds of goods that are imported and exported by developing countries, and their imports and exports often experience very different price movements. The aggregation of exportables and importables into one composite tradable good can be misleading if the terms of trade fluctuate significantly over time, as often happens in developing countries. Moreover, even if the terms of trade are constant, tariffs and other trade restraints tend to be applied in an asymmetric fashion to imports and exports in most developing countries so that domestic taxes on imports and exports may differ markedly. Because of these differences in exports and imports, the usefulness of lumping them into a single category of traded goods is sometimes questionable. Such an aggregation may obscure the effects

* Ms. Ingrid Ivins provided research assistance in the preparation of this chapter. The authors are grateful to Amparo Ballivian, Shanta Devarajan, Peter Montiel, Stephen O'Connell, and three anonymous reviewers for very helpful comments on earlier drafts.

1. See, for example, Dornbusch (1980), Chapter 6.

of changes both in the terms of trade and in trade policy, which are important concerns in many developing countries. Hence, as useful as the two-good internal RER framework is for analyzing the effects of productivity changes and macroeconomic policies, it has a major shortcoming for analytical work on developing countries—the inability to handle changes in the terms of trade and trade policy.

To explicitly take into account the foregoing effects, it is necessary to disaggregate tradables into importables and exportables and utilize a three-sector framework that permits the terms of trade to vary. This chapter introduces such a framework. The following section first discusses the definition and measurement of separate internal real exchange rates for exports and imports. The subsequent section then uses this three-good framework to analyze the effects of changes in the terms of trade and trade policy on the measured RER. The final section concludes the chapter, and Part I of this volume, with an overview and summary assessment of the two- and three-good internal RERs.

The Three-Good Internal RERs for Imports and Exports: Concepts and Measurement

This section defines the internal RERs for exports and imports in a three-good framework, compares this three-good framework with the two-good framework discussed in Chapter 3, briefly considers more complex multi-good approaches, and reviews alternative ways of directly measuring the internal RERs for exports and imports.

Definition of the Internal RER in a Three-Good Framework

In a three-sector framework consisting of importables, exportables, and nontradables, there are two internal real exchange rates: the relative price of exportables to nontradables ($IRERX_N$) and the relative price of importables to nontradables ($IRERM_N$). Let P^*_{Md} be the foreign currency border price of the home country's imports and P^*_{Xd} the foreign currency border price of the home country's exports with an * indicating the foreign currency price of a home country variable. For a small open economy, P^*_{Md} and P^*_{Xd} are assumed to be exogenous variables. If the law of one price holds for tradables, then for a given nominal exchange rate and trade taxes, the domestic prices of exportables (P_{Xd}) and importables (P_{Md}) will be determined by P^*_{Xd} and P^*_{Md}. The respective definitions of the internal RERs for exportables and importables are set out in equations 4.1 and 4.2:

$$(4.1) \qquad IRERX_N = \frac{P_{Xd}}{P_{Nd}} = \frac{E_{dc} \cdot P^*_{Xd}(1-t_x)}{P_{Nd}}$$

$$(4.2) \qquad IRERM_N = \frac{P_{Md}}{P_{Nd}} = \frac{E_{dc} \cdot P^*_{Md}(1 - t_m)}{P_{Nd}}$$

where t_x and t_m are the average ad valorem tax rates, net of subsidies, on exports and imports, respectively. The RER for exports can be related to the RER for imports by expressing it as the product of the internal terms of trade and the RER for imports, as shown in equation 4.3:

$$(4.3) \qquad IRERX_N = \frac{P_{Xd}}{P_{Nd}} = \frac{P_{Xd}}{P_{Md}} \cdot \frac{P_{Md}}{P_{Nd}} = \frac{P_{Xd}}{P_{Md}} \cdot IRERM_N = TOT_d \cdot IRERM_N.$$

$IRERX_N$ is an indicator of the *internal* price competitiveness of exportables in production and consumption relative to nontradables. It is a measure of the incentives guiding resource allocation between the domestic sectors producing these two categories of goods. As locally produced importables and imports are substitutes in this three-good framework, the real exchange rate ($IRERM_N$) for importables is similarly an indicator of the internal price competitiveness of importables in production and consumption relative to nontradables. The external and internal terms of trade, P^*_{Xd}/P^*_{Md} and P_{Xd}/P_{Md}, are also important relative prices, which influence both real incomes and the current account balance. Since these may move differently when trade taxes or policies are changed significantly, their movements are worth analyzing separately.

One disadvantage of the three-good framework is that there is no longer a single unique internal RER. A number of authors deal with this problem by computing the internal RER as the weighted geometric or arithmetic average of the RERs for exportables and importables as illustrated in equation 4.4:

$$(4.4) \qquad IRERT_N = IRERM_N^{\alpha} \cdot IRERX_N^{1-\alpha}$$

where α is the share of importables in total traded goods.[2]

---

2. See, for example, Edwards (1994) and Elbadawi (1994). An equivalent way to compute the RER in a three-good framework is to calculate P_{Td} as the weighted average of the prices of importables and exportables and the internal RER as the ratio of P_{Td} thus calculated to P_{Nd}. The domestic price index of domestically produced tradables (P_{Td}) is then:

$$P_{Td} = \left[E_{dc} \cdot P^*_{Md}(1 + t_m) \right]^{\alpha} \cdot \left[E_{dc} \cdot P^*_{Xd}(1 - t_x) \right]^{1-\alpha}$$

$$= E_{dc} \left[P^*_{Md}(1 + t_m) \right]^{\alpha} \cdot \left[P^*_{Xd}(1 - t_x) \right]^{1-\alpha}$$

where α is the share of importables in the tradable goods composite. $IRERT_N$ is then computed as the ratio of P_{Td} to P_{Nd}. This calculation yields a separate index for the prices of tradable goods as a by-product.

Under the above definition, however, the "single" internal RER is only the weighted average of the underlying RERs for exports and imports. These underlying RERs may move in opposite directions when the terms of trade change, and averaging them into one summary indicator will obscure such movements.

If for presentational purposes a single RER measure is required, the price of domestic goods in foreign exchange terms ($E_{fc} \cdot P_{Nd}$), which is the common term in the definitions of the internal RERs for exports and imports (equations 4.1 and 4.2), may be used as a single indicator of the RER as illustrated in Chapter 8. Since this indicator does not average two internal RERs that may move in opposite directions, it is a more transparent measure of the competitiveness of the domestic price level than is the weighted average of the internal RERs for exports and imports. Nevertheless, one still needs to bear in mind that the RER for exports, which is a very useful measure of the price incentives for existing export products, could behave quite differently from that for imports as a result of variations in the terms of trade or changes in trade taxes.[3]

Comparison of the Two- and Three-Good Frameworks

In the case of a small open economy, the external prices of exports and imports (P_{Xf} and P_{Mf}) are exogenously determined. Consequently, the home country cannot alter its external terms of trade, P_{Xd}^* / P_{Md}^*, through its policies, although it can change the internal prices of exports and imports, P_{Xd} and P_{Md}, and its internal terms of trade, P_{Xd}/P_{Md}, through trade taxes and similar policies.[4] If the external terms of trade and trade

---

3. In some cases, the RER for imports may be an alternative possible choice as a single indicator of the internal real exchange rate. Many developing countries export a narrow range of products (often primary commodities) but import a wide range of items so that their imports are usually much more diversified than their exports. Thus, the prices of a developing country's imports tend to be more broadly representative of the prices in its trading partners (including the prices faced by the developing country's own nontraditional exports) and of the trading opportunities open to the country than the prices of its traditional exports often are. For the same reason, in most developing countries import prices are usually less volatile than export prices. Hence, the RER for imports is usually a more representative measure than is the RER for exports and is a possible choice for use as a single indicator of the internal real exchange rate. However, if the RER for imports is used as a single indicator, one should be aware that the RER for exports could behave quite differently from the RER for imports and that the divergence between these two RERs could have important macroeconomic implications.

4. The internal terms of trade, P_{Xd}/P_{Md}, and the external terms of trade, P_{Xd}^*/P_{Md}^*, are denoted by TOT_d and TOT_d^* in the next section.

policies do not change, the aggregation of importables and exportables into one composite tradable good is reasonable for analytical purposes because, if the percentage change in export and import prices is the same, the change in the two-good internal RER (P_{Td}/P_{Nd}) will correctly indicate a proportionate change in the profitability of all tradables relative to nontradables.[5]

However, a distinction should be made between importables and exportables when an economy experiences changes in its external terms of trade or when changes in domestic policies, such as trade taxes, affect export and import prices differently. If the domestic prices of exportables and importables move in opposite directions or in the same directions but by different amounts, the aggregation of exportables and importables into one category of tradable goods, and the two-good RER, will give a misleading impression of the effect on incentives for producing and consuming them. For example, if the external terms of trade deteriorate, reflecting a decline in the external price of exportables and an increase in the external price of importables, the internal RER for exportables, P_{Xd}/P_{Nd}, will generally appreciate while the RER for importables, P_{Md}/P_{Nd}, will depreciate as explained in the next section. Whatever the net change in the ratio P_{Td}/P_{Nd}, it will not indicate that the profitability of exportables and importables has moved in opposite directions relative to nontradables as a result of the deterioration in the terms of trade.

Similarly, when, as often happens, trade taxes on imports are increased without a compensating change in the taxes or subsidies on exports, the domestic price of imports, P_{Md}, may increase; and the RER for imports, P_{Md}/P_{Nd}, may depreciate. The domestic price of exports, however, will not rise as a direct effect of this policy. The internal terms of trade, P_{Xd}/P_{Md}, will deteriorate; and the internal RER for exports, P_{Xd}/P_{Nd}, will appreciate to the extent that prices of domestic goods are indirectly increased by demand switching from the now more expensive imports to domestic goods.

---

5. For example, a devaluation or a uniform change in taxes on imports and exports may affect P_{Xd} and P_{Md} in the same way. In this case, the change in P_{Td} will accurately reflect what is happening to both exports and imports; and the two-good internal RER, the ratio P_{Td}/P_{Nd}, will give a good picture of the change in domestic price incentives. In such cases, the distinction between importables and exportables may be of little analytical importance; and the simpler two-good framework may be used. However, except in the special case when trade taxes or subsidies are changed uniformly for both exports and imports, the aggregation of exports and imports into tradables and the two-good internal RER are likely to obscure the different effects of the change in trade taxes on exportables and importables.

The law of one price usually plays an important role in both two-good and three-good models for determining the RER. As discussed in the preceding chapter, the law of one price is a reasonable hypothesis only when tradables are fairly homogeneous, but not when they are differentiated products. In some cases, particularly for commodity exports and imports such as food grains, it is reasonable to apply the law of one price to tradable goods in low-income developing countries. However, if a country trades differentiated products, the law of one price may not apply to its trade; and other functional relationships are then required to determine the domestic prices of importables and exportables from their external prices.

In practice, the three-good framework is often simplified somewhat for analytical or empirical reasons. To simplify the theoretical analysis, many economists assume, as in Chapter 8's constant elasticity model, that the home country consumes but does not produce importables and that it produces but does not consume exportables. Hence, although there are still three types of goods, the home country produces and consumes only two of these. In addition, data are usually available for exports, imports, and domestic goods rather than for exportables, importables, and nontradables. In the standard empirical case, aggregate price indexes will incorporate only two of these categories of goods: expenditure price indexes will include only imports and domestic goods; and production price indexes will include only exports and domestic goods. Although a number of the resulting theoretical and empirical analyses could be classified in an intermediate category between the two-good and the three-good approaches, they have been treated here as simplifications of the basic three-good framework because they differ fundamentally from a two-good framework, which has only tradable and nontradable goods.

Multi-Good Approaches

It is possible to allow for additional categories of goods in the analysis of internal prices to take into account the situation in a particular developing country. The most common additions are (a) adding a fourth category of goods by distinguishing between imports and import substitutes; (b) allowing for a separate RER for a particularly important export product or products; and (c) introducing additional RERs to allow for parallel exchange rates.

A Four-Good Framework. The three-good approach assumes that imports and import-competing goods are close substitutes so that the law of one price equalizes their domestic prices. Then imports and import-competing goods are indistinguishable for the consumer and may be aggregated. Since developing countries' imports are usually more diversified and differentiated than their exports, some analysts allow for differentiation of importables but not exportables. If import-competing goods and imports are not perfect substitutes, one needs a framework with at least four goods—imports, import-competing goods, exportables, and nontradables. In such a four-good framework, the law of one price applies to exportables and imports but not to import-competing goods. World prices influence but do not determine the domestic prices of import-competing goods. In this case, there is a third RER, that for import-competing goods. In order to determine the RERs in such a four-good framework, one needs to specify how the prices of both import-competing goods and nontradables are determined. A four-good framework also requires empirical price and output data for import-competing goods, which may be hard to come by except in countries that have exceptionally good statistical systems.

Disaggregated Analyses. In some countries the trade taxes on specific important imports or exports may differ substantially from the averages for imports or exports as a whole or the prices of these major products may behave differently from those of other exports or imports. Hence, it may sometimes be desirable analytically to allow for such differences in a multi-good framework. If such a disaggregated approach is used to take into account highly differentiated taxes, subsidies, or price movements for key subsectors, multiple internal RERs can be computed at the sector or subsector level using the formula for good i given in equation 4.5:[6]

$$(4.5) \qquad IRERi_N = \frac{E_{dc}P_{if}(1+t_i)}{P_{Nd}}.$$

The usefulness of this approach will depend upon (a) how important subsector i is in the economy, (b) whether the law of one price or some other known price determination mechanism applies to good i, and (c) whether or not domestic and external price data are available for it.

Parallel RERs. In countries with parallel foreign exchange markets, there are two possible border prices for exports and imports, one at the official exchange rate and another at the parallel rate. The relevant internal prices for both exports and imports will depend upon the degree of market segmentation and arbitrage between markets. In a three-good framework with a parallel foreign exchange market, there may be as

---

6. See Edwards (1989), page 7.

many as four internal RERs: two for exports, one each at the official and parallel rates, and two similar RERs for imports.

Parallel exchange rates may considerably complicate the analysis both conceptually and empirically. Conceptually, in order to measure the relevant RERs, it is now necessary to specify how the official and parallel exchange rates affect the domestic price or prices of imports and exports. Empirically, data may be needed on the types and volumes of transactions taking place at both exchange rates in order to assess their relative importance.

In specific circumstances it may be desirable to move from a three-good to a multi-good framework. If the required data are available, it is certainly worth analyzing empirically the behavior of the prices of import-competing goods, major import and export products, and the parallel RERs. However, incorporating additional RERs into the analysis will require using more complex models, the analytical and empirical feasibility of which will depend on what is possible for a particular country.

Direct Measurement of the Internal RER in a Three-Good Framework

The RERs for exports and imports may be measured at domestic prices, including tariffs and indirect taxes, or at border prices, excluding these taxes.

The Internal RERs at Domestic Prices (Including Taxes)

Separate RERs for imports and exports at domestic prices are easily calculated using the expenditure-based methodology set out in the appendix to Chapter 3. Figure 4.1 shows the import and export price indexes for Côte d'Ivoire together with the price index for domestic goods computed using this methodology. Figure 4.2 compares the RERs for imports and exports for Côte d'Ivoire with the internal RER for total trade. The RER for exports has been much more volatile than the RER for imports because of the much greater cyclical variations in export prices, which are predominantely those of primary commodities. As figure 4.2 shows, averaging these RERs together in calculating one internal RER for total trade obscures the significantly different incentives that have faced export- and import-substituting sectors as a result of the fluctuations in the terms of trade.

The foregoing direct measures of the internal RER are all based on internal national accounts price deflators, which include the effects of trade taxes and other home country trade and price policies. These measures are the appropriate indicators of domestic relative prices.

Figure 4.1 *Terms of Trade and Price Deflators for Domestic Goods, Imports, and Exports for Côte d'Ivoire, 1980–93 (1985=100)*

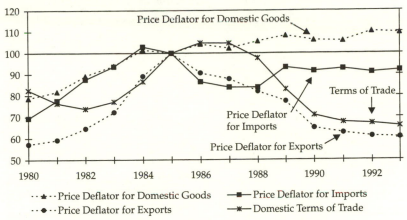

··▲··Price Deflator for Domestic Goods   ──■──Price Deflator for Imports
··●··Price Deflator for Exports   ──✳──Domestic Terms of Trade

Note: All deflators are measured in terms of final product prices. The final product price deflator for domestic goods has been calculated as the ratio of expenditures on domestically produced consumption and investment goods in current prices to that in constant prices as explained in the appendix to Chapter 3.
Source: Computed from World Bank data.

Figure 4.2 *Internal RERs for Imports, Exports, and Total Trade at Domestic Prices for Côte d'Ivoire, 1980–93 (1985=100)*

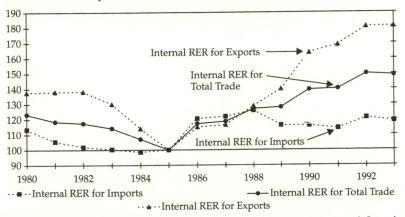

··■··Internal RER for Imports   ──●──Internal RER for Total Trade
··▲··Internal RER for Exports

Note: The internal RER for imports was calculated as the final product price deflator for domestic goods divided by the import deflator. The internal RER for exports was calculated as the final product price deflator for domestic goods divided by the export deflator. The internal RER for total trade was calculated as the final product price deflator for domestic goods divided by the price deflator for total trade. The final product price deflator for domestic goods is calculated as explained in the note to figure 4.1. The import, export, and total trade deflators are all final product price deflators. The three RERs are expressed here with the price of domestic goods in the numerator so that an upward movement is an appreciation.
Source: Computed from World Bank data.

Figure 4.3 *The Export Price Deflator from the National Accounts, UNCTAD Export Unit Value Index in CFA Terms, and the Effective Foreign Wholesale Price Index in CFA Terms at Official Exchange Rates for Côte d'Ivoire, 1980–93 (1985=100)*

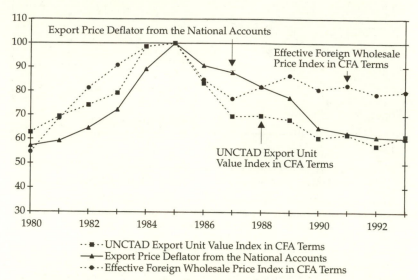

Note: The UNCTAD export unit value index in U.S. dollar terms was converted to CFA terms by multiplying it by an index of the CFA/$ exchange rate. The effective foreign WPI was converted to CFA terms by dividing it by the nominal effective exchange rate in foreign currency terms.
Source: Computed from World Bank data.

The Internal RERs at Border *Prices (Excluding Taxes)*

If data are available on border prices of traded goods measured in foreign currency, it may also be possible to construct a measure of the RER excluding taxes. Figures 4.3 and 4.4 compare the internal and border prices of exports and imports with their border prices in CFA terms calculated from UNCTAD import and export unit value indexes.[7] Figure 4.5 shows the internal and external terms of trade computed using the price indexes from figures 4.3 and 4.4.

Internal and border prices diverge partly because of trade taxes and other price policies and partly because of possible, but unknown, statistical discrepancies between the two series. The internal and border prices in

7. UNCTAD calculates dollar-based import and export value, volume, and unit value indexes for many developing countries. These data are available in the World Bank's central database (BESD).

Figure 4.4 *The Import Price Deflator from the National Accounts, UNCTAD Import Unit Value Index in CFA Terms, and the Effective Foreign Wholesale Price Index in CFA Terms at Official Exchange Rates for Côte d'Ivoire, 1980–93 (1985=100)*

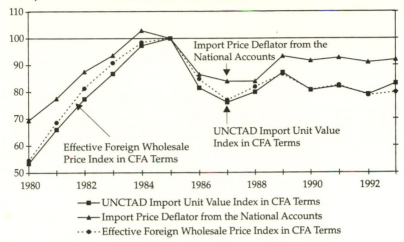

Note: The UNCTAD import unit value index in U.S. dollar terms was converted to CFA terms by multiplying it by an index of the CFA/$ exchange rate. The effective foreign WPI was converted to CFA terms by dividing it by the nominal effective exchange rate in foreign currency terms.
Source: Computed from World Bank data.

Figure 4.5 *The Internal Terms of Trade from the National Accounts and the External Terms of Trade from UNCTAD Data, 1980–93 (1985=100)*

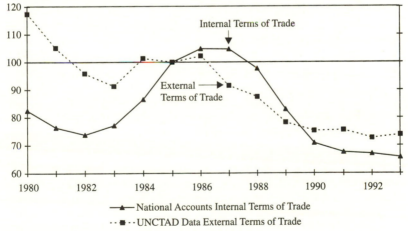

Note: The internal terms of trade is P_{Xd}/P_{Md}, and the external terms of trade is P_{Xf}/P_{Mf}.
Source: Computed from World Bank data.

figure 4.3 diverge for exports in the period 1986–89, when the domestic producer prices of cocoa and coffee were subsidized and export subsidies were paid for some other products that would have helped to maintain internal prices. The price series for imports in figure 4.4 diverge in 1989–93, when tariffs and trade barriers were increased. In addition, a statistical discrepancy may result from different coverage, computation procedures, and measurement errors in the internal and border price series. Ideally, it would be desirable to have independent estimates of the revenues from trade taxes, marketing board surpluses, and the effects of nontariff barriers to check the consistency of the internal and border price series. In the absence of such data, the analyst's only option is to use whatever information is available to assess the reliability and consistency of the two price series. As noted in the previous chapter, when a country is experiencing "import compression," particular attention will need to be paid to the divergence between border and internal prices.

Figure 4.6 shows the internal RERs, excluding taxes, for imports, exports, and total trade that can be calculated using the UNCTAD data for border prices and the price index for domestic goods. Figures 4.7, 4.8, and 4.9 compare the internal RERs for exports, imports, and total trade including and excluding taxes. They indicate that trade and price policies may have offset part of the appreciation in the RERs excluding taxes as the RERs including taxes appreciated less rapidly, although part of the difference may be attributable to statistical discrepancies discussed above.

The Terms of Trade, the Internal RERs for Imports and Exports, and the External RER

This section analyzes the effects of changes in the terms of trade on the relationships among the measured internal RERs for imports and exports and the external RER.[8]

The Relationship between the Internal and External RERs in a Three-Good Framework

In the three-good framework, the general price levels in the home and foreign country (or rest of the world) are weighted geometric averages

---

8. This section discusses the effects of variations in the terms of trade on the measured (or observed) RER. See Chapter 6 on the theory of the equilibrium RER for a discussion of the effects of the terms of trade on the equilibrium RER. For an alternative presentation of the theory and an empirical example for Australia, see Stein, Allen, and Associates (1995), Chapters 1 and 3. For a three-good model that incorporates the effects of both productivity and terms of trade changes, see De Gregorio and Wolf (1994).

Figure 4.6 *Estimated RERs for Imports, Exports, and Total Trade at Border Prices, Excluding Taxes, for Côte d'Ivoire, 1980–93 (1985=100)*

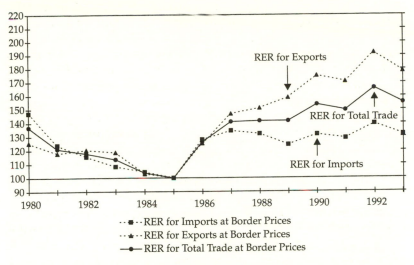

··■·· RER for Imports at Border Prices
··▲·· RER for Exports at Border Prices
—●— RER for Total Trade at Border Prices

Note: The estimated RER for imports at border prices was calculated as the final product price deflator for domestic goods divided by the UNCTAD import unit value index expressed in CFA terms. The estimated RER for exports at border prices was calculated as the final product price deflator for domestic goods divided by the UNCTAD export unit value index in CFA terms. The estimated RER for total trade at border prices was calculated as the weighted average of the estimated RER for imports at border prices and of the estimated internal RER for exports at border prices. The weights used are the shares of exports and imports in current total trade from the national accounts. An upward movement of the RERs represents an appreciation.
Source: Computed from World Bank data.

of the price of nontradables (P_N), importables (P_M), and exportables (P_X) as shown in equations 4.6 and 4.7:

$$(4.6) \qquad P_{Gd} = P_{Nd}^{\alpha} \cdot P_{Md}^{\beta} \cdot P_{Xd}^{\gamma}$$

where $0 < \alpha$, β, and $\gamma < 1$ and $\alpha + \beta + \gamma = 1$, and

$$(4.7) \qquad P_{Gf} = P_{Nf}^{a} \cdot P_{Mf}^{b} \cdot P_{Xf}^{c}$$

where $0 < a$, b, and $c < 1$ and $a + b + c = 1$.[9]

---

9. Note that the notation in this chapter, where the subscript f denotes a foreign country variable, is slightly different from that in the two preceding chapters, where the subscript f denoted the border price in foreign currency of a home country variable, which is denoted here by an *.

Figure 4.7 *The Internal RER for Exports at Domestic and Border Prices for Côte d'Ivoire, 1980–93 (1985=100)*

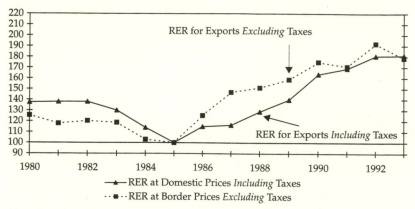

Note: The internal RER for exports at domestic prices, *including* taxes, was calculated as the national accounts final product price deflator for domestic goods divided by the export deflator. The internal RER for exports at border prices, *excluding* taxes, was calculated as the national accounts final product price deflator for domestic goods divided by the UNCTAD export unit value index expressed in CFA terms. An upward movement of the RERs represents an appreciation.
Source: Computed from World Bank data.

Figure 4.8 *The Internal RER for Imports at Domestic and Border Prices for Côte d'Ivoire, 1980–93 (1985=100)*

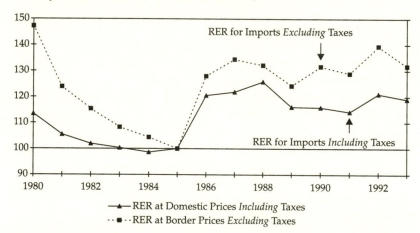

Note: The internal RER for imports at domestic prices, *including* taxes, was calculated as the national accounts final product price deflator for domestic goods divided by the import deflator. The internal RER for imports at border prices, *excluding* taxes, was calculated as the national accounts final product price deflator for domestic goods divided by the UNCTAD import unit value index expressed in CFA terms. An upward movement of the RERs represents an appreciation.
Source: Computed from World Bank data.

Figure 4.9 *The Two-Good Internal RER for Total Trade at Domestic and Border Prices for Côte d'Ivoire, 1980–93 (1985=100)*

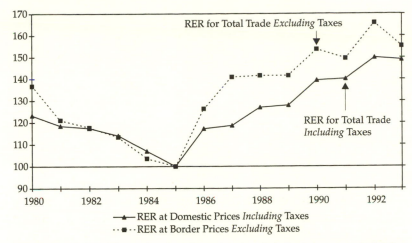

— ▲ — RER at Domestic Prices *Including* Taxes
· · ■ · · RER at Border Prices *Excluding* Taxes

Note: The internal RER for total trade at domestic prices, *including* taxes, was calculated as the national accounts final product price deflator for domestic goods divided by the deflator for total trade. The internal RER for total trade at border prices, *excluding* taxes, was calculated as explained in the note to figure 4.6. An upward movement of the RERs represents an appreciation.
Source: Computed from World Bank data.

Empirically, however, one will usually be working with data for imports, exports, and domestic goods rather than data for importables, exportables, and nontradables. Typically, an expenditure price index will contain only the price of imports and domestic goods so that for this index γ and c will both equal zero. Similarly, a production price index will contain only the prices of exports and domestic goods so that for it β and b will both equal zero.

The Internal RER for Imports

The bilateral external RER between the home and foreign countries is defined as in equation 4.8:

$$(4.8) \qquad BRER_{fc} = E_{fc} \cdot \frac{P_{Gd}}{P_{Gf}} = E_{fc} \cdot \frac{P_{Nd}^{\alpha} \cdot P_{Md}^{\beta} \cdot P_{Xd}^{\gamma}}{P_{Nf}^{a} \cdot P_{Mf}^{b} \cdot P_{Xf}^{c}}$$

where E_{fc} is the nominal exchange rate in foreign currency terms.

Multiplying and dividing the numerator of equation 4.8 by P_{Md} and its denominator by P_{Mf} gives equation 4.9:

$$(4.9) \qquad BRER_{fc} = E_{fc} \cdot \dfrac{\dfrac{P_{Nd}^{\alpha}}{P_{Md}^{\alpha}} \cdot \dfrac{P_{Md}^{\beta}}{P_{Md}^{\beta}} \cdot \dfrac{P_{Xd}^{\gamma}}{P_{Md}^{\gamma}} \cdot P_{Md}}{\dfrac{P_{Nf}^{a}}{P_{Mf}^{a}} \cdot \dfrac{P_{Mf}^{b}}{P_{Mf}^{b}} \cdot \dfrac{P_{Xf}^{c}}{P_{Mf}^{c}} \cdot P_{Mf}}$$

since $\qquad\qquad\qquad P_{Md}^{\alpha} \cdot P_{Md}^{\beta} \cdot P_{Md}^{\gamma} = P_{Md}^{\alpha+\beta+\gamma} = P_{Md}^{1}$

and $\qquad\qquad\qquad P_{Mf}^{a} \cdot P_{Mf}^{b} \cdot P_{Mf}^{c} = P_{Mf}^{a+b+c} = P_{Mf}^{1}.$

In equation 4.9 the terms P_{Nd}/P_{Md} and P_{Nf}/P_{Mf} are the internal RERs for importables for the home and foreign countries ($IRERN_M$); and the terms P_{Xd}/P_{Md} and P_{Xf}/P_{Mf} are their terms of trade (TOT_d and TOT_f). Thus we arrive at equation 4.10:

$$(4.10) \qquad BRER_{fc} = E_{fc} \cdot \dfrac{\left(IRERN_{Md}\right)^{\alpha} \cdot 1 \cdot \left(TOT_{d}\right)^{\gamma} P_{Md}}{\left(IRERN_{Mf}\right)^{a} \cdot 1 \cdot \left(TOT_{f}\right)^{c} P_{Mf}}.$$

Since the home country's imports are the foreign country's exports and vice versa, it is possible to derive a relationship between the home and foreign country's terms of trade. If t_{Md} and t_{Xd} are the home country's trade taxes on imports and exports[10] and the home country is price taker, then the law of one price for traded goods requires that equations 4.11 and 4.12 hold:

$$(4.11) \qquad\qquad P_{Md} = \dfrac{P_{Xf}\left(1+t_{Md}\right)}{E_{fc}}$$

and

$$(4.12) \qquad\qquad P_{Xd} = \dfrac{P_{Mf}\left(1-t_{Xd}\right)}{E_{fc}}.$$

As shown in appendix B, substituting equations 4.11 and 4.12 in equation 4.10 and manipulating the results algebraically yields the following expression (equation 4.13) for the home country's external RER:

---

10. The treatment of transport and other transactions costs is analogous. They have been omitted here to simplify the presentation.

(4.13) $BRER_{fc} = IRER_{Md}^{\alpha} \cdot IRERN_{Mf}^{-a} \cdot TOT_{d}^{*\gamma+c-1} \cdot (1-t_{Xd})^{\gamma} \cdot (1+t_{Md})^{1-\gamma}$

where (TOT_{d}^{*}) is the home country's terms of trade expressed in foreign prices and as shown by equation 4.14:

(4.14) $$TOT_{d}^{*} = \frac{1}{TOT_{f}} = \frac{P_{Xd}^{*}}{P_{Md}^{*}}.$$

Equation 4.13 relates the external RER to the product of the home country's internal RER for imports, the foreign country's internal RER for imports, the terms of trade, and trade taxes on exports and imports.

Taking the logarithm of equation 4.13 and then differentiating it yields the following expression (equation 4.15) for small changes in the home country's external RER:

(4.15)
$$\widehat{BRER}_{fc} = \underset{+}{\alpha \cdot \left(\widehat{IRERN}_{Md}\right)} - \underset{-}{a \cdot \left(\widehat{IRERN}_{Mf}\right)} + \underset{-/+}{(\gamma+c-1) \cdot \widehat{TOT}_{d}^{*}}$$
$$+ \underset{+}{\gamma \cdot \left(\widehat{1-t_{Xd}}\right)} + \underset{+}{(1-\gamma) \cdot \left(\widehat{1+t_{Md}}\right)}.$$

The equivalent expression for small changes in the home country's internal RER for imports is given by equation 4.16:

(4.16)
$$\widehat{IRERN}_{Md} = \underset{+}{\frac{1}{\alpha} \cdot \widehat{BRER}_{fc}} + \underset{+}{\frac{a}{\alpha} \cdot \widehat{IRERN}_{Mf}} + \underset{+/-}{\frac{(1-\gamma-c)}{\alpha} \cdot \widehat{TOT}_{d}^{*}} - \underset{-}{\frac{\gamma}{\alpha}\left(\widehat{1-t_{Xd}}\right)}$$
$$- \underset{-}{\frac{1-\gamma}{\alpha}\left(\widehat{1-t_{Md}}\right)}.$$

For an empirical expenditure price index, which contains imports but not exports, $\gamma = c = 0$; and equation 4.15 will simplify to 4.15.a:

(4.15.a)
$$\widehat{EBRER}_{fc} = \underset{+}{\alpha \cdot \left(\widehat{IRERN}_{Md}\right)} - \underset{-}{\alpha \cdot \left(\widehat{IRERN}_{Mf}\right)} - \underset{-}{\widehat{TOT}_{d}^{*}}$$
$$+ \underset{+}{\left(\widehat{(1+t_{Md})}\right)}$$

where $EBRER_{fc}$ is the expenditure-PPP bilateral external RER in foreign currency terms. Similarly, equation 4.16 will simplify to 4.16.a:

$$\widehat{IRERN}_{Md} = \frac{1}{\alpha} \cdot \widehat{EBRER}_{fc} + \frac{a}{\alpha} \cdot \widehat{IRERN}_{Mf} + \frac{1}{\alpha} \cdot \widehat{TOT}_d^*$$

$$+ \qquad\qquad + \qquad\qquad +$$

(4.16.a)

$$- \frac{1}{\alpha} \cdot \left(\widehat{1+t_{Md}}\right)$$

$$-$$

The Internal RER for Exports

Similarly, one can derive the following expression (equation 4.17) for the relationship between small changes in the home country's external RER, the home country's internal RER for exportables ($IRERN_{Xd}$), the foreign country's internal RER for exportables ($IRERN_{Xf}$), and the home country's terms of trade expressed in foreign prices ($\widehat{TOT}_d^*$):

$$\widehat{BRER}_{fc} = \alpha \cdot \left(\widehat{IRERN}_{Xd}\right) - a \cdot \left(\widehat{IRERN}_{Xf}\right) + (1-\beta-b) \cdot \widehat{TOT}_d^*$$

$$+ \qquad\qquad - \qquad\qquad +/-$$

(4.17)

$$+ \quad (1-\beta)\left(\widehat{1-t_{Xd}}\right) + \beta\left(\widehat{1+t_{Md}}\right)$$

$$+ \qquad\qquad +$$

The corresponding expression for small changes in the home country's internal RER for exports is given in equation 4.18:

$$\widehat{IRERN}_{Xd} = \frac{1}{\alpha}\left(\widehat{BRER}_{fc}\right) + \frac{a}{\alpha}\left(\widehat{IRERN}_{Xf}\right) - \frac{(1-\beta-b)}{\alpha} \cdot \widehat{TOT}_d^*$$

$$+ \qquad\qquad + \qquad\qquad -/+$$

(4.18)

$$- \left(\frac{1-\beta}{\alpha}\right) \cdot \left(\widehat{1-t_{Xd}}\right) - \frac{\beta}{\alpha}\left(\widehat{1+t_{Md}}\right)$$

$$- \qquad\qquad -$$

For an empirical production price index, which contains exports but not imports, $\beta = b = 0$; and equation 4.17 will simplify to 4.17.a:

$$\widehat{PBRER}_{fc} = \alpha \cdot \left(\widehat{IRERN}_{Xd}\right) - a \cdot \left(\widehat{IRERN}_{Xf}\right) + \widehat{TOT}_d^* + \left(\widehat{1+t_{Xd}}\right)$$

(4.17.a)

$$+ \qquad\qquad - \qquad\qquad + \qquad +$$

where $PBRER_{fc}$ is the production price bilateral external RER in foreign currency terms. Similarly, equation 4.18 will simplify to 4.18.a:

(4.18.a)

$$\widehat{IRERN}_{Xd} = \frac{1}{\alpha} \cdot \left(\widehat{PBRER}_{fc}\right) + \frac{a}{\alpha}\left(\widehat{IRERN}_{Xf}\right) - \frac{1}{\alpha}\left(\widehat{TOT}_d^*\right) - \frac{1}{\alpha} \cdot \left(\widehat{1-t_{xd}}\right).$$

$$+ \qquad\qquad + \qquad\qquad - \qquad -$$

The Effects of Including the Terms of Trade on the Interaction between the Internal and External RERs— Comparison to the Two-Good Case

Equations 4.15 and 4.17, which relate changes in the external RER to those in the internal RERs for imports and exports, are similar to equation 3.16.a in the preceding chapter, which gives the relationship between the two-good internal RER for tradable goods and the external RER. The differences resulting from changing from a two-good to a three-good framework are that:

a. The internal RERs for importables and exportables replace the internal RER for tradables on the right-hand side;
b. The home country's terms of trade in border prices now appear on the right-hand side in addition to the home country's internal RER and the foreign country's internal RER; and
c. Trade taxes on imports and exports are shown separately rather than being combined into a single aggregate tax on tradables.

The signs of the coefficients of all of the terms on the right-hand sides of equations 4.15 and 4.17, except for the terms of trade, can be readily determined from the conditions specified with equations 4.6 and 4.7 for the weights of the different categories of goods. The signs are shown beneath the two equations. Equations 4.15 and 4.17 are, however, for hypothetical price indexes containing importables, exportables, and nontradables. The empirical relationships for expenditure and production price indexes (equations 4.15.a and 4.17.a) are simpler. In particular, the ambiguity about the sign of the coefficient of the terms of trade disappears.

As in the two-good framework, changes in the external RER are related positively to the home country's internal RERs and negatively to the foreign country's internal RERs, with coefficients equal to the shares of nontraded goods in the two economies. For given (exogenous) values of the terms of trade, the foreign country's internal RER, and trade taxes, the home country's external RER is proportional to its internal RERs (equations 4.15.a and 4.17.a).

Since trade taxes on imports and exports are shown separately rather than combined into a single aggregate tax on tradables, the three-good framework makes it possible to see more clearly the different effects on the observed internal and external RERs of changes in the taxes levied on imports and exports. Changes in imports and export taxes have opposite effects on the internal and external RERs since they enter equations 4.16.a and 4.18.a for the internal RERs with signs opposite to those in equations 4.15.a and 4.17.a for the external RER. Thus, an increase in import tariffs will, other things being equal, depreciate the internal RER for imports but appreciate the expenditure price external RER. Conversely, an increase in export taxes will appreciate the internal RER for exports but depreciate the production price external RER. Note that it is the internal RERs that reflect the price incentives facing domestic industries and hence their movements are the ones that more accurately measure the resource allocation effects of trade taxes.

Although the sign of the coefficient on the change in the terms of trade is ambiguous in the hypothetical relationship, in the empirical relationships—in which either an expenditure or a production price index is used—an improvement in the terms of trade will always depreciate the measured internal RER for exports (equation 4.18.a) but appreciate that for imports (equation 4.16.a), since the change in the terms of trade enters the two empirical equations with opposite signs. There is a considerable literature that discusses the effects of movements in the terms of trade on equilibrium RERs in developing countries. In general, this literature finds that an improvement in the term of trade will also tend to depreciate the equilibrium internal RER for exportables but appreciate the equilibrium internal RER for importables. A deterioration in the terms of trade will usually have the opposite effect, appreciating the RER for exports but depreciating the RER for imports. The net effect of a change in the terms of trade on the weighted average of the two internal RERs, however, is theoretically ambiguous.[11]

In order to get around the problem of the internal RERs for imports and exports moving in opposite directions, some authors have suggested relying primarily on the external RER when the terms of trade change.[12] However, this approach does not solve the problem. The net effect of terms of trade movements on the external RER depends upon whether an expenditure-PPP measure (which excludes exports) or a production price (Mundell-Fleming) RER measure (which excludes imports) is used

---

11. Chapter 6 on the theory of the equilibrium RER examines the effects of variations in the terms of trade on the equilibrium RER. There Montiel finds that an improvement in the terms of trade will necessarily appreciate the equilibrium internal RER for importables but that the theoretical effect on the equilibrium RER for exportables is ambiguous. Chapters 7, 8, and 10 give methodologies for making quantitative estimates of the effects of movements in the terms of trade on the equilibrium RER and suggest that empirically an improvement in the terms of trade will almost always depreciate the internal RER for exports. De Gregorio and Wolf (1994) also give a theoretical model of a small open economy that integrates the effects of changes in both productivity and the term of trade on the RER in a three-good framework.

12. See, for example, Stein, Allen, and Associates (1995), Chapter 1, and appendix B to this chapter.

since the terms of trade have opposite signs in the empirical equations for the expenditure-PPP and production price RERs. An improvement in the terms of trade will depreciate the expenditure-PPP RER (equation 4.15.a) because it contains import prices, which decline in relative terms, but will appreciate the production price RER (equation 4.17.a) because it contains export prices, which increase in relative terms. Furthermore, when the terms of trade change, these two external RERs will move in the opposite direction from the corresponding internal RER. For example, when the terms of trade improve, the production price external RER will appreciate while the internal RER for exports depreciates and the expenditure-PPP external RER will depreciate while the internal RER for imports appreciates.

Qualifications and Limitations

As in the two-good case, the above equations set out the relationships between the measured or observed RERs, trade taxes, and the terms of trade. The shares of nontradables, importables, and exportables in production and expenditure at home (α, β, and γ) and abroad (a, b, and c) are taken here to be constant for small changes. For empirical price indexes these will actually be fixed weights until they are periodically updated. However, these shares are in fact variables that may, and generally will, change over time as a result of substitution and income effects of movements in the real exchange rate. Moreover, in some cases the terms on the right-hand sides of equations 4.15.a and 4.17.a may not be independent. For large trading partners, for example, a change in the terms of trade will generally be accompanied by offsetting changes in the foreign country's internal RER since an increase in the home country's export prices (an improvement in its terms of trade) is also an increase in the foreign country's import prices (a depreciation in the foreign country's internal RER for imports). To take into account the foregoing effects on the equilibrium RER in a systematic way, a full general equilibrium model needs to be used for the analysis, a task that Chapter 6 takes up.

Furthermore, the above quantitative relationships are all based on the assumption that the law of one price holds for tradable goods. While this assumption may be reasonable in some cases, particularly for commodity exports, in others it may be problematic. When the law of one price does not hold or holds only as a long-run tendency, the empirical relationships between the internal and external RERs and the terms of trade will be much looser and all of the caveats cited in Chapter 3 will apply.

Given the relationship between the external and internal RERs set out above, a theory that determines the equilibrium value of either the

external or internal RER should, in principle, also determine the equilibrium value of the others. However, changes in the terms of trade,
productivity, and trade policy will alter the relationship between the
internal and external RER. Empirically, consistent data on domestic
prices, border prices, and trade taxes necessary for fully reconciling
measures of the internal and external RERs will often be unavailable.
Hence, in practice one will often not know how much of the divergence
is explainable by changes in the terms of trade, productivity, and trade
policy and how much is just statistical noise. Consequently it is important that in estimating the equilibrium RER empirically, one use the
empirical measure of the actual RER—whether internal or external—
that is demanded by his theory of the equilibrium RER.

The Empirical Relationship between the External RERs and the Internal RERs for Exports and Imports

Analysis of the RER in a two-good framework can be obscured by movements in the terms of trade or differences in the taxation of imports and
exports, which a three-good framework handles more transparently.
However, the relationships between the different internal and external
RER measures are complex, and some care is needed in interpreting them.

Figures 4.10 and 4.11 provide a good illustration of some of the complexities, and potential confusion, involved when the terms of trade
change substantially. Figure 4.10 shows how the internal RERs for exports and imports can diverge from each other and from the expenditure-PPP and Mundell-Fleming external RERs, which also diverge. Because of the sharp decline in its export prices between 1985 and 1993,
Côte d'Ivoire's internal RER for exports appreciated by 80 percent, and
its Mundell-Fleming external RER actually depreciated by about 15 percent, while all of the other RER measures were appreciating. Although
the RER for imports and the expenditure-PPP external RER both appreciated, the RER for imports appreciated by almost twice as much as the
PPP external RER.

The effects of trade taxes and administered prices on the different
internal and external RERs can be seen by comparing the RERs measured in domestic and border prices in figures 4.10 and 4.11. At border
prices, the RER for exports appreciated more rapidly during 1985–88
than at domestic prices until administrative prices for cocoa and coffee
were cut. But, as domestic prices were aligned with border prices, the
domestic and border price RERs for exports eventually rose by the same
amount by 1993. In contrast, the RER for imports was about 10 percent
more depreciated at domestic prices than at border prices and diverged
that much more from the external RER. Thus, increased trade taxes and
restraints both protected the import-competing sector somewhat during

Figure 4.10 *The External REERs at Weighted Average Official and Parallel Exchange Rates and the Internal RER for Imports and Exports at Domestic Prices, and Terms of Trade, Including Taxes, 1980–93 (1985=100)*

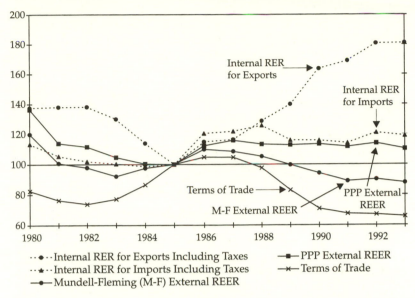

··●·· Internal RER for Exports Including Taxes   ──■── PPP External REER
··▲·· Internal RER for Imports Including Taxes   ──✕── Terms of Trade
──●── Mundell-Fleming (M-F) External REER

Note: The internal RER for imports-exports at domestic prices has been calculated as the final product price deflator for domestic goods divided by the import-export deflator at domestic prices. The PPP external REER has been calculated using foreign CPIs and adjusted IFS weights. The private consumption deflator has been used in lieu of the CPI for Côte d'Ivoire here and in the following graphs so that the inconsistency between the CPI and the private consumption deflator time series noted in footnote 40, Chapter 2, would not distort the comparisons between the internal and external RERs. The Mundell-Fleming external REER has been calculated using GDP deflators and adjusted IFS country weights. An upward movement represents an appreciation of the internal and external RERs.
Source: Computed from World Bank data.

this period and caused the RER for imports at domestic prices to track the expenditure-PPP external RER significantly better than it otherwise would have.

As noted in Chapter 2 on the external RER, developing-country imports tend to be more diversified than their exports and to reflect the movement in foreign countries' aggregate prices more closely than do the prices of developing-country exports. Consequently the internal RER for imports, as figures 4.10 and 4.11 illustrate, tends to track the expenditure-PPP external RER much more closely than does the internal RER for exports, which behaved quite differently from the other RER measures

Figure 4.11 *The External REERs at Weighted Average Official and Parallel Exchange Rates and the Internal RER for Imports and Exports at* **Border** *Prices, and Terms of Trade, Excluding Taxes, 1980–93 (1985=100)*

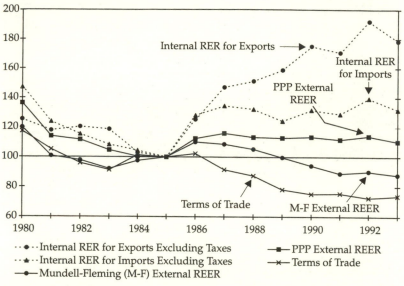

Note: The internal RER for imports-exports at border prices has been calculated as the final product price deflator for domestic goods divided by the UNCTAD import-export unit value index. The PPP external REER has been calculated using foreign CPIs and adjusted IFS weights. The private consumption deflator has been used in lieu of the CPI for Côte d'Ivoire for reasons explained in the note to figure 4.10. The Mundell-Fleming external REER has been calculated using GDP deflators and adjusted IFS country weights. An upward movement represents an appreciation of the internal and external RERs.
Source: Computed from World Bank data.

because of the sharp fluctuations in the export prices of cocoa, coffee, and other primary commodities. This greater similarity of commodity composition is an additional reason, when using a three-good framework, for comparing the expenditure-PPP external RER with the internal RER for imports and for considering separately what has happened to the RER for exports and the Mundell-Fleming external RER. However, the analyst still needs to pay attention to changes in trade taxes and administered prices that, depending upon the nature of the changes and the movements in the terms of trade, can increase or decrease the divergence between the internal RER for imports and the external RERs.

External Proxies for the Three-Good RERs

Because of a lack of timely data for computing the three-good internal RERs directly, external proxies are sometimes used for them as they are for the two-good internal RER discussed earlier. These proxies may be useful if no measurement problems are involved in computing the external RER but may be quite problematic if there are measurement errors.

As noted in the section in Chapter 3 on using external RERs as proxies for the two-good internal RER, the effective foreign WPI tracks import prices at the official exchange rate reasonably well. Hence, figure 4.12 compares the WPI-CPI proxy with the three-good internal RER for imports at border and internal prices expressed relative to the aggregate price level. The WPI-CPI proxy at official exchange rates does track the internal RER for imports at border prices fairly well. As expected, this proxy diverges significantly from the RER for imports at domestic prices when the latter diverges from the import RER at border prices.

Figure 4.12 *The Internal RER for Imports at Domestic and Border Prices Relative to the Aggregate Price Level and the WPI-CPI Proxy Calculated Using Official and Weighted Average Exchange Rates, 1980–93 (1985=100)*

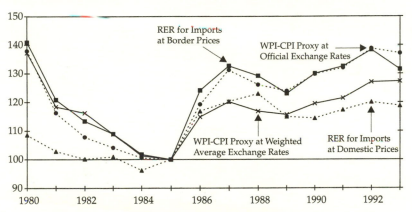

··▲·· RER for Imports at Domestic Prices, Including Taxes, Relative to the Aggregate Price Level

—■— RER for Imports at Border Prices, Excluding Taxes, Relative to the Aggregate Price Level

··◆·· WPI-CPI Proxy at Official Exchange Rates

—✕— WPI-CPI Proxy at Weighted Average Official and Parallel Exchange Rates

Note: The WPI-CPI proxy is calculated using adjusted IFS country weights. The private consumption deflator has been used as the aggregate price level in computing the internal RERs for comparability with the external RER measures. An upward movement represents an appreciation of both the internal RERs and the WPI-CPI proxy.
Source: Computed from World Bank data.

However, the existence of parallel exchange rates and unrecorded trade complicates the choice of an appropriate method for calculating the WPI-CPI proxy. As figure 4.12 shows, the correspondence between the WPI-CPI proxy and the RER for imports at border prices is less good if the proxy is calculated using weighted average parallel and official exchange rates. Figure 4.13 makes a similar comparison between the WPI-CPI proxy and the internal RER for imports using 1985 import weights for calculating the proxy rather than adjusted IFS country weights. It tells the same story as figure 4.12: the WPI-CPI proxy tracks the RER for imports at border prices reasonably well when calculated at official exchange rates but diverges significantly at weighted official and parallel exchange rates.

Figures 4.12 and 4.13 suggest two possibilities: (a) if the effect of the parallel exchange rates of some of Côte d'Ivoire's trading partners was actually negligible and may safely be ignored, then the CPI-WPI proxy should be measured at official exchange rates and would track the internal RER for imports at border prices quite well; or (b) if the effect of

Figure 4.13 *The Internal RER for Imports at Domestic and Border Prices Relative to the Aggregate Price Level and the WPI-CPI Proxy at Official and Weighted Average Exchange Rates, Calculated with 1985 Import Weights, 1980–93 (1985=100)*

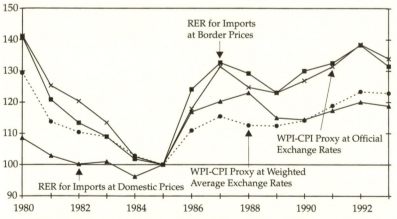

—▲— RER for Imports at Domestic Prices, Including Taxes, Relative to the Aggregate Price Level
—■— RER for Imports at Border Prices, Excluding Taxes, Relative to the Aggregate Price Level
··●·· WPI-CPI Proxy at Weighted Average Official and Parallel Exchange Rates
—×— WPI-CPI Proxy at Official Exchange Rates

Note: The WPI-CPI Proxy is calculated using 1985 import shares as weights. The private consumption deflator has been used as the aggregate price level in computing the internal RERs for comparability with the external RER measures. An upward movement represents an appreciation of both the internal RERs and the WPI-CPI proxy.
Source: Computed from World Bank data.

parallel rates was not negligible and should be taken into account, then the CPI-WPI proxy should be measured at weighted average parallel and official exchange rates and would not track the RER for imports well. Only further research in other countries on the empirical relationship between the WPI-CPI proxy and the RER for imports can answer the question of how well one can, on average, expect the proxy to track the RER for imports.

Summary and Conclusion

This chapter and the preceding one have discussed the two- and three-good versions of the internal RER, alternative ways of measuring these empirically, and the theoretical and empirical relationships among the external and internal RERs and the factors affecting these. This final section first summarizes the findings from the two chapters concerning the external and internal RERs and the relationship between these. It then concludes with some thoughts on the interpretation of changes in the various RERs and the need for improved data for measuring these. The various different measures of the internal RER are summarized in table 4.1.

Concepts and Measurement of the Internal RER

In selecting an appropriate measure of the internal RER, an analyst must choose between the use of a two-good vs. a three-good approach, domestic vs. border prices, and direct estimates vs. proxies.

A Three-Good vs. a Two-Good Approach

In choosing between a two-good and a three-good approach, the effects of three important factors should be borne in mind: (a) differential productivity growth in the traded and nontraded goods sectors; (b) trade taxes, import restraints, and domestic price policies; and (c) movements in the terms of trade.

The traditional two-good model was developed originally for analyzing the effects of productivity growth on trade between industrial countries. Balassa (1964) and Samuelson (1964) showed that faster productivity growth in the tradable than in the nontradable sector would lead to a decline in the relative price of tradables and hence to an appreciation of the two-good internal RER. Hence, in all countries experiencing more rapid productivity growth in traded goods than in the nontraded sector, the internal RER should follow an appreciating trend. However, in the absence of data on sectoral productivity growth rates, determining how much of an actual appreciation in the internal RER is attributable to the Balassa-Samuelson effect and how much to other real shocks (such as a decline in real export prices) is a difficult empirical

Table 4.1 Summary of Internal RER Measures

Internal RER Measure	Method of Calculation	Comments
1. Two-Good Approach: One RER for Traded Goods		
a. At Domestic Prices		
i. Expenditure-Based Estimate	Weighted average of *RERX* and *RERM* at *domestic* prices from three-good approach	The two-good RER for total trade is a common measure, but separate RERs for imports and exports are more useful than a single RER for total trade because import and exports prices may move in opposite directions.
ii. Production-Based Estimate	Ratio of value-added deflators for sectors producing traded and nontraded goods	This measure is not very useful in developing countries because the required disaggregated GDP data for value added by sector of origin often are not available. When the required data are available, the production-based estimate may provide a cross-check on the expenditure-based one, but it may as well differ significantly because of problems in separating sectors producing tradables and nontradables.
b. At Border Prices: Expenditure-Based Estimate	Weighted average of *RERX* and *RERM* at *border* prices from three-good approach	Since the external terms of trade and domestic commercial policies may affect imports and exports quite differently, averaging *RERX* and *RERM* at border prices into a single RER at border prices usually is not very useful.
2. Three-Good Approach: Separate RERs for Imports and Exports		
a. At Domestic Prices: Expenditure-Based Estimate	Ratios of national accounts deflators for imports and exports to deflator for domestic goods	These are direct measures that accurately reflect domestic resource allocation incentives.
b. At Border Prices: Expenditure-Based Estimate	Ratios of UNCTAD price indexes for imports and exports expressed in domestic currency to national accounts deflator for domestic goods	The difference between the RERs at border prices and at domestic prices gives a summary measure of effects of trade policies.
3. The External WPI-CPI REER Proxy	NEER multiplied by ratios of effective foreign WPI to domestic CPI.	This RER may be a reasonable proxy in some countries for the RER *for imports at border prices* expressed relative to the CPI. It should not be used as a proxy for the two-good internal RER or for the RER for imports at domestic prices.

Source: Computed from World Bank data.

problem. Furthermore, if productivity in the tradable goods sector grows relatively faster in the home country than in its trading partners, its external RER will also appreciate, although less rapidly than its internal RER. If the law of one price holds for traded goods, the external RER for traded goods will be a constant. If the law of one price does not hold for traded goods, the external RER for traded goods will depreciate as a result of more rapid productivity gains in the traded-goods sector at home than abroad.

The two-good RER was subsequently adapted to the developing-country context by Salter (1959) and Swan (1960). It is very useful for analyzing theoretically the effects of macroeconomic policies and productivity changes on the RER and is well established in the theoretical literature. Despite these advantages, the two-good internal RER has some serious conceptual and empirical limitations for use in developing countries. Conceptually, it is not suitable for analyzing variations in the terms of trade and commercial policy because it does not distinguish between imports and exports. Empirically, the two-good internal RER is difficult to measure accurately because of lack of data for accurately dividing goods into tradables and nontradables as described in Chapter 3.

The computation of separate internal RER indexes for imports and exports is still less common than calculating a single RER for traded goods. Nevertheless, when the terms of trade or trade policy change significantly, the internal RERs for imports and exports will behave quite differently. For a given price of domestic goods, an improvement in the terms of trade will depreciate the internal RER for exports but appreciate the RER for imports. A deterioration in the terms of trade will have the opposite two effects. Similarly, an increase in import tariffs will depreciate the internal RER for imports but may appreciate the RER for exports.

A single average RER for traded goods may thus obscure what is happening to relative prices. In fact, the internal RERs for exports and imports are the best measures for assessing the impact of changes in the terms of trade and trade policy in developing countries. Essentially the same data and amount of effort are required to compute these two RERs as are required to compute a single one for traded goods. Hence, it will usually be desirable to analyze the RERs for imports and exports separately rather than averaging them into a single RER for total trade. Calculation of separate internal RERs for imports and exports should become standard practice for low-income countries, and these should generally be used instead of a single internal RER for traded goods.[13]

---

13. If for presentational purposes a single internal RER measure is needed, the price of domestic goods in foreign currency terms may be used as discussed on page 178 and illustrated in Chapter 8.

In addition, in some cases it may be useful to have separate RER measures for traditional and nontraditional exports. Multi-good approaches that allow for additional RERs for parallel exchange rates, import-competing goods, or other major sectors are also worth calculating if the data are available for doing so. In addition, in a country with a specialized undiversified production structure, it may be worthwhile to compute separate disaggregated RERs for major export or import-competing subsectors to aid in the assessment of the loss or gain in the price competitiveness of these sectors.

Domestic Prices vs. Border Prices

When there are taxes or quantitative restraints on international trade, the internal RER may be measured either at domestic prices including taxes or at border prices excluding taxes. When trade taxes are important, the internal RERs at domestic and border prices may diverge significantly, both from each other and from the external RER. It is the internal RER inclusive of taxes that reflects relative domestic prices and affects domestic resource allocation. The RER excluding taxes, in contrast, reflects the tradeoffs between traded and nontraded goods actually available to the home country at border prices. A comparison of the RER excluding taxes with the RER including taxes gives a broad measure of the distortions resulting from a country's trade taxes and price policies.

Direct Estimates vs. Proxies

In analyzing exchange rates in developing countries, many economists have relied on external proxies for the internal RER rather than making direct estimates of it. This chapter presents a readily usable methodology for directly estimating the internal RER at domestic and border prices from commonly available national accounts and trade data. Whenever national accounts data are available, such direct estimates should be used for empirical analysis. It may also be possible to estimate the internal RER by disaggregating the CPI when the data required for doing so are available.

Although it can be distorted by strategic pricing behavior of importers, the commonly used WPI-CPI external proxy may track the internal RER for imports reasonably well at border prices (that is, excluding taxes) in some developing countries. However, the exports of many low-income developing countries are composed of a few primary products with volatile prices, which are given low weights in the WPIs of industrial countries. Hence, the WPI-CPI proxy is not likely to accurately reflect the export incentives faced by countries exporting primary commodities. It will not generally give an accurate indication of the internal

RER for total trade, either. Therefore, this proxy should be used to measure the internal RER at border prices (excluding taxes) rather than the internal RER at domestic prices (including taxes). This proxy should be compared to the direct measure of the internal RER for imports when this is available and used with caution when it is not. Calculation of the WPI-CPI proxy may also be quite sensitive to assumptions about unrecorded trade, parallel exchange markets, and appropriate country weights, which can make it hard to measure accurately in some cases.

The Relationship between Internal and External RERs

Competitiveness results from the interaction of domestic costs and international prices and may be defined in either internal or external terms as explained in the preceding chapter. The different internal and external RER concepts attempt to measure competitiveness in one or the other of these two ways. The relationship between them can be affected by a number of factors. Principal among these are the ones summarized above, namely:

a. Differential productivity growth in traded and nontraded sectors, which differently affects relative prices and the internal RERs both at home and abroad and the external RERs for all goods and traded goods;

b. Changes in trade taxes, administered prices, and other commercial policies that drive a wedge between internal and external prices and can cause the internal RERs for imports and exports to behave quite differently from each other and from external RER measures; and

c. Fluctuations in the terms of trade, which can shift relative prices much more sharply in developing countries than in their industrialized trading partners and cause the internal RERs for imports and exports to move in opposite directions.

The effects of changes in productivity, commercial policy, and the terms of trade on the measured internal and external RERs can be quantified. However, the quantitative relationships all depend upon the law of one price, the empirical validity of which is questionable. Deviations from the law of one price that result in changes in the nominal exchange rate or in foreign prices being reflected only partially in the domestic price of traded goods may lead to a considerably looser empirical relationship between the international external RERs and the factors affecting them than the theoretical quantitative relationships would suggest. In addition, the relative importance of homogeneous commodities and differentiated products in the exports of a particular low-income country will affect the behavior of its external RER for traded goods. Parallel markets, unrecorded trade, and large shifts in trade patterns may also complicate the measurement of the external RER in low-income countries as discussed in Chapter 2. Hence, in general, it is not appropriate to use external RERs to draw conclusions about movements in internal relative prices.[14]

As discussed in the survey of empirical research in Chapter 5, a significant amount of empirical work has been done on the statistical properties of external RERs, particularly on the question of the validity of purchasing power parity theory of equilibrium exchange rates. In contrast, relatively little work has been done on the statistical properties of internal RERs, except in the context of analyzing the Balassa-Samuelson effect in industrial countries, in part because of a shortage of data. Such questions as the effects of unrecorded trade and parallel exchange rates on the national accounts measures of the internal RER and the empirical relationship of the internal RER to the external RER have rarely been considered.[15] Even the relationship between the common external WPI-CPI proxy and the internal RER has hardly been analyzed.

A Combination of Measures

The natural question at this point is the one posed in the introduction: given the various factors affecting internal and external real exchange rates differently, which RERs can be measured most accurately and which RERs are the best to use in developing countries? Unfortunately, there is no simple answer to this question. Some external and internal RER measures are quite useful, but others are often misleading and should be avoided.

Despite the substantial amount of theoretical and empirical work that has been done on real exchange rates, measurement of the external RER unfortunately still involves as much art as science. Consequently, when an exchange rate appears to become overvalued, there may well be substantial controversy about what the different measures of the RER show and how the divergences between them can be explained. For typical low-income countries the most useful generally available RER measures are (a) the external RERs calculated using CPIs and, if available, labor costs and (b) separate internal RERs for exports and imports. When a particular low-income country is an exporter, or potential exporter, of

---

14. Wickham (1993) reaches a similar conclusion after examining evidence for Colombia and Kenya.

15. For one of the few examples known to the authors, see Guillaumont Jeanneney (1993).

differentiated manufactured products, external RERs for traded manufactured goods may be a useful additional indicator of competitiveness in this sector if the required data are available for calculating it. Conversely, averaging together the internal RERs for imports and exports obscures more than it reveals and should be avoided.

External RERs based on CPIs and labor costs and their components (the NEER and domestic and foreign price indexes) provide good indicators of movements in relative price and cost levels between countries and of nominal shocks to exchange rates and price levels. Internal RERs, in contrast, often provide only limited information about inflation since they are relative domestic prices, with inflation usually having largely offsetting, even if not exactly proportional, effects on both their numerators and denominators. Since internal RERs by themselves provide little information about nominal shocks, it is important to also look at available measures of the external RER. When domestic inflation that appreciates the observed RER relative to its equilibrium level is a primary concern, as in many Latin American and Eastern European countries, external RERs calculated using CPIs and labor costs are particularly useful.[16]

External RERs are of less use in analyzing real shocks that require adjustments in relative prices, since they provide little information about relative price movements within a particular country. Internal RERs, as measures of relative domestic prices, are quite useful in analyzing real shocks. It is particularly important to have separate RERs for imports and exports when the terms of trade fluctuate or trade taxes are changed.

External and internal RER measures provide different but related information about the nominal and real shocks affecting an open economy. However, because of data limitations, some of the measures may not be available for a given developing country. In addition, both the internal and external RERs may be subject to significant measurement errors. Therefore, to sort out as accurately as possible what is happening empirically, it is often useful to look at a both of them—at the external RER to see the effects of domestic inflation and the behavior of prices and exchange rates in competing countries and at the internal RER to analyze real shocks and domestic price incentives.

Since the various measures of the RER provide different but related information, one should calculate and interpret them together rather than concentrating exclusively on a single measure of either external or internal price competitiveness. Using a combination of them helps to

---

16. The potential usefulness of these external RERs is, however, not fully brought out by the empirical examples in Chapter 2 for Côte d'Ivoire, for which inflation was not an important problem in the 1980–93 period.

avoid potentially misleading signals provided by any one measure taken in isolation. Divergent movements in the different measures can sometimes be consistently interpreted, but the analyst needs to pay some attention both to the theoretical relationship among the different RERs and to data problems involved in their empirical measurement.

The Need for Improved Data

The availability of the data required for timely and accurate measurement of the internal RER is still problematic in many countries. Most low-income countries do not report price indexes for nontraded goods. In addition, price statistics on traded goods are usually limited to import and export prices, and little organized information typically is available on import substitutes and exportables. Furthermore, the data needed for computing the internal RER are usually available only annually. Hence, progress in improving the empirical measurement of the internal RER is likely to depend critically upon improved data collection.

Data required for accurately measuring and interpreting the external RER may also be hard to come by in some cases. Better data on the nature and size of transactions in parallel markets, unrecorded trade, and the impact of third-country competitors in export markets may be needed in countries in which these problems are important. Data on wages, productivity, and external competitiveness measures for the traded goods sector, which are quite important for distinguishing between real and nominal shocks, also tend to be quite scarce.

Data availability may have significant implications for the quality of the analysis that can be carried out in developing countries and possibly even for the feasibility of implementing some exchange rate policies—such as establishing an appropriate new fixed peg—that require reasonably accurate estimates of the actual and equilibrium RERs. Where data availability is a significant analytical or policy constraint, improving it is likely to be a priority for better economic management as the RER is a key macroeconomic variable that is critical for sustaining a successful development effort.

Appendix A

The Relationship between the Internal RER for Imports, the External RER, and the Terms of Trade

Substituting equations 4.11 and 4.12 in the main text in definition of the terms of trade yields equation 4.A.1:

(4.A.1)
$$TOT_d = \frac{P_{Xd}}{P_{Md}} = \frac{\dfrac{P_{Mf}\left(1-t_{Xd}\right)}{E_{fc}}}{\dfrac{P_{Xf}\left(1+l_{Md}\right)}{E_{fc}}}$$

$$= \frac{P_{Mf}\left(1-t_{Xd}\right)}{P_{Xf}\left(1+t_{Md}\right)} = \frac{1}{TOT_f} \cdot \frac{\left(1-t_{Xd}\right)}{\left(1+t_{Md}\right)}.$$

Since the foreign country's exports are the home country's imports and vice versa, if transportation and other transactions costs are negligible or the same percentage of import and export prices, the foreign country's terms of trade (TOT_f) are simply the inverse of the home country's terms of trade expressed in border prices, as shown in equation 4.A.2:

(4.A.2)
$$TOT_f = \frac{P_{Xf}}{P_{Mf}} = \frac{P_{Md}^*}{P_{Xd}^*} = \frac{1}{TOT_d^*}.$$

where the * notation indicates the border price of a home country variable. Equation 4.A.1 thus becomes equation 4.A.3:

(4.A.3)
$$TOT_d = TOT_d^* \left(\frac{1-t_{Xd}}{1+t_{Md}} \right).$$

Similarly, we can derive a relationship between the term $E_{fc} \cdot (P_{Md}/P_{Mf})$ in equation 4.10 of the main text and the home country's terms of trade expressed in foreign prices (TOT_d^*), as shown by equation 4.A.4:

(4.A.4)
$$E_{fc} \cdot \frac{P_{Md}}{P_{Mf}} = E_{fc} \cdot \frac{\dfrac{P_{Xf}(1+t_{Md})}{E_{fc}}}{P_{Mf}} = \frac{P_{Xf}}{P_{Mf}}(1+t_{Md})$$

$$= TOT_f (1+t_{Md}) = \frac{1}{TOT_d^*}(1+t_{Md})$$

Substituting the equivalent expressions in terms of the home country's terms of trade measured in foreign prices for TOT_d from equation 4.A.3 and for $E_{fc} \cdot (P_{Md}/P_{Mf})$ from equation 4.A.4 into equation 4.10 from the text gives equation 4.A.5:

(4.A.5)
$$BRER_{fc} = \frac{IRERN_{Md}^\alpha}{IRERN_{Mf}^a} \cdot \frac{1}{\left(\dfrac{1}{TOT_d^*}\right)^c} \cdot \left[TOT_d^* \left(\frac{1-t_{Xd}}{1+t_{Md}} \right) \right]^\gamma \cdot \left[\frac{1}{TOT_d^*} \cdot (1+t_{Md}) \right]$$

$$= \frac{IRERN_{Md}^\alpha}{IRERN_{Mf}^\alpha} \cdot TOT_d^{*c+\gamma-1} \cdot (1-t_{Xd})^\gamma \cdot (1+t_{Md})^{1-\gamma}$$

Taking the logarithm of equation 4.A.5 and differentiating it yields, for small percentage changes, equation 4.A.6:

(4.A.6)
$$\widehat{BRER}_{fc} = \alpha \cdot \widehat{IRERN}_{Md} - a \cdot \widehat{IRERN}_{Mf} + (c+\gamma-1) \cdot \widehat{TOT_d^*}$$
$$\underset{+}{} \qquad \underset{-}{} \qquad \underset{+/-}{}$$
$$+ \gamma \cdot \left(\widehat{1-t_{Xd}} \right) + (1-\gamma) \cdot \left(\widehat{1+t_{Md}} \right)$$
$$\underset{+}{} \qquad \underset{+}{}$$

Equation 4.A.6 is the result given in equation 4.15 in the text.

To obtain an equivalent expression for the home country's internal RER for imports, equation 4.A.5 is solved for $IRERN_{Md}$ (equation 4.A.7):

(4.A.7) $$IRERN_{Md}^\alpha = BRER_{fc} \cdot IRERN_{Mf}^a \cdot TOT_d^{*1-\gamma-c} \cdot (1-t_{Xd})^{-\gamma} \cdot (1+t_{Md})^{\gamma-1}.$$

Taking the logarithm of equation 4.A.7 and differentiating it yields, for small percentage changes, equation 4.A.8:

$$\widehat{IRERN}_{Md} = \frac{1}{\alpha} \cdot \widehat{BRER}_{fc} + \frac{a}{\alpha}\widehat{IRERN}_{Mf} + \frac{(1-\gamma-c)}{\alpha} \cdot \widehat{TOT_d^*} - \frac{\gamma}{\alpha}\left(\widehat{1-t_{Xd}}\right)$$

(4.A.8)
$$+ \qquad\qquad + \qquad\qquad +/- \qquad\qquad -$$

$$-\frac{1-\gamma}{\alpha}\left(\widehat{1+t_{Md}}\right)$$
$$-$$

which is the result given in equation 4.16 in the text.

Appendix B

An Additional Possible Proxy for the Three-Good Internal RER

An alternative way of computing proxies for the three-good internal RERs has been suggested by Stein, Allen, and Associates (1995).[17] For an empirical expenditure price index, which contains imports but not exports, $\gamma = c = 0$; and equation 4.13 for the expenditure-PPP external RER ($EBRER_{fc}$) simplifies to equation 4.B.1:

$$(4.B.1) \qquad EBRER_{fc} = IRERN_{Md}^{\alpha} \cdot IRERN_{Mf}^{-a} \cdot \frac{(1+t_{Md})}{TOT_d^*}.$$

If the foreign country (the rest of the world) is large and its internal RER does not change significantly when the home country's terms of trade change, equation 4.B.1 may be further simplified to equation 4.B.2:

$$(4.B.2) \qquad IRERN_{Md}^{\alpha} = k_1 \cdot EBRER_{fc} \cdot \frac{TOT_d^*}{(1+t_{Md})}.$$

Hence, if there are no changes in domestic trade taxes, the right-hand side of equation 4.B.2—the product of the terms of trade measured in border prices and the expenditure-PPP external RER—could be used as a proxy for the internal RER for imports.

An expression similar to equation 4.13 can be derived for the Mundell-Fleming external RER ($MFBRER_{fc}$). For an empirical production price index, which contains exports but not imports, $\beta = b = o$; and this expression will simplify to equation 4.B.3:

$$(4.B.3) \qquad MFBRER_{fc} = IRERN_{Xd}^{\alpha} \cdot IRERN_{Xf}^{-a} \cdot TOT_d^* \cdot (1-t_{Xd}).$$

---

17. See Stein, Allen, and Associates (1995), Chapter 3.

On the assumption, as above, that the foreign country's internal RER does not change, equation 4.B.3 may be further simplified to equation 4.B.4:

$$(4.B.4) \qquad IRERN_{Xd}^{\alpha} = \frac{k_2 \cdot MFBRER_{fc}}{TOT_d^* \cdot \left(1 - t_{Xd}\right)}.$$

If there are no changes in domestic trade taxes, the right-hand side of equation 4.B.4—the Mundell-Fleming external RER divided by the terms of trade measured in border prices—could be used as a proxy for the internal RER for exports.

We calculated the above proxies for the internal RERs for imports (*RER-M*) and exports (*RER-X*) for Côte d'Ivoire. The proxies performed very poorly (see figures 4.B.1 and 4.B.2), probably because of a combination of measurement errors in computing the REER, changes in Côte d'Ivoire's commercial policies, and changes in foreign countries' internal RERs resulting from productivity growth. Since these proxies may be problematic in other cases, too, we decided to include the discussion of them in an appendix rather than in the main text of the chapter.

Figure 4.B.1a *The PPP External REER, Terms of Trade at* **Border** *Prices, RER-M at Domestic Prices, and the RER-M Proxy, at Weighted Average Official and Parallel Exchange Rates and Adjusted IFS Weights, 1980–93 (1985=100)*

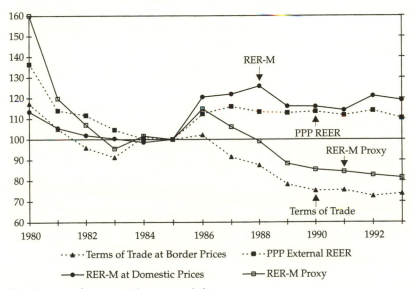

Note: An upward movement is an appreciation.
Source: Computed from World Bank data.

Figure 4.B.1b *The PPP External REER, Terms of Trade at* **Domestic** *Prices, RER-M at Domestic Prices, and the RER-M Proxy, at Weighted Average Official and Parallel Exchange Rates and Adjusted IFS Weights, 1980–93 (1985=100)*

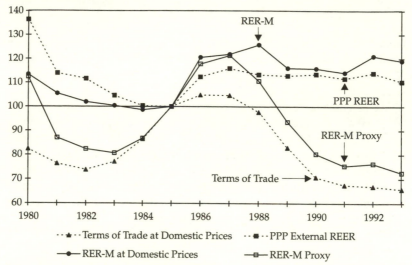

Note: An upward movement is an appreciation.
Source: Computed from World Bank data.

Figure 4.B.2a *The Mundell-Fleming External REER, Terms of Trade at* **Border** *Prices, RER-X at Domestic Prices, and the RER-X Proxy, at Weighted Average Official and Parallel Exchange Rates and Adjusted IFS Weights, 1980–93 (1985=100)*

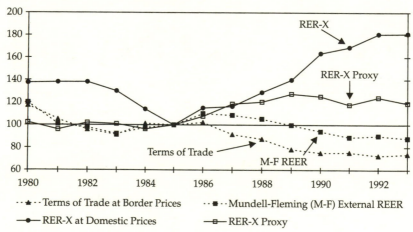

Note: An upward movement is an appreciation.
Source: Computed from World bank data.

Figure 4.B.2b *The Mundell-Fleming External REER, Terms of Trade at Domestic Prices, RER-X at Domestic Prices, and the RER-X Proxy, at Weighted Average Official and Parallel Exchange Rates and Adjusted IFS Weights, 1980–93 (1985=100)*

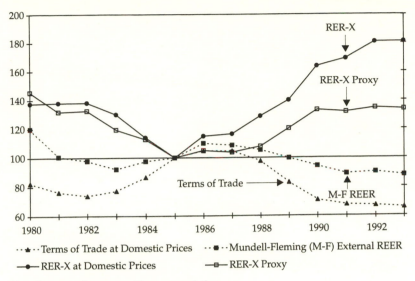

Note: An upward movement is an appreciation.
Source: Computed from World Bank data.

Part II

Determinants of the Equilibrium Real Exchange Rate

5

The Long-Run Equilibrium Real Exchange Rate: Conceptual Issues and Empirical Research

Peter J. Montiel

Following up on Part I's focus on definitions and measurement of the *actual* real exchange rate, Part II studies the definition and estimation of the *long-run equilibrium* real exchange rate (LRER). This chapter focuses on conceptual issues and a review of previous empirical research on the LRER, both for industrial as well as for developing countries. The next chapter builds an analytical model of the LRER suitable for identifying its "fundamental" determinants, as well as for exploring the qualitative direction of the effects of each of those determinants on the LRER.

There is a substantial degree of agreement on an LRER definition at the broad conceptual level. As originally described by Nurkse (1945), the LRER is that value of the real exchange rate that is consistent with the dual objectives of external and internal balance, for specified values of other variables that may influence these objectives.[1] The former refers to a situation in which the value of the current account deficit is one that can be financed by a "sustainable" level of capital inflows, while the latter refers to a situation in which the market for nontraded goods is in a "sustainable" equilibrium.[2] While this broad conceptual definition is

---

1. For a recent restatement by an authority on the subject, see Edwards (1989).

2. Alternatively, in the Mundell-Fleming framework more commonly applied in the industrial-country context, the market for domestically produced goods would be required to be in a sustainable equilibrium.

helpful, giving precise operational content to the term "sustainable" as well as to the "other variables that may influence these objectives" is not a trivial matter, and different approaches to these issues have resulted in markedly different empirical methodologies for measuring the LRER.

This chapter presents an overview of these alternative empirical methodologies, as applied in both industrial and developing countries. The objectives are both to describe the methodologies, as well as to place them in a common analytical framework within which they can be compared. To achieve these objectives, the chapter starts by setting out a broad conceptual framework and then describes in succession the alternative methodologies that have been used for estimating the LRER in industrial and developing countries. These are treated in separate sections, because the analytical approaches to the LRER, as well as the methods used to estimate it, have tended to differ in these alternative contexts.

Conceptual Issues

The appellation "long-run" attached to the equilibrium exchange rate concept under consideration arises from the provision in the Nurkse definition that the relevant external and internal balance outcomes should be "sustainable." The imposition of a sustainability requirement thus introduces a dynamic dimension into the definition of the equilibrium real exchange rate. Accordingly, to analyze the issues involved in defining the long-run equilibrium real exchange rate more precisely, it can help clarify matters to be as specific as possible about the dynamic structure of the economy at hand.

Sustainability in Theory

At any moment in time, an economy will exhibit a short-run equilibrium that can be thought of, in textbook fashion, as some combination of goods-market equilibrium and equilibrium in financial markets. This equilibrium may or may not feature full employment, a desirable rate of inflation, and a level of the current account deficit that external creditors are willing to finance indefinitely. The short-run equilibrium determines the values of the economy's endogenous variables—including that of the *actual* real exchange rate (which we can denote RER)—conditioned on the current values taken on by other variables that are not themselves determined as part of the short-run equilibrium, but that may be changing over time. These include macroeconomic variables of three types: predetermined, policy, and exogenous variables. Let X_1 represent the set of all current values of the relevant group of predetermined variables and X_2, the set of all current *and expected future* values of the group of relevant policy variables.[3] Concerning the exogenous variables, I will classify them into two types: "bubble" variables, denoted $B(t)$, are extraneous factors that affect the economy *only* through their influence on expectations, while "fundamental" factors are those that influence the economy at any given moment *independently* of any effects they may exert through expectations. I will use the symbol X_3 to denote the set of all current *and expected future* values of the "fundamental" exogenous variables. With this notation, a reduced-form expression for the real exchange rate that emerges from the economy's short-run equilibrium can be written as in equation 5.1:

$$(5.1) \qquad RER(t) = F(B(t), X_1(t), \mathbf{X}_2(t), \mathbf{X}_3(t))$$

where the argument t appearing in $\mathbf{X}_2$ and $\mathbf{X}_3$ indicates that expectations about the future values of the variables included in the sets are formed at time t. I will refer to this as the short-run equilibrium real exchange rate.

The formulation in equation 5.1 is quite broad. It is worth noting, in particular, that the inclusion of $B(t)$ makes it broad enough to encompass the role of so-called "rational bubbles," which are speculative factors that generate price increases of a self-fulfilling nature. Equation 5.1 states that the economy's short-run equilibrium depends on expectations about the future, consisting of expected future values of policy and exogenous variables, as well as extraneous bubble factors, if any.[4] By creating self-fulfilling price movements, such factors are capable of creating rational price "bubbles" and thus driving the real exchange rate away from the "fundamental" value that would be observed in the absence of such extraneous influences underpinning future price expectations.

A short-run equilibrium RER given by equation 5.1, but with no "bubble" term present among the exogenous variables, is often described as "fundamentals-driven," where the term "fundamentals" refers to the variables included in X_1, $\mathbf{X}_2$, and $\mathbf{X}_3$. For present purposes, however, I will use the more precise term "short-run fundamentals-driven" since, as will be shown presently, the definition of what constitutes "fundamentals" differs depending on the time horizon adopted. To avoid overburdening the discussion, in what follows I will abstract away from

---

3. Bold lettering is used to indicate that not just current, but also expected future variables are included in $\mathbf{X}_2$.

4. The future evolution of the predetermined variables is excluded from this list because it will itself depend on the expected future values of the exogenous and policy variables, through the influence of these on current endogenous variables, as explained below.

bubble factors altogether and restrict attention to "short-run fundamentals-driven" real exchange rate movements, given by equation 5.2:

(5.2) $RER(t) = F(0, X_1(t), \mathbf{X}_2(t), \mathbf{X}_3(t))$.

Since equation 5.2 determines the value of the real exchange rate at
any moment, the dynamics of the real exchange rate arise from move-
ments over time in X_1, $\mathbf{X}_2$, and $\mathbf{X}_3$. The factors that cause these variables
to change over time differ across the three types of variables.

Predetermined variables are those that, while they may be fixed at
any given moment, evolve endogenously over time, influenced not only
by the policy and exogenous variables, but also by the current and expected future values of the endogenous variables. Because each of the
latter will depend in turn on X_1, $\mathbf{X}_2$, and $\mathbf{X}_3$ through equations similar to
5.2, the change in the predetermined variables over time can be written
as in equation 5.3:

(5.3) $\dot{X}_1(t) = G(0, X_1(t), \mathbf{X}_2(t), \mathbf{X}_3(t))$.

The economy's stock of net international indebtedness and its capital
stock are such variables, for example, and if domestic nominal wages
are "sticky," so may be the aggregate nominal wage level.[5]

Unlike predetermined variables, policy variables follow a dynamic
path that may or may not be affected by the current state of the economy,
depending on the policy regime that is in place—in other words, on
whether the rules that guide policy incorporate feedback from actual
economic developments. If they do, then a set of equations similar to
equation 5.3 could be written for the policy variables. But even if they
do not, policy variables may be evolving over time as the result of policy
"gradualism"—that is, the undertaking of policy adjustments in a measured, rather than discrete, fashion. For example, the gradual liberalization of commercial policy, or the gradual removal of restrictions on

---

5. It is worth noting in passing that, to capture the notion of neutrality, it is
standard in textbook models to specify the variables on the right-hand side of
equations 5.2 and 5.3 in real terms. This means that predetermined variables that
are actually predetermined in nominal terms appear in equations 5.2 and 5.3
divided by some nominal variable. To retain their identity as predetermined variables, it is helpful to deflate these using exogenous or policy variables. For example, if it is predetermined in a particular model, the nominal wage may appear in equations 5.2 and 5.3 in the form of the real wage. To retain its predetermined character, in a fixed-exchange rate model we would want to think of it as
measured in units of traded goods, rather than in units of the domestic consumption bundle or some other real unit with an endogenous price.

capital movements, would generate such policy dynamics, with or without feedback. To incorporate either possibility, the policy variables are expressed as functions of time in equations 5.2 and 5.3.

Finally, the path followed by the exogenous variables (an important component of which, for example, consists of world economic conditions) is by definition independent of the current state of the domestic economy. Because these variables will typically be changing over time, they are also expressed as functions of time in the equations above.

With this framework in place, we can now be more precise about the meaning of sustainability, and thus of "long-run equilibrium." Suppose that we think of the policy and exogenous variables as being composed of "permanent" components that are constant over time—call these X_2^* and X_3^* respectively—and "transitory" components $\Delta X_2(t)$ and $\Delta X_3(t)$, where, as shown in equation 5.4:

(5.4)
$$\Delta X_2(t) = X_2(t) - X_2^*$$
$$\Delta X_3(t) = X_3(t) - X_3^* \ .$$

The "sustainable" values of the policy and exogenous variables can be identified by their permanent components.[6] Notice, however, that even if these two types of variables are set at their sustainable levels—that is, even if $X_2(t) = X_2^*$ and $X_3(t) = X_3^*$—the predetermined variables X_1 may be changing over time, according to equation 5.3. Sustainability for the predetermined variables requires that these variables have stopped evolving endogenously—that is, that they have reached their steady-state values. The steady-state value of the predetermined variables, denoted X_1^*, is that which satisfies equation 5.5:

(5.5)
$$0 = G(0, X_1^* , X_2^* , X_3^*).$$

In this context, a long-run equilibrium is simply a short-run equilibrium conditioned on particular values of the three types of "forcing" variables—specifically, on the permanent values of the policy and exogenous variables, as well as on steady-state values of the predetermined variables. The LRER is thus given by equation 5.6:

(5.6)
$$LRER = F(0, X_1^*(X_2^*, X_3^*), X_2^*, X_3^*)$$
$$= H(X_2^*, X_3^*)$$

---

6. In the case of the policy variables, the permanent component may or may not correspond to "desired" values, depending on whether policies that are not necessarily desired may nevertheless tend to be sustained.

where $X_1^*(X_2^*, X_3^*)$ is the implicit function defined by equation 5.5 that expresses the predetermined variables as functions of the policy and exogenous variables. Since the second line of equation 5.6 suggests that the LRER depends only on X_2^* and X_3^*, these are accordingly referred to as the "long-run fundamental" determinants of the LRER. This equilibrium described by equation 5.6 is "sustainable" in the sense that absent changes in the exogenous or policy variables, it can be expected to persist indefinitely.

Misalignment

The framework set out above can be useful in clarifying some controversial issues in the measurement of equilibrium real exchange rates. Isard and Faruqee (1998) point out that there are two schools of thought within the economics profession that question the usefulness of attempts to measure equilibrium real exchange rates. The first argues that real exchange rates can never become substantially misaligned—meaning that actual real exchange rates tend to reflect the underlying fundamentals—while the second accepts the concept of misalignment but is skeptical of the ability of any particular methodology to deliver accurate estimates of the degree of misalignment (that is, of the equilibrium real exchange rate) in practice.

The validity of the second of these views is an empirical issue. The usefulness of alternative methodologies for the measurement of equilibrium real exchange rates can be assessed in various ways—for example, by their ability to replicate historical episodes in particular countries during which informed observers agree that real exchange rate misalignment has been a serious problem, or by their ability to predict subsequent real exchange rate movements. Several of the methods described in this book have been evaluated favorably using such methods, as will be described below. At this point I focus instead on the first of these objections and consider it in the context of the conceptual framework described previously.

Isard and Faruqee (1998) characterize the first view as maintaining that real exchange rates are always "appropriate" conditional on the fundamentals and consequently that "inappropriate" exchange rates reflect unsustainable or otherwise undesirable macroeconomic policies. The implication is that under this view there is no separate welfare-enhancing role for exchange rate policy as such. The role of policy is simply to set the underlying real policy fundamentals at appropriate values. Given such policies, the observed real exchange rate will tend to be appropriate as well.

To interpret this in terms of our conceptual framework, it is useful to extend the framework slightly. Note first that the policy variables in X_2^*, though sustainable, may not be desirable. Suppose we call the "optimal" levels of the policy variables X_2^{**}. In general, X_2^{**} will depend on the values of the exogenous variables, specifically stated as: $X_2^{**} = J(X_3^*)$.

Substituting these values in equation 5.6, we end up with equation 5.7:

(5.7) $$DRER = H[J(X_3^*), X_3^*].$$

As indicated in equation 5.7, the solution to equation 5.6 with this set of policy variables can be referred to as the desired equilibrium real exchange rate (DRER).

Corresponding to each definition of "equilibrium" real exchange rate offered above (that is, SRER, LRER, and DRER) is a corresponding measure of misalignment—defined as the difference between the actual RER and its equilibrium value. The broadest of these is the gap between the RER and the DRER. This gap can be decomposed into three parts as follows:

$RER - DRER = (RER - SRER) + (SRER - LRER) + (LRER - DRER).$

Thus, misalignment defined as the gap between the actual real exchange rate and the desired long-run equilibrium real exchange rate can arise because of bubble factors (accounting for the difference between RER and SRER), slow adjustment of predetermined variables (accounting for the difference between SRER and LRER), and inappropriate policies (accounting for the gap between LRER and DRER). The view that the real exchange rate is always driven by fundamentals and that the only source of misalignment with policy implications is that which arises from inappropriate policies can now be rendered in the form of two statements about this decomposition:

a. RER – SRER = 0, so the real exchange rate is never influenced by speculative "bubble" terms; and
b. While deviations between LRER and DRER call for corrections in the policy fundamentals, deviations between SRER and LRER are optimal and, in particular, have no implications for exchange rate policy.

The first statement is an empirical statement about the behavior of the nominal exchange rate under a free float. The second statement is implied by the view that real exchange rates are always "appropriate" conditional on the fundamentals. If deviations of SRER from LRER are the (short-run) equilibrium outcomes of the optimizing behavior of agents operating in an undistorted environment, then such deviations are optimal and cannot be improved upon by exchange rate policy. The statement thus concerns the role of nominal rigidities in generating temporary deviations of the real exchange rate from its long-run equilibrium value and reflects the view that nominal rigidities do not help to account for such deviations.

Neither of these statements can be dismissed out of hand. The role that speculative bubbles may play in a variety of financial markets—including exchange rate markets—remains controversial and is an active topic of research in macroeconomics. For countries that maintain officially determined exchange rates, however—as is the case for the vast majority of developing countries—this issue does not directly arise, since the nominal exchange rate in such countries is not a market-determined asset price. The second statement is more fundamental. It amounts to an application to the exchange rate arena of the broader question of the role of nominal rigidities in explaining macroeconomic fluctuations. The maintained view among those who consider the estimation of equilibrium real exchange rates a worthwhile endeavor is that nominal rigidities have an important role to play in explaining such fluctuations, and consequently that temporary deviations of the RER from the LRER do indeed have implications for nominal exchange rate policies. Specifically, the presence of nominal rigidities implies that nominal exchange rate adjustments may often be useful in helping to guide the RER back to the LRER from an initial disequilibrium.

Sustainability in Practice

In principle, as defined above, "the" long-run equilibrium is that for which all of the conditioning variables—including both policy and predetermined—have reached their steady-state levels, given "permanent" values of the exogenous variables. In particular, this means that any transitory fluctuations in exogenous variables have been identified and discarded, that all policy variables have been set at their sustainable long-run values, and that *all* predetermined variables have been allowed to complete their endogenous adjustments and reach their steady-state levels. Unfortunately, however, a "purist" definition of this type would have little analytical or operational content. Translating this "purist" definition into a meaningful operational counterpart may be the most difficult problem that arises in the empirical measurement of the LRER. The key problem is specifying what we mean operationally by "sustainable" values of the exogenous, policy, and predetermined variables.

The issues that arise in doing so are different for each of the three types of variables. Things are perhaps most straightforward in the case of exogenous variables such as the terms of trade or world real interest rates. The issues in this regard are largely statistical, rather than conceptual. As assumed above, fluctuations in such variables will contain both permanent and transitory components. Thus, identifying the relevant "permanent" component X_3^* empirically involves implementing statistical techniques (or using any available ex ante information) to disentangle these two components so that such "permanent" values can be isolated. Since, as already indicated, the time-series properties of these variables are independent of anything that happens in the domestic economy, all that is required for the specification of the LRER is some technique for predicting the duration of shocks to such variables. This kind of exercise is of broad applicability in macroeconomics, and relevant techniques are not specific to this particular application.[7]

A more complicated set of issues arises in the case of policy variables, such as the level and composition of government spending and the restrictiveness of the trade and capital-account regimes. While the values of such variables are in principle determined by the authorities, their current and long-run values could differ if future policy adjustments are envisioned. A steady-state configuration for such variables is therefore one in which they have reached their *desired* values, conditional on all of the exogenous variables, so that no further change is envisioned. Both desired long-run values as well as the path of adjustment will in this case depend not only on the structure of the economy, but also on the objective function that guides the behavior of the policymakers. This makes the identification of the optimal long-run configuration of the policy variables an extremely complicated task.

The requirement that all relevant policy variables be set at their optimal levels, implied by the fact that only the optimal levels of policy variables can be "desired" to be permanent, would force the analyst to solve a hopelessly complicated dynamic optimization problem before specifying the LRER. Even if it were possible to do this in a way that would satisfy many observers, it would be far too ambitious an undertaking for most practical applications.[8] A far more practical alternative would be to define the LRER for given, *arbitrary* values of the policy variables—as long as such values are in principle sustainable—rather than for the optimal values of such variables to which welfare-maximizing policymakers would presumably eventually move them. Clearly, if

---

7. Because such techniques are widely discussed in other contexts, this issue is not pursued further here. By and large, with the exception of Chapter 10 by Baffes, Elbadawi and O'Connell in Part III of this volume, the chapters in this collection do not attempt to describe techniques for decomposing movements in relevant exogenous variables into permanent and transitory components.

8. Although, as we shall see below, some approaches to the estimation of the LRER take up this challenge.

we know how the LRER is related empirically to arbitrary values of the relevant set of policy variables, then we can say in particular how the long-run equilibrium value would change if those policy variables themselves change, perhaps in some direction defined as optimal.[9] In terms of equation 5.6, this would mean knowing the function $F(\ )$, but not necessarily the values of the arguments in X_2^*. Thus, although the ultimate LRER to which the economy is headed may be different from that which would be predicted on the basis of, for instance, the current values of policy variables—precisely because those values are expected to change—it may be sufficient to know how any such changes would affect the equilibrium value of the real exchange rate without necessarily specifying what such changes should be.

Finally, consider the case of predetermined variables. As indicated above, such variables evolve endogenously over time toward long-run equilibrium values that themselves depend on the long-run values of the policy and exogenous variables (as summarized in the function $X_1(X_2^*, X_3^*)$). The difficulty posed by such variables for the analysis of long-run equilibrium real exchange rates is that they tend to approach their steady-state values at different rates, raising the question of how close they are individually required to be to their steady-state values in an operational definition of long-run equilibrium. Requiring that *all* such variables reach their steady-state variables in our definition of the LRER may be unduly restrictive, in that the LRER that satisfies this condition may take so long to reach that it may be of little interest to policymakers.

How can widely different speeds of adjustment among the predetermined variables be handled in the formal framework described above? An asymmetry between fast-adjusting and slow-adjusting predetermined variables can be incorporated into the framework by defining the relevant *operational* concept of long run as requiring that only some subset of the predetermined variables—the relatively faster-adjusting ones—be at their sustainable equilibrium values. Suppose the set of predetermined variables X_1 is separated into two subsets: that of fast-adjusting variables X_{11} and slow-adjusting ones X_{12}. Then equation 5.2 could be written as 5.2':

$$(5.2') \qquad RER(t) = F(0, X_{11}(t), X_{12}(t), \mathbf{X}_2(t), \mathbf{X}_3(t))$$

and equation 5.3 becomes 5.3':

---

9. The first "if" in this sentence is not as innocent as it sounds, since it hides some deep Lucas-critique issues. These issues are treated here as they typically are in applied macroeconomics—acknowledged, then ignored. For further discussion, see Chapter 10 by Baffes, Elbadawi and O'Connell.

$$(5.3') \quad \begin{aligned} \dot{X}_{11}(t) &= G_1(0, X_{11}(t), X_{12}(t), \mathbf{X_2}(t), \mathbf{X_3}(t)) \\ \dot{X}_{12}(t) &= G_2(0, X_{11}(t), X_{12}(t), \mathbf{X_2(t)}, \mathbf{X_3(t)}). \end{aligned}$$

Since the variables in X_{11} adjust very rapidly compared to those in X_{12}, they will be relatively close to the equilibrium values defined implicitly by equation 5.4':

$$(5.4') \quad 0 = G_1(0, X_{11}^*, X_{12}(t), X_2^*, X_3^*)$$

that now replaces equation 5.4. Using this equation to solve for X_{11} and substituting the result, together with the long-run equilibrium values of the policy and exogenous variables, into equation 5.2 produces the new expression for the long-run equilibrium real exchange rate, equation 5.5':

$$(5.5') \quad \begin{aligned} LRER &= F(0, X_{11}^*(X_{12}(t), X_2^*, X_3^*), X_{12}(t), X_2^*, X_3^*) \\ &= H(X_{12}(t), X_2^*, X_3^*) \end{aligned}$$

Notice that this means that the LRER is now *conditioned* on specific values of the remaining, slower-adjusting predetermined variables $X_{12}(t)$, in addition to the policy and exogenous variables X_2^* and X_3^*. The slow-adjusting predetermined variables thus become part of the set of "long-run fundamentals." Because these variables do change over time, the implication is that the LRER itself changes over time, but with sufficiently slow adjustment in the conditioning variables, the gradual evolution of the LRER would not be of policy significance.

An Application

While slow-adjusting predetermined variables thus do not pose major conceptual difficulties, in practice one such variable has proven quite problematic in constructing estimates of the LRER. Return to the Nurkse definition of the long-run equilibrium real exchange rate as the value of RER that is compatible with the simultaneous attainment of "sustainable" internal and external balance, and consider again the set of predetermined variables mentioned previously—the nominal wage, the stock of net international indebtedness, and sectoral capital stocks. At one extreme, it may be realistic to suppose that adjustments in the nominal wage are completed relatively quickly, say within a 3 to 5 year horizon. At the other extreme, however, capital stock adjustment is likely to be substantially slower, and should perhaps be measured in decades. From the perspective of exchange rate policy, the former time horizon is clearly relevant; the latter is not. As will be shown below, most observers have therefore operationally defined "sustainable" internal balance as requiring full employment (that is, the absence of cyclical factors), but not full capital stock adjustment. In this context, the "long run" would consist of a period of time sufficient for nominal wage adjustments to be completed, eliminating cyclical unemployment associated with Keynesian nominal wage stickiness—if any. Thus, "internal balance" has been interpreted as referring to goods-market equilibrium at full employment for a given value of the capital stock.

While full nominal wage adjustment has invariably been required in operational definitions of the LRER, and full capital stock adjustment has typically not, analysts have differed sharply on how to treat the third predetermined variable in the list: the stock of net international indebtedness. The problem is that this variable probably adjusts over time at a pace that is intermediate between that of the nominal wage and that of sectoral capital stocks.

How this variable is treated determines the interpretation that is given to the Nurksian concept of "sustainable external balance." One option, assuming a policy-relevant speed of adjustment in the stock of net international indebtedness, is to treat the latter analogously with the nominal wage, thus requiring it to be in steady state in the operational definition of the long-run equilibrium. In this case, "external balance" requires the current account to be equal to the net capital inflow necessary to sustain the steady-state value of the economy's net international creditor position.[10] This flow need not be zero, of course, if the country's stock of net external liabilities would suffer inflationary erosion or would shrink relative to the size of the domestic economy in the absence of new borrowing or lending. At the other extreme, if the rate of adjustment of the stock of net international indebtedness is judged to be too slow for policy relevance, by analogy with the real capital stock the natural procedure is to condition the LRER on a predetermined value of the stock of net international indebtedness. In this case, once again the LRER would be moving over time as both types of state variables (the sectoral capital stocks and the stock of net international indebtedness) evolve, but again, this change may be sufficiently gradual as not to be of critical policy importance.[11,12] In this case, the concept of "external balance" is much looser, since the equilibrium level of capital inflow will presumably be different for each value of the economy's net international creditor position, and consequently will be changing over time.

---

10. This approach is adopted in Montiel (1997) and in the analytical model in the next chapter.

11. Stein (1994) adopts this approach, as do Faruqee (1995) and MacDonald (1997).

12. We may want to preserve the term ultra–long run to encompass full adjustment of sectoral capital stocks as well.

There is a relatively clear distinction between these alternatives, and they fit quite neatly into the conceptual framework just described. However, among those who do not define the LRER as requiring that the stock of net international indebtedness reach a steady-state value, many analysts adopt a very different approach from either of these. Rather than condition the LRER on a predetermined value of the stock of net international indebtedness, they condition it instead on an exogenously determined sustainable value of *net capital inflows only* (a flow, rather than a stock concept). This "flow" procedure obviously requires a specification of how the sustainable flow of external capital is to be determined. It also requires some rather strong assumptions about the structure of the economy.

The first of these is the absence of feedback from the cumulated stock of net international indebtedness to the level of net capital inflows. Since an ongoing capital flow will imply an ever-changing stock of net international indebtedness, the sustainability of that flow requires in particular that the net capital inflow not be affected by the cumulated stock of net international indebtedness. If it were, of course, it could not be treated as an exogenous variable.

Moreover, the sustainable net capital inflow must also be exogenous with respect to the other "fundamentals." Otherwise, the appropriate treatment for net capital inflows would be not as a separate "fundamental" but as yet another of the economy's endogenous variables that is determined simultaneously with the short-run equilibrium real exchange rate.[13]

The first two conditions must hold for the level of net capital inflows to be treated as an exogenous variable. In order to *also* omit the cumulated stock of external debt as a state variable, one or both of the following conditions must hold: either the flow of new debt has imperceptible effects on the stock over the relevant horizon, so the latter can be treated as constant, or the net stock of debt must have weak effects on the economy's short-run equilibrium real exchange rate through other macroeconomic mechanisms.[14] If one of these conditions does not hold, the

---

13. In this case, net capital inflows would be determined by a reduced-form equation similar to equation 5.1 and would not appear as a separate argument in equation 5.1.

14. Any predetermined macroeconomic variable that exerts at most very weak feedback effects on the economy's short-run equilibrium effectively does not enter equation 5.2—meaning that it is not a component of X_3—and consequently would not affect the LRER. Thus, the LRER would be the same whether such a variable is in steady state or not, and there would indeed be no reason to impose a steady-state condition on such a variable in a definition of the LRER.

"long-run equilibrium" real exchange rate defined in this way could be changing continuously and appreciably.

In other words, the "flow" approach amounts to omitting the stock of net international indebtedness from the vector X_3 and treating net capital inflows as an exogenous variable. The conditions listed above may well come close to being met for small low-income countries that receive external financing almost exclusively in the form of official credits with a large grant element. For such countries the level of net capital inflows can be considered a policy variable or an exogenous variable. But these conditions are unlikely to apply for countries that borrow and lend extensively on market terms, even if some component of the capital account (for example, public sector borrowing) is policy determined.

Nonetheless, acknowledging that in other countries net capital inflows may contain a *component* that is exogenous—at least over the period of time that is relevant for exchange rate policy—does not mandate the use of the pure "flow" approach, since the analyst may be unwilling to assume in addition that the stock of net international indebtedness is not a component of X_3. In this case, the exogenous component of net capital inflows can be treated as a "fundamental," and external balance can be interpreted as corresponding to equality between the current account and the exogenous component of net capital inflows, as in the "flow" approach described above. However, leaving the stock of net international indebtedness in X_3 would imply that the LRER in this case is determined for *given* values of the stock of net international indebtedness as well as of sectoral capital stocks. Thus, in practical terms, "long run" would mean in this context, as in the "stock" approach, that the nominal wage—but not the stock of net international indebtedness or sectoral capital stocks—has fully adjusted. Because this formulation shares with the "flow" approach the specification of an exogenous component of net capital inflows, and with the "stock" approach the treatment of the stock of net international indebtedness as a relevant predetermined variable, we can refer to it as a "hybrid" approach.

Operationally, then, the LRER can be conceptualized in alternative ways, depending on whether the "stock," "flow," or "hybrid" approach is adopted to treat the accumulation of net international indebtedness. In the "stock" approach, the LRER is the value of the short-run equilibrium real exchange rate that is conditioned on the *steady-state* values of all the predetermined variables other than sectoral capital stocks, as well as on *given* (not necessarily optimal) values of the policy variables, the exogenous variables, and the sectoral capital stocks. As implied by this discussion, the set of long-run fundamentals would include not just policy and exogenous values but also, for most policy applications, sectoral capital stocks. In the "flow" approach, the level of sustainable net capital inflows is added to the list of exogenous variables and the

stock of net international indebtedness is deleted from the set of predetermined variables. In this case, the set of long-run fundamentals includes the sustainable value of net capital inflows. In the "hybrid" approach, the exogenous component of net capital inflows is included
among the exogenous variables, but the stock of net international indebtedness is retained in the set of predetermined variables. In this case,
the long-run fundamentals include the exogenous component of net
capital inflows.

The next issue is how the LRER can be estimated empirically. As indicated previously, academic research on this issue has proceeded along
very different lines in industrial and developing countries. The key difference has concerned the specification of the LRER. In the industrial-
country context, research has focused on fairly simple specifications,
usually consisting of purchasing power parity (PPP) or a modification
of PPP adjusted for differences in sectoral productivity growth (the
Balassa-Samuelson effect, discussed below). Only very recently have
potential demand-side fundamental determinants of the LRER begun
to be accorded a role in academic research on the LRER for industrial
countries. Research on developing countries, by contrast, while not typically focused specifically on the issue of identifying the determinants of
the LRER, has nonetheless recognized for some time that factors such as
the terms of trade, commercial policy, and capital flows could alter the
value of the LRER. Because of these differences in perspective, these
two strands of research are considered separately in the two sections
that follow.

Empirical Estimation: Industrial Countries

Empirical research on the determination of the LRER in industrial countries has proceeded on two tracks. Academic researchers have focused
on testing the validity of the PPP hypothesis and some simple variants
using a single-equation methodology. The scope of this research has only
recently expanded to encompass the potential role that changes in fundamentals may play in explaining LRER behavior that deviates from
PPP. We can refer to this body of work as *reduced-form* estimation of the
LRER, since tests of PPP essentially assess the validity of a particular
method of estimating the LRER. Researchers at policy-oriented institutions, by contrast, have focused on structural approaches—including
the use of estimated macroeconomic models—to calculate LRERs that
respond to changes in a broad range of underlying fundamentals. The
common analytical framework underpinning this work has been some
variant of the Mundell-Fleming model. This section takes up each of
these components of industrial-country research in turn.

Single-Equation Reduced-Form Estimation of the LRER

Reduced-form estimation of the LRER for industrial countries has typically focused on tests of PPP. The failure of PPP has motivated the search for "fundamentals" that could account for sustained deviations of the real exchange rate from the value predicted by PPP. The next two subsections describe these two strands of industrial country research.

Tests of PPP

It is clear that the actual RER has not been an immutable constant in any country, industrial or developing. What is at issue in measuring the LRER, therefore, is whether fluctuations in the actual RER represent transitory movements away from a well-defined LRER and if so, what determines the relevant value of the LRER. The PPP hypothesis offers one set of answers to these questions. The hypothesis can be expressed in the form of equation 5.8 for the nominal exchange rate:

$$(5.8) \qquad\qquad s = \alpha_0 + (p - p^*) + \varepsilon$$

where s is (the log of) the nominal exchange rate, measured as the domestic-currency price of foreign currency; p and p^* are (the logs of) the domestic and foreign price levels, respectively (including both traded and nontraded goods); α_0 is a constant; and ε is a stationary random variable.[15] In this formulation, the (log of the) RER is given by $s + p^* - p$, and the (log of the) LRER is constant and equal to α_0. Thus, movements in the actual real exchange rate are indeed viewed as consisting of transitory departures from a well-defined—and *constant*—value of the LRER. Notice, in particular, that no "fundamentals" in the form of policy and exogenous variables appear to enter equation 5.8, as the conceptual discussion in the previous section suggests that they should. What has happened to them?

Observe first that equation 5.8 is a statement about the time-series properties of the RER. Specifically, since PPP requires that the deviations of the actual RER from a constant LRER be transitory (though possibly serially correlated), it implies that the RER must be a stationary time-series process. There are two ways to reconcile this with the conceptual framework described above. The first is that a broad set of fundamentals indeed affects the LRER, but all of these fundamentals are

---

15. This is actually the weaker, relative form of the PPP hypothesis, which just requires that the unconditional mean of the real exchange rate sp^*/p be a constant. In the stronger, absolute form, the unconditional mean is required to be unity.

stationary (or mutually cointegrated) in a time-series sense during the sample period. If so, a reduced-form expression for the LRER would indeed contain these fundamentals, but that expression would not be inconsistent with equation 5.8. The means of the fundamentals can be interpreted as being subsumed into the constant term α_0, and their random components into the error term e. If the exogenous and policy fundamentals are stationary in the conceptual framework described in the previous section, therefore, relative PPP should hold, and the real exchange rate should itself be a stationary variable. The other possibility is that some fundamentals are not stationary during the sample period, but the structure of the economy is such that any such nonstationary fundamentals do not affect the LRER. For example, suppose that among the set of potential fundamentals, the nonstationary ones are on the demand side of the economy, but that the structure of the economy makes the LRER supply-determined.[16] In that case as well, the behavior of the RER would be consistent with equation 5.8.

Traditionally, this hypothesis was tested by running the regression stated by equation 5.9:

$$(5.9) \qquad s = \alpha_0 + \alpha_1(p - p^*) + \varepsilon$$

and testing whether $\alpha_1 = 1$.[17] The general finding tended to be that, while this hypothesis held up fairly well for high-inflation episodes, it could be rejected for more normal periods, and specifically for industrial countries during the post–Bretton Woods period.[18]

Recent developments in time-series econometrics, however, have made it clear that this methodology was inappropriate. Since s, p^*, and p are all typically nonstationary, ε can only be stationary if s, p^*, and p are cointegrated. If they are not, then equation 5.9 is a spurious regression, and if they are, tests of the null hypothesis $\alpha_1 = 1$ in equation 5.9 cannot be based on the standard t distribution.

As a result, a new generation of empirical tests of PPP in industrial countries has emerged in recent years. One variant, which Froot and

---

16. This would be true, for example, under a two-sector (traded-nontraded) setup in which the production function in each sector exhibits constant returns to scale, capital is internationally and intersectorally mobile, and labor is intersectorally but not internationally mobile. With symmetric productivity growth in both sectors both at home and abroad, an expression such as equation 5.8 would hold, even if potential demand-side fundamentals were nonstationary.

17. See, for example, Frenkel (1981) and Hakkio (1984). Note that the stronger "absolute" version of PPP implies the additional restriction that $\alpha_0 = 0$.

18. See Froot and Rogoff (1994).

Rogoff (1994) label "stage two" tests to differentiate them from the simple ordinary least squares (OLS) procedure just described, focuses on detecting whether the real exchange rate $s + p^* - p$ is stationary, as required under equation 5.8. By and large, these tests have been unable to reject the hypothesis of a unit root for relatively short sample periods (for example, the floating-rate period), but have been more successful in doing so for samples covering much longer spans of time—for example, a century of annual data; see Edison 1987, Kaminsky 1988, and Mark 1990. A second variant (denoted "stage three" tests by Froot and Rogoff (1994)), has instead focused on detecting cointegration among s, p^*, and p.[19] Cointegration is necessary, but not sufficient, for equation 5.8 to hold. To see this, rewrite 5.8 to arrive at equation 5.10:

$$(5.10) \qquad s = \alpha_0 + \alpha_1 p + \alpha_2 p^* + \varepsilon.$$

Cointegration implies simply that ε is stationary. For equation 5.10 to be equivalent to equation 5.8, we require as well the "symmetry" restriction that $\alpha_1 = \alpha_2$ and the "homogeneity" restriction that $\alpha_1 = 1$. Overall, the results of this work have been mixed. The null hypothesis of no cointegration can often be rejected when long spans of data are used, but even in such cases the estimated values of α_1 and α_2 are often far from the required values of 1 and –1. Breuer (1994) summarizes the results of this research as follows:

> Cointegration between the exchange rate and domestic and foreign price series and stationarity of the real exchange rate are more likely to be confirmed for studies that met two of four conditions: When the span of data is long enough to capture a statistical equilibrium relationship, typically 70 or more years; when the trivariate specification that does not impose symmetry and proportionality is used; when bilateral exchange rate other than against the US dollar is used; and when the countries studied experienced rapid periods of inflation or deflation. (p. 268)

Of these conditions, the failure to reject PPP when the symmetry and homogeneity restrictions are not imposed, or when attention is restricted to high-inflation episodes, cannot be interpreted as providing strong support for the theory, since the symmetry and homogeneity restrictions are indispensable to it, and since the interpretation of PPP as a

---

19. Recent surveys of this literature are provided by Breuer (1994), Froot and Rogoff (1994), and MacDonald (1995).

statement about long-run neutrality is not controversial. The most important qualification to a negative verdict on the empirical performance of PPP is the relatively greater success of the theory when long spans of data are used.[20] This can be given two interpretations. One is that PPP holds in the *ultra–long term* but not over shorter horizons. Another is that the rejection of PPP in smaller samples may arise from the low power of the statistical tests employed.[21] The second interpretation is of greater potential policy significance, of course, since in contrast to the first, it bears directly on the validity of PPP as an estimate of the LRER over policy-relevant horizons.[22] However, even when adopting tests with greatly enhanced statistical power, only very weak additional support is provided for PPP among industrial countries in the post-Bretton Woods era (see Edison, Gagnon, and Melick 1994). Moreover, recent research suggests that the failure of cointegration tests to reject PPP over ultra-long-run horizons may itself be the result of problems with the statistical tests employed.[23] Overall, then, the "new generation" tests of PPP have not been very favorable to the hypothesis in industrial-country applications.

Testing the Role of "Fundamentals"

Since the real exchange rate is an endogenous macroeconomic variable, one way to interpret the failure of the "new generation" PPP tests to find stationarity for the real exchange rate is to view it as driven by nonstationary fundamentals. Accordingly, recent extensions of PPP-oriented research on the determination of the LRER in the industrial-country context has begun to enrich the implied specification of the LRER for such countries by incorporating both supply- and demand-side fundamentals that may cause the LRER to deviate from PPP, thereby moving industrial-country research in this area in the direction of the type of analysis more often conducted in the context of developing countries.

---

20. The fourth condition, that PPP tests are more successful for bilateral RERs that do not include the United States, is a puzzle that remains to be explained.

21. The latter interpretation is suggested as a possibility by Edison, Gagnon, and Melick (1994).

22. Williamson (1994) argues that even if PPP holds in the ultra–long term, that does not contradict the view that the equilibrium real exchange rate relevant for policy purposes can change over time.

23. Specifically, Engel (1996) shows that the "size" (probability of rejecting the null hypothesis when it is true) of the tests employed may have been understated substantially, implying too-frequent rejections of the null hypothesis of nonstationarity. In other words, the tests are overly favorable to ultra-long-run PPP.

The Balassa-Samuelson Effect. The methodology used in these recent extensions essentially involves single-equation estimation of equilibrium real exchange rates as a function of some set of fundamentals. This amounts to estimating a version of equation 5.8 in which the symmetry and homogeneity restrictions that the coefficient of $(p - p^*)$ is unity are imposed and that includes potential fundamentals as additional explanatory variables.[24] Among such fundamentals, the factor that has received the most attention is the Balassa-Samuelson effect, a supply-side phenomenon that, while long known, has recently undergone a revival of interest. This hypothesis provides the leading supply-side explanation for the empirical regularity that, when measured in a common currency, the price level tends to be higher in a high-income country than in one with a lower level of income per capita.[25] The specific mechanism that is relied upon to produce this effect is based on four assumptions:

a. Production in the traded- and nontraded-goods sectors is conducted under constant returns to scale, using capital and labor;
b. Higher per capita income reflects higher total factor productivity;
c. Productivity growth is faster in the traded-goods sector of the economy than in the nontraded-goods sector; and
d. Capital is highly mobile internationally and intersectorally. In particular, real interest parity holds.

As long as these conditions hold, the real exchange rate will be determined strictly by supply-side factors, and the key relevant variable is the rate of growth in total factor productivity.[26] Countries with fast

---

24. The work of this type described below has not delved into the time-series properties of the potential fundamentals. Consequently, if they are stationary we can interpret such equations as consistent with the PPP formulation, but simply fleshing out the contents of the error term ε in equation 5.8. If they are nonstationary, these regressions can be interpreted as estimates of cointegrating relationships.

25. See Kravis and Lipsey (1988). The leading demand-side explanation relies on a high income elasticity of demand for services, which tend to be nontraded.

26. The mechanism is as follows: real interest parity and constant returns to scale determine the capital-labor ratios, and thus the real wage, in the traded- and nontraded-goods sectors. The domestic-currency price of the traded good is determined by the law of one price, and given the real wage in the nontraded-goods sector, this determines the nominal wage of workers employed in that sector. With perfect intersectoral labor mobility, however, the nominal wage of workers in the nontraded-goods sector must be the same. Given the real wage of workers in that sector, the price of nontraded goods is determined, and therefore so is the real exchange rate.

productivity growth relative to their trading partners will experience a secularly appreciating LRER. Faruqee (1995a), for example, used this approach to explain the evolution of Japan's postwar real effective exchange rate (REER) as largely the product of differentially rapid productivity growth in Japanese traded-goods production.

The Balassa-Samuelson effect has been well-documented for industrial countries. The typical pattern seen in the RER data for industrial countries experiencing rapid productivity growth is a strong appreciation in the internal RER, a substantial but more modest appreciation in the external RER, and stability or depreciation in the external RER for traded goods. Rogoff (1996) reviews the empirical evidence and concludes that "overall, there is substantial empirical support for the Balassa-Samuelson hypothesis, especially in comparisons between very poor and very rich countries, and in time-series data for a select number of countries, including especially Japan."[27] He notes, however, that "whereas the relationship between incomes and prices is quite striking over the full data set, it is far less impressive when one looks either at the rich (industrialized) countries as a group, or at developing countries as a group."[28]

Canzoneri, Cumby, and Diba (1996) suggest a reason why the Balassa-Samuelson hypothesis may not explain very well some medium-term movements in external RERs between industrial countries.[29] They argue that the effect depends upon two key elements—first, that the production technology implies that the relative price of nontraded goods in each country (its internal RER) should reflect the relative productivity in the traded- and nontraded-goods sectors, and second, that the law of one price holds for traded goods. Using data from a panel of OECD countries, they find that internal relative prices generally do reflect relative labor productivities. However, they find that the law of one price (as discussed in the chapter in this volume on the external RER) does not explain the variations in traded-goods prices very well, especially for the U.S. dollar, although their results are more favorable for the German mark. Hence, Canzoneri, Cumby, and Diba conclude that the problems with the Balassa-Samuelson hypothesis for external RERs lie in the failure of the law of one price for traded goods.

27. Rogoff (1996), p. 660. See Clark and others (1994) for an example for Japan. Bennett (1995) notes that because of relatively more rapid productivity growth in the traded than the nontraded sector, developing countries such as Hong Kong and Estonia experienced higher inflation than the industrial countries (the United States and Germany) to which they successfully pegged their exchange rates.
28. Rogoff (1996), p. 662.
29. Gordon (1994) also makes this point.

Demand-Side Fundamentals. De Gregorio, Giovannini, and Wolf (1994) found, however, that while productivity growth in a sample of 14 OECD countries during 1970–85 was indeed faster in the traded-goods sector, and was indeed associated with an increase in the domestic relative price of nontraded goods (as predicted by the Balassa-Samuelson effect) in a sizable subset of the countries that they examined, the increase in the relative price of nontraded goods was associated with an increase in the relative size of the nontraded-goods sector. This caused them to speculate that demand-side factors may also have played a role in the determination of the RER for those countries. Baumol and Bowen (1966) had earlier hypothesized that if productivity in the goods-producing sector grows faster than in the service sector but demand for services is more income-elastic, the relative price of services would rise over time. Since services are concentrated in the nontradable sector, and the opposite is true for goods, such a "Baumol-Bowen effect" could cause a country's internal RER to appreciate. If two countries have different preferences and weightings of services in their consumption baskets, then a Baumol-Bowen effect on demand could cause the external RER between them to change. This speculation was supported by De Gregorio, Giovannini, and Wolf, who estimated a static panel regression in which the RER was affected by, in addition to the supply-side productivity variables, the level of per capita income as well as by that of government spending.[30] Increases in both of these variables were associated with RER appreciation. They interpreted the role of demand-side factors as reflecting the failure of real interest parity to hold among the countries they examined.

More recent research for industrial countries has tended to model the LRER as driven by both supply-side and demand-side fundamentals. For example, in subsequent work, De Gregorio and Wolf (1994) demonstrated formally that the failure of real interest parity can indeed create a role for demand-side factors. They showed, also for the same sample of 14 OECD countries, that the fundamental determinants of the LRER included sectoral productivity differentials, government spending, and the terms of trade. Inclusion of the latter rendered the level of per capita income insignificant. Similar results were derived by Feyzioglu (1997), who estimated the LRER for Finland using the terms of trade and the German long-term real interest rate as fundamentals, in addition to productivity differentials. MacDonald (1997) also combined supply- and demand-side factors to explain the real effective exchange rates of the United States, Germany, and Japan during the floating rate period. He

---

30. The empirical technique used was seemingly unrelated regression (SUR) in first differences.

found that differential productivity growth, the terms of trade, fiscal policy, and the stock of net foreign assets all helped explain the LRER for these industrial countries. As we shall see below, specifications of this type represent a point of convergence with LRER estimates for developing countries.

Estimation of the LRER Based on Structural Models

The other strand of research on the LRER that has recently surfaced in the industrial-country context has been directly motivated by policy issues—in particular, policy coordination among the G-7 countries and European monetary unification. This work has taken as its point of departure the view that PPP provides a poor estimate of the "equilibrium" real exchange rate relevant for policy purposes, essentially because the equilibrium real exchange rate is perceived as influenced by a variety of fundamental real determinants, including several of those mentioned above. Estimates of the LRER in this literature have typically been derived from one of two alternative methodologies: a partial-equilibrium specification based on estimated trade equations, and a general-equilibrium one based on simulations from empirical macroeconomic models. The main methodological difference between these estimates and those reviewed above is that the empirical links between the LRER and its fundamental determinants are estimated from (partial- or general-equilibrium) structural econometric models, rather than from a single reduced-form equation for the real exchange rate. The partial-equilibrium approach and two variants of the general equilibrium approach are reviewed below.[31]

The Partial-Equilibrium "Trade Equations" Approach

The partial-equilibrium approach has been the most frequently employed alternative to the use of PPP calculations in policy-oriented efforts to construct LRER estimates. This approach has the attraction that while it permits the calculation of the LRER to incorporate the potential influence of changes in fundamentals, it retains the virtues of simplicity, as well as of relying on a particular set of behavioral parameter estimates that are readily available for many countries. In the industrial-country context the partial-equilibrium approach is based on the standard Mundell-Fleming current account specification, as shown below in equation 5.11:

---

31. A detailed overview of the general-equilibrium approaches is available in Williamson (1994).

(5.11) $$CA = RB(RER, Y, Y_F, ...) + rD$$

where CA is the current account of the balance of payments, RB is the resource balance function, D is the country's stock of net international indebtedness, and r is the average interest rate that it pays on net external debt. The resource balance is taken to depend on the real exchange rate, on both domestic (Y) and foreign (Y_F) incomes, as well as potentially on other variables not specified above. The basic external input into the procedure is an exogenously determined target value of CA, determined from some estimate of "sustainable" net capital inflows. Given the target value of CA—which we will call CA^*—and an exogenous value of r, equation 5.11 can be used to determine a target value of RB as a function of D, as shown by equation 5.11':

(5.11') $$RB^* = CA^* - rD.$$

Let Y^* and Y_F^* denote the full-employment values of domestic and foreign incomes in the reference year for which the estimate of the LRER is being constructed. These values must be estimated independently.[32] Then, given estimates of the elasticities of RB with respect to the RER, as well as with respect to Y and Y_F (estimates of the function $RB(\ )$), the LRER can be calculated implicitly as equal to the value of RER that satisfies equation 5.12:

(5.12) $$RB^* = RB(RER, Y^*, Y_f^*).$$

This estimate of the LRER is consistent with internal balance in the form of full employment in both countries, as well as with external balance in the form of a current account balance equal to the value of "sustainable" net capital inflows.

In general, the LRER estimate derived from this methodology will not be consistent with PPP. It will be changing over time and thus will be different when computed for different years. There are two reasons for this. First, different growth rates and income elasticities in the home and partner countries will cause the value of RB associated with a given RER to change over time. And second, the sustained net capital inflow or outflow will cause D to change, thus causing the required value of

---

32. If the LRER estimate is not for the current year, this estimate can be derived for any future year using estimates of how far the current values of Y and Y_F are from their full-employment levels, as well as of the rate of growth of potential real GDP for both countries.

RB^* itself to change over time.[33] In addition, changes in world interest rates, or in the assumed value of sustainable net capital inflows, will result in discrete changes in the estimated LRER. Notice also that the resulting estimate of the LRER may be either a positive or a normative construct. Whether it is one or the other depends on how the values of the "sustainable" net capital inflows are estimated. The estimate has a normative aspect to the extent that it emerges from some optimizing procedure determining desirable net capital inflows, but is positive if based on some exogenous projection of available net capital inflows.

Bayoumi and others (1994) used the trade equations methodology to assess the Smithsonian realignments of 1971. They estimated dynamic trade volume equations for each of the major industrial countries (the G-7), and from them they derived long-run price and income elasticities. They used independent estimates of the trend rate of growth of potential real GDP and of the real output gap existing at a given point in time, to estimate the change in domestic and trade-weighted foreign output required to achieve internal balance in the domestic economy and in its trading partners in 1971. They then calculated the "long-run" trade balance for that year from the fitted values of the trade volume equations (a procedure that eliminates any residual in that year, taken to be a temporary phenomenon), using the long-run elasticities as well as the relevant full-employment levels of output at home and abroad. The estimated LRER for 1971 was that which would have been required to eliminate the gap between the estimated "long-run" trade balance and an independent trade balance target for that year. Bayoumi and others arbitrarily set the trade balance target so as to achieve a current account surplus of 1 percent of GDP for each of the G-7 countries in 1971.

A version of the "trade elasticities" approach has also been adopted by the International Monetary Fund (IMF) in its surveillance function for industrial countries. The Fund's methodology, which is dubbed the "macroeconomic balance" approach (see Isard and Faruqee 1998), differs from that described above with respect to the method used in the estimation of the sustainable level of net capital inflows. Rather than specify the volume of such flows in an ad hoc fashion, the Fund relies on the standard national income accounting identity, stated by equation 5.13:

(5.13) $$CA = S - I$$

---

33. Notice that, since the feedback on the LRER of changes in the stock of net international indebtedness is taken into account, this is an example of the "hybrid" approach to external balance discussed earlier.

(where S and I denote national saving and gross domestic investment, respectively) to derive an estimate of sustainable capital inflows based on the medium-term determinants of saving and investment. The current account is taken, as in equation 5.11, to depend on the real exchange rate, as well as on domestic and foreign income levels. For full-employment values of domestic and foreign incomes, and given any other current account determinants, this function generates a locus with a positive slope in RER-CA space, as depicted in figure 5.1 below.[34] The saving-investment balance is modeled as a function of the country's level of per capita GDP, its dependency ratio, its fiscal position, the gap between actual and potential GDP, and the level of world real interest rates. The parameters of this function are estimated from an industrial-country panel data set. Normal values of the saving-investment balance are derived for each country by setting per capita GDP at the level that would prevail at full employment, setting the output gap to zero, and setting the fiscal deficit at its "structural" level. The world interest rate is determined endogenously as that level required to equate world saving to investment. Given these "normal" values of the explanatory variables, a "normal"—or medium-term—level of the saving-investment balance is calculated for each country. This balance provides in effect an estimate of sustainable capital inflows. Because the medium-term saving-investment balance is taken to be independent of the real exchange rate, the right-hand side of equation 5.13 generates a vertical locus in RER-CA space. The intersection of the two loci, at a point such as B in figure 5.1, determines the LRER for each country.

An important property of the "macroeconomic balance" approach is its ability to model the effects of changes in a wide variety of fundamentals on the LRER. In particular, as distinct from the more traditional "trade equations" method with an ad hoc specification of sustainable capital inflows, this methodology can take account of changes in fundamentals—not only of the ones that drive the current account balance (such as productivity levels), but also of those that drive the sustainable level of capital inflows (in the form of the medium-term saving-investment balance). Such fundamentals include changes in the dependency ratio, structural fiscal balances, and world real interest rates. It is worth noting that the estimate of the LRER derived from the "macroeconomic balance" approach has no normative content. The LRER is driven by sustainable or "normal" values of the fundamentals, not necessarily by desirable ones.

Wren-Lewis and Driver (1998) recently applied the "trade equations" approach to generate LRER estimates for the G-7 countries for the years

---

34. The RER is expressed in domestic currency terms in figure 5.1 so that an upward movement in it represents a depreciation.

Figure 5.1 *The Macroeconomic Balance Approach*

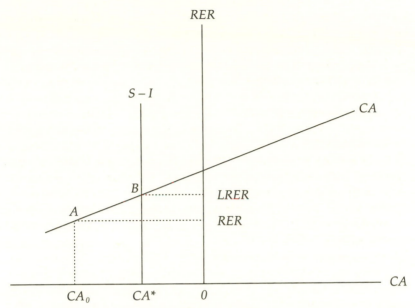

Note: An upward movement is a depreciation of the RER.

1995 and 2000. As in the cases of Bayoumi and others (1994) and Isard and Faruqee (1998), the procedure involved the estimation of dynamic trade balance equations and the calculation of "long-run" trade balances (fitted trade balances using long-run elasticities for the explanatory variables) at full employment for each of the two years in question, conditional on prevailing real exchange rates. An important difference from both Bayoumi and others and the IMF, however, was in the calculation of the trade balance targets to be reached by adjustments of real exchange rates to their long-run equilibrium values. The current account targets in Wren-Lewis and Driver (1998) for 1995 and 2000 were derived from an analysis of saving-investment balances by Williamson and Mahar (1998). As their point of departure for the estimation of sustainable current account balances, Williamson and Mahar use OECD projections in the case of industrial countries, and saving-investment balances for developing-country regions based on projections of changes in growth rates, dependency ratios, and public saving rates. Saving rates are based on estimated public and private saving functions that depend on these variables, and investment rate projections are derived from subjectively adjusted incremental capital-output ratios (ICORs) applied to the projected growth rates. These estimates are compared with updated versions of subjective estimates—derived based on optimizing principles in Williamson (1994) (described further below)—of sustainable current account balances for these countries. The estimated current account balances were adopted as the appropriate projections for the Wren-Lewis and Driver LRER estimation unless they were greatly at variance with the updated Williamson projections, in which case the projections were adjusted subjectively on a country-by-country basis on the basis of past history and optimizing considerations.

As indicated above, this partial-equilibrium approach to the estimation of the LRER has a number of virtues that make it attractive to use. However, it also has a number of limitations. The most obvious ones are its reliance on an ad hoc trade balance specification and its partial-equilibrium nature, even in the context of the Mundell-Fleming model from which the specification is drawn. The simple current account specification in equation 5.11, while based on a model that has been a workhorse of open-economy macroeconomics, ignores a number of complications that have been incorporated in more recent models of current account determination based on intertemporal considerations.[35] But even within the traditional Mundell-Fleming context, a number of general-equilibrium interactions that may be important in practice cannot be incorporated in a partial-equilibrium framework. Among these, as pointed out by Wren-Lewis and Driver (1998), there is no way to check the consistency between the exogenously estimated growth rates of potential output and the assumed sustainable net capital inflows; no feedback is allowed from the real exchange rate either to the levels of potential output or to the magnitude of the sustainable net capital inflows, and no allowance is made for potential effects on the LRER of alternative policies to move from actual to potential output.

Beyond these, there are empirical problems as well. Again as acknowledged by Wren-Lewis and Driver, estimated trade functions tend to involve large errors within the sample, and to be unstable out of sample. In general, trade elasticities tend to be estimated imprecisely, and real exchange rate elasticities do not tend to be large. Sampling errors in estimated trade elasticities imply large confidence intervals around LRER estimates based on such elasticities, as demonstrated by Kramer (1996). Small real exchange rate elasticities, however, make the point estimates for the LRER highly sensitive to the exogenously derived sustainable net capital inflow assumption. The upshot is that, while estimates of the

---

35. See, for example, Obstfeld and Rogoff (1996).

LRER derived using the "trade equations" approach may provide useful benchmarks, the range of uncertainty around them should probably be considered to be relatively large.

Approaches Based on General-Equilibrium Models

Some of the problems associated with the trade-elasticities approach can be handled by moving to an explicitly general-equilibrium framework. Both possible feedbacks from the RER to its determinants, as well as hysteresis effects operating through the stock of net international indebtedness, can be captured in this way. This section describes three applications of the general-equilibrium framework: Williamson's fundamental equilibrium real exchange rate (FEER), the IMF's desired equilibrium exchange rate (DEER), and the natural equilibrium real exchange rate (NATREX) of Stein and his associates.

FEER and DEER. Williamson's fundamental equilibrium real exchange rate (FEER) concept (described in Williamson 1994) is representative of the general-equilibrium alternatives to the partial-equilibrium trade-elasticities approach. Williamson's definition of the FEER involves the simultaneous attainment of external and internal balance, as in the simpler approach just described. In addition to using general-equilibrium structural models to simulate the LRER, however, he also explicitly adopts a normative perspective. Williamson gets around the general intractability of the optimization problem involved in finding the social welfare-maximizing LRER by restricting its scope, focusing only on the domestic rate of inflation and the steady-state value of the current account. In other words, for Williamson, the concept of internal balance has a normative element, in that it is interpreted as requiring not only full employment, but also noninflationary full employment. Similarly, external balance involves not just a current account deficit that is sustainable, but one that is desirable. He chooses the optimal value of the current account to GDP ratio for each country on the basis of past "normal" experience and a subjective judgment about the country's investment needs and its optimal saving rate. The former is derived from a framework that suggests that a country's desirable rate of investment is inversely related to the magnitude of its capital stock relative to the availability of complementary factors of production, and directly related to the rate of growth of the labor force, based on the standard intertemporal current account model. The latter is derived from demographic factors implied by the life-cycle saving hypothesis.[36]

---

36. See also the appendix by Williamson and Mahar in Wren-Lewis and Driver (1998).

Thus, the first step in the calculation of the FEER is making normative empirical judgments about the desirable rate of inflation and the desirable ratio of the current account to GDP. With these in hand, Williamson then derives the FEER by simulating a large macroeconometric model for the country concerned under the constraint that the path followed by the economy from its actual initial conditions must approach, within some specified period of time, a configuration with three characteristics. Those are (a) the level of output must be at its natural level; (b) the rate of inflation must have reached its previously identified low sustainable level; and (c) the external balance target must be reached. The endogenously determined RER generated by that simulation is the FEER.

Calculations of long-run equilibrium real exchange rates using general-equilibrium models have also been performed for industrial countries by the IMF's Research Department. These calculations have relied on simulations of the IMF's MULTIMOD econometric model, and the resulting estimate of the LRER for each country is referred to by the authors as that country's desired equilibrium exchange rate (DEER), to emphasize its normative content (see Bayoumi and others (1994), as well as Clark and others (1994)). The general-equilibrium procedure employed by the Fund to calculate DEERs is quite similar to that used by Williamson to compute FEERs. The particular exercise reported in Bayoumi and others (1994) brings out some important aspects of the simulation approach.

First, the results illustrate the fact that the general-equilibrium simulation approach cannot eliminate the uncertainty concerning the LRER associated with the simpler "trade equations" approach. Not only do the simulated models often tend to make use of the same elasticity parameters employed in the resource-balance approach, but in broadening the set of endogenous variables, they are forced to model many other aspects of economic behavior as well. While this is a virtue in the sense that the scope of economic interactions taken into account in the calculation of the LRER is greatly increased, it requires the estimation of a large number of additional behavioral parameters, to which the resulting estimates of the long-run equilibrium real exchange rate will be sensitive. Sensitivity analysis conducted by Bayoumi and others indeed suggests that plausible changes in the values of the underlying parameters can have large effects on the values of the estimated DEERs.

Second, as mentioned above, industrial-country model simulations tend to rely on models that essentially reflect a Mundell-Fleming analytical framework. Thus, they are in effect also based on equation 5.11. However, they have some important analytical advantages over the partial-equilibrium approach. Specifically, the use of the simulation model endogenizes both the full-employment values of Y and Y_F, as well as that of D. This means that general-equilibrium feedback effects caused by RER changes to all three variables—as well as separate effects on each of those variables of the particular set of policies adopted to move to full employment within some specified period of time—are taken into account in the resulting estimate of the LRER. This raises two sets of issues.

The first concerns the uniqueness of the FEER (or DEER). Presumably, any well-behaved macroeconometric model would eventually reach a steady state featuring full employment. To do so by a stipulated earlier date and with a stipulated current account balance, however, requires policy action. This raises the possibility that if the number of macroeconomic targets is small—as it is in the case of FEER and DEER calculations—relative to the set of effective instruments available to achieve them, then alternative combinations of policies that can achieve the targets when required may exist. These alternative ways of achieving the targets may have different implications for other endogenous macroeconomic variables, including the equilibrium real exchange rate. Simulations by Bayoumi and others employing alternative methods for achieving the internal and external balance targets confirmed that these methods matter for other macroeconomic variables as well as for the estimate of the DEER—as is to be expected. This problem arises from the attempt to restrict the dimensions of the optimization exercise, in the effort to make it tractable. To the extent that the other macroeconomic variables affected have social welfare implications, ranking these welfare consequences would allow the unique welfare-maximizing DEER to be identified. But constructing such a ranking obviously involves increasing the scope of the optimization problem.

The second set of issues has to do with the empirical magnitude of these feedback effects. Because the general-equilibrium approach is obviously more costly to implement than the trade-equations approach, an important question is how much empirical difference the analytical advantages of the general-equilibrium approach make. Bayoumi and others find that, given the internal and external balance targets, the trade-equations and general-equilibrium approaches often give similar values for the DEER, suggesting that feedback effects from the RER itself, as well as from the policy instruments that can be used to attain internal and external balance, on the proximate determinants of the LRER can be rather weak—at least in the particular model used for simulation.

In short, general equilibrium feedbacks matter both for the estimated value of the DEER itself and for the macroeconomic outcomes that accompany it, but they do not always matter enough—at least in the context of the MULTIMOD model and for the countries studied by Bayoumi and others—so as to generate LRER estimates that differ greatly from those derived using partial-equilibrium methods. The upshot is that, while adopting a structural general-equilibrium method can ensure that potentially important interactions have not been neglected in the estimation of the LRER, ex post the gain from employing full general-equilibrium simulation methods may not always turn out to be worth the cost.

Before leaving this section, it may be worth calling attention to the particular algorithm used to solve for the LRER in the normative model simulations discussed above, in light of the discussion in the chapter's first section. Empirical macroeconometric models typically converge to steady-state values over extremely long periods of time. Yet the simulations employed in calculating the FEER and DEER are required to hit their targets within a small number of years, and sustain them thereafter. This has the potentially important implication that, if the model's dynamics continue to play out after the particular targets spelled out in the calculation of the LRER have been reached—that is, if the model is not in a steady-state configuration when the targets are reached—sustaining the targets may require that policy variables continue to change after the target date. This means that to evaluate the desirability of the outcome, it would be necessary to look beyond the date when internal and external balances are reached. An alternative procedure would be to specify steady-state outcomes—rather than outcomes that emerge within a shorter period of time—as targets of policy and to define the FEER or DEER as the real exchange rate that emerges in the model's steady-state solution. If the model's dynamics are such that the steady state is reached too slowly to be of policy relevance, then the LRER can be defined as a dynamic concept—in other words, as the path followed by the RER on the way to a desirable steady state. In the terminology of the previous section, the LRER can be conditioned on non-steady state values of the slow-adjusting predetermined variables.[37]

The NATREX. Some of the difficulties in applying the FEER-DEER methodology are associated not with the use of structural general-equilibrium model simulations per se, but rather with the normative interpretation of the LRER and the particular solution algorithm adopted. An alternative approach adopted by Stein, Allen, and Associates (1995) defines the LRER in a positive rather than normative fashion and derives the simulation horizon endogenously. In addition, it bases estimation on a small medium-term model, rather than large, fully dynamic structural models. Stein (1994) and Allen (1995) define the "natural equilibrium real exchange rate," or NATREX, as the exchange rate that would

---

37. This is essentially what is done conceptually in the NATREX approach.

simultaneously be consistent with the domestic unemployment rate being equal to its natural rate and with the balance of payments being in equilibrium (that is, involving no reserve movements), exclusive of speculative and cyclical factors. In other words, it is the real exchange rate that is consistent with internal balance and a particular concept of external balance—one that sets the current account equal to actual long-term capital flows, defined as flows not motivated by cyclical and speculative factors.

The basic equations underlying the NATREX for a small open economy with high capital mobility are the following (5.14 through 5.16):[38]

$$(5.14) \quad I(K,r;Z) - S(K-D,r;Z) = RB(RER, K-D, K_F + D;Z) + rD$$
$$\quad\quad\quad - \;\; - \quad\quad\quad - \;\; + \quad\quad\quad\quad - \quad\quad + \quad\quad -$$

$$(5.15) \quad\quad\quad\quad\quad\quad dK/dt = I - nK$$

$$(5.16) \quad\quad\quad\quad\quad\quad dD/dt = RB + (r-n)D$$

where K, K_F, and D are respectively the stocks of domestic and foreign physical capital per effective worker and the domestic economy's net external debt, RB is the resource balance function, r is the world real interest rate, n is the rate of growth of effective labor, and Z is a vector of exogenous shocks. Signs below the variables in the behavioral relationships in equation 5.14 denote partial derivatives. The model is specified at full employment, so the functions $I(\ )$ and $S(\ )$ determine the levels of domestic investment and national saving that are forthcoming at full employment. The excess of investment over saving determines the long-term capital inflow, which is a function of the predetermined variables K and D as well as the exogenous variables r and Z. RB is the full-employment resource deficit, so the right-hand side of equation 5.14 is the full-employment current account deficit. Equation 5.14 is thus the "external balance" condition, and the value of RER that satisfies it is the medium-term NATREX. It is medium term in the sense that it is conditioned on K and D, which change over time according to equations 5.15 and 5.16.[39]

---

38. Alternative versions of the model, incorporating a "large country" financial assumption as well as the assumption of imperfect capital mobility for a small country, can be found in Stein, Allen, and Associates (1995).

39. Notice that, in the terms discussed in the first section of the chapter, adjustments in nominal wages are assumed to occur sufficiently rapidly to be of policy relevance, while the stock of net international indebtedness and the capital stock are grouped together as slow-adjusting predetermined variables.

Stein and his colleagues thus distinguish between a "medium-run" NATREX—one conditioned on predetermined values of both the stock of net international indebtedness and the capital stock—and a "long-run" NATREX, which holds when the capital stock and stock of net international indebtedness have settled at steady-state values—that is, when $dK/dt = dD/dt = 0$. The "long-run" NATREX obtained for steady-state values of the stock of net international indebtedness and the capital stock is viewed as ultimately determined by the set of exogenous fundamentals Z. The variables that make up Z may be country-specific. However, Stein and his colleagues assign pride of place among potential fundamentals in Z to domestic and foreign productivity and "social thrift" (essentially referring to the rate of time preference), which act in the model as shocks to the investment and saving functions. They note that for small countries the terms of trade and the world real interest rate would be exogenous, and thus would also be included among the fundamentals, though not for a large country like the United States.

To illustrate how the model works, consider the effects of a permanent negative shock to national thrift—that is, to the saving function. In the medium term, both K and D are given, so from the left-hand side of equation 5.14, the reduction in S is associated with a long-term capital inflow to finance an increase in consumption. The capital inflow must be associated with an increase in the current account deficit according to equation 5.14, so the RER must appreciate (fall). Thus, a permanent reduction in national thrift causes an appreciation in the medium-term NATREX. Since the investment function is not affected by this shock, the real capital stock does not change over any time horizon. The accumulation of external borrowing, however, increases D over time, and as a result of the associated reduction in national wealth $K - D$, saving will rise. In the long run, the increase in saving must be such as to restore $dD/dt = 0$ in equation 5.16. This means that D must be permanently higher in the long run. To finance the associated larger external interest payments, the long-run resource deficit must fall (or the surplus must rise). This requires a long-run depreciation of the NATREX.

To test the model, Stein (1994) examined its ability to account for short-run movements in the real effective exchange rate of the United States. He decomposed the change in the short-run equilibrium RER over time into two parts: the adjustment in the short-run RER to the medium-term NATREX (which is not described in the medium-term model above), and the evolution of the medium-term NATREX to its long-run value. The model above suggests that, for given values of the fundamentals in Z, the latter is driven by changes in the predetermined variables K, K_f, and D. Stein relies on a real interest parity argument to conclude that the adjustment of the short-run RER to the medium-term NATREX can be proxied by the long-term real interest rate differential.[40] Thus, he estimated a dynamic equation for the U.S. real effective exchange rate of the form shown in equation 5.17:

$$(5.17) \qquad RER = F[RER(-1), r - r_F, \Delta K, \Delta K_F, \Delta D]$$

where r and r_F are respectively the U.S. and foreign long-term real interest rates, and the symbol Δ denotes a change in a variable.[41] Other variables are defined as before.[42] The specification in equation 5.17 proved quite successful in tracking the recent evolution of the U.S. real effective exchange rate.

Equation 5.17 essentially models the implications of the NATREX model for the short-run equilibrium RER. To model empirically the medium-term NATREX itself, Stein took as his point of departure the regression shown in equation 5.18:

$$(5.18) \qquad RER = F[RER(-1), Z(-1), \Delta Z]$$

where Z is the vector of fundamentals introduced previously. In practice, however, Stein used the long-term real interest differential as a proxy for changes in the fundamentals in the estimation of equation 5.18. The estimated equation thus took the form shown in equation 5.18':

$$(5.18') \qquad RER = F[RER(-1), Z(-1), r - r_F].$$

Dynamic simulations based on this regression tracked the actual evolution of the RER for the United States quite well during 1976–89, in particular tracking the "long swings" in the U.S. dollar's real value during the decade of the 1980s fairly closely.

Unfortunately, the interpretations both of equation 5.18' and of the simulations based on it are problematic. The basic issue is that it is unclear whether the use of the real interest gap $r - r_F$ as a proxy for ΔZ in

---

40. The logic of the model implies that the relevant maturity should correspond to the time required for cyclical deviations from full employment to dissipate.

41. Since what is observed is the actual RER, while what is modeled in equation 5.15 is the evolution of the short-run equilibrium RER, the residuals of this regression presumably include the deviations of the actual RER from its short-run equilibrium value discussed in the first section of this chapter.

42. Notice that whether equation 5.15 accurately captures the dynamics of the short-run equilibrium RER depends on the validity of long-run real interest parity. If it does not hold, then the real interest gap will be a poor proxy for the gap between the short-run RER and the medium-term NATREX.

effect introduces short-run (for example, cyclical) factors as explanatory variables. Indeed, the rationale for the inclusion of the real interest differential in equation 5.17 was precisely to capture the dynamics of adjustment of the RER to the medium-term NATREX. The inclusion of cyclical factors in equation 5.18' would mean that simulations based on its fitted values would simply be tracking the short-run equilibrium real exchange rate, as in equation 5.17, rather than generating estimates of either the medium-term or long-run NATREX.[43]

Nonetheless, the key point is that there is very little difference between equation 5.18, derived from a structural general-equilibrium model, and the reduced-form estimation with fundamentals to which the research on PPP has led. Equation 5.18 amounts to an error-correction representation for the real exchange rate, linking it to its long-run fundamentals. This representation thus dovetails quite nicely with the single-equation cointegration estimates described at the end of the previous section (as represented, for example, by MacDonald 1997). If estimated directly, the "long-run" NATREX could be derived from fitted values of equation 5.18 by setting $RER = RER(-1)$, $DZ = 0$, and $Z(-1)$ equal to the "permanent" values of the long-run fundamentals. The difference in empirical implementation between the NATREX and the reduced-form approaches is precisely whether equation 5.18 is estimated directly. The reduced-form cointegration approach does so (for example, in the form of an error-correction equation), while Stein used equation 5.18' instead, replacing changes in the fundamentals with real interest differentials. The difference, therefore, amounts to different choices made with respect to the empirical modeling of short- and medium-run dynamics and does not concern the conceptual basis for the LRER and its determinants. Thus, following rather different routes, the two strands of industrial-country research have reached rather similar views about the role of the LRER in real exchange rate dynamics, as well as about the influence of real fundamentals on the LRER.

Empirical Estimation: Developing Countries

The active management of nominal exchange rates in the vast majority of developing countries and the consequent need to estimate the magnitude of possible misalignment—together with the frequent and occasionally large exogenous and policy shocks to which these economies

---

43. Black (1994) has made the same point about the use by Stein, Allen, and Associates (1995) of the "social consumption ratio" as a proxy for the rate of time preference, finding the former to be a cyclical variable.

have been subjected—have given the issue of estimating equilibrium real exchange rates a relatively greater urgency in the developing-country context than in the industrial-country context. While the PPP approach has often been used to estimate the equilibrium real exchange rate in practical policy applications, research on the determination of the LRER for developing countries has long acknowledged the potential role of real fundamentals. This research has often featured single-equation estimates such as those described in the previous section for industrial countries. A key difference, however, is that the developing-country variants have incorporated a richer menu of potential fundamentals for some time, reflecting the longer tradition, which was just mentioned, of recognizing the role of real variables in causing deviations from PPP.[44] I will discuss two variants of this single-equation approach: a traditional reduced-form version and a more recent version based on the estimation of a cointegrating equation linking the real exchange rate to its fundamental determinants. I will not consider practical applications, because the two techniques in most frequent use—PPP and the "trade equations" approach—have already been described in the industrial-country context and are discussed at length in the developing-country context in the chapter in Part III on operational approaches for estimating the LRER empirically.[45] Instead, I will focus on academic research on the LRER for developing countries.

Traditional Reduced-Form Studies

Both the traditional and cointegration approaches involve the estimation of a single reduced-form equation linking the real exchange rate to a set of fundamentals. The key difference between the two approaches concerns econometric methodology. Two applications of the traditional approach are described in this section, before turning to the cointegration approach in the section that follows.

Edwards (1989 and 1994). Perhaps the best known of the traditional single-equation reduced-form studies are those of Edwards (1989 and 1994). Edwards (1994) used panel data for 12 developing countries over the period 1962–84 to estimate a regression in which the actual real exchange rate was the dependent variable and the set of independent variables included both potential fundamentals—such as the rate of growth

---

44. A classic early reference is Diaz-Alejandro (1980).

45. A variant of the "trade equations" approach developed specifically for developing-country application by Devarajan, Lewis, and Robinson (1993) merits separate mention, but I do not take it up here because it is also covered in detail in Part III.

of total factor productivity, the terms of trade, the share of government consumption in GDP, a measure of the openness of the trade regime, and a measure of the severity of capital controls—and other variables interpreted as not affecting the LRER, but potentially causing the RER to deviate from the LRER. These primarily included proxies for temporary aggregate demand shocks and the change in the nominal exchange rate. Finally, the equation also included a lagged dependent variable to capture the dynamics of adjustment of the RER to the LRER. With the exception of the productivity variable, the estimation generally confirmed analytical results concerning the direction in which the included fundamentals affect the LRER. Transitory aggregate demand shocks in an expansionary direction tended to appreciate the LRER, while nominal depreciation proved capable of influencing the RER in the short run. Finally, the speed of adjustment of the LRER was found to be rather slow.

Edwards (1994) used his estimated regression to calculate estimates of the LRER. By setting the values of the transitory aggregate demand variables and of nominal exchange rate changes equal to zero, and setting the current and lagged RERs equal to each other, he solved for the coefficients of the fundamentals (essentially estimating the parameters of the function $H(\ )$ in equation 5.6). He then used five-year moving averages to estimate the permanent values of the fundamentals (X_2^* and X_3^* in equation 5.6) and, calculating the fitted values with coefficients and explanatory variables derived in this manner, produced estimated time series for the LRER for several of the countries in his sample. The central characteristic of these estimates is that, unlike PPP-based estimates or estimates that expand on PPP by including only smoothly trending fundamentals such as total factor productivity, these time series exhibited substantial variation over time, reflecting the effects of changes in real fundamentals on the LRER. It is precisely such temporal variation in the underlying value of the LRER that makes estimation of the LRER imperative to detect potential real exchange rate misalignment.[46]

Razin and Collins (1997). Similar in spirit to the work of Edwards, more recently Razin and Collins (1997) estimated reduced-form real exchange rate functions for a large country panel, including explanatory variables meant to capture both "fundamentals" that would affect the LRER (defined in their case as the flexprice solution of a Mundell-Fleming model with binding capital controls) and variables interpreted as driving the short-run equilibrium RER away from the LRER. The fundamental determinants of the LRER included familiar variables such as the terms of trade and the value of net long-term capital inflows as well as less familiar ones such as a proxy for the exogenous component of the trade

---

46. For a recent application of Edwards' model, see Mongardini (1998).

balance and the excess of money growth over GDP growth. As in Edwards, favorable terms of trade movements and increases in net long-term capital inflows were associated with an appreciation of the LRER. Transitory factors driving the RER away from the LRER were modeled as deviations of output and domestic absorption from estimated ARMA (1,1) processes. The LRER was estimated for each country as the fitted value of the panel regression with the transitory variables set equal to zero. Razin and Collins then went on to show that misalignment—measured as the difference between the RER and the estimated LRER—has a nonlinear relationship with long-run growth in a cross-country regression that controls for other growth determinants. Large average overvaluation of the domestic currency during the sample period is negatively associated with growth over the period, while undervaluation that is not excessively high has a positive relationship with growth.

Estimates Based on Cointegrating Equations

In recent years, researchers working in the context of developing countries have also begun to apply unit-root econometrics to the problem of estimating equilibrium real exchange rate for such countries, akin to the "stage three" research on PPP identified by Froot and Rogoff (1994) in industrial-country applications. In keeping with the flavor of developing-country research in this area, however, economists conducting "stage three" research for developing countries have not limited their attention to detecting the presence of cointegration among nominal exchange rates and national price levels—in other words, to testing PPP. Instead, they have sought to explain the failure of PPP to explain the behavior of long-run exchange rates in these countries by attempting to detect cointegration among real exchange rates and a variety of underlying "fundamentals" drawn from determinants of the LRER identified in earlier literature. To illustrate this approach, I will briefly describe a series of papers by Elbadawi (1994) and Elbadawi and Soto (1994 and 1995), as well as recent applications by Cardenas (1997) and by Loayza and Lopez (1997).

Elbadawi (1994) developed a model of the long-run equilibrium real exchange rate in which the "fundamentals" included the terms of trade, a measure of openness (as a proxy for commercial policy), the level of net capital inflows relative to GDP, the share of government spending in GDP, and the rate of growth of exports. His empirical estimation was based on annual data spanning the period 1967–90 for Chile and Ghana, and 1967–88 for India. He found that, in all three countries, the real exchange rate and all of the fundamentals identified in the model were nonstationary and cointegrated. The qualitative signs of the coefficients in the cointegrating regressions were in accord with those predicted by the theoretical model. Elbadawi used time-series techniques to estimate the permanent components of the fundamentals in each of the countries, and substituted these permanent values into the cointegrating equations to derive estimates of the long-run equilibrium real exchange rate over the sample in each of the countries. The differences between these estimated long-run equilibrium rates and the actual real exchange rates then were taken to represent estimates of misalignment. He found that such estimates fit the episodic descriptions of macroeconomic developments in these countries over the sample periods extremely well.

In the previous application, the actual level of net capital inflows was taken as a "fundamental." Two extensions of Elbadawi's original specification by Elbadawi and Soto (1994 and 1995) modified this assumption by distinguishing between long-term and short-term inflows. Elbadawi and Soto (1994) explored the Chilean case further, using annual data from 1960–90 and focusing specifically on the role of capital inflows. Separating the ratio of net inflows to GDP into long-term (portfolio and foreign direct investment (FDI)) and short-term flows, they found that the latter was stationary and consequently omitted it from the cointegrating equation, implicitly adopting an "external balance" criterion that interprets sustainable net capital inflows as long-term portfolio flows plus FDI. Using a specification otherwise similar to that of Elbadawi (1994), they found that an increase in long-term inflows tended to appreciate the LRER, and that the magnitude of the effect was large compared to that of government spending, implying that sustaining a depreciated equilibrium real exchange rate in the face of a large increase in long-term capital inflows through fiscal measures would have required very large reductions in government spending in Chile. Elbadawi and Soto also estimated a dynamic error-correction equation for the adjustment of the RER to the LRER, and found that episodes of short-term capital inflows tended to be associated with an appreciation of the RER relative to the LRER. Elbadawi and Soto (1995) extended this work to a larger sample of countries including—in addition to Chile—Côte d'Ivoire, Ghana, India, Kenya, Mali, and Mexico. In this exercise, the distinction between long-term (FDI and long-term net lending) and short-term capital inflows was retained, and the external nominal interest rate (corrected for a measure of country risk) was introduced as an additional fundamental. As in the previous work on Chile, long-term inflows played an important role in the cointegrating regression, with effects operating in the predicted direction.[47] The external interest rate also figured promi-

---

47. Interestingly, short-term inflows proved to be nonstationary in Mexico, where their large magnitude has been accorded an important role in the 1994 peso crisis.

nently and consistently in the cointegrating equations; an increase in the foreign interest rate was associated with a depreciation of the LRER. The effect of commercial openness was also consistent across countries; increased openness resulted in LRER depreciation in every case. Among the other fundamentals, the effects of the terms of trade, as well as of the size and composition of government expenditures, tended to vary across countries. However, the results previously obtained for Chile were duplicated in the broader sample: the magnitude of the coefficients on fiscal variables in the cointegrating equation suggested that offsetting the effects on the LRER of changes in sustained capital inflows through fiscal means would require very large changes in the fiscal variables. As in Elbadawi's earlier work, as well as in the previous study on Chile, estimates of misalignment derived from the cointegrating equation using "permanent" values of the fundamentals again accorded well with episodic experience in the countries concerned. In particular, an overvaluation of 18 percent was estimated for Mexico in 1994.

Other authors have applied this methodology using a more restricted set of fundamentals. Cardenas (1997), for example, estimated Colombia's LRER using quarterly data from the first quarter of 1980 to the third quarter of 1993. He considered fundamentals consisting of average labor as well as total factor productivity in the traded- and nontraded-goods sectors (to capture Balassa-Samuelson effects), the terms of trade, and government spending as a share of GDP disaggregated into various components. The Balassa-Samuelson hypothesis met with mixed success. An increase in total factor productivity (TFP) in the nontraded-goods sector was associated with real depreciation, as expected, but so was an increase in TFP in the traded-goods sector. Improvements in the terms of trade, as well as all components of government spending, resulted in appreciation of the LRER. Somewhat surprisingly, Cardenas found that the coefficients of the cointegrating equation—specifically those of the government expenditure variables—were altered by a change in the nominal exchange regime in Colombia in 1990, from a crawling peg to an exchange rate band. He acknowledges, though, that the instability may be reflecting omitted variables, perhaps associated with changes in the external financial environment that resulted in large capital inflows into Colombia beginning at the same time.

More recently, and somewhat closer in spirit to the industrial-country research in this area, Loayza and Lopez (1997) sought to measure the long-run equilibrium real exchange rate for seven Latin American countries by estimating cointegrating equations among the real exchange rate, the stock of net international indebtedness, and a Balassa-Samuelson relative sectoral productivity variable, using a sample of annual data from 1960 to 1995. For six of their seven countries, they found evidence that all three variables were nonstationary, and that a single cointegrating vector existed among them, contrary to PPP. Improvements in both the country's net international creditor position and in the relative productivity of its traded-goods sector relative to that of the nontraded-goods sector tended to appreciate the equilibrium real exchange rate. With a specification of "fundamentals" quite different from that of Elbadawi and Soto (1995), Loayza and Lopez estimated that the Mexican peso had become overvalued by 27 percent by 1994.

These cointegration-based estimates of the LRER for developing countries appear promising in at least two respects. First, despite the short samples (adversely affecting the power of the statistical tests involved), questionable data, and likely structural instabilities in these applications, cointegrating relationships are often found between RERs and a broad class of fundamentals suggested by theory. Moreover, estimates of the impacts of fundamentals on the LRER generally prove to be consistent with theoretical priors. Second, estimated LRERs are often capable of reproducing historical episodes of overvaluation as judged by other means. This type of confirmation supports the reliability of approaches to the estimation of the LRER based on unit-root econometrics. However, the application of this methodology is in its infancy, and it is not difficult to identify prospective problems in its implementation, despite the persuasive results of the studies listed above. Among potential pitfalls in their widespread application are the short span of data typically available for developing countries (especially for small low-income countries), the poor quality of some of the proxies that have to be employed for the relevant fundamentals, and the imperfect techniques currently available for estimating the "permanent" values of such fundamentals— which is a key step in the calculation of the LRER.

Summary

The intriguing observation that emerges from this overview is that, starting from very different positions, research on the empirical measurement of equilibrium real exchange rates in industrial and developing countries has tended to converge in methodology during recent years. Industrial-country research has tended to bifurcate into an academic branch primarily preoccupied with testing PPP, and a policy-oriented branch primarily focused on the evaluation of exchange-rate movements among G-7 countries as well as on the adequacy of exchange rate arrangements within the European Union. The failure of the PPP-implied restrictions to hold has led academic researchers to gradually expand the set of real "fundamentals" that may explain sustained deviations from PPP. The research has moved beyond Balassa-Samuelson productivity effects operating on the supply side of the economy, to encompass variables such as the terms of trade and government consumption, which may affect the LRER through both the demand and supply side or even strictly through the demand side of the economy. Policy-oriented researchers explicitly adopted Nurkse's definition of the LRER and have tended to implement it in two forms: through the traditional "trade equations" methodology and through the use of model simulations. One set of analysts working in this tradition (Williamson and the IMF's Research Department) has given the LRER an explicitly normative definition and has opted to simulate large existing models to measure the LRER, while others (Stein, Allen, and Associates) have specified the LRER in positive form and based estimation on a generic class of custom-built small models of much more limited scope. The implied reduced-form solutions for the LRER in these models essentially amount to cointegrating relationships linking the real exchange rate to a small set of real fundamentals, in effect quite similar to those that the PPP-based industrial-country research has begin to consider. The set of fundamentals emphasized in the reduced-form solutions of NATREX models for small countries—productivity, thrift, the terms of trade, and the external real interest rate—also have much in common with those that have long been considered in the developing-country literature, the key omissions from the list being commercial policy, fiscal variables, and capital flows. The work of De Gregorio and Wolf (1994) for OECD countries, for example, obviously has much in common with that of Cardenas (1997) for Colombia.

With the development of unit-root econometrics, a second type of convergence has begun to emerge, in the form of increased consistency between the statistical methodology applied in industrial- and developing-country research on determinants of long-run equilibrium real exchange rates. Estimation of the LRER has clearly been advanced by the development of unit-root econometrics. This has, on the one hand, facilitated meaningful tests of PPP (the "stage two" tests of Froot and Rogoff 1994). On the other hand, it has freed the estimation of the long-run relationship between the RER and its fundamental determinants from dependence on appropriate specification and estimation of short-run macroeconomic dynamics. Estimation of the LRER on the basis of cointegrating equations appears to be a promising avenue for research at present. Particularly in the developing country context, such estimates have yielded measured effects of fundamentals consistent with theoretical predictions, and the fitted values of the LRER derived from such equations have produced estimates of misalignment that have tended to correspond well with commonly accepted features of the recent macroeconomic histories of the countries involved. Moreover, the statistical significance of lagged error-correction terms in dynamic real exchange rate equations implies that estimated LRERs are significant predictors of future movements in actual RERs—a key test of whether the methodology has succeeded in capturing an important aspect of real exchange rate dynamics.

Where does all of this leave us? Conceptually, monetary neutrality implies that relative PPP should hold in the face of nominal shocks, but theory does not require that PPP hold in response to real shocks. The issue depends on the persistence of those shocks. Empirically, the evidence suggests that PPP may or may not hold as an extremely long-run proposition (that is, over spans of time in excess of half a century) in industrial countries. Over shorter periods of time—including over the complete span of data that tend to be available for developing countries—the real exchange rate tends to be nonstationary, and PPP provides a poor approximation of the equilibrium real exchange rate. Since the real exchange rate is an endogenous macroeconomic variable, the nonstationarity of the real exchange rate suggests nonstationarity in some subset of its underlying real fundamental determinants. There is a substantial amount of agreement on the eligible set of such fundamentals. They consist of sectoral total factor productivity levels, the economy's terms of trade, commercial policy, the level and composition of government spending, and some indicator of the external financial environment.

The last of these fundamentals raises an important unresolved issue on the conceptual side of LRER measurement. Specifically, just how long is the relevant long run? The literature has taken different positions on this question. While all observers take the long run as being long enough to eliminate speculative and cyclical phenomena, the majority of the papers reviewed here do not go to the extent of defining the long run as sufficiently long as to eliminate capital-stock dynamics. The issue is whether the relevant time frame should allow for full adjustment of the country's stock of net international assets. Most writers have not been explicit on this, and their implicit assumptions have to be inferred from the way they treat external financial variables in the estimation of the LRER. At one extreme, allowing for full adjustment in the economy's net creditor position involves conditioning the LRER on the external interest rate, and not on net capital inflows or the stock of net international debt. At the other extreme, conditioning the LRER on the stock of net international debt implies adopting a relatively shorter-run horizon. The common procedure of conditioning the LRER on a "sustainable" level of net capital inflows can be understood as a special case of the latter in which the adjustment in the economy's net creditor position implied by the ongoing net capital inflow is small (in other words, the rate of adjustment of the net creditor position is slow). The empirical challenge in this case is how to measure this exogenous component of net capital inflows. No single method that commands wide agreement has emerged.

On the empirical side, the reliability of approaches to the estimation of the LRER based on unit-root econometrics remains to be established. Among potential pitfalls in their application are the short span of data typically available for developing countries (which adversely affects the power of the statistical tests involved), the poor quality of some of the proxies that have to be employed for the relevant fundamentals, and the imperfect techniques currently available for estimating the "permanent" values of such fundamentals, a key input into the calculation of the LRER. Overall, these methods offer the promise of improving on PPP when the nonstationarity of the RER suggests that the latter is a poor empirical hypothesis. However, they have not yet been shown to deliver the robustness and precision that would be required for a nonstructural approach such as this to dominate more traditional structural approaches to the estimation of the LRER in policy applications.

In short, the single-equation approach appears to be the most promising avenue for further research; but data problems can limit its usefulness in specific policy applications, particularly in low-income and transition economies. Simulations from large macroeconomic models have not proved very tractable or reliable in either industrial or developing countries. Hence, the trade-equations approach, which is less appealing theoretically, but more feasible to implement empirically, is likely to continue for some time as the policy workhorse. Even the trade-equations approach, however, is too time consuming to implement in multicountry studies, and for these the PPP-based approach to estimating misalignment remains the only feasible one, despite its limitations.

6

Determinants of the Long-Run Equilibrium Real Exchange Rate: An Analytical Model

*Peter J. Montiel**

In the previous chapter, the long-run equilibrium real exchange rate (LRER) was defined as the value of the real exchange rate that emerges from the economy's macroeconomic equilibrium when policy and exogenous variables are at sustainable "permanent" levels and when the operationally relevant subset of the economy's predetermined variables have settled into their steady-state configurations. As indicated there, the sustainable values of the policy and exogenous variables, as well as the actually prevailing values of the slower-adjusting predetermined variables, together constitute the set of "long-run fundamentals" that determine the long-run equilibrium real exchange rate.

Identifying these fundamentals precisely and concretely is an important step in estimating the LRER, because the dynamic behavior of these variables is what ultimately determines the path followed by the real exchange rate over time. Making this identification requires the use of a specific analytical model that is capable of explaining the time path followed by the real exchange rate in response to macroeconomic shocks. In the context of such a model, those shocks that alter the value of the real exchange rate in the economy's long-run equilibrium constitute the

* I would like to thank Pierre-Richard Agenor, Betsy Brainerd, Jonathan Conning, Larry Hinkle, Earl McFarland, Steve O'Connell, and three anonymous reviewers for their comments on earlier drafts. They are not responsible for any errors that remain.

relevant set of long-run fundamentals. A wide variety of such shocks, operating on both the demand and supply sides of the economy, have been identified by economists at different times, using diverse analytical frameworks.[1] The purpose of this chapter is to present a unified treatment, within a single analytical framework, of the problem of identifying the long-run fundamentals for the real exchange rate.

As indicated in the previous chapter, an important step in identifying the fundamentals is determining how the economy's net international creditor position is to be treated. The issue is whether adjustment in the net creditor position is sufficiently rapid as to be completed within the policy horizon (in which case the net creditor position is endogenously determined and does not constitute a "fundamental") or whether slow adjustment in this variable makes it more appropriate to condition the LRER on a given value of the net creditor position (in which case that value becomes one of the fundamentals). The model described in this chapter is one in which the LRER is defined as the real exchange rate that is compatible with steady-state equilibrium for the economy's net international creditor position, conditioned on the permanent values of a variety of policy and exogenous variables. Thus, of the alternative definitions of "external balance" discussed in the previous chapter, the model developed here adopts the "stock" rather than "flow" approach, implying that the economy's international net creditor position does not appear among the set of conditioning long-run fundamentals. This set consists instead only of exogenous and policy variables.

The chapter's objectives are to identify the relevant set of variables, and to explore the direction of their influence on the LRER, in the context of an analytical model that is intended to be familiar and transparent, yet sufficiently general so as to accommodate a wide variety of factors that could potentially influence the LRER. The model adopted for the purpose is an extended version of a well-known model by Dornbusch (1983), which has become a familiar analytical tool for macroeconomists working on developing countries. By specifying a comprehensive set of "fundamental" LRER determinants in this familiar framework, and analyzing their effects on the long-run equilibrium real exchange rate, this chapter will set the stage for the empirical ones that follow.

The chapter is organized as follows: The first two sections describe the analytical framework and how the model can be solved for the long-run equilibrium real exchange rate. Then comes the heart of the chapter, titled "Long-Run Fundamentals," which explores the properties of the

---

1. The most comprehensive treatment of equilibrium real exchange rates in the developing-country context is in Edwards (1989). See also Mussa (1986), Montiel (1986), Khan and Lizondo (1987), as well as Khan and Montiel (1987).

long-run equilibrium using a graphical presentation relying on the concepts of internal and external balance that have become familiar in the literature on real exchange rate determination.[2] The focus of that section is specifically on how changes in exogenous variables affect the equilibrium value of the real exchange rate. A recap of the results in that section is then presented under "Summary and Conclusions."

The Analytical Framework

This section describes an analytical framework designed to identify the determinants of the long-run equilibrium real exchange rate in a "representative" developing country. The model is highly stylized and will obviously be a poor representation of any particular developing economy. However, it represents a common analytical framework used by many observers in thinking about real exchange rate issues in the context of such countries. Indeed, the model described below essentially adds several extensions to a framework originally developed by Dornbusch (1983).[3] The framework is not only a familiar one, but as illustrated in "Long-Run Fundamentals" below, it also has the virtue of ready adaptability to incorporate a variety of phenomena not built into its basic structure, but that may be empirically important in the circumstances of specific countries.

The model is intended to analyze the determination of the real exchange rate in a small open economy with a predetermined nominal exchange rate and flexible domestic wages and prices.[4, 5] The economy is given a two-

2. The formal dynamic solution to the model is not directly relevant to the narrow purpose of understanding the properties of its long-run equilibrium, so readers are referred to Montiel (1998), which also establishes the stability of the long-run equilibrium and describes how its qualitative properties can be established formally.

3. The key extensions are the introduction of money and of an endogenous country risk premium. Less importantly, the model is specified in continuous time, in contrast with the discrete-time formulation in Dornbusch (1983).

4. The assumption of wage-price flexibility merits some comment. The issue is problematic in the developing-country context. A review of evidence is presented in Agenor and Montiel (1999). The assumption of full wage-price flexibility is innocuous as long as the focus is on the long-run results of the section on long-run fundamentals, since the long run will be characterized by full employment in any event. It becomes very important, however, in the analysis of short-run misalignment and optimal management of the nominal exchange rate.

5. Officially determined exchange rates remain the rule for the vast majority of developing countries. Fully flexible rates are rare, and more exotic arrangements such as dual rates have become less common in recent years (see Agenor and Montiel 1999). The assumption of predetermined rates will be implemented in the form of a crawling peg below, which includes a fixed exchange rate as a special case.

sector "dependent economy" production structure, and is assumed to be financially open.[6] Trade restrictions are absent in the reference model described in this section, but are incorporated in the section on long-run fundamentals.

Production

The economy in question is assumed to be a price taker in the world market for what it buys and sells. Its domestic production structure is of the Swan-Salter variety, consisting of traded- and nontraded-goods sectors that produce outputs y_T and y_N respectively.[7] Output in each sector is produced with a fixed, sector-specific factor and homogeneous, perfectly mobile labor, and is subject to diminishing marginal returns to the variable factor.[8] Letting w denote the real wage measured in terms of *traded* goods and e the real exchange rate measured as the relative price of traded goods in terms of nontraded goods, employment in the two sectors is determined by the profit-maximizing conditions $y_T'(L_T) = w$ and $y_N'(L_N) = we$, which imply labor demand functions $L_T(w)$ and $L_N(we)$ with the usual properties. Labor market equilibrium is given by equation 6.1 below:

$$(6.1) \qquad\qquad L_T(w) + L_N(we) = L$$

where L denotes the fixed labor force. This condition implies that the equilibrium real wage is a decreasing function of the real exchange rate, as shown by equation 6.2:

$$(6.2) \qquad\qquad \begin{aligned} w &= w(e), \text{ with} \\ w' &= -wL_N' / (L_T' + L_N'e) < 0 \ . \end{aligned}$$

Aggregate real output in this economy, measured in terms of traded goods and denoted y, is thus given by equation 6.3:

---

6. For evidence that financial openness with imperfect substitutability has been the relevant empirical assumption for a "representative" developing country, see Montiel (1995).

7. To capture the effects of terms-of-trade changes and commercial policy on the equilibrium real exchange rate, a three-good structure (with exportables, importables, and nontraded goods) would be more appropriate. Rather than complicate the notation at this point, however, I will describe the model with the two-good dependent-economy framework and then indicate at the appropriate point how these phenomena can be incorporated into the analysis (see the subsection "Changes in the Terms of Trade" in the section on long-run fundamentals).

8. This assumption implies that the economy possesses a standard concave production possibilities frontier relating maximum values of y_T and y_N.

$$y(e) = y_T \left[L_T(w(e)) \right] + y_N \left[L_N(w(e)e) \right] / e$$

(6.3) $= y(e)$, with:

$$y' = -y_N / e^2 < 0.$$

Household Behavior

The demand side of the model reflects the actions of households and of the consolidated public sector. Households receive income from production, out of which they pay taxes, consume, and save. Their saving can be allocated to the accumulation of net foreign bonds or domestic money, and portfolio equilibrium is assumed to hold continuously.

The problem faced by the representative household can be described as follows: At each instant, it allocates its net worth, denoted a, between net bond holdings f_H and domestic money m (both measured in terms of traded goods), subject to the balance sheet constraint (equation 6.4):

(6.4) $$a = f_H + m.$$

Bonds may be denominated in domestic or foreign currency. Foreign currency–denominated bonds pay the nominal interest rate i^*, while domestic currency–denominated bonds pay the interest rate i, and the two are related through the uncovered parity condition, defined by equation 6.5:

(6.5) $$i = i^* + \varepsilon,$$

where ε is the rate of depreciation of the domestic currency.[9]

The holding of money is motivated by a desire to avoid the transactions costs associated with consumption. Such costs are given by equation 6.6:

(6.6) $$T(m,c) = \tau(m/c)c; \ \tau' < 0, \tau'' > 0,$$

where c is total consumption expenditure measured in terms of traded goods. This specification postulates that transactions costs per unit of consumption are a decreasing function of the stock of money per unit of consumption, but that the productivity of money in reducing transactions costs is subject to diminishing returns. The accumulation of net

---

9. Adding an exogenous currency risk premium to this condition would not affect any of the properties of the model.

worth over time is the sum of household saving and net real capital gains or losses. It can be expressed in the form of the budget constraint shown by equation 6.7:

$$(6.7) \qquad \dot{a} = y + (i^* + \varepsilon)f_H - t - (1 + \tau)c - \pi^* a$$

where t denotes real (lump-sum) taxes, and π^* is the rate of increase in the domestic-currency price of traded goods. The latter, in turn, is the sum of the rate of depreciation of the domestic currency and the external inflation rate, denoted π_W:

$$\pi^* = \varepsilon + \pi_W.$$

The path of consumption expenditure is determined by the maximization over an infinite horizon of an additively separable utility function in which future felicity (that is, the future flow of utility) is discounted at the constant rate of time preference ρ. Consumption of traded goods, denoted c_T, and of nontraded goods c_N, are the only direct sources of utility for the household. Thus the representative household will seek to maximize a function of the form:

$$\int u(c_T, c_N)e^{-\rho t} dt$$

To make the analysis more tractable, I will give the felicity function $u(c_T, c_N)$ a specific form. Following Dornbusch (1983), I will assume that the felicity function is of the constant relative risk aversion (CRRA) type in total consumption, while the intratemporal elasticity of substitution between the two types of goods is unity. This means that the felicity function can be written as equation 6.8:

$$(6.8) \qquad u(c_T, c_N) = \frac{[c_T^\theta c_N^{1-\theta}]^{1-\sigma}}{1-\sigma}$$

The parameter θ represents the share of traded-goods consumption in total consumption expenditure (see below), while σ is the inverse of the intertemporal rate of substitution. The Cobb-Douglas specification for intratemporal substitution between the two types of goods implies that consumption expenditure is allocated in constant shares between the two types of consumption goods as shown in equation 6.9:

$$(6.9) \qquad \begin{aligned} c_T &= \theta_c \\ c_N &= (1-\theta)ec \end{aligned}$$

where total consumption expenditure c is given by $c = c_T + c_N/e$. Using these in equation 6.8 permits us to express the felicity function in the indirect form in equation 6.10:

$$(6.10) \qquad u(c_T, c_N) = v(e, c) = \frac{\kappa[e^{1-\theta}c]^{1-\sigma}}{1-\sigma}$$

where κ is a constant. The term in square brackets is the ratio of the price of traded goods to the "true" consumption price index $P_T^\theta \, P_N^{1-\theta}$ (where P_T is the domestic-currency price of traded goods, and P_N is the domestic-currency price of nontraded goods) times total consumption measured in terms of traded goods. Thus this term measures total consumption in units of the consumption bundle, which is the direct source of utility for the household.

The household's problem can thus be stated as follows: it chooses paths for consumption expenditure c and money m so as to maximize:

$$(6.11) \qquad \int_0^{\cdot \cdot} \frac{[\kappa e^{1-\theta}c]^{1-\theta}}{1-\sigma} \exp(-\rho t)dt$$

subject to the flow-budget constraint (equation 6.7) and a transversality condition. These constraints can conveniently be written as equation 6.12:

$$(6.12) \qquad \begin{array}{c} \dot{a} = y - t + ra - im - (1 + \tau(m/c))c \\[6pt] \lim a \, \exp(-\int rdt) \succeq 0 \end{array}$$

where r is the real interest rate earned by domestic residents on their holdings of foreign bonds, measured in terms of traded goods ($r = i - \pi^*$). This is equivalent to the external nominal interest rate i^* faced by domestic residents, minus the foreign-currency rate of inflation in the price of traded goods:

$$r = i - \pi^* = (i^* + \varepsilon) - (\pi_W + \varepsilon) = i^* - \pi_W.$$

The present-value Hamiltonian for this problem can be written as:

$$H = (\frac{[\kappa e^{1-\theta}c]^{1-\sigma}}{1-\sigma} + \lambda \dot{a})\exp(-\rho t)$$

where λ is the costate variable for the household's financial wealth a, with economic interpretation as the marginal utility of wealth. The solution of this problem is characterized by the first-order conditions shown in equations 6.13.a through 6.13.b:

(6.13.a) $$\kappa e^{\gamma} c^{-\sigma} = \lambda(1 - \tau(m/c) - \tau'(m/c))c$$

(6.13.b) $$-\tau'(m/c) = i$$

(6.13.c) $$\lambda(\rho - r) = \dot{\lambda}$$

as well as the budget constraint and transversality conditions given in equation 6.12. These conditions have intuitive interpretations. Equation 6.13.a describes the necessary condition for the level of consumption to be at its optimal level at each instant, conditional on the marginal utility of wealth. It states that the marginal utility gain from an extra unit of consumption must be equal to its marginal utility cost—that is, the loss arising from forgone saving. The latter is the product of the marginal utility of wealth λ and the reduction in saving associated with an extra unit of consumption, given by the quantity $(1 + \tau + \tau')$, which includes the transaction costs associated with each extra unit of consumption. Equation 6.13.b is the necessary condition for the allocation of the household portfolio between money and bonds to be at its optimal level, conditional on the level of consumption expenditure. It states that the marginal gain from holding an extra unit of money, in the form of reduced transaction costs, must be equal to its marginal cost, in the form of forgone interest. Finally, equation 6.13.c is necessary for wealth to be allocated optimally over time. It states that since wealth should be drawn down more quickly (through increased consumption) when the household is more impatient (that is, when ρ is large relative to r), the marginal utility of wealth should rise more rapidly under those conditions.

These equations can be used to describe the household's demand for money, the path of its consumption expenditure, and its rate of accumulation of financial assets at each moment in time. Equation 6.13.b implicitly defines a relationship between money and consumption that resembles a standard money-demand equation, shown in equation 6.14:

(6.14) $$m = h(i)c, \ h' < 0.$$

Thus the demand for money depends in familiar fashion on the interest rate and the level of transactions. To derive an expression for the path of consumption expenditure, differentiate equation 6.13.a with respect to time. Using equations 6.13.b, 6.13.c, and 6.14, we can derive the time path of consumption. It is given by equation 6.15:

(6.15) $$\dot{c} = \sigma^{-1}\left[r + \gamma\dot{e}/e - \frac{h(i)\dot{i}}{1 + \tau(h(i)) + ih(i)} - \rho\right]c$$

where $\gamma = (1 - \sigma)(1 - \theta)$. This represents a generalization of the familiar Euler equation for the optimal time path of consumption under constant relative risk aversion, to incorporate changing relative prices of the two consumption goods as well as the role of the transactions technology. Note that, given the real interest rate measured in terms of traded goods r:

a. An expected real depreciation makes consumption cheaper in the future (since it implies a lower relative price of nontraded goods). This increases the consumption-based real interest rate (the opportunity cost of current consumption), which steepens the consumption path (thereby discouraging current consumption), and
b. A steepening of the path of the future nominal interest rate (a positive value of $\dot{i}$) would tend to increase the transactions costs associated with future consumption, thus decreasing the consumption-based real interest rate, which tends to tilt the consumption path toward the present, making it flatter.

The Consolidated Public Sector

The consolidated public sector includes both the government and the central bank. The economy operates with a predetermined exchange rate, administered as a crawling peg in which the domestic currency depreciates continuously at the policy-determined rate ε. The central bank's functions consist of maintaining the parity (by exchanging domestic and foreign currency for each other on demand in unlimited amounts at the official exchange rate) and providing credit to the government. The latter, in addition to credit from the central bank, receives lump-sum taxes from the private sector and spends by purchasing both traded and nontraded goods, in the amounts g_T and g_N, respectively. Thus the consolidated period-by-period (flow) budget constraint of the public sector can be expressed as equation 6.16:

$$(6.16) \qquad \dot{f}_c = t + r f_c + (\dot{m} + \pi^* m) - (g_T + g_N / e)$$

where $\dot{f}_c$, which may be positive or negative, is the stock of bonds held by the consolidated public sector. Like the private sector, the government has to respect an intertemporal budget constraint, given by $\lim \dot{f}_c \exp(-^* r \, dt) > 0$.

For concreteness, I shall assume that it does so in a particularly simple way—by levying taxes in an amount sufficient to keep $\dot{f}_c - \dot{m} = 0$. Notice that this does not imply a balanced budget, but rather a reliance on the inflation tax to finance fiscal deficits.

Equilibrium Conditions

The model is closed with two equilibrium conditions. The first is an arbitrage relationship describing the terms on which the rest of the world will lend to the domestic economy, and the second characterizes equilibrium in the market for nontraded goods.

The Supply of Funds

Though the home country is a price taker in the world goods market, its financial liabilities are not perfect substitutes for those of the rest of the world, and thus the interest rate at which residents of the country can borrow abroad reflects a risk premium, which is an increasing function of the share of the country's liabilities held in world financial portfolios. This is incorporated in the model in the form of an upward-sloping supply-of-funds schedule relating the external interest rate confronted by the country's residents, i^*, to the country's net international indebtedness, as well as to world financial conditions, measured by the world interest rate i_w. The specific formulation expresses i^* as the sum of the world interest rate and a risk premium p, which is inversely related to the country's aggregate net creditor position, as expressed by equation 6.17:

$$(6.17) \qquad i^* = i_w + p(f), \, p(0) > 0, \, p' < 0.$$

The supply-of-funds schedule described by equation 6.17 is depicted as the curve i^* in figure 6.1.[10] The external interest rate faced by the economy is determined by the height of this schedule above the relevant value of the net external asset position f.

Equilibrium in the Market for Nontraded Goods

Finally the equilibrium condition in the market for nontraded goods can be expressed as equation 6.18:

$$(6.18) \qquad \begin{aligned} y_N(e) &= c_N + g_N \\ &= (1 - \theta)ec + g_N \, . \end{aligned}$$

For future reference, it is worth noting that the specification of equilibrium in the nontraded-goods market (equation 6.18) implies that all

---

10. For a similar specification, see Bhandari, Haque, and Turnovsky (1990). Agenor (1997) provides more detail on this specification and how it relates to alternative approaches to modeling international capital market imperfections.

Figure 6.1 *The Supply-of-Funds Schedule*

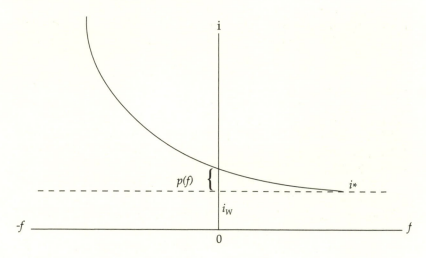

production of nontraded goods is available for consumption, either by the households or by the government. This has the consequence that the transactions costs associated with consumption must absorb traded goods only. This assumption is not necessary and is discussed further below.

Equation 6.18 can be solved for the value of the real exchange rate that clears the nontraded-goods market, conditional on the values of c and g_N. This short-run equilibrium real exchange rate is given by equation 6.19:

$$e = e(c, g_N)$$

(6.19) $$e_1 = (1-\theta)e / (y'_N - (1-\theta)c) < 0$$

$$e_2 = 1/(y'_N - (1-\theta)c) < 0 \, .$$

The real exchange rate that solves equation 6.19 is a *short-run* equilibrium one in the sense that it clears the market for nontraded goods for a *given* value of private consumption expenditure c. Thus, this real exchange rate will be sustainable only to the extent that c is itself sustainable.

The Long-Run Equilibrium Real Exchange Rate

As shown in Montiel (1998), the model of the previous section can be solved to derive the entire dynamic path of the real exchange rate and other endogenous macroeconomic variables in response to a variety of macroeconomic shocks, be they transitory or permanent, occurring in the present, or expected to occur in the future. A key characteristic of the model is that the economy it describes tends to settle into a steady-state equilibrium after a shock in which the stock of net international indebtedness and the real exchange rate are both unchanging.[11]

This section examines the properties of that equilibrium. Since the focus is specifically on the determination of the long-run equilibrium real exchange rate, the solution method chosen in this section is one that focuses specifically on that variable and links up with the traditional literature that views the equilibrium real exchange rate as that value of the real exchange rate that is consistent with the simultaneous attainment of internal and external balance.

To solve the model, we first reduce it to a smaller number of key relationships. The first step is to consolidate the budget constraints of the household and public sectors. To do so, we differentiate the household balance sheet constraint (equation 6.4) and substitute into the flow-budget constraint (equation 6.12). This permits equation 6.12 to be written as equation 6.12′:

$$(6.12') \qquad \dot{f}_H = y - t + rf_H - (\dot{m} + \pi^* m) - (1 + \tau(m/c))c .$$

Adding equations 6.12′ and 6.16 together, and using the definitions of y and c as well as the equilibrium condition in the nontraded-goods market (equation 6.18), we have equation 6.20:

$$(6.20) \qquad \dot{f} = y_T(e) + rf - (\theta + \tau(m/c))c - g_T .$$

This is the flow-budget constraint for the economy as a whole. Recalling that $c_T = \theta c$, and that transactions costs are assumed to be incurred in traded goods, aggregate demand for traded goods is given by $(\theta c + g_T)$, and aggregate supply is $(y_T - \tau c)$. Thus, aggregate excess supply of traded goods, equal to the real trade balance surplus, is $(y_T - \tau c) - (\theta c - g_T) = y_T - (\tau + \theta)c - g_T$. Adding the receipt of real interest payments from abroad (recall that f is the country's international net creditor position) yields the inflation-adjusted current account surplus, measured in units of traded goods, which is the right-hand side of equation 6.20. This is equated to the change in the economy's real net creditor position $(\dot{f})$. This equation thus determines how the real net creditor position evolves over time.

---

11. As is common with models of this type, that equilibrium is unique and saddlepoint stable.

Private spending, in turn, evolves over time according to the Euler equation 6.15, reproduced here for convenience:

$$(6.15) \qquad \dot{c} = \sigma^{-1} \left[r + \gamma \dot{e}/e - \frac{h(i)\dot{i}}{1 + \tau(h(i)) + ih(i)} - \rho \right] c \,.$$

As is evident from equation 6.15, the evolution of private expenditure over time is itself dependent on the paths of the real exchange rate and domestic nominal interest rates. These are determined respectively by the nontraded-goods market equilibrium condition (equation 6.19, reproduced below for reference) and the arbitrage condition (equation 6.5), reproduced below as equation 6.5′:

$$(6.19) \qquad\qquad e = e(c, g_N)$$

$$(6.5') \qquad\qquad i = (r + \pi_W + p(f)) + \varepsilon$$

where equation 6.5 has been modified to take into account the foreign Fisher relationship and the supply-of-funds schedule (equation 6.17).

To analyze the properties of the long-run equilibrium real exchange rate, begin by imposing the long-run equilibrium conditions $\dot{c} = \dot{e} = \dot{i}$ in the Euler equation 6.15. This implies the steady-state condition equation 6.21:

$$(6.21) \qquad\qquad \begin{aligned} \rho &= r \\ &= r_W + p(f). \end{aligned}$$

Since r_W and ρ are both exogenous, this equation determines the long-run equilibrium value of the net international creditor position for this economy, f^*.[12] Because the premium p is a decreasing function of the net creditor position f, the equation implies that countries with a high rate of time preference will be driven to have a smaller stock of net external claims in long-run equilibrium than those with lower rates of time preference.

Next, to derive the long-run equilibrium value of the domestic *nominal* interest rate, substitute equation 6.21 in 6.5′, yielding equation 6.22:

$$(6.22) \qquad\qquad \begin{aligned} i &= (\rho + \pi_W) + \varepsilon \\ &= \rho + \pi^*. \end{aligned}$$

---

12. This value can be positive or negative, without violating the transversality conditions on the private and public sectors.

This value of i pins down the long-run values of consumption velocity h and transactions cost per unit of consumption τ, as expressed in equations 6.23 and 6.24:

$$(6.23) \qquad\qquad h^* = h(i) = h(\rho + \pi^*)$$

$$(6.24) \qquad\qquad \tau^* = \tau[h(i)] = \tau[h(\rho + \pi^*)].$$

With these results in hand, the conditions that characterize the long-run equilibrium real exchange rate in this model can be described. Using equations 6.22 and 6.24 in 6.21 yields equation 6.25:

$$(6.25) \qquad 0 = y_T(e) + \rho \dot{f} - (\tau[h(\rho + \pi^*)] + \theta)c - g_T.$$

This is the long-run external balance condition in the model. It states that for the economy's real external net creditor position to reach an equilibrium value, the inflation-adjusted current account balance must be zero. An alternative and more useful formulation, however, focuses on the conventional (non-inflation-adjusted) current account balance. Adding the inflation adjustment $\pi_w f^*$ to both sides, we can write equation 6.25 as 6.25′:

$$(6.25′) \quad \pi_w f^* = y_T(e) + (\rho + \pi_w)f^* - (\tau|\, h(\rho + \pi_w + \varepsilon\,) + \theta)c - g_T.$$

Condition 6.25′ states that in long-run equilibrium the real current account balance, which is equal to real national saving, must be equal to the inflationary erosion of the real value of the country's net claims on the rest of the world.[13] The latter represents the sustainable value of the country's capital account balance. A net creditor country (with a positive value of f^*) would run a sustainable current account surplus and capital account deficit that would enable it to acquire claims on the rest of the world that are sufficient to offset the inflationary erosion of its existing claims. By contrast, a net debtor country would run a sustainable current account deficit and capital account surplus, accumulating

---

13. The model from which equation 6.25 was derived does not feature growth of productive capacity. In a growth context—for example, with constant Harrod-neutral technical change at the rate n—steady-state equilibrium would require constancy of the country's net international creditor position per effective worker, so the left-hand side of equation 6.25 would be modified to $(n + \pi_w)f$. In a growth context, a net debtor country would be able to run larger sustainable current account deficits than in the static case.

new debt sufficient to offset the effective amortization of its existing debt through the inflation component of its nominal interest payments.

Since y_T is increasing in the real exchange rate e, and since an increase in consumption expenditure reduces the trade surplus, the set of combinations of e and c that satisfies equation 6.25´ is plotted as the positively sloped external balance locus EB in figure 6.2. Internal balance is, of course, given by the nontraded-goods market clearing condition 6.19. As suggested by equation 6.19, the locus traced out by the set of combinations of e and c that are consistent with internal balance (IB) has a negative slope in figure 6.2. The long-run equilibrium real exchange rate is that which is simultaneously consistent with external and internal balances in the long run. It is defined by the intersection of the two loci at point A in figure 6.2, and is labeled e^*.

Long-Run Fundamentals

The response of the long-run equilibrium real exchange rate to its fundamental determinants can be established by examining the effects of permanent changes in the various exogenous variables included in the

Figure 6.2 *Determination of the Long-Run Equilibrium Real Exchange Rate*

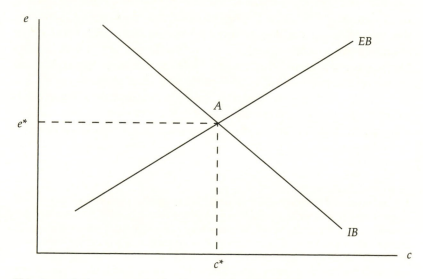

Note: An upward movement is a depreciation of the real exchange rate.

model on the location of the long-run equilibrium point A. In this section, I take up these fundamentals one at a time, identifying individual fundamentals as well as the qualitative nature of their influence on the long-run equilibrium real exchange rate.

Fiscal Policy

I begin by considering changes in government spending, holding the fiscal deficit constant. As is well known, effects on the long-run equilibrium real exchange rate depend on the sectoral composition of these changes.[14]

Changes in Government Spending on Traded Goods

An increase in government spending on traded goods has no effect on the internal balance locus, but it shifts the external balance locus upward—to EB' in figure 6.3. The increase in government spending creates an incipient trade deficit, which requires a real depreciation in order to maintain external balance. As indicated in figure 6.3, at the new long-run equilibrium B, the equilibrium real exchange rate depreciates, and private consumption of traded goods falls.[15] The reduction in private consumption of traded goods is smaller than the increase in government consumption, however, because the real depreciation induces an increase in the production of traded goods, allowing the accommodation of an increase in total spending on traded goods.

Changes in Government Spending on Nontraded Goods

In contrast to the previous case, the locus affected in this case is the internal balance locus IB. The increased demand for nontraded goods requires an increase in their relative price to maintain equilibrium in the nontraded-goods market, and the IB schedule thus shifts downward, to

---

14. For earlier work on the effects of the composition of government spending on the long-run equilibrium real exchange rate see Montiel (1986) and Khan and Lizondo (1987).

15. In contrast, Penati (1987) finds that an increase in government spending on traded goods has no effect on the long-run equilibrium real exchange rate. The aspect of model specification that accounts for this difference is that in the present model, a steady-state equilibrium is ensured by an endogenous risk premium, while in Penati's model the same result is achieved by endogenizing the rate of time preference. This feature makes Penati's model block-recursive and permits external balance to be restored after an increase in government spending on traded goods through an increase in the economy's net claims on the rest of the world, with no repercussions for relative prices.

Figure 6.3 *Effects of Changes in Government Spending on the Long-Run Equilibrium Real Exchange Rate*

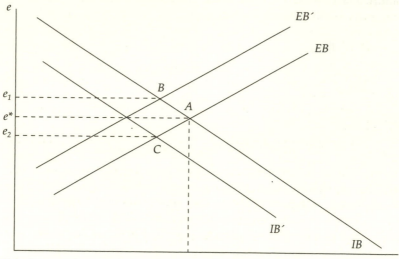

Note: An upward movement is a depreciation of the real exchange rate.

IB´ in figure 6.3. The new equilibrium is at point C. As in the previous case, private consumption expenditure is crowded out in long-run equilibrium, but in this case the equilibrium real exchange rate appreciates. The upshot of this exercise and the previous one is that the long-run equilibrium real exchange rate is a function of the sectoral composition of government spending.

A Reduction in the Fiscal Deficit

Consider a reduction in the fiscal deficit, in the form of a tax increase. Since taxes are actually endogenous in the model under the assumptions made in the section on the analytical framework, this shock is equivalent to a reduction in the rate of monetary emission by the central bank, which in turn is equivalent to a reduction in the rate of crawl of the nominal exchange rate. The gain from a lower fiscal deficit in this model comes in the form of a reduction in the distortions associated with the inflation tax. A reduced rate of depreciation lowers the domestic interest rate, increases the demand for money, and reduces the transactions costs associated with consumption—in other words, τ^* falls. This has the effect of increasing the supply of real output. Whether the long-run equilibrium real exchange rate will appreciate or depreciate depends on whether transactions costs are borne in the form of traded or nontraded goods.[16] This will determine the form that the increase in real output takes. As currently specified, the model assumes that these costs are borne in the form of traded goods. The reduction in τ^* will thus increase the supply of such goods, shifting the external balance locus downward and resulting in a real appreciation, together with an increase in consumption. On the other hand, if transactions costs are incurred in nontraded goods, the external balance locus would remain fixed, and the internal balance locus would shift to the right. In that case, the equilibrium real exchange rate would depreciate, and consumption would rise.[17]

It may be worth noting that the effects of a reduction in the fiscal deficit brought about by changes in spending would simply be a combination of one of the first two shocks described above with the third. The effects would depend on whether the reduction in spending fell on traded or nontraded goods, as well as on the composition of transactions costs.

Changes in the Value of International Transfers

The other demand-side variable that enters the model is the external real interest rate r_w. Before analyzing the effects of changes in external financial conditions, however, it is useful as a point of reference to consider the effects on the equilibrium real exchange rate of changes in the level of international transfers received by the domestic economy. These will provide an interesting contrast with the case of interest rate changes. As formulated above, the model does not explicitly consider the role of international transfers. It is straightforward to add them, however. Such transfers would simply represent an addition to household incomes equal to the amount of the transfer. They would appear as an additive term in the household's budget constraint equation 6.7, in the dynamic equation 6.20 for f, and in the long-run equilibrium condition equation 6.25′.[18] Accordingly, the effect of a permanent increase in the receipt of transfer income would be to shift the external balance locus to the right—the

---

16. This property that the long-run equilibrium real exchange rate is affected by a change in the rate of monetary expansion—that is, the failure of superneutrality—also characterizes the model of Penati (1987).

17. A change in the foreign inflation rate π_w affects the model in exactly the same way as a change in the rate of depreciation ε, since the two variables enter only in the additive form $\pi^* = \varepsilon + \pi_w$ in equation 6.25.

18. It makes no difference in this model whether the transfer is received directly by the private sector or whether it goes to the government, since under the fiscal regime assumed above, the latter would transfer the proceeds to the private sector.

receipt of additional transfer income permits an expansion of consumption to be consistent with external balance at an unchanged exchange rate. There are no direct effects on the *internal balance* locus, so the equilibrium is at B in figure 6.4, with an equilibrium real *appreciation* and an increase in private absorption.

Changes in International Financial Conditions

The analysis of transfers is instructive because many observers' intuition about the effects of changes in capital inflows on the long-run equilibrium real exchange rate is derived from the corresponding effects of transfers. Capital inflows and transfers have in common the feature that they permit an expansion of absorption relative to income in the short run. However, the two phenomena differ in two important respects. First, the volume of capital inflows is an endogenous variable that can arise from a variety of changes in domestic and external economic conditions. Presumably, the change in the long-run equilibrium real exchange rate associated with a particular capital-inflow episode depends on the source of the shock that triggers the inflow. Second, unlike transfers, capital inflows create repayment obligations in the long run. These also will affect the long-run equilibrium real exchange rate.[19]

Consider, then, a particular shock that has been associated with the emergence of capital inflows: a reduction in world real interest rates.[20] Again, this shock directly affects only the external balance locus. To see in which direction the locus moves, differentiate equation 6.25′:

$$de / dr_W \Big|_{\dot{f}=0} = \frac{\rho + \pi_W}{p' y'_T} < 0.$$

Thus, the real exchange rate consistent with external equilibrium moves in a direction *opposite* to the world interest rate. In this case, when the world real interest rate falls, the external balance locus thus shifts

---

19. Such obligations will affect the long-run equilibrium real exchange rate under the "stock" approach to the definition of external balance described in the previous chapter, which is the approach adopted here. If the "flow" approach were adopted instead, the effects of capital inflows on the LRER would resemble those of transfers, except that the endogenous nature of capital inflows would cause those effects to depend on the source of the shock triggering the inflows.

20. The view that the capital-inflow episode affecting several large developing countries during the early 1990s was triggered by a reduction in interest rates in the United States, first put forward by Calvo, Leiderman, and Reinhart (1993), is now widely accepted. For a review of this episode, see Fernandez-Arias and Montiel (1996).

Figure 6.4 *Effects of Changes in Foreign Transfers and World Real Interest Rates on the Long-Run Equilibrium Real Exchange Rate*

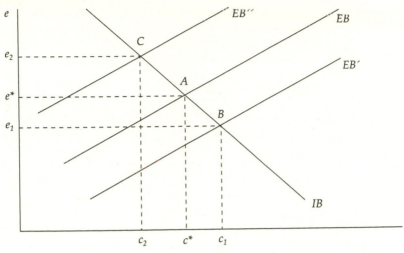

Note: An upward movement is a depreciation of the real exchange rate.

upward, to a position similar to *EB″* in figure 6.4, and the equilibrium real exchange rate, determined at point C, actually *depreciates*, contrary to what happens in the case of an increase in the level of transfer receipts.[21]

Why is this the case? Equation 6.25′ suggests that the effect of a change in world interest rates on the real exchange rate consistent with external balance depends on the effect of this change on the country's long-run net interest receipts. Thus, like those of a transfer, the effects of a change in external interest rates on the long-run equilibrium real exchange rate depend on their long-run implications for national income. In this model, however, the implications of a reduction in world interest rates for

21. Notice that de/dr_w does not depend on f^*. Thus, the direction of the shift in the external balance locus, and therefore the result that a change in r_w causes the long-run equilibrium value of e to move in the opposite direction, does not depend on whether the economy is initially a net external creditor or debtor. This result is also derived, with a different approach to modeling imperfect asset substitutability, by Agenor (1996). However, the dynamics of adjustment to the new equilibrium do indeed depend on the economy's initial international net creditor position, as shown in Montiel (1998).

national income are *negative* in the long run, unlike those of transfers. This is precisely because of the capital inflows induced by the change in world financial conditions. In the new long-run equilibrium, the country's net creditor position with the rest of the world deteriorates, reflecting the effects of net external borrowing (capital inflows) during the transition from one long-run equilibrium to the next.[22] The change in the external real interest rate has no other direct effects on the country's long-run current account balance (equation 6.25′). In particular, the interest rate that the country actually faces in world capital markets is unchanged from one long-run equilibrium to the next, because changes in the country's net external creditor position drive that interest rate to equality with the domestic rate of time preference. A higher risk premium, associated with a reduced net international creditor position, reconciles the constant effective interest rate faced by domestic residents in the long run with the lower world interest rate. Since, unlike in the case of transfers, the borrowing has to be repaid, this is reflected in a reduction in long-run equilibrium national income.[23]

The Balassa-Samuelson Effect

To capture the effects of differential productivity growth in the traded-goods sector, the production function in this sector can be respecified as shown by equation 6.26:

(6.26) $$y_T = y_T(L_T, \alpha); \quad y_{T1} > 0, \quad y_{T2} > 0$$

where α is a productivity parameter. Since the demand for labor in the traded-goods sector will now be a function of this productivity parameter, labor market equilibrium becomes equation 6.27:

(6.27) $$L_T(w, \alpha) + L_N(w) = L$$

and the equilibrium real wage can be written as equation 6.28:

$$w = w(e, \alpha), \quad \text{with}:$$

(6.28)

$$w_2 = \frac{L_{T2}}{L_{T1} + L_N'e} > 0.$$

This means that output in the traded- and nontraded-goods sectors are given respectively by equations 6.29 and 6.30:

---

22. The transition is described in Montiel (1998).
23. For a more extensive discussion of this issue, see Agenor (1996).

(6.29)
$$y_T = y_T[L_T[w(e,\alpha),\alpha],\alpha]$$

$$\frac{dy_T}{d\alpha} = y_{T1}L_{T2}\frac{L_N'e}{L_{T1}+L_N'e} + y_{T2} > 0.$$

(6.30)
$$y_N = y_N[L_N[w(e,\alpha)]], \quad \text{with:}$$

$$\frac{dy_N}{d\alpha} = y_N'L_N'w_2 < 0.$$

Thus, the effect of the productivity shock in the traded-goods sector is to increase the demand for labor in that sector, thereby increasing the equilibrium real wage. In turn, this causes the nontraded-goods sector to release labor, which is absorbed by the traded-goods sector. At a given real exchange rate, the traded-goods sector expands, while the nontraded-goods sector contracts.

To examine the effects on the long-run equilibrium real exchange rate, notice that the productivity shock α enters the internal and external balance equations 6.19 and 6.25′ only through its effects on y_N and y_T, respectively. Since, according to equation 6.30, an increase in α reduces y_N, it creates excess demand in the nontraded-goods market, requiring a real appreciation to restore internal balance. In figure 6.5, the *IB* locus shifts downward. At the same time, however, by increasing production of traded goods (see equation 6.29), the shock gives rise to an incipient trade surplus, so a real appreciation is also required for the restoration of external balance. Thus, *EB* shifts downward as well. Both effects operate in the direction of equilibrium real appreciation, as proposed by the Balassa-Samuelson analysis. Thus, differential productivity growth in the traded-goods sector creates an appreciation of the equilibrium real exchange rate.[24]

Changes in the Terms of Trade

As indicated previously, the model as specified is not suitable for analyzing changes in the terms of trade, since exportable and importable goods are not distinguished from each other in the traded-goods sector. To make the necessary modifications, split up total traded-goods output into output of exportables y_X and importables y_Z, both produced under conditions described previously for y_T, that is, with a fixed

---

24. It can be shown that the downward shift in *EB* exceeds that in *IB*. The implication is that the favorable productivity shock results in an increase in real private absorption in equilibrium, as one would expect.

Figure 6.5 *Effects of Differential Productivity Shocks and Terms-of-Trade Changes on the Long-Run Equilibrium Real Exchange Rate*

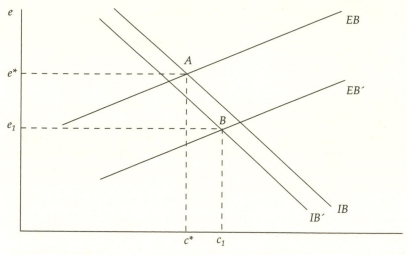

Note: An upward movement is a depreciation of the real exchange rate.

sector-specific factor and mobile labor, with sectoral employment levels L_X and L_Z. Let ϕ denote the terms of trade, defined as the price of exportables in terms of importables, and redefine the real exchange rate e as the relative price of *importables* in terms of nontraded goods. To keep the demand side of the model simple, assume that the exportable good is not consumed at home.

The analysis of the effects of terms-of-trade changes is, as might be expected, quite similar to that of productivity shocks to the traded-goods sector. Labor market equilibrium is now given by equation 6.31:

(6.31) $$L_X(w/\phi) + L_Z(w) + L_N(we) = L$$

where w is now the real wage in terms of importables. The real wage that clears the labor market becomes:

$$w = w(e, \phi), \quad \text{with}$$
(6.32) $$w_2 = \frac{L'_X w / \phi^2}{L'_X / \phi + L'_Z + L'_N e} > 0.$$

An improvement in the terms of trade increases the real wage, because this permits labor to be transferred from the importables and nontraded sectors to the expanding exportables sector. Sectoral supplies are now as expressed in equations 6.33, 6.34, and 6.35:

(6.33)
$$y_x = y_x[L_x[w(e,\phi)/\phi]]$$
$$\frac{dy_x}{d\phi} = y'_x L'_x (w_2/\phi - w/\phi^2) > 0$$

(6.34)
$$y_z = y_z[L_z[w(e,\phi)]]$$
$$\frac{dy_z}{d\phi} = y'_z L'_z w_2 < 0$$

(6.35)
$$y_N = y_N[L_N[w(e,\phi)e]]$$
$$\frac{dy_N}{d\phi} = y'_N L'_N w_2 e < 0.$$

The internal balance equilibrium condition remains as before, with the exception that output of nontraded goods is now specified as in equation 6.35. The external balance condition (equation 6.25′), however, has to be modified to take into account that traded-goods production now involves output of both exportables and importables, yielding equation 6.36:

(6.36) $$\pi_w f^* = \phi y_x(e,\phi) + y_z(e,\phi) + (\rho + \pi_w)f^* - (\tau^* + \theta)c - g_z .$$

As shown above, an improvement in the terms of trade results in a contraction in output of nontraded goods. The resulting excess demand in the nontraded-goods market causes the internal balance schedule to shift downward. The effects on the external balance schedule depend on whether the real value of total traded-goods output increases or decreases. This effect is given by:

$$\frac{\partial(\phi y_x + y_z)}{\partial\phi} = y_x - \phi y'_x L'_N e w_2 > 0 .$$

The value of traded-goods output increases through two channels: a valuation (income) effect arising from the higher relative price of exportables and an output effect arising from the absorption in the exportable sector of labor released by the nontraded-goods sector. The implication is that, as in the case of the favorable productivity shock, the external balance locus will shift downward—the incipient improvement in the trade balance requires a real appreciation to keep the trade balance at its sustainable level. Thus, the effects of a terms-of-trade improvement can also be represented as in figure 6.5.[25, 26]

Commercial Policy

Finally, consider the effects on the long-run real exchange rate of a liberalization of commercial policy, modeled as a reduction in export subsidies. This is the simplest case to model in the present context, because it makes using several of the results derived for the analysis of the effects of terms-of-trade shocks possible. Consider, in particular, an export subsidy set at the rate $(\phi - 1)$. In this case, the *internal* terms of trade will be ϕ, and the previous analysis can be repeated, at least on the supply side of the economy. In particular, an increase in the subsidy would pull labor out of the importable and traded-goods sectors into the exportables sector, just as would an equivalent favorable terms-of-trade shock. A direct implication is that effects of subsidy changes on the internal balance schedule *IB* are the same as those of an equivalent terms-of-trade shock. A subsidy increase causes *IB* to shift downward by creating an excess demand for nontraded goods, and a subsidy decrease causes it to shift upward.

Where matters differ is in regard to the effects of export subsidies on the external balance schedule. Because changes in the internal terms of trade have the same output effects whether brought about by external terms-of-trade changes or by subsidy rate changes, an increase in the subsidy rate would create an expansion in the output of traded goods and cause an incipient trade balance improvement, just as before. Again, the reason is because a subsidy increase draws labor from the nontraded to the exportables sector. However, the income effect is absent in this case. The reason is that, unlike in the case of an external terms-of-trade improvement, the increase in the price of exportables brought about by a subsidy increase has to be financed. In the case of the subsidy, a tax liability is created for the private sector in an amount equal to the subsidy rate times the output of exportables—that is, in the amount $(\phi - 1)y_x$. When this tax liability is taken into account in equation 6.36, the result is equation 6.37:

---

25. Just as before, it can be shown that the downward movement in *EB* exceeds that in *IB*, so the sustainable level of private absorption increases as a result of this shock.

26. As figure 6.5 suggests, an improvement in the terms of trade is associated with an appreciation of the long-run importables real exchange rate. Whether the long-run exportables real exchange rate, given by $e\phi$, depreciates or appreciates, however, is ambiguous in the model.

(6.37)

$$\pi_w f^* = \phi y_x(e,\phi) + y_z(e,\phi) + (\rho + \pi_w)f^* - (\phi - 1)y_x(e,\phi) - (\tau + \theta)c$$
$$= y_x(e,\phi) + y_z(e,\phi) + (\rho + \pi_w)f^* - (\tau + \theta)c.$$

The implication is that a given change in the export subsidy rate would cause the external balance schedule to shift in the same direction, *but by a smaller amount*, than a terms-of-trade change that has an equivalent impact on the internal terms of trade.

In the case at hand, the issue concerns the effect on the real exchange rate of liberalization of commercial policy—that is, a reduction in the export subsidy rate. The results just established imply that a shock of this type would shift both the internal and external balance schedules upward, with the implication that commercial liberalization results in a depreciation of the equilibrium real exchange rate.

Summary and Conclusions

The objective of this chapter has been to analyze the determination of the long-run equilibrium real exchange rate in the context of a simple analytical framework that is flexible enough to accommodate a broad variety of potential influences on the real exchange rate. The long-run equilibrium real exchange rate was defined as the rate consistent with the steady-state value of a country's international net creditor position, given the paths of all relevant policy and exogenous variables.

The determinants of the long-run equilibrium real exchange rate identified here consisted of the following:

Domestic Supply-Side Factors. The most venerable theory regarding long-run real exchange rate determination is the Balassa-Samuelson effect. This was incorporated in the analysis in the form of an asymmetric productivity shock favoring the traded-goods sector. The equilibrium real exchange rate appreciates, both because excess demand is created in the nontraded-goods sector and because the trade balance tends to improve.

Fiscal Policy. Changes in the composition of government spending between traded and nontraded goods affect the long-run equilibrium real exchange rate in different ways. Additional tax-financed spending on nontraded goods creates incipient excess demand in that market, requiring a real appreciation to restore equilibrium. By contrast, tax-financed increases in spending on traded goods put downward pressure on the trade balance, and require a real depreciation to sustain external balance. The effects of a tax-based fiscal adjustment depend on the form in which transactions costs are incurred.

Changes in the International Economic Environment. The aspects of the world economic environment analyzed here consisted of the terms of trade for the domestic economy, the availability of external transfers, the level of world real interest rates, and the world inflation rate. Improvements in the terms of trade and increases in the flow of transfers received tend to appreciate the equilibrium real exchange rate, the former both by improving the trade balance and creating excess demand for nontraded goods, and the latter through positive effects on the current account. Reductions in world real interest rates and increases in world inflation, by contrast, cause the long-run equilibrium real exchange rate to depreciate. Lower world interest rates cause capital inflows, which reduce the country's net creditor position over time, and the long-run loss of net interest receipts requires a real depreciation to maintain external balance. Changes in world inflation affect the equilibrium real exchange rate through effects on transactions costs associated with changes in real money balances. In the case of an increase in world inflation, the long-run real exchange rate tended to depreciate in this model, though this conclusion is sensitive to an essentially arbitrary assumption about the form in which transactions costs are incurred.

Commercial Policy. Finally, trade liberalization, analyzed here in the form of a reduction in export subsidies, is associated with long-run real depreciation. The effect works by channeling resources into the nontraded-goods sectors. The emergence of incipient excess supply in the nontraded-goods market dictates the nature of the adjustment in the real exchange rate.

Part III

Methodologies for Estimating the Equilibrium RER: Empirical Applications

7

Estimating the Equilibrium RER Empirically: Operational Approaches

*Theodore O. Ahlers and Lawrence E. Hinkle**

The estimation of long-run equilibrium RERs (LRERs) and measurement of misalignment have traditionally relied on two approaches with strong operational advantages: a relative purchasing power parity-based methodology that assumes a stationary LRER and a target resource balance methodology that employs trade equations or elasticities.[1] In addition, in cases of split or multiple exchange rates, the parallel market rate has sometimes been used as an indicator of misalignment.

The two traditional approaches are still widely used in operational applications in both industrial and developing countries, particularly when the data or time required for implementing more complex methodologies are not available. Even when it is feasible to employ the general-equilibrium methodologies discussed in the subsequent chapters in Part III of this volume, the traditional operational approaches still provide good starting points for the analysis, and transparent reference points for cross-checking the plausibility, of the results from the more complex methodologies. Most of the input data required to implement

* Ms. Ingrid Ivins provided research and computational assistance in the preparation of this chapter. The authors are grateful to Peter Montiel, Fabien Nsengiyumva, and three anonymous readers for very helpful comments on earlier drafts.

1. The term resource balance is used in this chapter to refer to the difference between exports of goods and nonfactor services, and imports of goods and nonfactor services. The resource balance equals the current account balance exclusive of net interest and other factor service payments.

the two operational approaches are needed for the other methodologies in any case.

When the RER is stationary in a time-series sense, long-run equilibrium exchange rates may be estimated on the basis of relative purchasing power parity (PPP) by using either a base-year or a trend approach. The base-year approach first establishes a base period in which the observed RER is believed to be at its equilibrium level. Misalignment is then measured as the difference between the observed RER and its base-period value, on the implicit PPP assumption that the LRER has remained at its base level. The utility of this PPP-based methodology is limited because of its inability to allow for permanent changes in the LRER that would cause the RER to be nonstationary. The methodology is, however, still useful for analyzing situations where the LRER is believed to have remained unchanged, such as when shocks to the economy have primarily affected nominal variables or when shocks to the "real" fundamentals have been transitory. In both cases, relative PPP would hold during the sample period. Alternatively, the LRER may be estimated as the trend or mean value to which the RER tends to return in the long term under PPP theory; and misalignment is then measured as the deviation from this trend or mean value.

Since all the other methodologies for measuring misalignment, including the trade-equations approach, are much more time-consuming to implement than the above relative PPP–based approaches, these are often the only feasible methodologies for multicountry studies in which the amount of time that can be devoted to individual country cases is limited. For the same reason, PPP-based graphical analysis is also widely used for making initial diagnoses of individual countries and for identifying hypotheses for analysis using more sophisticated techniques.

The trade equations–elasticities methodology is the second of the standard operational approaches for estimating the LRER. Although there are a number of variations of this methodology, the key quantitative relationships in each are relatively straightforward and transparent. Each of the variants of this methodology involves the same three basic analytical tasks. First, trade equations or trade elasticities are used to establish a quantitative relationship between the RER, imports, exports, and, hence, the resource balance. Second, a target, norm, or equilibrium resource balance is determined using independent projections of the saving-investment balance or of sustainable capital flows. And, third, the actual resource balance in the initial year is adjusted for changes in cyclical, exogenous, and policy variables that affect it in order to estimate the underlying structural balance and provide an appropriate basis for computing the change required in the initial RER. The quantitative relationship between the RER and the resource balance established in the first step is then used to calculate the appreciation or depreciation in the initial RER required to move the resource balance from its adjusted level in the initial year to the target level, everything else remaining the same. The estimated long-run equilibrium RER is the one that corresponds to the target or equilibrium resource balance.

The trade-equations-elasticities methodology permits taking into account permanent changes in some of the fundamental determinants of the RER. The methodology can directly address the relative price effects of changes in the terms of trade and tariff rates, and cover, at least in a back-of-the-envelope fashion, permanent changes in most of the other fundamental exogenous and policy variables in which one may be interested. Like the relative-PPP-based approach, the trade-equations methodology can also provide useful inputs for more complex ones. For example, adjusting the initial resource balance, determining a target resource balance, and projecting exogenous variables are steps common to many of the approaches used for estimating equilibrium real exchange rates. The analytical techniques for carrying out these steps, which are set out in this chapter, are used both with the trade-equations methodology and with some of the other methodologies discussed in the subsequent chapters of Part III of this book.

As noted above, a parallel exchange rate has sometimes been used as an additional indicator of distortions in the foreign exchange market and potential misalignment. However, because exchange rate misalignment does not necessarily lead to the development of a parallel market and parallel rates are much less common than they were a decade ago, opportunities to apply this approach are limited. Moreover, the approach turns out to be fraught with analytical difficulties. For both reasons, the existence of a parallel foreign exchange market is considered as a special case in Part IV of this volume. There the chapter by Ghei and Kamin examines the relationship between the parallel and the unified equilibrium exchange rates and considers the usefulness of the parallel rate as a guide for determining a unified exchange rate.

This chapter discusses the two standard operational approaches for estimating the LRER. The structure of the chapter is as follows. The following section first sets the PPP-based approach in the context of recent theoretical and empirical work on the determination of equilibrium RERs and then discusses the interpretation and usefulness of PPP-based estimates of misalignment. The remainder of the chapter goes on to consider alternative ways of carrying out the three basic analytical tasks involved in implementing the trade-equations methodology. Since the trade-equations methodology is more complex than the PPP-based approach, the rest of the chapter is considerably longer than the discussion in the following section on the PPP-based approach. The first section on the trade-equations approach discusses the use of trade equations and trade elasticities to establish quantitative relationships between the RER and the resource balance. It also presents a specific example of a trade-elasticities methodology employing a three-good framework (with exports, imports, and domestic goods) that is suitable for use in low-income countries with minimal data in which changes in the terms of trade and commercial policy are important considerations. Then come two sections on the resource balance. The first of these examines alternative methods of determining a target resource balance using saving-investment balance and sustainable capital flows approaches. The second then considers techniques for adjusting the initial resource balance to reflect changes in cyclical, exogenous, and policy variables affecting it in order to estimate the underlying structural balance. The final section concludes with a brief discussion of the advantages and limitations of the trade-equations methodology. The various analytical techniques are illustrated with empirical examples for Côte d'Ivoire at the time of the devaluation of the CFA francs in 1994.

The Relative PPP-Based Approach to RER Misalignment

As noted above, the simplest methods of estimating the long-run equilibrium RER are based on relative PPP. Although more sophisticated methodologies that take into account variations in the fundamentals determining the LRER have been developed, the PPP-based approaches are still widely used in both graphical analyses of individual countries and in econometric analyses of large multicountry samples because of the relative ease with which these can be implemented.

The use of a relative-PPP-based methodology can be justified in either of two ways. On the one hand, the analyst may simply adopt ex ante the traditional relative-PPP view on the determination of the long-run equilibrium real exchange rate, which essentially takes the LRER to be a constant. On the other hand, the analyst may view the LRER as being determined by a broad set of fundamentals, which may turn out ex post to be stationary in a time-series sense for the specific country concerned. In the first case, the decision to apply the PPP approach would be made without considering the data. In the second case, the PPP approach would be adapted only after the RER for the country concerned passes a test of stationarity.

Whichever justification for using relative PPP is adopted in a specific case, theoretical and empirical work on PPP has suggested that the equilibrium RER may be estimated in two ways—using either a base-year or a long-term trend value. This section gives an updated presentation of these two standard techniques for estimating the LRER and then discusses the interpretation of such PPP-based analyses.

Base-Year Estimates of the Equilibrium RER

When relative PPP is assumed to hold ex ante, measuring the equilibrium real exchange rate essentially involves removing the effects of nonsytematic transitory shocks. In practice, these are eliminated by identifying a base period in which such shocks are believed, on the basis of independent evidence, to have been negligible—a procedure that ensures that the actual RER coincided with its equilibrium-PPP value in the base period. Thus the actual RER in the base period represents the estimate of the equilibrium rate, and the nominal exchange rate consistent with the LRER from that moment on can be calculated by simply adjusting the nominal exchange rate for the cumulative difference between domestic and foreign inflation.

The alternative case is that the LRER is interpreted as subject to change in response to changes in underlying fundamentals but turns out empirically to be stationary for a particular country. In this case, the stationarity of the RER forces the analyst to take the position that its fundamental determinants are either individually stationary—that is, their "permanent" values have not changed during the sample period although the fundamentals may have been subject to transitory variations—or that any nonstationary fundamentals must be cointegrated among themselves. In either situation, the LRER can still be measured using a base-year value, although the identification of a suitable base year is more complicated under their interpretation. In this case, the base-year method for estimating the equilibrium RER involves analyzing the movements in the fundamental variables determining the LRER to identify a base year in which, on average, these fundamentals, and hence the RER, were at sustainable levels. If the fundamental variables do not change after the base year, or return to their level in that year, then the LRER should also remain at the base-year level. Misalignment is then measured as the difference between the actual RER in the current year and its (unchanged) equilibrium value in the base year.[2] Note that the expenditure-PPP version of the external RER (usually computed with CPIs) should be used both in the base-year analysis and in the trend analysis discussed below since this RER concept is the one employed in relative-PPP theory.

---

2. Appreciations, depreciations, and misalignment may be expressed in either domestic- or foreign-currency terms. Formulas for converting from one to the other are given in appendix C.

The base-year approach is most useful in cases in which all movements after the base year result from either nominal shocks (which temporarily cause the actual RER to diverge from its equilibrium level) or from transitory movements in the fundamentals. However, if the fundamentals change permanently after the base year, so too will the LRER.[3] In this case, the base-year approach will provide little guidance on the RER's new equilibrium value until a new base year has been established. In the base-year approach everything thus depends upon the identification of a suitable base year.

The definition of the long-run equilibrium RER in Part II suggests the criteria for selecting a representative base or equilibrium year. Recall that this definition requires that the current account deficit can be financed by a "sustainable" level of capital flows and that the market for nontraded (or domestic) goods also be in a sustainable equilibrium for given values of the predetermined, exogenous, and policy variables that influence these objectives. As mentioned above, the procedure for choosing the base year also depends upon whether the rationale underlying the procedure is a simple ex ante relative-PPP-based one or a more sophisticated one in which the real exchange rate is driven by stationary fundamentals. In the simple PPP case, the "independent evidence" of equilibrium referred to previously is likely to concern the behavior of a particular outcome variable, such as the resource balance.

In contrast, from the "stationary fundamentals" perspective, the base year chosen should be a recent year in which the actual exchange rate is believed to have been close to its equilibrium value because all the fundamentals were close to their sustainable values. As explained in the survey of empirical estimation in Chapter 5, the set of fundamentals to be considered in choosing a base year may include both exogenous and policy variables. In practice, when selecting base years, one usually focuses first on the external balance criteria, typically interpreted as choosing a year with a reasonable or normal current account (or resource) deficit for the country concerned. For assessing the sustainability of exogenous variables, the analyst looks for terms of trade that are reasonably close to their likely long-term trend levels and capital flows that are consistent in amount and terms both with the likely longer-term availability of capital and with the country's debt-servicing capacity. For assessing the sustainability and desirability of policy or objective variables, one looks at growth, investment, employment, and inflation performance and compares these to the country's long-run policy targets.

---

3. In addition, if the law of one price does not hold or only holds loosely, the return to a base-year value could be quite slow even after a purely nominal shock to the exchange rate, as domestic prices may be quite sticky and the actual RER will tend to follow the nominal RER.

Other things being equal, it is also desirable to select as recent a base year as possible to minimize the changes in the economy's structure taking place between the base year and the current year. Because a year that is appropriate as a base for a particular country may not be appropriate for another, country-specific rather than standardized base years should be used when measuring misalignment relative to a base year.[4]

The Devarajan-Lewis-Robinson (DLR) constant-elasticities model, the econometric model, and the reduced-form econometric methodology presented in Chapters 8, 9, and 10, respectively, also employ base periods, like those used here, in which the observed RER equals the equilibrium RER. The criteria for selecting these base periods are essentially the same under these methodologies so that the base period used for the relative-PPP-based analysis may also be used with the more sophisticated methodologies.

A common problem in determining an appropriate base year is that, because of policy shortcomings and external constraints, years in which exogenous variables are at sustainable levels are not always years in which policy variables were at desirable levels. For example, historically, desirable growth and investment levels have sometimes been attained only when the terms of trade have been temporarily inflated or capital flows have been unsustainable. Conversely, sustainable terms of trade and capital flows have often been associated with undesirable growth and investment outcomes. Hence, in determining when the RER was near its long-run equilibrium value and selecting a corresponding base year, one is often forced to make tradeoffs between sustainability and desirability and to take these tradeoffs into account in an ad hoc way in subsequent qualitative analysis. Moreover, in both historical and forward-looking analysis, some care is needed in analyzing the movements of the fundamentals to identify shifts in these or breaks in time series that could indicate that a change in the base year is needed. As a result, the choice of a base year may be subjective; and reasonable alternatives should be considered when they are available.

For the Côte d'Ivoire examples shown in the graphs in this section, the RER was nonstationary, as explained in Chapter 10, and 1985 was chosen as the base or equilibrium year for analytical purposes. This was the most recent year before the devaluation year of 1994, in which both the terms of trade and capital flows were at broadly sustainable levels and there was reasonable growth and low inflation. This choice, however,

---

4. The standard procedure is to select the RER for the base year as its equilibrium value. However, because of lags in the effects of the RER on the economy, one could also argue that the RER for the preceding year or a three-year moving average centered on the preceding year would be a more accurate estimate of the rate that actually generated the base-year equilibrium.

has elements of both unsustainability and undesirability. The situation in 1985 was unsustainable in that the debt service burden was too heavy for the long term and the terms of trade were more favorable than their historical trend. It was also undesirable in that the investment level was too low to support the desired long-term growth rate and trade policy was too restrictive to promote accelerated export and productivity growth. Hence, even in 1985 the actual RER was probably overvalued relative to the equilibrium RER in normative terms and even somewhat overvalued in positive terms. Furthermore, as a result of the sharp decline in the terms of trade in subsequent years, the equilibrium RER probably depreciated in the 1986–93 period rather than remaining constant at the 1985 base-year level as assumed in the PPP-based analysis.

The effect that choosing different base years can have on PPP-based analysis is illustrated in figure 7.1. In the long debate over the overvaluation of the CFA franc, most of those arguing for a devaluation chose 1985 as the best available base year. This choice indicated that on the eve of the devaluation in 1993 Côte d'Ivoire's actual real effective exchange rate (REER) had appreciated by 37 percent relative to the equilibrium base year. In contrast, some of those arguing for maintaining the existing parity chose 1980 as a base year, a choice which showed that Côte d'Ivoire's actual REER in 1993 was close to its base-year level. Note, in addition, that the use of either year as a base assumes that the equilibrium RER remained constant at the level of that year. If, however, as discussed in the preceding paragraph, the sustainable values of the terms of trade or other fundamentals in fact deteriorated after the base year, the equilibrium RER would depreciate. The use of either base year would thus give an underestimate of the misalignment.

Means for Short Base Periods

For sustainability of predetermined variables, theoretically it would be desirable to have an equilibrium period, rather than just a single equilibrium year, so that the predetermined variables have time to approach their steady-state values. In addition, in practice all of the fundamentals will not necessarily be at sustainable levels in precisely the same year. One way of dealing with these problems is to use the average value of the RER over a short equilibrium period as a base. However, the utility of this alternative empirically depends very much on the situation in the particular country concerned. In some circumstances, particularly when an appropriate choice of base year is not obvious or when a country has a market-determined exchange rate that fluctuates significantly year to year, a mean for a short time period may be a more representative indicator of the equilibrium value of the RER than a single base-year estimate. In other cases, equilibrium periods may be limited to little

Figure 7.1 *The REER for Côte d'Ivoire, 1970–95 (Base Years 1985=100 and 1980=100)*

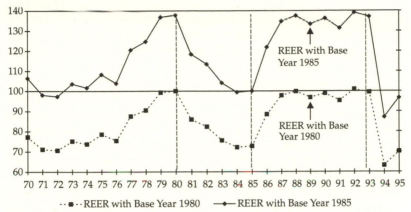

--■--REER with Base Year 1980   --◆--REER with Base Year 1985

Note: The REER has been calculated using CPIs, weighted average parallel and official exchange rates, and adjusted IFS country weights. An upward movement is an appreciation of the REER.
Source: Computed from World Bank data.

more than a year or two by the volatility of the terms of trade, capital flows, or other fundamentals. In Côte d'Ivoire, for example, the longest period in the 1980s that might reasonably have been used as a base was 1985–86. If this two-year period had been used as a base together with a one-year lag in the RER, the results would have been similar to those from using 1985 because the average RER for 1984–85 was almost equal to that in 1985. However, when, as in this case, some exogenous or policy variables diverge in the same direction from sustainable levels for the entire period, the mean value of the RER for the period may not reflect the sustainable values of these variables any better than does the RER for a single year.

Long-Period Mean and Trend PPP Estimates of the Equilibrium RER

One way of dealing with fluctuations in the fundamentals during the sample period is to estimate their sustainable values on the basis of their sample means or, in the trend-stationary case, as their trend values within the sample. In effect, this procedure amounts to estimating the LRER as the sample mean or the trend value of the RER within the sample, rather than as the particular value of the RER in a specified base year. Hence, instead of trying to identify a particular year or short span of years in which the RER is believed to be at its equilibrium level, one tries to identify the long-term trend value toward which the actual RER tends. Thus, the LRER could be estimated as being the mean value of the RER over a long period of time or as evolving along a deterministic or stochastic trend. Justification for both procedures can be found in the literature.

However, as discussed in the survey of empirical research on PPP in Chapter 5, the evidence supporting relative PPP is not that strong; and, hence, some care is needed in using this procedure. For example, according to Clark and others (1994): "Empirical evidence suggests that PPP-based indicators may be useful to explain *long-run* movements in exchange rates among industrial countries, but less so to explain movements of these exchange rates in the short run, or of exchange rates between industrial and developing countries, either in the long or the short run." Hence, before deciding whether to use a long-period mean or a trend as a base for a particular developing country, time-series data for its RER should be analyzed to determine, if possible, whether its RER has been stationary for the sample period as illustrated for Côte d'Ivoire and Burkina Faso in Chapter 10 on the single-equation methodology. Unfortunately, sometimes the short time period for which RER data are available and the weak power of unit-root tests will make it impossible to determine whether the RER is stationary or nonstationary for the sample period. Both possibilities should then be considered.

Means for Long Time Periods.

The *long-run* referred to in the above citation for which relative PPP has been found to hold for a few industrial countries is in fact very long—specifically, periods of 70 to 100 years, over which both nominal and real shocks to the external RER may prove transitory. In addition, ultra-long-term relative PPP has been shown to hold only for a small group of industrial countries with fairly similar income levels. The long-term behavior of RERs between developing and industrial countries at quite different income levels, which is our primary interest here, could be equally different. If a sufficiently long data series is available for a particular developing country, the equilibrium value of the RER in the very long term could be determined as its mean; and RER misalignment could be measured accordingly. However, data for 70 to 100 years are only rarely available for developing countries. Data for even 20 to 30 years are hard to come by for many low-income and transition economies. Since PPP theory permits extended periods of misalignment during which the actual RER diverges from its long-term equilibrium value and empirical studies of PPP have found substantial volatility in RERs and only very slow convergence toward the mean, the significance of a mean for anything other than a very long period is not clear. Despite the weakness of the theoretical and empirical support for PPP, it is entirely possible that, as in the Burkina Faso case in Chapter 10, the RER for a particular country will be stationary for a given sample period. In this case, the mean value of the RER for the sample period will be the best estimate of its equilibrium value. However, when available time-series data are long enough neither for determining with any accuracy whether the RER for a particular country is stationary or nonstationary nor for computing a meaningful long-term mean, a base-year estimate of the equilibrium RER is likely to be preferable.

Trend Estimates of the Equilibrium RER

As discussed in the chapter on the two-good internal RER and the survey of empirical research, the Balassa-Samuelson effect provides theoretical justification for observing persistent long-term trends in the equilibrium RER. Countries experiencing significantly higher or lower productivity growth than their trading partners should show a statistically significant long-term trend appreciation or depreciation in their external RER. Demand factors (for example, a high-income elasticity of demand for services and other nontraded goods) or long-term trends in other fundamentals (for example, a sustained deterioration in the terms of trade) can also generate trends in the RER. In samples for which the RER is nonstationary, such trends are more meaningful measures of the equilibrium RER than the mean; and misalignment should be measured relative to the trend value of the RER rather than relative to its mean. Such time trends can be either deterministic or stochastic. Figure 7.2 shows the time trends in the RER for Côte d'Ivoire and compares these to the mean and 1985 base-year values of the equilibrium RER. Since empirically it is very hard to distinguish between deterministic and stochastic time trends with short noisy time-series data, deterministic trends have been used in figure 7.2 for simplicity.

Interpretation of PPP-Based Analyses

Five points concerning the interpretation of analyses based on relative PPP are worth noting: (a) the alternative of measuring competitiveness only in terms of goods that are internationally traded, (b) the relationship between the expenditure-PPP external RER and the internal RER, (c) the effects of structural breaks in the RER series, (d) statistical indicators of misalignment from multicountry studies, and (e) measures of misalignment based on data for standardized baskets of goods from the International Comparison Programme (ICP).

Figure 7.2 Côte d'Ivoire: The REER—Actual Values, Average Values, and Time Trends, 1967–85 and 1986–93 (1985=100)

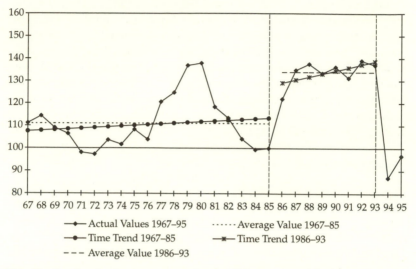

———Actual Values 1967–95   ⋯⋯⋯Average Value 1967–85
———Time Trend 1967–85   —✻—Time Trend 1986–93
– – – Average Value 1986–93

Note: The time trend value was computed as an OLS regression of the logarithm of the REER and a time trend. The annual growth rate is 0.3 percent in 1967–85 and 1.0 percent in 1986–93. The REER was computed using CPIs, adjusted country weights, and weighted average official and parallel exchange rates. An upward movement of the REER is an appreciation. *Source:* Computed from World Bank data.

Competitiveness in Internationally Traded Goods: An Alternative Approach

The base-year and trend approaches for measuring RER misalignment were originally developed for use with the expenditure-PPP version of external RER. However, they can be used equally well with the external RER for traded goods since relative PPP can be applied to traded goods as an interpretation of the law of one price. As discussed in the chapter on the external RER, it can, in fact, be quite reasonably argued that the entire foregoing analysis should be in terms of the external RER for traded goods rather than the expenditure-PPP version using CPIs.

Theoretically, somewhat different behavior should be expected in the prices of homogeneous and differentiated traded goods, with the external RER for homogeneous traded goods obeying relative PPP more closely than the RER for differentiated traded goods.[5] Unfortunately,

---

5. Although the theoretical basis for expecting relative PPP to hold for internationally traded goods is stronger than for all goods (both traded and nontraded), Isard and Faruquee (1998) note that the hypothesis that the relative price of traded

data on the relative prices of internationally traded goods are only available for recent years for industrial countries and often not available at all for developing countries. Because of the shortage of data, relatively little empirical research has been done for industrial countries, and even less research for developing countries, on whether relative PPP holds for traded goods.

When the required data are available, it is useful to examine the behavior of the external RERs for both homogeneous and differentiated traded goods. Unfortunately, only limited data are available for the prices of traded goods in Côte d'Ivoire. Since these data have already been presented in figures 2.12 and 2.13 in Chapter 2 on the external RER and the application of the techniques presented above to traded goods is straightforward, the external RER for traded goods is not shown here.

Relationship to the Internal RER

Because of the Belassa-Samuelson effect and highly income-elastic demand for nontraded goods, all countries in which productivity grows faster in the traded-goods sector than in the nontraded-goods sector, the common experience, should experience a sustained trend appreciation in the equilibrium internal RER. This pattern is in fact what has been observed in studies of the internal RER in industrial countries. De Gregorio, Giovannini, and Wolf (1994), for example, find that for 14 industrial countries the internal RER appreciated almost uniformly at an average rate of more than 1 percent per year in the period 1970–85. Furthermore, as explained in earlier chapters, it is entirely possible and consistent for the external RER for all goods, the external RER for traded goods, and the internal RERs to follow different trends. The typical pattern for a country experiencing more rapid productivity growth than its trading partners is a rapidly appreciating internal RER, a more slowly

---

goods should remain constant over time can still be questioned on the following grounds: "(1) the composition of tradable goods across countries can change over time; (2) changes over time in the relative prices of different tradables can contribute to deviations from PPP insofar as the weights of different categories of tradable goods in national price or cost indices differ across countries; and (3) the scope for arbitraging price or cost differentials across countries can be affected by the liberalization of trade and foreign exchange restrictions, reductions in transportation costs, or changes in other components of the costs of market penetration." But they conclude that "these limitations notwithstanding, calculations of different measures of international price and cost competitiveness can often be helpful when judging whether exchange rates are reasonably close to medium-run equilibrium levels."

appreciating external RER for all goods, and a constant or depreciating external RER for traded goods. The internal RER is, in addition, generally more useful than the external RER in assessing the magnitude of real shocks.

Although relative PPP is not directly applicable to the internal RERs, analytically it is still useful to know how the internal RERs have behaved both relative to trend and to their values in the last equilibrium (base) year. Figures 7.3 and 7.4 thus look separately at the internal RERs for imports and exports for Côte d'Ivoire. Figure 7.3 indicates that the internal RER for imports behaved in a similar fashion to the expenditure-PPP external RER, jumping upward by 20 percent during 1985–86 because of the appreciation of the nominal effective exchange rate (NEER) and then remaining relatively stable until the 1994 devaluation. As figure 7.4 shows, the export sector was more severely affected than the import competing sector. Because of the sustained decline in the prices of its major export commodities (primarily coffee and cocoa) and devaluations by competing developing-country exporters, Côte d'Ivoire's internal RER for exports appreciated strongly throughout the entire period, rising by almost 80 percent during 1986–93, four times the appreciation in the RER for imports.

Structural Breaks

Large external shocks and major regime shifts can cause structural breaks in the RER data for developing countries and create significant problems in interpreting these. Such structural breaks can cause nonstationarity in the RER and lead to significant shifts in means, trends, and base years.

The data for Côte d'Ivoire provide a good example of the possible effects of structural breaks. The combination of the large drop in Côte d'Ivoire's terms of trade after 1985 and the strong appreciation in its NEER shown in figure 7.5 caused a marked change in the external environment that the country faced, and its RER was nonstationary as discussed in Chapter 10. Since figure 7.5 shows that the NEER and the terms of trade behaved in significantly different ways in the periods 1967–85 and 1986–93, figures 7.2–7.4 take 1985 as the dividing point between two different time periods and give the means and time trend values separately for the 1967–85 and the 1986–93 periods. During 1967–85, the average value of the expenditure-PPP external RER was 10 percent more appreciated than the 1985 base-year level but showed little trend movement over the period. In the 1986–93 period, in contrast, the external RER appreciated strongly and was, on average, nearly 30 percent more appreciated than in the 1985 base year.

Figure 7.3 Côte d'Ivoire: The REER and the Internal RER for Imports—Actual Values, Average Values, and Time Trends, 1970–85 and 1986–93 (1985=100)

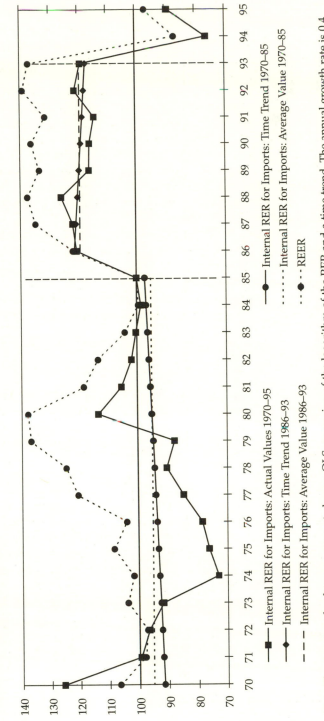

— Internal RER for Imports: Actual Values 1970–95
■ Internal RER for Imports: Time Trend 1986–93
- - Internal RER for Imports: Average Value 1986–93

— Internal RER for Imports: Time Trend 1970–85
···· Internal RER for Imports: Average Value 1970–85
····● REER

Note: The time trend value was computed as an OLS regression of the logarithm of the RER and a time trend. The annual growth rate is 0.4 percent in 1970–85 and –0.5 percent in 1986–93. The REER was computed using CPIs, adjusted country weights, and weighted average official and parallel exchange rates. An upward movement is an appreciation.

Source: Computed from World Bank data.

307

Figure 7.4 Côte d'Ivoire: The REER and the Internal RER for Exports—Actual Values, Average Values, and Time Trends, 1970–85 and 1986–93 (1985=100)

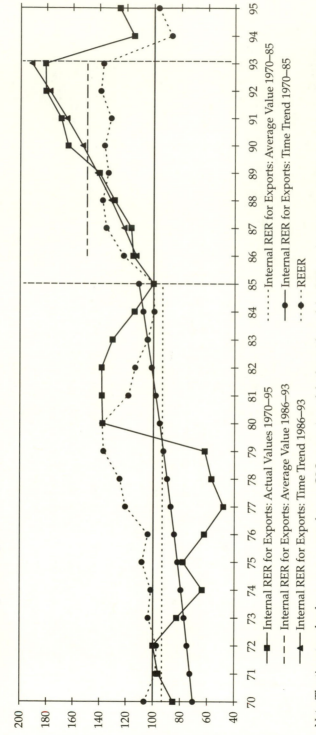

── Internal RER for Exports: Actual Values 1970–95

- - - Internal RER for Exports: Average Value 1986–93

─▲─ Internal RER for Exports: Time Trend 1986–93

········· Internal RER for Exports: Average Value 1970–95

─●─ Internal RER for Exports: Time Trend 1970–85

·····●····· REER

Note: The time trend value was computed as an OLS regression of the logarithm of the RER and a time trend. The annual growth rate is 3.1 percent in 1970–85 and 7.9 percent in 1986–93. The REER was computed using CPIs, adjusted country weights, and weighted average official and parallel exchange rates. An upward movement is an appreciation.
Source: Computed from World Bank data.

Statistical Indicators of RER Misalignment

Because of the availability of CPIs for calculating the expenditure-PPP version of the RER in most developing countries and the relative ease of computing PPP-based measures of misalignment, these measures have been used in numerous multicountry econometric studies. These studies have noted some empirical regularities that are useful in assessing RER misalignment in individual countries. Since selection of appropriate base years requires detailed knowledge of individual countries and can be criticized as subjective, most large multicountry studies have measured misalignment of the RER relative to its long-term mean or trend value; and hence their insights apply to misalignment measured in this way. In Chapter 12, for example, in analyzing parallel market exchange rates for a sample of 24 developing countries, Ghei and Kamin use a simple relative PPP-based measure for the equilibrium unified RER—the average of the official real exchange over long periods of time during which a county's exchange markets were unified.

Large appreciations of the actual RER relative to its trend value, which are easily detectable in a PPP-based analysis, are often warning signs of serious exchange rate misalignment and potential currency crises. For

Figure 7.5 *Côte d'Ivoire: The Real Effective Exchange Rate (REER), the NEER, and the Terms of Trade, 1970–95 (1985=100)*

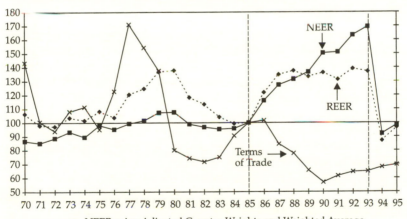

—■—NEER using Adjusted Country Weights and Weighted Average
     Official and Parallel Exchange Rates

··◆··REER using CPIs, Adjusted Country Weights, and Weighted
     Average Official and Parallel Exchange Rates

—×—Terms of Trade

Note: An upward movement is an appreciation of the REER.
Source: Computed from World Bank data.

example, Milesi-Ferretti and Razin (1996, 1998) use the degree of appreciation of the RER relative to its 25-year average (median) as a benchmark for assessing the sustainability of current account deficits and find
that even this crude measure of misalignment is a useful predictor of
currency crises. Kaminsky, Lizondo, and Reinhart (1997) find that substantial appreciation of the RER above its trend value is a warning sign
of a future devaluation and that the 10 percent of RER observations that
are the farthest from the trend are accurate leading indicators of a currency crisis within the next 24 months. Similarly, Goldfajn and Valdes
(1996, 1997) analyze a large set of RER appreciations for 93 countries
from 1960 to 1994 and find that for large real appreciations of 15 percent
to 35 percent relative to trend the probability of a subsequent devaluation ranged from 68 percent for real appreciations of 15 percent or more
to 100 percent for appreciations exceeding 35 percent. Hence, even if
there is some uncertainty about the precise level of the equilibrium RER,
large appreciations in a short period of time are a warning sign of misalignment. Finally, volatility of the real exchange rate, which is readily
measurable, implies that the RER spends more time farther away from
its equilibrium level. Volatility is, as noted in Chapter 11 on the effect of
the RER on trade flows, a deterrent to export growth; and, as Razin and
Collins (1997) have observed, volatility has served in effect as a reasonable proxy for misalignment in some multicountry studies.

Measures of Misalignment Based on International Comparison Program Data

Equilibrium exchange rates can be based on absolute as well as relative
PPP. As explained in the chapter on the external RER, measurement of
absolute PPP requires the use of standardized baskets of goods. For example, the "Big Mac Index" is a simple one-good absolute-PPP exchange
rate, which *The Economist* uses as an informal indicator of the equilibrium nominal exchange rate. It is simply the ratio of the domestic-currency
price of a Big Mac in the home country to its price in the numeraire
country.[6] However, data for more comprehensive measures of absolute
PPP have been hard to come by.

Because relative-PPP-based measures of misalignment have various
theoretical shortcomings and estimating equilibrium exchange rates
using the more sophisticated methodologies discussed later in this vol-

---

6. See *The Economist* (1995, August 26) and (1996, April 27). In a lighter vein,
Cumby (1996) analyzes data for 14 countries for the "Big Mac Index" and finds
that their exchange rates converge to "Big Mac parity" twice as fast as to relative
PPP.

ume is quite time-consuming, researchers have long sought a methodology simple enough to use in measuring misalignment for panel data for a large number of countries. Until recently, the lack of price data for representative standardized baskets of goods had inhibited the empirical use of absolute PPP for this purpose. Hence, as the Summers-Heston data for standardized baskets of goods has become available for 90 or so countries from the International Comparison Programme (ICP) described in appendix A to Chapter 2, some researchers have utilized these to develop alternative simplified procedures for estimating equilibrium exchange rates.

Aggregate ICP exchange rates have themselves occasionally been used to analyze trade distortions and exchange rate misalignment. Nominal exchange rates for developing countries derived from the ICP data are generally lower (less appreciated) than nominal market exchange rates with the U.S. dollar because of the Balassa-Samuelson effect discussed in Chapters 3, 5, and 6. Figure 7.6, which compares the aggregate ICP dollar exchange rate for GDP for Côte d'Ivoire with the official rate, illustrates this point. The magnitude of the differences between aggregate ICP exchange rates and nominal exchange rates also tends to vary inversely with per capita income.[7]

A predictable tendency in the ICP data for the relative price levels of countries to vary positively with their relative income levels as a result of the Balassa-Samuelson effect has been exploited by a number of researchers to derive estimates of the equilibrium RER. Dollar (1992) regresses the relative price levels of the standardized baskets of goods from the ICP data on relative per capita GDP. This regression gives him a norm that he considers as the equilibrium relationship between the free trade RER and per capita income. Deviations from this norm give a measure of the combined effects of trade and exchange rate policy on outward orientation. Bosworth, Collins, and Chen (1996) employ a procedure similar to Dollar's to derive a measure of exchange rate misalignment that they then use in analyzing the factors affecting growth in an 88-country sample. Razin and Collins (1997) use data on the relative international price of the standardized basket of consumption goods and services in different countries as a measure of the real exchange rate. This measure is then regressed on the fundamental variables determining the RER using panel data, and the fitted values are used as an estimate of the equilibrium RER.

---

7. See, for example, Rogoff (1996) for data and regression results documenting these stylized facts.

Figure 7.6 *Côte d'Ivoire: The International Comparison Programme and Official Exchange Rates with the U.S. Dollar*

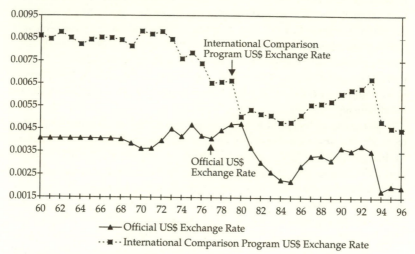

Note: An upward movement is an appreciation.
Source: Computed from World Bank data.

Such statistical analyses of ICP exchange rates may give broad indications of misalignment suitable for use in general multicountry studies and provide country-specific information that is useful in particular cases. However, more research is needed on the relationship between these general measures of misalignment and those from the methodologies discussed elsewhere in this volume before basing policy recommendations for individual countries on ICP exchange rates.

Conclusion: Advantages and Limitations of the Relative-PPP-Based Approach

The relative-PPP-based approach set out above has a number of practical advantages in estimating the equilibrium RER in low-income developing countries. Its data requirements are limited. The methodology is both straightforward and transparent. With simple computer spreadsheets it is easy to run extensive sensitivity analyses of the results assuming different base years or means. A number of multicountry statistical analyses of misalignment are also available for comparative purposes. These are significant practical advantages for balance-of-payments management in a developing country in which data and professional manpower may both be limited. Relative-PPP-based measures of misalignment can also be quite useful in high-inflation countries where shocks to the external RER are primarily nominal ones. Thus, for example, the implementation of real exchange rate targeting has often relied on simple relative-PPP-based rules.[8]

The PPP-based approach does have some major limitations, however. In developing countries, lack of data on the prices of internationally traded goods usually forces one to use the external RER for all goods (computed with CPIs) rather than the theoretically preferable external RER for traded goods. The PPP-based analysis also relies on relatively simple base-year or mean-trend estimates of the equilibrium RER. If there are structural breaks in the time-series data for the RER or permanent changes in the fundamentals and hence in the equilibrium RER, base-period or mean estimates of misalignment may no longer be relevant, and PPP analysis is of little help in determining the new equilibrium RER. Moreover, real exchange rates can be quite volatile—and convergence to the mean, if it occurs at all, is typically quite slow. Hence, the RER may diverge from a PPP-based equilibrium for long periods, and it may be of little practical use for policy purposes.

However, all of the other methodologies for measuring misalignment, including the trade-equations approach discussed below, are much more time-consuming to implement than the relative-PPP-based approaches. Thus the relative-PPP-based approaches are often the only feasible methodologies for multicountry studies in which the amount of time that can be devoted to individual country cases is limited. For the same reason, PPP-based analysis is also widely used for making initial diagnoses of individual countries and for identifying hypotheses for analysis using more sophisticated techniques. A comparison of the movements of the fundamentals with movements of the RER since the last equilibrium may also be useful for detecting cases of possible misalignment. The PPP-based methodology thus provides a starting point—it may be used alone, when nothing else is available, or as a reference point when more sophisticated methodologies are also used.

The Trade-Equations Approach: Establishing the Quantitative Relationship between the RER and the Resource Balance

The second of the established operational methodologies for measuring exchange rate misalignment is the trade-equations approach. The

---

8. See, for example, Calvo, Reinhart, and Vegh (1995).

general rubric "trade-equations approach" is used here to cover a group of similar methodologies, all of which involve three basic analytical tasks:

a. Using trade equations or trade elasticities to establish a quantitative relationship between the RER, imports, exports, and, hence, the resource balance;
b. Independently determining a target, norm, or equilibrium resource balance using projections of the saving-investment balance or sustainable capital flows; and
c. Estimating the underlying or structural resource balance by adjusting the actual resource balance in the initial year for cyclical, exogenous, and policy changes that affect it.

The quantitative relationship between the RER and the resource balance established in task (a) is then used to calculate the appreciation or depreciation in the initial RER required to move the resource balance from its adjusted level in the initial year to its target level, everything else remaining the same. The estimated long-run equilibrium RER is the one that corresponds to the target or equilibrium resource balance. The following section of this chapter discusses task (a). Tasks (b) and (c) are taken up in the subsequent two sections.

Because of the different structures of industrial and low-income developing economies and the greater availability of data in the former, trade is usually modeled in somewhat different fashions for the two groups. In industrial countries, trade equations based on the Mundell-Fleming production structure, the subject of the first part of this section, are usually used. In developing countries, in contrast, a trade-elasticities approach based on a three-good production structure, the subject of the last part of this section, is often employed.

The Mundell-Fleming Framework—Industrial Countries

The general analytical framework used in the trade-equations methodology in industrial countries usually employs equations 7.1 through 7.3:

(7.1) $$\log M = \varepsilon_M \log RER + \eta_M \log Y_D + f(Z_M)$$

(7.2) $$\log X = \varepsilon_X \log RER + \eta_X \log Y_F + g(Z_X)$$

(7.3) $$\Delta RB = \Delta X - \Delta M$$

where M and X are the quantities of imports and exports, Y_D and Y_F are domestic and foreign real income, Z_M and Z_X are vectors of whatever predetermined or exogenous variables (for example, lagged values of the RER, the terms of trade, commercial policy) are relevant in a particular case, and the resource balance (RB) is expressed in real terms. The two trade equations are usually estimated econometrically to obtain values for ε_M and ε_X, the price elasticities of import and export demand, and for η_M and η_X, the income elasticities of import and export demand.

To solve the above system of three equations, domestic and foreign income are determined exogenously by setting them at full employment or some other desired level. The change in the resource balance is also set exogenously as the difference between the target and the adjusted resource balances, which are determined separately in tasks (b) and (c). One is thus left with three variables—M, X, and RER—to be determined endogenously; and the three equations are solved for these.

A number of general points about the application of the trade-equations approach to industrial economies are worth noting. First, the analytical framework used for industrial countries is usually based on the Mundell-Fleming production structure. In this framework, complete specialization of both the domestic and foreign economies in producing one composite good (their own GDPs) makes export supply functions perfectly elastic, while the domestic and foreign goods are taken to be imperfect substitutes in demand. Export and import quantities are thus demand-determined. The RER exerts its effect on the trade balance through the price elasticities of domestic demand for imports and of foreign demand for exports. Second, since industrial-country trade models focus primarily on competitiveness in the domestic and foreign markets for differentiated traded goods, the traded-goods version of the external RER (computed using relative wholesale prices or unit labor costs in the traded-goods sector) is commonly used in equations 7.2 and 7.3. Third, the estimated equilibrium exchange rates for large industrial countries like the G-7 that account for large shares of world trade need to be mutually consistent since one country's economy can have important income and relative price effects on the others', a fact that considerably complicates the estimation of equilibrium exchange rates for large industrial economies. Fourth, if the RER is quite volatile and subject to large random fluctuations, these could be reflected either in similar volatility in the resource balance or in significant statistical noise in the empirical relationship between the RER and the resource balance, either of which could complicate empirical analysis and policy making.[9]

---

9. See Knight and Scacciavillani (1998).

Both the International Monetary Fund (IMF) and the Institute for International Economics (IIE) employ the trade-equations approach for estimating equilibrium exchange rates for the G-7 countries. Major papers by Wren-Lewis and Driver (1998) for the IIE and Isard and Faruqee (1998) for the IMF documenting their approaches have been published within the last year. Since both of these papers have already been reviewed in the survey of empirical research in Chapter 5, they are not discussed further here. The reader is referred, instead, to the previous survey for a review of the papers and to the papers themselves for detailed presentations of industrial-country applications of the trade-equations methodology.

The Three-Good Framework—Developing Countries

The General Analytical Framework

An alternative analytical framework is usually adopted for small developing countries whose production structures are less flexible and whose exports are dominated by undifferentiated primary products. For these countries, imports could still reasonably be modeled by equation 7.1, in which the demand for imports depends upon the domestic price and income elasticities of demand. However, equation 7.2 for exports is more problematic in a developing-country context. For a small open developing economy that accounts for a tiny fraction of world trade, it is more appropriate to consider export demand as being infinitely price-elastic and to drop foreign income from the export equation but to allow for a finite elasticity of export supply.[10] Then the quantity of exports is determined by the elasticity of export supply. Hence, *export supply* elasticities are conventionally employed in modeling developing countries rather than export demand elasticities used in equation 7.2.

For example, Wren-Lewis and Driver (1998) follow the Mundell-Fleming tradition of modeling trade in industrial countries in terms of differentiated products that are imperfect substitutes. They estimate price elasticities of demand for exports ranging from –0.23 for Canada to –1.36 for Japan, with a median of –0.96. In contrast, the empirical evidence on RERs and trade flows in developing countries cited by Ghei and Pritchett in Chapter 11 suggests that the standard assumption of an infinite price elasticity of demand for developing-country exports is reasonable. Conversely, Wren-Lewis and Driver assume an infinite price elasticity of export supply for the G-7 countries rather than supply

---

10. Conceptually, this approach also implies supposing that the home country produces at least one other type of good besides the exportable good and, hence, requires adopting a three-good framework.

elasticities in the 1.0–2.0 range suggested for developing countries by Ghei and Pritchett.

The differences in approach to modeling trade in industrial and developing economies also lead to differences in view about the relevance of the Marshall-Lerner condition. This condition for a real depreciation to improve the resource balance measured in domestic currency terms, starting from a zero balance, requires that the sum of the absolute values of the price elasticities of *demand* for imports and exports exceed unity.[11] The Marshall-Lerner condition is satisfied for industrial countries by the average values of the price elasticities of demand for imports (–0.9) from Ghei and Pritchett and of the demand for exports (–1.0) from Wren-Lewis and Driver (1998). Although the Marshall-Lerner condition would also be satisfied by the representative values of demand elasticities for developing countries, it is not directly applicable to them for two reasons. First, the condition assumes an infinite price elasticity of export supply, whereas the empirical evidence suggests a supply elasticity of 1.0 to 2.0 for developing countries. Second, many developing countries are capital importers and start from a resource deficit rather than from the balanced position assumed in deriving the simplest version of the Marshall-Lerner condition.

Because trade models of developing countries focus on domestic resource allocation incentives, the internal RER rather than the external RER for traded goods is usually the appropriate RER measure for them. The use of the internal RER also has the advantage that the effects of changes in some fundamentals on the equilibrium RER that are difficult to handle in the Mundell-Fleming framework can easily be handled in a three-good framework with importables, exportables, and domestic goods. Because of its assumed production structure, the Mundell-Fleming framework cannot distinguish between the terms of trade and the RER. Thus, it cannot be used to analyze the impact of changes in the terms of trade and commercial policy whereas these can be readily incorporated in a three-good framework.

Finally, for analyzing small economies it is not necessary to determine a set of mutually consistent multicountry RERs as is done in modeling the G-7 economies. Rather, a simpler partial-equilibrium approach that ignores the impact of a developing country's RER and trade flows on the rest of the world can be used. Because of the relative ease with which it can be implemented and the availability of estimated elasticities from the large amount of empirical work on trade reviewed in

---

11. The resource balance measured in foreign-currency terms will almost always improve for reasons explained in footnote 40 in Chapter 11 on trade flows and the RER.

Chapter 11, the trade-elasticities approach has been widely used in operational applications in developing countries. This chapter and the subsequent one on the DLR model give two examples of trade-elasticity methodologies. Both chapters utilize three-good frameworks with exports, imports, and domestic goods and constant-elasticities assumptions. In this chapter, the relationship between the three goods is in terms of constant price elasticities of the supply of exports and of the demand for imports. The DLR model also assumes constant elasticities—but in this case they are elasticities of transformation in production between exports and domestic goods and of substitution in consumption between imports and domestic goods.[12]

A Specific Three-Good Methodology

The remainder of this section presents a specific trade-elasticities methodology that is suitable for use in low-income countries in which only limited data are available. The relationship between the resource balance, trade elasticities, and the internal RER is set in an explicit three-good framework. This formulation allows for different RERs for imports and exports and facilitates the analysis of the relative price effects of changes in the terms of trade and commercial policy.[13] Essentially, the approach involves using the definitions of the price elasticities of demand for imports and the supply of exports to replace the trade equations 7.1 and 7.2 above for imports and exports.[14] The procedure for calculating the equilibrium RER is otherwise the same as that set out above for the trade-equations approach.

Appendix A gives the detailed derivation of the basic RER, trade-elasticities, resource balance equation in a three-good framework. As shown there, the RER for imports (*RERM*) may be expressed as in equation 7.4:

$$(7.4) \qquad \frac{\Delta RERM}{RERM} = \frac{\Delta RB - \sigma_x \cdot X \left(\frac{\Delta ITT}{ITT} \right)}{\sigma_x \cdot X - \varepsilon_M \cdot M}$$

---

12. The elasticities of transformation and substitution are ratios of relative changes in the quantities of two goods rather than—as in the case of standard trade elasticities—the ratio of the relative change in the quantity of a single good to the change in its own relative price. Although these elasticities can be derived from each other mathematically, their values will generally differ.

13. This formulation requires the assumption that the elasticities of export supply and import demand are the same for changes in relative prices as for changes in the real exchange rate. This assumption is quite natural when using separate internal RERs for exports below but less so when using the PPP external RER.

14. Alternatively, a trade equation similar to equation 7.1 could also be used to express imports as a function of *RERM* and real income with the trade-elasticities formula being used for *RERX*.

where σ_X is the price elasticity of export supply; ε_M is, as above, the price elasticity of import demand; and the change in the resource balance is measured in real terms. The internal terms of trade, ITT, is defined as the domestic price of exports relative to the domestic price of imports—that is, P_{Xd}/P_{Md}. If the law of one price holds, ITT is determined exogenously by the foreign prices of imports and exports (P_{Mf} and P_{Xf}) and the home country's average trade taxes on them (t_M and t_X) as shown in equation 7.5:

$$(7.5) \qquad ITT \;=\; \frac{P_{Xd}}{P_{Md}} \;=\; \frac{P_{Xf}\left(1-t_X\right)\cdot E_{dc}}{P_{Mf}\left(1+t_M\right)\cdot E_{dc}} \;=\; \frac{P_{Xf}\left(1-t_x\right)}{P_{Mf}\left(1+t_M\right)}.$$

The RER for exports ($RERX$) is given by equation 7.6:

$$(7.6) \qquad\qquad\qquad RERX = RERM \cdot ITT.$$

Equation 7.3 for the change in the resource balance remains as stated above.

The system now contains four equations (numbers 7.3, 7.4, 7.5, and 7.6) and four endogenous variables (M, X, $RERM$, and $RERX$). It contains only the parameters, σ_X and ε_M; initial values of X, M, and ITT; and two exogenously determined variables, ΔRB and ΔITT. The determination of the change in the internal terms of trade, ΔITT, from equation 7.5 is straightforward. Exogenous projected values are used for the external prices of exports and imports, P_{Xf} and P_{Mf}. Average trade taxes on exports, t_X, and imports, t_M, are policy variables, for which assumed values are used for future years.[15]

The other exogenous variable on the right-hand side of equation 7.5 is the targeted or required change in the resource balance, ΔRB. Adjusting the initial resource balance for cyclical, exogenous, and policy changes and determining the sustainable or target resource balance are similar in the Mundell-Fleming and three-good frameworks. These two tasks, however, are considerably more complicated than determining ΔITT and are discussed separately in the following two sections of this chapter.

Once the adjusted and target resource balances have been determined, the trade-elasticity relationships are used in place of the trade equations employed in industrial countries to calculate the change in the RER needed to move it from its actual level to its equilibrium level. Thus, the computed values of ΔITT and ΔRB are plugged into the right-hand side of equation 7.4 to calculate the change in the RER for imports necessary

---

15. See the section below on adjusting the initial resource balance for a further discussion of projecting the terms of trade and trade taxes.

to achieve the required change in the resource balance. The RER for exports can then be computed using equation 7.6. After the RERs for imports and exports have been calculated, the supply response to the change in the RER (that is, the corresponding changes in the volume of imports and exports) can also be computed using the equations in appendix A.

Note, however, that equations 7.4 and 7.6 only permit determining relative prices, not nominal ones. The definitions of the internal RERs, in fact, contain two endogenous variables, the nominal exchange rate, E_{dc}, and the price of domestic goods, P_{Dd}, as well as the exogenously determined prices of exports or imports.[16] In order to determine separate values for these two endogenous variables, either the nominal exchange rate or the domestic-currency price of domestic goods needs to be exogenously specified as a nominal anchor for domestic prices.[17]

The accuracy of the equilibrium RER calculated using the trade-elasticities methodology depends upon that of the elasticity estimates used. Econometrically estimating country-specific elasticities can be both a time-consuming and problematic process in developing countries with inadequate data. However, a considerable amount of empirical work has been done on trade elasticities for a wide range of countries and products; and one of the advantages of the trade-elasticities methodology is that empirical estimation of the elasticities is not necessary in cases where data or time constraints do not permit it. Chapter 11 on trade flows and the RER summarizes the results of this empirical work and gives a good idea of what are reasonable values to assume for import and export elasticities in developing countries.

Three additional points concerning the parameters in the relationship between the internal RER, trade elasticities, and the resource balance merit further explanation and possible modification in particular applications, namely: (a) the empirical trade-elasticity estimates to be used in equation 7.4; (b) the numeraires used in measuring the elasticities and the RER; and (c) the problem of price-inelastic export demand. These are discussed in appendix A.

---

16. These two endogenous variables may be compressed into one variable (the price of domestic goods expressed in foreign-currency terms) by multiplying them together to arrive at an alternative single measure of the internal RER that is used by some authors. See, for example, the related concept of the equilibrium GDP deflator in the DLR constant elasticity model in the next chapter.

17. For a further discussion of the nominal anchor problem and a methodology for calculating consistent nominal and relative prices, see Chapter 13 on devaluations and inflation.

Determining the Target Resource Balance

Establishing a reliable quantitative relationship between the real exchange rate and the resource balance is only the first of the three major analytical tasks involved in implementing the trade-equations methodology. The second and third tasks are to determine a reasonable target for the resource balance and to adjust the initial resource balance so that it provides a satisfactory basis from which to calculate the change in the resource balance required to achieve its target level. Since the approach that one takes to adjusting the initial resource balance depends, among other things, upon how the target resource balance is determined, this section first examines the alternative methods for determining the target resource balance. The next section then considers the problem of making appropriate adjustments in the initial resource balance.

Determining an appropriate target for the resource or current account balance is an analytical step that is common to the trade-equations methodologies as a group and is also encountered when using macroeconomic models and the single-equation methodology for estimating the equilibrium RER. The trade-equations methodologies employed for industrial countries by the IMF and the IIE in the studies by Isard and Faruqee (1998) and Wren-Lewis and Driver (1998) cited earlier established target current account balances in order to calculate the equilibrium RER required to achieve these. Similarly, for developing countries, the DLR constant-elasticities model in the next chapter relies on establishing target resource balances.

The analytical problem of determining an appropriate target for the resource balance is not, however, limited just to the trade-equations methodologies. As discussed in the survey of empirical research in Chapter 5, some analysts (such as Williamson 1994 and Bayoumi and others 1994) who use large macroeconomic models must also determine target current account balances. Similarly, the reduced-form single-equation methodology set out in Chapter 10 uses a target resource balance in order to estimate the equilibrium RER in in-sample counterfactual simulations and in forward-looking out-of-sample policy applications. Hence, much of the discussion here and in the next section is relevant both to the trade-equations methodologies as a group and to a number of other methodologies for estimating the equilibrium RER.

The simplest approach to targeting is to aim at returning to the situation existing in a base year that is deemed to be satisfactory. In this case, one must chose, as in the relative-PPP-based analysis discussed earlier, an appropriate base year in which the resource or current account balance is believed to have been an equilibrium or desirable level. This approach is illustrated by Devarajan for his constant-elasticities model in the next chapter. However, the usefulness of the base-year approach in a specific application depends upon having a fairly recent base year that constitutes a reasonably satisfactory equilibrium in both positive and normative terms. Since, for the reasons explained earlier, appropriate base years are often not available, alternative methods for establishing appropriate targets for the resource balance are usually needed.

This section reviews the two basic alternative ways of determining targets for the resource or current account balance—the saving-investment balance and the sustainable capital flows approaches. It then examines the cases of aid-dependent, fully and partially creditworthy developing countries.

The National Accounts Identity and Alternative Approaches to Targeting

The basic national accounting identities (equations 7.7 and 7.8) relate GDP (Y), consumption (C), saving (S), investment (I), and exports, imports, and the resource balance. They require that the resource balance equals the saving-investment balance:

$$(7.7) \qquad Y = C + S = C + I + X - M = C + I + RB$$

$$(7.8) \qquad S - I = X - M = RB$$

where S and I are defined to include both private and public saving and investment and the identities hold in both nominal and real terms. Thus, exports, imports, and the resource balance can potentially be affected by changes in Y, C, I, or S as well as by the movements in relative prices discussed in the previous section.[18]

The resource balance is also the mirror image of the net resource transfers needed to finance it. The standard balance-of-payments accounting identities require that the resource balance equal the net resource transfer between the home country and abroad, plus the change in reserves, (with the opposite sign) as shown in equation 7.9:

---

18. Saving and investment may be further subdivided into their government and private components if a more detailed analysis (for example, of the effects of a fiscal deficit) is desired:

$$RB = S_P + S_G - I_G - I_P = S_P - I_P + FB$$

where FB is the fiscal balance. See, for example, Knight and Scacciavillani (1998).

(7.9) $RB = -(NFI + NT + NCF + \Delta RES) = -(NRT + \Delta RES)$

where *NFI* is net factor income payments or receipts (including interest on debt), *NT* is net transfers, *NCF* is net capital flows, *ΔRES* is the change in external reserves, and *NRT* is the net resource transfer.

Hence, a target resource balance can be determined either by using projections of the savings-investment balance in equation 7.8 or projections of sustainable net resource transfer and a targeted change in reserves in equation 7.9.[19] In either case, the equilibrium RER is the one that corresponds to the target resource balance. A three- to five-year time horizon is usually adopted for targeting in order to allow adequate time for the medium-term effects of changes in the RER to work through the economy as discussed in Chapter 11 on the relationship between trade flows and the RER.

Whether using the saving-investment balance or the sustainable capital flows approach in deriving a resource balance target, the trade-equations methodology employs a partial-equilibrium recursive approach in the analysis. That is, the saving-investment balance or sustainable capital flows determine the target resource balance, which then determines the target (equilibrium) RER. Any feedback effects from the RER to saving-investment and capital flows are not explicitly taken into account in the methodology.[20]

In operational applications, one also has to decide whether the resource or the current account balance is the appropriate target. The resource and current account balances are related through the balance of payments accounting identities shown in equation 7.10:

(7.10) $CAB = RB + NFI + NT = -(NCF + \Delta RES) = \Delta NFA$

where *CAB* is the current account balance and *NFA* is an economy's net stock of foreign assets broadly defined.[21] While the resource and current account balances are related, they differ in their treatment of net

---

19. Note that in both cases projections in real terms are needed since the change in the resource balance in equation 7.3 is measured in real terms.

20. See Wren-Lewis (1992) for a discussion of the implications of such recursiveness. Ideally, it would be desirable to have a full macroeconomic model to capture all the interactions and the net effects of the changes in prices and expenditures in a full general equilibrium setting such as in the macroeconomic model discussed in Chapter 9. However, as noted there, the full general-equilibrium approach is much more difficult to implement in operational applications.

21. Defined here to include the change in external reserves.

factor income and net transfers.[22] A current account balance of zero implies no change in a country's net foreign assets or liabilities, whereas a zero resource balance implies that a debtor country is borrowing to finance interest payments and its indebtedness is therefore increasing.

Whether the resource or current account balance is the appropriate variable to target depends upon the nature of the financial flows to a particular country and the approach taken to modeling these. Typically, the resource balance approach, which in effect treats interest payments as an item to be financed, is used for noncreditworthy developing countries in which an equilibrium is specified in terms of a sustainable level of capital flows. By contrast, the current account balance is usually used with the equilibrium debt stock approach. In this approach, interest payments are generally determined by the stock of the debt and an assumed interest rate, and are treated as an item to be paid on a current basis. This relationship may be written in a stylized form (abstracting from other factor service payments and transfers) as equation 7.11:

$$(7.11) \qquad\qquad CAB = RB - rD = \Delta D$$

where D is the debt stock, r is the average interest rate paid on the debt, and ΔD is the change in the debt stock. This approach is often used for creditworthy countries to allow for feedback between interest payments and the debt stock.

The Saving-Investment Balance Approach

For creditworthy industrial countries, current practice is to project the saving-investment balance to determine a target resource balance through the national accounts identity (equation 7.8). These countries typically have full access to capital markets, and both the public and private sectors usually borrow almost entirely from private sources. The standard assumption for such countries is that capital markets will provide whatever financing is required for a sustainable current account deficit. Even for these countries, however, after projecting the saving-investment balance separately, analysts typically use the rules of thumb

---

22. Note that saving measure in the saving-investment balance in equation 7.8 is domestic saving, that is, GDP minus total consumption. If total saving (domestic saving plus NFI plus NT) is used, $S - I$ will equal the current account balance rather than the resource balance. Hence, when choosing whether to target the resource or current account balance, one needs to work with the corresponding saving measure.

discussed in the capital flows section below to verify that the corresponding current account deficit is in fact sustainable.

The analytical procedures used in determining the target current account balance have evolved in the 1990s from ad hoc adjustments to trend current account balances taking into account theories of saving and investment to more systematic econometrically based projections of the saving-investment balance. For example, in using macroeconomic models to estimate equilibrium RERs for the G-7 countries in 1994, Williamson (1994) examined past current account balances in terms of (a) an analysis of investment needs based on the relative availability and growth rate of labor and other complementary factors of production and (b) a demographic life-cycle analysis of saving in order to determine whether the balances reflected rational economic behavior or misguided government policies. In cases in which the current account reflected inappropriate policies, he adjusted the balances to more appropriate levels as suggested by the saving and investment theories. These current account balances were then used as targets in the macroeconomic models to compute the equilibrium RER. Similarly, to compare the use of dynamic trade equations and the IMF's MULTIMOD model for calculating equilibrium REERs, Bayoumi and others (1994) simply assumed that all of the G-7 countries needed to aim at current account surpluses of 1 percent of GDP. A few years later when providing target current account deficits for the G-7 as inputs for Wren-Lewis's and Driver's (1998) estimates of the LRER using the trade-equations methodology, Williamson and Mahar (1998) draw on available macroeconomic projections of saving and investment from the OECD to determine target saving-investment and current account balances for the G-7 countries. Subsequently, in the IMF study by Isard and Faruqee (1998), a more systematic approach is adopted for the G-7 countries. In that study, each country's saving-investment balance is modeled econometrically as depending on its relative per capita income, relative dependency ratio, fiscal position, the gap between its actual and potential output levels, and the level of world interest rates.

Similar procedures may be used for determining current account targets for creditworthy developing countries. In cases in which reliable macroeconomic projections are not available, one often has to make ad hoc projections of the saving-investment balance. Thus, Williamson and Mahar (1998) utilize the results of recent econometric studies of the determinants of saving in developing countries to project private saving on the basis of relative per capita GDP, changes in the growth rate of real GDP, the dependency ratio, government saving, and changes in current account balances. Government saving is projected separately on the basis of changes in real GDP growth per capita and in current account balances. Williamson and Mahar project investment using incremental capital output ratios (ICORs). The resulting saving-investment balance and interest payments on the country's debt determine the target current account balance.

One stylized fact worth noting in this regard is the relationship between changes in the fiscal deficit and the resource balance. A reduction in the current fiscal deficit, an increase in public saving, will tend (assuming Ricardian equivalence does not hold and the increase in public saving is not matched by an offsetting reduction in private saving) to reduce the resource deficit. One way of allowing for this effect is to use the rule of thumb that 50 percent of the net change in the structural fiscal deficit will be reflected in the external resource balance and the other 50 percent in the crowding out or in of domestic private-sector activity. A ratio of about 50 percent has been observed in a wide range of open economies and is a reasonable standard for judging the effects of fiscal changes in economies with fully employed resources.[23]

In cases in which country-specific targets for the saving-investment balance are available separately, or can be developed, these may be utilized in the analysis. Some countries have macroeconomic plans or multiyear programs, such as those reflected in Policy Framework Papers (PFPs), which set out saving-investment and current account targets that can be used in estimating LRERs. The World Bank's revised minimum-standard model (*RMSM–X*) can also be used to establish a target for the saving-investment balance (World Bank, 1997a). In this model, a target level of investment is determined from an assumed medium-term ICOR, a target ratio of investment to GDP, or a combination of the two. The determination of a target saving rate is more problematic, in part because the effects of government policies on private sector saving are quite difficult to predict. Saving is thus usually calculated as a residual in the projection process. Numerous iterations of the projections are made until the analyst arrives at a scenario that is consistent both with the projected behavior of other variables and his judgment about the likely behavior of saving in the country concerned.

---

23. See, for example, Williamson (1994, p. 198), who writes: "The stylized fact to have emerged from the econometric modeling of recent years is that about half of the counterpart to a lower fiscal deficit is to be found in a lower current account deficit. . . ." Faruqee and Debelle (1998) confirm this finding in a study of data for 21 industrial countries. Note that this finding applies to the structural fiscal deficit: when there are substantial unemployed resources and an increase in the fiscal deficit leads primarily to increased demand for and output of nontraded goods, the effect of a change in the fiscal deficit on the resource balance will be limited.

Sustainable Capital Flows Approaches

The definition of the long-run equilibrium RER requires that the current account or resource balance be at a level that can be financed by sustainable financial flows. As discussed in the survey of empirical research in Chapter 5, there are two approaches to determining what constitutes sustainable financial flows: a flow approach and a stock approach. The flow approach examines the level and composition of capital and other financial flows to determine a sustainable medium-term trend or pattern of flows. The stock approach takes a longer-term view, deriving sustainable flows from a sustainable debt level. The flow approach is the simpler of the two and is widely used, particularly for noncreditworthy countries. The stock approach is used primarily for creditworthy countries with full access to capital markets. However, in practice the distinction between the stock and flow approaches is often blurred as analysts utilizing the flow approach usually check to ensure that the projected flows are consistent with realistic debt levels.[24]

With the medium-term flow approach, the simpler target resource balance is often used, with interest payments netted against other financial flows in determining the projected net resource transfer as noted above. With the longer-term stock approach, in contrast, the current account balance—with interest payments determined by the level of the debt and an assumed interest rate—is used to allow for feedback between interest payments and the debt stock via equation 7.11 above.

Different developing countries have different mixes of public and private flows, and the choice of methodologies for projecting financial flows usually depends upon whether a country's capital flows come primarily from the public or the private sector. At the limit, there are two polar ways of establishing sustainable capital flows: one for noncreditworthy countries that must rely entirely on public aid flows and the other for creditworthy countries that borrow entirely on private market terms. The simpler case of aid-dependent countries is discussed first.

Noncreditworthy Aid-Dependent Countries

For aid-dependent countries, sustainability of the resource balance is essentially a question of aid availability—that is, the amount of aid available

---

24. Another consideration in determining sustainable capital flows is to ensure consistency between the assumptions about capital flows and those about policy targets (such as investment and saving rates) used to determine the adjusted resource balance.

to a country on a sustained basis determines the resource deficit that
can be financed. Thus, for these countries, the analysis normally starts
by projecting the sustainable net resource transfer and a target external
reserve level in order to determine the target resource balance from the
balance-of-payments identity (equation 7.9). The internal saving-investment balance (equation 7.8) is assumed to adjust to the external balance.
An implicit assumption under this approach is that aid flows are on
appropriately concessional terms so that they pose no debt-servicing
problem. Hence, the country should draw on the aid to the extent that it
is available. For example, in the counterfactual simulations in Chapter
10, the target resource balance for Burkina Faso was determined primarily by an estimate of the sustainable level of concessional aid flows
likely to be available to the country in the long term.

In aid-dependent low-income countries, private capital flows are often such a small part of total net resource transfer that the overall result
is relatively independent of the accuracy of the projections of private
flows. In these circumstances, the projection procedure for private flows
is often simply to make a reasonable assumption about the level of private capital flows that is consistent with the projected behavior of investment. Alternatively, private capital flows may be subject to government controls, in which case they are, in effect, a policy-constrained variable that can be limited to desired levels.

Different analytical techniques are sometimes used in backward- and
forward-looking analyses of financial flows in aid-dependent countries.
Historical analyses often use the same statistical techniques employed
for determining sustainable values of other exogenous variables, namely:
moving averages or procedures for decomposing changes in financial
flows into permanent and transitory components. These techniques are
illustrated in the backward-looking analysis of misalignment in Burkina
Faso and Côte d'Ivoire in Chapter 10. Such statistical techniques can
also be used for forward-looking analysis of financial flows by assuming a continuation of trend or a return to base-year levels. Alternatively,
independent projections can be made of financial flows. Independent
projections are employed in determining the adjustment, λ, to the base-
year resource balance in the DLR constant-elasticities methodology in
Chapter 8 and in making the counterfactual simulations for the single-
equation methodology in Chapter 10.

Creditworthy and Partially Creditworthy Countries

The other polar extreme in analyzing capital flows is that of creditworthy countries with full access to private markets. Operational applications in creditworthy industrial countries originally started with ad hoc

estimates of sustainable capital flows.[25] But, as discussed above, recent analyses have increasingly adopted the saving-investment balance approach.

However, even creditworthy industrial countries face long-term borrowing constraints and cannot indefinitely finance excessive current account deficits. Large current account deficits can lead to a rapid buildup in debt and debt service obligations. Unless the initial deficit is eliminated spontaneously (for example, because an adverse terms-of-trade shock proves temporary), policy actions will be needed to reverse the initial current account deficit, including possibly an eventual depreciation of the RER. If capital markets do not perceive the required policy actions as likely, sources of financing may dry up. Lenders' concerns about creditworthiness and debt-servicing capacity thus set limits on the maximum level of sustainable borrowing. Hence, even if the analysis starts by projecting the saving-investment balance, one still needs to check that this balance can in fact be financed on a sustained basis. Moreover, for countries already having high debt levels, the analysis can often simply start with the question of what is a sustainable level of borrowing because that may be the effective constraint on the current account deficit as larger saving-investment deficits cannot be financed.

Creditworthiness Indicators. Standard creditworthiness analysis typically utilizes a maximum sustainable debt to GDP or debt to export ratio.[26] When this limit on borrowing has been reached, the growth rate of nominal debt is subsequently limited to that of nominal GDP or nominal exports so that the debt to GDP or debt to export ratio stabilizes. Williamson (1994) and Williamson and Mahar (1998) follow this approach, noting that common rules of thumb for dangerous levels of debt are 40 percent of GDP and 200 percent of exports.[27] Similarly, the World Bank's debt reduction initiative for highly indebted poor countries (HIPC) sets a limit of 200 percent to 250 percent for the ratio of the net

---

25. Isard and Faruqee (1998).

26. See Cuddington (1997) for a derivation of the accounting formulas for the equilibrium deficit that will yield a constant debt to GDP ratio. Cuddington also describes the more sophisticated present-value constraint approach and notes the difficulties in implementing it empirically. A problem with both approaches is that temporary large deficits are financeable only if there will be a future turnaround in them and lenders believe that such a turnaround is likely. Neither approach addresses the problem of what causes such turnarounds.

27. A debt to GDP ratio of 40 percent is equivalent to a debt to export ratio of 200 percent when exports account for 20 percent of GDP. Williamson and Mahar (1998, p. 87) argue that "in some sense, the debt/GDP ratio may be considered the more fundamental long-term criterion, in as much as adjustment policies can transform domestic output into exports should the need arise."

present value of the public and publicly guaranteed foreign debt to exports.[28] Assuming a 3 percent world inflation rate and 5 percent growth rate of real GDP, Williamson and Mahar estimate that a current account deficit of 2–3 percent of GDP is consistent with these rules of thumb. Sustained growth rates of real GDP of 7–8 percent would permit somewhat higher sustained current account deficits of 3–4 percent of GDP. A persistent current account deficit of 5 percent or more of GDP has, in contrast, traditionally been viewed as a warning sign of unsustainable policies, particularly if it reflects a consumption boom or is financed by building up short-term debt or drawing down external reserves.[29]

In reality, many developing countries are partially creditworthy, borrowing on both concessional and quasi-commercial terms, and fall in between the two extremes of aid dependency and full market access. In such cases, one first assumes the utilization of available aid flows. Remaining debt-servicing capacity then sets a limit on the amount of commercial borrowing that can be undertaken. Total capital flows are determined as the sum of aid flows and commercial borrowings.[30]

The Composition of Capital Flows. A similar type of creditworthiness analysis can be carried out for the public sector separately and used to establish limits for public-sector borrowing.[31] Creditworthy countries,

---

28. The following two additional criteria are also considered: a ratio of external debt service to exports within the range of 20–25 percent and, "for very open economies with a heavy fiscal debt burden despite strong efforts to generate fiscal revenue, a net present value of the debt to export ratio below 200% and a net present value of the debt to fiscal revenue ratio no higher than 280%."

29. See, for example, Milesi-Ferretti and Razin (1996).

30. Alternatively, a limit on the current account deficit may be based on an assessment of the total interest payments that an economy can bear over the long term considering its income level and growth prospects. This approach was used for projecting external capital flows for Côte d'Ivoire and for the counterfactual simulations in Chapter 10. The target resource balance for Côte d'Ivoire was based on the assessment that its debt burden at the time of the devaluation in 1994 was unsustainable. The basic assumptions at the time were that 4 percent of GDP was the maximum amount that Côte d'Ivoire could pay in interest on its outstanding debt given its income level and growth prospects and that the outstanding debt would eventually be restructured or canceled as necessary to reduce it to a sustainable level reflecting this assumption. To cover interest charges of 4 percent of GDP, other net factor service payments, and private transfer outflows (workers' remittances, primarily to Burkina Faso), a target resource balance of 6 percent of GDP was established as explained in appendix C to Chapter 10.

31. This approach is followed in the Maastricht Treaty, which sets a limit on total public-sector borrowings of 60 percent of GDP as one of its fiscal convergence criteria for prospective European Monetary Union members.

however, also usually have large private-private capital flows, which increasingly are overshadowing private-public flows. Although the consequences of a private sector default may be somewhat different from one by the public sector, private sector borrowing still creates future debt service obligations with balance of payments implications just as public sector borrowing does.

Data on private capital flows are often inadequate. Improved data on these flows, particularly short-term ones, may in many cases be essential for sustainability analysis. Private capital flows are notoriously difficult to predict in any case, and determining "sustainable" levels of these may be one of the most hazardous steps in estimating the equilibrium RER empirically. Because of the size and volatility of private capital flows in some countries, estimating the equilibrium RER in these cases may essentially be a problem of determining what constitutes a sustainable level of private flows.

Public borrowing from private capital markets is under direct government control and is thus a policy variable. For countries with controls on private capital flows, these too may be subject to policy limits. However, liberalization of the capital account may both appreciate the RER by encouraging larger capital inflows and increase the volatility of these flows.[32] In the absence of direct controls on private capital flows, government influence over private-private flows is an indirect one through monetary, fiscal, exchange rate, and financial-sector policies. Hence, if an aggregate target for debt is to serve as a basis for exchange rate policy, the government must manage its macroeconomic policies to stay within this limit.

Because of the volatility of private capital flows, the composition of these flows and the maturity structure of a country's external debt, as well as the overall level of debt relative to GDP, are concerns in analyzing creditworthiness. As Bacchetta and van Wincoop (1998) note, private outflows have been relatively stable, most of the volatility has been associated with changes in inflows, and the story of net flows has largely been that of variations in inflows.

Short-term debt is, in particular, subject to rollover risk if credit market conditions change because of such factors as increases in interest rates in industrial countries or contagion effects from a financial crisis in a neighboring country. In view of the role of excessive levels of short-term borrowing in the Mexican and East Asian currency crisis, credit markets have started to monitor the ratio of short-term foreign debt to

---

32. See World Bank (1997b), Bacchetta and van Wincoop (1998), and Isard and Faruqee (1998), p.37.

external reserves, typically looking for a ratio below 1.0 to ensure that short-term debt can be repaid in the event of a crisis.[33] Hence, in determining sustainable debt levels, at the least, assumptions about the reliance on short-term debt need to be consistent with the target for external reserves. Elbadawi and Soto (1994, 1995) in the papers reviewed in the research survey in Chapter 5, go even farther: they exclude short-term debt altogether when determining sustainable long-term flows.

Liquid private portfolio investment can also be quite volatile and may be subject to bubble effects. However, although private direct investment flows have to be serviced, they tend to be long-term in nature and have been the most stable component of private flows to developing countries. Hence, Williamson and Mahar (1998) suggest counting only 50 percent of private direct investment against the debt limit but counting a higher percentage of portfolio investment.

Current Account Sustainability. The above analytical techniques and assumptions about sustainable debt and current account limits are commonly used and do provide a starting point for the analysis. However, they are somewhat arbitrary. A given current account deficit may be financeable in some circumstances but not in others, a fact that complicates the determination of a sustainable level of capital flows. Concern about the arbitrariness of the traditional rules of thumb and the need for a better understanding of the volatility of capital flows and exchange rate crises has led to some recent research on the sustainability of current account deficits. Milesi-Ferretti and Razin (1996, 1998) find that current account deficits significantly larger than 5 percent of GDP can be financed for extended periods if a country has ample investment opportunities and markets are confident that external resources are being productively used. Nevertheless, at some point a country that has been running a large current account deficit and amassing a large external debt must reach a turning point where the resource balance shifts from deficit to surplus in order to pay the interest on this debt. Moreover, even smaller current account deficits of significantly less than 5 percent of GDP can be unfinanceable if markets view a country's policies as inconsistent and do not believe that they will lead to an eventual turnaround in its balance of payments position. Milesi-Ferretti and Razin conclude that in assessing the sustainability of current account deficits, a number of factors, rather than a single indicator, need to be considered, in particular: "A 5 % or so current account deficit becomes worrisome when a

---

33. If data on short-term debt are inadequate, as was the case in some of the East Asian countries, improved data are likely to be needed for effective exchange rate management.

nation's export sector is small, debt service is large, savings are low, the financial sector is dominated by banks with weak regulatory oversight, and equity financing is small."

Adjusting the Initial Resource Balance

After establishing a quantitative relationship between the RER and the resource balance and determining the target resource balance, the remaining analytical task in the trade-equations methodology is to adjust the resource balance for the initial year for cyclical, exogenous, and policy changes (for example, lagged effects of changes in the RER, a return to full employment, exogenous movements in the terms of trade, changes in the fiscal deficit) so that it provides an appropriate basis for computing the change required in the RER to move the resource balance to its target level. This analytical task is often referred to as detecting the structural or "underlying" current account balance.[34]

There are several ways of handling the problem of how to adjust the initial resource balance, ranging from fairly simple to quite complex. This section both discusses general approaches to the problem and sets down some simple analytical procedures that can be used to adjust the initial-year resource balance in low-income developing countries with limited data. It first sets out the relationship between the adjusted and the target resource balances. The section then discusses positive adjustments for changes in cyclical, predetermined, and exogenous variables and subsequently considers normative adjustments for policy actions and targets.

The Adjusted Resource Balance

The trade-equations methodology can be used in either of two ways to determine the relationship between the actual and equilibrium RER: (a) to estimate the change in the equilibrium RER required to move from one long-run equilibrium to another or (b) to estimate the change in the actual RER in any given initial year required to move from the initial situation to long-run equilibrium. As noted in the previous section, the simplest, although often not very satisfactory, procedure is to start with a base year in which the resource balance and RER are believed to be at their equilibrium levels. Equations 7.4 to 7.6 are then used to determine the change in the equilibrium RER since the base year is needed to offset the changes in the resource balance that have been caused by movements in the fundamental variables that affect it.

---

34. See Isard and Faruqee (1998), pp. 9–11.

The trade-equations methodology does not, however, require starting with a base year for which the actual and equilibrium RERs are assumed to be equal. The alternative, and more common, approach is to work with data for almost any recent initial year and adjust these data as discussed below to take into account deviations from trend, spontaneous exogenous changes, and policy measures. This procedure permits establishing an adjusted initial resource balance from which one can determine the real appreciation or depreciation required to attain a targeted resource balance and move the RER from its initial level to its equilibrium level.

Because of the absence of satisfactory base years, in most cases it is desirable to work with an adjusted resource balance. The adjustment to the initial resource balance to take into account factors other than the appreciation-depreciation of the RER needed to achieve a particular target resource balance can be expressed algebraically as in equation 7.12:

$$(7.12) \qquad\qquad \Delta RB_0 = RB_a - RB_0$$

where RB_0 is the initial- or reference-year resource balance in real terms, ΔRB_0 is the change in the resource balance, and RB_a is the adjusted or underlying resource balance. The change in the adjusted resource balance (ΔRB_a) required to achieve the target resource balance (RB^*) can similarly be expressed as in equation 7.13:

$$(7.13) \qquad\qquad \Delta RB_a = RB^* - RB_a.$$

The total required change in the resource balance (ΔRB_r) is the sum of the adjustments to the initial resource balance and the desired change in the adjusted resource balance as shown in equation 7.14:

$$(7.14) \qquad\qquad \Delta RB_r = \Delta RB_0 + \Delta RB_a = RB^* - RB_0.$$

In most cases one is, in fact, interested in separating the total required change in the initial resource balance into ΔRB_0 and ΔRB_a, as different policy actions (or nonactions) are needed to achieve these. In some cases (for example, to allow for lagged effects of changes in the RER), it may also be desirable to use an adjusted RER for the initial year, RER_a, rather than the actual RER in the initial year, RER_0.[35]

---

35. See the discussion of the components of misalignment in Chapter 5. Clark and MacDonald (1998) refer to the change in the RER required to move from RER_0 to RER_a as "current misalignment" and that which is required to move from RER_a to the LRER as "total misalignment." In the same vein, the difference between RER_a and the LRER could be referred to as structural misalignment.

Two types of factors other than the RER may affect the initial resource balance: (a) positive changes in predetermined, cyclical, and exogenous variables; and (b) normative policy actions and targets. The procedure for estimating the effects of these two groups of changes on the initial resource balance in order to determine ΔRB_0 are discussed below. As explained there, in some cases the adjustment procedure will depend upon whether the target resource balance, RB^*, has been determined through the saving-investment balance or the sustainable capital flows approach.

Positive Adjustments for Changes in Predetermined, Cyclical, and Exogenous Variables

To arrive at the underlying current account deficit in industrial countries, the IMF uses trade equations to adjust imports and exports in the initial year for the lagged effects of changes in the RER in the preceding two years and for the gaps between current and full employment output at home and abroad.[36] Wren-Lewis and Driver (1998) follow a similar procedure, using the fitted values of imports and exports from their trade equations and full employment output in calculating the adjusted resource balance for the initial year. For developing countries, additional adjustments in the initial resource balance may be needed to allow for exogenous shocks to import and export quantities and for significant movements in the terms of trade. Positive adjustments for these factors are discussed below, the effects of quantity changes first and then those of relative price movements.

Quantity Changes

Underutilized Productive Capacity or Return to Trend Growth Rate of GDP. The trade-equations methodology may be used equally well for economies that are on the production frontier with fully employed resources and for those that are inside it. When, as in the CFA zone prior to the 1994 devaluation, the RER has been overvalued for a significant period and nominal wages and prices in the nontradable sector are sticky downwards, internal relative prices change at best very slowly. As a result, resources may not shift quickly enough from the production of nontradables to tradables. In such cases, a country may experience a significant recession or a period of below-trend GDP growth. Imports may then be depressed below their full employment level through cyclical income effects. In these cases, a return either to full utilization of the existing capital stock or to the trend level of GDP growth may lead to a cyclical increase in the demand for imports as expanding production

---

36. See Isard and Faruqee (1998).

and incomes lead to higher absorption and imports and a deterioration of the resource balance.[37] However, there may also be cases where absorption is excessive, inflation is accelerating, the economy is overheated, and the current account deficit is too large, requiring a reduction in GDP, and imports, in the initial year from their actual levels to trend.

The standard procedure for determining output gaps in industrial countries is to estimate a production function for GDP and calculate the output gap as the difference between output given by the production function and actual output.[38] In developing countries, the data necessary for estimating production functions are often not available; and simpler approaches have to be used. Typically, the size of the gap between potential and actual GDP is estimated from an analysis of trend growth rates and deviations from them. When the required data are available, the trend analysis can be supplemented by examining capacity utilization and unemployment figures. Once the estimated GDP gap has been determined, it is multiplied by an estimated or assumed income elasticity of demand for imports to calculate the additional imports needed to allow for a return to full employment. Appendix B summarizes representative estimates of income elasticities of demand for imports that may be used for this purpose when country-specific estimates are not available.[39]

Exogenous Quantity Changes. In addition to cyclical income effects, the initial resource balance may also be affected by exogenous variations in export or import quantities that are not caused by changes in incomes or the RER. Such exogenous changes in quantities may reflect corrections for unusual circumstances or deviations from trend in the initial year (for example, higher-than-normal food imports because of a drought or lower-than-normal exports because of a strike or civil unrest). Alternately, they may take account of projected new developments that would occur without any change in the RER—such as additional exports from completion of an investment already in progress in a major mining project, or adoption of improved agricultural technology. Such projected changes in import and export volumes are added to the initial-year val-

---

37. The above formulation assumes that it is not profitable to shift resources to the production of tradable goods without a depreciation of the internal RER so that the excess capacity is in the nontradable sector. If output in the export sector is demand- rather than supply-constrained and there is excess capacity in this sector, then a return to full employment or trend growth levels of GDP could also lead to an expansion of exports that could offset part or all of the increased demand for imports.

38. See, for example, Demasi (1997).

39. If investment is also cyclically depressed, an additional allowance should be made for its recovery as discussed below.

ues to determine the adjusted resource balance. In the Burkina Faso example in Chapter 10, new zinc exports of 2.6 percent of GDP and additional imports of 0.9 percent of GDP were projected as the result of the completion of a mining project that was already being implemented before the 1994 devaluation and would have started production any case.

Changes in Relative Prices

Lagged Effects of Changes in the RER. As discussed in Chapter 11 on the effects of the RER on trade flows, on average it takes approximately three years for all the effects of changes in the RER to work their way through an economy. The trade equations used by Isard and Faruqee (1998) thus model imports and exports as functions of the RER in the current and preceding two years, with average weights of 0.6, 0.25, and 0.15 assigned to the RERs in these years. The underlying current account deficit is then calculated assuming that the RER remains at its current level indefinitely. When trade-elasticity equations 7.4 through 7.6 are used, a simpler adjustment may be made when appropriate, that is: imports and exports in the initial year can be assumed to reflect the weighted average of the RER in the current and preceding two years, with whatever adjustments to Isard's and Faruqee's weights are merited in light of country-specific data. The resulting three-year weighted average RER is then used as the base for calculating its equilibrium level.[40]

Projected External (International) Prices. Although recently a great deal of attention has been focused on the volatility of capital flows, fluctuations in the terms of trade can—as in the case of the devaluation of the CFA francs—be equally or more important concerns for commodity-exporting low-income countries with limited access to private capital markets. Hence, for developing countries with highly variable terms of trade, determining sustainable values for the exogenous external prices of their imports and exports is a key step in the estimation of the equilibrium RER.[41] The central analytical problem is to distinguish between temporary and permanent (or sustained) changes in what are often quite volatile export prices. Different approaches to this problem are usually taken in historical and forward-looking analyses. In historical analyses,

---

40. Using this procedure for the internal RERs also takes into account changes in the terms of trade and commercial policy in the preceding two years since these are reflected in the internal RER.

41. Fluctuations in the terms of trade are normally much less of a concern for industrial countries that export a range of manufactured products. Isard and Faruqee (1998, p. 38) note that for most of these countries, variations in the terms of trade have typically been a temporary phenomenon.

moving averages of the annual values or econometric techniques for decomposing changes into permanent and transitory components are usually used in order to reduce the random fluctuations in what are normally quite volatile annual data. These techniques are illustrated in Chapter 10 for the single-equation reduced-form methodology.

Forward-looking analysis may also assume that external prices continue to follow historical trends and simply extrapolate these trends into the future. Alternatively, they may employ available projections of international prices of primary commodities and manufactured goods such as those regularly produced by the World Bank. In this case, the changes in the real (inflation-adjusted) prices of exports and imports are multiplied by the corresponding price elasticities of supply and demand to calculate the adjustment to the initial resource balance.

Adjustments for Policy Actions and Targets

The above adjustments to the initial resource balance for changes in cyclical, predetermined, and exogenous variables are all positive ones needed to estimate the underlying or structural resource balance. In addition, the initial resource balance may need to be adjusted for the effects of policy actions and targets other than changes in the RER. As explained in the discussion of conceptual issues in Chapter 5, numerous different assumptions about policy actions and targets can be made when estimating the equilibrium RER; and these will generally lead to somewhat different estimates of the LRER. These assumptions may be classified broadly into two groups: (a) positive assumptions specifying the policies that one thinks are likely to be implemented and (b) normative assumptions specifying the policies that one thinks should be implemented.[42] The principal policies that need to be taken into account in a developing-country context are those affecting trade and the import intensity of absorption.

Trade Taxes

Developing countries often undertake devaluations, at least in part, to permit dismantling of protective barriers against competition. Hence, devaluations are commonly accompanied by reforms, often extensive, in trade policy; and the effects of these on the initial resource balance need to be taken into account. Equation 7.5 above contains the average trade taxes on imports and exports, t_M and t_X. These should be broad

---

42. In addition, in considering the effects of a devaluation and alternatives to it, it may also be helpful analytically to distinguish between the effects on the initial resource balance of those policy measures that could be implemented without a devaluation and those that would require a devaluation.

measures of the *average* trade taxes (net of subsidies) on imports and exports. In principle, t_M and t_X should also include the tariff equivalent of nontariff barriers, differential domestic taxes on traded goods, profits of marketing boards, and effects of administered pricing schemes, although quantifying these effects empirically may be difficult. Since the structure of protection in developing countries is often highly differentiated with a wide dispersion of effective trade tax rates, it is sometimes possible to achieve a general leveling of incentives (particularly through the elimination of exemptions and non-tariff barriers) while maintaining or even increasing revenues from trade taxes. In such cases, historical changes in average trade tax rates may give a vague or even a misleading idea of the changes in the incentives facing key subsectors; and ad hoc adjustments, based on whatever data are available in a particular case, may be needed.

As in the case of exogenous external prices, different approaches are usually utilized for historical and forward-looking analyses of changes in commercial policy. Accurate historical measures of commercial policy are hard to come by.[43] Hence, changes in openness to trade are sometimes used as a proxy for changes in commercial policy as in Chapter 10, in which alternative empirical measures of trade openness are examined. Forward-looking analyses, on the other hand, typically start by making an ad hoc estimate of the average tariff rates in the initial or base year and an assumption about how this rate will change as a result of future policies. The effects on the initial resource balance are then calculated using equations 7.4 to 7.6.

Policies Affecting the Import Intensity of Absorption

In a particular country application, the previous trend rate of GDP growth may be satisfactory; and the policy objective associated with the equilibrium RER may simply be a return to this growth rate. Or, the previous trend rate of GDP growth may have been too low; and the equilibrium RER may need to be estimated assuming an acceleration in growth. In the former case, the adjustment to the initial resource balance for a return to trend growth described in the previous subsection will be sufficient. If, however, an acceleration of the growth rate is desired, a higher level of investment will generally be required.[44]

---

43. See Pritchett (1996). Pritchett finds that there is no reliable robust measure of commercial policy orientation that can be used in cross-country regression analyses and suggests that the issue may be too complex and opaque to be analyzed with a single standardized measure.

44. This subsection discusses the effects of an increase in the *growth rate* of GDP whereas the preceding subsection on the GDP gap discusses the effects of a one-time increase in the *level* of GDP. In empirical applications, care needs to be taken to ensure consistency in the treatment of these effects.

Since the target resource balance (and hence the $S - I$ balance) is determined independently by the level of sustainable capital flows, a higher investment rate will require increased saving. An additional important consequence of higher investment for present purposes, however, is that the resulting change in the composition of absorption may have implications for the equilibrium level of the real exchange rate. Because investment tends to be relatively more import-intensive than consumption in most low-income countries, even an equal increase in the levels of investment and saving may tend to raise the import intensity of expenditure. Consequently, for a given resource balance (and thus for a given $S - I$ balance), the higher the level of investment, the more depreciated the RER may need to be to offset the greater ex ante import intensity of absorption.[45] In the Côte d'Ivoire case, for example, the import intensity of investment was estimated at 0.6 and that of consumption at 0.3 so that a balanced increase in investment and saving would, other things being equal, require an increase in imports. Hence, to offset the resulting tendency for the composition of expenditure to become more import intensive because of increased investment, a depreciation of the RER would be required.

The initial resource balance can be adjusted to allow in a rough way for the differential effects on imports of projected increases in the levels of investment and saving. This adjustment is computed by multiplying the projected increase in investment, as a share of GDP, from its initial level by the import intensity of investment and then subtracting from this product the projected increase in saving from its initial level multiplied by the import intensity of consumption.[46]

---

45. An important assumption underlying the above approach is that public and private saving behavior have little direct impact on exports. Low-income countries typically do not consume a significant share of their export production, which usually consists largely of export crops (for example, coffee, cocoa, cotton), mineral products (for example, phosphates, petroleum), or nontraditional products (for example, horticulture, garments) produced for foreign markets. (Another type of export on which saving behavior would have little direct effect is the exportable surplus of a basic consumption good, such as rice, with a low-income elasticity of demand.) Hence, the effects of changes in saving and consumption fall primarily on imports and domestic goods.

46. The import intensities of both private and public consumption and investment may also differ, with private investment being relatively more equipment (import) intensive and public investment being relatively more construction (nontraded good) intensive, making it desirable to split investment and saving into their public and private sector components. However, in practice the data on the import intensities in the public and private sectors are often so sketchy that, as in the Côte d'Ivoire case, it is difficult to quantify these differences.

Significant compositional effects requiring an adjustment in the initial resource balance can also arise from projected changes in the composition of government expenditures. For a given fiscal deficit, a shift in government expenditure between traded and nontraded goods will tend to affect the resource balance. As discussed in Chapter 6 on the theory of the equilibrium RER, switching government expenditures from domestic (nontraded) goods to imports will tend in the first instance to widen the resource deficit.[47] When the switching of government expenditure between traded and nontraded goods is important in a specific case, a rough adjustment can be made, similar to that made for a balanced increase in investment and saving, using whatever data are available on the import intensities of the categories of expenditure involved. Because data decomposing government expenditures into those on traded and nontraded goods are often not available, in practice data for government investment and consumption expenditures (particularly wages) are often used as proxies for these.[48]

Limitations of the Adjustment Procedures

The recursive approach used in the trade-equations methodology does not explicitly allow for feedback from the RER to the variables that determine the target resource balance.[49] Investment and saving behavior, both public and private, may, however, be affected by changes in the RER. As discussed in appendix B of Chapter 2 on the external RER, a depreciation of the RER (an increase in competitiveness) will tend to raise returns to capital and thereby increase both investment and saving. A depreciation of the RER may also have important effects on government revenues—particularly if the government is highly dependent on trade taxes—and on the real value of nominal government expenditures.

---

47. For a further discussion and empirical evidence, see Khan and Lizondo (1987) and Lane and Perotti (1996).

48. Likewise, changes in government revenues may also have somewhat different effects on imports from changes in government expenditures. In this case the adustment to the initial resource balance for equal changes in government revenues and expenditures would be computed by multiplying the change in government expenditure by the average import intensity of the expenditures involved and subtracting from this product the increase in government revenues multiplied by the import intensity of private consumption (assuming that the increased taxes fall on private consumption).

49. Isard and Faruqee (1998) hypothesize that the determinants of the saving-investment balance in the G-7 countries are independent of the RER and, hence, do not make some of adjustments to the initial resource balance discussed above. See Chapter 5, Figure 5.1, and the discussion of it on pp. 244–246.

Alternative monetary and fiscal policies for closing an output gap may have differing implications for the RER. Movements in the RER and in investment, saving, and fiscal variables can also affect lenders' perceptions of a country's creditworthiness and hence the level of sustainable capital flows. Ad hoc adjustments can be made for some of these effects, as discussed above, when they are important in particular cases and the required data are available.[50] For other effects, it may not be possible to make adjustments in a specific case. Moreover, a devaluation and accompanying policy measures need to be designed to adjust both the external resource balance $(X - M)$ and the saving-investment gap $(S - I)$ in equation 7.8 in a consistent way to achieve the targeted resource balance. While rough adjustments can be made in specific cases for some of the more important interactions, theoretically it would be desirable to have a full general-equilibrium framework that takes into account all of the important feedbacks in a fully consistent manner.

Conclusion: Advantages and Limitations of the Trade-Equations Methodology

The trade equations–elasticities methodology set out above has a number of practical advantages in estimating the equilibrium RER in low-income developing countries. First, its data requirements are limited. One needs only GDP, CPI, and balance of payments statistics for the home country. Reasonable estimates of the price elasticities of export supply and import demand needed for the methodology are also readily available even if trade elasticities have not previously been estimated for the particular country concerned. Second, the methodology is reasonably straightforward and transparent. With simple computer spreadsheets it is easy to run extensive sensitivity analyses of the results from the methodology assuming different parameter estimates and structural changes, projections of exogenous variables, policy targets, and so forth. Minimal data requirements, readily available parameter estimates, and transparency are significant practical advantages at the time of a balance of payments crisis in a developing country in which data, time, and professional manpower are all likely to be limited. Third, in cases of shifts in the fundamentals, the trade equations–elasticities methodology can provide a measure of the new equilibrium RER that cannot be

---

50. The trade-equations methodology also does not explicitly take into account such short-term factors as speculative stocking and destocking and the relationship between the seasonality of the cropping cycle and the timing of RER movements. It does not consider possible expansionary or contractionary monetary effects on real balances, either. Again, it is sometimes possible to make ad hoc adjustments for these effects in cases in which they are important.

estimated using the simpler relative-PPP-based approach. The methodology is thus a useful base-line approach that may be used by itself, when nothing else is available, or as a cross-check when other methodologies are also used.

However, the trade-equations methodology does have some significant limitations. First, the errors involved in the parameter estimates could be substantial and suggest large confidence intervals around the estimated LRER. The methodology is, in principle, valid only for marginal changes. Large nonmarginal changes caused by major RER realignments may lead to structural changes affecting the parameters.[51] Although sensitivity analyses can be readily made for alternative parameter estimates and changes in these as illustrated in the next chapter, outcomes of large changes in the RER are often hard to predict.

Second, the three-good framework utilized in the developing-country version of the methodology assumes that the law of one price holds for internationally traded goods. If the law of one price does not hold or holds only loosely, the relationship between domestic and foreign prices will be much looser, and the internal RERs for exports and imports may change less or more slowly than assumed.

Third, the trade-equations methodology employs a recursive partial-equilibrium approach. Given required changes in the resource balance, it determines new equilibrium values for the RER, imports, and exports but not for other important macroeconomic variables that may also change simultaneously. Nor does it explicitly allow for feedback from the RER to the factors (for example, saving, investment, capital flows) determining the target resource balance. While rough adjustments are possible for some of the more important income and feedback effects, one would be more confident of the results if they were determined in a complete general-equilibrium framework that takes into account all important interactions in a fully consistent manner.

Fourth, the methodology is one of comparative statics. It projects long-term changes but not the dynamic time path of the adjustment process, although by repeated applications of the methodology, year by year, it is also possible to generate a time series for the equilibrium RER as illustrated with the DLR constant-elasticities model in the next chapter. The volatility of exchange rates implies that the RER may diverge from its equilibrium value for significant time periods and the path by which it converges to this value may in some cases have significant policy implications (for example, for the level of debt or the length of the adjustment period).

---

51. For example, the elasticities or the various import ratios used in computing the adjustments in the target resource balance may change.

Finally, forward-looking analyses of the LRER using the trade-equations methodology require projections of the fundamental variables determining the LRER. If some important fundamentals such as the terms of trade or private capital flows are completely unpredictable or subject to repeated shocks to their "permanent" values, the LRER will also be unpredictable or volatile.

How accurate then are estimates of misalignment from the trade equations–elasticities methodology likely to be? Little research has been done on this question. The methodology was not fully articulated until 1994–98. Before that, it was applied in different forms as it evolved and was typically used, often in informal unpublished internal analyses, for operational purposes without systematically looking back years later to see how accurate the results were. Isard and Faruqee (1998) present a historical analysis of what the methodology would have revealed about the major exchange rate misalignments of the 1980s and 1990s in industrial countries *if* it had been used then in its present form and find that, if applied ex ante, it could have identified these misalignments. In the absence of formal statistical measures of accuracy, they suggest, based on the IMF's experience, a 10–15 percent confidence interval for industrial countries.[52] That is, estimated misalignments of 10 percent or less are probably not significant given all of the uncertainties involved. Misalignments of 15 percent or more are likely to merit further careful investigation, and the significance of misalignments between 10 percent and 15 percent can only be judged in light of country-specific knowledge of the factors likely to affect their accuracy.[53] This rule of thumb also seems reasonable for developing countries until further experience provides better guidance.

---

52. See also Kramer (1996) for a more formal statistical analysis of a case study for the Canadian dollar.

53. For a further discussion of the interpretation of apparent misalignment, see Isard and Faruqee (1998), pp. 1–3 and 16–17.

Appendix A

The RER, Trade-Elasticities, Resource Balance Relationship in a Three-Good Framework

This appendix derives the relationship between the resource balance, trade elasticities, and the internal RER in a three-good framework with exports, imports, and domestic goods.[54] This formulation allows for different RERs for imports and exports and facilitates more explicit treatment of the relative price effects of changes in the terms of trade and commercial policy than does the expenditure-PPP external RER. Both formulations require the assumption that the elasticities of export supply and import demand are the same for changes in relative prices as for changes in the real exchange rate. This assumption is quite natural when using separate internal RERs for exports and imports but less so if the PPP external RER is used. The approach developed below uses the definitions of the price elasticities of imports and exports to calculate the equilibrium RER from a target value for a sustainable resource balance and estimates of the home country's import and export elasticities.

Derivation of the Basic RER, Trade-Elasticities, Resource Balance Equation

The Definition of Trade Elasticities

The price elasticity of export supply, σ_X, is defined as shown in equation 7.A.1:

---

54. For earlier discussions of the trade-elasticities methodology see E. Bacha and L. Taylor (1971) and A. Kreuger and others (1988).

345

$$(7.A.1) \qquad \sigma_x = \frac{\dfrac{\Delta X}{X}}{\dfrac{\Delta\left(\dfrac{P_{Xd}}{P_{Dd}}\right)}{\dfrac{P_{Xd}}{P_{Dd}}}} \qquad \sigma_x > 0$$

where X is the quantity of exports, P_{Xd} is the domestic price of exports, and P_{Dd} is the domestic-currency price of domestic goods. Similarly, the price elasticity of import demand, ε_M, is defined as in equation 7.A.2:

$$(7.A.2) \qquad \varepsilon_M = \frac{\dfrac{\Delta M}{M}}{\dfrac{\Delta\left(\dfrac{P_{Md}}{P_{Dd}}\right)}{\dfrac{P_{Md}}{P_{Dd}}}} \qquad \varepsilon_M < 0$$

where M is the quantity of imports and P_{Md} is the domestic price of imports. Note that the domestic-currency price of domestic goods, P_{Dd}, is used as the numeraire for measuring relative prices in both equations.

As in the chapter on the three-good internal RER, domestic goods are defined here as goods that are both produced and consumed in the home country. They are semitradable in the sense that they are substitutes in consumption for imports via the price elasticity of import demand and in production for exports via the price elasticity of export supply. This formulation has the advantages of corresponding directly to the format in which data are actually collected and making it possible to estimate the equilibrium RER empirically using only standard national accounts and balance of payments statistics.

The Definition of the Internal RERs

In the above three-good framework, the internal RER is the domestic price of exports or imports relative to the price of domestic (nontraded) goods. The internal RERs for exports, RERX, and for imports, RERM, are defined as shown in equation 7.A.3:

$$(7.A.3) \qquad RERX = \frac{P_{Xd}}{P_{Dd}} \qquad \text{and} \qquad RERM = \frac{P_{Md}}{P_{Dd}}.$$

If the home country is a price taker in international trade, its exports and imports are subject to the law of one price. The domestic prices of exports, P_{Xd}, and imports, P_{Md}, are then determined by their international (border) prices and trade taxes as shown in equations 7.A.4 and 7.A.5:

(7.A.4) $$P_{Xd} = P_{Xf}(1-t_x) \cdot E_{dc}$$

(7.A.5) $$P_{Md} = P_{Mf} \cdot (1+t_M) \cdot E_{dc} .$$

P_{Xf} and P_{Mf} are the foreign-currency border prices of exports and imports, t_X and t_M are the average trade taxes on exports and imports, and E_{dc} is the nominal exchange rate in domestic-currency terms. The definitions of the internal RERs may then be written as in equations 7.A.6 and 7.A.7:

(7.A.6) $$RERX = \frac{P_{Xd}}{P_{Dd}} = \frac{P_{Xf}(1-t_x) \cdot E_{dc}}{P_{Dd}}$$

(7.A.7) $$RERM = \frac{P_{Md}}{P_{Dd}} = \frac{P_{Mf}(1+t_M) \cdot E_{dc}}{P_{Dd}} .$$

The trade elasticities may be expressed in terms of the RERs for exports and imports by substituting the definitions of the internal RERs from equations 7.A.3 into equations 7.A.1 and 7.A.2 as shown in equations 7.A.8 and 7.A.9:

(7.A.8) $$\sigma_x = \frac{\frac{\Delta X}{X}}{\frac{\Delta RERX}{RERX}}$$

(7.A.9) $$\varepsilon_M = \frac{\frac{\Delta M}{M}}{\frac{\Delta RERM}{RERM}} .$$

The Resource Balance

The resource balance and its first difference measured in real terms are given in equation 7.A.10:

(7.A.10) $$RB = X - M \quad \text{and} \quad \Delta RB = \Delta X - \Delta M.$$

Expressions for ΔX and ΔM in terms of the internal RERs and trade elasticities may be derived by rearranging equations 7.A.8 and 7.A.9 to obtain equations 7.A.11 and 7.A.12:

$$(7.A.11) \qquad \Delta X = \sigma_X \cdot X \cdot \frac{\Delta RERX}{RERX}$$

$$(7.A.12) \qquad \Delta M = \varepsilon_M \cdot M \cdot \frac{\Delta RERM}{RERM}.$$

Subtracting equation 7.A.11 from 7.A.12 yields equation 7.A.13 for the change in the resource balance, ΔRB:

$$(7.A.13) \qquad \Delta RB = \Delta X \ - \ \Delta M = \sigma_x \cdot X \cdot \frac{\Delta RERX}{RERX} \ - \ \varepsilon_M \cdot M \cdot \frac{\Delta RERM}{RERM}.$$

Solution for the Internal RERs

The Relationship between the Internal RERs for Imports and Exports

In order to solve equation 7.A.13 for either $RERX$ or $RERM$, we need an expression for the relationship between them. Dividing the definition of $RERX$ by that for $RERM$ (equation 7.A.3) gives equations 7.A.14 and 7.A.15:

$$(7.A.14) \qquad \frac{RERX}{RERM} = \frac{\dfrac{P_{Xd}}{P_{Dd}}}{\dfrac{P_{Md}}{P_{Dd}}} = \frac{P_{Xd}}{P_{Md}} = ITT$$

$$(7.A.15) \qquad RERX = RERM \cdot ITT$$

where the internal terms of trade, ITT, are defined as the domestic price of exports relative to the domestic price of imports, that is: P_{Xd}/P_{Md}. Note, for future reference, that the numeraire, P_{Dd}, cancels out in equation 7.A.14 (see page 351).

Substituting for P_{Xd} and P_{Md} from equations 7.A.4 and 7.A.5 yields equation 7.A.16:

$$(7.A.16) \qquad ITT = \frac{P_{Xd}}{P_{Md}} = \frac{P_{Xf}(1-t_X) \cdot E_{dc}}{P_{Mf}(1+t_M) \cdot E_{dc}} = \frac{P_{Xf}(1-t_x)}{P_{Mf}(1+t_M)}.$$

Since all of the variables on the right-hand side of equation 7.A.16 are exogenously determined if the law of one price holds, so are the internal terms of trade, ITT. Hence, $RERX$ can be calculated from $RERM$ and the exogenously determined internal terms of trade using equations 7.A.15 and 7.A.16.

The Internal RERs

By substituting for from equation 7.A.15 in equation 7.A.13 and rearranging the terms, equation 7.A.17 for the internal RER for imports can be obtained:

(7.A.17)
$$\frac{\Delta RERM}{RERM} = \frac{\Delta RB - \sigma_x \cdot X\left(\dfrac{\Delta ITT}{ITT}\right)}{\sigma_x \cdot X - \varepsilon_M \cdot M}.$$

The above system contains four equations (numbers A.10, A.15, A.16, and A.17) and four endogenous variables (M, X, $RERM$, and $RERX$). It also contains the parameters σ_x and ε_M; initial values of X, M, and ITT; and the exogenously determined variables ΔRB and ΔITT. The determination of the change in the internal terms of trade, ΔITT, from equation 7.A.16 is straightforward. Exogenous projected values are used for the external prices of exports and imports, P_{xf} and P_{Mf}. Average trade taxes on exports, t_X, and imports, t_M, are policy variables.

The other exogenous variable on the right-hand side of equation 7.A.17 is the targeted or required change in the resource balance, ΔRB. Determination of both the adjustments to the initial resource balance for cyclical, exogenous, and policy changes and determination of the sustainable or target resource balance is similar in the trade-equations and the trade-elasticities approaches. This process is considerably more complicated than calculating ΔITT and is discussed separately in the sections of the text on the adjusted and target resource balances.

Once the adjusted and target resource balances have determined, as in the trade-equations approach, the trade-elasticity relationships are used to calculate the change in the RER needed to move it from its actual level to its equilibrium level. Thus, the computed values of ΔITT and ΔRB are plugged into the right-hand side of equation 7.A.17 to calculate the change in the RER for imports necessary to achieve the required change in the resource balance. The RER for exports can then be computed using equation 7.A.15. After the RERs for imports and exports have been calculated, the supply response to the change in the RER (that is, the corresponding changes in the volume of imports and exports) can also be computed using equations 7.A.8 and 7.A.9.

Note, however, that equations 7.A.15 and 7.A.17 only permit determining relative prices, not nominal ones. The definitions of the internal RERs, in fact, contain two endogenous variables, the nominal exchange rate, E_{dc}, and the price of domestic goods, P_{Dd}, as well as the exogenously set prices of exports or imports.[55] In order to determine separate values

---

55. These two endogenous variables may be compressed into one variable (the price of domestic goods expressed in foreign-currency terms) by multiplying

for these two endogenous variables, either the nominal exchange rate or the domestic-currency price of domestic goods needs to be exogenously determined as a nominal anchor for domestic prices.[56]

Parameter Estimates

Three points concerning the parameters in the relationship between the internal RER, trade elasticities, and the change in the resource balance merit further explanation and possible modification in particular applications. These are (a) the empirical trade-elasticity estimates to be used in equation 7.17; (b) the numeraire used in measuring the elasticities and the RER; and (c) the problem of inelastic export demand. Each of these is discussed in turn below.

Trade-Elasticities Estimates

The accuracy of the equilibrium RER calculated using the trade-elasticities methodology depends upon that of the elasticity estimates used. Econometrically estimating country-specific elasticities can be both a time-consuming and problematic process in developing countries with inadequate data. However, a considerable amount of empirical work has been done on trade elasticities for a wide range of countries and products. Chapter 11 by Ghei and Pritchett on trade flows and elasticities summarizes the results of this empirical work and gives a good idea of what are reasonable values to assume for import and export elasticities.

The elasticity estimates used in equation 7.A.17 may either be aggregate elasticities for imports and exports or a weighted average of the commodity-specific elasticities for major product groups.[57] The definition of trade elasticities (equations 7.A.1 and 7.A.2) and the law of one price (equations 7.A.4 and 7.A.5) used in deriving equation 7.A.17 implicitly assume that there is no import compression through exchange

---

them together to arrive at an alternative single measure of the internal RER that is used by some authors. See, for example, the related concept of the equilibrium GDP deflator used in the DLR model discussed in Chapter 8.

56. For a further discussion of the nominal anchor problem and a methodology for calculating consistent nominal and relative prices, see Chapter 13 on devaluations and inflation.

57. Nonfactor service receipts and payments should be treated as imports and exports in order to allow for the possibility that they may change in response to a change in the RER. In some cases, it may also be desirable to treat some factor service flows and private transfers as "imports" and "exports" and allow for a non-zero price elasticity for these. The elasticities of different product groups should be weighted by the ratios of imports or exports of these to GDP to determine the aggregate import and export elasticities.

controls or nontariff barriers and no smuggling of either exports or imports. Hence, the quantities of imports and exports are determined entirely by foreign prices, trade taxes, and the market or official exchange rate. If one or more of the foregoing distortions are present, the average tax rate on imports and exports needs to be adjusted to allow for these as discussed below.

The Numeraire for the Trade Elasticities and the RER

In the formulas for import and export price elasticities (equations 7.A.1 and 7.A.2) relative prices are expressed in terms of the price of domestic goods. Relative prices are, however, more often expressed in terms of the aggregate price level, P_{Gd}. Because of the ready availability of data for aggregate price indexes, the common practice when estimating elasticities empirically is, in fact, to express import and export prices relative to the aggregate price level rather than to the price of domestic goods.

The relationship between the aggregate price level and the prices of imports, exports, and domestic goods are given by equations 7.A.18 and 7.A.19:

(7.A.18)
$$P_{GDP} = P_{Xd}^{\tau_x} \cdot P_{Dd}^{1-\tau_x}$$

(7.A.19)
$$P_{GDA} = P_{Md}^{\tau_m} \cdot P_{Dd}^{1-\tau_m}$$

where P_{GDP} is the deflator for GDP, P_{GDA} is the deflator for gross domestic absorption, τ_x is the share of value added in exporting in GDP, and τ_m is the share of imports of final goods in absorption. If, as often happens, the prices of traded goods vary more than those of domestic goods, elasticities with respect to the aggregate price level, which includes traded goods, will be higher than with respect to the price of domestic goods.

Fortunately, however, as long as the elasticities for imports and exports *and the RER* are expressed relative to the same numeraire,[58] equation 7.A.17 can be used for any numeraire as the numeraire cancels out in its derivation as noted above. Hence, standard elasticity estimates expressed relative to the general price level may be used as long as the same numeraire (for example, the deflator for GDP or GDA or the CPI) is used for estimating the elasticities for both imports and exports. However, *in this case the RER will also be expressed relative to the general price level rather than to the price of domestic goods.* If the equilibrium RER

---

58. The composition of the numeraire must also not change during the period for which the elasticities are measured empirically. That is, τ_x and τ_m must be constant.

expressed relative to the general price level is calculated using equation 7.A.17, then equations 7.A.18 and 7.A.19, which relate the price of domestic goods to the general price level, may subsequently be used to calculate the RER expressed relative to the price of domestic goods as discussed in Chapter 13 on devaluations and inflation.

The Elasticity of Foreign Exchange Supply

The above formulations assume that the home country's imports and exports are small relative to the world markets for these goods and services and that it is a price taker for both imports and exports. Hence, it faces infinitely elastic import supply and export demand curves. However, if the home country's exports of a particular commodity represent a large share of world exports and foreign demand for them is not highly price elastic, the quantity of the home country's exports will affect the price at which they can be sold. Whenever the absolute value of the price elasticity of demand for a particular country's exports of a given product is less than infinite but greater than unity, the elasticity of foreign exchange earnings will be less than the elasticity of export supply, although still positive. In this case, the elasticity of the supply of exports, ε_x, should be replaced in equation 7.A.17 by the elasticity of the supply of foreign exchange, σ_f, given by equation 7.A.20:

$$(7.A.20) \qquad \sigma_f = \frac{\sigma_x \left(-\varepsilon_f - 1\right)}{\sigma_x - \varepsilon_f} \qquad \varepsilon_f < 0$$

where ε_f is the price elasticity of foreign demand for the home country's exports and σ_f is the price elasticity of export supply. ε_f is equal to the price elasticity of demand in the world market for the commodity concerned divided by the home country's share of the world market.

Consider, for example, the case of exports of cocoa and coffee from the entire CFA zone at the time of the devaluation of the CFA franc in 1994. Together these accounted for 24 percent of total CFA zone exports, and the zone's cocoa exports were a large enough share of the world market (36 percent) that inelastic demand was a reasonable policy concern.

Since the price elasticity of world demand for cocoa was estimated at –0.35, an increase in the quantity of cocoa exported by the CFA countries would lower the world price and total revenues from cocoa sales. Using the rule of thumb (from Chapter 11 on trade flows and the RER) that the elasticity of demand for an individual country's exports is the world elasticity divided by the country's market share, the price elasticity of demand for cocoa exports from the CFA countries was approximately –1.0 (that is, (–.35)/(–.36)). Using the estimated long-term supply elasticity for the CFA countries' cocoa exports of 1.0 from Ghei and

Pritchett, the estimated elasticity of foreign exchange earnings from equation 7.A.20 is 0.

By contrast, for coffee, the estimated price elasticity of world demand was higher (–0.5 for coffee vs. –0.35 for cocoa); and the CFA zone's market share was much lower (8 percent for coffee vs. 36 percent for cocoa). Hence, the price elasticity of demand for its coffee exports, although not infinite, was much larger (–6.2 = (–0.5)/(–.08)) than for cocoa. Consequently, the elasticity of foreign exchange earnings from equation 7.A.20 was only slightly lower (0.6) than the estimated long-term elasticity of export supply for coffee (0.8).

Appendix B

Representative Estimates of the Income Elasticity of Demand for Imports

Empirically, import demand functions are usually estimated as log linear functions of the relative price of imports and real income. Recent studies (see table 7.B.1) have found that on average, income elasticities of import demand are somewhat higher in industrial countries than in developing countries, another possible reflection of the difference in import structure discussed earlier.[59] As with price elasticities, income elasticities are lower in the short run than in the long run.

As Wren-Lewis and Driver (1998) point out, differences in income elasticities can, other things being equal, lead to changes in equilibrium RERs. They note, for example, that even if the trend growth rates of GDP in the United States and Japan are the same, U.S. imports will grow more rapidly than Japanese imports because the income elasticity of import demand in the United States is 2.0 compared to 1.2 in Japan. More rapid growth of imports will put pressure on the U.S. equilibrium RER to depreciate over time relative to Japan's. Similarly, a low-income elasticity will create pressure on a country's equilibrium RER to appreciate over time relative to its trading partners'. However, it is important to bear in mind that, as discussed elsewhere in Parts II and III of this volume, the income elasticity of import demand is only one of many factors determining intertemporal movements in the equilibrium RER.

---

59. Senhadji (1997) gives individual elasticity estimates for 48 developing countries.

Table 7.B.1. *Estimated Income Elasticity of Import Demand*

Study	Average Income Elasticity	Number of Countries
Industrial Countries		
Bayoumi and Faruqee (1998)	1.50	—
Wren-Lewis and Driver (1998)	1.82	7
Senhadji (1997)	1.67	19
Reinhart (1995)	2.05	—
Developing Countries		
Senhadji (1997)	1.25	48
Reinhart (1995)	1.22	—

Source: Studies cited in table.

Appendix C

Formulas for Exchange Rate Appreciation, Depreciation, and Misalignment in Domestic- and Foreign-Currency Terms

A presentational question involved in measuring exchange rate misalignment empirically is whether to express the required appreciation or depreciation in domestic- or foreign-currency terms. Although each of these may be calculated from the other, the two expressions are not equal and may differ substantially in the case of large misalignments.

Exchange rates may be expressed in either domestic-currency (E_{dc}) or foreign-currency terms (E_{fc}), where these are the reciprocals of each other, as shown in equation 7.C.1:

$$(7.C.1) \qquad E_{dc} = \frac{1}{E_{fc}}.$$

Thus, for example, an exchange rate for the CFA franc in domestic-currency terms of CFAF 50 = FF 1.0 is equivalent to an exchange rate in foreign-currency terms of FF 0.02 = CFAF 1.0. Similarly, a depreciation from 50 CFA francs per French franc to 75 CFA francs per French franc (or FF 0.0133 = CFAF 1) represents a depreciation of 50 percent in domestic-currency terms and 33 percent in foreign-currency terms.

Equations 7.C.2 and 7.C.3 give the formulas for converting a given percentage depreciation (d_{fc}) or appreciation (a_{fc}) in foreign-currency terms into the corresponding depreciation (d_{dc}) or appreciation expressed in domestic-currency terms:

$$(7.C.2) \qquad d_{fc} = 1 - \frac{1}{1 + d_{dc}} \qquad \text{and} \qquad d_{dc} = \frac{1}{1 - d_{fc}} - 1$$

356

(7.C.3) $a_{fc} = \dfrac{1}{1 - a_{dc}} - 1$ and $a_{dc} = 1 - \dfrac{1}{1 + a_{fc}}.$

Note that depreciation and appreciation are expressed relative to the actual exchange rate. Hence, an appreciation (depreciation) of x percent followed by a depreciation (appreciation) of x percent would not return the exchange rate to its original level. An appreciation of X_a percent requires a depreciation of $X_a/(1+X_a)$ to return to the original level of the exchange rate. Similarly, a depreciation of X_d would require an offsetting appreciation of $X_d/(1-X_d)$. For example, an appreciation of 20 percent (a movement of the exchange rate index from 100 to 120 in foreign-currency terms, appreciation of 20/100=20 percent) requires a depreciation of 16.7 percent to return to the original level (movement of the index from 120 back to 100, depreciation of 20/120=16.7 percent).

Exchange rate misalignment itself may be expressed relative to the actual or the equilibrium value of the RER. Theoretically, misalignment, MA, is usually expressed as the percentage divergence of the actual rate from its equilibrium value and is calculated as shown in equation 7.C.4:

(7.C.4) $$MA = \left(\frac{ARER}{ERER} - 1 \right) \cdot 100$$

where $ARER$ is the actual RER and $ERER$ is the equilibrium RER. Empirically, however, the actual RER is usually known; but the equilibrium RER, the numeraire in the above formulation, is uncertain. Hence, empirically it is often clearer to use the known actual RER as the numeraire and indicate the estimated depreciation or appreciation required, RD, to bring the actual RER to the equilibrium level as shown in equation 7.C.5:[60]

(7.C.5) $$RD = \left(\frac{ERER}{ARER} - 1 \right) \cdot 100 .$$

As explained in the chapters in Part I of this book, different RER measures may diverge because of fluctuations in the terms of trade, differential productivity growth in the traded and nontraded sectors, changes in trade taxes, differences in the behavior of the prices of standardized and differentiated products, parallel markets, and unrecorded trade. Furthermore, as the actual value of the RER may vary with the concept employed, so too may its equilibrium value and the resulting estimate

---

60. See, for example, Clark and MacDonald (1998), p. 30.

of misalignment. Hence, it is important that misalignment be calculated using the same measures for both the equilibrium and the actual RERs. Given the relationship between the internal and external RERs set out in Part I, the equilibrium value of either the internal or the external RER should, in principle, also determine the equilibrium value of the other. However, because of the theoretical and empirical limitations of the various methodologies, it is desirable to look separately at the behavior of the internal and external RERs, estimate the misalignment in both of them, and then cross-check the results, utilizing the relationships discussed in Part I of this volume.

8

Estimates of Real Exchange Rate Misalignment with a Simple General-Equilibrium Model

*Shantayanan Devarajan**

In addition to the damage they cause the economy, misaligned real exchange rates (RERs) can be a serious problem for economists. When the RER in a country is overvalued, everyone turns to economists for a quantitative estimate of the degree of misalignment. The usual response of suggesting a multiyear research project to answer the question often will not do, as urgent policy decisions—such as the magnitude of currency devaluation—hinge on this estimate. Instead, the economist has to make use of available data and other information, often without the aid of a model or other consistency check, to develop quick estimates of the degree of RER misalignment.

The situation in the CFA franc zone prior to the January 12, 1994, devaluation illustrates this problem. Most observers agreed that the RER was overvalued, but they disagreed on the extent of the overvaluation. Since data were scarce, robust estimates, let alone formal models, were hard to come by. But the particular nature of the franc zone made the problem even more complicated. Since the CFA franc was convertible, there was no parallel market in foreign exchange, which is often used as

* I am grateful to Larry Hinkle for suggesting this chapter and to him, Peter Montiel, and three anonymous readers for helpful comments at various stages. Valuable assistance was provided by Fabien Nsengiyumva and Ingrid Ivins.

a guide for estimating RER misalignment.[1] The fact that 13 countries shared the same currency (across two monetary unions) meant that the degree of misalignment could be (and was) different across the countries of the zone. Finally, the CFA franc had never been devalued before, so the implication of an estimate of extreme misalignment could be quite profound. It could signal the need for a nominal devaluation that would, in turn, call the credibility of the zone's fixed exchange rate regime into question.

Theoretically, it would be desirable to estimate the equilibrium exchange rate using a full macroeconomic model that simultaneously takes into account all of the important interactions of the key variables affecting the exchange rate. However, as discussed in the following chapter by Haque and Montiel, constructing and estimating such models is so data- and time-intensive that it is not feasible in many cases in which estimates of the equilibrium exchange rate are needed for policy purposes. Fortunately, there are other approaches to estimating RER misalignment that do not require a full econometric model. This chapter illustrates one such approach.

There is a long tradition of using multisector computable general equilibrium (CGE) models to calculate equilibrium real exchange rates (See Dervis, de Melo, and Robinson (1982), Lewis and Urata (1984)). The model developed in this chapter is a miniature version of these large-scale models. As shown in Devarajan, Lewis, and Robinson (1993), these tiny models can approximate the larger models quite closely for real exchange rate calculations. Consequently, recent efforts have concentrated on these smaller models—see, for example, Abdelkhalek and Dufour (1997), Sekkat and Varoudakis (1998), and Tokarick (1995).

The purpose of this chapter is to show how RER misalignment such as that observed in the CFA zone can be estimated using one such simple general-equilibrium model of an open economy. The model by Devarajan, Lewis, and Robinson (1993) presented here permits a quick calculation of RER misalignment using minimal data. Hence, it is feasible to estimate the extent of RER misalignment for a number of countries in a limited amount of time. The model is used here to gauge the extent of misalignment in 12 of the CFA zone countries prior to the January 1994 devaluation. The model captures some of the salient features of such economies, particularly the effects of volatile terms of trade. At the same time, as we will show, the model incorporates the purchasing power parity (PPP) estimate of RER misalignment as a special case.

---

1. For a cautionary note on this procedure, see Chapter 12 by Ghei and Kamin on the use of the parallel exchange rate as a guide for setting the official rate.

The following section of this chapter describes the basic model and its relationship to the other methods of calculating RER misalignment. The next section applies the model to 12 of the (then) 13 CFA zone countries to calculate the degree of RER overvaluation just before the devaluation. For each country, it also shows how RER misalignment evolved over time. Then comes a section that discusses the sensitivity of the calculation to the choice of base-year and model parameters and presents extensions of the model to allow for changes in commercial policy and sustainable capital flows. The final section contains some concluding remarks.

The DLR Model

The DLR method extends the Salter-Swan model by dividing the economy into three goods:[2] exports, imports, and "domestic goods." The latter are goods produced and consumed in the country. Exports are substitutes for domestic goods in production but are assumed not to be consumed domestically. The relationship between exports (E) and domestic goods (D) can be expressed as a transformation function, with a constant elasticity of transformation, W. Profit maximization implies that the ratio of E to D is given by equation 8.1:

$$(8.1) \qquad\qquad E/D = k(P_E/P_D)^{\Omega}$$

where P_E and P_D are the prices of exports and domestic goods, respectively, and k is a constant. Assuming the country's exports are small in relation to world markets and are subject to the law of one price, the domestic price of exports is equal to the border price, P_E^* multiplied by the nominal exchange rate in domestic-currency terms, s.

Imports (M) are (imperfect) substitutes for domestic goods in consumption. This relationship is expressed as a constant elasticity of substitution (CES) utility function with elasticity of substitution, σ, giving rise to a first-order condition expressed in equation 8.2:

$$(8.2) \qquad\qquad M/D = k'(P_D/P_M)^{\sigma}$$

where P_M is the price of imports. On the assumption again that the law of one price holds, P_M is equal to sP_M^*, with P_M^* being the border price of

---

2. This subsection gives a summary description of the DLR model. The model's equations are given in the appendix. Readers interested in applying the DLR model should see Devarajan, Lewis, and Robinson (1993) for a fuller presentation of it.

imports. There are two real exchange rates in the model: the ratio of the price of domestic goods (P_D) to either the price of imports (P_M) or to the price of exports (P_E), expressed in domestic-currency terms. Note that the DLR model retains the Salter-Swan notion of the real exchange rate's being a ratio of the internal prices of tradables to nontradables—although here "nontradables" are all domestic goods, which are imperfectly sub-stitutable with traded goods, and traded goods are divided into imports and exports. The advantages of this approach are that P_D, P_M, and P_E are readily obtained from national accounts data and that the effects of changes in the terms of trade can be analyzed.[3]

The *equilibrium* real exchange rate in the DLR approach is that rate which is consistent with a specified current account target, given changes in import and export prices—that is, the terms of trade. Equations 8.1 and 8.2 provide two equations for the three unknowns E/D, M/D, and P_D. The current account target provides the third equation, a relation-ship between E/D and M/D. If, relative to a year in which the current account was in balance, import prices have risen and export prices fallen, for a given nominal exchange rate, P_D would most likely have to fall to restore the balance. If the nominal exchange rate were flexible, the re-quired adjustment could also occur through numerous combinations of changes in this rate and in domestic prices.

The amount by which P_D would have to fall depends not just on the changes in import and export prices but also on the elasticities of trans-formation and substitution. For small changes, the relationship between the required adjustment in P_D and the size of the terms-of-trade shocks and elasticities can be derived by log-differentiating equations 8.1 and 8.2. Denoting the log-derivative by a hat ("$\wedge$"), we obtain equation 8.3 (equation 16 in DLR):

(8.3) $$\hat{P}_D = [(\sigma - 1)\hat{P}_M + (\Omega + 1)\hat{P}_E]/(\sigma + \Omega).$$

To understand the economic intuition behind equation 8.3, it is useful to rewrite it as equation 8.4:

(8.4) $$\hat{P}_D = (\sigma\hat{P}_M + \Omega\hat{P}_E)/(\sigma + \Omega) + (\hat{P}_E - \hat{P}_M)/(\sigma + \Omega).$$

The first term on the right-hand side of equation 8.4 is a weighted aver-age of changes in world prices facing the country, in which the weights are elasticities. This term is similar to the adjustment implied by the

---

3. See below and Chapter 4 on the three-good internal RER, which explains the calculations of these different RER measures.

purchasing power parity approach: domestic prices should proportionately rise with world prices, in order to keep the real effective exchange rate at its equilibrium level. The second term on the right-hand side of equation 8.4 is the terms-of-trade change divided by a factor representing the "multiplier effect" of world prices on domestic prices. Equation 8.4 says, therefore, that domestic prices have to adjust not just to changes in the overall level of world prices but also to changes in the relative price of exports to imports (the terms of trade). Put another way, the purchasing power parity base-year approach is consistent with the DLR approach when there are no terms-of-trade shocks.

There is also some similarity between the DLR method and the trade-elasticities approach, since both use constant elasticity assumptions and aim at a specified current account target. However, note that the elasticities in equations 8.1 and 8.2 are constant elasticities of transformation and substitution, whereas the trade-elasticities approach in Chapter 7 uses constant elasticities of export supply and import demand. In the DLR model the equilibrium price in the specification of the domestic-goods market, P_D, and hence the real exchange rate, is that price which clears the nontraded (domestic) goods market.

Finally, the basic DLR model can be viewed as a special case of the reduced-form single-equation approach, inasmuch as both calculate the response of the equilibrium real exchange rate to terms-of-trade shocks. The reduced-form approach, though, postulates that the equilibrium RER is also a function of other variables, such as real income, openness, fiscal policy, and a time trend. Furthermore, while the DLR approach estimates only the equilibrium real exchange rate, the reduced-form approach also models the adjustment of the actual exchange rate to its equilibrium value.

The bare-bones version of the DLR model described above can, however, be extended to take into account several additional fundamental variables. Two such variables—which are particularly relevant for RER misalignment in the CFA countries—are changes in (a) sustainable capital flows and (b) trade policy. The remainder of this section describes how the basic DLR model can be extended to incorporate these. The section on sensitivity analyses and extensions subsequently provides illustrative calculations of the impact of these two effects on the estimates of RER misalignment for one country, Côte d'Ivoire.

The calculation of the equilibrium real exchange rate in equations 8.3 and 8.4 assumed that there were no changes in the levels of sustainable capital flows; the only changes were the shifts in world import and export prices. Yet in many cases, the source of the RER misalignment is not just a terms-of-trade shock but also a change in the sustainable capital inflow. For example, in the early 1980s many developing countries—

including those that faced no major terms-of-trade shocks—found themselves with reduced access to financing in world capital markets following the "debt crisis." To incorporate the impact of a change in the sustainable capital flow on the equilibrium real exchange rate, we add a
variable, λ, which represents the ratio of total imports to total exports.
When capital inflows are positive, zero, or negative, λ is greater than,
equal to, or less than 1, respectively. The effect of a change in λ on the
equilibrium real exchange rate is given by the following extension of
equation 8.4, equation 8.4′:

$$(8.4')\qquad \hat{P}_D = (\sigma\hat{P}_M + \Omega\hat{P}_E)/(\sigma+\Omega) + (\hat{P}_E - \hat{P}_M)/(\sigma+\Omega) + \hat{\lambda}/(\sigma+\Omega).$$

Thus, a drop in the level of sustainable capital inflows (λ declining) will
lead to a depreciation of the equilibrium real exchange rate. The magnitude of this depreciation is a function of the two elasticities, σ and Ω.

To estimate the response of the equilibrium domestic price to a change
in the tariff rate, we incorporate the tariff into the definition of the domestic price of the import, so that $P_M = sP_M^*(1+t)$, where t is the tariff rate
on imports. We make the additional simplifying assumption that tariff
revenues are rebated to the consumer in a lump-sum fashion. With this
assumption, the change in the equilibrium domestic price for a given
change in the tariff rate is expressed by equation 8.5:

$$(8.5)\qquad\qquad\qquad \hat{P}_D = \sigma\hat{\tau}/(\sigma+\Omega)$$

where, as shown in equation 8.6:

$$(8.6)\qquad\qquad\qquad \hat{\tau} = t\hat{t}/(1+t).$$

Note that, as σ approaches infinity, the change in the domestic price
level approaches the change in the tariff rate. (This result makes sense
since in this case imports and domestic goods are almost perfect substitutes.) However, for relatively small values of σ, the response of the domestic price level to tariff changes is also small.

The relationship between trade policy and the equilibrium real exchange rate is a complex one, and occasionally a source of confusion in
the literature. By raising the domestic price of importables (part of the
tradable sector), an import tariff also causes the internal real exchange
rate for imports to depreciate. However, the internal RER for exports
may remain constant or appreciate as a result of an induced increase in
the price of domestic goods. The explicit distinction among imports,
exports, and domestic goods made in the DLR model clarifies the confusion. The effect of an import tariff is to raise the price of imports and

also to raise the price of domestic goods, but not to the same extent as the price of imports (because imports and domestic goods are imperfect substitutes). Thus, the relative price of imports to domestic goods rises, so that the real exchange rate for imports depreciates. In contrast, the relative price of exports to domestic goods falls, so that the real exchange rate for exports appreciates, moving resources away from the export sector. The sign of the net effect of the depreciation of the internal RER for imports and of the appreciation of the internal RER for exports on the weighted average internal RER for all tradable goods and on the external RER is theoretically ambiguous. Empirically, however, the weighted average internal RER for traded goods will usually depreciate like the internal RER for imports because (a) the RER for imports will normally depreciate by much more than the RER for exports will appreciate and (b) if the country is a net capital importer like most developing countries, imports are usually larger than exports (see Chapter 4 on the three-good internal RER).

As with sustainable capital flows, we provide illustrations of the role of the tariff policy in real exchange rate misalignment for the case of Côte d'Ivoire.

Applying the DLR Model to the Pre-1994 CFA Zone

We now estimate the extent of RER misalignment in the CFA zone just before the January 1994 devaluation. The model's underlying equations 8.1 and 8.2 are applied to 12 of the 13 member countries of the zone in 1994 for which adequate data were available. Since many of the terms-of-trade shocks these countries faced were large, the linear approximation given by equations 8.3 and 8.4 cannot be used (although these equations will help in interpreting the results). Instead, we solve the full-blown nonlinear model, which consists of equations 8.1 and 8.2 and the set of accounting identities set out in appendix A.

The calculation of RER misalignment proceeds in several steps. First, we decide on a base year in which the actual RER was equal to the equilibrium RER so that we can estimate the amount by which domestic prices should have changed in order to preserve equilibrium. Column 2 of table 8.1 lists the base year chosen. In most cases, this choice was based on the last year in which the current account in those countries was thought to be in equilibrium in the sense that it could be financed by sustainable capital flows. For most countries, the base year is in the mid-1980s, the period after which terms of trade began moving sharply against the CFA countries. Since the choice of base year is somewhat arbitrary, we subsequently perform sensitivity tests around the selected year as discussed in the next section on sensitivity analyses and extensions.

Second, we decide on the values of the export transformation and import substitution elasticities to be used (columns 3 and 4, table 8.1). These parameter values are based on informed estimates or, in some cases such as Cameroon, may come from larger models of the country (Devarajan, Lewis, and Robinson (1993)). Again, the following section tests the sensitivity of the results to the assumptions about the parameters. Recent econometric evidence (Devarajan, Go, and Li, (1998)) suggests that these elasticities are less than 1 for most developing countries and are considerably lower for low-income primary-exporting economies. The base case export transformation elasticities were, therefore, assumed to be slightly higher (0.5) for the more diversified middle- and former middle-income economies, such as Côte d'Ivoire, Cameroon, and Senegal, than for the low-income countries (0.3). The elasticity of import substitution, in contrast, was assumed to be the same (0.4) in all the countries.

We turn now to the data. Table 8.2 presents first the changes in import and export prices between the base year and 1993. With a fixed nominal exchange rate in the CFA countries, if there had been no change in domestic prices, the real exchange rate would almost surely have been out of equilibrium in the wake of these terms-of-trade shocks. But, of course, domestic prices did change (column 3 of table 8.2), so the empirical question we attempt to answer is whether they changed enough—and in the right direction—to restore equilibrium.

Table 8.1 *Assumptions*

Country	Base Year	Sigma	Omega
Benin	1986	0.4	0.3
Burkina Faso	1985	0.4	0.3
Cameroon	1984	0.4	0.5
Central African Republic	1981	0.4	0.3
Chad	1984	0.4	0.3
Congo	1984	0.4	0.5
Côte d'Ivoire	1985	0.4	0.5
Gabon	1984	0.4	0.5
Mali	1984	0.4	0.3
Niger	1984	0.4	0.3
Senegal	1977	0.4	0.5
Togo	1984	0.4	0.3

Source: Author's judgment.

Table 8.2 *Changes in Prices between Base Year and 1993 (in percent)*

Country	Base Year	Import Prices	Export Prices	Terms of Trade	Domesticprices (GDP Deflator)
Benin	1986	25	18	–7	12
Burkina Faso	1985	–14	–13	1	14
Cameroon	1984	–32	–60	–28	15
Central African Republic	1981	97	67	–30	66
Chad	1984	–28	–16	12	–16
Congo	1984	10	–60	–70	–27
Côte d'Ivoire	1985	–3	–32	–29	–11
Gabon	1984	15	–43	–58	–7
Mali	1984	–9	–31	–22	17
Niger	1984	10	–15	–25	–11
Senegal	1977	–3	15	18	56
Togo	1984	–15	–36	–21	20

Source: World Bank data.

Table 8.2 shows that 3 of the 12 CFA countries did not suffer a negative terms-of-trade shock between their base year and 1993. Of these, Senegal experienced the largest improvement in its terms of trade. However, as we will show later, this does not necessarily mean that the real exchange rate was undervalued even in that country. The reason is that the observed 56 percent increase in domestic prices in the same period could have been excessive, given the terms-of-trade changes that occurred. Similarly, five countries experienced a decline in domestic prices during the period in question. Yet, some of these (such as Gabon) will turn out to be among the most overvalued in 1993 because the decline in their export prices was much sharper. The variations in the terms-of-trade change can be largely attributed to the differences in the composition of the countries' exports.[4]

Having spelled out the assumptions and presented the basic data, we are now in a position to calculate the degree of RER misalignment in each of the 12 countries. We solve the DLR model using the elasticities in

4. At first glance, it may seem surprising that the import price deflator varied so much across these countries, even though they import roughly the same basket of goods. There are two reasons for this variation. First, the base from which the price change was calculated varied substantially across countries. Second, some countries import petroleum products whereas others export them.

table 8.1 and import- and export-price changes in table 8.2. The model calculates the domestic price level that, for a fixed nominal exchange rate, is consistent with those price changes, given the elasticities and structure of the economy. The economic structure, in turn, is determined by the levels of real GDP, imports, and exports only—hence the claim that the model is economical in its demands on data. We then compare this model-calculated price level with the actual price level in 1993 to determine the extent of RER misalignment in that year.

Before discussing the results, two presentational issues must be addressed. First, the essence of the DLR model is the notion that the price of domestic goods adjusts to restore equilibrium in the economy. The calculations assume that the nominal exchange rate is fixed—as it is in the CFA economies. While the adjusting domestic price is precisely defined, and can be easily calculated using national accounts data, it is not always reported in standard price statistics. Instead, these statistics usually report the consumer price index (CPI) and the GDP deflator. Since there is a straightforward relationship between the price of domestic goods and the GDP deflator (the latter is a weighted average of the former and the export price deflator) in the national accounts and the DLR model,[5] we will report the results in terms of the GDP deflator in order to make them more readily comparable to available price statistics. That is, we use the model first to calculate the equilibrium domestic price and subsequently compute the equilibrium GDP deflator. We then compare the latter to the actual level of the GDP deflator to determine the degree of price level overvaluation.

It may seem curious that, while we have stressed the advantage of the DLR model as capturing the two real exchange rates, we use neither in our estimation of price misalignment. We have adopted this procedure in order to simplify the presentation and focus it on the model's endogenous price variable—the domestic price level. Recall that the RERs for imports (RERM) and for exports (RERE) are defined as shown in equations 8.7 and 8.8:

$$(8.7) \qquad RERM = \frac{P_M}{P_D} = \frac{sP_M^*}{P_D} = \frac{P_M^*}{\left(\frac{1}{s}\right) \cdot P_D}$$

$$(8.8) \qquad RERE = \frac{P_E}{P_D} = \frac{sP_E^*}{P_D} = \frac{P_E^*}{\left(\frac{1}{s}\right) \cdot P_D}.$$

---

5. See the appendix to Chapter 3 on the two-good internal RER.

In the DLR model, P_M^* and P_E^* are specified exogenously; and $(1/s) \cdot P_D$, the price of domestic goods in foreign currency terms, is the model's endogenous price variable. If s is also fixed as in the CFA countries, P_D becomes the model's single endogenous price variable and the endogenous determinant of the RERs for both exports and imports. The equilibrium RERs for imports and exports can, however, be readily computed with equations 8.7 and 8.8 using the equilibrium domestic price level and the exogenously determined border prices of imports and exports.

A second presentational issue, which all studies of real exchange rates have to confront, is the question of whether the measure should be expressed in domestic- or foreign-currency terms. In the figures in this chapter, the results are presented in foreign-currency terms, so that an upward movement of the RER or domestic price level is an appreciation and a downward one is a depreciation. Since we are comparing price levels, our measure of overvaluation is *the degree to which domestic prices will have to fall in order to restore equilibrium*.

With these clarifications in mind, figure 8.1 presents the degree of overvaluation of the GDP deflator in the CFA countries in 1993. For example, the domestic price level in Cameroon, the most overvalued country, needed to fall by 78 percent because the equilibrium price level was only 22 percent of the actual price.

Several points about these results are worth noting. First, the degree of real overvaluation in 1993 was substantial—an unweighted average of 31 percent for the CFA countries as a group. Second, the variation in RER misalignment across countries was also substantial: the middle- and former middle-income countries, and within that group the oil producers (Cameroon, Gabon, Congo), were the most overvalued, while some of the low-income countries were only slightly overvalued or, in one case (Chad), undervalued.[6] Third, the comparable calculation using the PPP base-year method yields much lower degrees of real overvaluation. The reason, as mentioned earlier, is that the PPP base-year approach leaves out the effects of changes in the terms of trade on the country's equilibrium real exchange rate. To the extent that CFA countries suffered adverse terms-of-trade shocks during this period, such an omission will lead to an underestimate of the degree of overvaluation (see equation 8.4).[7]

---

6. The large variation in RER misalignment does not necessarily imply that a uniform nominal devaluation was unwarranted, since a nonuniform devaluation would have necessitated introducing multiple currencies and, therefore, undermined the zone's two monetary unions.

7. In addition, the PPP base-year approach usually uses the country's overall price level (CPI). Since this index reflects tradable as well as nontradable prices (import prices in the CPI), it is not directly comparable to the price of domestic goods.

Figure 8.1 *Overvaluation of the GDP Deflator in the CFA Zone, 1993*

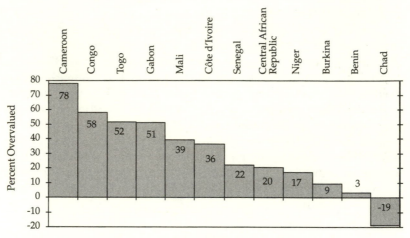

Source: Computed from World Bank data using the DLR model.

Figure 8.1 summarizes the extent of price overvaluation on the eve of the devaluation. Was this overvaluation persistent, or had it arisen in the last few years? To answer this question, we examine the evolution of misalignment over time for each of the 12 countries. We do so first by using the DLR model to compute the level of the GDP price deflator required to restore equilibrium for every year after the base year and then by comparing the equilibrium level to the actual levels of those years. Such an exercise helps answer another question: How much of the overvaluation was due to changes in the equilibrium price level, and how much to changes in the actual domestic price level?

The results of this exercise for three representative countries are presented in figure 8.2. The picture painted in the previous discussion now comes into sharper view. Cameroon, a major oil producer, suffered a major terms-of-trade shock in 1986 (when the price of oil plummeted) and remained severely overvalued subsequently. Even though the price level in the country rose only slightly, it was still far above the equilibrium level, which declined sharply. Similarly, in another highly overvalued country, Côte d'Ivoire, the gap between the equilibrium and actual price levels started growing in the mid-1980s and continued to grow until the end of 1993. By contrast, in one of the low-income countries, Niger, the GDP deflator was either in equilibrium or even undervalued for most of the 1980s. Niger's GDP deflator became overvalued only

Figure 8.2 *Equilibrium vs. Actual GDP Deflators*

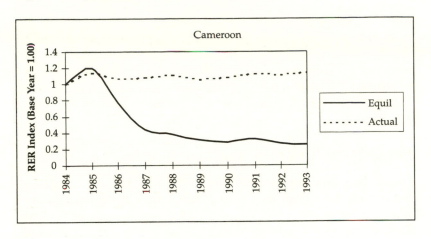

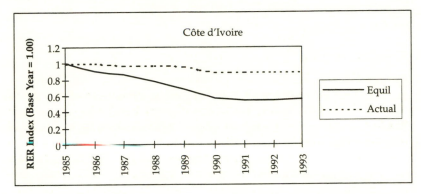

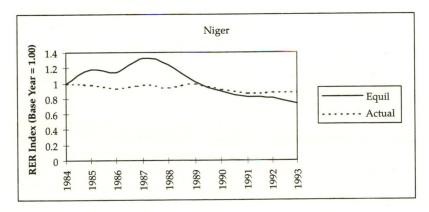

Note: An upward movement is an appreciation.
Source: Computed from World Bank data using the DLR model.

after 1990, when uranium prices fell. Nevertheless, by the early 1990s, a significant gap between the equilibrium and actual GDP deflator rate had appeared in 10 of the 12 CFA countries, with the gaps becoming ominously large (more than 30 percent) in six countries. Most of the countries were subject to adverse terms-of-trade shocks for their primary export commodities; and the appreciation of the French franc (to which the CFA franc was pegged) relative to the U.S. dollar following the 1985 Plaza Accords exacerbated the decline in their export earning in CFA terms.

Sensitivity Analyses and Extensions

This section discusses the sensitivity of the estimates of misalignment to the model's assumptions. The two most crucial are the choice of base year and the assumed elasticities of transformation and substitution. The section goes on to give an example of an extension of the basic analysis to incorporate changes in sustainable capital flows and commercial policy.

Sensitivity to Choice of Base Year

As mentioned earlier, the choice of base year for the calculation of RER misalignment is somewhat arbitrary. The analyst has to decide in which year the actual RER equaled the equilibrium RER and the resource balance of the economy reflected a sustainable level of capital flows. Significantly, that level of capital flows need not be zero: a country may have a current account deficit, or a negative resource balance, and still be in a sustainable equilibrium. Indeed, the resource deficit could be larger in the base year than in a current (disequilibrium) year if the external capital inflows have fallen. In this case the smaller current resource deficit would not be sustainable, although the larger one in the equilibrium base year was sustainable. In short, the choice of a base year does not lend itself to some simple, mechanical formula, such as "the year in which the resource balance was x percent of GDP." Hence, we based our choice of base years on the knowledge of economists familiar with the particular situation of the individual countries. Given that this is a subjective method for determining a potentially crucial component of the analysis, we examined the sensitivity of the price misalignment estimates to the choice of base year.

Figure 8.3 reports on simulations with the DLR model using different candidates for the base year from 1980 to 1990 for three representative countries. For each different base year, both the terms-of-trade shock (with respect to 1993) and the structure of the economy (in the base year) are different. The resulting patterns are quite revealing. For one of the

Figure 8.3 *Sensitivity of the 1993 Equilibrium GDP Deflator to Choice of Base Year*

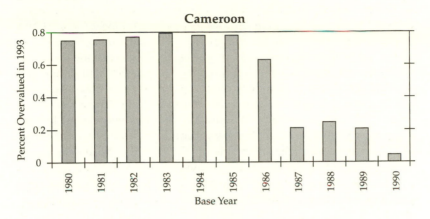

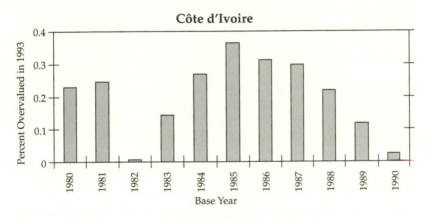

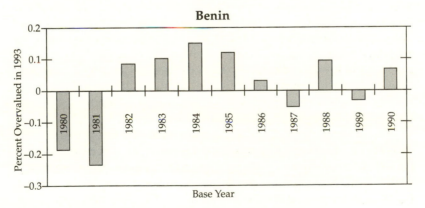

Source: Computed from World Bank data using the DLR model.

most overvalued former middle-income countries, Cameroon, the degree of price misalignment is quite robust to the choice of base year up to 1986–87. This pattern is not surprising. Cameroon faced the largest terms-of-trade shocks in the mid-1980s. Yet, after 1986–87 export and import prices were not that different from the level in 1993. Hence, if one of the years after 1986–87 is chosen as the base year, the degree of misalignment is much lower. Yet no economist familiar with Cameroon would suggest that 1988, for example, was a reasonable base year for it. The country was then in the middle of a major adjustment period because of the oil-price shock. In contrast, for a less overvalued low-income country such as Benin, the magnitude, and possibly even the sign, of the price misalignment depends on the choice of base year. Benin could be considered undervalued or overvalued depending on which year in the 1980s was picked as its base year. To be sure for the years after 1982, the degree of misalignment would range only from +10 percent to –5 percent so that Benin would still be close to equilibrium in any case. Finally, note that for Côte d'Ivoire—which is often thought to be the leader in the CFA zone—the degree of price overvaluation is quite sensitive to the choice of base year even if the choice is restricted to the first half of the 1980s because of sharp swings in its terms of trade. For instance, if 1982 were to be chosen, the country was hardly out of equilibrium in 1993. But if 1985 were the base year, Côte d'Ivoire was above the CFA average in overvaluation. These results provide a partial explanation of why observers of Côte d'Ivoire may have disagreed on whether the country's RER was misaligned: they may have been thinking in terms of different base years.

Sensitivity to Elasticities

As the DLR model relies on assumed values of two key parameters, it is also important to investigate how robust the results are with respect to assumptions about these parameters. The results of sensitivity tests using values of these elasticities below and above the base case values are reported below.

As figure 8.4 indicates, for the most overvalued country, Cameroon, the degree of price overvaluation is not very sensitive to either elasticity. The range of price overvaluation between the high elasticity case (both elasticities equal to 2, four to five times the base case levels) and the low elasticity case (0.2 and 0.25, one half the base case levels) is only between 66 percent and 81 percent. This result is not surprising since, as we saw earlier, Cameroon suffered a sharp terms-of-trade decline, which (with a fixed nominal exchange rate and downward price rigidity) would lead to a substantial overvaluation for any reasonable substitution and

Figure 8.4 *Sensitivity of Price Misalignment to Elasticity Assumptions*

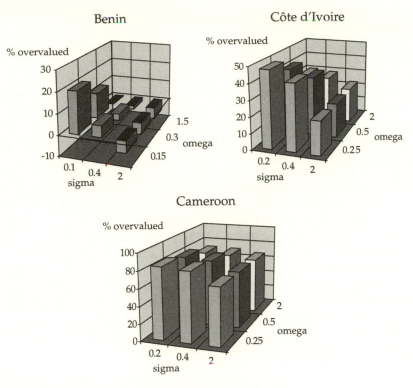

Source: Computed from World Bank data using the DLR model.

transformation elasticities. This result is repeated for all the highly overvalued oil-producing countries. However, as with the choice of base year, assumptions about the elasticities can affect the sign of the misalignment for less overvalued low-income countries such as Benin. Again, though, the range between the high and low cases is not very large—around 20 percentage points. In Côte d'Ivoire's case, the degree of misalignment, while somewhat sensitive to the choice of base year, is less sensitive to the elasticities: the range between the high and low cases is around 20 percentage points, with very little variation in the intermediate values. Again, this outcome is driven by the fact that Côte d'Ivoire's overvaluation was the result of the large terms-of-trade shocks it suffered in the mid-1980s. These shocks were sufficiently large that they dominated the effect of reasonable variations in the assumed elasticities.

Extensions

Finally, as anticipated in the section that introduced the DLR model, we now present some illustrative calculations for Côte d'Ivoire of the RERs for exports and imports, and the two extensions to the DLR model discussed in this chapter—namely, changes in sustainable capital flows and in tariffs. Figure 8.5 shows the evolution of the actual and equilibrium RERs for exports and imports expressed relative to the GDP deflator in Côte d'Ivoire. Note that the two RERs behaved somewhat differently. The actual RER for exports appreciated by about 35 percent, while the equilibrium export rate depreciated by almost 20 percent. For imports, in contrast, the actual RER changed little, whereas the equilibrium rate depreciated by nearly 40 percent.

As for the first of the two extensions, estimating sustainable capital flows and determining target current account deficits is a significant analytical problem in its own right, which is discussed further in the preceding chapter on traditional methodologies and operational techniques by Ahlers and Hinkle. Recall that the assumption in figure 8.1 that there was no change in the level of sustainable flows yielded a degree of overvaluation for Côte d'Ivoire of 36 percent. How does this estimate vary with changes in the level of sustainable capital flows? We can use equation 8.4′ to obtain an approximation of the additional overvaluation for a given reduction in the level of sustainable capital flow. Note that *since λ allows us to adjust for changes in capital flows, the critical factor in choosing a base year is that, taking into account all of the fundamentals, the actual RER be as close as possible to the equilibrium RER.*

The calculation proceeds in the following steps. First, we translate a 1 percent of GDP reduction in the level of capital inflow (or increase in the level of outflow) into a change in the ratio of total imports to total exports. Given the levels of GDP, imports, exports, and the resource balance in Côte d'Ivoire in the base year (1984), this 1 percent of GDP reduction is equivalent to a 3 percent decrease in λ. Second, from (8.4′), we determine that a 3 percent reduction in λ would require an additional decline in the domestic price of 3.3 percent to restore equilibrium (given elasticities of 0.4 and 0.5). Third, this 3.3 percent decline in the domestic price would lower the overall price level by an additional 2 percentage points (exports are about 40 percent of GDP). The next result is that if Côte d'Ivoire was overvalued by 36 percent when capital flows return to the base-year level, it is overvalued by 39 percent when they are 1 percent of GDP lower than in the base year. In sum, for every 1 percent of GDP decline in the level of sustainable capital inflow from the 1984 level, Côte d'Ivoire's degree of price overvaluation goes up by 3 percentage points.

Figure 8.5.a *Côte d'Ivoire: RER for Exports*

Export RER (*Px/Pe*)

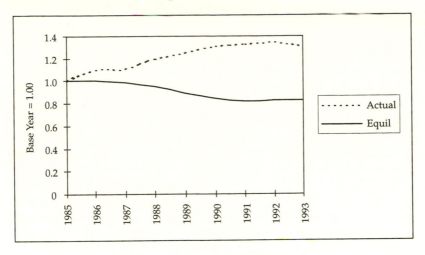

Figure 8.5.b *Côte d'Ivoire: RER for Imports*

Import RER (*Px/Pm*)

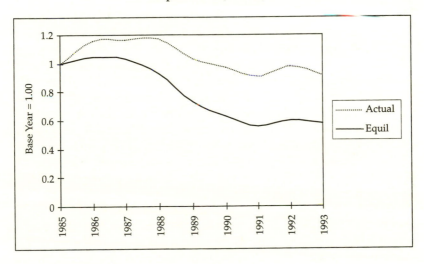

Note: An upward movement is an appreciation.
Source: Computed from World Bank data using the DLR model.

The calculation for a change in tariffs proceeds along similar lines. For example, if the initial effective tariff rate (tariff revenues collected as a share of imports) in Côte d'Ivoire was 20 percent, then a 30 percent reduction in the effective tariff rate (that is, the effective tariff rate being reduced to 14 percent) would have implied a reduction in the equilibrium domestic price of 2.2 percent (using equation 8.5). However, the domestic price of imports including tariffs would also have fallen by 5 percent, while the domestic price of exports would have remained constant. If we go back to the definitions of two real exchange rates—the relative prices of imports to domestic goods and of exports to domestic goods—the former would have appreciated by 2.8 percent, while the latter would have depreciated by 2.2 percent. If one were using a weighted average of the two real exchange rates for the internal RER, the net effect would probably be an appreciation, given the greater change in the import RER and the fact that for most capital importing countries (like Côte d'Ivoire) imports exceed exports. Hence, a reduction in protection is likely to lead to an appreciation of the equilibrium RER but to have asymmetric effects on the RERs for imports and exports, appreciating the former but depreciating the latter.

Conclusion

This chapter has demonstrated the use of a simple general-equilibrium model that captures some salient features of RER misalignment in developing countries (specifically, the change in the equilibrium RER in response to changes in the terms of trade and capital flows) but requires only minimal data for the calculations. The analysis has shown that neglecting changes in the equilibrium RER can be seriously misleading in determining the extent of RER overvaluation. Several CFA countries experienced a decline in their domestic price levels over the late 1980s and early 1990s; yet some of these same countries were still the most overvalued as the equilibrium RER declined even further because of adverse terms-of-trade shocks. Two extensions of the basic model—one that allowed for changes in the level of sustainable capital inflows, the other for changes in the tariff regime—were also presented and used to calculate the impact of each of these changes on the degree of RER overvaluation in Côte d'Ivoire.

The simplicity of the DLR model permits a range of sensitivity analyses of the estimates of misalignment. While the choice of base year is often controversial, we find that our estimates of misalignment do not change significantly for a wide range of base years. Specifically, for the most overvalued countries, any base year in the early- to mid-1980s before the adverse terms-of-trade shock would give more or less the same estimate of overvaluation, since the terms of trade of these countries fell sharply in the mid-1980s and have not recovered since.

The estimate of domestic price overvaluation for the countries experiencing large terms-of-trade shocks is similarly robust to assumptions about the model's elasticities. The terms-of-trade shocks were so severe that for a wide range of elasticities the gap between the equilibrium and actual real exchange rate in 1993 was substantial. In contrast, for the countries where the terms-of-trade shocks were smaller, the estimates are quite sensitive to the elasticities. However, insofar as the economies of these countries are relatively simple, we can attach more confidence to our "base case" levels of the elasticities (which were quite low) and therefore to our initial estimates of RER overvaluation in those countries.

Two limitations of the approach in this chapter should be highlighted here. First, being an equilibrium model but not a dynamic one, the model only calculates the gap between the actual and equilibrium real exchange rates. It is silent about the path that the economy should take to achieve equilibrium, or even how long it should take. Second, as a model of relative prices, it is better suited for analyzing countries with fixed exchange rates, as the domestic price level can be uniquely determined only if the nominal exchange rate is predetermined or exogenously specified. In addition, in countries with fully flexible exchange rates, changes in the nominal exchange rate can affect real variables through the monetary sector. These effects are left out of the present model. That said, if the situation calls for the rapid calculation of the equilibrium real exchange rate in a country subject to terms-of-trade shocks, the general-equilibrium model presented in this chapter can help put the estimate of RER misalignment on a firmer analytical footing.

Appendix

The DLR Model

Equations

(8.A.1)	$X = G(E, D; \Omega)$
(8.A.2)	$Q = F(M, D; \sigma)$
(8.A.3)	$E/D = g(P_D, P_E; \Omega)$
(8.A.4)	$M/D = f(P_D, P_M; \sigma)$
(8.A.5)	$P_M = sP_M^*$
(8.A.6)	$P_E = sP_E^*$
(8.A.7)	$P_M^* M = P_E^* E$
(8.A.8)	$s = 1.$

Endogenous variables

E	Exports
M	Imports
D	Domestic goods
Q	Composite goods
P	Price of domestic goods
P_M	Domestic price of imports
P_E	Domestic price of exports
s	Nominal exchange rate

Exogenous variables

X	Aggregate output
P_M^*	World price of imports
P_E^*	World price of exports
λ	Ratio of value of imports to value of exports
Ω	Elasticity of transformation of supply
σ	Elasticity of substitution in demand

9

Long-Run Real Exchange Rate Changes in Developing Countries: Simulations from an Econometric Model

Nadeem Ul Haque and Peter J. Montiel

This chapter describes a methodology for the empirical estimation of the impact on the long-run equilibrium real exchange rate (LRER) of permanent policy changes and external shocks. Because the real exchange rate is one of two key macroeconomic relative prices (the other being the real interest rate), it is endogenous to a wide variety of potential macroeconomic disturbances. A variety of techniques, reviewed elsewhere in this book, are available for deriving approximate estimates of the reaction of the long-run equilibrium real exchange rate to shocks, using simplified models that focus on the particular aspects of the adjustment process believed to be most important in specific applications. However, the full general-equilibrium interactions can only be studied in the context of larger models. Consequently an empirical judgment about where the prevailing real exchange rate in a given country stands relative to its sustainable long-run value would ideally be formed by working out the economy's full dynamic adjustment in the context of such a model. Thus, numerical simulation experiments with macroeconomic models are—at least in principle—the tool of choice for understanding both the "real time" and long-run effects of policy measures and external shocks on real exchange rates in developing countries.

Such experiments have been conducted for industrial countries by international institutions that maintain large multicountry economic models.[1] Whether this methodology can in fact be applied more generally in other country circumstances, however, depends on the availability of a reliable empirical macroeconomic model for the country in question. Unfortunately, this is rarely available for such countries, and the construction and simulation of custom-made models for the purpose of estimating long-run equilibrium real exchange rates is expensive and time consuming.

One approach to this problem is to adapt an existing model, which is broadly applicable to the country in question, to the application at hand. The usefulness of the results from such a procedure, however, would depend on how closely the model chosen for the purpose can replicate the macroeconomic behavior of the country under study.

In this chapter, we describe how the long-run behavior of the real exchange rate can be explored using a particular empirical developing-country macroeconomic model that may be suitable for many such applications. The model used for this purpose is one developed by Haque, Lahiri, and Montiel (1990). The Haque-Lahiri-Montiel (HLM) model was designed for the purpose of estimating representative developing-country values for the parameters of standard macroeconomic behavioral functions typically used by policymakers in such countries for the quantitative formulation of fiscal, monetary, and exchange rate policies. This feature makes it a likely candidate for use in the manner just described. Other characteristics of the model make it specifically suitable for the study of real exchange rate dynamics. In particular, while the behavioral relationships incorporated in it are of the ad hoc variety typically found in models of this type, the model was specified with careful attention to dynamic considerations, and is reasonably comprehensive in its incorporation of dynamic macroeconomic adjustment mechanisms. Among other features, it was estimated and simulated under the assumption of rational expectations, and it allows for full adjustment of the capital stock to its long-run equilibrium value. The various adjustment mechanisms incorporated in the model can be shown to yield a stable long-run equilibrium, in which the real exchange rate plays an important macroeconomic equilibrating role.

Our specific purpose in this chapter is to explore the predictions of the HLM model for the adjustment of this long-run equilibrium real exchange rate to permanent changes in the "fundamentals"—namely, domestic policy shocks and changes in the external environment—as an illustration of how macroeconometric models can be used in a developing-country setting to extract estimates of equilibrium real exchange rates

---

1. See, for example, Williamson (1994) and Bayoumi and others (1994).

that reflect full general-equilibrium interactions. As indicated above, the model described here can be used as a template for the specification and estimation of country-specific versions in particular applications in which its general properties match those of the country under study. It can also be used as a source of representative value estimates of key behavioral parameters for simulation purposes, in applications in which country-specific parameter estimation is not feasible.

The chapter is organized as follows: The next section presents a brief description of the model and some of its relevant properties. The section titled "Domestic Policy Shocks" examines the effects of a variety of permanent policy shocks on the long-run equilibrium real exchange rate, while the effects of permanent external shocks are analyzed in the subsequent section. A final section summarizes the findings, and an appendix describes an application of the methodology to the estimation of the equilibrium real exchange rate for Thailand.

A Brief Description of the Model

The structure of the HLM model (equations 9.1 through 9.19) is described in table 9.1. A detailed equation-by-equation description is contained in Haque, Lahiri, and Montiel (1990), so the exposition in this section is deliberately brief. We focus on several features of the model that make it particularly suited for the purpose at hand. First, it is designed to be applied to an open economy with a Mundell-Fleming production structure operating under a fixed exchange rate.[2] Despite the prevalence of the alternative Swan-Salter "dependent-economy" production structure in analytical macroeconomic models for developing countries, data limitations described in Part I of this volume have implied that the vast majority of empirical macroeconomic models for developing countries have incorporated the Mundell-Fleming production structure. Thus the HLM model is reasonably representative of the class of models used for quantitative policy formulation and evaluation in such countries.[3] Second, as mentioned above, the model's individual behavioral equations reflect conventional, widely used specifications. For example, as described in equations 9.2 and 9.5, respectively, private consumption depends on current and lagged values of disposable income and the domestic real interest rate, while private investment depends on the real

---

2. Fixed exchange rate arrangements are common among developing countries, and were even more so during the sample period over which the model was estimated.

3. See Montiel (1993) for a survey of such models.

Table 9.1 *Structure of the HLM Model*

Equation Description	Equation Formula
Goods market equilibrium condition (Equation 9.1)	$Y = C_t + I_t + G_t + (X_t - [(e_t P_t^* Z_t)/P_t])$
Consumption function (Equation 9.2)	$\log C_t = \alpha_o - 0.12\, r_t + 0.99 \log C_{t-1} + 0.34 \log Y_t^d$ $- 0.33 \log Y_{t-1}^d$
Disposable income (Equation 9.3)	$Y_t^d = Y_t + [i_t^* e_t F_{p,t}/P_t] - [i_t DC_{p,t}/P_t] - T_t$
Household budget constraint (Equation 9.4)	$Y_t^d = C_t + I_t + \{(M_t - M_{t-1}) + e_t(F_{p,t} - F_{p,t-1}) - (DC_{p,t} - DC_{p,t-1})\}/P_t$
Investment function (Equation 9.5)	$\log I_t = k_o - 0.207\, r_t + 0.199 \log Y_t - 0.815 \log K_{t-1}$
Export demand function (Equation 9.6)	$\log X_t = \tau_o + 0.054\,(e_t P_t^*/P_t) + 0.106 \log Y_t^*$ $+ 0.927 \log X_{t-1}$
Import demand function (Equation 9.7)	$\log (e_t Z_t/P_t) = d_o - 0.129 \log (e_t P_t^*/P_t) + 0.135 \log Y_t$ $+ 0.847 \log [(e_{t-1} Z_{t-1})/(P_{t-1})]$
Production function (Equation 9.8)	$\log Y_t = q_o + 0.162 \log K_t + 0.838 \log L_t$
Capital stock accumulation (Equation 9.9)	$K_t = I_t + 0.95\, K_{t-1}$
Central bank balance sheet (Equation 9.10)	$M_t = e_t R_t + DC_t$
Domestic credit identity (Equation 9.11)	$DC_t = DC_{p,t} + DC_{G,t}$
Money market equilibrium (Equation 9.12)	$\log M_t/P = m_o - 0.055 i_t + 0.203 \log Y_t$ $+ 0.796 \log (M_{t-1}/P_{t-1})$

Uncovered parity *condition* (Equation 9.13)	$i_t = i_t^* + (E_t e_{t+1} - e_t)/e_t$
Current account identity (Equation 9.14)	$CA_t = p_t X_t - e_t p_t^* Z_t + i_t^* e_t (F_{p,t-1} + F_{G,t-1})$
Balance of *payments identity* (Equation 9.15)	$e_t \Delta R_t = CA_t - e_t(\Delta F_{G,t} + \Delta F_{p,t})$
Definition of the domestic *real interest rate* (Equation 9.16)	$r_t = i_t - (E_t P_{t+1} - P_t)$
Government budget *constraint* (Equation 9.17)	$\Delta F_{G,t} - \Delta DC_{G,t} = P_t(T_t - G_t - (e_t P_t^*/P_t)GZ_t)$ $+ i_t^* e_t F_{G,t-1} - i_t DC_{G,t}$
Expectations formation (Equation 9.18) (Equation 9.19)	$e_{t+1} = E_t(e_{t+1} \mid \Omega_t) + \varepsilon$ $P_{t+1} = E(P_{t+1} \mid \Omega_t) + \eta$

Note: Definition of Variables

Y	= Real GDP.
C	= Real private consumption expenditure.
I	= Total real investment expenditure.
G	= Government expenditure on domestic goods.
X	= Real exports.
e	= Nominal exchange rate (price of foreign currency in domestic-currency terms).
P^*	= Foreign-currency price of imports.
P	= Domestic-currency price of domestic goods.
Z	= Real (private) imports measured in terms of the foreign good.
r	= Real rate of interest.
Y^d	= Real disposable income.
F_p	= Stock of foreign assets held by the private sector (measured in foreign-currency terms).
DC_p	= Stock of domestic bank credit held by the private sector.
i	= Nominal interest rate.
T	= Real tax receipts.

(table continues on next page)

(Table 9.1 continued)

M = Nominal money supply.
K = Aggregate capital stock.
Y^* = Foreign real GDP.
R = Stock of foreign exchange reserves.
DC = Stock of total domestic credit.
DC_G = Stock of domestic credit to the public sector.
CA = Current account of the balance of payments.
F_G = Foreign assets held by nonfinancial public sector.
L_t = Labor force.
GZ_t = Real government expenditure on foreign goods (measured in foreign-
        currency terms).
ε, η = White noise error terms.

interest rate, the level of economic activity, and the lagged value of the capital stock. The demand for money is also conventional, depending on the domestic nominal interest rate and the level of real GDP, with partial adjustment allowed for the real money stock (equation 9.12). Third, the behavioral parameters were estimated using a large pooled cross section-time-series sample of countries, a consistent data set, and empirical techniques appropriate for the estimation of rational expectations models with panel data.[4] The objective was to extract "representative" estimates from the data for the parameters involved in these conventional specifications. Fourth, the model was designed to test empirically for the degree of effective capital mobility exhibited by the countries in the sample. The degree of capital mobility applicable among developing countries is an issue on which there is little agreement, even for specific countries, and consequently any particular assumption adopted on a priori grounds would essentially be arbitrary. As it happens, the estimation proved unable to reject the hypothesis of perfect capital mobility (uncovered interest parity) over the sample period.[5]

---

4. The parameters were estimated using an error-components three-stage least squares technique for a pooled cross-section time-series sample of 31 developing countries covering various regions of the world and levels of income per capita. Details of the estimation, including diagnostic statistics, are provided in Haque, Lahiri, and Montiel (1990).

5. Consistent with this result, Haque and Montiel (1990, 1991) conducted tests for capital mobility for several developing countries and found a surprisingly high degree of financial openness among developing countries over the 1970s and the 1990s, in panel data tests of the capital mobility hypothesis in isolation as well as for many individual countries in this sample.

The HLM model assumes flexible prices and thus is characterized by continuous full employment. Unlike other features of the model, such as the production structure and behavioral specifications, this assumption is not characteristic of empirical developing-country macroeconomic models. The full-employment assumption is controversial, but the question of the existence of Keynesian unemployment in developing countries arising from sluggish price adjustment is unsettled and is obviously likely to be country-specific. While short-run nominal wage and price stickiness will make an important difference to the dynamic path that the economy follows from one long-run equilibrium to another, it will not affect the nature of the long-run equilibrium itself. Consequently this issue is not central for the purpose at hand.

The assumption that expectations are formed rationally is also more important for the dynamics of adjustment than it is for the nature of the long-run equilibrium. Rational expectations enter the model in two ways. First, expectations of devaluation of the official nominal exchange rate enter the interest-parity condition (equation 9.13 in table 9.1), which determines the domestic nominal exchange rate. Second, the real interest rate, which affects both consumption and investment behavior and is given by equation 9.16, is assumed to incorporate a rational forecast of next period's price level. As mentioned previously, the assumption that expectations are formed rationally also played a role in determining the technique used to estimate the model.

Steady-State Properties

The long-run properties of the policy simulations, which are the subject of this chapter, are better understood if we first examine analytically the steady-state version of the model. The steady-state version of the HLM model is presented in table 9.2. It has been broken into four recursive blocks, according to its solution algorithm. This algorithm works as follows: since in this chapter we work with steady states for which the nominal exchange rate (e) is fixed, we have $E_t (e_{t+1} | \Omega_t) = e_{t+1} = e_t$, where Ω_t denotes the set of information available at time t and E is the expectations operator. Since the real exchange rate must be constant in the steady state, constancy of the nominal exchange rate implies that the domestic price level must be constant as well, so $E_t (P_{t+1} | \Omega_t) = P_{t+1} = P_t$.[6] With these conditions, equations 9.13 and 9.16 of table 9.1 yield the steady-state values of the domestic nominal (i_t) and real (r_t) interest rates, both of which equal the foreign nominal interest rate i^*. These equations appear in block I of table 9.2. The solution for r derived from block I, together

---

6. For the purpose of the simulations, foreign inflation is set equal to zero.

Table 9.2 *Structure of the Steady-State Model*

Equation Description	Equation Formula
I. Interest Rate Block	
(Equation 9.13)	$i_t = i_t^*$
(Equation 9.16)	$r_t = i_t$
II. Output-Capital Block	
(Equation 9.5)	$\log I = k_o - 0.207\, r + 0.199\, \log Y + 0.815\, \log K$
(Equation 9.8)	$\log Y = q_o + 0.162\, \log K + 0.838\, \log L$
(Equation 9.9)	$I = 0.05K$
III. Monetary Block	
(Equation 9.10)	$M = eR + DC$
(Equation 9.11)	$DC = DC_p + DC_G$
(Equation 9.12)	$\log (M/P) = b_0 - 0.27\, i + \log Y$
IV. Demand Block	
(Equation 9.1)	$Y = C + I + G + X - eP^*Z/P$
(Equation 9.2)	$\log C = a_o + 12\, r + \log Y^d$
(Equation 9.3′)	$Y^d = Y + ieF^*/P - i\, DC_p/P - T$
(Equation 9.6)	$\log X = t_o + 0.74\, \log (eP^*/P) + 1.45\, \log Y^*$
(Equation 9.7)	$\log Z = d_o + 0.84\, \log (eP^*/P) + 0.882\, \log Y$
(Equation 9.8)	$CA = PX - eP^* (Z + GZ) + i^*e\, (F_P + F_G + R)$
(Equation 9.9)	$CA = 0$
(Equation 9.17)	$eP^*GZ = P(T - G) + i^*e\, (F_G + R) + iDC_p$

with the steady-state condition for the capital stock $K_t = K_{t-1}$ in table 9.1 (equation 9.9), permits block II (consisting of the equations 9.5, 9.8, and 9.9) to be solved for real GDP (Y), the capital stock (K), and investment (I). The solutions take the form $Y = Y(i^*)$, $K = K(i^*)$, and $I = I(i^*)$, with Y', K', $I' < 0$.

The third block contains the monetary equations 9.10, 9.11, and 9.12. The steady-state version of equation 9.12 reflects the condition that $Y_t = Y_{t-1} = Y(i^*)$, with its implication that the money supply (M) is constant— that is, $M_t = M_{t-1} = M$.

Substituting equations 9.10 and 9.11 into this version of equation 9.12 yields an equation of the form 9.12′:

$$(9.12') \qquad \log[(eR + DC_p + DC_G)/P] = \beta_0 + \beta_1 i^* + \beta_2 Y(i^*)$$

where R is the foreign-currency value of international reserves and DC_P and DC_G denote central bank credit to the private and public sectors, respectively. Since i and Y are determined in blocks I and II respectively, and since e, DC_p, and DC_G are exogenous, this equation contains only two endogenous variables—R and P. To display the solution of the steady-state model diagrammatically, we can depict the combinations of R and P that satisfy (9.12′) as the locus MM in figure 9.1. The slope of this locus is:

$$\left.\frac{dR}{dP}\right|_{MM} = M/eP > 0$$

Since reserve growth results in an increase in domestic money supply, which, in the absence of other measures, will lead to an increase in the price level, this locus is positively sloped. The remainder of the model is grouped into the fourth block, which we have termed the demand block. Using equations 9.14, 9.15, and 9.17 of table 9.1 in 9.3′ we can rewrite private disposable income (Y^d) as:

$$Y^d = Y + \frac{eP^* Z}{P} - (G + X)$$

where P^* is the level of foreign prices, Z is the volume of imports measured in units of the foreign good, G is real government spending on domestic goods, and X denotes real exports. Substituting this in equation

Figure 9.1 *Steady-State Equilibrium*

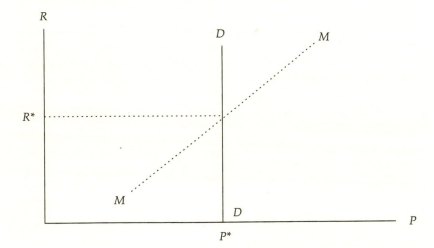

9.2 and then using equations 9.2, 9.6, 9.7, and 9.9 in equation 9.1, we have equation 9.1′:

$$Y(i^*) = C\{i^*, Y(i^*) + (eP^*/P)Z(eP/P, Y(i^*))\}$$

(9.1′)

$$+ I(i^*) + G + X(eP^*/P, Y^*) - \frac{eP^*}{P} Z\left(\frac{eP^*}{P}, Y(i^*)\right).$$

Since e, G, i^*, and Y^* are exogenous, this equation only contains the endogenous variable P. Block IV therefore also generates a locus in (R, P) space, which is given by equation 9.1′. This locus is denoted by DD in figure 9.1. Since R does not appear in equation 9.1′, this locus is vertical.

The key endogenous variables in the steady-state version of the model are thus the stock of international reserves R and the domestic price level P. The solution of the model is depicted by the intersection of the MM and DD loci at point A in figure 9.1. The model's exogenous variables consist of policy variables—namely, the nominal exchange rate e, the stocks of credit to the private and government sectors, respectively (DC_p and DC_G), and government spending on home goods G, as well as external variables consisting of the external interest rate i^*, foreign demand Y^*, and the foreign price level P^*. Once the solution values for R and P are determined as in figure 9.1, the values of the remaining endogenous variables in block IV (C, X, Z, Y^d, F_p, CA, and GZ) can be found. Given the fixed exchange rate and the exogenous value of the international price level, the real exchange rate can then be determined.

The stability of the steady-state equilibrium at A was verified in Haque, Lahiri, and Montiel (1990) by calculating the model's characteristic roots. These roots were computed using the parameter estimates in table 9.1 and linearizing around an artificial steady state generated by values of the exogenous variables intended to capture a "representative" developing-country configuration.[7] The model has a single root with modulus above unity. Since it also contains a single "jump" variable (the domestic price level), it thus exhibits saddlepoint stability (see Blanchard and Kahn 1980).

Neutrality to Nominal Shocks

Before considering the simulated economy's long-run response to domestic policy shocks taken individually, it is useful to verify the model's neutrality by examining the effects of a particular combination of nominal shocks—specifically, an equiproportional exchange rate devaluation and increase in both (private and public) domestic credit stocks. Notice

---

7. The roots were computed through the subroutine LIMO in TROLL.

that an x percent increase in e, DC_p, and DC_G would continue to satisfy equation 9.12′ if P also increased by x percent. The same is true of equation 9.1′, where DC_p and DC_G do not appear. Thus, the model is homogeneous of degree one in e, DC_p, and DC_G—since all nominal values change in the same proportion, real variables are unaffected, and the model's neutrality is verified. In terms of figure 9.1, both the MM and DD loci shift to the right by x percent, increasing the equilibrium price level by this amount, but leaving the equilibrium stock of reserves and all other real variables unchanged.

Domestic Policy Shocks

With the nature of the steady state described and the model's neutrality established, we now turn to an examination of the long-run effects of policy and external shocks. In this section we examine responses to shocks in the domestic policy variables (the exchange rate, the stock of credit, and government spending on domestic goods), while in the following section we turn to the effects of shocks in the external environment—specifically changes in world interest rates and foreign demand.

Devaluation

For our first exercise we consider a nominal exchange rate devaluation of 10 percent, taken in isolation—that is, with credit stocks unchanged. The steady-state effects of this shock are depicted analytically in figure 9.2 and the results of the simulation are presented in the second column of table 9.3. Since the stock of domestic credit does not affect equation 9.12′, the DD curve shifts horizontally to the right (to $D'D'$, for example), in proportion to the devaluation (that is, by 10 percent), as in the case of the neutral shock. The immediate implication is that the domestic price level must rise by 10 percent, so that the steady-state real exchange rate is unaffected by this nominal shock. Because DC_p and DC_G are unchanged, however, the proportional shift in MM, which can be derived from (9.1′), amounts to:

$$\frac{dP}{de}\frac{e}{P}\Big|_{MM}\hat{e} = \frac{R/P}{(M/P)^2}\frac{e}{p}\hat{e}$$

$$= (eR/M)\hat{e} < \hat{e}$$

since $eR/M < 1$.[8] Thus, the shift of MM to $M'M'$ in figure 9.2 falls short of the neutral shift. As a result, the steady-state stock of reserves increases

---

8. The symbol "∧" denotes a proportionate rate of change.

Figure 9.2 *Steady-State Effects of Nominal Devaluation*

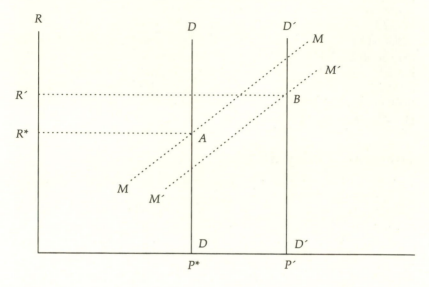

(which would presumably have been the motive behind the devaluation in the first place). The stock of reserves increases by 17.4 percent, and the reserve to GDP ratio increases by 1.7 percentage points. Because the public sector is assumed to use the interest income from its larger stock of net foreign assets to increase spending on foreign goods, the trade balance deteriorates by an offsetting amount (note that the interest rate applicable to reserve assets is unchanged).

Thus, a change in the nominal exchange rate has no effect on the long-run equilibrium real exchange rate. The nominal exchange rate change simply results in reserve accumulation until the money stock has increased in proportion to the change in the nominal exchange rate, restoring the original real equilibrium with a changed composition of the assets backing the monetary base.

It may be worth pointing out that the only endogenous variables whose steady-state values are affected by devaluation are those determined in blocks III and IV of table 9.2. Specifically, real output, which emerges from block II, is not affected. Thus, devaluation is neither expansionary nor contractionary in the long run (see table 9.3). The reason is that the domestic real interest rate, which determines the capital stock, continues to be determined by the unchanged foreign interest rate. Thus, the output effects of devaluation are temporary, appearing only during the process of adjustment.

Domestic Credit Shock

As a second exercise, we consider an alternative domestic nominal shock, in the form of a permanent increase in the stock of domestic credit to the private sector of 10 percent, announced and implemented simultaneously in the first period. Since this economy is characterized by perfect capital mobility—in the sense that uncovered interest parity holds continuously—the standard "monetary approach to the balance of payments" (MABP) analysis would suggest that the credit expansion would displace an equivalent amount of reserves in the central bank's balance sheet, leaving all else (including the domestic price level and thus the long-run equilibrium real exchange rate) unaffected.

This is exactly what happens in the HLM model. The steady-state configuration is summarized in figure 9.3 and the model simulation results are given in the third column of table 9.3. Since DC_p only appears in equation 9.12′, only the locus MM is affected by the credit expansion. Since 9.12′ would continue to hold if $edR = -dDC_p$, the MM locus shifts downward by the amount of the credit expansion, to a point such as B at the original domestic price level P^*. The consequent loss of reserves at B, amounting to $(R^* - R')$ in figure 9.3, is that which would be observed in the MABP case. Since the locus DD is vertical, it passes through both A and B and results in a new steady-state equilibrium at B. The domestic

Table 9.3 *Long-Run Effects of Domestic Policy Shocks*

	10 Percent Nominal Devaluation	10 Percent Expansion in the Stock of Credit	Shift in Government Spending toward Domestic Goods*
Real Exchange Rate (percent change)	0	0	–6.7
Real GDP (percent change)	0	0	0
Trade Balance/GDP Ratio (level change)	–1.7	2.0	–3.1
Reserves/GDP Ratio (level change)	1.7	–2.0	2.1

Note: * Total government spending on domestic goods increases by 10 percent, financed by an equivalent reduction of spending on foreign goods.

Figure 9.3 *Steady-State Effects of a Domestic Credit Expansion*

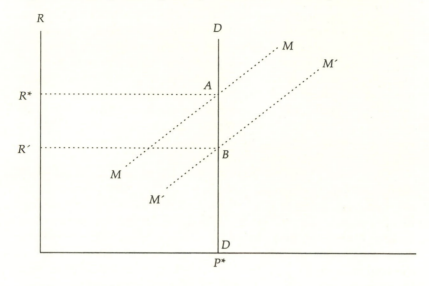

price level is unchanged, and so therefore is the long-run equilibrium real exchange rate. Real GDP and the domestic real interest rate are both unchanged, but the stock of reserves falls, in this case, by a total of 21.5 percent, causing the reserve-GDP ratio to decrease by 2 percentage points. Since the loss of interest income on reserves means that government spending on imports falls in this case, the trade balance improves.

A Permanent Increase in Government Spending on Domestic Goods

Consider the effects of an increase of 10 percent in the amount of government spending on domestic goods, financed by an equivalent reduction in government imports. The steady-state effects of an increase in government spending on home goods are depicted in figure 9.4, while the results of the simulation are summarized in column 4 of table 9.3. Since the level of government spending on such goods affects only the demand block (equation 9.12′) and not the monetary block (equation 9.1′), only the DD curve is affected. Because the change in the spending mix is expansionary, the domestic price level must increase at a given value of R—that is, the DD curve must shift to the right, while the MM curve is stationary. The new equilibrium will thus be found at a point such as B, with higher reserves and a higher domestic price level—in

Figure 9.4 *Steady-State Effects of a Shift in the Composition of Government Spending toward Home Goods*

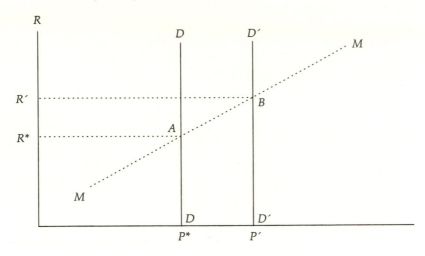

other words, the shock will result in a real exchange rate appreciation (of about 6.7 percent, as shown in table 9.3). The reason for the reserve increase is that the higher domestic price level increases the demand for money. Since the spending increase on home goods is financed by curtailing government imports and not by domestic credit expansion, the increased demand for money can be satisfied only by a reserve inflow.[9] In this case, the close association between the effects on the reserve-GDP ratio and the trade balance ratio that existed in the case of the nominal shocks is broken by effects of the change in spending itself and of changes in the real exchange rate on the government budget.

External Shocks

The economy modeled in table 9.1 is affected by changes in both foreign interest rates and incomes. Because the country is small and uncovered interest parity holds continuously, the fixed nominal exchange rate implies

---

9. It may be worth noting that the spending shift has no effect on domestic interest rates or output in the long run. Again, this is a consequence of the interest parity condition and the determination of output in block II, which is unaffected by the composition of government spending.

that the domestic nominal interest rate must adjust to the nominal interest rate that prevails externally. Also, since domestic output is an imperfect substitute for the output of the rest of the world, foreign incomes affect the foreign demand for domestic output.[10] In this section we examine the effects of permanent shocks in both of these variables.

An Increase in External Demand

An increase in external demand (Y^*) affects the demand block (block IV) in the steady-state model, but not the monetary block (block III). An increase in export demand is expansionary, requiring an increase in domestic prices (and thus an appreciation of the real exchange rate), at a given value of R to restore equilibrium in the domestic commodity market. Thus the DD curve shifts to the right. Qualitatively, the situation is similar to that which arises from the permanent shift in government spending toward home goods depicted in figure 9.4—international reserves rise and the real exchange rate appreciates in steady state. The effects of an equivalent percentage increase in Y^* are larger, however, for two reasons. First, the elasticity of demand for exports exceeds unity. Second, the openness of the "representative economy" in this simulation (in other words, the relatively large share of exports in GDP) causes the impact of a 1 percent change in exports to exceed that of a 1 percent change in exhaustive government spending on home goods. The actual simulation results are summarized in column 2 of table 9.4.

Permanent Increase in the External Real Interest Rate

Unlike the previous shocks, an increase in the external real interest rate affects both of the steady-state loci described above, because the foreign interest rate enters both equation 9.12′ and 9. 1′.[11] An increase in i^* reduces the real demand for money, requiring an increase in the price level and appreciation of the real exchange rate to clear the money market, thus causing MM to shift to the right, to a position such as $M'M'$ in figure 9.5. In this case, unlike all the others analyzed in this chapter, the long-run level of output is affected. The increase in the steady-state interest rate depresses investment, which in turn implies a reduction in the size of the capital stock that can be maintained in the long run, and consequently in the level of output produced.

---

10. A third link to the rest of the world, through foreign prices, is also present in the model. To save space, however, we will not describe the effect of shocks to this variable.

11. Since the external rate of inflation is exogenous, this is equivalent to an increase in the external nominal interest rate.

Table 9.4 *Long-Run Effects of External Shocks*

	10 Percent Increase in Partner-Country Incomes	Increase in Foreign Interest Rate
Real Exchange Rate (percent change)	–35.6	8.1
Real GDP (percent change)	0	–0.02
Trade Balance to GDP Ratio (level change)	–11.7	3.8
Reserves to GDP Ratio (level change)	16.6	–2.4

Figure 9.5 *Steady-State Effects of an Increase in the Foreign Real Interest Rate*

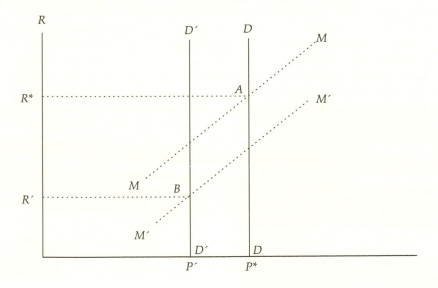

Since the steady-state output contraction is small in the HLM model (column 3 of table 9.4) the demand-side effect dominates in the goods market, creating incipient excess supply. This causes DD to shift to the left, to a position such as $D'D'$ in figure 9.5. The implication is that the long-run equilibrium real exchange rate must depreciate to stimulate demand for domestic goods and restore goods market equilibrium. The estimated depreciation in the long-run equilibrium real exchange rate amounts to about 8 percent.

Regarding the other endogenous variables, the combination of lower domestic output, a higher domestic interest rate, and lower domestic price level (required to generate the real depreciation) results in a reduced nominal demand for money. The steady-state effect on the stock of international reserves is therefore negative. The trade balance improves, primarily as the result in the import contraction implied by the deterioration in the economy's net international creditor position.

Summary and Conclusions

In each of the simulations described above, the long-run response of the economy to a permanent shock emerges from the interaction of several important features of the model employed. These include, in addition to the general Mundell-Fleming structure, specific a priori characteristics of the specification, such as the absence of wealth effects on aggregate demand. Certain estimated parameter values are also quite important. In particular, the imposition of perfect capital mobility on the simulation model was based on an estimated capital mobility parameter. The implication is that the model used here, as well as versions that retain these general features, will be suitable for use in countries with structures that reflect these basic characteristics—for example, in middle-income developing countries with diversified manufactured and other exports (for which the Mundell-Fleming structure is relevant) and with open capital accounts and substantial capital inflows. For undiversified primary exporters with closed capital accounts that rely on large aid flows, however, the framework applied here would be less useful.

The methodology described in this chapter can be adapted readily for use in individual country applications. The equations and structure of the model are simple enough—with 6 estimated behavioral equations and 13 identities—for it to be used in most developing-country settings to which the general analytical framework is applicable. Since it relies on conventional macroeconomic data of the type frequently used in developing-country macroeconometric models, data constraints will not generally pose an insurmountable problem in the middle-income developing countries for which the framework is designed. Where estimation is not feasible, the "representative" parameters reported here, or parameters derived from other sources, can be used for simulation purposes. To illustrate the application of the model to an individual middle-income developing country using "representative" parameter estimates, an appendix to this chapter uses the model to derive an estimate of the equilibrium real exchange rate for Thailand in 1995.

Moreover, certain important aspects of the model can readily be modified to capture country-specific circumstances. Central among these, the assumption of financial openness can be tested for the country in question and the appropriate degree of openness embedded into the model.[12] Once the model has been adapted to the particular situation at hand, simulated policy experiments can be used, as illustrated in this chapter, for the purpose of estimating the impacts of permanent "fundamental" shocks on the long-run equilibrium real exchange rate.

Since the analytical framework used is a well-established one, it is not surprising that the simulation results reported here reveal effects on the LRER of the various shocks considered that are quite conventional. For example, equiproportionate changes in the nominal exchange rate and the stock of domestic credit are neutral with respect to *all* real variables in the model. Independent changes in the nominal exchange rate and in the stock of domestic credit, however, are neutral with respect to the long-run equilibrium real exchange rate, but have other real effects. Since both nominal devaluations and changes in the stock of domestic credit affect the steady-state stock of interest-bearing reserves, they have real effects that are transmitted to the trade balance through the government budget.

Certain real variables, by contrast, play the role of long-run real exchange rate "fundamentals" in this model, because permanent changes in their values, unlike in the case of the nominal variables mentioned previously, result in changes in the long-run equilibrium real exchange rate. The fundamentals in this model consist of a domestic policy variable (the composition of government spending) and two variables that characterize the external macroeconomic environment (the world interest rate and the level of external demand). What is gained in the simulation approach, of course, is the quantification of the effects of these "fundamentals" on the LRER. The individual effects of each of these variables on the LRER in this model are summarized for convenience in table 9.5.

12. For details see Haque and Montiel (1991) and Haque, Lahiri, and Montiel (1990).

The effects of these variables on the long-run equilibrium real exchange rate fall into two categories. The effects of two of these variables (namely, the levels of government spending on home goods and of external demand), fall into the first category. While quantitatively conditional on the specified model and the form of the simulation experiments, they have familiar qualitative properties that would not be overturned with other theoretically admissible parameter estimates. In other words, they both result in long-run equilibrium real appreciation. Even in these cases, however, without a model at hand of the type we have employed, the effects of "fundamentals" such as these would be difficult to quantify in a general-equilibrium setting.

The remaining real fundamental—the external interest rate—falls into a different category. Under perfect capital mobility and fixed exchange rates, the domestic interest rate moves in step with the foreign rate. Because long-run equilibrium in this model allows for full capital stock adjustment, an increase in the foreign interest rate lowers the steady-state capital stock and with it the steady-state level of real output. However, this effect turns out to be dominated empirically in our model by the depressing effects of higher interest rates on demand for domestic goods, implying that long-run equilibrium requires a reduction in their price—in other words, a long-run real depreciation. This result is likely

Table 9.5 *Long-Run Changes in the Real Exchange Rate*

Fundamentals	Value of Change[a]
Domestic Policy Shock	
Permanent shift in the composition of government spending toward domestic goods by (10 percent increase)	–6.7
Shocks to the External Environment	
Permanent increse in the external interest rate by one percentage point	8.1
Permanent increase in partner-country incomes by 10 percent.	–35.6

Note: a. Percent differences from preshock steady-state values.

to be parameter-specific, even qualitatively. It arises in this application because of the empirical magnitudes of estimated parameters—specifically, a relatively high sensitivity of demand to changes in real interest rates—and it could in principle go the other way in specific applications in which this sensitivity is reduced. Thus, assessing even the direction of the effects of external interest rate changes on the long-run equilibrium real exchange rate will require the use of an estimated general-equilibrium model such as the one described here.

Appendix

An Application to Thailand

The model described in this chapter can readily be applied to the estimation of LRERs for individual developing countries. As indicated in the text, the model is best suited for middle-income developing countries that export differentiated products and are well integrated with international financial markets. Ideally, the parameters of the model would be re-estimated for each application. However, where the data or time constraints render this infeasible, the model can be used with the "representative" parameters reported here to provide at least a rough indication of the effects that changes in "fundamentals" may have exerted on the LRER in the case of a specific country, as a correction to simple PPP calculations.

To illustrate this use of the model, we have applied it to the calculation of Thailand's LRER in 1995, using the "representative" parameter estimates reported in the text. Thailand is a middle-income country with a diversified export structure that, at least until 1997, was well integrated with international financial markets. Indeed, Thailand led the way in the renewed access to external finance by developing countries after the international debt crisis of the 1980s and was one of the largest recipients of external funds (relative to GDP) among developing countries through the early 1990s. The behavior of Thailand's real effective exchange rate (REER) over the 1980–96 period is shown in figure 9.A.1. As is evident from the figure, the country underwent a large REER depreciation during the mid-1980s, but the REER stabilized in the early 1990s. After some mild appreciation in 1991, the REER began to depreciate again—very moderately—in subsequent years. Yet, many accounts of the crisis that broke out in that country in the summer of 1997 assign an important role to real exchange rate misalignment. The role that real exchange rate overvaluation may have played in generating the foreign exchange crisis that afflicted Thailand in July of 1997 makes this an interesting application of the methodology described in this chapter.

402

Figure 9.A.1 *Thailand Real Effective Exchange Rate, 1980–96*

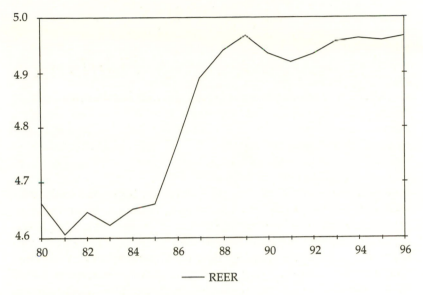

— REER

Note: An upward movement is a depreciation of the REER.
Source: Computed from World Bank data.

In principle, if the model were to be re-estimated for Thailand, the procedure for estimating the LRER would be to solve the steady-state version of the estimated dynamic model for the LRER conditional on "permanent" values of the real fundamentals (government spending, the external real interest rate, and external economic activity), setting the residuals in the behavioral equations equal to zero in doing so. Because we have used parameter estimates that were not estimated for Thailand, however, we are forced to make ad hoc adjustments to our behavioral equations to correct for nonzero average residuals. Our procedure was thus as follows:

First, we identified a "base" year in which Thailand's actual real exchange rate was judged to be close to the LRER. We chose 1991 for this purpose, on the basis of evidence in Montiel (1997) suggesting that the Thai real exchange rate was approximately in long-run equilibrium at that time.

Using Thai macroeconomic data for 1991 and the estimated "representative" parameter values for the behavioral equations of the model, we calculated residuals for each of the behavioral equations of the model.

Using the estimated residuals to rebase the model's behavioral equations (that is, adjusting the constants in each of those equations by adding the 1991 Thai residuals to them), we solved the model for the equilibrium real exchange rate using the 1995 values of the real "fundamentals." This yielded an estimate of the LRER conditioned on the dual assumptions that the RER was equal to the LRER in *1991, and* that the real "fundamentals" were at sustainable "permanent" values in 1995.

Thailand's fundamentals evolved in ways that had conflicting effects on the LRER during 1991–95. The share of government spending on domestic goods in GDP increased moderately over the period, while external interest rates (as measured by the London interbank offered rate; LIBOR) fell quite sharply. Together, these factors would have contributed to an appreciation of the LRER. However, at the same time the growth in the real GDP of Thailand's main trading partners was substantially slower than that of Thailand itself. Relatively slower partner-country growth would have contributed to a depreciation of the LRER. As indicated above, we simulated the net effects of the changes in fundamentals between 1991 and 1995 on the assumption that these changes were permanent. Our central result was that the Thai LRER depreciated by approximately 17 percent from 1991 to 1995. Since Thailand's real effective exchange rate actually depreciated by a little less than 4 percent over the same period, the methodology suggests an overvaluation of the baht amounting to approximately 13 percent by 1995. This contrasts with what would be derived from a simple PPP "base year" calculation that, using 1991 as the base year, would imply an *under*valuation equal to the change in the real exchange rate from 1991 to 1995—in other words, an undervaluation of about 4 percent. Subsequent events in Thailand suggest that the model-based prediction—even as crudely applied as it was applied here—may have been closer to the mark.

10

Single-Equation Estimation of the Equilibrium Real Exchange Rate

John Baffes, Ibrahim A. Elbadawi, and
Stephen A. O'Connell*

Estimating the degree of exchange rate misalignment remains one of the most challenging empirical problems in open-economy macroeconomics (Edwards (1989), Williamson 1994). A fundamental difficulty is that the equilibrium value of the real exchange rate is not observable. Standard theory tells us, however, that the equilibrium real exchange rate is a function of observable macroeconomic variables, and that the actual real exchange rate approaches the equilibrium rate over time (Edwards (1989), Devarajan, Lewis and Robinson (1993), Montiel (1997)). A recent strand of the empirical literature exploits these observations to develop a single-equation, time-series approach to estimating the equilibrium real exchange rate (Edwards (1989), Elbadawi and O'Connell (1990), Elbadawi (1994), Elbadawi and Soto 1994, 1995). Drawing on this earlier work, we outline an econometric methodology for estimating both the equilibrium real exchange rate and the degree of misalignment, and illustrate the methodology using annual data from Côte d'Ivoire and Burkina Faso.

* We are grateful to Chris Adam, Neil Ericsson, Philip Jefferson, Lant Pritchett, and Luis Serven for helpful advice, to Peter Montiel for very thorough comments on an earlier draft, and to Ingrid Ivins for assistance with data. Larry Hinkle provided invaluable comments and advice throughout and constructed the counterfactual simulations for Côte d'Ivoire and Burkina Faso. Any errors are our own responsibility.

The procedure involves three steps. In the first step, the investigator identifies the long-run relationship to be estimated, adapting existing theory as necessary to key features of the country in question. This relationship is then embedded in a dynamic model whose long-run parameters are estimated in the second step, using techniques appropriate to the time-series characteristics of the data. In the third step, the investigator uses the estimated long-run parameters to calculate the equilibrium rate and the degree of misalignment under alternative assumptions regarding the sustainability of the fundamentals.

The chapter is organized accordingly. In the next section, we define the real exchange rate and derive an equilibrium relationship between the real exchange rate and a set of macroeconomic "fundamentals," including government spending patterns and the terms of trade. International credit constraints and changes in trade policy are potentially important features of the Côte d'Ivoire and Burkina Faso cases; and we show how these modify the list of fundamentals. We present the comparative statics and discuss the sources of short-run misalignment and dynamic adjustment. The section that follows, on motivating the single-equation approach, concludes the first step by embedding the long-run equilibrium in a single-equation, error-correction specification for the real exchange rate. This section provides a bridge to steps two and three by placing our approach in a broader stochastic context, discussing the relationship of our methodology to the standard PPP approach.

We then implement step two, starting in the section on estimation with an investigation of the time-series properties of the data. Côte d'Ivoire and Burkina Faso prove to be polar cases, with all variables nonstationary in Côte d'Ivoire and all variables (trend-) stationary in Burkina Faso. We focus particularly on Côte d'Ivoire, in which cointegration between the real exchange rate and its fundamentals opens up a menu of possible estimation approaches. We present the econometric results for both countries and discuss them in light of the existing empirical literature.

The section on calculating the equilibrium real exchange rate takes up the final step of the methodology. We discuss alternative ways of identifying "sustainable" values for the fundamentals and illustrate the alternatives for the cases at hand. Our preferred point estimates are based on counterfactual simulations for the fundamentals; these estimates suggest that by the end of the sample period (1993), Côte d'Ivoire was overvalued by roughly 30 percent while Burkina Faso had a small undervaluation.

In the end, of course, ongoing developments in time-series econometrics and the inevitable complexity of applied work leave us well short of attempting a "cookbook" in this chapter. Our more modest aim

is to provide sufficient detail—including pointers to the relevant literature and two extended illustrations—to encourage application of the
methodology "in the field." The final section concludes the chapter with
an assessment of the practical value of the single-equation, time-series
approach.

Step One: Modeling the Equilibrium Real Exchange Rate

The concept of the real exchange rate (RER) that has been most heavily
used in analyses of external adjustment by developing countries is the
domestic relative price of traded to nontraded goods (for example,
Dornbusch 1983).[1] This is shown in equation 10.1:

$$(10.1) \qquad RER \equiv e \equiv \frac{EP_T^W}{P_N}.$$

Although the world price of traded goods, P_T^W, is exogenous for a small
country, the domestic price of nontraded goods is endogenous except
over short periods of wage-price rigidity. The RER is therefore endogenous even under a predetermined nominal exchange rate. In this section we use a simplified model to illustrate the determination of the real
exchange rate and derive an expression for its long-run equilibrium
value. Since the relevant theory is well covered by Montiel in Chapter 5,
we use his model as a basis for the discussion (see also Edwards (1989)
and Rodriguez 1994).

The literature defines the long-run equilibrium real exchange rate as
the rate that prevails when the economy is in internal and external balance for sustainable values of policy and exogenous variables. Internal
balance holds when the markets for labor and nontraded goods clear.
This occurs when the following equation 10.2 holds:

$$(10.2) \quad y_N(e,\xi) = c_N + g_N = (1-\theta)ec + g_N, \quad \partial y_N / \partial e < 0, \quad \partial y_N / \partial \xi < 0$$

where y_N is the supply of nontraded goods under full employment, c is
total private spending measured in traded goods, q is the share of this
spending devoted to traded goods, and g_N is government spending on
nontraded goods. The variable ξ is a differential productivity shock that
raises the output of traded goods and lowers the output of nontraded

---

1. This is what Hinkle and Nsengiyumva call the "internal" real exchange
rate in Chapters 2 and 3.

Figure 10.1 *Internal and External Balance*

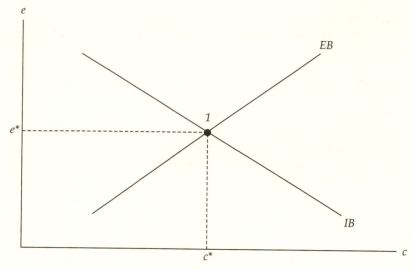

Note: The *EB* schedule is drawn for steady-state values of the service account and transaction costs. A rise in *e* is a real depreciation.

goods at given relative prices (see below). Equation 10.2 is shown as the schedule *IB* in figure 10.1. Starting in a position of internal balance, a rise in private spending creates an excess demand for nontraded goods at the original real exchange rate. Restoration of equilibrium requires a real appreciation that switches supply toward nontraded goods and demand toward traded goods. A rise in government spending on nontraded goods shifts the *IB* schedule downward; a productivity shock in favor of traded goods shifts it upwards.

To define external balance, we begin with the current account surplus, which is given by equation 10.3:

$$(10.3) \qquad \dot{f} = b + z + rf = y_T(e, \xi) - g_T - (\theta + \phi)c + z + rf,$$
$$\partial y_T / \partial e > 0, \quad \partial y_T / \partial \xi > 0$$

where f is total net foreign assets, b is the trade balance, z is net foreign grants received by the government, all measured in traded goods, and r is the real yield on foreign assets. The trade balance is the difference between domestic production of traded goods, y_T, and the sum of government (g_T) and private spending on these goods. The equation is standard except for the term ϕ, which measures the transactions costs associated with private spending. In Montiel's model of optimizing households, these costs motivate the holding of domestic money, which would otherwise be dominated in rate of return by foreign assets.[2] They are assumed to be incurred in the form of traded goods (at the rate ϕ per unit of spending) and therefore appear as an outflow in the trade balance.

External balance has been defined in various ways in the literature, with earlier approaches tending to focus directly on sustainable net capital *flows* and more recent work focusing on long-run *stock* equilibrium. We take the latter approach, following Montiel and others (for example, Khan and Lizondo (1987), Edwards (1989), and Rodriguez 1994). External balance therefore holds when the country's net creditor position in world financial markets has reached a steady-state equilibrium. We can solve for the combinations of private spending and the real exchange rate that are consistent with this notion of external balance by holding f at its steady-state level and setting the right-hand side of equation 10.3 to 0. This traces out a second relationship between the real exchange rate and private spending, labeled *EB* in figure 10.1. Starting at any point on this schedule, a rise in private spending generates a current account deficit at the original real exchange rate. To restore external balance, the real exchange rate must depreciate, switching demand toward nontraded goods and supply toward traded goods; the *EB* schedule is therefore upward-sloping. We will see below that this stock equilibrium concept of external balance is consistent with a sequence of "flow" restrictions on the trade balance when countries are rationed in the international financial market.

A fully specified macroeconomic model must also satisfy fiscal balance in the long run. Since the predetermined rate of crawl of the nominal exchange rate ties down seigniorage revenue as a function of predetermined money holdings (both measured in traded goods), some fiscal variable must ultimately adjust to guarantee fiscal balance. Government spending is being held fixed, so the adjustment falls to tax revenue. Montiel assumes that any incipient public sector deficit is financed continuously via lump-sum taxes or rebates. Fiscal balance therefore holds at each point in time in this model, with the required adjustments taking place behind the scenes. It is worth noting that if the exchange rate were freely floating rather than managed, the rate of crawl would become endogenous and choices regarding lump-sum taxation would help

---

2. Montiel assumes that transactions costs are a decreasing function of the ratio of money holdings to spending: $\phi = \phi(m/c)$, $\phi' < 0$.

tie down the long-run inflation rate; but in other respects the long-run schedules would be unchanged.[3]

The equilibrium real exchange rate, e^*, is given by the intersection of the *IB* and *EB* curves, which occurs at point 1 in the diagram. Setting the right-hand side of equation 10.3 to zero and combining this with equation 10.2, we obtain equation 10.4:

(10.4)
$$e^* = e^*(g_N, g_T, [r^*f^* + z], \phi^*, \xi)$$
$$\quad\quad - \quad + \quad\quad - \quad\quad + \;\; -$$

where " * " superscripts denote steady-state values of endogenous variables and the signs below the equation are those of the corresponding partial derivatives of e^*. The signs of the partial derivatives in equation 10.4 are easily verified, either graphically or algebraically, using equations 10.2 and 10.3.

Montiel solves for the steady-state service account r^*f^* by assuming that the country faces an upward-sloping supply curve of net external funds and that households optimize over an infinite horizon.[4] Transactions costs per unit, f, are also endogenous; they depend on the ratio of money holdings to private spending and therefore on the nominal interest rate, which is the opportunity cost of holding domestic money. Since the nominal interest rate is tied down in the long run by the time preference rate and the domestic inflation rate, the final expression for the equilibrium real exchange rate takes the form

(10.5)
$$e^* = e^*(g_N, g_T, z, r_W, \pi_T, \xi)$$
$$\quad\quad - \quad + \quad - \quad - \quad + \;\; -$$

where r_W is the world real interest rate and π_T is the rate of inflation in the domestic price of traded goods.[5] Note that the nominal exchange rate does not appear among the fundamentals in equation 10.5. This is

---

3. See Agenor and Montiel (1999) for an analysis of the effect of exchange rate regime (managed versus floating) on macroeconomic dynamics in a model similar to the one analyzed here. Note that taxes are assumed to be lump-sum and therefore nondistortionary in our model; otherwise tax rates would enter the long-run balance schedules.

4. The latter feature ties the domestic real interest rate to the time-preference rate in any steady state. Given r^*, the value of f^* is then determined uniquely by the external supply function.

5. Since $\pi_T = \pi_W + \pi_e$ where π_W is the world inflation rate and π_e is the rate of crawl of the nominal exchange rate, we can think of the latter two variables as among the fundamentals. Note also that we have suppressed the time-preference

because the underlying behavioral relationships are all homogeneous of degree 0 in nominal variables. A nominal devaluation therefore has at most a transitory effect on the real exchange rate.

Equation 10.5 emphasizes that the real exchange rate consistent with internal and external balance is a function of a set of exogenous and policy variables. In practical applications, this relationship between e^* and its macroeconomic "fundamentals" differentiates the modern approach to equilibrium real exchange rates from the earlier purchasing power parity (PPP) approach. Under PPP, the analyst would identify a reference period of internal and external balance and use the real exchange rate that prevailed during that period as an estimate of the equilibrium for other periods. Equation 10.5 implies that this is only legitimate if the fundamentals did not change between the reference and comparison periods. This criticism of the PPP approach is now widely accepted.[6]

The analysis underlying equation 10.5 can be readily modified to accommodate features that are important in particular applications. For our purposes, important extensions involve rationing of foreign credit, changes in the domestic relative price of traded goods, and short-run rigidities in domestic wages and prices. We discuss these extensions briefly in what follows.

Rationing of Foreign Credit

Equation 10.6 is derived under the assumption that the country faces an upward-sloping supply curve of external loans. The current account and trade balances are therefore endogenously determined at each moment by the saving and portfolio decisions of households. An extreme version of this view, more relevant for countries without access to commercial international borrowing on the margin, is that the country faces a binding credit ceiling (or equivalently, a floor on its international net

---

rate in writing equation 10.5. Finally, note that while the impact effect of a rise in the world real interest rate depends on whether the country is initially a net debtor or a net creditor, the steady-state *domestic* real interest rate is constant in this model (see previous footnote) and the long-run effect of a rise in r is independent of the country's (endogenous) net creditor position.

6. The period of macroeconomic balance used in PPP calculations can be a single year or a group of years; elsewhere in this volume these alternatives are referred to as the "PPP base-year approach" and the "PPP average or trend approach." In the section on the relationship of the PPP approach to the single-equation approach below we discuss further the distinction between these PPP approaches and our econometric approach.

creditor position). Since a binding credit ceiling shuts down the capital account and also determines net interest payments, the trade surplus becomes an exogenous function of aid flows both in the short run and in the long run provided the ceiling remains binding.[7] Credit ceilings thereby generate a natural link between "stock equilibrium" concepts of external balance and "flow" approaches that define external balance as holding when the trade deficit is equal to exogenously given net resource transfers. With a binding credit ceiling equation 10.4 takes the simpler form (10.6):

$$
(10.6) \qquad e^* = e^*(g_N, g_T, b, \phi^* \xi,)
$$
$$
\qquad\qquad\qquad\quad -\quad +\ +\ + -
$$

In our empirical work below, we treat the trade surplus $b = -(rf + z)$ as one of the fundamentals, consistent with this interpretation.

The Terms of Trade, Trade Policy, and Productivity Differentials

The domestic relative price of exports and imports is given by equation 10.7:

$$
(10.7) \qquad \frac{P_X}{P_M} = \frac{\tau}{\eta}, \qquad \tau \equiv \frac{P_X^W}{P_M^W}, \qquad \eta \equiv \frac{1 + t_M}{1 - t_X}
$$

where τ is the external terms of trade and η is a parameter summarizing the stance of domestic trade policy. If either τ or η changes over time, the analysis must be disaggregated to accommodate different real exchange rates for imports and exports—a point well emphasized elsewhere in this volume. The equilibrium real exchange rates for imports and exports can then be written as functions of the set of fundamentals identified above, along with τ and η. Since the real exchange rate for tradables is itself a geometrically weighted average of the real exchange rates for imports and exports, it will depend on the same set of fundamentals, and elasticities will depend on the relative weight (α) of imported goods in the tradables price index.[8] Equation 10.6 then becomes equation 10.8:

---

7. The domestic real interest rate, in contrast, becomes endogenous. Movements in the domestic real interest rate reconcile private spending decisions with the exogenous credit constraint; and the spread between the domestic and foreign real interest rates captures the shadow price of the credit constraint.

8. Defining real exchange rates for imports and exports as $e_M = EP_M^W/P_N$ and $e_X = EP_X^W/P_N$ and the price index for traded goods as $P_T^W = (P_M^W)^\alpha (P_X^W)^{1-\alpha}$, the

(10.8)
$$e^* = e^*(g_N, g_T, b, \phi^*, \xi, \eta, \tau)$$
$$\quad\quad -\ \ +\,+\,+\ \ -\,-\ \ ?$$

An improvement in the terms of trade increases national income measured in imported goods; this exerts a pure spending effect that raises the demand for all goods and appreciates the real exchange rate. This effect can in principle be overcome by substitution effects on the demand and supply sides, leading to an overall real depreciation. A tightening of trade policy appreciates the real exchange rate in the long run.

As outlined in the subsection on specifying an empirical model below, our fundamental task in this chapter will be to estimate the parameters of equation 10.8. To measure the real exchange rate we will use the ratio of foreign wholesale price indexes to domestic consumer prices (a measure of the "external RER," in the terminology of Chapter 1 of this volume). This has two important implications for the interpretation of equation 10.8. First, as discussed at length in Chapter 1, the external RER tends to move more closely with the internal real exchange rate for imports than with the internal real exchange rate for traded goods, e. While the magnitude of estimated elasticities will reflect this fact, the qualitative predictions indicated in equation 10.8 remain unchanged if the dependent variable is the internal real exchange rate for imports. This includes the ambiguity of the terms-of-trade effect, although there is a stronger tendency toward a real appreciation. The external RER has been widely used in empirical applications, and the spending effect has indeed proved dominant in most cases (for example, Edwards (1989), Elbadawi 1994).

The second implication of using an external RER measure is that the interpretation of the differential productivity shock ξ must be adjusted accordingly. A tendency for productivity to advance more rapidly in the production of traded goods than in nontraded goods is the basis of the celebrated Harrod-Balassa-Samuelson (HBS) explanation for why nontraded goods are systematically cheaper in poor countries than market exchange rates would suggest (see Obstfeld and Rogoff 1996). Equation 10.4, of course, focuses on the internal real exchange rate rather than on international comparisons of nontraded goods prices. A rise in ξ depreciates the internal equilibrium real exchange rate by increasing the relative output of traded goods. When using an external real exchange rate, however, the HBS effect comes into play. To the degree that

---

real exchange rate is $e = (e_M)^\alpha (e_X)^{1-\alpha}$. In our empirical work we use the ratio of foreign WPIs to the domestic CPI as our measure of the real exchange rate. As indicated elsewhere in this volume, this "external real exchange rate" tends to be a closer proxy to e_M than to the "internal real exchange rate for tradables."

differences between foreign and home productivity are concentrated in traded goods, these differences will show up in nontraded goods prices that are systematically higher in richer countries than purchasing power parity would suggest. This in turn means a more depreciated external real exchange rate for the home country, other things being equal. The sectoral shock ξ *therefore captures the* difference *between trading part-* ners and the home country in the relative productivity of labor in traded and nontraded goods. In our empirical work we use a ratio of foreign to domestic overall labor productivity as a proxy for ξ.

Nominal Rigidities and Short-Run Dynamics

In Montiel's model, domestic wages and prices are perfectly flexible and internal balance prevails continuously. If we consider the case of a bind- ing credit ceiling, so that the trade balance is exogenous, we conclude that as long as changes in the fundamentals are permanent, the actual real exchange rate *never* deviates from its long-run equilibrium. This is apparent from the inspection of the internal and external balance sched- ules: with b tied down exogenously, e and c are free to adjust immedi- ately to their new long-run equilibrium values when one of the funda- mentals changes. This is illustrated in figure 10.2, in which we show the adjustment to an increase in the world real interest rate by a net debtor country facing a binding credit ceiling. For a given aid inflow, the rise in r_w increases the required trade surplus, shifting EB to the left (to EB') and depreciating the equilibrium real exchange rate. The adjustment from point 1 to point 2 is immediate; with a predetermined path for the nominal exchange rate the adjustment takes place through a fall in do- mestic prices and wages. Given wage-price flexibility, therefore, the bind- ing credit constraint removes the model's only source of internal dy- namics. The only remaining source of a divergence between the actual real exchange rate and its long-run equilibrium is a temporary change in one of the fundamentals.

If domestic wages and prices are sticky in the short run, a second important source of internal dynamics comes from disequilibrium in the labor market and the market for nontraded goods. As long as these markets eventually clear, the equilibrium real exchange rate is unaffected by the short-run nominal rigidity. But any shock that alters the equilib- rium real exchange rate will now give rise to an adjustment process during which the actual real exchange rate will deviate from its new equilibrium. In figure 10.2, sticky wages and prices prevent the real ex- change rate from moving to point 2 in the short run, so that output and spending take the burden of the external adjustment. The short-run equi- librium is at point 3, at which unemployment and inventory accumula- tion gradually push nominal wages and the prices of nontraded goods

Figure 10.2 *Adjustment to an Increase in* r_w *(under a Binding Credit Constraint)*

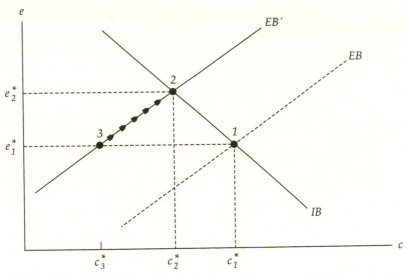

Note: A rise in r_w shifts *EB* upward to *EB'*. With flexible wages and prices, adjustment to the new long-run equilibrium at point 2 is immediate. With nominal rigidities, the economy jumps to point 3 and then converges gradually to point 2 along *EB'*. An upward movement is a depreciation of e.

down relative to the prices of traded goods. The real exchange rate depreciates over time, bringing the economy to point 2 in the long run. The process illustrated in figure 10.2 is often viewed as providing the primary role of nominal devaluation in macroeconomic adjustment: that of speeding an otherwise excessively slow and contractionary adjustment to an adverse external shock (Corden 1989).

As the foregoing observations suggest, the long-run relationship given by equation 10.8 is consistent with a variety of sources and patterns of short-run dynamics, including not only wage-price stickiness and gradual asset adjustment but also costs of labor mobility and other frictions not present above. In the section on specifying an empirical model we incorporate this feature by embedding equation 10.8 in a flexible specification of short-run dynamics.

Interpreting Real Exchange Rate Misalignment

In this chapter we follow Edwards (1989) and Montiel (1997) in using the term "misalignment" to denote the gap between e and e^*. There are two important differences, however, between this descriptive use of the term and its more normative use in most policy discussions. The first is illustrated by our discussion of nominal rigidities. In the absence of nominal rigidities or other market imperfections, deviations between e and e^* are market-clearing responses to temporary movements in the fundamentals or to permanent movements that alter the long-run equilibrium level of net foreign assets. In such cases the gap between e and e^* has no clear normative significance, and in particular there is no presumption in favor of "corrective" policy intervention. The second difference stems from the observation that the real exchange rate may well be misaligned from a normative perspective even when the economy is in a steady-state equilibrium. Dollar (1992), for example, argues that African real exchange rates were systematically overvalued in the 1970s and 1980s, as a result of highly inward-looking trade regimes. In the theory developed here, the equilibrium real exchange rate is conditional on trade policies and other government interventions. Given these policy settings (whether socially optimal or not) misalignment is necessarily a temporary phenomenon, generated by short-run macroeconomic forces that prevent an immediate movement to the long-run equilibrium.[9]

Specifying an Empirical Model

In equation 10.8 we defined the equilibrium real exchange rate as the steady-state real exchange rate conditional on a vector of permanent values for the fundamentals. Given this structure, our task is to construct a time series for this unobserved variable (within sample and potentially out of sample), using data on the actual real exchange rate and fundamentals. As a first step we assume that the long-run relationship delivered by theory is linear in simple transformations (for example, logs) of the variables. Equation 10.8 therefore becomes equation 10.9:

$$(10.9) \qquad\qquad \ln e_t^* = \beta' F_t^P$$

where e^* is the equilibrium real exchange rate and F^P the vector of permanent values for the fundamentals. Our task, therefore, is reduced to one of estimating the vector β of long-run "parameters of interest" and choosing a set of permanent values for the fundamentals appropriate to period t.

To estimate β we need an empirical model that is consistent with equation 10.9 but relates observable variables. We obtain such a model by translating into stochastic terms two straightforward and general fea-

---

9. For a more extensive discussion, see Chapter 5 by Montiel in Part II.

tures of the theory. The first is that equation 10.9 comes from a steady-state relationship between actual values of the real exchange rate and fundamentals. To capture this relationship we assume that the disturbance ω_t in the following equation 10.10

$$(10.10) \qquad \ln e_t = \beta'F + \omega_t$$

is a mean-zero, stationary random variable.[10]

The second general feature of the theory is that the steady state is dynamically stable.[11] Shocks that cause the exchange rate to diverge from its (possibly new) equilibrium in the short run should produce eventual convergence to the relationship in equation 10.9 in the absence of new shocks (or equivalently, in conditional expectation). A specification that captures this notion while retaining consistency with both equation 10.9 and 10.10 is the general error-correction model expressed in equation 10.11:

$$(10.11) \quad \Delta \ln e_t = \alpha(\ln e_{t-1} - \beta'F_{t-1}) + \sum_{j=1}^{p}\mu_j\Delta\ln e_{t-j} + \sum_{j=0}^{p}\gamma_j'\Delta F_{t-j} + \upsilon_t,$$

where Ft = $[g_N, g_R, b, f, x, h, t]'$ is the vector of fundamentals and υ_t is an independent and identically distributed, mean-zero, stationary random variable. Assuming that all variables are either stationary or I(1) (see below) in levels, equation 10.11 implies equation 10.10; and for $-2 < \alpha < 0$ the corresponding long-run equilibrium is stable.

Equation 10.11 embodies the central insight of the single equation approach: that the equilibrium real exchange rate can be identified econometrically as *that unobserved function of the fundamentals towards which the actual real exchange rate gravitates over time* (Kaminsky (1987), Elbadawi (1994), Elbadawi and Soto (1994, 1995)). Note that in contrast to the long-run relationship, the short-run dynamics are not heavily restricted since equation 10.11 is just a re-parameterization of the unrestricted p^{th}-order autoregressive distributed lag (ADL) representation of $\ln e_t$, as shown in equation 10.12:

$$(10.12) \qquad \ln e_t = \sum_{i=1}^{p}\mu_j^a\ln e_{t-j} + \sum_{j=0}^{p}\gamma_j^a F_{t-j} + \upsilon_t,$$

10. Note that equation 10.9 follows directly from equation 10.10 if $\ln e^*$ and F^p are interpreted as long-run conditional expectations of the relevant variables.

11. This does not rule out theoretical models that exhibit instability in certain directions (for example, rational expectations models); the key assumption is that the economy "chooses" a convergent path for given values of the fundamentals.

under the stability restriction $|\Sigma_j \, \mu_j^a| < 1$ and the assumption that the real exchange rate enters the long-run relationship.[12] For different parameter values, the unrestricted error-correction representation (equation 10.11) encompasses a wide variety of commonly used dynamic models (Hendry, Pagan, and Sargan (1984), Ericsson, Campos, and Tran 1991). This flexibility is an advantage, because although the dynamic structure of any *particular* theoretical model may place restrictions on the parameters in equation 10.11, these restrictions will depend on the nature of nominal and real rigidities, on whether households optimize or use rules of thumb, and on other model-dependent features that have little or no effect on the set of variables that enter the long-run equilibrium. With unrestricted dynamics, we allow the data maximum scope for determining their actual pattern, while retaining consistency with the long-run specification.

Much of our econometric work will take place in versions of equation 10.11. It is straightforward to incorporate variables that in theory do not belong among the long-run fundamentals, but that may affect the short-run dynamics. An example is the nominal exchange rate. Denoting such variables by a vector s, we would capture long-term effects by adding the term $\delta's$ inside the parentheses in equation 10.11 (allowing a test of the hypothesis $\delta = 0$) and short-term dynamics by adding $\Sigma_j \varphi_j' \Delta s_{t-j}$ to the right-hand side. Equation 10.12 would then include the corresponding term $\Sigma_j (\varphi_j^a)' \Delta s_{t-j}$, with $\delta = 0$ corresponding to a particular set of restrictions on the ADL parameter vectors $(\varphi_j^a)'$. Equation 10.11 can also accommodate an intercept or deterministic trend and we can readily include dummy variables for potentially important exogenous events (for example, the Sahel drought of the early 1980s).

A Brief Detour: Motivating the Single-Equation Approach

Before moving to estimation we take a brief detour to place our approach in a broader context. This section can be skimmed without loss of continuity, although we encourage the reader to return to it when evaluating the overall methodology. We address three questions here. First, why restrict attention to equation 10.11 rather than studying the full joint

---

12. In terms of the ADL parameters, the adjustment speed α and long-run parameters β_i in the error-correction representation are given by $\alpha = \Sigma_j \, \mu_j^a$ (so that the stability restriction implies $\alpha < 0$) and $\beta_i' = -(\Sigma_j \gamma_j^a)/\alpha$. Note that we are also restricting the long-run impacts of the s variables to be zero.

distribution of the real exchange rate and its fundamentals? While information is generally lost by conditioning, we argue in the first subsection below that the alternative of systems-based estimation is unrealistic in small samples. Second, what is the role of econometric exogeneity in the single-equation approach? If the fundamentals are weakly exogenous, conditioning is without loss of relevant information and fully efficient estimation and inference can proceed in a single-equation setting. We introduce weak exogeneity in the first subsection (with technical details in appendix A). Weak exogeneity is testable. When it fails, the investigator faces a choice between systems estimation and instrumental variables. Strong and super-exogeneity also have natural applications in our approach, as outlined in the second subsection, on sustainable fundamentals and exogeneity requirements. Finally, a question of fundamental interest to practitioners: why go the econometric route at all, rather than relying on the standard PPP approach? The answer is more subtle than expected (see the last subsection, on the relationship to the PPP approach) and reveals the fundamental strengths and weaknesses of the two approaches.

Small Samples, Limited Information, and Weak Exogeneity

With reasonable generality the joint distribution of the real exchange rate, its fundamentals, and short-run variables can be represented by an n-variable vector autogression (VAR) of finite order p, which in turn has a vector error-correction representation of the form shown in equation 10.13:

$$(10.13) \qquad \Delta x_t = \Gamma x_{t-1} + \sum_{j=1}^{p} A_j \Delta x_{t-j} + \varepsilon_t$$

where $x_t = [\ln e_t, Ft', s_t']'$ is the $n \times 1$ vector of variables and ε_t is the vector of reduced-form innovations (see appendix A). In general, efficient estimation of the parameters of equation 10.11 requires an analysis of the full joint distribution of the variables. A fundamental difficulty, however, is that sample sizes are likely to be very small. This is partly because the historical reach of developing-country data is typically short, and partly because models of the type considered here call for national accounts or fiscal data that are available only annually. For Côte d'Ivoire we have 29 annual observations; for Burkina Faso, 24. A general implication of small sample size is that the statistical properties of estimators may be poor and that testing procedures are likely to have low power. Existing Monte Carlo evidence can in some cases help discriminate between alternative choices of estimator, but we will often have to make informal judgments about robustness to sample size. A second implication is that we are virtually forced into assuming that the parameters are constant over the sample. This assumption rules out structural changes that may in fact be present and, if incorrect, can produce misleading inferences about the stationarity properties of the data (see the section on the I[1] case below) and the values of the parameters.[13]

For our purposes, however, a more definitive effect of small samples is to limit the scope for systems-based estimation. The number of unknown parameters in the full joint distribution of the real exchange rate and its fundamentals rises roughly geometrically with the number of fundamentals and the lag length. With three or four variables among the fundamentals and fewer than 30 observations, this "curse of dimensionality" tends rapidly to overwhelm any attempt to estimate the full joint distribution. We will see below that the dimensionality problem is somewhat alleviated if the variables are nonstationary and cointegrated (and only the long-run parameters are of direct interest), but that even here the small sample size exerts a serious limitation on systems estimation. Our analysis will therefore generally take place in a single-equation context, in which we implicitly condition on the current values of at least a subset of the fundamentals and the lagged values of all variables.

Conditioning is at some potential cost, because efficient statistical inference regarding the parameters of interest—which may go beyond β to include the adjustment speed α and the short-run parameters μ_i and γ_j—generally requires analysis of the full joint distribution of $\ln e_t$, F_t and s_t. As shown by Engle, Hendry, and Richard (1983), however, fully efficient estimation and inference can take place conditional on the fundamentals if these variables are *weakly exogenous* for the parameters of interest. As outlined more fully in appendix A, weak exogeneity holds when the parameters of interest can be directly recovered from the

---

13. On the positive side, the shocks to developing-country data often appear to have high variance, thereby generating substantial variation over time; and temporal length of sample (as opposed to number of observations, which may increase because of a move from annual to quarterly data without lengthening the sample) has the same effect when the real exchange rate and its fundamentals are nonstationary variables. A relatively small sample may therefore contain substantial information, particularly regarding the long-run parameters. In the end, of course, this high variability is useful only if it can be parameterized in a sufficiently parsimonious manner; hence our caveat about ruling out structural changes.

distribution of the real exchange rate conditional on the fundamentals (and the past) *and* there are no cross-equation restrictions linking the parameters of this conditional model with those of the marginal model for the fundamentals. In this case the marginal distribution of the fundamentals holds no information of use to estimating the parameters of interest.

Weak exogeneity is testable (see appendix A), though generally at the cost of moving to systems estimation. Failure of weak exogeneity limits the scope for fully efficient conditional inference but need not undermine the ability to perform valid (though inefficient) inference in an essentially single-equation context. For regressions involving stationary variables, limited-information approaches such as two-stage least squares (or instrumental variables more generally) are available subject to sufficient identifying restrictions.[14]

For Côte d'Ivoire and Burkina Faso, the "small country" assumption suggests that variables such as the terms of trade and the foreign price level are determined outside the country.[15] The same is true for the trade-weighted nominal exchange rate, since the CFA franc was pegged to the French franc at an unchanged parity throughout the sample. The trade balance is in this category if borrowing constraints are exogenous and binding. For these variables, weak exogeneity seems a reasonable assumption. Unfortunately, however, it is not guaranteed if behavior is affected by conditional expectations of these variables; for example, forecast errors will be jointly determined with the real exchange rate, potentially violating weak exogeneity. Variables such as government spending and the investment share may also be jointly determined with the contemporaneous real exchange rate. In what follows we test for weak exogeneity in the Côte d'Ivoire case and treat it as a maintained hypothesis for Burkina Faso.

---

14. When the the original variables are stationary, one option is to specify a dynamic simultaneous model or even a just-identified "structural VAR" along the lines of Bernanke (1986). This would require more identifying information than we are willing to impose, however. Moreover, system-based estimates that exploit this information are known to be less robust to mis-specification than limited-information approaches that ignore identifying information outside of the equation being estimated. Note also that limited information estimates can also support inference in cointegrated systems under failure of weak exogeneity, provided the equations being estimated involve only stationary variables and stationary combinations of nonstationary variables (that is, after the process Hendry 1995 calls "mapping to stationarity").

15. Côte d'Ivoire may well be large enough in the world cocoa market to affect its terms of trade.

Sustainable Fundamentals and Exogeneity Requirements

If we begin with equation 10.10, the equilibrium real exchange rate in equation 10.9 has a natural interpretation as the limit (as k goes to infinity) of a k-period-ahead conditional forecast of the real exchange rate. This suggests two broadly alternative ways of tying down the permanent values of the fundamentals. The first is using the sample information to generate long-run forecasts of the fundamentals conditional on information available in period t (or in some earlier period if t is out-of-sample). The second is combining theory and a priori information into a counterfactual simulation for the fundamentals. These correspond closely to the use of a single equation for conditional forecasting and "policy analysis." We argue below that the investigator will generally want to consider both alternatives. Here we briefly comment on the relevant exogeneity requirements (see Engle, Hendry and Richard 1983).

The requirements for valid single-equation forecasting and simulation generally go beyond those for valid estimation and inference. When using conditional forecasts of the fundamentals, the implicit assumption is that there is no feedback from the real exchange rate to the fundamentals. The appropriate concept is *strong exogeneity*, which combines weak exogeneity with lack of Granger casualty from the real exchange rate to the fundamentals. Given weak exogeneity, strong exogeneity can be readily tested by determining whether lagged values of the real exchange rate enter the marginal model for the fundamentals.

When using counterfactual simulations of the fundamentals, the relevant issue is whether β can be treated as a constant in the face of shifts in the marginal distribution of the fundamentals. The problem here is the Lucas critique of econometric policy analysis: the counterfactual exercise implicitly alters the joint distribution of the fundamentals and the real exchange rate, thereby invalidating the original parameter estimates unless the corresponding parameters are invariant to the class of distributional shifts being considered. The appropriate concept in this case is *super-exogeneity*, which combines weak exogeneity with invariance of the parameters of interest to the class of distributional shifts under consideration. The invariance property is sensitive to the particular class of interventions under study and we will treat it as a maintained hypothesis rather than attempting formal testing.[16]

---

16. See Hendry (1995) and Ericsson and Irons (1995) on tests of super-exogeneity. Not surprisingly, such tests generally require intensive study of the relationship between the estimated equation and the associated reduced form for the fundamentals. One natural test (given weak exogeneity) relies on establishing parameter constancy in the estimated model given a sample break in the associated reduced form for the fundamentals.

Relationship to the PPP Approach

A hallmark of the PPP approach to equilibrium real exchange rates was the choice of a single equilibrium rate for all periods, without reference to movements in the fundamentals. The standard theory-based criticism, as embodied in our theoretical model, was that the notion of equilibrium delivers a *relationship* between the real exchange rate and fundamentals, not a single value for the real exchange rate. Since the fundamentals are themselves time-varying, this criticism has often been summarized in the claim that the equilibrium real exchange rate should move over time.

This way of stating the criticism, however, may miss the fundamental distinction between the PPP and econometric approaches. Consider the case in which the real exchange rate itself is stationary. Stationary variables have time-invariant means, implying that all movements away from the mean are ultimately temporary. In such a situation the best sample-based estimate of the equilibrium real exchange rate for any period is simply the sample mean. To put this another way, the quantity $\beta'F_t$ in equation 10.10 is the difference between two stationary variables and is therefore stationary, so that while the individual fundamentals may have permanent movements (that is, while they may be nonstationary), the relevant *function* of the fundamental—in our case, the long-run forecast of a linear combination of these fundamentals—*never* moves permanently. When forecasted at successively distant horizons, $\beta'F_{t+k}$ simply reverts to the mean of $\ln e_t$.[17] An equilibrium relationship between the real exchange rate and other macroeconomic variables is therefore consistent with a time-invariant equilibrium real exchange rate, or in the trend-stationary case, with a deterministically trending equilibrium.

The more fundamental distinction between the two approaches resides in their contrasting use of sample and a priori information. The PPP approach requires a set of judgments that are informed both by theory and data but that remain largely implicit and a priori from an econometric perspective. The econometric approach, in contrast, uses theory sparingly but powerfully to extract information about the equilibrium real exchange rate from the entire data sample. A priori information becomes relevant when the analyst is interested in counterfactual simulations for the fundamentals, but such information is combined with

---

17. Estimation of long-run parameters appears superfluous in this case. The investigator will typically be interested, however, not only in a good conditional forecast of the real exchange rate but also in various characteristics of the short-run dynamics. Uncovering the relevant parameter values requires estimation even in the stationary case. Moreover, estimates of β are also required to apply counterfactual simulations for the fundamentals.

the sample information (used to estimate the parameters) in a restricted and transparent manner.

The econometric approach has clear advantages in reasonably large samples, where the high quality of the sample information should outweigh the loss of potentially sophisticated but implicit judgments central to the PPP approach. To give the PPP approach its due, however, we consider a problem that is peculiar to samples that are not necessarily small but are short in duration. We have just pointed out that in the stationary case, the sample mean provides a natural estimator of the long-run equilibrium real exchange rate. This implies, however, that the average misalignment within the sample is constrained to be zero. A similar though not identical outcome will tend to prevail in the nonstationary case: although the equilibrium rate itself is time-varying in this case, an important test of empirical success is that the equilibrium error is stationary. The resulting estimates of misalignment will then also tend to have a mean near zero if data-based forecasts for the fundamentals are used.

In other words, the econometric methodology tends by construction—except when counterfactual simulations of the fundamentals are used—to deliver an average misalignment of zero within the sample. This is in strong contrast to the PPP approach, which embodies no such restriction. In large samples, the restriction of a near-zero average misalignment is an unambiguous virtue, since it imposes the structure required to uncover the long-run parameters. But there may be severe problems in small samples, particularly if adjustment speeds are slow. Côte d'Ivoire's real exchange rate, for example, is thought by some to have been substantially overvalued for much of the post-WWII period. *Our methodology, when applied using data-based permanent values for the fundamentals, is essentially incapable of reproducing this finding.*

One response to this short-sample difficulty is to "rebase" the fitted equilibrium real exchange rates ex post by simply shifting their mean; this preserves their rates of change while altering the estimated degrees of misalignment. Despite its obvious appeal, however, rebasing has two important shortcomings. First, it leans very heavily on loosely structured a priori information, a feature of the PPP approach that the present approach is trying to avoid.[18] Second, it embodies an implicit assumption

---

18. There is a sense in which rebasing can be characterized as imposing impossibly *tight* prior information: if the equilibrium rate is estimated via a static regression, rebasing by x percent is equivalent to imposing exact prior information of the form that the average degree of misalignment in the sample is x (since minimizing the sum of squared residuals subject to this constraint produces a shift only in the constant term)! There may be ways of making rebasing more palatable, however, without assuming either loosely structured or tightly structured

of super-exogeneity with respect to potentially substantial and largely implicit interventions in the marginal distribution of the fundamentals. Our use of counterfactual simulations for the individual fundamentals is a close cousin to the rebasing approach, but has the advantages of greater structure and transparency and, in particular, of exploiting the maintained super-exogeneity assumption more fully.

Viewed in this light, the PPP approach can be reinterpreted not primarily as an assumption that the equilibrium rate is a constant, but rather as an assumption that when samples are short and super-exogeneity *fails*, loosely structured a priori information (for example, "the economy was in internal and external balance in 1985") is of greater value to the policy analyst than the information contained in the sample distribution of the real exchange rate and fundamentals—even when the latter is combined with structured a priori information about the fundamentals.

Step Two: Estimation

Steps Two and Three involve estimating the long-run parameters in equation 10.11 and combining them with sustainable fundamentals to calculate the equilibrium real exchange rate. In what follows we outline these steps in detail and illustrate their implementation using data from Côte d'Ivoire and Burkina Faso. We begin with a discussion of the data and an investigation of the stationarity properties of the variables. Next we provide a brief overview of econometric considerations in the nonstationary and stationary cases. We end this section by presenting the econometric results.

The Data

As always in applied work, the documentation of definitions and sources of data (provided in appendix B) is fundamentally a list of compromises. We begin here with the real exchange rate, the measurement of which is treated comprehensively in Part I of this volume. We followed the bulk of the literature in using an external real exchange rate, the numerator of which is a trade-weighted average of foreign wholesale prices converted

---

omniscience. Elbadawi and Soto (1995), for example, determine time-varying sustainable values for the fundamentals and then let the data "choose" the reference period by identifying the quartile of sample years in which the vector of fundamentals is "closest" to the vector of permanent values. The entire set of equilibrium rates is then rebased to make the average misalignment in these years zero. A potential drawback is that this approach ignores misalignment associated with slow error correction (see equation 10.15 below).

at official exchange rates. An internal real exchange rate would have been preferable on theoretical grounds, and in the case of Côte d'Ivoire we experimented extensively with measures of the internal real exchange rate and also with the use of black market exchange rates in converting Ghanaian and Nigerian prices. The results were not robust across alternative measures, and those presented here are the strongest of the lot in terms of the plausibility of long-run parameters and the evidence of cointegration (see below). We return to the issue of robustness in our concluding section.[19]

To capture a possible Harrod-Balassa-Samuelson (HBS) effect associated with the use of an external real exchange rate, we used internationally comparable real GDP data to construct the ratio of real GDP per worker in the OECD to real GDP per worker in the home country. Since average labor productivity may be highly sensitive to demand-side influences in the short run, we used a three-year-lagged moving average of this ratio (with linearly declining weights). This variable performed poorly in preliminary stages for Côte d'Ivoire, however, and we dropped it for that country while retaining it for Burkina Faso.

Data limitations forced two further compromises worth discussing here. The first is that we were unable to separate government spending into traded and nontraded goods. Data were available, however, for the share of government consumption and investment in total spending, and we used these to proxy for the composition of spending. A rise in government spending appreciates the real exchange rate if government spending is more intensive in domestic goods than is private spending. A rise in the share of investment in aggregate spending is likely to shift spending toward traded goods, other things equal, given the high import content of investment, and therefore to depreciate the real exchange rate. The second compromise is that in lieu of direct measures of the stance of trade policy, we had to construct proxies for this variable. It is common in this literature to use various ratios of trade to GDP, on the argument that a more liberal trade regime, other things being equal, means higher trade volumes. We experimented with three such proxies: the ratio of current imports to current GDP, the ratio of constant-price imports to constant-price GDP, and the ratio of total trade (imports plus

---

19. Annual data were used for all variables. Although monthly data were available for the external RER measure used, data for most of its fundamental determinants were available only on an annual basis. Moreover, use of monthly data for the RER would have introduced seasonal and other transitory fluctuations, increasing the noise in the time series without improving the accuracy of the statistical estimates. (For a further discussion of this point, see MacDonald 1995).

exports) to constant-price GDP. All three performed adequately for Burkina Faso, but in Côte d'Ivoire the ratio of current imports to current GDP was clearly superior to the other proxies. We therefore retained only this proxy in the analysis reported here. For the case of Côte d'Ivoire we also included a drought dummy variable that takes the value of one for 1983 and 1984 and zero otherwise. Since agriculture is primarily a traded-goods sector, this supply shock should depreciate the real exchange rate.

Determining the Order of Integration

Macroeconomic data often appear to possess a stochastic trend that can be removed by differencing once. Since the presence of such a trend influences the statistical behavior of alternative estimators, a key preliminary step is to determine the order of integration of the data. Variables that are best characterized as nonstationary in levels but stationary after differencing once are integrated of order 1, or $I(1)$. Other variables may be stationary ($I(0)$) or trend-stationary (that is, $I(0)$ after removing a deterministic trend component), or they may require repeated differencing before achieving stationarity ($I(d), d > 1$). These properties can readily be revealed using standard tests for the presence of a unit root.[20] The appropriate unit-root tests are well known; in our applications we use the Dickey-Fuller (DF), augmented Dickey-Fuller (ADF), and Phillips-Perron (PP) tests. Although there are concerns about the low power of these tests against stationary but persistent alternatives, the ADF test appears to perform satisfactorily on this score even when (as in our case) the number of observations is small (Hamilton 1994). We also supplement the unit-root tests with variance ratio tests (Cochrane 1988); these tests exploit the fact that the variances of conditional forecasts explode for nonstationary series and converge for stationary series as the forecast horizon grows.

---

20. Hamilton (1994) emphasizes the difficulty of distinguishing truly nonstationary processes from processes that are stationary but persistent. The problem is that the finite-sample autocovariances of any nonstationary series can be reproduced arbitrarily closely by those of a suitably persistent stationary series. The usual tradeoff between consistency and efficiency is therefore present even at this preliminary stage. If we correctly characterize the order of integration, we gain efficiency in estimation and inference by applying the appropriate estimation technique; but a misclassification typically means that these techniques will deliver inconsistent estimates or standard errors. Unfortunately the alternatives are non-nested and we see no generally robust way of proceeding in marginal cases. Hamilton (p. 447) suggests comparing estimates obtained under alternative classifications; if they differ widely the investigator may sometimes see ancillary statistical or other grounds for preferring one over the other.

Table 10.1 *Stationarity Statistics—Levels without and with Time Trend*

	Côte d'Ivoire			Burkina Faso		
	DF	ADF	PP	DF	ADF	PP
Levels without Time Trend						
log(REER)	−0.59	−1.26	−1.89	−2.25	−4.25	−2.25
log(TOT)	−1.42	−1.54	−1.78	−1.95	−1.82	−1.87
RESGDP	−2.11	−2.57	−2.25	−3.84	−2.22	−4.07
log(OPEN1)	−1.06	−1.39	−1.42	−4.02	−3.04	−4.30
log(OPEN2)	−2.35	−1.99	−2.48	−3.23	−3.02	−3.35
log(OPEN3)	−2.52	−2.16	−2.69	−3.63	−2.99	−3.82
log(HBS3)	n.a.	n.a.	n.a.	−1.21	−2.05	−1.67
log(ISHARE)	−1.01	−0.78	−0.68	n.a.	n.a.	n.a.
Levels with Time Trend						
log(REER)	−1.83	−2.46	−2.09	−4.89	−2.76	−5.35
log(TOT)	−1.51	−1.56	−1.69	−2.30	−2.08	−2.34
RESGDP	−2.05	−2.50	−2.24	−4.27	−2.69	−4.64
log(OPEN1)	−1.02	−1.32	−1.29	−3.84	−2.94	−4.20
log(OPEN2)	−2.81	−2.30	−3.02	−3.12	−2.95	−3.31
log(OPEN3)	−2.47	−1.99	−2.72	−3.47	−2.91	−3.75
log(HBS3)	n.a.	n.a.	n.a.	−3.65	−3.75	−3.68
log(ISHARE)	−2.42	−2.19	−2.42	n.a.	n.a.	n.a.

Note: DF, ADF, and PP refer to Dickey-Fuller, augmented Dickey-Fuller, and Phillips-Perron stationarity statistics. The number of observations is 29 for Côte d'Ivoire and 24 for Burkina Faso. The variables are defined in appendix B (ISHARE is not available for Burkina Faso).
Source: Computed from data from sources listed in appendix B.

Table 10.1 shows the results of unit-root tests for all stochastic variables. Côte d'Ivoire and Burkina Faso represent two extremes. For Côte d'Ivoire, all three tests indicate nonstationarity for all variables. Moreover, we can reject the unit-root hypothesis for the first difference of the variables (not reported), so we conclude that these are $I(1)$ variables. For Burkina Faso, all variables appear to be trend-stationary, with the possible exception of the terms of trade, which is bordering on nonstationarity. Figures 10.3 and 10.4 provide some additional information in the form of variance ratio tests.[21] These tests corroborate the unit-root

---

21. This ratio is defined as $(1/k)Var\ (X_t - X_{t-k})/Var\ (X_t - X_{t-1})$, where X_t is the variable of interest and k is the lag length (Cochrane, 1988).

Figure 10.3 *Variance Ratio Tests for Côte D'Ivoire*

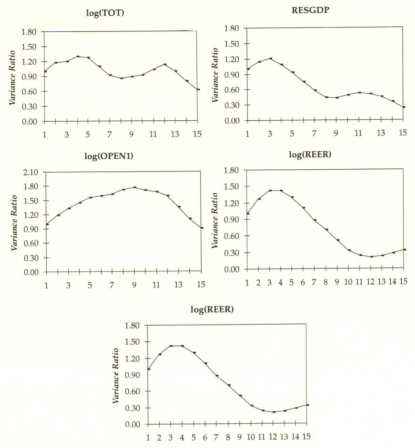

Source: Computed from data from sources listed in appendix B.

tests, and for Burkina Faso's terms of trade the variance ratios decline at longer horizons, consistent with a persistent but stationary variable. We therefore proceed under the assumption that the terms of trade are stationary. In principle, of course, the vector $[\ln e_t, F_t', s_t']'$ may contain an arbitrary combination of $I(0)$ and $I(1)$—or even $I(2)$—variables. We focus our exposition, however, on the two cases represented by our examples.[22]

22. Methods have recently been developed that allow consistent estimation and inference in regressions that involve mixtures of integrated processes. See Phillips (1995) and Phillips and Chang (1995).

Figure 10.4 *Variance Ratio Tests for Burkina Faso*

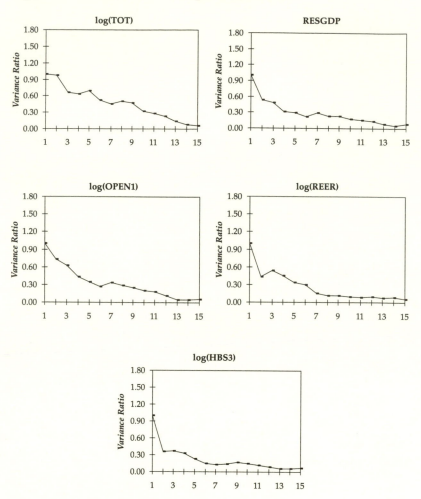

Source: Computed from data from sources listed in appendix B.

The I(1) Case

When the variables are all $I(1)$, as for Côte d'Ivoire, stationarity of the residual ω_t in equation 10.10 implies that the real exchange rate and its fundamentals are *cointegrated* (Granger 1981). This property is extremely useful econometrically, and a massive literature has developed in the wake of Engle and Granger (1987). As shown by Johansen (1988), cointegration is a restriction on the reduced form or VAR representation of the joint distribution of the real exchange rate and its fundamentals, equation 10.13. If the number of linearly independent stationary combinations of the variables is r $(0 < r < n)$, then the matrix Γ in equation 10.13 is of reduced rank $r < n$. We can then write $\Gamma = ab'$, where a and b are two nxr matrices of rank r.[23] The columns of b span the "cointegrating space" of stationary combinations of the x_{it}; the rows of a give the weights with which these combinations enter the individual equations of the reduced form. Equation 10.13 becomes equation 10.14:

$$(10.14) \qquad \Delta x_1 = ab'x_{t-1} + \sum_{j=1}^{p} A_j \Delta x_{t-j} + \varepsilon_t$$

where as before $x_t = [ln\ e_t, F_t', s_t']'$ is the $nx1$ vector of variables in the system. Since the cointegrating vectors are identified only up to a normalization, we are free to impose r restrictions on the b matrix; for example, we might choose the normalization $b_{ii} = 1$, $i = 1, ..., r$. We will restrict attention in this chapter to the case in which $r = 1$, so that there is a single cointegrating vector. The normalization on $ln\ e_{t-1}$ (which assumes only that $ln\ e_{t-1}$ actually enters the long-run relationship) then exactly identifies the remaining components of the cointegrating vector.[24] With a single cointegration vector, then, a and b are $nx1$ vectors of the form $a = [a_1, a_2]'$ and $b = [1, \beta']'$, where 1 is the scalar weight on the equilibrium error bx_{t-1} in the first row of equation 10.14. Note that if the st are truly short-run variables, their long-run coefficients will be zero.

---

23. Since each of the variables in x is either $I(0)$ or $I(1)$, all of the first differences in equation 10.14 are stationary. Stationarity of ε_t then implies that each row of Γx_{t-1} must also be stationary (since it is a linear combination of stationary variables) although the individual x_{it}'s are all nonstationary. This is accomplished if the rows of Γ induce stationary linear combinations of the nonstationary variables x_t: hence the decomposition of Γ. Note that if there are n stationary combinations, then the individual x_{it}'s must all be stationary.

24. If there are multiple cointegrating relationships, normalization alone is insufficient to relate the long-run parameters uniquely to their counterparts in any particular economic theory—that is, to obtain interpretable parameter estimates. In addition we require further identifying restrictions (see, for example, Johansen and Juselius 1994). In this case the single-equation approach is likely to pick up a weighted combination of the cointegration vectors (Johansen, 1992). This lack of identification may not be highly damaging for forecasting purposes, but it raises a variety of issues that go beyond the scope of single-equation approaches. The closest counterpart to our approach in the $r > 1$ case is the "structural error correction model" of Boswijk (1995; discussed in Ericsson 1995), which is obtained by premultiplying equation 10.14 by a square matrix and then imposing a set of restrictions.

Determining the Cointegrating Rank

The cointegrating rank is a property of the full system, and a system estimator is required to test for it. Table 10.2 reports the results of Johansen's likelihood ratio tests for the cointegrating rank in Côte d'Ivoire. We use a lag length of one for the underlying VAR system; this is very restrictive even for annual data, but longer lag length leaves us with very few degrees of freedom. The null hypothesis for these tests is that the number of cointegrating vectors relating the n nonstationary variables is less than or equal to r (where $r < n$). Comparing the estimated likelihood ratios in column 2 to the asymptotic critical values in column 3, we see (row 1) that the hypothesis of no cointegration ($r = 0$) can be rejected in favor of at most one cointegrating vector. In row 2, the hypothesis of one vector cannot be rejected in favor of more than one. The asymptotic tests therefore indicate one cointegrating vector.

Likelihood ratio tests of cointegration are known to be sensitive to small-sample bias, tending to reject low values of r too often. In columns 3 and 5 we show a set of critical values that adjust for small-sample bias using a method suggested by Cheung and Lai (1993). Using these critical values it is difficult to distinguish between zero and one

Table 10.2 *Johansen's Maximum Likelihood Test of Cointegration Rank for Côte d'Ivoire*

		10 Percent Critical Value		5 Percent Critical Value	
	L-Max	*Unadjusted*	*Adjusted*	*Unadjusted*	*Adjusted*
With the drought dummy variable					
$r = 0$	45.01	36.35	48.34	39.43	52.44
$r \leq 1$	30.05	30.84	41.02	33.32	44.31
Without the drought dummy variable					
$r = 0$	32.65	30.84	39.17	33.32	42.32
$r \leq 1$	18.63	24.78	31.47	27.14	34.47

Note: The first row ($r = 0$) tests the null hypothesis of no cointegration; the second ($r \leq 1$) tests the null of at most one cointegration vector. The first column (L-Max) gives the estimated Johansen likelihood value in each case. The second and fourth columns give the 10 percent and 5 percent critical values taken from Osterwald-Lenum (1992, table 1.1). The third and fifth columns give the small-sample-adjusted critical values. The adjustment factor is calculated as $T/(T-nk)$, where T is the number of observations (28), n is the number of variables including the intercept (6) and drought dummy variable where included, and k is the number of lags (1). When the dummy is included (upper panel), the adjustment factor is 1.33; when it is excluded, this becomes 1.27. See Cheung and Lai (1993) for discussion of the adjustment factor.
Source: Computed from data from sources listed in appendix B.

cointegrating vector. We will proceed under the assumption that there is one vector, although we are marginally unable to reject the hypothesis of zero at the 10 percent level using the adjusted critical values.[25]

Alternative Estimators

There are a number of potential approaches to estimating the cointegrating parameters. The simplest and earliest is the Engle-Granger (1987) "two-step" method, which applies OLS to a static regression relating the levels of the real exchange rate and its fundamentals (equation 10.10). Cointegration implies that the residuals from this regression are stationary, and this restriction provides a test for cointegration. Because of the dominance of the common stochastic trend, the estimates of β from the static regression are super-consistent, approaching the true parameters at a rate proportional to the sample size rather than the square root of the sample size; and they remain so even in the absence of weak exogeneity. In the second step, lagged residuals from the static regression are used in place of the equilibrium errors on the right-hand side of a reduced-form error-correction equation. Again OLS provides consistent estimates, this time of the adjustment speed α and short-run parameters of the error-correction specification.[26]

While the Engle-Granger method is extremely simple to implement, the estimates of the cointegrating vector are biased in small samples. The degree of bias depends on the degree of persistence in the residual, suggesting that superior estimates might be obtained by accounting for the short-run dynamics (Bancrjee and others 1993). We therefore also report OLS estimates of β taken directly from the error-correction specification (equation 10.9). These control for the short-run dynamics—which may be of interest themselves—and, like the static regression estimates,

---

25. We include the drought variable in the long-run relationship, on the grounds that it picks up a supply shock that is highly asymmetric between traded and nontraded goods. Unfortunately, the critical values of Dickey-Fuller tests and the majority of the tests used in the Johansen procedure are sensitive to the exact specification of deterministic variables in the cointegrating relationship. We do not attempt the Monte Carlo simulations that would be required to establish critical values for our case.

26. Engle and Granger (1987) demonstrated an equivalence between cointegration and error correction for nonstationary variables. In the nonstationary case, therefore, equation 10.10, which implies cointegration, also implies that the real exchange rate has a reduced-form error-correction representation—that is, one that is similar to equation 10.11 but with contemporaneous values of the fundamentals excluded. It is this reduced-form error-correction equation that is estimated in the second step of the Engle-Granger method.

remain consistent even with a failure of weak exogeneity.[27] Moreover, in line with our earlier discussion, a second and potentially decisive advantage emerges under weak exogeneity: estimates of β taken from the conditional error-correction model are equivalent to full-information maximum-likelihood estimates. They are therefore asymptotically efficient, and the t-ratios generated by OLS are asymptotically normal, allowing standard inference. This is in contrast to the static regression case, where the t-ratios have nonstandard distributions even asymptotically.

A third natural alternative is the Johansen (1988) procedure, which is a systems approach based on estimation of the full VAR in equation 10.13. The "curse of dimensionality" is a serious limitation here, however. Monte Carlo evidence suggests that the Johansen procedure deteriorates dramatically in small samples, generating estimates with "fat tails" (in other words, frequent outliers) and sometimes substantial mean bias. Moreover, the procedure is less robust than the single-equation alternatives to mis-specification of system parameters such as lag length and to practical features such as serial correlation in the equilibrium error (Hargreaves 1994). Because of these small-sample problems, we limit our use of the Johansen procedure to determination of the number of cointegration vectors and investigation of weak exogeneity, both of which are features of the entire system of equations 10.13. For estimation purposes we restrict attention to the single-equation methods.

The I(0) Case

In the case of Burkina Faso, we find that all variables are stationary in levels. We pointed out above that in this case, the long-run "equilibrium" value of ln e_t, like that of any stationary variable, is simply its mean. A consistent and efficient estimator of the equilibrium real exchange rate is therefore the sample mean, corrected for any deterministic trend. This implies that the long-run parameters need not be estimated for the purpose of tying down the long-run equilibrium. If the fundamentals are super-exogenous with respect to these parameters, however, a structural shift in the marginal process generating the fundamentals (for example, a shift in the mean of F_t) will produce a corresponding change in the mean of ln e_t, with the slope of the effect given by the associated long-run parameter. Moreover, the long-run parameters and the short-run dynamics may be of theoretical interest even in

---

27. A failure of weak exogeneity, however, means small-sample bias and invalid inference regarding the long-run parameters. Recall also that the conditions for weak exogeneity with respect to short-run parameters are stronger.

the absence of super-exogeneity; and the investigator may have a practical interest in generating short-to-medium-term conditional forecasts of the real exchange rate. For all of these reasons, we proceed with estimation in the stationary case, even though it is not strictly necessary for assessment of the long-run equilibrium.

The theory of specification and estimation in the stationary case is well developed and we will not review it here; see Hendry 1995. What is clear is that the existence of a long-run relationship no longer exerts the kind of statistical leverage that it does when the variables are individually nonstationary. This is apparent in equation 10.10 since all the dynamics have been pushed into the residual ω_t, which is therefore likely to be correlated with the right-hand side variables. OLS estimates of the static regression are therefore inconsistent in the $I(0)$ case, even though (as emphasized above) they are super-consistent when the variables are nonstationary and cointegrated.[28] The error-correction model addresses this problem to some degree by incorporating dynamics; but the contemporaneous values of the fundamentals still raise issues of predeterminedness. Lacking identifying information on equation 10.11, one way to obtain consistent estimates of the parameters in that equation is to use higher lags of the fundamentals as instruments.[29]

Empirical Results

Tables 10.3 and 10.4 contain estimation results for Côte d'Ivoire while table 10.5 contains results for Burkina Faso. For Côte d'Ivoire, table 10.3 shows long-run parameters obtained from OLS regressions in levels (the first step of the Engle-Granger two-step method), using three alternative

---

28. The standard sufficient condition for consistency of OLS in the stationary case is that the right-hand side variables are *predetermined*—that is, that the residual is uncorrelated with contemporaneous and lagged right-hand side variables. In equation 10.10 the condition is $Cov(\omega_t, F_{j, t-k}) = 0$ for $k > 0$ and for each of the fundamentals F_j. In the stationary case, predeterminedness corresponds closely (but not exactly) to weak exogeneity (Engle, Hendry, and Richard 1983; Monfort and Rabemanajara 1990).

29. The lack of a clear statistical distinction between the individual and joint variation of the variables carries over to the conditions for weak exogeneity, which now make no general distinction between the short- and long-run parameters. A sufficient condition in the present limited information context (that is, in which identifying restrictions on the marginal model are not available) is that equation 10.11 and the marginal model form a block-recursive system (which guarantees predeterminedness and obviates the need for instrumental variables). We do not formally test for weak exogeneity in the $I(0)$ case (Burkina Faso), treating it instead as a maintained hypothesis where necessary (see Monfort and Rabemanajara 1990).

Table 10.3 *Long-Run Parameter Estimates for Côte d'Ivoire Using Alternative Proxies for Openness*

	OPEN1	OPEN2	OPEN3
Constant	–3.61	–4.29	–4.30
	(–16.71)	(–22.01)	(–12.22)
log(TOT)	–0.04	–0.16	–0.15
	(–3.03)	(–1.06)	(–0.94)
RESGDP	2.67	1.47	1.45
	(5.49)	(3.25)	(3.71)
log(OPEN)	0.78	0.08	0.03
	(3.68)	(0.34)	(0.12)
log(ISHARE)	0.27	0.31	0.30
	(5.83)	(4.63)	(5.15)
D8384	0.22	0.30	0.30
	(3.01)	(3.43)	(3.49)
Adjusted R^2	0.72	0.56	0.56
Q	14.32	13.80	14.21
	(0.05)	(0.05)	(0.05)
DW	1.16	1.14	1.15
DF	–3.55	–3.31	–3.31
ADF	–3.54	–3.84	–3.89
PP	–3.61	–3.30	–3.29

Note: The numbers in parentheses are *t*-ratios (note that these have nonstandard distributions even asymptotically). The period of estimation is 1965–93. The three regressions use the alternative openness variables discussed in appendix B. The dependent variable is *log (REER)*.
Source: Computed from data from sources listed in appendix B.

versions of the openness variable. There is strong evidence of cointegration in each case, as indicated by the unit-root tests applied to the estimated residuals: in each case the calculated values reject nonstationarity in favor of stationarity at standard levels.[30] Since the OPEN1 results are generally strongest, we use this variable in what follows. Except where otherwise noted, in the following discussion we focus on columns 1 and 3 of table 10.4 for Côte d'Ivoire and column 3 of table 10.5 for Burkina Faso. For Côte d'Ivoire, the selected columns

---

30. Note that the critical values for this test are more demanding than when testing for a unit root in a single variable, since the OLS estimation tends to induce stationarity in the residual.

Table 10.4 *ECM Parameter Estimates for Côte d'Ivoire*

	Two-Step ECM		Unrestricted ECM	
	OLS	IV	OLS	IV
Constant	5.60	5.69	5.54	5.53
	(25.99)	(25.28)	(15.02)	(9.13)
Adjustment Speed				
$\log(REER_{t-1})$ or $Error_{t-1}$	−0.34	−0.39	−0.45	−0.37
	(−2.05)	(−2.09)	(−2.32)	(−1.63)
Long–Run Parameters				
$\log(TOT_{t-1})$	−0.40	−0.50	−0.54	−0.75
	(−3.03)	(−3.24)	(−2.83)	(−2.21)
$RESGDP_{t-1}$	2.67	2.81	2.60	1.53
	(5.49)	(5.58)	(3.04)	(1.04)
$\log(OPEN_{t-1})$	0.78	0.81	0.64	0.46
	(3.68)	(3.69)	(1.87)	(0.82)
$\log(ISHARE_{t-1})$	0.27	0.30	0.33	0.43
	(5.83)	(5.38)	(4.97)	(3.56)
$D8384_{t-1}$	0.22	0.23	0.31	0.44
	(3.01)	(3.07)	(3.03)	(2.51)
Short–Run Parameters				
$\Delta\log(TOT_t)$	−0.38	−0.43	−0.37	−0.33
	(−2.86)	(−2.97)	(−1.78)	(−1.44)
$\Delta RESGDP_t$	1.47	1.86	0.95	0.76
	(3.29)	(3.72)	(1.27)	(0.90)
$\Delta\log(OPEN_t)$	0.38	0.49	0.29	0.28
	(1.99)	(2.59)	(0.95)	(0.87)
$\Delta\log(ISHARE_t)$	0.10	0.10	0.18	0.11
	(1.72)	(1.40)	(2.37)	(0.96)
$\Delta\log(PFOR_t)$	0.30	0.14	0.21	0.14
	(2.39)	(1.06)	(0.97)	(0.58)
$\Delta D8384$	0.05	0.05	0.07	0.04
	(1.04)	(1.01)	(0.97)	(0.43)
Adjusted R^2	0.49	0.55	0.42	0.36
Q	14.32	7.21	7.16	4.68
	(0.30)	(0.31)	(0.59)	(0.05)
DW	1.11	1.14	2.22	2.15

Note: The numbers in parentheses are *t*-ratios. The period of estimation is 1965–93. In columns 3 and 4, the long-run parameters and associated standard errors are obtained by estimating the Bewley transform of the ECM. In columns 1 and 2, we use the lagged residual from the static regression as the error-correction term. Columns 2 and 4 are instrumental variable estimates, using two lags of all right-side variables as instruments for ISHARE. The dependent variable is *log(REER)*.
Source: Computed from data from sources listed in appendix B.

correspond to the two-step Engle-Granger method and an unrestricted ECM. For Burkina Faso, where the sample is shorter and long-run coefficients are estimated imprecisely in the unrestricted ECM, we focus mainly on a parsimonious parameterization (column 3) obtained by eliminating short-run variables with statistically insignificant coefficients from the unrestricted ECM. Except when using the Engle-Granger method, long-run parameters and associated standard errors were obtained by estimating by OLS the appropriate transform of the ECM.[31]

Long-Run Parameters and Adjustment Speed

For both countries, the estimated long-run parameters strongly corroborate the theoretical model. We begin with the estimated coefficients on the resource balance to GDP ratio (RESGDP), which are positive as expected for both countries, suggesting that an increase in net capital inflows (inducing a decrease in the resource balance) raises domestic absorption and shifts the composition of potential output toward nontraded goods. The implied elasticities of the real exchange rate with respect to the resource balance (0.26 for Côte d'Ivoire and 1.02 for Burkina Faso) are comparable in magnitude to those obtained in Elbadawi and Soto (1995) for Côte d'Ivoire and Mali.

The effects of shocks to the terms of trade (TOT), as pointed out in the first main section of this chapter (on modeling the equilibrium exchange rate), are theoretically ambiguous. However, consistent with the bulk of the empirical literature (for example, Edwards (1989), Elbadawi and Soto 1995), we find that an improvement in the terms of trade appreciates the real exchange rate, suggesting that the spending effects of this variable dominate substitution effects. The estimated elasticities are plausible in light of the existing literature. Perhaps most strikingly, the magnitude of the estimated effect is very similar in the two countries despite their differences in economic structure. A 10 percent improvement in the terms of trade appreciates the real exchange rate by 4 percent in Côte d'Ivoire and 3 percent in Burkina Faso.

In both countries the estimated coefficient on the openness variable is positive, supporting the notion that trade-liberalizing reforms depreciate the equilibrium real exchange rate. The size of the elasticity differs,

---

31. For example, we obtain the long-run parameter estimates and their standard errors by applying instrumental variables to the Bewley transform of the ADL representation, using the ADL variables as instruments. This gives numerically equivalent results to applying OLS to the ADL, but with the advantage that the long-run parameters and associated standard errors can be read directly from the estimated equation. See Banerjee and others (1993), pp. 55–64.

Table 10.5 *ECM Parameter Estimates for Burkina Faso*

	1	2	3
Constant	8.94	7.01	6.12
	(2.96)	(2.80)	(3.43)
Adjustment Speed			
$\log(REER_{t-1})$	–0.94	–0.70	–0.76
	(–2.83)	(–2.77)	(–3.89)
Long-Run Parameters			
$\log(TOT_{t-1})$	–0.10	–0.50	–0.30
	(–0.29)	(–2.02)	(–2.27)
$\log(OPEN_{t-1})$	–0.17	0.18	0.22
	(–0.45)	(0.62)	(1.13)
$RESGDP_{t-1}$	2.28	4.06	3.89
	(1.34)	(3.53)	(4.48)
$\log(HBS3_{t-1})$	–1.27	–0.96	–0.72
(–3.22)	(–2.84)	(–3.48)	
$\log(PFOR_{t-1})$	0.14	n.a.	n.a.
	(0.99)		
Short-Run Parameters			
$\Delta\log(TOT_t)$	0.28	0.03	n.a.
	(0.97)	(1.16)	
$\Delta\log(OPEN_t)$	–0.13	–0.02	n.a.
	(–0.53)	(–0.10)	
$\Delta RESGDP_t$	1.87	2.46	2.73
	(2.01)	(3.20)	(4.34)
$\Delta\log(HBS3_t)$	–1.19	–0.68	n.a.
	(–2.09)	(–1.36)	
$\Delta\log(PFOR_t)$	0.07	0.14	n.a.
	(0.36)	(0.74)	
Adjusted R^2	0.78	0.77	0.75
Q	7.60	9.02	7.29
	(0.18)	(0.11)	(0.21)
DW	2.34	2.83	1.99

Note: Numbers in parentheses are *t*-ratios. The period of estimation is 1970–93. The first column (unrestricted ECM) corresponds to equation 10.11 in the text. The long-run parameters and associated standard errors are obtained by estimating the Bewley transform of the ECM. The dependent variable is $\Delta\log(REER)$.
Source: Computed from data from sources listed in appendix B.

however: it is 0.78 for Côte d'Ivoire and 0.22 for Burkina Faso. While these elasticities are not precisely estimated, they are consistent with evidence obtained by M'Bet and Madeleine (1994) and Elbadawi and Soto (1995), suggesting that the effects are stronger in the larger CFA countries.

For Côte d'Ivoire, a 10 percent increase in the share of investment in GDP (ISHARE) depreciates the real exchange rate by at least 2.7 percent, consistent with the view that this shifts the composition of spending toward traded goods. This evidence is consistent with that of Edwards (1989), but reveals an effect substantially lower than his estimates, which are in the range of 7 percent for a group of 12 developing countries. For Burkina Faso, the negative coefficient on HBS3 is consistent with a Harrod-Balassa-Samuelson effect: a 10 percent increase in domestic labor productivity compared to OECD labor productivity appreciates the real exchange rate by 7.2 percent.

To test the long-run homogeneity property—that the foreign price level, converted to CFA francs using the nominal exchange rate, does not affect the equilibrium real exchange rate—we include the log of PFOR in the specification and test the null hypothesis of a zero long-run coefficient. We use the dynamic regression results for this test since the t-statistics from the static regression have nonstandard distributions even under weak exogeneity. For Burkina Faso, homogeneity cannot be rejected at any reasonable level of significance (table 10.5). For Côte d'Ivoire, inclusion of the change in PFOR (or just the change in the trade-weighted nominal exchange rate) in the ECM causes a marked deterioration in the results. Thus, while long-run homogeneity cannot be rejected, the remaining results are unsatisfactory.[32] For the purposes of subsequent calculations, we impose long-run homogeneity for both countries by restricting the long-run parameter on PFOR to be zero.

Short-Run Dynamics

Tables 10.4 and 10.5 show the short-run parameters from the estimated ECMs for Côte d'Ivoire and Burkina Faso. For Côte d'Ivoire (table 10.4) we show two alternatives, corresponding to the second step of the Engle-Granger procedure and the unrestricted ECM. Column 1 uses the lagged residual from the static regression in column 1 of table 10.3, so that the short-run parameters are estimated conditional on the cointegration

---

32. When Δlog(PFOR) is included in the regression, it soaks up much of the explanatory power of other variables. The remaining coefficients, including the long-run coefficient on LPFOR, are estimated imprecisely and often with the "wrong" signs.

vector from the static regression.[33] In column 2 we estimate the short-run parameters jointly with the long-run parameters using the unre-stricted ECM.

The dynamic estimates provide direct evidence on the short-run ef-fects of nominal devaluations on the real exchange rate. We emphasized earlier in this chapter that even under long-run homogeneity, nominal devaluations may play an important macroeconomic role if nominal ri-gidities prevent the price of nontraded goods from responding quickly to shocks that alter the equilibrium real exchange rate. This role requires that movements in the nominal exchange rate not be fully offset in the short run by domestic inflation. Our estimates are consistent with a tran-sitional role for the nominal exchange rate if the coefficient on Δlog(PFOR) in the error-correction representation is positive (note also that since we are using an external real exchange rate, the upper boundary for this coefficient is not 1 but the share of traded goods in the domestic price index). For Côte d'Ivoire, the point estimates in columns 1 and 3 of table 10.4 suggest that over 20 percent of a nominal devaluation passes through to the real exchange rate over a one-year horizon. The elasticity is high-est (at 0.3) in the Engle-Granger ECM (column 1), in which it is also statistically significant. An elasticity of 0.3 implies that a 50 percent nomi-nal devaluation (as implemented in 1994: note that PFOR rises by 100 percent) will depreciate the real exchange rate by 30 percent in the short run. For Burkina Faso, the point estimates are uniformly smaller and have large standard errors. Wage-price rigidity therefore appears to give some role to the nominal exchange rate in macroeconomic adjustment in Côte d'Ivoire, but there is little evidence here of such a role for Burkina Faso.

Turning to the fundamentals, for Côte d'Ivoire we find short-run ef-fects that are generally appreciable in size, statistically significant, and in the same direction as the long-run effects. For Burkina Faso, the short-run impact effects are substantially less than the size of their correspond-ing long-run coefficients, and in most cases are statistically insignificant.

A crucial parameter in the estimation of these short-run dynamic models is the coefficient of the error-correction term, which measures the speed of adjustment of the real exchange rate to its equilibrium level. The adjustment speeds estimated for Côte d'Ivoire in table 10.4 are lower (at −0.30 and −0.45, respectively, in the two-step and unrestricted ECM) than the corresponding estimate for Burkina Faso in table 10.5 (at −0.76).

---

33. Note that this is not the same as the error-correction representation re-ferred to in the Granger Representation Theorem (Engle and Granger, 1987). The latter is a reduced-form equation that omits contemporaneous changes of the fundamentals.

The adjustment speed for Côte d'Ivoire is somewhat higher than that obtained for Côte d'Ivoire by Elbadawi and Soto (1995) using a similar framework. From these estimates the number of years required to eliminate a given misalignment can be derived.[34] For example, eliminating 95 percent of a shock to the real exchange rate would take slightly more than three years in Burkina Faso and could take as long as eight years in Côte d'Ivoire. Elbadawi and Soto (1995) find a similar difference in adjustment speed for Côte d'Ivoire and Mali. In this respect the smaller economies in the zone appear to be more adaptive to shocks than the larger ones. This conclusion is consistent with the widely held view that the latter group experienced a much higher degree of overvaluation during the 1986–94 period than the former. The results just discussed for PFOR suggest one reason for this: adjustment may be slower in these countries because nominal rigidities are more important. Slower adjustment of wages and nontraded-goods prices is consistent with a larger formal sector in Côte d'Ivoire than in Burkina Faso (here we would include both government and medium- to large-scale private enterprises) and also, for any given degree of nominal rigidity, with a larger share of nontraded goods in domestic prices. By the same token, while adjustment in Burkina Faso is relatively rapid, convergence to the new equilibrium is not immediate, suggesting the existence of some source of real rigidity of the type alluded to in the subsection on nominal rigidities and short-run dynamics.

Adjustment speeds for both countries, however, are substantially larger than the –0.19 figure obtained by Edwards (1989) using a partial adjustment model for a group of 12 developing countries with predetermined nominal exchange rates. To the degree that these adjustment speeds can be legitimately compared, they provide some support for the view that membership in a monetary union increases the credibility of monetary policy, thereby producing greater flexibility of nominal wage settlements in the private sector (Rodrik 1993).

Finally, a note on weak exogeneity for the case of Côte d'Ivoire. As discussed earlier, weak exogeneity holds with respect to the long-run parameters if the cointegrating vector does not enter the marginal model for the fundamentals. Engle and Granger (1987) suggest testing for weak exogeneity by introducing the error-correction term (the lagged residual from the static regression) into the equations of the marginal model and applying asymptotic t-tests to the hypothesis that the coefficients are zero. Using this test we are not able to reject weak exogeneity of the

---

34. The time required to dissipate x *percent* of a shock is determined according to $(1-|\alpha|^t) = 1 - x$, where t is the number of years and α the speed of adjustment parameter.

variables individually at reasonable significance levels, with the exception of ISHARE in which we reject weak exogeneity at the 5 percent level. Rejection for ISHARE suggests problems with inference in the error-correction specification: the long-run parameter estimates remain super-consistent, but standard errors are biased and inconsistent. To handle this we re-estimate the ECM via instrumental variables, using two lagged differences of all fundamentals as instruments for ISHARE (see columns 2 and 4 of table 10.4). Inference can proceed from the IV version of the ECM, conditional on legitimacy of the chosen instruments.[35] The results of the IV estimation do not alter the conclusions reported above.

Step Three: Calculating the Equilibrium Real Exchange Rate

In the subsection on the relationship of the single-equation approach to the PPP approach we distinguished conditional forecasts and counterfactual simulations as two alternative approaches to constructing sustainable values for the fundamentals. Here we broaden the first of these alternatives to consider various alternatives based on the time-series behavior of the data. For policy purposes, concern often centers about the current or prospective situation rather than the historical episodes that make up the data sample. While our discussion focuses on within-sample estimates or simulations, the considerations outlined below apply equally to the construction of projected sustainable values for the fundamentals.

Sustainable Fundamentals: Time-Series-Based Estimates

When the fundamentals are stationary, their movements are inherently temporary and the conditional long-run forecast is simply the sample mean (as corrected for any deterministic trend). At the other extreme all movements in the fundamentals are permanent. In this case, the fundamentals are individually random walks and the equilibrium real exchange rate in period τ is simply $\beta' F_t$.

In practice, the fundamentals are likely to include both transitory and permanent components. This is clear for nonstationary fundamentals, in which the permanent component corresponds to the underlying stochastic trend.

---

35. Although these results are encouraging, weak exogeneity may be a more serious problem than is indicated by our variable-by-variable tests. Using Johansen's system-based chi-squared test, we strongly reject joint weak exogeneity for the fundamentals taken together.

The Beveridge-Nelson (B-N) method, which we use below in the Côte d'Ivoire case, assumes that the fundamentals each follow a univariate ARIMA$(p,1,q)$ process, with the autoregressive and moving average parts generating stationary fluctuations about an underlying random walk (Beveridge and Nelson 1981). Movements generated by the unit-root part are permanent and are extracted to construct F_t^p, the permanent component of F_t. The equilibrium rate is then given by $\hat{\beta}'F_t^p$, where $\hat{\beta}$ is the vector of estimated long-run parameters. This will tend to be a somewhat smoother series than $\hat{\beta}'F_t$, reflecting the elimination of transitory shocks to the fundamentals.[36]

We will also calculate sustainable values using centered moving averages of the fundamentals in both the stationary and nonstationary cases. This approach can be defended by appealing to the judgmental nature of the decomposition exercise and noting the disadvantages imposed by small samples. Moving averages mechanically smooth the data, to a greater degree the larger the number of periods used. In the nonstationary case, even a narrow moving average typically smoothes the individual series more substantially than a B-N decomposition and may therefore yield results that are more appealing economically. The B-N approach is particularly problematic in small samples, where the results can be highly sensitive to the underlying ARIMA specification and can often exacerbate turning points in economically implausible ways. This problem can affect the resulting equilibrium rate even more dramatically: if the fundamentals are all smoothed with a moving average, the resulting equilibrium rate is simply the corresponding moving average of $\hat{\beta}'F_t$. The weighted sum of permanent components, in contrast, can easily be substantially more variable than F_t itself (as in our Côte d'Ivoire example below). Small samples also increase the possibility that stationary but persistent series are misidentified as nonstationary, in which case the B-N decomposition presumes a permanent component that in fact is not present.

In the stationary case, the moving average approach provides a way of acknowledging that even stationary fundamentals may have long-lasting movements. When a stationary variable is highly persistent, its conditional expectation at policy-relevant horizons can easily be relatively far from its unconditional mean. Using a moving average allows the long-run equilibrium rate to move in response to the current values

---

36. Any set of cointegrated variables has a common trend representation; this could be the basis of a joint decomposition of the real exchange rate and fundamentals into a stochastic trend component and a stationary (moving average) component (see Banerjee and others 1993). The B-N approach approximates this by treating the variables one by one.

of the fundamentals, even though these movements are thought ultimately to be temporary.

Sustainable Fundamentals: Counterfactual Estimates

Ex ante modeling of the permanent components of the fundamentals
provides an important alternative to ex post approaches that rely on the
underlying data-generating processes of the fundamentals. There are
both positive and normative reasons for pursuing this extension. On the
positive side, small samples can make it virtually impossible, when using time-series decomposition methods or moving averages, to distinguish persistent but unsustainable changes in the fundamentals from
genuinely sustainable changes. The accumulation of international arrears by Côte d'Ivoire starting in the early 1980s provides an example:
by this indicator, trade balances in that country appear to have been
unsustainably large for over a decade. A natural approach in such a case
is to construct a counterfactual path for the fundamental(s) in question
that is more in line with a plausible notion of sustainability. For example,
one might construct a path for the trade balance that would have kept
arrears reasonably low given "voluntary" capital inflows. The exercise
will often require a sequence of judgments; in this case, one needs a
plausible description of voluntary inflows, and one may be as interested
in the sensitivity of the estimated misalignment to changes in assumptions as in the overall change relative to the baseline.

The second, more normative use for counterfactual simulations is in
addressing the "what if" questions that are of central interest to
policymakers, particularly when the fundamentals include variables
potentially under policy control. Again using the Côte d'Ivoire case,
policymakers might want to know the implications for the real exchange
rate of a trade liberalization or change in government spending patterns. Preserving the relative simplicity of the single-equation approach,
a natural way of handling these concerns is to construct counterfactual
simulations of desirable values for selected fundamentals. As in the positive case, the construction of "desirable" values for the fundamentals is
not a trivial exercise. Theory can often provide loose guidelines (for example, in the proposition that the optimal tariff is zero for a small open
economy with no other distortions), but translating these into alternative values for the fundamentals will require an additional set of judgments (in this case, assessing what freer trade would have meant for the
openness ratio, which is our proxy for trade policy).

As pointed out in appendix C, a potentially important side effect of
counterfactual simulations, whether the underlying motivation is positive or normative, is to break the restriction implicit in the methodology
that the average degree of misalignment be near zero within sample.

The reason is straightforward: the misalignment calculation is now done using time paths for the fundamentals that were not used estimating the long-run parameters. The implicit super-exogeneity assumption, as emphasized earlier, is that the β vector estimated using sample information is relevant for assessing the effect of alternative paths for the fundamentals.

In appendix C, we construct counterfactual simulations for the resource balance, openness, and investment share variables for both Côte d'Ivoire and Burkina Faso. For Côte d'Ivoire, the simulations incorporate the following judgments (using "unsustainable" and "undesirable" to distinguish essentially positive rationales from essentially normative ones):

- The actual resource balance was unsustainably low after 1979;
- Trade policy was undesirably restrictive, particularly after 1979; and
- The investment to GDP ratio was undesirably low, particularly after 1979.

For Burkina Faso, in which the investment to GDP ratio does not enter the model, the key judgments are:

- The resource balance is determined by the volume of concessional inflows, and drought-year levels are unsustainable; and
- Trade policy was undesirably restrictive throughout the sample.

The details of these calculations appear in appendix C.

Estimating the Degree of Misalignment

The estimated degree of misalignment, m_t, is simply the percentage difference between the real exchange rate and its computed equilibrium value, as expressed in equation 10.15:

$$(10.15) \qquad m_t = \ln e_t - \ln e_t^* = [\ln e_t - \hat{\beta}'F_t] + \hat{\beta}'(F_t - F_t^p).$$

For within-sample estimates, e_t is simply the actual real exchange rate. For out-of-sample estimates, e_t can be forecasted using a dynamic simulation that feeds projected paths for the fundamentals through the estimated short-run parameters of the model.

The degree of misalignment is decomposed mechanically in equation 10.15 into an error-correction term that captures the deviation of the exchange rate from the "fitted" real exchange rate using long-run parameters (the term in square brackets) and a term that captures the deviation of the current fundamentals from sustainable values. Expressing m_t this way brings out the role of sustainability calculations for the fundamentals. Suppose, for example, that the long-run parameter for the terms of trade is negative, implying that a sustained terms-of-trade improvement appreciates the real exchange rate. If most movements in the terms of trade are temporary, however, and households optimize without borrowing constraints, then the short-run impact of a change in the terms of trade should be substantially below the estimated long-run impact (as in our theoretical model). A temporary improvement in the terms of trade would then produce offsetting changes in the components of m_t. The second component would be large and negative, reflecting the temporary nature of the terms of trade boom; the first would be large and positive, reflecting the very modest response of the actual real exchange rate to the substantial short-run movement in F_t. Misalignment calculated using the actual rather than sustainable value of the terms of trade (that is, setting $F_t^p = F_t$) would pick up only the second of these effects, producing the mistaken impression of a badly undervalued real exchange rate.

What the decomposition cannot do, of course, is identify the source of misalignment relative to plausible values for F^p. As discussed earlier, e_t may differ from F_t^p for reasons of real or nominal rigidities or, equivalently, equilibrium or disequilibrium dynamics; or it may be pushed by random shocks.

Empirical Results: Equilibrium Real Exchange Rates and Misalignment

Tables 10.6 and 10.7 show alternative measures of the equilibrium real exchange rate while figures 10.5 and 10.6 depict the observed and sustainable RERs as well as the fitted (for Côte d'Ivoire) and trend (for Burkina Faso) real exchange rates.[37] For Côte d'Ivoire, we use the long-run parameters derived from the static regression in column 1 of table 10.3. For Burkina Faso, we use the long-run parameters from the unrestricted ECM in column 1 of table 10.5.

We report four measures of the equilibrium real exchange rate for Côte d'Ivoire: the fitted RER, its corresponding five-year moving

---

37. Figures 10.5 and 10.6 could have been supplemented by confidence intervals based either on the standard errors of the estimated parameters or (via bootstrapping) on the empirical distribution of the data. Bootstrapping confidence intervals, however, are in general quite wide and, given the imprecision of our parameter estimates, are likely to be so in our case.

Figure 10.5 *The RER for Côte d'Ivoire, 1965 to 1993 (1985 Actual RER=100)*

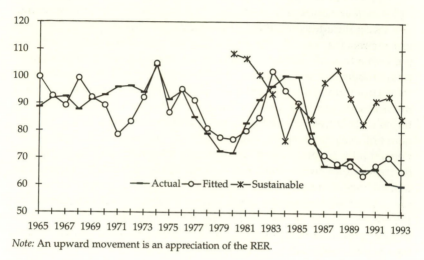

Note: An upward movement is an appreciation of the RER.

Figure 10.6 *The RER for Burkina Faso, 1970 to 1993 (1985 Actual RER=100)*

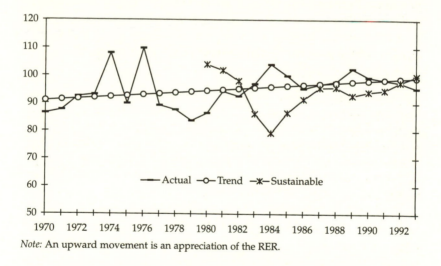

Note: An upward movement is an appreciation of the RER.

average, an equilibrium rate based on Beveridge-Nelson decompositions of the fundamentals, and one based on the counterfactual simulations described in appendix C. For Burkina Faso, we replace the B-N decomposition with the fitted trend for the real exchange rate; as discussed earlier, this represents the most natural long-run forecast for a trend-stationary variable.

Recall that when we generate long-run "forecasts" of the real exchange rate using time-series-based estimates of the "permanent" fundamentals, we require not only adequate estimates of the long-run parameters but also a lack of Granger causality from the real exchange rate to the fundamentals. With a lag length of one, weak and strong exogeneity coincide and the partial tests reported earlier for Côte d'Ivoire therefore provide some support for these calculations. As an additional check, we tested the multivariate generalization of Granger noncausality from the real exchange rate to the fundamentals and were unable to reject noncausality at any reasonable levels, using a lag length of either one or two. As argued earlier, the use of counterfactual simulations for the fundamentals involves an assumption that the long-run parameters are invariant to the interventions being constructed; we treat this as a maintained hypothesis.

The last columns of tables 10.6 and 10.7 show the percentage gap between the observed and equilibrium real exchange rates, using the counterfactual simulations for the equilibrium rate. The gap between these two series provides a measure of real exchange rate misalignment. The figures show a remarkable success on the part of the computed index in reproducing well-known overvaluation (and undervaluation) episodes in the recent macroeconomic history of these countries and the CFA zone more generally. In particular, note that Côte d'Ivoire managed to reverse substantial real overvaluation by 1985–86. While some of this was generated by contractionary macroeconomic policies that fell heavily on investment, a substantial contribution came from the steady depreciation of the French franc against the U.S. dollar and other major currencies and an ultimately temporary recovery in the terms of trade. When the French franc moved in the reverse direction following 1986, the fiscal laxity and structural rigidities that characterized the Côte d'Ivoire economy all along were fully exposed; our calculations imply that during the 1987–93 period the real exchange rate was overvalued by 34 percent on average. By 1994 a set of corrective measures, including a zone-wide 50 percent devaluation, were implemented. Using a constant elasticity model, Devarajan (Chapter 8) finds a somewhat larger degree of overvaluation in Côte d'Ivoire for 1993 (56 percent in domestic-currency terms) than our estimates based on counterfactual simulations of the fundamentals.

For Burkina Faso, in contrast, our results for 1980–93 do not indicate any major overvaluation (last column of table 10.7 and figure 10.6). Indeed, according to our estimates, Burkina Faso's real exchange rate was undervalued by 1 percent on average between 1980 and 1986 and by

Table 10.6 Observed and Equilibrium RER Indexes for Côte d'Ivoire— 1980 to 1993 (1985 Observed RER=100)

Year	Observed	Fitted	5-year MA	B-N	"Sustainable"	Overvaluation
					Equilibrium RER	
1980	72	77	85	74	108	51
1981	83	80	93	81	107	29
1982	91	85	94	86	101	10
1983	96	102	95	83	94	−3
1984	100	95	87	82	76	−24
1985	100	90	76	96	90	−10
1986	79	76	82	87	84	6
1987	67	71	85	83	98	46
1988	67	68	80	96	103	54
1989	70	67	75	54	92	32
1990	66	64	79	52	83	26
1991	66	68	76	60	91	38
1992	61	71	81	60	93	52
1993	60	65	80	64	85	41

Note: The observed RER is the one used in the econometric analysis. The long-run parameter vector is taken from the static regression in column 1 of table 10.3. "Fitted" values are obtained directly from that regression; "5-year MA" refers to five-year moving averages for all fundamentals; "B-N" refers to Beveridge-Nelson decompositions of all fundamentals; and the "sustainable" RER is defined as the fitted RER with all fundamentals replaced by counterfactual sustainable values, as determined in appendix C. Overvaluation is defined as 100·(sustainable RER − observed RER)/(observed RER).
Source: Computed from data from sources listed in appendix B.

nearly 14 percent during 1987–93.[38] The estimated undervaluation may be on the high side for the latter period.[39] Burkina Faso is generally regarded, however, as having adjusted more successfully to the adverse shocks that affected the entire zone after 1986, especially in comparison with the larger CFA countries (Devarajan and Hinkle 1995). Substantially milder overvaluation (or even undervaluation) is one measure of this success; another is the absence in Burkina Faso of the deep reces-

38. The apparent overvaluation in 1980 was eliminated by the depreciation of the actual REER in the early 1980s that was caused largely by the depreciation of the French franc to which the CFA franc was linked.

39. For example Elbadawi and Soto (1995), using a similar methodology, estimate that the RER in Mali was virtually in equilibrium (on average) during the 1987–94 period, while the CGE estimates of Devarajan in Chapter 8 suggest that the RER in Burkina Faso was overvalued by about 9 percent in 1993.

Table 10.7 *Observed and Equilibrium RER Indexes for Burkina Faso—1980 to 1993 (1985 Observed RER=100)*

Year	Observed	Fitted	Trend	5-year MA	"Sustainable"	Overvaluation
				Equilibrium RER		
1980	86	100	94	101	104	17
1981	94	100	95	101	102	7
1982	93	103	95	104	98	6
1983	97	103	96	103	86	−13
1984	104	113	96	102	79	−31
1985	100	98	96	101	87	−16
1986	95	93	97	100	91	−4
1987	97	100	97	98	96	−1
1988	98	99	97	100	96	−2
1989	102	102	98	101	93	−10
1990	99	106	98	100	94	−6
1991	98	99	98	101	95	−4
1992	98	98	99	100	98	0
1993	96	99	99	99	100	−4

Note: The observed RER is the one used in the econometric analysis. The fitted RER is the one estimated from the cointegration regression (see table 10.6). "Trend" refers to a fitted linear trend for the RER. "5-year MA" refers to five-year moving averages. The "sustainable" RER is the fitted RER in which the fundamentals (RESGDP and OPEN) have been replaced by their sustainable counterparts as outlined in appendix C. Overvaluation is defined as 100·(sustainable RER − observed RER)/(observed RER).
Source: Computed from data from sources listed in appendix B.

sion experienced by Côte d'Ivoire during the 1980s and early 1990s. Both observations suggest a more flexible domestic wage and price structure in the smaller of the two countries, and therefore significantly milder nominal rigidities.

Conclusions

The decision to devalue depends fundamentally on the degree of misalignment of the real exchange rate and the speed with which internal adjustment mechanisms are likely to restore macroeconomic balance. Measuring the degree of misalignment is difficult, however, given that the equilibrium real exchange rate is unobservable whenever the economy is not in internal and external balance. The standard PPP approach is to identify a period in which the economy is judged to have been in balance, and to take the real exchange rate of that period as the equilibrium rate for all years. But this fails to account for the effect of changes in the fundamentals on the equilibrium real exchange rate.

Once the endogeneity of the equilibrium real exchange rate is recognized, however, a second problem arises: restricting attention to plausible candidates for years of macroeconomic balance, there will rarely be enough observations to estimate the elasticities of the equilibrium rate with respect to even a small list of fundamentals. In this chapter, we addressed these problems by imposing the relatively mild (and testable) restriction, drawn from standard theories of the equilibrium real exchange rate, that the distance between the actual and equilibrium real exchange rates is a stationary random variable. When the variables are $I(1)$, this leads naturally to the use of cointegration methods for estimating the long-run relationship between the real exchange rate and its fundamentals. When the variables are stationary, standard procedures of dynamic specification and estimation apply. We illustrated the methodology using annual data for Côte d'Ivoire and Burkina Faso.

How useful an addition is this methodology to the standard toolbox for assessing the equilibrium real exchange rate and the degree of misalignment? Our view is that this methodology belongs in the analyst's toolkit as a clear advance over PPP and a useful complement to other methods. There are three fundamental reasons for this.

- First and foremost, this approach provides a natural way of incorporating the reality that the fundamentals will sometimes move permanently. In such a case our approach extracts maximal leverage from the theoretical proposition that the real exchange rate will not stray indefinitely from a function of the fundamentals.
- Second, estimating the equilibrium real exchange rate is typically motivated by policy concerns. The analyst may therefore be particularly interested in the relationship between the equilibrium real exchange rate and hypothetical changes in individual fundamentals. For out-of-sample exercises, interest would center on how changes in the fundamentals would alter both the actual and the equilibrium rates, and thereby the degree of misalignment. Under super-exogeneity of the fundamentals, our approach delivers a set of parameters that can be used for such policy analysis in a transparent and straightforward manner.
- Third, this approach takes a partial step toward imbedding the determination of the long-run relationship in the overall dynamic relationship between the real exchange rate and its fundamentals. Under weak exogeneity with respect to the short-run parameters, fully efficient estimation and inference on these parameters can take place conditional on the current and lagged fundamentals. The resulting information on short-run dynamics may be of interest in its own right and if Granger noncausality also holds, can be

used to generate short-term forecasts of the real exchange rate and degree of misalignment.

From the viewpoint of dynamic specification, there are various directions in which the approach advocated here might be extended. One is to allow both $I(0)$ and $I(1)$ variables in the long-run relationship. In this case, the theory still implies cointegration among the $I(1)$ variables, but the Engle-Granger two-step method will produce inconsistent estimates of the long-run parameters on the stationary variables. We are therefore pushed toward allowing explicitly for the short-run dynamics, whether via the error-correction model, the Johansen procedure, or some alternative. A second extension would be allowing multiple long-run relationships between the variables. Such a case might arise, for example, from the existence of a reaction function relating fiscal policy to the trade balance or the real exchange rate. Moreover, since most of our variables are already measured in ratios (the real exchange rate, the openness variable, and so on), we may already be reducing the order of integration of underlying nonstationary variables (such as the domestic price level). The structural error-correction model of Boswijk (1995) represents the closest counterpart to our analysis in the case of multiple cointegrating relationships. Finally, we have chosen not to impose any theoretical structure on the short-run dynamics. In cases where particular sources of short-run dynamics are of interest, there may be a substantial return to developing a theoretical structure to capture these dynamics, and imposing the resulting identifying restrictions; for an interesting attempt to incorporate rigidity of domestic prices, see Kaminsky (1987). An important challenge along these lines is that of separating misalignments caused by price rigidities from those caused by internal real dynamics or temporary movements in the fundamentals. Naturally, most of these extensions will bring out a tension between maintaining the simplicity of a single-equation approach—an important feature if this approach is to be used "in the field"—and allowing the overall dynamic relationship(s) to emerge from the data.

As a final extension of the single-equation approach, we note the possible usefulness of cross-country data in tying down the long-run elasticities. A version of our static regression could easily be run on a pure cross-section or panel of countries. The obvious advantage of this approach lies in its expansion of the sample size. The resulting increase in degrees of freedom is conditional on the validity of pooling restrictions, but with multiple time periods some of these will be testable. The handling of dynamics remains a difficult problem in panel data, however, and in this area there is a clear tradeoff between the flexibility associated with our single-country approach and the restrictions required to support dynamic estimation in a panel. Our theoretical model and empirical results suggest that pooling restrictions are at least as likely to fail with respect to short-run parameters and error structure as with respect to the long-run parameters. Strategies such as using nonoverlapping time-averaged data (for example, five-year averages) may help minimize some of these difficulties but to our knowledge a consensus has not yet emerged on how to handle nonstationarity in panel data.

In the field, of course, the virtue of cross-sectional or panel results is that the long-run parameters can be "borrowed" from existing studies without requiring new estimation. Such parameters could be combined with data on changes in a given country's fundamentals to derive changes in the equilibrium real exchange rate for that country and therefore changes in the degree of misalignment. Identifying the *level* of misalignment in any particular year would then require a "rebasing" exercise of some sort, and in this respect the use of borrowed cross-country parameters is a kind of hybrid of the PPP approach and econometric approaches.

Our aim in this chapter has been to give a self-contained presentation of a methodology that we consider to be applicable at reasonably low cost in the field. The chapter is not a cookbook, however. In the end, the effective use of the single-equation, time-series approach requires a balanced sense of both its virtues and its limitations and—as always in econometric practice—some attention to the evolving state of time-series econometrics. We close by identifying three particular cautions regarding the use of our methodology in the policy arena.

First, the econometric approach is data intensive and inherits all the limitations of developing-country data. Our empirical findings for Côte d'Ivoire and Burkina Faso are broadly consistent with the empirical literature on equilibrium real exchange rates in developing countries, and they line up well with estimates obtained by other methods. But they are not robust. We noted above that the econometric results were quite sensitive to the choice of proxies for the fundamentals and to the estimation procedure. The choice of real exchange rate index also made a difference empirically, and although changes in long-run elasticities are to be expected, we found that the overall statistical performance was highly sensitive to whether an internal or external real exchange rate concept was employed and whether the nominal exchange rate was adjusted for black market transactions. While such conditions define the art of econometric practice, they may be particularly acute when the notion of long-run equilibrium is required to carry so much weight in short samples.

The reality of short samples brings out a second potential weakness in this approach, even relative to the PPP approach. In effect, the single-equation methodology assumes that the economy was in internal and external balance *on average* over the sample period. This avoids the need for a priori and possibly ad hoc claims about macroeconomic balance in any particular year, providing instead a systematic way of bringing the whole sample to bear in determining the path of the equilibrium rate. But it implies that unless the analyst is prepared to undertake counterfactual simulations for the fundamentals, the average degree of misalignment in the sample will tend, by construction, to be small. There will be little scope for uncovering episodes of overvaluation or undervaluation that last more than a few years. In the CFA zone, where the real exchange rate was widely thought to be overvalued for most of the period between 1978 and 1994, the implicit "balance on average" assumption may be seriously misleading. The PPP approach, of course, does not require such an assumption; the result is that the real exchange rate can in principle be overvalued (or undervalued) in every period other than the benchmark one. We suggested that a natural way of handling this within our methodology was to construct counterfactual simulations for the fundamentals. In our counterfactuals for Côte d'Ivoire, freer trade, higher domestic investment, and smaller trade deficits all produced a depreciation of the equilibrium rate and therefore tended to increase the estimated degree of misalignment.

Finally, the methodology relies on concepts of equilibrium and misalignment that are conditional on policies or structural features that can reasonably be treated as predetermined, whether or not those policies or features generate welfare losses. In this view, short-run misalignments may well reflect market-clearing responses to shocks, and long-run movements in the real exchange rate may well reflect highly suboptimal macroeconomic policy choices. For both reasons the misalignments most readily identified using single-equation time-series methods—those not requiring counterfactual simulations—may not be the most interesting from a policy perspective. While we have seen that policy content can be imposed in the form of normative counterfactual simulations for the fundamentals, the implicit assumption of super-exogeneity places an additional burden on the data that may or may not be justified in the sample at hand.

Appendix A

Conditioning and Weak Exogeneity

Weak exogeneity is (potentially) a property of the joint distribution of the real exchange rate and the fundamentals. In this appendix we introduce the concept of conditional and marginal models and explore the relationship between the single-equation model (equation 10.11) and the full distribution of the $(n \times 1)$ vector $x_t = [\ln e_t, F_t', s_t]'$, conditional on its own past (see also Ericsson 1992). With reasonable generality we can describe this distribution as the pth-order Gaussian vector autoregression (VAR), as expressed by equation 10.A.1:

$$(10.A.1) \qquad x_t = \sum_{j=1}^{p} \Pi_j x_{t-j} + \varepsilon_t, \qquad \varepsilon_t \sim IN(0, \Sigma)$$

where the Π_j are $(n \times n)$ matrices of reduced-form coefficients and Σ is the $n \times n$ symmetric and positive definite matrix of contemporaneous covariances between the innovations ε_{it}. Equation 10.A.1 can be written equivalently as equation 10.A.2:

$$(10.A.2) \qquad \Delta x_t = \Gamma x_{t-1} + \sum_{j=1}^{p} A_j \Delta x_{t-j} + \varepsilon_t$$

where $\Gamma = [(\Sigma_{j=i,p} \Pi_j) - I]$ and $A_j = -\Sigma_{i=j+1,p} \Pi_i$. The first row of equation 10.A.2 is a *reduced-form* error-correction model for $\Delta \ln e_t$; it is similar to equation 10.11 but excludes contemporaneous values of F and s. To obtain the distribution of $\Delta \ln e_t$ conditional on lagged x_t and contemporaneous F and s, we first partition the vector x_t into $x_t = [\ln e_t, w_t']'$, where $w_t = [F_t', z_t]'$ is the vector of macroeconomic determinants of the real exchange rate. Without loss of generality, we can then factorize the joint distribution represented by equation 10.A.2 into the distribution of $\Delta \ln e_t$ conditional on contemporaneous $w_t's$ and lagged $x_t's$ and the associated marginal distribution of the $w_t's$ given lagged $x_t's$. Under normality of ε_t, the conditional and marginal models take the form shown in equation 10.A.3.a:

(10.A.3.a)
$$\Delta \ln e_t = \Sigma_{12}(\Sigma_{22})^{-1}\Delta w_t + (\Gamma_1 - \Sigma_{12}(\Sigma_{22})^{-1}\Gamma_2 x_{t-1} + \sum_{j=1}^{p}(A_{1j} - \Sigma_{12}(\Sigma_{22})^{-1}A_{2j})\Delta x_{t-j} + \xi_t$$

(10.A.3.b)
$$\Delta w_t = \Gamma_2 x_{t-1} + \sum_{j=1}^{p} A_{2j}\Delta x_{t-j} + \varepsilon_{2j}$$

where the numerical subscripts refer to the blocks of appropriately partitioned matrices (so that, for example, Γ_1 is the first row of Γ and Σ_{22} the $n - 1 \times n - 1$ lower-diagonal bloc of Σ). By construction, the disturbance term in (10.A.3.a), $\xi_t = \Sigma_{11} - \Sigma_{12}(\Sigma_{22})^{-1}\Sigma_{21}$ is uncorrelated with all of the variables on the right-hand side of that equation. That this representation is simply a reparameterization of (10.A.2) can be confirmed by premultiplying equation 10.A.2 by the $n \times n$ nonsingular matrix

$$B = \begin{bmatrix} 1 & \Sigma_{12}(\Sigma_{22})^{-1} \\ 0 & I_{n-1} \end{bmatrix}$$

which results in equation 10.A.3.

Equation 10.A.3.a is a single-equation conditional error-correction model whose form mimics that of equation 10.11. Although it is often assumed in writing an equation like 10.11 that the disturbance is uncorrelated with the right-hand side variables, this is true *by construction* for equation 10.15.a. To the degree that the parameterizations differ, therefore, OLS estimation of equation 10.11 will tend to uncover the parameters of equation 10.A.3.a (in which orthogonality holds by construction), yielding inconsistent estimates of the parameters of equation 10.11. Moreover, even if the parameters of equation 10.11 can be recovered from those of equation 10.A.3.a, the latter are potentially complicated functions of the underlying VAR parameters. There may therefore be cross-equation restrictions linking these parameters to those of the marginal model (equation 10.A.3.b). In such a case efficient estimation of the conditional model requires that these restrictions be imposed; and failure to impose them may produce inconsistent standard errors, invalidating inference.

These considerations motivate a search for conditions under which estimation and inference regarding particular parameters of equation

10.11 can proceed successfully in the conditional model alone (in other words, without analyzing the full system). In such cases the subvector w_t is said to be *weakly exogenous* for the parameters of interest (Engle, Hendry, and Richard 1983). In the context of the above discussion, weak exogeneity requires (a) that the parameters of interest can be directly recovered from those of the conditional model and (b) that there be no cross-equation restrictions linking these parameters to those of the marginal model.

Weak exogeneity is testable, though generally at the cost of moving to systems estimation. For the case of nonstationary but cointegrated variables (see the section on the $I(1)$ case), Urbain (1992) and Johansen (1992) show that w_t is weakly exogenous for the long-run parameters and adjustment speed if $\Gamma_2 = 0$, or equivalently if the cointegration vector does not enter the marginal model. In our empirical section we test this restriction for the case of Côte d'Ivoire. With respect to the short-run parameters of equation 10.11, matters are more complicated. The condition for weak exogeneity with respect to the long-run parameters of equation 10.11 also guarantees weak exogeneity with respect to the short-run parameters *of the conditional model itself* (that is, of equation 10.A.3.a). Recall, however, that the long-run parameters of interest were derived not from conditioning but from a theoretical model. If the short-run parameters (equation 10.11) have similar structural interpretations, then the conditions for weak exogeneity are more demanding. A set of sufficient conditions (Urbain 1992) when the variables are nonstationary and cointegrated is $\Gamma_2 = 0$ and $\theta = 0$, where θ is the vector of covariances between the disturbance in equation 10.11 and the vector of disturbances from the marginal model (equation 10.A.3.b). (Under these conditions, equations 10.A.3.a and 10.A.3.b form a block-recursive system.) We do not test for weak exogeneity of the short-run parameters in this chapter.

When the variables are stationary, the lack of a clear statistical distinction between their individual and joint variation carries over to the conditions for weak exogeneity, which now make no general distinction between the short- and long-run parameters. A sufficient condition in the limited information context of this chapter (that is, the context in which identifying restrictions on the marginal model are not available) is that equation 10.11 and the marginal model form a block-recursive system. As is well known, this guarantees predeterminedness and obviates the need for instrumental variables. We will not formally test for weak exogeneity in the $I(0)$ case (see for example, Monfort and Rabemanajara 1990), treating it instead as a maintained hypothesis where necessary.

Appendix B

Data Description

The data were taken from three sources: (a) IMF, International Financial Statistics; (b) UNCTAD; and (c) the World Bank's Unified Survey. The variables were constructed as follows:

Real Exchange Rate (RER). The ratio of the trade-weighted index of foreign wholesale prices each expressed in CFA (local currency) terms by converting at the relevant bilateral official exchange rate to the home country's consumer price index (CPI). The price and exchange rate indexes (WPI and NER) are calculated as geometric averages across the home country's n largest trading partners, with bilateral total (import plus export) trade shares (normalized to unity) as weights. We use official data for the trade weights; these are not corrected for unrecorded trade: $RER = (WPI \cdot NER)/CPI$.

Terms of Trade (TOT). The external terms of trade are P_X^w/P_M^w, where P_X^w and P_M^w are export and import price indexes (expressed in dollars) from UNCTAD. The macroeconomic impact of a change in the terms of trade is proportional to the share of international trade in economic activity. If the export share is relatively constant over the sample there is little point in adjusting the relative price measure. Our data for Côte d'Ivoire, however, show what appears to be a major structural increase in exports starting in 1984. To capture this feature we multiply Côte d'Ivoire's external terms of trade by an export share dummy variable, defined for observations between 1965 and 1983 inclusive as the average export share for that period and for later observations as the average export share after 1984.

Openness (OPEN). OPEN1 is the import to GDP ratio (IMPGDP), and is defined as the value of imports at current prices (IMPCP) over GDP at current prices (GDPKP): $OPEN1 = IMPCP/GDPCP$. OPEN2 is the ratio of the value of imports at constant prices (IMPKP) plus exports

459

at constant prices (EXPKP) to GDP at constant prices (GDPKP): OPEN2 = (IMPKP + EXPKP)/GDPKP. OPEN3 is the ratio of imports at constant prices to domestic absorption at constant prices: OPEN3 = IMPKP/ (GDPKP − (EXPKP − IMPKP)).

Resource Balance to GDP Ratio (RESGDP). Value of exports at constant prices (EXPKP) minus value of imports at constant prices (IMPKP), divided by GDP at constant prices (GDPKP). EXPKP has been adjusted by the domestic terms of trade (TOTD), which are defined as the ratio of export to import deflator. Thus RESGDP = (EXPKP·TOTD − IMPKP)/ GDPKP.

Investment Share (ISHARE). Ratio of gross investment at constant prices (IGROSS) to the sum of private consumption (PCONK), government consumption (GCONK), and gross investment, all at constant prices: ISHARE = IGROSS/(PCONK+GCONK + IGROSSK).

Foreign Price Level (PFOR). Trade-weighted index of foreign wholesale prices expressed in CFA terms (that is, in home-country currency). Thus PFOR = WPI · NER (and RER = PFOR/CPI; see definition of RER above).

Harrod-Balassa-Samuelson Proxy (HBS3). A lagged 3-year weighted moving average of the ratio of home country GDP per worker to OECD GDP per worker, using the Penn World Tables (Heston-Summers) data for these variables. OECD GDP per worker was constructed by summing OECD GDP and dividing by total OECD workers. Weights decline linearly. Denoting the ratio of GDPs per worker in year t by R(t): HBS3(t) = (3/6) · R(t − 1) + (2/6) · R(t − 2) + (1/6) · R(t − 3).

Appendix C

Sustainable Fundamentals

Time-Series Measures: TOT and LPFOR

Both Burkina Faso and Côte d'Ivoire are very small economies by world standards and are therefore price takers in the markets for both their exports and imports. Moreover, the nominal exchange rate for the CFA francs was fixed throughout the 1970–93 sample period and could not be changed by individual CFA countries. The terms of trade (TOT) and the foreign price level converted to CFA francs (LPFOR) are therefore exogenous variables. While these variables fluctuate substantially from year to year, we have no basis on which to question the sustainability of their longer-run movements. We therefore use five-year centered moving averages as the sustainable values of these variables (extrapolating out of sample using the first- and last-year values). We also generate alternative sustainable values for Burkina Faso and Côte d'Ivoire using sample means and Beveridge-Nelson decompositions, respectively.

Counterfactual Simulations: RESGDP

RESGDP is the ratio of the resource balance to GDP, both in constant prices. Since Burkina Faso relied heavily on concessional aid flows in 1970–93, determining a sustainable resource balance is essentially a problem of determining sustainable levels of financial inflows. These inflows can be divided into net factor income, net transfers, and net capital flows. We used five-year moving averages for the first two (interest payments were small and changed very slowly over the sample, so we ignored the feedback from borrowings to interest payments). We then divided net capital flows into its dominant component—net long-term concessional borrowing—and "other" flows (net direct investment, net portfolio investment, net short-term borrowing, net errors and omissions), using five-year moving averages for the latter. The government of Burkina

461

Faso attempted to maximize net concessional borrowing during the sample period, so this component was ultimately determined by the foreign donors. To smooth out year-to-year fluctuations in net concessional borrowing, we used the smaller of the five-year moving average of the actuals or 3.5 percent of GDP (the highest level reached except in drought years). The sustainable resource balance is then the sum of these sustainable components. Note that the World Bank's debt stock and flow data are not consistent with the national accounts and balance-of-payments data for Burkina Faso and Côte d'Ivoire. Since the balance of payments and national accounts data are consistent with each other and essential for the analysis, we used balance-of-payments data when there were conflicts between these and the Bank's debt data.

The Côte d'Ivoire case is both more complicated and more representative of the problems likely to emerge in developing-country applications. Côte d'Ivoire avoided balance-of-payments and debt problems in the 1970s. We therefore treated actual flows as essentially sustainable during the 1965–79 period, using five-year moving averages to smooth out temporary fluctuations. After 1980, the country was unable to meet its debt service payments. Moving averages therefore seem unlikely to capture sustainable movements in net borrowing and interest payments after 1980, and we cannot ignore the feedback from higher debt levels to higher interest payments. For 1980–93 we proceed as follows.

To proxy the sustainable level of borrowing, we used zero net repayments and net disbursements after 1979 (in other words, no change in the debt stock other than through write-downs). Côte d'Ivoire's debt ratio jumped from 47 percent in 1979 to 62 percent in 1980, then climbed to 115 percent in 1985, after which the country defaulted. The Maastricht Treaty, after which the fiscal guidelines for the West African Monetary Union are modeled, sets 60 percent of GDP as the maximum desirable debt level for the EU countries. A developing country might be able to target a somewhat higher debt level than 60 percent depending upon its rate of growth and its access to financing on concessional terms; so 1979 is by these criteria the last year of sustainable debt levels.

We calculate sustainable direct and portfolio investment as assumed percentages of total sustainable investment as determined below; together with the sustainable borrowing figures, these yield a sustainable level of total capital inflows.

To proxy sustainable interest payments, we use 4 percent of GDP. This represents a kind of compromise between a normative scenario in which interest payments are capped at 2.5 percent of GDP and a positive scenario (essentially feasibility calculation) that caps them at 5 percent. For comparison, the Maastricht debt ceiling, with an inflation rate of 3 percent and a real interest rate of 3 percent, implies interest payments of 1.8 percent of GDP for the EU countries. Côte d'Ivoire was unable to sustain the service payments on its debt after interest payments reached 3.5 and 5.2 percent of GDP in 1981 and 1982.

The sustainable resource deficit for 1980–93 is then calculated as the sum of net transfers, net factor income, and net capital inflows, using five-year moving averages of the actuals for transfers and factor income flows other than interest payments.

Counterfactual Simulations: ISHARE and OPEN1

ISHARE is the ratio of investment to GDP in constant prices; OPEN1 is the ratio of imports to absorption in current prices. The sustainability criterion we use for these variables is consistency with a 3 percent long-run growth rate of GDP per capita.

With population growth estimated at about 3 percent for both countries over the sample, GDP growth of 6 percent is required to achieve 3 percent growth in GDP per capita. Using ICORs of 4 for Côte d'Ivoire and 5 for Burkina Faso, this would in turn require investment ratios of about 25 percent and 30 percent of GDP, respectively. The 25 percent ratio is in line with those actually achieved during the 1960s and 1970s in Côte d'Ivoire; it is also the target that the World Bank has suggested as a guideline for Africa as a whole (World Bank 1989). For Côte d'Ivoire, therefore, we use a moving average of the actual investment levels for 1965 to 1981, which were reasonably close to 25 percent, and 20 percent for 1982–93 when investment was depressed far below this level. For Burkina Faso, in which the investment to GDP ratio is used only as an input to calculate the target import to absorption ratio (see below), we assume a sustainable investment ratio of 25 percent.

For both countries, we assume that increases in the import to GDP ratio were required to deliver the import content of additional investment and also support a more liberal trade regime. We estimate an import content of investment of roughly 0.6 for both countries. To incorporate trade liberalization, we assume increases in the import ratio of 3 percent and 2 percent of GDP, respectively, for Côte d'Ivoire and Burkina Faso. The target import ratio is then estimated as the actual import ratio plus 3 percent of GDP plus 0.6 times the difference between the target investment ratio and the actual investment ratio. This target import to absorption ratio is used for the entire sample period, as a more open trade policy would have been desirable throughout.

A Caveat

As the above discussion suggests, determining target values for particular countries requires considerable country-specific knowledge and a number of assumptions based on partial information and analysis. These assumptions are open to question—and different ones (regarding either the key parameters or the underlying notion of sustainability) would yield different results. It may therefore be important in specific cases to consider alternative plausible assumptions and to compare the results of the various alternatives to those from using moving averages for the target variables.

Part IV

Policy and Operational Considerations

11

The Three Pessimisms: Real Exchange Rates and Trade Flows in Developing Countries

Nita Ghei and Lant Pritchett [*]

The preceding chapters in this volume have argued that the real exchange rate is one of the primary determinants of the resource balance. This chapter turns to the question of how, empirically, the RER actually affects trade flows and the resource balance in developing countries.

A significant strand of the development literature of the 1950s and 1960s, based on the work of Myrdal, Prebisch, and Singer, was pessimistic about the trade elasticities faced by low-income countries. Some economists disputed the ability of changes in the real exchange rate to improve the trade balance of developing countries, even in the medium to long run. They argued that import and export elasticities are so low that the required changes in the RER would be neither feasible nor desirable and that structural policies rather than real exchange rate adjustment should be pursued for dealing with balance-of-payments deficits. Pessimism about the long-term trends in the terms of trade and the prospects for export-led growth also led this group of economists to advocate inward-looking industrialization.[1] More recently, some authors have reopened this debate, citing new empirical evidence on unit roots and nonstationarity of key variables to reassert that depreciation of the real exchange rate is not strongly associated with a significant improvement

* The authors are grateful to Peter Montiel, Larry Hinkle, and three anonymous reviewers for helpful comments on earlier drafts of this chapter.
1. See Meier (1995) for a succinct discussion of this literature.

in the trade balance.[2] These arguments are still echoed in policy debates over devaluations in low-income countries, such as that of the CFA franc in 1994.

The view that the real exchange rate is unimportant for trade performance and external balance is derived from three pessimistic assessments of the responsiveness of trade in low-income developing countries (LIDCs) to shifts in the RER and relative prices. The first, "import demand pessimism," is based on the view that the import structure in LIDCs is such that most imports are inputs into production and that the elasticity of substitution in production between imports and domestic value added is essentially zero. "Export supply pessimism," in turn, holds that LIDC exports are concentrated in a few products with a very low domestic supply response so that changes in relative prices will not induce domestic producers to change marketed output by much. Finally, "export demand pessimism" maintains that world demand is inelastic, with respect to both income and prices, for the products in which LIDC exports are concentrated.

Conventionally, adjustment of overvalued real exchange rates is considered an essential element in improving the trade balance of an economy; and an expansion of trade is seen as an important element of a growth strategy. However, if true, the above three pessimisms would imply that there is little role for the RER in achieving internal and external macroeconomic balance and would suggest that much of the concern about the effects of RER misalignment on macroeconomic stability and growth is irrelevant or even misguided. This chapter undertakes a critical evaluation of these three pessimisms in low-income countries.

In addition, accurate estimates of import and export price elasticities are quite useful for applied policy analysis, and this chapter provides a summary of the best available estimates of these. Such estimates may be used, among other things, in calculating the value of the RER required to achieve a target trade or resource balance. They provide a "back of the envelope" way of estimating the equilibrium RER for small low-income countries in which limited data availability and frequent changes in policy make more sophisticated techniques problematic.[3] Trade elasticities may also be used with estimates of required RER adjustment made with other methodologies to calculate and cross-check the impact of a proposed RER realignment on exports and imports. However, for such methodologies to yield meaningful results, import and export price elasticities must be high enough that the trade balance is reasonably

---

2. See, for example, Rose (1990, 1991) and Rose and Yellen (1989).
3. See Chapter 7 for a discussion of this methodology.

responsive to changes in the RER; and one must be able to estimate the elasticities with reasonable precision.

A few preliminary comments are in order before proceeding. First, the analysis in this chapter relies solely on a partial-equilibrium relative price approach. That is, we assume that changes in the relative prices of imports and exports take place and examine only how the markets for imports and exports respond to such changes. This relative price approach is in contrast to, although not in conflict with, the absorption approach of treating the current account as an element of the fundamental macroeconomic identity and focusing on the changes in saving and investment necessary to accommodate reductions in the current account deficit. The focus in the relative price approach is on only the expenditure and resource switching component of adjusting an imbalance. The two perspectives, macroeconomic consistency and relative price, are mutually consistent, as both must hold in short- and long-run equilibrium.

Nor does this chapter address the question of *"nominal* exchange rate pessimism." It considers neither whether a nominal devaluation will be able to achieve a change in the RER nor what complementary policies are necessary to sustain a real depreciation. It simply assumes that a policy package that changes the RER is adopted and then examines the implications for imports and exports of such a change.[4]

The third caveat is that the chapter concentrates primarily on the components of the merchandise trade balance. The reason for the lack of attention to the nonmerchandise trade components of the current account is not that the exchange rate effect on these flows is believed to be negligible, but only that relatively less empirical work has been done on the determinants of nonfactor service flows.[5]

Fourth, the chapter does not explore the short-run adjustments surrounding an exchange rate change. Some short-run effects of devaluations can be empirically important, such as a speculative rise in imports and a withholding of exports preceding an anticipated devaluation. These effects are noted but not dealt with in depth here.

Finally, unless otherwise noted, the RER concept cited here is, depending upon the study, either the bilateral or multilateral expenditure-PPP version of the external RER. This is the best established of the various internal and external RER concepts and has been widely used in

---

4. See Chapter 13 for a discussion of nominal exchange rate pessimism and the role of devaluations in depreciating the RER.

5. Empirical evidence, in fact, suggests that earnings flows from tourism, for instance, are quite responsive to the RER. (See, for example, Wren-Lewis and Driver (1998) and Zanello and Desruelle 1997).

empirical work in developing countries, although the external RER for traded goods is now sometimes used in studies of industrial countries.

The chapter takes up each of the three pessimisms in turn and summarizes the best estimates of the corresponding import and export price elasticities. The next section, on the import response to a real depreciation, analyzes import demand pessimism and the response of imports to devaluations. The subsequent section examines export demand pessimism. The following section on the export supply response to RER movements then discusses export supply pessimism and elasticities. The final section summarizes and concludes. Since some of the original work for this chapter was done at the time of the devaluation of the CFA franc in 1994, the CFA countries are used as examples in a number of places.

The Import Response to a Real Depreciation

"Import demand pessimism" and the expected response of imports to a real depreciation are examined in three steps. First, we review the empirical literature. Much of this literature, in fact, does not find much evidence of a strong response of imports to exchange rate changes in developing countries, a finding that has been taken to support the pessimists' view. Second, we argue that this apparent lack of import response to devaluations is attributable to an "import compression" (or rationing) syndrome. Import restrictions have often been imposed or tightened in response to a balance-of-payments deficit in developing countries. Therefore, even though a devaluation, other things being held constant, would reduce imports, a devaluation accompanied by an easing of import restrictions may or may not lead to reduced imports. Finally we examine the likely magnitude and speed of import adjustment in countries that are not starting from a predevaluation import compression situation.

Evidence of the Apparent Failure of Imports to Respond to Changes in the Real Exchange Rate

Both episodic and econometric evidence suggest that exchange rate adjustment and changes in import flows have historically been weakly associated, *on average*, in developing countries. Kamin (1988a), for example, compared the evolution of a number of macroeconomic variables (imports, exports, trade balance, inflation) in countries that experienced discrete devaluations with a comparator group of nondevaluing countries. He found that, although the trade balance improved in the devaluing group, the group's imports actually grew more rapidly in the years following a devaluation than in the years preceding it—contrary to what one would expect if a devaluation increased the relative price of imports and imports were price sensitive. Similarly, Rose (1991) was among the earliest to consider the possibility that, because of the nonstationarity of the variables, previous statistical estimates of import elasticities may have been invalid. He analyzed data for 30 developing countries using unit-root techniques and was unable to find a strong, stable effect of the RER on the trade balance.

The statistical evidence in Pritchett (1991) tells the same story. In a sample of 60 non-oil-exporting developing countries for the period 1965–88, the trade balance did not have any consistent empirical relationship to the real exchange rate, whether comparing across countries or in individual countries over time. When the trade balance effect was decomposed into exports and imports separately, the expected negative relationship was found between exports and the RER,[6] but an appreciating RER was associated with *decreasing*, rather than increasing, imports. Pritchett's findings are consistent with the previous econometric evidence from the estimation of import functions. In the past, multicountry studies that estimated simple import quantum RER elasticities rarely got more than half of the coefficients with the "right" sign.

The Import Compression Syndrome

However, the lack of an empirical association *on average* between RER depreciation and reductions in imports does not necessarily imply that imports are not affected by the exchange rate as was conventionally assumed. Three strands of empirical evidence suggest that the common failure to find an impact of devaluation on import levels in developing countries is attributable to the fact that devaluations typically take place after an episode of import compression and are often accompanied by an easing of import restrictions. Hence, the impact of a devaluation alone is difficult to isolate statistically.

Often, as the exchange rate becomes overvalued and imports become relatively cheap, developing countries have resorted to rationing imports through quantitative restrictions on them, foreign exchange, or both. Therefore, even though "notional" import demand increases as imports become cheaper relative to domestic goods, actual import quantities do not increase, as these notional import demands are not realized.[7] Hence, an overvalued exchange rate may lead to apparently

---

6. Using the "depreciation is down" convention of measuring the RER in foreign-currency terms, an increase in the RER in foreign-currency terms is an appreciation and should reduce exports.

7. Neary and Roberts (1980) provide a framework for analyzing rationing in which demands may or may not be realized and the "notional" demand is the demand if the good were in fact available at that price. There is a price along their notional demand schedule such that the rationed quantity would be the quantity demanded at that "virtual" price.

"cheap" imports at border prices and the official exchange rate while import rationing (either through foreign exchange controls or quantitative restrictions) actually makes imports quite expensive domestically by generating rents for those controlling rationed imports. The variable that adjusts to "clear" the markets in this case is the implicit rationing premium on imports, which is usually unobservable by the econometrician. A devaluation may not increase (and even may decrease) the "true" price of importables (that is, including the implicit rationing premium) if accompanied by reductions in rationing that lower the implicit premium.

To put this point algebraically, the internal real exchange rate for imports in domestic currency terms ($IRERM_N$) may be expressed as in equation 11.1:

$$(11.1) \qquad IRERM_N = \frac{P_{Md}}{P_{Nd}} = \frac{E_{dc} \cdot P_{Mf}(1+t_m)}{P_{Nd}}$$

where t_m is the implicit average ad valorem trade tax on imports, taking into account both tariffs and the tariff equivalent of nontariff barriers (NTBs).[8] Import compression increases NTBs and their tariff equivalents and, like a nominal devaluation, depreciates the internal RER for importables. Similarly, a trade liberalization, which reduces import compression and t_m, appreciates the internal RER for imports and will offset, partially or entirely, an accompanying nominal devaluation.

Krueger (1978) provided early empirical evidence on the import compression syndrome. She found that trade regimes generally move through different phases of control over imports. Initial moves to reduce quantity rationing of imports and foreign exchange licensing were generally associated with large nominal devaluations that wiped out the rents associated with the divergence between border and domestic prices. However, since true internal relative prices did not change much in spite of the depreciation of the external RER, the volume of imports was not much affected by such devaluations cum liberalizations.

The second strand of evidence comes from Edwards' study (1989, Chapter 6) of devaluation episodes. This study documented the evolution of payments restrictions before and after devaluation episodes, showing clearly the typical accumulation of administrative import controls in the period leading up to a devaluation.[9]

---

8. See Chapter 4 on the three-good internal RER.

9. Edwards' episodic evaluation of nominal devaluations also showed no effect on the current account for the devaluing countries, even for those that maintained a depreciated RER.

The final strand of evidence on changes in import compression surrounding devaluations comes from studies of the parallel market premium and its response to devaluations. The parallel market premium is not a perfect indicator of import compression since asset markets and capital controls, as well as the rationing of foreign exchange for imports, may play an important role in determining its value. However, in many cases the marginal price of imports is a function of the price of foreign exchange available through the parallel market.[10] Episodic and econometric studies (Kamin 1988b, Edwards 1989) confirm that the parallel market premium tends to grow in the period prior to a devaluation and fall immediately after a devaluation.

Import Response without Import Compression

In the absence of import compression, the expected response of imports to a real depreciation depends on (a) the response of the domestic price of imports to a change in the exchange rate and (b) the aggregate long-run price elasticity.

Exchange Rates and Domestic Prices

Since the supply of imports represents the willingness of the rest of the world to sell goods to a given country, the import supply curve is likely to be infinitely elastic for small low-income countries. For this reason there are three, not four pessimisms. No one has argued that small countries can lower the price of their imports by reducing their own demand for them. Hence, the border price of imports in domestic-currency terms should rise one for one with a devaluation; and, unless trade restrictions are simultaneously relaxed, the internal price of imports should increase accordingly.[11] Such price responsiveness is indeed confirmed by the empirical evidence for nearly all developing countries. The evidence indicates that import prices respond one for one (generally within at most two quarters) to exchange rate changes (Goldstein and Khan, 1985). A more recent study of the impact of exchange rate movements on domestic prices in developing countries (Feinberg 1997) confirms that

---

10. In cases in which smuggling is pervasive, the level of domestic prices of importables (especially easily smuggled items with low weight to value ratios, such as consumer electronics) may be determined more by the parallel rate of exchange than the official rate as discussed in Chapter 12.

11. Simultaneous reductions in a country's tariffs or nontariff barriers would tend to offset a devaluation. If part of a devaluation is offset by accompanying changes, the response to it will be accordingly muted as indicated by equation 11.1 above.

exchange rate changes are passed through to the domestic prices of traded goods. The behavior of prices of imported goods in high-inflation countries, in which price increases are passed through almost instantaneously after a devaluation, is also consistent with these findings. Therefore, a discussion of the responsiveness of imports to real exchange rate changes becomes essentially a discussion of price elasticities, which must be augmented by distinctions between small and large, and transitory and permanent, changes in prices.[12]

However, for large industrial countries there is considerable evidence that the domestic price of imports rises less than proportionately after a devaluation and that the response of import prices to changes in the exchange rate is often quite delayed. There is in fact a substantial literature on the question of the applicability of the law of one price to large industrial countries, particularly the United States and Japan. Goldberg and Knetter (1997) recently reviewed this literature. They noted the considerable empirical evidence of widespread, prolonged, substantial divergences of the prices of imported manufactured products from the law of one price, incomplete partial pass-through of exchange rate changes to the prices of imported manufactures, and strategic pricing-to-market behavior by firms selling in large industrial countries. Goldberg and Knetter find that in the United States typically only half of a change in the nominal exchange rate is passed through to the domestic prices of imports of manufactures.

In light of the above findings about pricing behavior in large industrial countries, it is also possible that foreign firms selling in a few large developing countries with large import-competing sectors may engage in strategic pricing to market for selected important differentiated manufactured products. Feinberg (1997) warns that monopolistic behavior is a potentially important problem in developing countries, but there is little empirical evidence of pricing to market in these countries. Hence,

---

12. The empirical literature notes only one important exception to full pass-through of exchange rate movements to the prices of imports in developing countries. This concerns import-competing firms protected by quantitative restrictions. Such firms may not raise their prices proportionately after a devaluation as the existing quantitative restriction may have already permitted them to set their predevaluation prices at as high a level as the market would bear. The existence of such binding import quotas can also affect the attitude of import-substituting industries toward devaluations. These industries may view devaluations as raising the cost of their imported inputs without giving them any further protection—or scope to raise their output prices—than was already provided by the import quotas.

in most circumstances, the most realistic assumption would still appear to be that, despite widespread violations of the law of one price in large industrial countries, in small developing countries exchange rate adjustments are usually fully and quickly passed through to domestic prices unless trade restrictions are simultaneously relaxed.

Price Elasticity of Import Demand

What is the "typical" aggregate price elasticity of import demand in a small, developing, non-import-compressed economy? Three sources of evidence can be used to generate estimates: developing-country estimates of the price elasticity of import demand, industrial-country estimates of the import price elasticities, and industrial-country price elasticity estimates that are adjusted to take into account the different structure of imports in developing countries. Each source has its difficulties, but together they suggest that the long-run price elasticity to a permanent change in relative import prices is around −0.7 to −0.9.

Industrial Countries. Table 11.1 summarizes the price elasticity estimates from a number of studies that estimate import price elasticities

Table 11.1 *Price Elasticity of Import Demand: Average Estimates for* **Industrial** *Countries*

Study	Average Elasticity	Number of Countries (of Which Positive)
Houthakker and Magee (1969)	−.81	13 (3)
Adams and others (1969)	−.72	9 (3)
Armington (1970)	−1.35	14 (0)
Samuelson (1973)	−.92	14 (7)
Taplin (1973)	−.79	13 (0)
Beenstock Minford (1976)	−1.51	7 (2)
Stern, Francis, and Schumacher (1976)	−.99	17 (0)
Gylfason (1978)	−1.24	10 (3)
Geraci and Prewo (1980)	−.73	5 (0)
Marquez (1990)	−.74	6 (0)
Senhadji (1997)	−.64	19 (0)
Driver and Wren-Lewis (1997)	−.71	7 (0)
Mean (median) of the study averages	−.93 (−.80)	

Source: Updated from Pritchett (1988a).

for *industrial* countries.[13] The grand mean (median) of the averaged estimates is –93 (–80). The range of the averaged estimates is from –64 to –1.51. The two most recent of these studies (Senhadji (1997) and Wren-Lewis and Driver (1998)), which test and adjust for unit roots, yield estimates at the low end of this range. Bayoumi and Faruqee (1998), however, use an import elasticity of –0.92 as a representative value for the G-7 countries. The advantage of these industrial-country estimates is that they are, on average, much less likely to be contaminated by import compression episodes that would result in underestimation of the price response. But the more advanced economic structure of the industrial countries may create greater import substitution possibilities, in which case their elasticities may overestimate price responsiveness in a developing country.

Developing Countries. Table 11.2 below summarizes estimates of price elasticities for *developing* countries.[14] The mean of these averaged estimates is –79, with a range from –51 to –1.07. Some of the estimates for developing countries should be considered as underestimates of the (absolute value of the) price elasticity, since the presence of import compression as described in the preceding subsection historically tended to bias the estimates toward low values.[15] Moreover, Pritchett (1988b) shows that different estimation techniques can make a large difference in the price elasticity estimates. Price elasticity estimates using instrumental variables for developing countries are almost 50 percent higher on average than the traditional ordinary least-squares estimates and are similar to the estimates for the industrial countries.[16] Bayoumi and Faruqee (1998) suggest a representative value of –0.69 for the price elasticity of import

---

13. Most empirical estimates of trade elasticities are made using external expenditure-PPP real exchange rate measures, either REERs or bilateral RERs with the country's major industrial trading partner. A few recent estimates, such as those from Wren-Lewis and Driver (1998), use the external RER for traded goods. Senhadji (1997) uses the import price index divided by the GDP deflator as the internal RER for imports. Unless otherwise noted, all elasticity estimates presented in this chapter are with respect to the expenditure-PPP external RER.

14. See footnote 13.

15. Pritchett (1988a) actually uses a barrage of specification tests in an attempt to eliminate country estimates in which periods of import compression lead to an unstable import demand function. Prichett (1996) also finds that there is no reliable, robust measure of trade policy orientation that can be used in cross-country regression analyses. The issue is, in effect, too complex and opaque to be analyzed with a single standardized measure.

16. The instrumental variables' estimates differ from ordinary least-squares estimates because with endogenous import, rationing the "supply" of imports given by foreign exchange availability is not the usual horizontal supply of goods assumed for a small country.

Table 11.2 *Price Elasticity of Import Demand, Average Estimates for Developing Countries from Multicountry Studies*

Study	Average[a]	Number of Countries (Number Positive)
Senhadji (1997)	–.88	48 (0)
Reinhart (1995)	–.51	12 (1)
Pritchett (1988a)	–.77	28 (4)
Bahami-Oskooee (1986)	–.69	7 (0)
Moran (1986)	–.81	5 (1)
Khan (1974)	–1.07	5 (1)
Mean (median) of the averages	–.79 (–.79)	

a. This average excludes positive estimates.
Source: Studies cited in this table.

demand in developing countries.

The problem of low price elasticity might be considered particularly important for Africa, given its relatively low level of industrialization and capacity to produce import substitutes. However, in the existing studies African countries do not have particularly low estimated import demand elasticities compared to other developing countries. Table 11.3 gives estimates of the typical price elasticities for sub-Saharan African (SSA) countries; again, the price elasticity estimates are near to or greater than one.[17] The studies cited in table 11.3 do find substantial instability in the estimated parameters of simple import demand equations in SSA, as one would expect from import compression episodes.

In light of the above estimates, a best guess of the typical aggregate import demand elasticity for low-income developing countries would be somewhere between –0.7 and –0.9. The estimates for developing countries, once adjusted for the attenuating bias created by import controls, are in the low range of the estimates for the industrial countries.

The Structure of Imports in Developing Countries

The concern that import demand in developing countries may be price-inelastic stems in part from the belief their structure of imports is such that there is very little scope for substitution. Such inflexibility could be attributable to two causes.

---

17. See footnote 13.

Table 11.3 *Price Elasticity of Demand for Imports in African Countries*

Study	Median Estimate	Number of Countires (Number Positive)
Arize and Afifi (1986)	–.88	23 (3)
Pritchett (1988a)	–1.40	4 (0)
Ghurra and Grennes (1994)	–1.06	—
Reinhart (1995)	–1.36	—
Senhadji (1997)	–0.98	15 (0)

Note: Positive estimates are excluded from the medians. The estimates from Arize and Afifi are for the 1972–82 period. The estimates by Ghurra and Grennes and Reinhart were made using pooled data and are for an average African country.
Source: Studies cited in this table.

First, in imposing direct controls on imports, governments may have forced their countries' import structures into inflexibility by administratively eliminating all imports deemed nonessential. Such artificial price inelasticity is an aspect of the overall experience of import compression discussed above. Removal of import controls and accompanying reforms will over time eliminate this source of "inelasticity."

A second possible cause of inflexibility is that the natural import structure in many developing countries, even absent controls, could consist primarily of goods such as petroleum and intermediate inputs, which are intrinsically price insensitive and for which few domestic substitutes exist. Developing countries may also tend to have a low share of imports in the nonfood consumer goods category, which are usually the most price elastic. Hence, even if import price elasticities by sector were equal across industrial and developing countries, the aggregate price elasticity would be lower in developing countries because of their import structure.

How important a factor is the structure of imports in developing countries? This issue can be examined through a counterfactual statistical experiment of estimating what the aggregate import elasticity of a typical developing country would be if the country had its own import structure (proportions of fuels, food, manufactures) but had industrial-country sectoral import price elasticities. This experiment is useful because, since industrial countries generally have better data and fewer import controls, estimates of sectoral import price elasticities are more accurate for them.

In the experiment, synthetic estimates of aggregate import price elasticities were constructed using estimates of the price elasticities of the disaggregated components of imports from the *industrial* countries, weighted by the actual import structure of a sample of *developing* countries. The results of the exercise are reported in table 11.4. The table suggests that the magnitude of the difference in elasticities between developing and industrial countries that would be created by their differing import structure is small, only about 20 percent. Therefore, if we take –0.9, the overall average from the studies of industrial countries, as a plausible estimate of import price elasticity in industrial countries, then –0.7 would be the estimate for a developing country with roughly the same import structure as the average for the sample group in table 11.4 if the price elasticities were the same within sectors in industrial and developing countries.[18] Hence, the results of our counterfactual statistical experiment are consistent with the average price elasticities for developing countries reported above.

The calculations in table 11.4 would obviously be affected if the price elasticities within sectors differed between industrial and developing countries. Sectoral price elasticities may be higher in industrial countries because of the existence of a broader range of domestic substitutes for imports. Unfortunately, there is very little reliable empirical evidence on sectoral import elasticities in developing countries to resolve this question.[19] Furthermore, the most recent comprehensive analysis of import elasticities for 77 industrial and developing countries using econometric techniques that take into account unit roots (Senhadji 1997) actually finds, counterintuitively, that the average price elasticity is greater in developing countries (–0.88) than in industrial countries (–0.64).

---

18. Note that the synthetic aggregate elasticities in table 11.4 are somewhat higher than the averages reported in tables 11.1 and 11.2 for industrial and developing countries. However, the point of this exercise is to illustrate the *differences* between industrial and developing countries attributable to import structure. A general characteristic of price elasticity estimates is that, the broader the category, the lower the estimate, as there is less scope for substitution the fewer the categories. For example, the import demand and export supply elasticities will be lower for all cereals together than for a single cereal.

19. See De Rosa (1990) for a summary of the fragmentary estimates that are available. An additional concern, especially for low-income countries, is that a large fraction of imports are donor-financed capital goods. Since donor decisions are not primarily driven by the domestic costs of capital goods, a devaluation would probably not reduce such capital goods imports by much. However, since these imports are in effect self-financing, reducing them may also not be a practical policy concern.

Table 11.4 *The Effect of Import Structure on Aggregate Import Price Elasticities: A Simulation*

Country	Calculated Aggregate Elasticity	Share of Sector in Total Imports[c]				
		Food (−0.75)[a]	Fuels (−0.75)[a]	Capital Goods (−1.5)[a]	Inter-mediates (−0.5)[a]	Non-food Consumer (−2.5)[a]
CFA Countries						
Cameroon	−1.12	17.9	2.2	40.4	31.3	8.3
Congo	−1.04	19.1	3.1	35.9	35.7	6.2
Ivory Coast	−0.94	17.3	22.2	23.1	32.0	5.4
Senegal	−1.00	28.2	9.6	29.7	26.8	5.6
Togo	−0.98	26.1	5.5	23.1	36.7	8.7
Niger	−0.95	16.9	4.2	26.7	45.7	6.6
Other Developing Countries						
Argentina	−0.97	3.8	9.4	35.7	46.9	4.2
Bangladesh	−0.83	24.3	16.6	18.3	38.6	2.2
Burundi	−1.08	10.3	15.4	37.6	29.4	7.2
Pakistan	−0.94	16.0	14.3	33.0	34.9	1.9
Morocco	−0.88	12.7	13.2	25.0	45.9	3.2
Industrial Countries						
Belgium–Lux	−1.18	11.8	7.7	25.5	36.5	18.6
Denmark	−1.13	13.0	6.5	29.5	36.5	14.4
USA	−1.37	6.1	9.9	43.6	20.6	19.9
Means						
Developing Countries	−.098	17.5	10.5	29.9	36.7	5.4
Industrial Countries	−1.23	10.3	8.0	32.9	31.2	17.6

Note: a. Figures in parentheses are assumed sectoral elasticities. The assumed elasticities are taken from the review by Stern, Francis, and Schumacher (1976), which reports the "best" estimates of the elasticities for each product category for 14 different developed countries assembled from a complete review of the literature. The assumed elasticity for each category is taken from the middle of the range of the estimates across the countries. b. The calculated elasticity is simply the import-share weighted average of the elasticities in the row (for example, for Cameroon −1.12 = .179 · (−.75) + .022 · (−.75) + .404 · (−1.5) + .313 · (−.5) + .083 · (−2.5)). c. The import shares are calculated from the United Nations Statistical Office's COMTRADE database.
Source: See notes a-c.

Speed of the Import Response

The remaining question about the expected import response concerns the speed of the adjustment. Goldstein and Khan (1985) reviewed five studies of the speed of the adjustment of imports to relative price changes and found that 50 percent or more of adjustment tends to take place in the first year. They also found, however, that the estimates of the adjustment speed were quite imprecise.[20] More recently, Senhadji (1997) finds that the lags involved can be substantial. His estimate of the average price elasticity is close to zero in the short run and reaches 90 percent of its long-run value only after five years. Bayoumi and Faruqee (1998), however, suggest a shorter three-year lag for the G-7 countries, with 60 percent of the full effect occuring during the first year, 25 percent in the second, and 15 percent in the third.

Wilson and Tackacs (1979) and Bahmani-Oskooee (1986) found (for industrial countries and for seven developing countries, respectively) that adjustments in response to exchange rate changes were faster than adjustments in response to relative price changes arising from other sources. That adjustment is faster for exchange rate changes is consistent with the plausible conjecture that large and well-publicized price changes (as would result from once-off nominal devaluations) will be immediately perceived and change expectations of future price ratios, whereas individual changes in international prices of particular traded goods are less noticeable and their implications for future relative profitability may be less clear. The more rapid recognition of relative price shifts and greater perception of the permanence of the shifts could lead to a faster (and potentially larger) short-run response to exchange rates than to changes in import prices generally.[21]

Overall Import Response

Overall, the foregoing analysis of the literature suggests that, in the absence of import compression, the long-run aggregate import price elasticity is most likely about –0.9, although it maybe as low as –0.7, for

---

20. One factor affecting the speed of the response in different countries is that imports tend to recover quickly after a period of import compression. Typically, imports of countries that have had large drops in imports under administrative controls spring back rapidly when those controls are lifted.

21. The existence of binding import quotas can also affect the attitude of import-substituting industries toward devaluations. These industries may view devaluations as raising the cost of their imported inputs without giving them any further protection, or scope to raise their output prices, than was already provided by the import quota.

small developing economies, and that full adjustment to devaluation-induced changes in relative prices should occur over the medium term (two to four years). If econometric estimates for individual countries differ significantly from these price elasticity figures, then those estimates themselves need to be examined carefully. Using the short time series and noisy data generally available for the typical developing country, it is difficult to estimate an elasticity with any precision or robustness and easy to get misleading results.[22]

If a country's merchandise balance is in large deficit, import adjustment may actually be quantitatively more important than export adjustment. Arithmetically, an equal percentage change in imports will have a greater absolute influence on reducing the deficit than an equivalent change in exports for the simple reason that in a country with a trade deficit imports are larger than exports.

Export Demand Pessimism

Export demand pessimism is based on the beliefs that (a) developing countries' traditional exports are concentrated in products with low world price and income elasticities of demand facing declining long-run terms of trade and that (b) the expansion of their nontraditional exports is constrained by trade barriers in industrial countries. Typically, exports with low elasticities of demand are agricultural commodities such as wheat, cotton, tea, cocoa, and coffee. Low world income elasticities imply that a country's exports of such commodities will grow at best slowly in the absence of increases in its market share. Low world price elasticities imply that large reductions in world prices of these commodities would be necessary to increase aggregate world export quantities. Hence, if all developing countries were to expand their exports of such commodities because of the high price elasticity of demand facing each country separately, the group's total export earnings would decline because of the resulting price reductions. This conundrum is known in the literature as the "adding up problem."[23] Export demand pessimism, which the adding up problem has fed, has been reinforced by industrial countries erecting nontariff barriers to nontraditional developing-

---

22. Wren-Lewis and Driver (1998), for example, found that the empirical results for a number of G-7 countries were unsatisfactory or unusable; and parameter estimates for these countries had to be based on results from other similar countries.

23. For reviews of the adding up problem for Africa, see Akiyama and Larson (1994) (for primary commodities), Chhibber (1991), and World Bank (1993) (for cocoa, coffee, and tea).

country exports in a few conspicuous cases (for example, textiles and footwear) in which such exports have expanded rapidly.

The poor export performance of most sub-Saharan African countries has, for example, often been blamed on the countries' dependence on a few key commodity exports facing inelastic aggregate world demand. Relative prices of many of these commodities have been drifting downward over the long term (in spite of their recent surge).[24] Export earnings of many SSA countries have declined along with prices, and this decline has engendered considerable pessimism about prospects for export-led growth.

Declining real prices for some primary commodities and inelastic world demand raise two issues: whether individual countries acting alone can increase their export revenues and whether countries producing similar goods can gain by coordinating their policies. The key point, however, is that even if the *world* price elasticity is low, the price elasticity of export demand for standardized commodities for individual countries with *small* market shares may still be quite high. Hence these countries can expand their market shares rapidly if they can produce at low cost.[25] A simple rule of thumb is that the demand elasticity for one country is the world price elasticity of demand multiplied by the inverse of the country's market share.[26] Even with a low world price elasticity of demand of 0.4, for example, a single country's price elasticity is still 8 when its market share is 5 percent, implying that a 20 percent rise in its exports would cause only a 2.5 percent decline in the world price.

Still, individual efforts by a number of countries to expand their exports in response to such price incentives could potentially lead to a significant decline in the world price. However, in most cases a number of countries produce a given commodity; and the market shares of individual countries are too small to confer any significant market power on small groups of them. Coordinating policies is feasible only in the few cases in which production is concentrated in a few countries and short-run supply elasticity is low (as in the case of tree crops, which take

---

24. Volatility of real commodity prices, as distinct from unfavorable long-term trends in them, has also been considered an obstacle to export-led growth. See Dupont and Juan-Ramon (1996).

25. See the example (page 492) of the growth of textile, clothing, and footwear exports from Korea and Taiwan.

26. This simple rule of thumb assumes that the entire increase in world demand via the world price elasticity would accrue to the country expanding its exports. The rule does not take into account, among other factors, the supply response of other producers to lower world prices or strategic behavior on the part of rivals and assumes that goods are perfect substitutes across countries.

several years to mature) so that it would take time for potential competitors to enter the market. Larson, Akiyama, and Lau (1996) found
that large market shares and low price elasticity of demand make policy
coordination a realistic possibility for only a few commodities produced
by a few low-income countries. Those are cocoa in Cote d'Ivoire and
Ghana, tea in Kenya, and burley tobacco in Mali.[27] For virtually all other
exports from low-income countries, market shares of individual countries are small enough that each country can gain substantially from
independently increasing its exports.

However, even if individual developing countries are small in international trade and the notional price elasticity of export demand facing
them is very large,[28] trade barriers to exports to industrial countries may
provide an additional rationale for export demand pessimism. Industrial-
country trade barriers are indeed a significant obstacle to exports of a
few selected primary (for example, sugar and bananas) and nonprimary
(for example, textiles and footwear) products from developing countries. For countries relying heavily on these products, such barriers can
be a significant constraint to expansion of these particular exports, and
the price elasticity of demand for such exports may be low. It is important, however, not to overstate the magnitude of this constraint. Despite
existing constraints, a number of developing countries have expanded
nontraditional exports rapidly as discussed in the next section. Similarly, it has been well documented that Africa's poor historical trade
performance was not caused by export barriers, particularly not by barriers to nontraditional exports (Amjadi, Reinke, and Yeats 1996). The
trade barriers facing other small low-income countries in today's

---

27. See also Akiyama and Larson (1994). Devarajan and others (1996) discuss
the optimal export tax that should be imposed by those countries facing inelastic
export demand.

28. Most economists have assumed that, in the absence of trade barriers, the
export demand elasticity facing small industrial and developing countries is effectively infinite. Until recently, there was little statistical evidence to support
this assumption. However, Panagariya, Shah, and Mishra (1996) in a study using highly disaggregated data for Bangladeshi textile exports to the United States
found consistently high demand elasticities, exceeding 65 in all cases. Exports
from major industrial countries, on the other hand, are large enough to affect
prices in other countries; and export demand functions are usually estimated for
these countries. Thus, for example for the G-7 countries, Wren-Lewis and Driver
(1998) find price elasticities of export demand ranging from –0.23 (Canada) to
–.36 (Japan) with a median of –0.96 and income elasticities ranging from 0.58
(Germany) to 1.12 (the United States) for exports with a median of 0.91. Similarly, Bayoumi and Faruqee (1998) use a price elasticity of export demand for the
G-7 countries of –0.71.

globalizing economy are no worse than the barriers that these two groups of countries faced.

The Export Supply Response to RER Movements

Before discussing the magnitude of the potential response of aggregate exports to changes in the RER, the path by which the relative price movements are expected to work should first be considered. For an RER adjustment to affect exports, it must first alter the relative profitability of factors (for example, land, labor, capital) in producing exportables versus other domestic goods. There are some instances in which a devaluation may not improve the relative profitability of exports. First, a devaluation increases the border price of export crops in domestic-currency terms (that is, the border price in foreign currency multiplied by the nominal exchange rate).[29] However, if the increase in border prices is not passed through the marketing system to producers, then no supply response should be expected. In some African countries, devaluations have been completely absorbed by increased margins of the marketing agencies, and the real prices received by farmers have not changed. Second, if changes in the relative prices of other inputs occur simultaneously (for example, if fertilizer subsidies are cut or interest rates raised) then the net improvement in relative prices may be less than the increase in export prices.

The non-pass-through of devaluations to the domestic producer prices of export products—or "export repression"—can cause empirical problems in estimating export supply elasticities that are similar to those caused by the relaxation of import compression at the time of a devaluation. That is, the exchange rate changes, but the domestic price changes (much) less, so that in some cases it maybe difficult to detect the empirical effects of a devaluation on exports.[30] Export repression is an important consideration in analyzing the effects of devaluations but is not treated in depth here. We ask only, "assuming a real depreciation or appreciation changes the relative profitability of exports, by how much would export quantities change?"

The Mundell-Fleming and other industrial-country models typically assume that the elasticity of export supply is effectively infinite. In developing countries, however, inelasticity of aggregate export supply is

---

29. Because of the importance of homogeneous primary commodities and fairly standardized nontraditional products in developing-country exports, there is less reason to question whether the law of one price holds for their exports than for their imports.

30. See the discussion below of Bond's results for sub-Saharan Africa.

an important concern, the evidence on which is reviewed below. The price responsiveness of individual primary commodities and the potentially rapid expansion of nontraditional exports are then considered.

Aggregate Export Elasticities

The elasticity of aggregate exports to changes in relative prices has been the subject of several studies using econometric techniques as well as episodic analysis. Both types of study are reviewed in this subsection.

Episodic Analysis

Kamin (1988a) found evidence of large export responses to nominal devaluations. Table 11.5 shows that between the year prior to a devaluation and the year following a devaluation, the median growth of exports in U.S. dollars for devaluing countries accelerated by 11.5 percentage points per annum (an increase in the export growth rate of 100 percent). Devaluing countries went from export growth 4.4 percentage points below the average of nondevaluing countries in the year preceding a devaluation, to export growth 7 percentage points above in the year following the devaluation. This export response is large when one considers that the median real depreciation in Kamin's sample was only 15 percent. This large effect on the growth rate of exports continued for several years after the devaluation (even though in Kamin's sample the effect of the nominal devaluation on the real exchange rate was typically eroded after three years).

Kiguel and Ghei (1993) obtained similar results for a sample of devaluations in low-inflation countries. They found that the share of exports in GDP fell prior to a major devaluation and then rose. The ratio of exports to GDP was significantly higher statistically three years after the devaluation (mean value of 17.4 percent), compared with the year before the devaluation (a mean of 15.4 percent).

With the episodic analysis of exports the mystery is not why the export supply response to a devaluation is so small but rather why it is so large and swift. At least part of the large effect on export may come from (a) complete or partial elimination of smuggling and underinvoicing of exports and switching of some exports from parallel to official markets; (b) speculative stockpiling of exports in anticipation of a devaluation; or (c) delays in remitting export receipts, again in anticipation of devaluation. The degree of smuggling and underinvoicing of exports (that is, the amount by which a country's reported exports are understated relative to the world's reported imports from the same country) is also likely to be related to the black market premium, which generally increases before a devaluation and drops back after one.

Table 11.5 The Response of Export Growth in Nominal Devaluation Episodes

Year relative to devaluation	Devaluing countries' growth rate of exports, percent per annum	Total sample, growth rate of exports, percent per annum	Difference between devaluers and nondevaluers
T-3	8.5	7.3	1.2
T-2	8.2	8.6	-0.4
T-1	3.8	8.2	-4.4
T (Year of devaluation)	12.8	9.4	3.5
T+1	16.7	9.6	7.1
T+2	13.2	9.2	4.0
T+3	8.2	6.5	2.0
Difference predevaluation (T1) to postdevaluation (T2)	12.9	1.4	11.5

Source: Adapted from Kamin (1988a), table 3.

Econometric Analyses

Econometric studies typically find large effects of devaluations on export volumes, consistent with large elasticities of export supply with respect to the real exchange rate if, as with imports, exchange rate changes are passed through the domestic prices of exportables. Many of these studies have focussed on African countries, where the question of supply response has been the most contentious. Table 11.6 summarizes estimates of price elasticities of aggregate export supply for various countries.[31] Most of these estimates fall in the range between 0.8 and 2.0. The only estimates that were significantly lower than this range were two of those for sub-Saharan African countries for the 1960–85 period (Bond 1985 and Ghurra and Grennes 1994). During this period, export repression—excessive taxation of exports and policies of not permitting the effects of devaluations to pass through to the domestic producer prices of major export products—was widespread. Overall, the studies summarized in table 11.6 suggest that if the effects of RER movements are passed through fully to domestic prices, the elasticity of aggregate export supply is at least 1.0 in non-oil-exporting developing countries and may be as high as 2.0 in some cases.

Studies of Supply Elasticities for Individual Commodities

Since some primary commodity exporting countries are highly specialized in a few products, another way of approaching the export response problem is to consider the likely supply elasticities of their major commodity exports. For example, as noted earlier, the CFA countries, like many other low-income countries, tend to have exports that are quite concentrated: for each country just four products account for 70–90 percent of total trade.[32] Since a few products are so important, a separate analysis of the producer and export supply elasticity of the major products may be useful.

Earlier work has suggested that the price elasticity of supply for the agricultural sector as a whole may be quite low because substitution possibilities between broad sectors are more limited than those between individual crops or industries and significant time lags are involved in increasing aggregate resource availability.[33] However, price elasticities

---

31. See footnote 13.

32. This ratio is much lower in some other developing countries, for example: India, 31 percent; Korea, 20 percent; Argentina, 35 percent; Brazil, 26 percent; Philippines, 31 percent. But the CFA ratio is typical for sub-Saharan Africa, for example: Nigeria, 98 percent; Zambia, 91 percent; Kenya, 67 percent; and Tanzania, 65 percent.

33. See for example Killick (1993). Petroleum may be a special case of particularly inelastic supply if most production costs are in foreign exchange so that a devaluation does not significantly affect profitability.

Table 11.6 Econometric Studies of Aggregate Export Supply Response

Study	Countries, Exports, and Period Covered	Estimated Price Elasticity of Aggregate Export Supply
Ghurra and Grennes (1994)	Aggregate export supply, pooled data for 33 SSA countries, 1970-87	0.65
Balassa (1990)	Pooled SSA countries, total merchandise exports, 1965–82	1.01
Balassa and others (1989)	Korea and Greece	2.4 and 2.1
Bond (1987)	Average for all non-oil-exporting developing countries using pooled data, total merchandise exports 1963–81	2.01
Khan and Knight (1986)	Pooled developing countries, total exports, 1971–80	0.845
Bond (1985)	Average African country using pooled data for 1963–81; separate estimates for major product groups with one year lag	Range from 0.09 to 0.32
Goldstein and Kahn (1978)	Seven developed countries, total exports	Range from 1.1 to 6.6, median 1.9

Source: Studies cited in this table.

of supply for individual agricultural commodities, which allow for switching resources from nontraded to traded crops, are typically higher. Considerable analytical work has been done by the World Bank on major individual commodities, and representative supply elasticities are available for a number of them on request from the staff that prepare commodity price projections.[34]

An Example: Cocoa and Coffee Exports from the CFA Countries

Coffee and cocoa are tree crops, and the time from planting to first production is several years. In the short run, the production response is entirely at the intensive margin, and supply elasticities can be expected to be low. Akiyama and Varangis (1988) and Imran and Duncan (1988) estimate short- and long-run supply elasticities for coffee and cocoa. However, their estimates did not take into account the effect that low world prices and a highly overvalued exchange rate together can have, making it unprofitable even to harvest much of the crop. An analysis of the potential export response to a devaluation in the CFA countries (World Bank 1991) reviewed the literature on crop supply elasticities and estimated the short-run (first-year) elasticity for cocoa at about 0.2 and the long-run elasticity at about 1.0. For coffee, the elasticity estimates were 0.5 in the short run and 0.8 in the long run, with the short-run estimate being fairly high because of the neglect of routine crop care and the abandonment of harvesting in some areas during the period of low prices.

The Role of Nontraditional Exports

A persistently overvalued RER raises foreign currency–denominated unit labor costs relative to other countries and makes it difficult for a country to establish export potential in anything other than resource-intensive products. One important element in a decision to adjust the RER is to create conditions for export diversification and the rapid expansion of nontraditional exports.[35] Nontraditional exports are not just manufactures. Many countries have expanded into higher value–added natural resource and agricultural or horticultural products. Higher value–added products in this case mean more labor intensity and more labor embodied in the exports. Without RER adjustment such export activities are not attractive compared with nontradables production for the local market.

---

34. See also Bond (1985) for a summary of supply elasticity estimates available for individual commodities as of 1985.

35. Note also that the RER for nontraditional exports, which tends to follow the RER for imports, can be significantly less favorable than the overall RER for exports when the terms of trade for primary commodities improve. See Chapter 4 on the three-good internal RER.

The experiences of many countries indicate that under the right conditions the expansion of nontraditional exports can be both extremely rapid in percentage terms *and* sustained for very long periods. Table 11.7 shows the expansion of manufactured exports for seven countries during prolonged periods of rapid export growth. In many cases (for example, Brazil in 1967, Mexico in 1982, Turkey in 1980), the rapid increases in exports were preceded by trade reforms that accompanied a large adjustment of the RER. In the early stages of export take-off, it is not unusual for exports to grow at rates exceeding 40 percent per year. World trade has seen numerous instances of exports rising from a few hundred million dollars to more than a billion dollars within five years. Even as nontraditional exports mature, sustained growth rates well over 30 percent per year are possible. Because of the relatively small changes in the importing-country markets such expansions of small new exports entail, these gains are unlikely to be stymied in the near term by protectionist barriers raised in response, except in special cases such as textiles, in which NTBs are already well established.

Table 11.7 *Episodes of Sustained Rapid Expansion of Manufacturing Exports*

Country	1970	1975	1980	Mid-1980s[a]
Thailand ($ mn)	32	317	1,604	n.a.
(% per year)		58	38	
Brazil ($ mn)	361	2,193	7,489	n.a.
(% per year)		43	28	
Malaysia ($ mn)	109	665	2,433	n.a.
(% per year)		44	30	
Mexico ($ mn)	n.a.	n.a.	1,837	10,384
(% per year)				41
Turkey ($ mn)	n.a.	n.a.	782	4,854
(% per year)				44
Mauritius ($ mn)	n.a.	n.a.	115	623
(% per year)				23
Indonesia ($ mn)	n.a.	n.a.	503	5,228
(% per year)				34

a. The final year is 1987 for Mexico, 1985 for Turkey, 1988 for Indonesia and Mauritius.
Source: Computed from UNCTAD. 1990. *Handbook of International Trade and Development Statistics,* table 4.1.

Even if the income elasticity for a given product is low, a country's exports of this product will grow if the country is cost-competitive and expands its share in the world export market. In fact, in the analysis of export performance, the initial composition of exports tends to be an unimportant long-term factor. Studies using "constant market share" analysis decompose the growth of a country's exports into that component that would have occurred because of the general increase in the size of the market and that which is attributable to changes in market share. Changes in the types of the products exported and in market shares explain most of the differences in long-term export performance across countries, with little explained by the growth of the overall markets for the exports (income elasticities) of the particular products initially exported.

For instance, the annual growth rate of world exports of textiles, clothes, and footwear (TCF) in 1962–82 was 11.7 percent. However, total world exports of all products grew more rapidly at 14.2 percent, so that TCF actually fell as a percent of world trade from 10.1 percent to 6.5 percent. Even though TCF were not growing as rapidly as exports overall, Korean and Taiwanese (China) exports of these products increased at 40 percent and 28 percent per year, as Korea's exports grew from $8 million to $7.2 billion, a thousandfold increase. Taiwan (China) and Korea were able to achieve these rates of growth by increasing their shares of the world market from 0.07 percent to 6.8 percent (Korea) and .4 percent to 5.9 percent (Taiwan, China). These and other "success cases" were not particularly well situated in the early 1960s in products whose overall markets had rapid subsequent growth, and they did not move into markets that were rapidly growing. Rather they maintained their cost-competitiveness and increased their market shares of the nontraditional exports rapidly in order to achieve high overall export growth rates.

Successful diversification into nontraditional exports and rapid export growth need not come only in manufactures. Chile's movement away from dependence on copper exports has seen sustained export success, with exports more than doubling from 1985 to 1990, while the share of exports in "manufactures"[36] has remained roughly constant. This diversification has been accomplished by moving into higher value–added agricultural and horticultural products such as off-season temperate fruits (for example grapes, apples), processed vegetable products,

---

36. "Manufactures" is in quotes because the usual definition of manufactures according to the trade classification, SITC categories 5 through 8 less 68, excludes a number of goods with substantial processing value added that are included in the definition of manufactures used by the United Nations Industrial Development Organization (UNIDO) (for example, alcoholic beverages [beer and wine], chocolate preparations, and shaped wood).

and wines (Jafee, 1992). Chile's exports of food items doubled from $897 million to $1,988 million from 1985 to 1990. Brazil's exports of frozen concentrated orange juice grew from $82 million in 1975 to $338 million in 1985 to over $1 billion in 1988, becoming Brazil's fifth largest export product (Braga and Silber, 1991). Exports of cut flowers from Colombia grew from a very small base in the 1970s to $111 million in 1982 to $228 million in 1990. In sub-Saharan Africa, Kenya has been successful in establishing diversified agricultural exports. Kenyan horticultural exports were $133 million in 1990. The Kenyan cut-flower industry is internationally competitive as exports grew from almost nothing in the 1970s to more than $40 million in 1990. Kenya has also managed to move into the supply of fresh fruit and vegetables to the European market.

Many cases of nontraditional export growth of countries with competitive real exchange rates have come at the expense of countries that allowed their currencies to become overvalued. Madagascar dominated the market for vanilla beans in the 1960s and 1970s with 80 percent of the market by volume but has seen its share of the market shrink to 35 percent as Indonesia developed the crop and expanded its share from almost nothing to 35 percent of the market. Ghana and Nigeria together accounted for 50 percent of the volume of cocoa bean exports in the early 1950s but less than 20 percent of the market in 1990. In the 1960s and 1970s Côte d'Ivoire moved into cocoa production and increased its share from less than 10 percent to 30 percent of the market by the early 1980s. In the 1980s, however, Malaysia and Indonesia entered the cocoa market. Their shares of the market have risen rapidly, from 3 percent and 1 percent in the early 1980s to almost 10 percent and 6 percent, respectively, of the market today.

Overall Export Response

In sum, three strands of empirical literature show very strong export responses to devaluations in developing countries generally. Appreciating countries tend to suffer a large deterioration in export performance, losing market share. Exports typically have increased substantially following large devaluation episodes, and export supply elasticities are generally one or greater.[37] The export response has also been quite rapid,

---

37. Short-term supply elasticities for some primary commodities are, however, low. Hence, for countries specializing in a few such products, near-term elasticities might be lower than the average estimates for low-income countries. In these cases, it is worth considering the supply elasticity estimates for the particular products involved and checking the resulting estimates of the aggregate export supply elasticity against aggregate estimates for commodity-exporting countries.

much of it occurring within a year or two. Finally, although nontraditional exports are unlikely to contribute substantially to overall export growth in the near term, experience suggests that a competitively valued exchange rate maintained over an extended period is a necessary, if not a sufficient, condition for diversifying exports successfully and sustaining their rapid growth.[38] In fact, in countries where secular deterioration in the terms of trade and export diversification are long-term issues, the growth of nontraditional exports is an important indicator of the appropriateness of the RER and trade policy.

However, there is no guarantee that a change in relative prices alone will be sufficient to stimulate rapid growth of nontraditional exports. Nonprice factors are undoubtedly important in creating the climate for a rapid export expansion in response to a depreciation of the real exchange rate. The elasticity estimates cited above do not control for differences in the structural reforms that may accompany a devaluation. One of the reasons for the wide range of estimates of elasticities for both aggregate exports and individual commodity is probably differences in accompanying measures that could enhance the export supply response, such as provision of adequate transport, marketing, and credit facilities.[39]

Summary and Conclusion

To return in concluding to the question posed at the start of this chapter, how, empirically, does the real exchange rate affect trade flows and the resource balance in developing countries?

In some circles "real exchange rate elasticity pessimism" has been a predominant view for developing countries. This view, that the real exchange rate is unimportant for trade performance and external balance, is founded on three empirical pessimisms about developing countries' trade:

- *Import demand pessimism:* that LIDCs' import structure is such that most, if not all, inputs are required for producing output so that the elasticity of substitution between imports and domestic value added is essentially zero (the Leontief case);

---

38. See, for example, World Bank (1993).

39. Excessive volatility in the RER, which creates uncertainty and increases risks for exporters, has also been shown to negatively affect exports (Caballero and Corbo 1989). Dell'Ariccia (1998) also finds, using panel data for the European Union, that an increase in exchange rate volatility depresses international trade, although the effect is not large. Empirically, volatility in the RER has sometimes served, in effect, as a proxy for RER misalignment because of the difficulty in measuring the latter (Collins and Razin 1997).

- *Export demand pessimism:* that world demand for the products in which LIDC exports are concentrated is inelastic, both with respect to incomes and prices; and
- *Export supply pessimism:* that LIDC exports are concentrated in a few products with very low supply responses and that changes in relative prices will not induce domestic producers to change output by much.

However, a substantial amount of empirical work has been done on exchange rates, trade elasticities, and trade flows in low-income countries. The international evidence suggests the trade response to an RER adjustment should be substantial in low-income developing countries; and reasonably reliable estimates of trade elasticities are available as summarized below.

Price elasticity of import demand. The response of producers of import substitutes is typically strong as the rise in the price of imports increases the supply of import substitutes. Unless trade is liberalized at the time of a devaluation, low-income countries should expect an elasticity of imports with respect to the RER of roughly –0.7 to –0.9, with the full adjustment occurring over two to four years. For countries with large trade deficits, the near-term response of imports may be quantitatively more important than the export response.

Price elasticity of export demand. Because of the small size of most low-income economies and their small shares of the markets for their exports, general export demand pessimism is not warranted. Gains in market shares offer possibilities for substantial export expansion even in slowly growing markets for low-income elasticity products.

Price elasticity of aggregate export supply. If the effects of exchange rate changes are passed through to domestic producer prices, aggregate exports typically respond fairly strongly and swiftly (within a year or two) to real exchange movements. The price elasticity of supply of aggregate exports from non-oil-exporting countries is at least 1.0 and may be as high as 2.0 in some cases.

Commodity exports. The supply response of some primary commodity exports may tend to be rather small in the near term and so may be a significant concern in countries specializing heavily in a few of these products. But the supply response can be much larger in the long term.

Nontraditional exports. Analysis of growth in nontraditional exports suggests that supply pessimism is not generally valid for these and that the potential response of these exports to economic incentives is enormous. An appropriately valued exchange rate has been a necessary condition for creating the types of dramatic export expansions witnessed in some developing countries. Furthermore, in countries in which

deteriorating terms of trade for traditional exports and export diversification are long-term issues, the growth of nontraditional exports is an
important indicator of the appropriateness of the RER and trade policy.

The above estimates of the aggregate price elasticity of demand for
imports (–0.7 to –0.9) and of the supply of exports (1.0 to 2.0) in developing countries, together with the quite high world price elasticity of demand for exports from *individual* countries except in a few isolated cases,
suggest that RER movements have quite significant effects on trade balances. Because of the speed of both the import and export responses,
any J-curve effects (that is, the tendency of the trade balance in domestic-currency terms to worsen after a depreciation before it improves)
should be limited to the first year after a depreciation.[40] Only in unusual
cases, such as a tiny economy entirely dependent on oil exports, are the
effects of RER depreciation on the trade balance likely to be limited.

---

40. The J-curve effect is a phenomenon that may occur after a devaluation in
the balance of payments measured in domestic-currency terms and may be an
important consideration for short-term macroeconomic management. For small
countries that are price takers in international trade, a devaluation raises both
import and export prices in domestic currency proportionately. If import and
export volumes are fixed in the short term (or slow to respond) and imports
initially exceed exports (a deficit in the trade balance), the initial arithmetic effect of a devaluation will be to widen the trade deficit measured in domestic-
currency terms. A J-curve effect can also occur between industrial countries that
invoice their exports in their own currencies so that initially their export revenues are unaffected by a devaluation whereas the domestic currency cost of
their imports rises, causing a deterioration in their balance of payments.

For small countries, however, a devaluation has no effect on import and export prices in foreign-currency terms. Unless import and export volumes respond
perversely to a devaluation because of a simultaneous relaxation of import compression or an increase in export repression policies, the trade deficit will at worst
remain constant in *foreign*-currency terms. Hence, the J-curve phenomenon is
not usually observed in the balance-of-payments data in foreign-currency terms,
which are commonly reported for many developing countries.

12

The Use of the Parallel Market Rate as a Guide to Setting the Official Exchange Rate

Nita Ghei and Steven B. Kamin [*]

Determining the appropriate level at which to set the exchange rate is a challenging problem for any country pursuing a managed or fixed exchange rate policy. Ideally, a country would set its exchange rate at the long-run equilibrium real rate, that is, the rate consistent with internal and external balance (the latter referring to balance between the current account and sustainable capital account flows). Even in relatively stable and mature industrial economies, however, the long-run equilibrium level of the real exchange rate is usually difficult to identify. In developing countries subject to macroeconomic instability or structural change, this identification is even more difficult. The determination of the equilibrium real exchange rate is especially uncertain if the economy is in the midst of trade liberalization and other reforms that promise to change previously existing relations between trade performance and the exchange rate.

The issue of how to estimate long-run equilibrium real exchange rates has been addressed from a variety of different empirical perspectives by other chapters in this volume. This chapter rounds out that coverage by extending the analysis to a particular context not specifically considered elsewhere in this book: that of countries that maintain multiple exchange rate arrangements. Such arrangements, formal and informal,

* We are grateful to Larry Hinkle, Peter Montiel, Steve O'Connell, and three anonymous readers for helpful comments and suggestions.

legal and illegal, were the norm for developing countries until very recently. Even though an increasing number of countries have unified their exchange rates, often as part of a larger liberalization effort, parallel foreign exchange markets have not disappeared as yet. Nigeria, which has never successfully unified its exchange rate, is a prominent example in Africa. In Venezuela, which unified its exchange rate in 1989, a parallel market emerged in 1994 following the reimposition of capital controls. Because parallel exchange rates continue to exist in important countries and because specific analytical issues in estimating the long-run equilibrium real exchange rate (LRER) that do not arise in the context of unified rates present themselves in this case, the implications of parallel rates merit separate attention.

The key question to be addressed in this context is the extent to which the free exchange rate in a parallel exchange market can provide guidance in identifying the long-run equilibrium real exchange rate. In cases in which a parallel market for foreign exchange exists, it may appear natural to consider the parallel exchange rate as a proxy for the "underlying" equilibrium real exchange rate—that is, the rate that would tend to prevail over the long run in a unified exchange market. This interpretation suggests itself because the parallel exchange rate usually has the benefit of being determined in a free market and hence may not appear to be obviously contaminated by the distortionary effects of government policy.

Notwithstanding the appeal of a parallel market determined exchange rate as a guide to setting the official exchange rate, however, we will argue that various factors complicate the relationship between the parallel market rate and the long-run equilibrium real exchange rate. First, while the parallel market for foreign exchange may not itself be controlled by the government, conditions in that market are likely to be affected by government policy. Relative supplies and demands for foreign currency in the parallel market will be altered by the level of the official exchange rate, the extent to which exchange and trade controls are enforced, and the government's formula for rationing foreign exchange receipts to importers. Second, because the parallel exchange market represents an asset market as well as a trade-related market, the parallel market rate is likely to reflect expectations, political concerns, capital flight, and other speculative factors not directly associated with the equilibrium real exchange rate. Hence, only under a relatively narrow set of circumstances may the parallel market rate serve as a useful guide to determining the equilibrium value of the official exchange rate.

The structure of this chapter is as follows. The following section on the essential characteristics of parallel exchange markets provides the requisite background information on multiple exchange rate arrangements. It also defines parallel exchange markets more precisely and describes their key characteristics.[1] In the subsequent section we review a simple theoretical model of parallel exchange markets to shed light on how parallel exchange rates are determined in relation to both official exchange rates and equilibrium exchange rates. Then comes a section that brings some empirical evidence to bear on the analysis, comparing the evolution of parallel and official real exchange rates over time to provide a feel for the applicability of the theoretical results derived in the previous section. The final section summarizes the chapter's analytical and empirical findings concerning the relation between the parallel exchange rate and the long-run equilibrium real exchange rate.

Essential Characteristics of Parallel Exchange Markets

This background section sets out the essential characteristics of parallel exchange markets. It begins by defining more precisely what we mean by a parallel exchange market and describing its key features. The section then considers alternative ways in which governments have managed parallel markets, distinguishing broadly between the Latin American and African models. The section concludes with a review of trends in parallel markets in the 1990s.

Basic Concepts

A parallel foreign exchange market system is one in which transactions take place at more than one exchange rate and at least one of the prevailing rates is a freely floating, market-determined rate (the parallel exchange rate).[2] Parallel market systems represent a subset of the broader category of multiple exchange rate regimes, which refer to any regimes in which two or more exchange rates are applied to the same currency. Many developing countries have applied separate, fixed exchange rates to different types of transactions, but this practice is, in essence, equivalent to a single exchange rate coupled with different taxes or subsidies (depending on the transaction). By contrast, a parallel market for foreign exchange is distinguished by the fact that the parallel exchange rate is determined freely in the market. Usually, the official exchange rate in parallel market systems is pegged by the authorities at a particular

---

1. For general surveys of the issues associated with parallel markets for foreign exchange, see Agenor (1992) and Kiguel and O'Connell (1995).

2. Kiguel and O'Connell (1995).

fixed (or crawling) rate, although in principle the official rate could be floating as well. Additionally, it is frequently—although not always—the case that the official exchange rate applies to current account transactions, while the parallel market rate, whether legal or illegal, applies to capital account transactions.

Parallel markets for foreign exchange can emerge only when the government imposes exchange controls, that is, restrictions on the volume of certain foreign exchange transactions or on the price at which such transactions are made. Trade barriers, quantitative restrictions, or high tariffs alone are not in themselves sufficient to give rise to a parallel exchange market. While such controls may affect the demand or supply of foreign currencies, they will not drive a wedge between exchange rates for different transactions as long as foreign exchange is freely available for all transactions at an official or market-determined exchange rate. A parallel market arises when the government limits the amount of foreign exchange that can be bought or sold for particular transactions, causing excess demand or supply to spill over into a parallel market, or authorizes that exchange rates for certain transactions be pegged and for other transactions be floating.

Parallel exchange rate systems may be legal or illegal. When the parallel market for foreign exchange is legal, it is often referred to as a dual exchange rate (DER) system. In these cases, most current account transactions take place at a pegged commercial rate, and capital account transactions at a market-determined financial rate. A number of countries have experimented with DER systems of varying duration. Some countries maintained official dual exchange rates for long time periods, such as Belgium (from 1957 to 1990) and the Dominican Republic (until 1993). The parallel market in these countries was used to insulate the rest of the economy from short-term capital flows. France (1971–74) and Italy (1973–74) adopted dual rates for a short period following the collapse of the Bretton Woods system as a transitory measure. Argentina, Mexico, and Venezuela adopted DER regimes in the 1980s in the wake of balance-of-payments crises and huge capital outflows.

Illegal parallel market systems emerge when private agents attempt to evade restrictions on the price or quantity of foreign exchange transactions. Illegal parallel markets were the norm in most of Africa and South Asia, as well as in several Latin American countries, especially through the 1980s. The authorities, with some exceptions, generally tolerated the parallel markets. For example, the threat of enforcement and penalties was significant in Ghana before 1983, but these efforts fell by the wayside later on, and the coverage of the parallel market grew, as did the parallel premium (Kiguel and O'Connell, 1995). In Sudan, trading on the parallel market was a capital offense, and enforcement was attempted between 1970 and 1990. But even the threat of capital punishment did not totally wipe out the parallel market, though it may have been a factor in the very high premium observed in Sudan.

In principle, there is little difference, in terms of macroeconomic implications, between legal and illegal systems. In either case, free-market transactions in foreign exchange take place alongside controlled price transactions. In either legal or illegal systems, there are incentives for transactions to spill over or "leak" from one market into the other. These leakages may tend to undermine the dual exchange rate systems, depending upon how rigidly exchange controls are enforced.

Observers frequently view the incidence of restrictions on international transactions as evidence of the prevalence and importance of parallel exchange markets. According to IMF reports, about one-half of the member countries impose restrictions on payments on transaction on the current account; more than three-quarters do so on capital account payments (See table 12.1). However, the mere existence of restrictions does not necessarily imply the existence of significant parallel markets since the IMF data are qualitative, with only two values (yes and no), and so do not capture either the intensity of restrictions or the effectiveness of their enforcement. Therefore, considering the existence of payments restrictions alone would result in an overestimate of the prevalence of parallel markets for foreign exchange. In fact, only 46 (33 percent) out of the 138 countries in table 12.1 having some form of payments restrictions in 1994 actually had parallel market premiums exceeding 15 percent in that year. Of these 46 countries, 40 had restrictions on both current and capital account transactions, with the other 6 having restrictions only on capital account transactions. Of the 46 countries with significant parallel premiums, 20 were in Africa, 14 were socialist or formerly socialist economies, and the other 12 were in Latin America, Asia, or the Middle East.[3]

Parallel markets are likely to be unimportant, and the parallel premium low, when payments restrictions and capital controls are either minimal or not enforced. For example, South Africa imposed capital controls in 1985, following massive capital outflows, and reintroduced a dual exchange rate system at that time. But the parallel premium has remained modest enough—the median premium was 4.4 percent for

---

3. Comprehensive data on parallel exchange rates used to be published in *Pick's World Currency Yearbook* and by its successor, *International Currency Analysis, Inc.* However, since these ceased publication in the mid-1990s, no single public source of comprehensive data on parallel rates after 1994 has been readily available. Data on parallel rates now have to be obtained on an ad hoc country-by-country basis from whatever official or unofficial sources may be available.

Table 12.1 *Incidence of Payments Restrictions among IMF Member Countries*

Transaction Type	Year	
	1980	1994
Current Account[a]	51.8%	51.7%
Capital Account	78.0%	77.5%

a. All countries with payment restrictions on current transactions also had restrictions on capital account transactions
Source: "Exchange Restrictions and Exchange Arrangements: Annual Report of the IMF," various issues.

the period 1980–89 and declined to 2.3 percent during the period 1990–94 (Ghei, Kiguel, and O'Connell 1996)—that South Africa would be considered to have a unified exchange rate regime under the definition adopted in the section below on trends in official and parallel real exchange rates. There are several other examples of countries that have had extremely low premiums, including Thailand, Malaysia, and Indonesia, with median premiums varying from –1.5 to 3.4 per cent (Ghei, Kiguel, and O'Connell 1996).

Management of Parallel Markets

Parallel market systems emerge for different reasons in different countries. There is one legitimate rationale for a system in which current account transactions are conducted at a pegged rate and capital account transactions are conducted at a floating rate: to insulate domestic prices and economic activity from exchange rate fluctuations deriving from transitory shocks in the financial market.

In practice, the implementation of parallel market systems in developing countries rarely has been consistent with this rationale. In certain Latin American countries, dual exchange rate systems were indeed adopted in response to strong, temporary capital outflows resulting from balance-of-payments crises in the 1980s. These did, to a certain extent, protect their economies from excessive, transitory depreciations of the exchange rate. There was very little rationing in the official market for trade transactions, as foreign exchange supply was usually enough to satisfy demand. On average, the premium of the parallel rate relative to the official rate was quite moderate in these cases—though there were occasional spikes when the premium was very high. But these spikes reflected temporary macroeconomic crises, not a drastic and persistent misalignment of the real exchange rate. However, these dual market arrangements were retained long after the financial crises had passed. Moreover, even after the crises had passed, the parallel rates continued to be more depreciated than the official rates. In a dual rate system designed to protect an economy from exchange rate variability—as opposed to a system designed to target the official rate at a level persistently more appreciated than the one that the market would set—the parallel rate would be expected to fluctuate both above and below the official rate.

In African countries, parallel markets were even less consistent with the one legitimate rationale for maintaining a dual rate system. In these countries, exchange controls were frequently tightened as progressive overvaluation of the official exchange rate led to excess demand for foreign exchange at the official rate. This tightening, in turn, led to the creation of parallel markets to evade exchange controls, even in the absence of strong capital account pressures. Hence, exchange controls were used to prop up persistently misaligned official exchange rates, not to insulate the domestic economy from transitory fluctuations. In the prototypical case, foreign exchange rationing grew more stringent over time as the official exchange rate became increasingly overvalued. Importers who lacked access to ever scarcer foreign exchange through the official channels turned to the parallel market to obtain foreign exchange for trade transactions. The parallel premium grew to very high levels, and stayed there, as the official rate became more and more overvalued. In Ghana, which is the textbook example of this phenomenon, the official exchange rate was so overvalued by the end of the 1980s that it became irrelevant for most transactions; even domestic prices and inflation reflected the parallel, not the official rate (Chhibber and Shaffik, 1991).

Parallel Markets in the 1990s

Although a great many countries have experimented with parallel exchange arrangements at various times, the incidence of such arrangements has been declining in the 1990s, since an increasing number of developing countries have sought to unify their exchange rates, often as part of a larger structural reform effort, which includes liberalization of the external accounts. The breakup of the former Soviet Union temporarily added a number of new countries that initially had parallel exchange markets. However, the trend among the new transition economies has also been toward unification (Halpern and Wyplosz 1997).

Observers have identified various negative consequences of exchange controls and the parallel markets that they engender. A nonexhaustive list would include, first, the fact that exchange controls allow the authorities to maintain a persistently misaligned official exchange rate— perhaps coupled with inappropriate fiscal, monetary, and commercial policies—without losing all their international reserves, thereby distorting relative prices in the economy and inhibiting the growth of exports. Second, because parallel market regimes often involve the rationing of foreign exchange at subsidized rates to those with preferential access to the authorities, exchange controls encourage the development of rent-seeking behavior among private entrepreneurs. Finally, the introduction of exchange controls, which by their nature are hard to enforce and profitable to evade, tends to promote a culture of law evasion among private entrepreneurs that may spill over into other areas such as tax compliance or adherence to other economic and financial regulations.

In response to these and other adverse effects of exchange controls, many countries have moved to dismantle exchange controls and unify their exchange markets. Parallel exchange rate arrangements are now found in developing countries only; Belgium, which was the last developed country with dual exchange rates, moved to a unified exchange rate in 1990. Some parallel markets were abandoned either because they were no longer needed (for example, when the crisis that led to them ended) or because they were no longer effective (for example, when rampant evasion of exchange controls undermined the dual exchange rate system). Argentina, Mexico, and Venezuela had legal dual rates that were expected to be temporary. All three created dual rates and then unified within the period 1980 to 1994, though a parallel market did re-emerge in Venezuela in 1994, as discussed above. Other Latin American countries moved to multiple rates or unified within the same period. In the African and Asian countries, in contrast, parallel markets have tended to be more long lived. A few of these countries unified their exchange rates in the 1990s. Others (including Tanzania, Ghana, and India) moved to legalize their parallel markets as a transitional measure while easing restrictions on current account transactions—as a step on the path to unification of the exchange rate. In those cases, unification has been part of a larger structural reform effort aimed at liberalizing markets overall.

However, the trend toward unification has not been universal. Major exceptions remain—mostly in Africa, including Nigeria, Kenya, and Zambia. To assess the extent to which the survival of parallel markets has been more widespread, we gathered data on the official and parallel exchange rates for a sample of 24 developing countries listed in table 12.2.[4] Our sample includes countries in which significant parallel markets existed for some time. It includes most of the more important

4. The sample is drawn from the World Bank research project on the macroeconomic implications of multiple exchange rates in developing countries, the findings of which are reported in Kiguel, Lizondo, and O'Connell (1996). The basic data set used here is from Ghei and Kiguel (1992). We added three African countries—Algeria, Malawi, and Sudan—and extended the data set to the end

developing countries outside Eastern and Central Europe and the former Soviet Union. The sample is otherwise fairly representative geographically, with 11 countries from Latin America, 10 from Africa, 2 from South Asia, and Turkey. Parallel exchange rates were still present in half of these countries at the end of 1994 (see table 12.2).[5]

The evolution over time of the official and parallel real exchange rates in the sample group of countries is shown in figure 12.1.a and 12.1.b. The level of the parallel premium has decreased, on average, in the countries that have retained parallel exchange rate arrangements. For a selected group of high-premium countries, Ghei, Kiguel, and O'Connell (1996) find that the median premium for the period 1990 to 1994 was 49 percent, compared with a figure of 100 per cent for the period 1980 to 1989.[6] Similar trends have been observed for moderate and low-premium countries as well. For our sample, we find lower premiums in 1994 relative to 1985 in many cases.

Overall, then, there are indications that developing countries are moving in the direction of unified exchange rates. The number of countries with significant parallel markets has declined, and the gap between the official and the parallel rate is steadily decreasing in most of the countries that still have parallel rates. Nonetheless, parallel exchange rates continue to exist in a significant number of developing countries around the world.

A Simple Model of Parallel Exchange Rate Determination

As we have just seen, unification of parallel exchange markets has been on the policy agenda of many developing countries in recent years. When the unification of parallel exchange rates is intended to result in a single exchange rate that is officially determined—as is generally the case—the authorities will need to identify the long-run equilibrium value of the real exchange rate, and, as noted in the introduction, this task will

---

of 1994, the last year for which consistent data are available as explained in footnote 3. A number of transition economies also had parallel rates in 1994 but were not part of the sample studied.

5. However, documenting the trend toward unification, parallel exchange rate arrangements had been even more widespread in developing countries in the 1980s—every country in our sample had more than one exchange rate in 1985.

6. A high-premium country is one in which the median premium exceeds 50 percent. The term "moderate premium" is applied to countries with a median premium between 10 percent and 50 percent. A median level of less than 10 percent puts a country into the low-premium category. The time period examined is 1970–94.

Table 12.2 *Status of the Parallel Market and Level of the Parallel Premium (%)*

Country	Year			
	1980	*1985*	*1990*	*1994*
Latin America and Turkey				
Argentina	Unified	30.79	29.93	Unified
Bolivia	19.85	223.60	Unified	Unified
Brazil	8.90	30.12	14.28	Unified
Chile	6.03	25.39	16.78	8.67
Colombia	Unified	11.42	9.24	6.12
Dominican Rep.	38.00	7.69	68.01	Unified
Ecuador	11.45	76.90	23.53	5.45
Mexico	Unified	28.46	7.41	Unified
Peru	36.25	29.53	104.80	Unified
Uruguay	Unified	9.41	10.93	16.51
Venezuela	Unified	104.00	Unified	4.73
Turkey	9.98	–7.17	Unified	Unified
Africa and South Asia				
Algeria	193.25	375.23	248.81	253.95
Egypt	7.77	122.90	89.47	Unified
Ethiopia	35.02	127.66	192.75	113.26
Ghana	485.92	143.48	9.84	Unified
Kenya	9.38	4.51	3.11	19.78
Malawi	92.27	49.51	17.51	14.62
Nigeria	67.67	306.22	19.40	231.87
Sudan	92.40	27.14	955.45	53.13
Tanzania	174.00	271.89	56.36	Unified
Zambia	70.27	65.39	279.56	–6.15
India	9.58	15.12	9.10	Unified
Pakistan	26.26	–0.67	8.72	Unified
# Parallel Markets	*19*	*24*	*21*	*12*

Note: The premium is defined as $(e^p/e^o - 1) \cdot 100$. The exchange rate is expressed as domestic currency/U.S. dollars. Data are annual averages calculated using ending of quarter values. *Source: IFS* and *World Currency Yearbook, Currency Analysis,* various issues.

be fraught with considerable uncertainty. Under these circumstances, the prevailing preunification parallel exchange rate appears as an obvious proxy for the postunification equilibrium rate, and the authorities might naturally consider the parallel rate to be an appropriate target toward which to move the official rate, either gradually or all at once. However, there are many factors that could cause the parallel rate to diverge significantly from the long-run equilibrium value of a unified rate, making it, in many instances, an inappropriate target for the official exchange rate.

Figure 12.1.a *Latin America and Turkey: Official and Parallel Bilateral Real Exchange Rates with the U.S. Dollar, 1970–94 (First Quarter of 1985=100)*

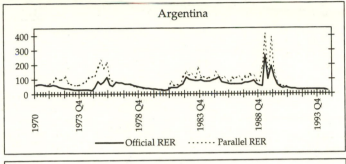

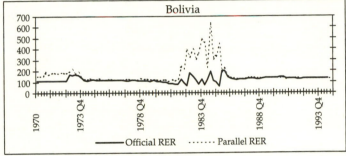

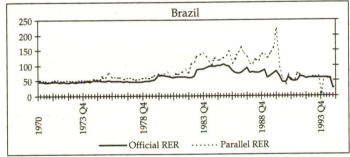

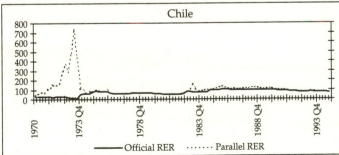

Note: Quarterly figures with year marking fourth quarter. An upward movement is a depreciation of the RER.

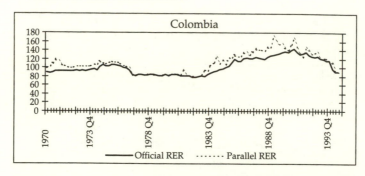

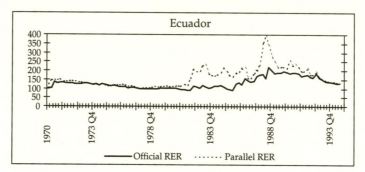

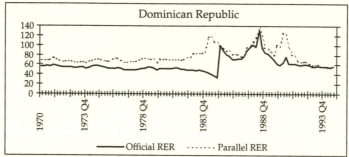

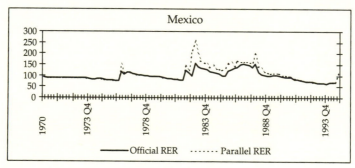

Note: Quarterly figures with year marking fourth quarter. An upward movement is a depreciation of the RER.

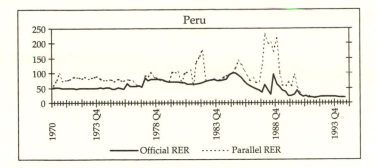

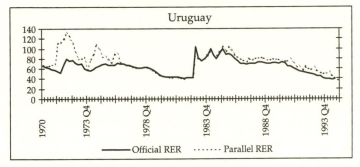

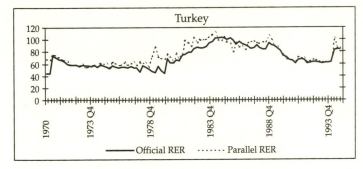

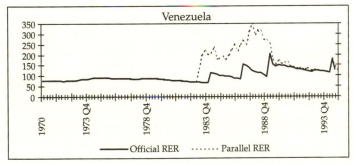

Note: Quarterly figures with year marking fourth quarter. An upward movement is a depreciation of the RER.

Figure 12.1.b *Africa and South Asia: Official and Parallel Bilateral Real Exchanges with the U.S. Dollar, 1970–94 (First Quarter of 1985=100)*

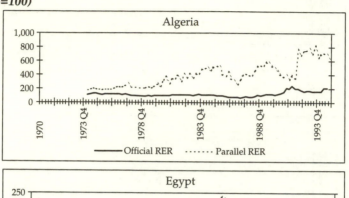

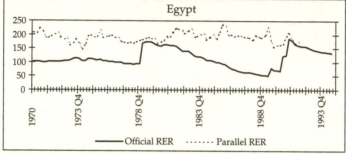

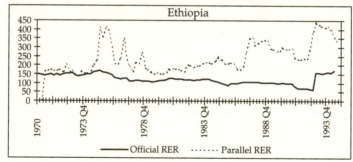

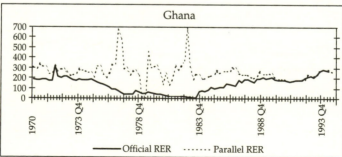

Note: Quarterly figures with year marking fourth quarter. An upward movement is a depreciation of the RER.

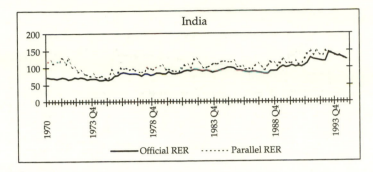

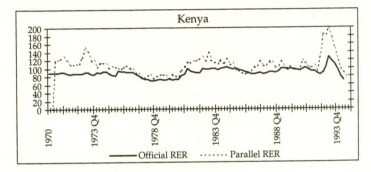

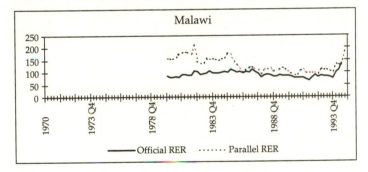

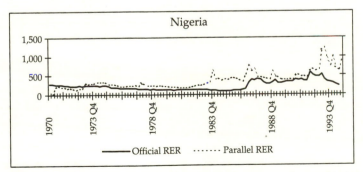

Note: Quarterly figures with year marking fourth quarter. An upward movement is a depreciation of the RER.

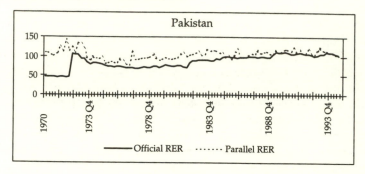

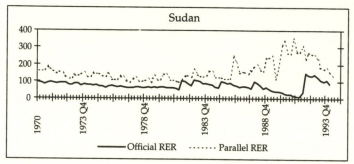

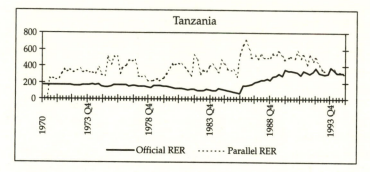

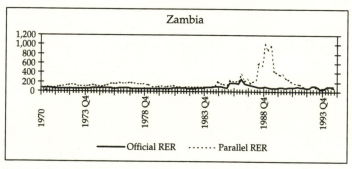

Note: Quarterly figures with year marking fourth quarter. An upward movement is a depreciation of the RER.

To develop this argument, this section presents a simple partial-equilibrium model to illustrate how the parallel market exchange rate is determined in relation both to the official exchange rate and to the long-run equilibrium exchange rate—that is, the rate that would produce equilibrium in the balance of payments under normal, sustainable policy conditions.[7] There is no consensus regarding the most appropriate model to use in explaining the parallel market rate, just as there is no agreement as to which model best explains the movement of floating exchange rates among industrial countries. The model illustrated below has the advantage of being relatively straightforward and intuitive, while hopefully highlighting the most important features influencing the parallel market rate.

Basic Setup

Consider a small open economy trading in two goods, a nondomestically consumed export good and a nondomestically produced import; the world prices of both goods are fixed and set to unity. To focus on developments in the external sector, we assume it to be small relative to the domestic economy, so that the analysis describes the operation of the parallel exchange market in partial equilibrium. Therefore, the output of a nontraded good and its price are considered fixed as well. We assume for convenience that the U.S. dollar is the only foreign currency traded.

Turning to the parameters of government policy, it is assumed that monetary and fiscal policies are at their long-run, sustainable levels, and moreover, for analytical convenience, that there are no tariffs, subsidies, or other commercial policy interventions. (The role of import barriers will be examined later.) The official exchange rate E (measured in terms of domestic currency per dollar) is pegged at an overvalued level relative to the equilibrium rate. Therefore, at that level of the exchange rate, the flow demand for U.S. dollars (to be elaborated below) exceeds their flow supply. Unlike other models considered in this book, we assume here that the overvaluation is supported by foreign exchange rationing—that is, exporters are required to surrender their dollar earnings to the central bank at the official rate E, and the central bank rations dollar sales to importers, restricting them to the amount OS, based on the amount of export revenues surrendered to the central bank OX, according to a central bank rationing function as shown in equation 12.1:

(12.1) $$OS = OS(OX), \quad OS'() > 0.$$

---

7. The model and its exposition are based on the analysis presented in Kamin (1993, 1995).

Private capital flows are assumed to take place in the parallel market with the central bank supplying foreign exchange only for imports to the official market.

In response to the prevailing excess demand for dollars at the official rate E, a parallel market for dollars priced at the parallel market rate E^p emerges. We follow the conventional stock-flow approach to exchange rate determination in positing that in the long run, the parallel rate moves so as to equate flow demands for dollars by importers with flow supplies for dollars by exporters. That is, in the long run E^p is set so as to balance the private sector's current account. In the short run, in contrast, the parallel market rate is assumed to move exclusively to set the portfolio demand for dollars equal to the stock of dollars outstanding, so that at any given moment the private current account may be out of balance.

The Equilibrium Parallel Market Rate

We now analyze the determination of the parallel market rate when the private current is in account equilibrium. The private-sector current account is defined as the difference between private dollar inflows or supplies, S, and outflows or demands, D. We assume that foreigners hold no domestic assets, so that changes in the stock of dollars held by the private sector, B, occur exclusively through imbalances in the private sector's current account, as shown by equation 12.2:

$$(12.2) \qquad\qquad dB = S - D.$$

The current account (or flow) demand for dollars is a derived demand for imported goods. Arbitrage ensures that the price of the import will be the same, whether purchased from a legal importer with access to official foreign exchange or from a smuggler using dollars purchased in the parallel market.[8] In either case, the price of imports will be set equal to its marginal cost, the parallel market rate E^p (since by assumption, the foreign-currency price is set to unity). Therefore, the private demand for imports, as indicated in equation 12.3 below, depends (negatively) upon the domestic currency price of imports E^p relative to the price of nontradables P^n.[9]

---

8. We assume that there are no tariffs and that restrictions on smuggling are evaded at no cost. The latter assumption is relaxed below.

9. In principle, import demand is a function of income as well. Since, in this partial equilibrium model, income is considered to be fixed, we do not include it explicitly in the demand function.

(12.3) $D = D(E^p/P^n) = D(e^p), \quad D'() < 0$

where e^p is the real parallel exchange rate.

The current account (or flow) supply of dollars derives both from underinvoiced dollar earnings—that is, export receipts not turned over to the central bank—and from official dollar sales to importers, OS. Note that while holders of import licenses have an incentive to overinvoice, this does not add to the total supply of dollars to the private sector, which is fixed by the central bank's rationing function (equation 12.1). Let X represent the quantity of total exports and total dollar revenues as well (since the world price is set to unity), while f represents the share of total export proceeds diverted to the parallel market. Then, as shown by equation 12.4:

(12.4) $S = \phi X + OS(OX) = \phi X + OS((1-\phi)X).$

Exporters maximize domestic-currency profits subject to rising marginal costs of production—which we assume to be related to the price of nontraded goods—as well as rising costs associated with the underinvoicing share f. We can derive the supply curve for total exports as a function of the weighted average of the real (nontradables price deflated) official (e) and parallel (e^p) market exchange rates as shown in equation 12.5:[10]

(12.5) $X = X(\phi e^p + (1-\phi)e), \quad X'() > 0.$

The underinvoicing share f can be shown to positively depend upon the real parallel market premium as indicated by equation 12.6:

(12.6) $\phi = \phi(e^p - e), \quad \phi'() > 0.$

For a given value of the real official rate e, a unique real parallel market rate e^p will equate dollar demands and supplies in equilibrium as shown in equation 12.7:

(12.7) $D(e^p) = \phi X + OS(OX).$

This equation can be further simplified if we posit that, on average and over a long enough time period, the central bank will have roughly stable

---

10. See Kamin (1993) for details.

international reserves. Therefore, we can assume that over a long time period, the central bank will resell all surrendered export receipts $OX = (1-f)X$ to licensed importers, after it extracts any foreign exchange needs of the government (assumed to be invariant to the exchange rate), D^g.[11] This relationship is expressed in equation 12.8:

$$(12.8) \qquad OS\,(OX) = OX - D^G = (1-\phi)X - D^g.$$

Therefore, equation 12.7 can now be rewritten as 12.9:

$$(12.9) \quad D\,(e^p) = \phi\,X + (1-\phi)\,X - D^g = X - D^g = X\,(\phi\,e^p + (1-\phi)\,e) - D^g.$$

Figure 12.2 below depicts various different equilibria in the parallel exchange market, depending upon the value of e set by the authorities. The DD curve depicts equation 12.3, the private demand for foreign exchange as a function of the real parallel rate e^p. The SS curve depicts the supply of foreign exchange to the market as a function of e^p; its location also is a function of e, since both e^p and e affect the total quantity of exports supplied. The variable e^* is the long-run equilibrium real exchange rate. It is the level of the real exchange rate that would clear the market (that is, set total demands for foreign exchange equal to total supplies) in a unified foreign exchange market. Note that when the official exchange rate is set equal to e^*, the parallel rate also must equal e^*.[12] In other words, when the official exchange rate is set at its equilibrium value, there is no current account motive for the emergence of a parallel foreign exchange market, since there is no excess demand for foreign exchange at the official rate. We now consider the effects on the real parallel rate of a real appreciation of the official rate. Assume that the authorities allow the official rate e to appreciate to an overvalued level $e_1 < e^*$. Because this lowers the profitability of exports, the supply curve SS shifts inward, creating an excess demand for foreign exchange at that rate. This puts upward pressure on the foreign exchange value of the dollar in the (now emergent) parallel market, causing the parallel exchange rate to depreciate from e^* to e_1^p.[13]

Hence, in cases in which the emergence of the parallel market reflects the overvaluation of the official commercial exchange rate, the parallel

---

11. This formulation is consistent with the assumptions in Sheik (1976) and Nowak (1984).

12. This equality must hold because if $D(e^*) = X(e^*) - Dg$ in a unified exchange market and if in a parallel market system $D(ep) = X(fep + (1-f)e^*) - Dg$, then it is obvious by inspection that the second equation is satisfied for $ep = e^*$.

13. This result is consistent with that found by Nowak (1984).

Figure 12.2 *Flow Supply and Demand for Foreign Exchange in the Parallel Market*

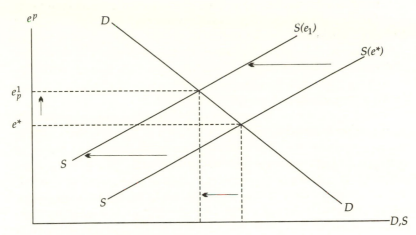

Note: An increase in e^p is a depreciation.

market rate, on average, is likely to be more depreciated not only than the commercial rate but probably also than the long-run equilibrium exchange rate. Various factors are likely to determine the extent to which the parallel rate is more depreciated than the equilibrium exchange rate. As figure 12.2 makes obvious, the more overvalued the official exchange rate—and so the greater the extent to which the SS curve shifts inward— the greater will be the gap between the parallel rate and the equilibrium rate. It also is straightforward to show that the more elastic exports are and the less elastic imports are with respect to the exchange rate, the greater the gap will be.

The extent to which export surrender requirements are enforced plays a key role in determining the value of the parallel exchange rate as well. Recall that total exports are a function of a weighted average of the real official and parallel exchange rates. If foreign exchange regulations are tightly enforced, underinvoicing of exports will be limited, reducing the underinvoicing ratio f and thereby increasing the weight placed on the official exchange rate. In this case, the overvaluation of the official exchange rate depresses total exports significantly, reducing the supply of foreign exchange to the parallel market, and depreciating the real parallel market exchange rate substantially relative to the equilibrium rate.

Conversely, if foreign exchange regulations are poorly enforced and widely evaded, the underinvoicing ratio will be higher, the weighted average exchange rate will be more favorable for exporters, and total exports will not be as severely depressed. This will lead to less pressure on the parallel market exchange rate and a smaller gap relative to the equilibrium rate. At an extreme, as to some extent occurred in some African countries, the official exchange rate becomes so widely evaded that it becomes irrelevant to most economic decisions. In this context, most trade is routed through the underground economy, and the parallel exchange rate may become a reasonably accurate guide to the long-run equilibrium rate.

Finally, the value of the parallel exchange rate in long-run equilibrium is likely to be influenced by the extent to which short-run barriers to imports (above and beyond merely rationing official sales of foreign exchange through exchange controls) are enforced.[14] The above analysis assumes that once importers acquire foreign exchange, whether officially or from the black market, they may use that financing to freely import goods. However, if the authorities temporarily impose high import barriers and the barriers are well enforced so that smuggling is costly, these barriers will reduce the demand for foreign exchange in the black market—that is, the *DD* curve shown in figure 12.2 will shift inward and to the left. This reduced demand, in turn, would cause the real parallel exchange rate to appreciate relative to the long-run equilibrium value of the real exchange rate. For sufficiently tight controls on imports, the real parallel rate could even be more appreciated than the long-run equilibrium real rate.

The Parallel Market Rate in Short-Run Portfolio Equilibrium

The results described above are likely, at best, to hold on average over relatively long periods of time. In the very short term, the stock of dollars held by the private sector is considered to be fixed, since it takes time to accumulate or dissipate dollars through current account imbalances. During this short run, the parallel market rate, at which all private capital flows are assumed to take place, is conventionally modeled as being determined by the portfolio-based demand for dollars. This portfolio demand depends upon the relative expected rates of return to holding dollars and domestic assets—which are influenced by anticipated inflation, other aspects of macroeconomic performance, and political events as well. The volatility of such expectations largely explains

---

14. We consider the case of short-run barriers only, since these leave the long-run equilibrium real exchange rate e^* unchanged.

the high volatility exhibited by most freely floating exchange rates, including parallel market exchange rates.

For a simple theoretical exposition, assume that private-sector agents hold two assets in their portfolio, dollars and domestic currency. Following Dornbusch and others (1983), the desired ratio of the domestic-currency value of private-sector dollar holdings to the nominal domestic money supply (M) is modeled as a function of the expected rate of depreciation of the black market rate (the ^ denotes percentage change), as shown in equation 12.10:

$$(12.10) \qquad \frac{E^{p}B}{M} = \Phi(\hat{E}^{p}), \quad \Phi'() > 0$$

where B is the stock of dollars held by the private sector. Dividing the numerator and the denominator on the left side of equation 12.10 by the price of nontraded goods yields equation 12.11:

$$(12.11) \qquad \frac{e^{p}B}{m} = \Phi(\hat{E}^{p}), \quad \text{where} \quad m = \frac{M}{P^{n}}.$$

The notation for the rate of depreciation, $\hat{E}^{p}$, omits an expectational term to reflect the assumption of perfect foresight. The portfolio demand for dollars (when the parallel market rate is stable) traces out a downward-sloping curve in (e^{p}, B) space as shown in figure 12.3. Given that B is considered fixed at any one moment, the level of B determines the level of e^{p} at that moment.

In the long run, the parallel market rate and the private stock of dollar holdings are determined by the requirements of both portfolio and current account equilibrium. In addition to the portfolio equilibrium condition described above, figure 12.3 depicts the locus of points for which the private current account is in equilibrium, so that the stock of dollars (B) held by the private sector is unchanging. This curve, denoted dB = 0, is vertical, since for any given official exchange rate, a single value of the parallel market rate e^{p} clears the private current account.[15] The point where the two curves cross—the steady-state equilibrium—is

---

15. For simplicity, this analysis abstracts from the interest payments associated with net asset holdings, as well as from the wealth effects of asset holdings on import demand. In the presence of interest payments or wealth effects, the dB = 0 curve would not be vertical, since the value of the parallel market exchange rate that cleared the private current account would depend upon the stock of dollar holdings B.

Figure 12.3 *Current Account and Portfolio Equilibrium in the Parallel Market*

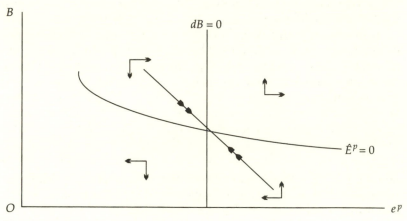

Note: An increase in e^p is a depreciation.

the only point at which both the current account is in equilibrium and the stock of dollars held by the private sector equals its portfolio demand. Finally, the vertical and horizontal arrows represent the direction of movement of B and e^p outside of equilibrium, while the diagonal line—the "stable saddle path"—indicates the path by which B and e^p converge toward equilibrium, should they start out outside of equilibrium.

We now consider the effects on the parallel market rate of a rise in inflation—for example, from 0 to 20 percent—leading to higher rates of nominal depreciation of the official and parallel exchange rates. This example is an important one because many countries that imposed exchange controls experienced increases in inflation and other measures of macroeconomic volatility at about the same time, particularly in Latin America (and Turkey).

As shown in figure 12.4, the increased expected level of inflation—and hence of nominal depreciation of the parallel market rate—leads agents to desire to hold a higher ratio of dollars to domestic currency, causing the portfolio balance curve to shift upward. Equilibrium dollar holdings shift from B_0 to B_1, while the equilibrium real parallel market rate remains unchanged. However, in order to accumulate additional dollars, the private current account must shift into surplus temporarily, which in turn requires a temporary depreciation of the real parallel exchange rate. Hence, at the moment of increased inflation expectations, the parallel market rate jumps from initial equilibrium at (1) to the new stable saddle path at (2). After this, the accumulation of dollars through the current account surplus reverses the depreciation of the real parallel market rate until the system returns to equilibrium at (3).

In the example depicted above, the real parallel exchange rate becomes, for a time, more depreciated than its own equilibrium level, conditional on the value of the real official rate. (As a result of these temporary capital outflows, the short-run equilibrium exchange rate in a unified market also would depreciate relative to its long-run equilibrium level.) Since the equilibrium level of the parallel exchange rate is likely (as shown above in the previous subsection) to be more depreciated than the long-run equilibrium rate in a unified exchange market, the accumulation of dollar balances during periods of macroeconomic volatility and capital outflows will cause the parallel rate to be even more depreciated at such times. Hence, during periods of macroeconomic volatility and heavy capital outflows, the parallel rate is likely to be a particularly biased guide to setting the appropriate level of the official exchange rate.

In fact, because of the asset market function of the parallel exchange market, the parallel market rate can trade at a large premium over the official rate, even when the official rate is close to its long-run equilibrium value—that is, the value that equilibrates the balance of payments in "normal" macroeconomic circumstances. As noted above, during periods of heavy capital outflows the short-run equilibrium real exchange

Figure 12.4 *Effect of Increased Inflation on the Parallel Exchange Rate*

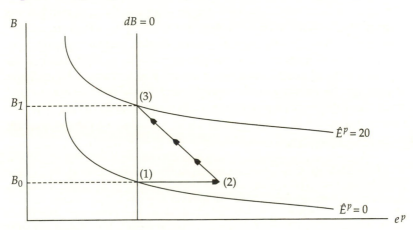

Note: An increase in e^p is a depreciation.

rate in a unified exchange market may depreciate relative to its long-run level. If the official exchange rate remains at its equilibrium long-run level, a temporary excess demand for foreign exchange will develop that will cause a parallel market premium to emerge. The Latin American countries' experiences with exchange controls may fit this scenario. As will be discussed further below, in several of these countries a combination of factors led to a balance-of-payments crisis in the 1980s. The governments responded to this crisis by depreciating the official exchange rate, but because of the size of the capital outflows triggered by the crises, the parallel market rates in these countries depreciated still further.

Finally, we should underscore the fact that even if the real parallel market exchange rate, on average over long periods of time, were a good indicator of the long-run equilibrium real exchange rate, the value of the real parallel market rate at any single point in time would likely be an extremely unreliable proxy for that equilibrium rate. This is because the parallel market exchange rate, like any other asset price, depends upon highly volatile portfolio demands, and hence is itself highly volatile. This volatility may be seen quite easily in the figures showing the official and parallel exchange rates at the end of this chapter. Hence, aside from the fact that the parallel rate is likely to be a *biased* indicator of the long-run equilibrium exchange rate, it is also—unless averaged over very long periods—likely to be a highly *volatile and inaccurate* indicator of the equilibrium rate as well.[16]

Trends in Official and Parallel Real Exchange Rates

The theoretical model described above suggests that the parallel exchange rate is likely to be more depreciated than the long-run equilibrium real exchange rate unless (a) macroeconomic factors inducing capital flight are not present, (b) exchange controls are poorly enforced, or (c) there are high import barriers that are well enforced. To evaluate these hypotheses, we would, ideally, compare the path of the parallel exchange rate in various countries to that of the long-run equilibrium real exchange rate in order to gauge the extent to which the parallel rate

---

16. On the basis of an optimizing model of the parallel market exchange rate, Montiel and Ostry (1994) come to much the same conclusion. They find that in the transition between steady-state equilibria in response to a productivity shock, the parallel market premium may move both above and below zero, and hence is "an unreliable indicator of the sign and magnitude of real exchange rate misalignment."

may serve as a useful guide to determining the equilibrium exchange rate and, therefore, in setting the official rate.

Unfortunately, the equilibrium real exchange rate is a theoretical construct that must be estimated, not a directly measurable quantity for which data exist. Moreover, even in a unified market, the empirical estimation of the equilibrium real exchange rate is no easy task. Estimating the equilibrium rate is a highly involved process requiring strong assumptions about the operation of the current and capital accounts, as well as the estimation of stable trade and payments relationships over time.

Estimation of the long-run equilibrium real exchange rate for a wide set of countries, in order to compare those exchange rates to actual parallel rates, would go beyond the limited scope of this chapter. As a first step toward identifying where parallel market rates stand in relation to long-run equilibrium real exchange rates, however, it makes sense to compare levels of the parallel rate to levels of the official rate, averaged over long periods of time. This comparison may be informative, since over sufficiently long periods, the balance of payments must on average be at a sustainable level. Additionally, it may be useful to compare the level of the real official exchange rate during periods in which exchange controls are in effect—and hence parallel markets exist—to periods during which exchange markets are unified. Such comparisons may shed light on the factors that motivated the imposition of exchange controls, which in turn may have implications for the relationship between the parallel and equilibrium real exchange rates.

A complicating factor in using averages of actual exchange rates as proxies for equilibrium exchange rates is that for most countries, the process of development and structural change will cause the long-run equilibrium real exchange rate to change over time.[17] In that sense, a long-period average of actual real exchange rates may yield, at best, an average of long-run real equilibrium exchange rates over that period. With this caveat in mind, however, we still believe that empirical comparisons of actual official and parallel exchange rates can yield useful insights.

First, our analysis will focus on averages of exchange rates across a large set of different countries. Therefore, even if long-run real equilibrium exchange rates follow particular trends in each individual country, the average long-run real equilibrium exchange rate for the sample as a whole may be more stationary. Second, our analysis focuses upon

---

17. This problem is in essence the one, highlighted in Chapters 5 and 7 of this book, of using PPP-based estimates of the long-run equilibrium real exchange rate when the real exchange rate proves to be nonstationary.

comparison of different types of exchange rates—official and parallel—during regimes with and without exchange controls. Therefore, our results will be vulnerable to misinterpretation if the timing of exchange control periods in the sample coincide with particular movements in long-run equilibrium real exchange rates. While we believe, as discussed above, that exchange control periods are likely to coincide with systematic movements in *short-run* equilibrium real exchange rates, as a result of temporary shocks to capital flows or the terms of trade we have less cause to believe that exchange controls have been associated with particular trends in *long-run* equilibrium real exchange rates.

Methodology

Our statistical analysis is based on the 24-country sample described in the first section of this chapter on the essential characteristics of parallel exchange markets. To meaningfully compare levels of exchange rates in these countries over time, we first corrected the nominal (parallel and official) exchange rate data for changes in prices by calculating real exchange rates. There are a number of different empirical definitions of the real exchange rate as set out in Part I of this volume. Here we use the bilateral real exchange rate between the country that we are examining and the United States (units of local currency per U.S. dollar so that an increase in the exchange rate indicates a depreciation). The consumer price index (CPI) is used as a proxy for domestic prices, and the U.S. producer price index is used for world prices.

$$(12.12) \qquad\qquad e = \frac{E \cdot P^{us}}{P}$$

where e is the real exchange rate; E, the nominal exchange rate, is the local-currency value of U.S. dollar; P^{us} is the U.S. producer price index; and P is the domestic CPI.[18]

The data used are end-of-quarter, for the period from 1970 through 1994. The real official exchange rate is indexed so that its value in the first quarter of 1985 is equal to 100. The real parallel market exchange rate is indexed so that its value in the first quarter of 1985 is equal to 100 plus the premium (in percent) of the parallel rate over the official rate in

---

18. It is possible that the use of a bilateral exchange rate, using the U.S. producer price index as a proxy for world prices, may bias our results, in view of the significant movements of the U.S. dollar relative to the currencies of other industrial countries during the 1980s. Results of tests for sensitivity with respect to choice of foreign price index are presented in the appendix for a subsample of countries for the period 1979–94.

that base quarter. For each country, the mean and median average values are calculated for the following: e, the official real exchange rate for the entire period; e^p, the parallel real exchange rate for the entire period of its existence, that is, when exchange controls were in effect; e^{nu}, the nonunified official real exchange rate for the periods when exchange controls were in effect and exchange markets were not unified; and e^u, the unified official real exchange rate during periods, if any existed, when exchange markets were unified. A unification of exchange markets is defined to have taken place if the absolute value of the parallel rate deviates by less than 3 percent from the official rate for at least four quarters. The nonzero number is to take into account measurement errors, since the official and parallel rates are from different sources (see tables).[19]

A cross-country summary of our calculations of the four real exchange rate categories described above, based on mean averages of the exchange rate data for each separate country, is presented in columns 1 through 4 of table 12.3. Results are presented in table 12.3 for the whole sample, as well as two subsets. For the countries in each subset, we present the mean, median, and standard deviation of the real exchange rate. In columns 5 though 9 of table 12.3, we calculate various ratios of the data shown in columns 1 through 4, and perform binomial sign tests to determine whether these ratios differ significantly from one. The "Pr (H_0 is true)" row indicates the probability that the observed configuration of ratios would be observed, if the null hypothesis—that the ratio is equal to 1—were true.

The regional groupings were chosen in order to test our hypotheses concerning the different motivation and function of parallel markets in different regions set out above in the section on the essential characteristics of parallel markets. In Latin America and Turkey, exchange controls were imposed, particularly in the 1980s, in situations of macroeconomic and balance-of-payments crisis leading to strong capital outflows. In these countries, pressures from capital flight are likely to have caused the parallel rate to depreciate well above the long-run equilibrium real rate, even if the official exchange rate was not especially overvalued relative to its long-run equilibrium value. African and South Asian countries, in contrast, experienced much less macroeconomic distress. In those countries, exchange controls were more likely to have arisen as a means of rationing foreign exchange receipts in the context of a progressive overvaluation of the official exchange rate. As described in the subsection above on the equilibrium parallel market rate, the parallel rate is

---

19. The official exchange rates and prices are from the IMF, *International Financial Statistics*. The parallel exchange rates are from *World Currency Yearbook* and *International Currency Analysis, Inc.*

Table 12.3 *Average Official and Parallel Real Exchange Rates, 1970–94, for Sample Group Countries, Ratios, and Binomial Sign Tests*

Country	1 Official real ER 1970–94 e	2 Parallel Real ER e^p	3 Official ER with par. mkt. e^a	4 Official ER when unified e^{nu}	5 Ratio, e^p/e 2/1	6 Ratio, e^{nu}/e 3/1	7 Ratio, e^p/e^{nu} 2/3	8 Ratio, e^p/e^u 2/4	9 Ratio, e^{nu}/e^u 3/4
Latin America and Turkey									
Mean	82.52	121.02	85.13	76.91	1.46	1.03	1.42	1.58	1.12
Median	69.10	115.01	69.43	64.66	1.24	1.06	1.36	1.32	1.10
Std Dev	26.17	24.29	47.71	27.28	0.36	0.26	0.34	0.39	0.16
Number < 1	n.a	n.a	n.a	n.a	0	3	0	0	3
Number > 1	n.a	n.a	n.a	n.a	12	9	12	12	9
Pr (H_0 is true)	n.a	n.a	n.a	n.a	0.0002	0.019	0.0002	0.0002	0.019
Africa and South Asia									
Mean	120.04	222.82	117.94	195.24	1.82	0.98	1.85	1.05	0.65
Median	103.56	186.64	101.56	267.03	1.78	1.00	1.81	0.97	0.57
Std Dev	45.99	111.76	45.03	85.81	0.58	0.02	0.58	0.18	0.12
Number < 1	n.a	n.a	n.a	n.a	0	12	0	3	5
Number > 1	n.a	n.a	n.a	n.a	12	0	12	2	0
Pr (H_0 is true)	n.a	n.a	n.a	n.a	0.0002	0.0002	0.0002	0.500	0.031
All countries									
Mean	101.28	171.92	101.53	111.71	1.64	1.01	1.64	1.43	0.99
Median	91.38	131.33	91.10	86.24	1.52	1.00	1.54	1.36	1.07
Std Dev	41.60	99.81	40.40	74.67	0.50	0.04	0.51	0.38	0.25
Number < 1	n.a	n.a	n.a	n.a	0	15	0	3	8
Number > 1	n.a	n.a	n.a	n.a	24	9	24	14	9
Pr (H_0 is true)	n.a	n.a	n.a	n.a	0.000	0.153	0.000	0.006	0.500

Source: IFS; *World Currency Yearbook,* and *International Currency Analysis Inc.,* various issues; authors' calculations.

likely to be more depreciated than the long-run equilibrium rate in this context as well, unless exchange controls are poorly enforced or well-enforced import barriers effectively curtail the demand for foreign exchange.

Comparisons of Period Averages

We now compare the real parallel rate e^p to various proxies of the equilibrium real exchange rate. The first possible proxy for the equilibrium RER we consider is e, the average RER for a period of 25 years. As may be seen in column 5, e^p/e, on average, is greater than 1, with a mean of 1.64 for the entire sample. In fact, there is no country in our sample for which the average real parallel market exchange rate was more appreciated than the average real official rate (calculated for periods in which the exchange market was unified as well as nonunified). To the extent that the average official rate, when averaged over a sufficiently long period, is a good proxy for the equilibrium real rate, this suggests that the parallel rate is a biased indicator of the equilibrium rate.

However, using the average RER for the entire period may be misleading, since it includes periods with exchange controls as well as periods in which the exchange market is unified. When exchange controls are in place, the nominal price of foreign exchange is set by the authorities, and access to foreign exchange is determined by quantitative rationing. Hence, the official real exchange rate during periods of exchange control is likely to be more appreciated than the equilibrium real rate. It may be more appropriate to use the RER averaged over periods of unified exchange markets—that is, e^u—as a proxy for the long-run equilibrium RER.

For the whole sample, the parallel rate is, on average, more depreciated than the unified official RER; as indicated in column 8, the mean of the ratio, e^p/e^u, is 1.43 for all countries. However, this result masks strong differences between Latin America and Turkey, with a mean of 1.58, and Africa and South Asia, with a mean value of 1.05 (which is not significantly different from 1). Hence, to the extent that e^u is a good proxy for the long-run equilibrium real exchange rate, e^p appears, on average, to have been close to the long-run equilibrium exchange rate in Africa and South Asia, but much more depreciated than the long-run equilibrium level in Latin America and Turkey. This may seem surprising, given the far higher average parallel premiums that have been observed in much of Africa; as shown in column 7, the ratio of the parallel market rate to the official rate during periods of exchange control averaged 1.85 for Africa and South Asia but only 1.42 for Latin America and Turkey.

The strong differences in e^p/e^u, the ratio of the parallel rate to the unified official rate, between Latin America and Africa appear to be related to equally marked differences in the evolution of the official exchange rate between the two regions. As indicated in column 9, in Latin America and Turkey, the real official exchange rate tended to be more depreciated during periods of exchange controls than during periods in which the exchange markets were unified; the mean ratio of e^{nu}/e^u was 1.12, with 9 of the 12 countries having ratios greater than 1. This is consistent with our view that in Latin America and Turkey, unsustainable policies resulted in macroeconomic disequilibrium, which, in turn, triggered capital outflows that depreciated the short-run equilibrium real exchange rate (a relationship that would hold in a unified exchange market) relative to its long-run level. The government did depreciate the official exchange rate, but not by as much as the short-run equilibrium rate depreciated. Therefore, an excess demand for foreign exchange developed, causing the parallel rate to depreciate as well. As macroeconomic pressures eased, capital outflows moderated and reversed themselves, leading to an appreciation of the short-run equilibrium exchange rate and facilitating the unification of exchange markets.

In contrast to Latin America and Turkey, in the African and South Asian countries in our sample, the real official exchange rate tended to be more appreciated when exchange controls were in place than when exchange markets were unified. As shown in column 9, for Africa and South Asia, the ratio of e^{nu}/e^u was only .65, with all five countries in this grouping showing ratios less than 1. This evidence, while qualified by the low number of observations in the subsample, supports our speculation that the emergence of a parallel market in Africa and South Asia was typically the result of an appreciation of the real official exchange rate relative to the long-run equilibrium rate. Authorities chose, for a variety of reasons, to ration foreign exchange while maintaining an overvalued real exchange rate. As the extent of overvaluation increased, often foreign exchange rationing tightened, and the parallel market grew, as did the premium.

Considering how overvalued the real official exchange rate was in the South Asian and many African countries, relative to its long-run equilibrium value, it is surprising that parallel rates in those countries were not more depreciated compared with average official exchange rates during the periods when exchange markets were unified. The subsection above on the equilibrium parallel market rate showed that, all else being equal, the more overvalued was the official exchange rate, the more undervalued would be the parallel rate relative to the long-run equilibrium rate. Therefore, unification presumably would have required African and South Asian governments to devalue their official exchange rates to a level that was *not* as depreciated as the prior level of the parallel rate.

In addressing this issue, it is important to point out that we have a very small sample to examine—only five countries in our sample in the subset consisting of Africa and South Asia unified their exchange rates. In two of these five cases (Egypt and Tanzania), the ratio is greater than 1. Additionally, as pointed out earlier in the discussion of the equilibrium parallel market rate, there are factors that may lower the parallel rate relative to the level predicted by the basic model. First, consider the case when underinvoicing, f, is high because exchange controls are not effective because enforcement is lackadaisical and evasion widespread. Then, for all practical purposes, the relevant rate for the economy becomes the parallel rate, which may, in this case, be close to the equilibrium rate. Thus, when exchange markets are unified, the official rate would need to be depreciated to the level of the former parallel rate, and e^p/e^u would be close to one. Ghana is an excellent illustration of this possibility (Chhibber and Shaffik 1991).

A second factor that might appreciate the parallel market rate relative to the level predicted by the basic model might be the strong enforcement of import controls. This would cause the premium to be low, even if the official exchange rate is maintained at a substantially overvalued level compared with the long-run equilibrium exchange rate, since effective import controls reduce the demand for foreign exchange and thereby appreciate the short-run equilibrium exchange rate. Then, if unification is associated with import liberalization, thereby depreciating the short-run real equilibrium exchange rate, the official exchange rate will have to depreciate by a large amount if excess demands for foreign exchange are to be eliminated. This scenario would lead to a ratio, e^p/e^u, that would be low compared with the predictions of the basic model outlined in the subsection on the equilibrium parallel market rate. India is the best example of this scenario: unification of the exchange rate took place in 1993 as part of a larger liberalization effort, requiring a greater devaluation of the official exchange rate than would have been the case in the absence of import liberalization.

The Official Exchange Rate after Exchange Market Unification

The issues related to unification can be further examined by considering what happens to the official exchange rate at that time. We have 20 observations of unifications. In some cases, a country has two episodes of dual exchange rates, with a period of unified exchange rates in the interim; these are treated as two separate observations. Some countries have never unified, and therefore are not represented (see the appendix for the complete list). The composition of the unification data set is quite different from that used in table 12.1. First, three-quarters of the observations are from the experience of unification in Latin America; only 3 out of the 20 observations are for Africa, with the 2 South Asian countries completing the count. The small sample means that the subset results are to be interpreted with caution for the Africa and South Asia subset.

In table 12.4, we look at the mean, median, and standard deviation of three variables: the average official RER for the year before the unification (column 10), the average official RER in the year following unification (column 11), and the average parallel rate for the year preceding the unification (column 12). We calculate two ratios of the postunification official RER to the preunification RER, e^u_{t+1}/e^{nu}_{t-1}, and the ratio of the postunification official (and sole) RER to the preunification parallel rate, e^u_{t+1}/e^p_{t-1}. As before, we report the mean, median, and standard deviation for all variables as well as the results of binomial sign test for the ratios.

The results are consistent with the findings reported in table 12.3. The ratio of the post- to preunification official exchange rate, e^u_{t+1}/e^{nu}_{t-1}, is approximately equal to 1 for the whole sample. Again, aggregation obscures the difference in results between the two subsets. The ratio e^u_{t+1}/e^{nu}_{t-1} is (very) slightly less than 1 for Latin America and Turkey, suggesting a small appreciation in the RER following unification. This is consistent with the idea that capital inflows resumed as the macro crisis was alleviated, appreciating the short-run real equilibrium exchange rate and allowing the authorities to appreciate the real official exchange rate while simultaneously unifying the exchange markets. The ratio is slightly greater than 1 on average for Africa and South Asia, as the exchange rate was devalued following unification. Again, this is consistent with the observation that in these countries, official exchange rates during the exchange control period were overvalued relative to their long-run equilibrium rates, so that unification required the devaluation of the official rate.

The relationship between the unified official rate and the prior parallel rate also differs somewhat among the subsamples. The ratio e^u_{t+1}/e^p_{t-1} clearly is less than 1 for the entire sample, indicating that in general, the official rate is not depreciated all the way to the level of the former parallel rate. With the exception of Ghana and Bolivia, the average ratio is less than 1 for all countries. This result also is unambiguous for the Latin America and Turkey subset. On the other hand, the ratio e^u_{t+1}/e^p_{t-1} does not appear to be significantly different from 1 for the African and South Asian sample, which is consistent with results described above—average unified official exchange rates appear to be close to the average level of the parallel rate in South Asia and Africa.

Table 12.4 *Unification Episodes—Statistics, Ratios and Binomial Sign Tests*

Country	10	11	12	13	14
	Official RER, year, unif −1, e^{ou}_{t-1}	Official RER, year, unif +1, e^u_{t+1}	Parallel RER, year, unif −1, e^p_{t-1}	e^u_{t+1}/e^{ou}_{t-1} 11/10	e^u_{t+1}/e^p_{t-1} 11/12
Latin America and Turkey					
Mean	85.15	85.62	109.31	1.00	0.83
Median	81.99	75.74	101.98	0.98	0.87
Std Dev	29.89	33.19	54.88	0.09	0.15
Number < 1	n.a.	n.a.	n.a.	9	15
Number > 1	n.a.	n.a.	n.a.	7	1
Pr (H_0 is true)	n.a.	n.a.	n.a.	0.576	0.001
Africa and South Asia					
Mean	183.67	201.50	203.81	1.08	0.98
Median	172.71	155.21	180.99	1.11	0.94
Std Dev	71.92	87.56	85.81	0.12	0.13
Number < 1	n.a.	n.a.	n.a.	1	4
Number > 1	n.a.	n.a.	n.a.	4	1
Pr (H_0 is true)	n.a.	n.a.	n.a.	0.188	0.188
All Countries					
Mean	108.61	113.21	131.81	1.02	0.86
Median	99.42	83.77	118.08	1.00	0.90
Std Dev	60.60	71.42	75.28	0.11	0.16
Number < 1	n.a.	n.a.	n.a.	10	19
Number > 1	n.a.	n.a.	n.a.	11	2
Pr (H_0 is true)	n.a.	n.a.	n.a.	0.500	0.0001

Source: IFS; *World Currency Yearbook*, and *International Currency Analysis Inc.*, various issues; authors' calculations.

Summary and Conclusions

This section now summarizes the most important findings presented in this chapter. To begin with, our theoretical analysis indicated that when the emergence of a parallel exchange market is motivated by the over-valuation of the official exchange rate relative to the long-run equilibrium real exchange rate, the parallel market rate is likely, on average, to be more depreciated than the long-run equilibrium real exchange rate. The gap between the parallel rate and the long-run equilibrium rate is likely to be smaller to the extent that export receipt surrender requirements *are not* well enforced and to the extent that barriers to imports and other commercial policies that tend to appreciate the short-run equilibrium real exchange rate *are* well enforced.

Moreover, our theoretical analysis indicated that even if the official exchange rate is set at its long-run equilibrium level, a parallel market may arise in order to meet the demands of residents seeking to augment their holdings of foreign assets. During the period in which foreign assets are being accumulated—that is, when capital flight is occurring—the parallel exchange rate will be more depreciated than its own equilibrium value, and hence probably more depreciated than the long-run equilibrium exchange rate for the economy as a whole. Additionally, because the parallel market rate is an asset price, and exhibits the volatility that is characteristic of all asset prices, the value of the parallel rate at any given moment is likely to be a particularly poor indicator of the long-run equilibrium exchange rate.

These considerations suggest that on balance, the parallel rate is likely to be more depreciated than the long-run equilibrium real exchange rate, and hence the official exchange rate in a unified exchange market will in general best be set at a level that is more appreciated than the prior parallel rate (averaged over a suitably long period).

In this chapter, we did not compare actual parallel exchange rates to estimates of the long-run equilibrium rate in different countries, owing to the difficulty of estimating equilibrium rates for a large sample. However, we compared multiyear averages of real parallel rates to real official rates in a sample of 24 developing countries and made a number of empirical observations.

First, we found that for the sample as a whole, the real parallel market rate was generally more depreciated than the official exchange rate, even when the official rate was measured only during periods in which the exchange markets were unified. During periods in which the exchange market is unified and there are no exchange controls to bridge the gap between supplies and demands for foreign exchange, the official exchange rate is more likely to be close to the long-run equilibrium rate on average. Hence, these two observations constitute partial evidence that the parallel rate tends to be undervalued relative to the long-run equilibrium exchange rate.

Second, we found important differences in the relationship between parallel and official exchange rates among different subsets of our country sample. In Latin America and in Turkey, the emergence of parallel exchange markets appears to have reflected a sharp depreciation of the short-run equilibrium exchange rate relative to its long-run value, *not* the appreciation of the official exchange rate from its long-run equilibrium value. In those countries, the parallel rate was clearly depreciated compared with the official exchange rate during periods in which the exchange markets were unified. However, the undervalued nature of the parallel rate does not appear to have reflected the overvaluation of the official exchange rate relative to the long-run equilibrium real exchange rate during periods of exchange controls, since the official exchange rate in this subset was on average more depreciated during the periods in which exchange controls were in effect than in the periods in which markets were unified.

We surmise that a combination of internal and external shocks led to macroeconomic turbulence and capital flight in Latin America and Turkey, mainly in the 1980s. These developments, in turn, depreciated the short-run equilibrium real exchange rate relative to its long-run level. While the authorities depreciated their official exchange rates—possibly even to levels more depreciated than the long-run equilibrium rate—they did not do so by enough to resolve excess demands for foreign exchange. That is, even if official exchange rates during the exchange control period were undervalued relative to the long-run equilibrium rate, they were overvalued relative to the short-run equilibrium rate, thereby giving rise to parallel exchange markets. As a result, the parallel rates probably were even more undervalued relative to the long-run equilibrium rate than were the official rates.[20]

Third, we found that the African and South Asian countries in our sample better fit our preconception that the emergence of parallel exchange markets reflects the overvaluation of the official exchange rate relative to its long-run equilibrium value. Among the few countries in this subset that experienced periods of unified exchange rates, the real official exchange rate clearly was more appreciated during periods in

---

20. Although they were not included in our sample, the situation in the transition economies appears to have been similar to that in the Latin American countries with the parallel rates significantly undervalued relative to the long-run equilibrium rate. Hence, a policy of unifying at the parallel rate would have led to an initial RER that was significantly undervalued relative to the long-term equilibrium. (Halpern and Wyplosz 1997).

which exchange controls were in effect than in periods in which exchange markets were unified. This suggests that in contrast to the Latin America and Turkey case, the real appreciation of official exchange rates in Africa and South Asia, relative to long-run equilibrium values, was the main factor underlying the emergence of parallel markets.

However, in Africa and South Asia, the parallel exchange rate was not significantly more depreciated than the official exchange rate during periods in which markets were unified—put another way, when exchange markets were unified, the authorities had to depreciate the official rate all the way to the level of the former parallel rate. The relative similarity of parallel and unified official exchange rates underscores the fact that in the case of some African countries, exchange controls may have been so poorly enforced that the parallel rate effectively mimicked the role of the official rate in a unified exchange market. Additionally, in some Asian countries, well-enforced import barriers constrained the demand for foreign exchange when exchange controls were in effect, thereby appreciating both the short-run equilibrium exchange rate and the parallel rate; exchange markets were unified at about the same time as import barriers were lowered, making it necessary to depreciate the official exchange rate substantially in order to maintain the balance of payments in a unified market.

Our findings for some African and South Asian countries suggest that in some cases, the parallel rate might indeed be reasonably close to the long-run equilibrium real exchange rate that would prevail in a unified market. However, this finding cannot be relied upon to support the use of the parallel rate as a proxy for the long-run equilibrium unified rate more generally because somewhat special factors were operative in these countries—specifically, very poorly enforced exchange controls in some African countries, and very well-enforced import controls in some South Asian countries. More generally, the parallel market rate would seem to represent an upper bound, in terms of local currency per dollar, on the appropriate level of the unified official exchange rate.

Appendix

Sensitivity of Results to Choice of Real Exchange Rate

In order to simplify the calculations, the empirical analysis in this chapter was carried out with bilateral RERs computed using the U.S. producer price index as a proxy for world prices. This procedure may bias the results, particularly for time periods in which movements in the U.S. real exchange rate diverge significantly from those of other industrial countries, as they did over much of the 1980s. We estimate the same ratios as in table 12.3, using trade-weighted multilateral real exchange rates (see tables 12.A.1 and 12.A.2 below).

Data were available in the International Financial Statistics database of the IMF for only 10 of the 24 countries in our sample, for the time period of 1979–94. While it would be possible to calculate multilateral real exchange rates for all the countries in the sample, for the period under consideration this computation would be a laborious process. Further, this data set covers a shorter time period than the one used in the study (1970 to 1994). However, the real U.S. dollar bilateral rate would have diverged significantly from the trade-weighted multilateral rate primarily in the 1980s; this data set includes the period of interest. Therefore we use the smaller readily available data set to compare the values obtained for the ratios we calculate using the bilateral real exchange rate with those for available trade-weighted, multilateral real exchange rates.

The use of multilateral exchange rates yields estimates of the ratios under consideration that are remarkably similar to those obtained using bilateral results. The one result that is different is the binomial sign test for the ratio e^{nu}/e^{u}. The probability that H_0 is true is much higher when the multilateral rate is used. This is probably due to the very small sample: just five observations. The orders of magnitude do not differ markedly for the measures of central tendency.

535

Table 12.A.1 Comparison of Bilateral and Multilateral Exchange Rates

Variable	1 Official real ER 1979–94 e	2 Parallel real ER e^p	3 Official ER w/ par. mkt. e^{mu}	4 Official ER when unified e^u	5 Ratio, e^p/e 2/1	6 Ratio, e^{mu}/e 3/1	7 Ratio, e^p/e^{mu} 2/3	8 Ratio, e^p/e^u 2/4	9 Ratio, e^{mu}/e^u 3/4
Summary statistics									
Mean									
Bilateral	118.09	191.01	118.69	87.68	1.55	1.01	1.55	1.62	1.19
Multilateral	175.73	279.88	172.69	149.36	1.53	1.00	1.56	1.50	1.10
Median									
Bilateral	106.28	168.57	104.21	72.18	1.36	1.00	1.36	1.60	1.19
Multilateral	132.80	186.09	124.66	103.88	1.38	1.00	1.40	1.54	1.12
Standard deviation									
Bilateral	54.66	116.71	54.10	35.74	0.37	0.06	0.42	0.25	0.31
Multilateral	120.95	230.58	117.96	104.42	0.37	0.07	0.43	0.30	0.33
Binomial sign tests									
Number <1									
Bilateral	n.a.	n.a.	n.a.	n.a.	0	6	0	0	2
Multilateral	n.a.	n.a.	n.a.	n.a.	0	8	0	1	3
Number >1									
Bilateral	n.a.	n.a.	n.a.	n.a.	10	4	10	6	4
Multilateral	n.a.	n.a.	n.a.	n.a.	10	2	10	5	3
Pr (H_0 is true)									
Bilateral	n.a.	n.a.	n.a.	n.a.	0.0001	0.377	0.0001	0.0156	0.3438
Multilateral	n.a.	n.a.	n.a.	n.a.	0.0001	0.055	0.0001	0.1094	0.6563

Source: IFS, *World Currency Yearbook,* and *International Currency Analysis, Inc.,* various issues; authors' calculations.

Table 12.A.2 Basic Statistics for All Countries in Sample

Country	ER Type	1 e: Official real ER 1970–94 median	2 e^p: Parallel real ER median	3 e^{nu}: Offical ER with parallel market median	4 e^u: Official ER when unified median	5 e^p/e: 2/1 median	6 e^{nu}/e: 3/1 median	7 e^p/e^{nu}: 2/3 median	8 e^p/e^u: 2/4 median	9 e^{nu}/e^u: 3/4 median
Bolivia	Multilateral	289.00	319.34	244.85	381.72	1.10	0.85	1.30	0.84	0.64
	Bilateral	138.10	152.84	123.30	151.38	1.11	0.89	1.24	1.01	0.81
Chile	Multilateral	136.00	151.50	136.56	91.01	1.11	1.00	1.11	1.66	1.50
	Bilateral	90.36	101.73	91.50	59.75	1.13	1.01	1.11	1.70	1.53
Colombia	Multilateral	157.97	186.99	176.03	102.45	1.18	1.11	1.06	1.83	1.72
	Bilateral	121.17	145.01	133.40	74.55	1.20	1.10	1.09	1.95	1.79
Ecuador	Multilateral	141.94	182.46	141.94	None	1.29	1.00	1.29	n.a.	n.a.
	Bilateral	150.82	189.93	150.82	None	1.26	1.00	1.26	n.a.	n.a.
Uruguay	Multilateral	93.58	110.32	98.84	64.97	1.18	1.06	1.12	1.70	1.52
	Bilateral	71.04	82.95	75.26	40.40	1.17	1.06	1.10	2.05	1.86
Venezuela	Multilateral	143.79	268.09	114.39	181.20	1.86	0.80	2.34	1.48	0.63
	Bilateral	111.29	231.37	100.74	139.19	2.08	0.91	2.30	1.66	0.72
Zambia	Multilateral	104.58	162.84	104.58	None	1.56	1.00	1.56	n.a.	n.a.
	Bilateral	91.50	129.10	91.50	None	1.41	1.00	1.41	n.a.	n.a.
Dom. Rep.	Multilateral	102.28	115.52	100.32	102.86	1.13	0.98	1.15	1.12	0.98
	Bilateral	67.31	84.22	67.71	67.21	1.25	1.01	1.24	1.25	1.01
Malawi	Multilateral	113.53	156.98	113.53	None	1.38	1.00	1.38	n.a.	n.a.
	Bilateral	95.08	132.03	95.08	None	1.39	1.00	1.39	n.a.	n.a.
Nigeria	Multilateral	516.72	806.06	516.72	None	1.56	1.00	1.56	n.a.	n.a.
	Bilateral	252.61	435.02	252.61	None	1.72	1.00	1.72	n.a.	n.a.

Source: IFS, World Currency Yearbook, and International Currency Analysis, Inc., various issues; authors' calculations.

The choice of a bilateral real exchange rate would not seem to affect the results in any significant way. At the same time, using the bilateral real exchange rate has other advantages. In particular, using the bilateral rate permits analysis for a larger sample of countries for a longer time period. However, there are some instances in which the differences in the values using the different real exchange rates are more than trivial (see table 12.A.2, particularly Uruguay and Nigeria (columns 8 and 9). If the analysis is to be done for a single country, the use of the trade-weighted multilateral real exchange rate would be preferable. For a sample as large as the one in this study, the computational advantages of using the bilateral real exchange rate are greater.

13

A Note on Nominal Devaluations, Inflation, and the Real Exchange Rate

Nita Ghei and Lawrence E. Hinkle [*]

Difficult as it may be to accurately estimate the degree of RER misalignment, doing so is only the first step in designing the policies to correct a misalignment. The RER is not a policy variable or instrument. It is an endogenous variable, the level of which is determined by other fundamental macroeconomic variables. Policy makers cannot change the RER directly. Rather, they can only adjust the official nominal exchange rate and other nominal variables, such as monetary and fiscal policy instruments, that may affect the domestic price level.

In industrial countries with relatively low inflation and market-determined exchange rates, short- to medium-term movements in both nominal and real exchange rates are extremely hard to distinguish empirically from driftless random walks. Nominal exchange rates are on average six times more volatile than domestic relative prices. Nominal and real exchange rates are also highly correlated so that there is a pronounced tendency for the real exchange rate to follow the nominal one, particularly in the short to medium term.[1]

---

[*] Ms. Ingrid Ivins provided research and computational assistance in the preparation of this chapter. The authors are grateful to Emmanuel Akpa, Steve Kamin, Peter Montiel, Fabien Nsengiyumva, and three anonymous reviewers for very helpful comments on the drafts of this chapter.

1. See Taylor (1995), p. 31; Frankel and Rose (1995); Stein, Allen, and Associates (1995), pp. 6, 84; Mark (1995); and Chari, Kehoe, and McGrattan (1997).

In developing countries, however, the relationship between the nominal and real exchange rates may be complicated by large fluctuations in the external terms of trade and domestic relative prices, by high or highly variable inflation rates, and by relatively large and volatile capital flows. Nevertheless, a devaluation of the nominal exchange rate appears empirically to be a necessary condition for achieving a large depreciation of the real exchange rate. In fact, empirical research has shown that virtually all large real depreciations have required nominal devaluations.[2] Wages and prices in the formal sector in developing countries generally tend to be fairly rigid downward in nominal terms and at best tend to decline only slowly in relative terms; and, in most circumstances, it is unrealistic to assume a substantial decline in nominal prices and factor costs. Hence, when a substantial depreciation of the RER is required, nominal devaluations are often necessary to accelerate the adjustment in relative domestic prices and factor costs.

A devaluation is not, however, a sufficient condition for achieving a real depreciation as the effects of many devaluations have been quickly eroded by inflation. In addition, in cases of small misalignments (10 percent or less) a devaluation may not be necessary. For example, with a fixed nominal exchange rate, overvaluation of the RER may be gradually eliminated over time if the domestic inflation rate is held below the foreign inflation rate so that the actual RER depreciates to eliminate the initial misalignment or if productivity rises faster at home than abroad so that the equilibrium RER appreciates to eliminate the misalignment.

A devaluation can, nevertheless, facilitate the adjustment of the real exchange rate to its equilibrium level under two conditions. First, the RER must in fact be overvalued before a devaluation so that a devaluation moves the economy toward equilibrium rather than away from it. And, second, a devaluation must be accompanied by a stance of macroeconomic demand management policies that supports the required adjustments in absorption and relative prices rather than frustrates these adjustments.

In many cases, a devaluation is likely to unleash general inflationary pressures on domestic prices as a result of the rapid increase in the prices of tradable goods. In addition, the exchange rate itself sometimes serves as a nominal anchor for a country's monetary and price policies; and a

---

2. See Kiguel and Ghei (1993) and Goldfajn and Valdes (1996). Kiguel and Ghei find that, for low-inflation developing countries, *all* large real depreciations were preceded by large nominal devaluations. Goldfajn and Valdes find for a broad sample of 93 countries that 90 percent of real appreciations of 25 percent or more and 100 percent of real appreciations of 35 percent or more were corrected by nominal devaluations.

devaluation may affect the credibility of monetary policy. Hence, in order to determine the size of a nominal devaluation required to correct a given overvaluation of the RER, one needs to determine to what extent a nominal devaluation will depreciate the RER (and bring about the desired changes in relative domestic wages and prices) and to what extent it will simply raise, or be "passed through" to, the domestic price level.

Achieving a successful depreciation of the RER through a devaluation requires *both* raising the relative price of tradable goods and containing the rise in the general price level. For a devaluation to succeed in depreciating the external RER, the aggregate domestic price level must rise less than the foreign price level rises in domestic-currency terms as a result of the devaluation. To depreciate the internal RER, the price of tradable goods must increase relative to the price of nontradables.[3]

While a number of methodologies are available for determining the change required in the RER as discussed in Part III, the literature on developing countries has devoted much less attention to the problem of determining the change required in the *nominal* exchange rate.[4] The importance of accurately determining the size of the required nominal depreciation, as well as the size of the required real depreciation, depends, in part, upon the type of exchange rate policy that a country plans to pursue after devaluing.

In cases in which a country will need to maintain its new nominal exchange rate for a significant period after a devaluation, it is important to establish accurately the size of the necessary *nominal* change as well as that of the real change. Although the number of countries that are able to sustain a fixed exchange rate policy has declined dramatically in recent years because of increasing capital mobility and financial market integration, there are still some cases, such as the CFA countries, of adjustments from one fixed rate to another.[5] A reasonably accurate

---

3. See Chapters 2 to 4 for the definitions of the external and internal RERs and a discussion of the theoretical and empirical relationships between them. As explained there, in general, the internal and external RERs will move in the same direction unless there are significant changes in the terms of trade, commercial policy, or relative productivity in the tradable and nontradable sectors.

4. The authors are aware of only three papers that deal with the problem of determining the equilibrium nominal exchange rate. For developing countries, Khan and Lizondo (1987) present a model that determines the equilibrium RER and corresponding nominal rate. For industrial countries, Mark (1995) estimates a monetary model of the nominal U.S. dollar, Canadian dollar, Deutschemark, Swiss franc, and yen exchange rates using relative money stocks and relative real incomes. A similar monetary model is employed in MacDonald (1995).

5. See Obstfeld and Rogoff (1995).

estimate of a new equilibrium nominal rate is also required for exchange rate–based stabilization programs, although in this case the new nominal rate may be easier to revise subsequently than when the new rate is intended to be quasi-permanent.[6]

For countries following a flexible postdevaluation exchange rate policy (such as a managed float or a crawling peg), accurately determining the size of the required nominal change may be less critical. A country may simply devalue by the amount corresponding to the required real depreciation, subsequently adjust the nominal exchange rate to offset any inflation in the prices of domestic goods, and thus maintain the initial real depreciation. The stronger a country's monetary discipline and the greater the tendency of its real rate to follow its nominal rate as in industrial countries, the more advantageous such a policy will be.[7] However, even in such cases accurate estimates of the initial changes required in the nominal as well as the real exchange rate will facilitate policy design and minimize unintended inflationary or recessionary consequences of changes in the nominal exchange rate and other nominal policy variables.

Ideally, it would be desirable to have a macroeconomic model that simultaneously determines both the real and nominal values of the equilibrium exchange rate and other key variables in a full general-equilibrium setting. This approach is the one followed for industrial countries

6. Although the new exchange rates introduced under exchange rate–based stabilization programs are often billed as permanent, Caramazza and Aziz (1998) find that these new pegs have typically been short-lived, with a median duration of about 10 months.

7. Several plausible explanations of why the real exchange rate tends to follow the nominal one in industrial countries have been suggested. Large immediate effects of monetary policy on nominal exchange rates coupled with long lags in its effects on domestic economic activity and prices is one such explanation. Downward rigidities in nominal prices and wages could also cause the speed of relative price changes to depend upon the inflation rate, contributing to the observed greater relative price and RER variability in developing countries with higher inflation rates and causing monetary policy to have persistent effects on some real variables in industrial countries. As noted in the chapters on the external RER and trade flows, there is considerable empirical evidence that the law of one price at best holds only loosely in industrial countries for trade in differentiated products, and prices of traded goods respond only very slowly to movements in the nominal exchange rate. Faruqee (1995) and Chari, Kehoe, and McGrattan (1997) argue that such deviations from the law of one price for traded goods and the resulting stickiness in domestic prices of traded goods could cause changes in the nominal exchange rate—and hence in monetary policy, which often drives these—to have long-lasting effects on the real exchange rate in industrial countries.

in Williamson (1994), which uses existing large macroeconomic models for the G-7 countries. However, the required models are not available for most low-income countries; and neither the time nor the data needed for developing them are typically available when a devaluation is being considered. Even in industrial countries it is sometimes necessary to adopt simpler approaches. For example, in estimating equilibrium bilateral nominal exchange rates for the year 2000, Wren-Lewis and Driver (1998) simply assume that inflation rates in the G-7 countries will be roughly similar and that the nominal and real exchange rates will move in parallel.

In the absence of a macroeconomic model that determines nominal as well as relative prices, two sources of guidance are available on the relative sizes of the nominal and real changes that are likely to follow a devaluation: the experience of other developing countries that have devalued and the accounting relationships between the nominal and real changes. This chapter examines the usefulness of these two sources of information for estimating the relationship between changes in the nominal and the real exchange rates. It assumes that an estimate of the required change in the RER is available from one or more of the methodologies discussed in Part III and addresses the problem of how to make practical empirical estimates of the size of a nominal devaluation required to achieve a given depreciation in the internal and external RERs and how to establish consistent targets for the required adjustments in nominal and relative domestic wages and prices.

The next section of the chapter begins by briefly reviewing the inflationary experiences of developing countries after large devaluations and summarizes the stylized empirical facts about the relationship between nominal devaluations, inflation, and the external RER. The subsequent section then sets out a simple accounting framework linking the nominal exchange rate, the internal and external RERs, the general price level, relative prices of tradables and nontradables, and nominal and real wages in domestic- and foreign-currency terms. The use of this framework is illustrated by an analysis of the changes in wages, prices, the real exchange rate, and related variables in Côte d'Ivoire as a result of the January 1994 devaluation of the CFA franc. Although the accounting framework is relatively simple, it can provide, in the absence of a more sophisticated methodology, a starting point for determining a realistic and consistent set of nominal and real prices *if* reasonable assumptions can be made about the postdevaluation behavior of a nominal anchor on the basis of either the stylized facts from experience elsewhere or of the specific policy program accompanying a devaluation. The final section of the chapter concludes with a discussion of the advantages and limitations of the accounting framework.

Devaluations, Inflation, and the External RER: the Stylized Facts

As noted above, the domestic price level nearly always rises after a devaluation of the nominal exchange rate as a consequence of higher local-currency prices of both final and intermediate traded goods. Increases in the price level and the redistributional effects of changes in relative prices are the reasons why devaluations are often approached with trepidation.

Historically, devaluations have had a decidedly mixed impact on inflation and real exchange rate alignment in developing countries. During the 1950s and 1960s, a period of relatively low world inflation and stable nominal exchange rates, devaluations were fairly successful in depreciating RERs without excessive inflation. In the more inflationary 1970s and 1980s, on the other hand, inflation-devaluation-inflation cycles that resulted in little change in the RER were much more common and led to considerable pessimism (known as "nominal exchange rate pessimism") about the usefulness of devaluations for realigning relative prices.

There are three sources of concern about devaluations and inflation: (a) the relationship between the devaluation and the actual misalignment, if any, of the exchange rate; (b) the effectiveness of a nominal devaluation in depreciating the internal RER by achieving the required increase in the relative price of traded goods; and (c) the possible longer-term impact of a devaluation on price stability and the trend inflation rate. First, only if the RER is initially overvalued will a devaluation depreciate the RER toward its equilibrium level. If, in fact, the RER is correctly aligned initially, a devaluation will move the RER away from equilibrium and create excess demand in the market for nontraded goods (by reducing their relative price from the equilibrium level) that will appreciate the RER back toward the original equilibrium. Second, even if the exchange rate is initially overvalued, it is still often feared that an increase in the price of traded goods due to a devaluation will also lead to an increase in the price of nontraded goods as well through inadequate monetary and fiscal discipline, indexation of wages and prices, or market power and demonstration effects. If the increase in the price of nontraded goods is large enough to offset most of the impact of a nominal devaluation on relative prices, a devaluation will then merely result in raising the general price level, without achieving the desired depreciation of the internal RER and change in relative domestic prices. Third, even if a devaluation is successful in realigning relative prices, it could, by changing expectations about the future path of prices, result in a permanent increase in the trend inflation rate. A country could, in a worst-case scenario, get trapped in an accelerating inflation-devaluation spiral without ever depreciating its RER except temporarily.

Since theoretically many combinations of changes in the general price level and relative prices are possible after a devaluation, it is desirable to have some measure of the effectiveness of a nominal devaluation in achieving a real depreciation. To measure the effects of a devaluation on domestic inflation and the external RER, both a "pass-through co-efficient" and an "effectiveness index" are often calculated.[8] The external RER is defined in domestic-currency terms as shown by equation 13.1:

$$(13.1) \qquad ERER_{dc} = E_{dc} \cdot \frac{P_{Gf}}{P_{Gd}}.$$

Assuming for convenience that the initial foreign price level is 1.0 and log differentiating equation 13.1 above yields the following approxima-tion (equation 13.2) for small changes in the variables:

$$(13.2) \qquad \widehat{ERER_{dc}} \cong \widehat{E_{dc}} - \widehat{P_{Gd}}$$

where the hat operator ("^") applied to any variable x has the standard meaning of $\Delta x/x$. Dividing by E_{dc} and rearranging the terms yields equa-tion 13.3:

$$(13.3) \qquad \frac{\widehat{ERER_{dc}}}{\hat{E}_{dc}} + \frac{\widehat{P_{gd}}}{\hat{E}_{dc}} \cong 1.$$

The first term $\widehat{ERER_{dc}} / \hat{E}_{dc}$ is what Edwards (1989) defines as the effec-tiveness index of a devaluation. It indicates how much of a nominal devaluation is translated into a depreciation of the external RER. The second term $\hat{P}_{gd} / \hat{E}_{dc}$ is the pass-through coefficient. It indicates how much of devaluation is simply reflected in increased prices.[9] Note that the term "pass-through coefficient" is used in the literature with two slightly dif-ferent meanings. Sometimes it is used, as here, to refer to the pass-through

---

8. Virtually all of the empirical work on devaluations and inflation has fo-cused on the aggregate domestic price level and the external RER because data on internal RERs, domestic relative prices, and wages are not readily available for many developing countries. For this reason, the discussion of the stylized facts in this section is also largely in terms of the external RER.

9. The additive linear approximation in equation 13.3 of the relationship be-tween the pass-through coefficient and the effectiveness index is, however, only valid for small (marginal) percentage changes. For "maxi" devaluations and other large percentage changes in the variables, it is necessary to use the actual multi-plicative relationship between the pass-through coefficient and the effectiveness index.

of the effects of a nominal exchange rate change to the general domestic price level; and sometimes it refers more narrowly to the pass-through of changes in foreign prices, tariffs, or the exchange rate just to the domestic prices of traded goods.

Nominal Devaluation Pessimism

Pessimism about a nominal devaluation's effectiveness in achieving a real depreciation was fed by the experiences of a number of developing countries in the 1970s and 1980s—a period characterized by accelerating global inflation in which the initial depreciation of the real exchange rate achieved by a devaluation often appeared to be eroded quite rapidly by inflation. The Philippines, for example, undertook large devaluations in the early 1980s but achieved almost no depreciation in its RER as most of the nominal devaluation was negated by domestic price increases. In other countries such as Argentina, which experienced high inflation and repeated devaluations, indexation or dollarization often became widespread and changes in the exchange rate were quickly reflected in domestic prices.[10]

However, subsequent, more systematic analysis of the empirical evidence produced less pessimistic conclusions. Kamin (1988) examined a sample of about 70 large or maxi-devaluations of 15 percent or greater that took place between 1953 and 1983 and for which data were available. Kamin found that, relative to nondevaluing countries, the RERs of the devaluing countries were significantly more depreciated three years after a devaluation.

Edwards (1989) reached similar conclusions. He examined a sample of 29 devaluations under fixed exchange rate regimes and 9 devaluations by countries that adopted crawling pegs after the devaluation. Edwards defined a devaluation as successful if, after three years, it had resulted in a depreciation of the external RER of 30 percent or more of the nominal devaluation expressed in domestic-currency terms—that is, if it had an effectiveness index of at least 30 percent or, equivalently, if the pass-through coefficient was 54 percent or less.

Edwards found that about one-third (10) out of the 29 cases of stepwise devaluations under fixed exchange rate regimes were successful and that on average in these countries two-thirds of the nominal devaluation was translated into a depreciation of the external RER (that is, an average effectiveness index of 67 percent). However, in the other two-thirds of the cases of devaluations under fixed exchange rate regimes either the initial effect of the nominal devaluation on the external RER

---

10. See Inter-American Development Bank (1995), p. 234.

was completely wiped out within three years or less (8 cases) or less than 30 percent of the nominal devaluation was ultimately reflected in the depreciation of the external RER (12 cases).

Countries with crawling pegs achieved larger real depreciations on average, as one would expect, but this relative success was purchased at the price of higher inflation. As in the case of fixed exchange rates, in only one-third of the cases of crawling pegs was more than 30 percent of the cumulative nominal devaluation translated into a real depreciation. In the other two-thirds of the crawling peg cases, only a small real depreciation was achieved at the expense of accelerating inflation. Edwards concluded by stressing the importance of monetary and fiscal discipline and other accompanying measures to restrain inflation for successfully translating a nominal devaluation into as large a real depreciation as possible. [11]

Additional evidence suggests that, in the right circumstances, devaluations can be quite effective in achieving a real depreciation. Kiguel and Ghei (1993) examined the hypothesis that low-inflation countries might be more successful in controlling the inflationary effects of large devaluations because of the continuation of the very policies and institutional arrangements that had led them to have low predevaluation inflation rates to start with. They analyzed a sample of *all* 33 large or maxi-devaluations (specifically, those between 20 percent and 200 percent in domestic-currency terms) since the 1950s in low-inflation countries (specifically, countries with an annual inflation rate of 15 percent or less for the three years preceding the devaluation). They found that about 60 percent of the initial depreciation in the external RER was maintained three years after the event—about the same average effectiveness index as in Edwards' cases of *successful* devaluations.

Most of the devaluation episodes in low-inflation countries took place in the 1950s and 1960s, when fixed exchange rates were prevalent and global inflation was low. Devaluations then were regarded as discrete events and therefore appear to have had a higher probability of success than in the more inflationary 1970s and 1980s. This relatively greater success rate was partly due to less indexation of wages and other prices then. The infrequency of devaluations at that time probably also meant that they were not as likely to generate expectations of further devaluations, and economic agents with market power did not act immediately to offset the full impact of the devaluation by increasing prices. However, some of the episodes in Kiguel's and Ghei's sample of low-inflation countries did take place in the higher-inflation 1970s (Pakistan in 1972 and Egypt in 1979) yet were still successful in depreciating the real

---

11. See also Kiguel (1992).

exchange rate. Experiences such as those of Chile and Morocco also suggest that in successful devaluations 30 to 65 percent of the nominal devaluation is typically translated into a depreciation of the external RER, with the overall increase in the price level offsetting anywhere from 20 percent to 55 percent of the devaluation.

Chhibber (1991) notes that nominal devaluation pessimism in Africa resulted mainly from the experiences of Ghana and Zimbabwe although he also cites some other cases. In simulations of devaluations, Chhibber found that the pass-through effect of a devaluation on inflation is generally larger than the share of imports in GDP even for successful devaluations. For Ghana, for which the share of imports in GDP is 0.20, Chhibber found a pass-through coefficient of 0.40. On the other hand, Chhibber also found that if the fiscal deficit is not kept under control, the resulting additional inflation can completely wipe out the initial effect of the nominal devaluation on the external RER. In a best-case scenario with more optimistic assumptions about postdevaluation fiscal performance and supply response in Zimbabwe, Chhibber found that only one-third of a nominal devaluation would be offset by inflation and a real depreciation of 50 percent would be achieved.

More recently, Kamin (1998) in a study of 38 Asian, Latin American, and industrialized countries examines the relationships between exchange rate competitiveness, changes in the nominal exchange rate, and inflation. Although Kamin is constrained by the size of his sample to using an imperfect relative-PPP-based measure of misalignment, he does find that, statistically, a depreciated (undervalued) RER leads to higher inflation and an appreciated (overvalued) RER to lower inflation. This tendency is particularly strong in Latin American countries with a history of higher inflation and rigidities to depreciating the RER, in which the responsiveness of inflation to nominal depreciations is significantly higher than in Asian and industrialized countries. Kamin also finds some evidence that "prior inflation, by raising the sensitivity of institutions and expectations to inflationary shocks, raises the responsiveness of inflation to exchange rate changes." Thus, high-inflation countries may tend to have higher pass-through coefficients than low-inflation ones.[12]

The Time Path of Inflation

Thus, some increase in the price level is usually unavoidable after a devaluation since the rise in the domestic-currency price of traded goods

---

12. See also Calvo, Reinhart, and Vegh (1995) for a further discussion of the theory and empirical evidence that excessive devaluations and undervaluation lead to higher inflation.

to reflect the new nominal exchange rate leads to a one-time upward shift in the general price level. What is the typical time profile of the increase in prices? Kamin (1988) examined this question for all developing countries that implemented large devaluations, and Kiguel and Ghei (1993) looked at the experiences of a subgroup of low-inflation countries. Although the beginning and ending inflation rates were, of course, higher in the larger sample than in the subgroup of low-inflation countries, inflation followed a broadly similar pattern in both groups of devaluing countries as shown in table 13.1. The prices of final and intermediate traded goods usually rise quickly after a devaluation; but wages, other factor costs, and the prices of nontraded goods generally respond with various lags to a devaluation. Most of the adjustment in prices typically takes place in the 12 months after the devaluation. The inflation rate normally rises sharply right after the devaluation and remains higher than the trend level for the two years after the devaluation as the changes in domestic-currency prices of tradable goods work themselves through the economy. The inflation rate then typically falls back toward historical levels by the third year after the devaluation. Some acceleration in inflation is also likely in the year preceding a devaluation, particularly if the devaluation is anticipated.

Effect on the Long-Term Inflation Rate

The evidence on the long-term impact of a devaluation on trend inflation rates is mixed. Kamin (1988) found that the trend inflation rate in devaluing countries increased. However, nondevaluing countries in

Table 13.1 *The Time Path of Inflation after Large Devaluations in Developing Countries*

	Median inflation rates in percent					
	Years				Difference between years	
Countries	D − 3	D − 1	D	D + 3	D + 3 and D − 3	D + 3 and D − 1
All Devaluing Countries	9.9	14.0	17.3	13.9	4.0	−0.1
Low-Inflation Countries	3.6	4.7	5.6	5.1	1.5	−0.4

Sources: Kamin (1988) for all devaluing countries and Kiguel and Ghei (1993) for low-inflation countries.

Kamin's control group also experienced rising inflation rates, and the evidence from the study suggests that there was no difference in the inflation performance of the two sets of countries. Kiguel and Ghei (1993) find that the effect of a nominal devaluation on long-term inflation was quite limited in low-inflation countries as the data in table 13.1 above indicate. In their sample, inflation rates three years after a devaluation were, on average, very close to those prevailing before the event.

The Importance of Disciplined Accompanying Policies

The effects of a particular devaluation on the real exchange rate and inflation depend ultimately on the policies that accompany a devaluation, not just on the devaluation itself. Hence, one's ability to predict the outcome of a devaluation depends, among other things, on the ability to predict the policies that will accompany it. If monetary growth is kept in check, demand management (particularly fiscal policy) is appropriate, and wage push is avoided, there is no reason why a devaluation that moves the RER in the direction of its long-run equilibrium value cannot result in a long-term depreciation of the RER without permanently increasing the inflation rate. On the other hand, as experience has shown, if these conditions are not met, inflation will quickly offset the initial depreciation of the RER.

While it is important to find a firm nominal anchor for monetary policy, and a fixed exchange rate may play this role, empirical evidence suggests that neither the adoption of a flexible exchange rate policy nor a devaluation under a fixed exchange rate regime by themselves necessarily need trigger higher inflation. Edwards, Kiguel, and Ghei, and Chhibber all conclude that the success of a devaluation ultimately depends on the accompanying polices. Chhibber credits the low inflation rates of the CFA zone countries not to their fixed exchange rate per se, but to the monetary discipline imposed by the conditions of membership in the zone. Similarly, the external RER tracked the nominal exchange rate closely in the 1980s and early 1990s in Malaysia, which had a flexible exchange rate regime, because it also had disciplined macroeconomic policies and low inflation. In contrast, countries such as Zambia and the Philippines in the 1980s that devalued often or moved to crawling pegs typically failed to adopt disciplined monetary and fiscal policies. The results were not surprising: higher inflation without any marked reduction in the overvaluation of the real exchange rate.[13]

---

13. The implications of fixed vs. flexible exchange rate regimes for inflation and growth have also been a subject of continuing research interest. For a summary of the historical evidence, see Ghosh and others (1996), who use a

Summary of the Stylized Facts

Both theoretically and empirically, any combination of RER realignment and inflation is possible after a devaluation: a depreciation, an appreciation, or no change in the external RER accompanied by an acceleration of inflation or a return to predevaluation price trends. The empirical evidence shows that the effectiveness index and pass-through coefficient are both variables, not fixed parameters, that may take on quite different values in different circumstances.

In general, the pass-through coefficient is likely to be higher, and the effectiveness index lower, in high-inflation countries such as those in Latin America than in lower-inflation countries such as those in Asia and Africa. The key to a successful devaluation is monetary discipline and appropriate demand management policies. The probability of success is also higher in countries with a history of low inflation because of the policy traditions and institutional arrangements that led these countries to have low predevaluation inflation rates in the first place. Successful devaluations (those accompanied by appropriate macroeconomic policies) in open developing economies have typically led to a depreciation of the external RER of 30 to 70 percent of the nominal devaluation

comprehensive database to study the link between exchange rate regimes, inflation, and growth. They find that: "Two sturdy stylized facts emerge. First, inflation is both lower and more stable under pegged regimes, reflecting both slower money supply and faster money demand growth. Second, real volatility is higher under pegged regimes. In contrast, growth varies only slightly across regimes, though investment is somewhat higher and trade growth somewhat lower under pegged regimes. Pegged regimes are thus characterized by lower inflation but more pronounced output volatility." Lane (1994) finds that inflation is inversely related to openness (controlling for country size) and that more open economies were more able to choose and more likely to maintain fixed exchange rates. However, in an analysis of the recent experience with increasing capital market integration and the replacement of fixed by flexible exchange rates in the 1990s, Caramazza and Aziz (1998) find that the differences in inflation and output growth between fixed and flexible regimes are no longer significant. They also find that misalignment and currency "crashes" are equally likely under pegged and flexible exchange rate regimes, in part because relatively few developing countries have had truly floating exchange rates and some of those that had an officially declared flexible policy were in fact pursuing an unofficial target rate. Caramazza and Aziz conclude that: "The average inflation rate for countries with flexible exchange rates has fallen steadily to where it is no longer significantly different from that of countries with fixed rates. The perceived need for greater [exchange rate] flexibility has probably resulted from increasing globalization of financial markets—which has integrated developing economies more closely into the global financial system. This in turn imposes an often strict discipline on their macroeconomic policies."

in domestic-currency terms, with the RER depreciating on impact by the full amount of the devaluation and then gradually appreciating as the domestic price level shifts upward. The aggregate price level has typically shifted upward by 20 to 55 percent of the amount of the nominal devaluation—two to three times the share of imports in GDP. Most of the upward shift in the price level has occurred in the first year, with the inflation rate dropping back to its trend level over the course of the second year. No increase in the long-term trend inflation rate has typically resulted from successful devaluations.

Because of the numerous different possibilities, unsuccessful devaluations are more difficult to characterize. They often lead to increased inflation and a depreciation of the external RER that is less than 30 percent of the cumulative change in the nominal exchange rate—and may, under a fixed exchange rate regime, result in no change in, or even an appreciation of, the external RER. The probability of success is lower in high-inflation countries in which frequent devaluations have generated expectations of further inflation, and devaluations and economic agents with market power act immediately to offset the full impact of a devaluation by increasing prices. In addition, in cases in which the exchange rate is appropriately aligned to start with, a devaluation will move the RER away from, rather than toward, equilibrium and generate inflationary pressures tending to appreciate it back to its original level.

An Accounting Framework for Determining Consistent Nominal and Relative Prices

The above stylized facts indicate that a wide range of outcomes is possible after a devaluation and that the policies accompanying a devaluation play a critical role in determining which of the many possible outcomes actually occurs in a particular case. However, the stylized facts say little about the changes in key nominal and relative prices that must take place to realign the internal RER. Because of lack of data very little empirical work has been done on the changes in internal relative prices that take place after a devaluation.

Because of the multiplicity of factors affecting the pass-through coefficient, the lack of time-series data for measuring many of these, and the key role played by accompanying policies, it would be difficult to construct a predictive model accurate enough for policy analysis in a range of different country cases. Hence, the remainder of this chapter takes a different approach: it sets out a simple accounting framework that can be used for analyzing alternative policy scenarios and calculating consistent sets of nominal and relative prices that will result from these.

The following section first summarizes the accounting framework, the individual equations of which are discussed in more detail in the appendix. It then illustrates the use of this consistency framework for analyzing alternative devaluations and policy scenarios.

The Consistency Framework

The full accounting system is based on a two-good framework with a tradable and nontradable sector. It is is composed of the following eight equations (13.4 to 13.11) set out in the appendix.

1. The definition of the external RER:

(13.4)
$$ERER_{dc} = E_{dc} \cdot \frac{P_{Gf}}{P_{Gd}}.$$

2. The law of one price:

(13.5)
$$P_{Td} = E_{dc} \cdot (1+t) \cdot P_{Tf}$$

where t is the average tariff on final goods.

3. The definition of the internal RER for traded goods expressed relative to the general domestic price level:

(13.6)
$$IRERT_G = \frac{P_{Td}}{P_{Gd}} = \frac{E_{dc} \cdot P_{Tf}(1+t)}{P_{Gd}}.$$

4. The definition of the general price index:

(13.7)
$$P_{Gd} = \tau \cdot E_{dc} \cdot P_{Tf}(1+t) + (1-\tau)P_{Nd}$$

where τ is the weight of tradables in the index.

5. The allocation of the cost of nontraded goods between imported inputs and domestic factor costs (F_N):

(13.8)
$$P_{Nd} = \alpha \cdot E_{dc} \cdot P_{Tf}(1+t_m) + (1-\alpha)F_N$$

where α is the share of imported inputs in the cost of producing nontraded goods.

6. The allocation of factor payments in the nontraded sector between wages (W_d) and profits (π):

(13.9)
$$F_N = \lambda \cdot W_d + (1 - \lambda) \cdot \pi$$

where λ is the share of wages.

7. An assumption about the rate of increase in nominal wages and profits after a devaluation:

(13.10)
$$\frac{\Delta W_d}{W_d} = \frac{\Delta \pi}{\pi}.$$

8. The definition of the real wage:

(13.11)
$$w_G = \frac{W_d}{P_{Gd}}.$$

The above system of 8 equations contains 14 variables, of which 4 are exogenous and 10 endogenous. The 4 exogenous variables are the foreign price of traded goods, P_{Tf}, the aggregate foreign price level, P_{Gf}, and the 2 home country trade tax rates on imports of final goods, t, and inputs, t_m. The first 2 of the exogenous variables are determined by assumptions about the international economic environment, and the latter 2 are policy variables.

The first 3 of the 10 endogenous variables are exchange rates: the nominal exchange rate (E_{dc}), the external RER ($ERER_{dc}$), and the internal RER ($IRERT_G$). The other 7 endogenous variables are the general domestic price level (P_{Gd}), the domestic price of nontraded goods (P_{Nd}), the domestic price of traded goods (P_{Td}), payments to domestic factors of production (F_N) in the nontraded sector, nominal wages (W_d), nominal profits (π), and the real wage (w_G).

The above system also has three structural parameters—τ, the weight of traded goods in the aggregate home country price index; α, the share of traded inputs in the cost of producing nontraded goods; and λ, the share of wages in value added in producing nontraded goods. The empirical values of these in Côte d'Ivoire were estimated at 0.22, 0.11, and 0.7, respectively, as explained in the appendix. Variations in the structural parameters will cause a given nominal devaluation to have a greater or lesser inflationary impact (and effect on real wages), depending upon whether they are higher or lower. The sensitivity of the calculations to different assumptions about these parameters is analyzed in scenarios 2 and 4 below.

Since the accounting framework has 8 equations but 10 endogenous variables, the values of 2 of the 10 endogenous variables need to be specified to solve for the other 8 variables. A target for 1 real variable can be specified ex ante—for example, the postrealignment internal or external RER. But a target for the RER is only enough to solve for relative prices. A nominal variable—for example, the domestic price level, nominal wage rate, or nominal exchange rate—also needs to be specified in order to solve for nominal prices. Fixing the value of such a nominal variable is the "nominal anchor" problem. Thus, the values of 2 variables need to be determined outside the system to obtain a solution: a real variable and a nominal anchor or 2 nominal variables (such as the nominal exchange rate and wage rate).

To briefly illustrate the interaction of the above equations, a nominal devaluation (an increase in E_{dc}) will, other things being equal, raise the domestic-currency price of traded goods relative to nontraded goods and initially depreciate the internal RER accordingly. A 100 percent nominal devaluation would double the price of foreign exchange in domestic currency and thus double the price of traded goods (both final and intermediate) in domestic currency if there are no changes in taxes and subsidies on traded goods (equation 13.2). A reduction in import tariffs or export subsidies would attenuate the domestic price increase. A devaluation would also result in some increase (equation 13.8) in the domestic price of nontraded goods, proportionate to the share of traded inputs, α, even if there are no changes in nominal profits and nominal wages. The increase in the domestic-currency price of traded goods will also raise the general level of domestic prices, proportionate to the share of traded goods in output or absorption, τ, (equation 13.7) and to the share of traded goods as inputs in the production of nontraded goods, α (equation 13.8). Any increase in nominal wages or profits will further raise the price of nontraded goods and the general price level (equation 13.9), offsetting some or all of the rest of the initial depreciation in the RER.

A key assumption underlying the use of the above framework is that the RER is initially overvalued and the objective is to depreciate it by no more than the amount required so that a devaluation and the corresponding changes in relative prices will reflect a movement back toward equilibrium. The behavior of nominal wages and profits in the nontraded sector after a devaluation is also critical. Equations 13.9 and 13.10 assume that producers of nontraded goods can raise their prices only to the extent that their costs increase. That is, they behave competitively and do not have the market power to automatically increase the price of nontraded goods by the full amount of the realignment in the nominal exchange rate. A change in the relative prices of traded and nontraded goods and a depreciation of the RER are not possible if nominal wages and profits in the nontraded sector rise in proportion to a devaluation.

The ability to make reasonably accurate assumptions about the postdevaluation behavior of wages, profits, and prices is the key to the usefulness of this framework empirically. Monetary and fiscal policies also need to be designed to achieve the target value for the chosen nominal anchor and the required behavior of nominal wages. The approach used in the devaluation of the CFA franc in 1994 was to make the change in nominal wages the critical policy target of the economic policies accompanying the devaluation.[14]

The consistency framework, however, permits one to model the behavior of wages and prices in a number of different ways. For example, nominal wages may be assumed to respond to movements in the domestic price level, as shown in equation 13.12:

(13.12) $$\Delta W_d = \rho_1 \cdot \Delta P_{Gd}, \quad O \le \rho_1 \le 1$$

where ρ_1 is a reaction coefficient. When $\rho_1 = 1$, there is full indexation, and no adjustment in the real wage is possible. For countries that have undergone repeated nominal devaluations, nominal wages may be assumed to respond to movements in the nominal exchange rate, as shown by equation 13.13:

(13.13) $$\Delta W_d = \rho_2 \cdot \Delta E_{dc}, \quad O \le \rho_2 \le 1$$

where ρ_2 is again a reaction coefficient. Alternatively, the new real wage may be specified as a percentage of the initial one (equation 13.14):

(13.14) $$\frac{W_d}{P_{Gd}} = \rho_3 \cdot \left(\frac{W_{dc}}{P_{Gd_o}} \right)$$

where ρ_3 is the ratio of the new real wage to the initial one.[15] Equation 13.10 can also be modified to allow for differential changes in wages and profits. Numerous alternative scenarios can be analyzed, as

---

14. Standard methodologies exist for using monetary and fiscal policies to target nominal variables such as the domestic price level or the nominal exchange rate. In order to design an appropriate policy package to accompany a devaluation, such a methodology is required to complement the consistency framework presented here. A discussion of these methodologies, however, is beyond the scope of this chapter. For an example of an application of such a methodology for a CFA country, see Callier (1992).

15. The reaction coefficients could be estimated when data availability permits doing so or assumed when it does not. Note that these coefficients could take on quite different values in low- and high-inflation countries as suggested by the stylized facts about devaluations and inflation.

illustrated below, to explore different options and the range of possible outcomes.[16]

The accounting framework set out above can be used in operational applications to determine consistent sets of changes in the nominal exchange rate, the internal and external RERs, and key nominal and relative domestic prices and factor costs. Using a computer spreadsheet for the accounting framework, numerous scenarios can be run quickly on alternative assumptions. The key to getting reasonably accurate results is the ability to make realistic assumptions about the reaction of wages and prices to a devaluation.

Although the framework computes the immediate adjustments in the endogenous variables in response to changes in the exogenous variables, it does not allow for full general-equilibrium repercussions that might occur over a longer time period. The framework is also one of comparative statics and does not calculate the time path of the adjustments, although it can be used iteratively. If reasonable assumptions can be made about the time path of exogenous variables, then a time series for the resulting adjustments in endogenous variables can be calculated.

Examples of Alternative Scenarios

There are two basic ways of approaching the question of how much to devalue: a strictly technical approach and a political economy approach. The technical approach is to estimate the size of the required real depreciation using the methodologies set out in Part III of this volume and then determine the size of the nominal devaluation that is necessary to achieve this real depreciation under alternative assumptions about the accompanying policies and the response of wages and prices. However, many devaluations follow balance-of-payments crises when governments are forced, often against their will, to devalue. In such cases policymakers usually do not have the luxury of taking a strictly technical approach to the question of how much to devalue. Hence, the political economy approach typically starts by identifying a specific nominal devaluation that is both politically acceptable, given the crisis situation, and large enough to be credible with financial markets. For this specified devaluation, one then explores how much inflation and real depreciation are likely to result under alternative policy scenarios.

---

16. Alternatively, in a specific case an equation such as (13.11), (13.12), or (13.13) could be included in the framework to endogenize an additional variable. This approach has not been followed here, however, in order to preserve the flexibility of the framework for analyzing different possibilities about the postdevaluation behavior of wages and prices.

The following subsections give examples of alternative scenarios about the outcome of the 1994 devaluation in Côte d'Ivoire. The political economy approach, assuming the nominal devaluation of 100 percent in domestic-currency terms (50 percent in foreign currency) that was actually implemented, is discussed first since the presentation of it is more straightforward. In the discussion of both the political economy and the technical approaches, a real depreciation in $IRERT_G$ of 40 percent in domestic-currency terms (29 percent in foreign currency) is assumed to be optimal as was suggested by the analysis carried out before the devaluation.

Because the consistency framework does not endogenously determine how wages and profits will react to a nominal devaluation, the change in wages and profits, and hence in the overall price level, has to be specified in some other way. There are several ways of handling this problem, three of which are illustrated below. One way of pinning down the behavior of wages and prices is to assume that the government adopts accompanying economic policies that hold the percentage increase in them to a given rate that is considered politically feasible. This rate is then specified exogenously so that the resulting increase in the prices of nontraded goods can be determined. Alternatively, equation 13.12 or 13.13 above may be used to relate the change in wages to either the nominal devaluation or the resulting change in prices. Given any of these assumptions about the postdevaluation behavior of wages and prices and a specific nominal devaluation or targeted real depreciation, the accounting framework may be used, as illustrated in the scenarios below, to calculate a consistent set of nominal and relative prices.

The Political Economy Approach: Analyzing the Implications of a Specified Nominal Devaluation

Table 13.2 examines the implications of a specified nominal devaluation of 100 percent, the one actually implemented in Côte d'Ivoire, for the RER nominal and relative prices. Four different scenarios are analyzed to consider the effects of (a) a reduction in trade taxes, (b) alternative distributions of the change in nominal factor payments between labor and capital, (c) the responsiveness of wages to prices, and (d) the sensitivity of the calculations to the assumptions about the size of the tradable sector.

Reduction in Trade Taxes. Scenarios 1.a and 1.b look at the effects of a reduction in trade taxes. The effects of a 100 percent devaluation are shown with and without the planned reduction in the average tariff on imported final products from 0.13 to 0.07 and in the average tariff on imported inputs from 0.16 to 0.11. When trade taxes are held constant in scenario 1.a, the external RER, $EXRER_{dc}$, and the internal RER, $IRERT_G$, depreciate by the same amount, 50 percent. But, when trade taxes are cut, the resulting somewhat smaller increase in the domestic price of traded goods reduces the depreciation of the internal RER from 50 percent to 44 percent. The effect of the trade tax cut on the external RER is the opposite—the smaller increase in the domestic price of traded goods reduces the increase in the general domestic price level from 33 percent to 32 percent and increases the depreciation in the external RER from 50 percent to 51 percent.[17] Since a reduction in trade taxes was actually both planned and implemented at the time of the devaluation, all the remaining scenarios assume a reduction in trade taxes.

A Freeze on Wages Profits. Scenarios 1.a and 1.b also assume that nominal wages and profits are frozen. They illustrate the maximum potential real depreciation that could be achieved with downward rigidity in nominal wages, one reason why a devaluation was needed to help guide the economy back to a full employment equilibrium. Together scenarios 1.a and 1.b suggest that a real depreciation of 40 percent to 50 percent was the largest that might be achieved by a 100 percent nominal devaluation and, conversely, that a pass-through coefficient of 0.3 was the smallest likely to be feasible.

Establishing a Target for Wages and Prices. As noted above, the key analytical problem in analyzing the effects of a nominal devaluation is to determine how much it depreciates the real exchange rate and how much it simply increases the price level. One way of pinning down the rate of inflation is to establish an inflation target for the monetary fiscal policies accompanying the devaluation that seems plausible in light of both the stylized facts about devaluations and inflation and the historical experience of the particular country concerned. In the accounting framework there are three domestic prices that could be targeted: the general price level, the price of nontraded goods, and total domestic factor costs (F_N). Of these, the price of nontraded goods contains the price of imported inputs. The general price level contains the price of imported final goods as well as the price of nontraded goods and, thus, of imported inputs. Domestic factor costs, in contrast, are a pure measure of domestic costs and prices. Hence, the following scenarios are based on assumptions about the changes in nominal factor payments. In other cases, however, one may wish to use the general price level instead of nominal factor payments because data on the general price level are more readily available or because it has been previously used for inflation targeting in the country concerned.

---

17. This divergence is an example of the contrary movements in the internal and external RERs that can be caused by changes in commercial policy or the terms of trade as described in Chapters 3 and 4.

Table 13.2 Implications of a Nominal Devaluation of 100 Percent

					Percentage change in variable						
Scenario	$IRERT_G$	$ERER_{dc}$	P_{Gd}	P_{Nd}	P_{Td}	W_d	π_d	$\dfrac{W_d}{P_{Gd}}$	$\dfrac{W_d}{P_{Nd}}$	*p.t.c..*	*e.i.*
1. Freeze in nominal factor payments with											
a. No change in trade taxes	50.3	50.3	33.1	12.4	100.0	0.0	0.0	−24.9	−11.1	.33	.50
b. Reduction in trade taxes[a]	43.5	51.3	32.2	11.3	89.7	0.0	0.0	−24.4	−10.2	.32	.5
2. 15 percent increase in nominal factor payments with a reduction in trade taxes[a]											
a. Equal percentage increase in wages and profits	35.7	43.0	39.8	24.5	89.7	15.0	15.0	−17.8	−7.6	.40	.43
b. Entire increase goes to capital	35.7	43.0	39.8	24.5	89.7	0.0	50.0	−28.5	−19.6	.40	.43
c. Entire increase goes to labor	35.7	43.0	39.8	24.5	89.7	21.4	0.0	−13.2	−2.4	.40	.43
3. Nominal factor payments increase by 50 percent of the increase in prices[a]	28.5	35.5	47.6	34.6	89.7	23.8	23.8	−16.1	−8.0	.48	.36
4. Sensitivity analysis of scenario 2a with a 50 percent larger traded-goods sector	21.3	27.9	56.4	29.7	89.7	15.0	15.0	−29.4	−11.4	.56	.28

(table continues on next page)

560

(table 13.2 continued)

Variables:

$IRERT_g$ = Internal RER (relative to the domestic price of traded goods)

W_d = Nominal wage rate with respect to the general price level

$ERER_{dc}$ = External RER in domestic-currency terms

P_d = Domestic general price index

P_d = Domestic price of nontraded goods

P_{Td} = Domestic price of traded goods

$e.i.$ = Effectiveness index

π_d = Nominal profit rate

$\dfrac{W_d}{P_{Gd}}$ = Real wage in terms of the general price level

$\dfrac{W_d}{P_{Nd}}$ = Real wages in terms of nontraded goods

$p.t.c.$ = Pass-through coefficient

a. Assumed reduction in average trade taxes on final goods from 0.13 to 0.07 and in average trade taxes on imported inputs from 0.16 to 0.11.

Source: Computed using the equations given in the appendix.

Since a large real depreciation was required in Côte d'Ivoire and it had been a low-inflation country, with a declining price level in the early 1990s, it was assumed in planning for the 1994 devaluation that the increase in nominal wages and other domestic factor costs could be held to 10–15 percent in the 12–18 month period after a 100 percent nominal devaluation. Scenario 2.a illustrates this option.[18] It predicts an increase in the general price level of 40 percent, a real depreciation in $IRERT_G$ of 36 percent, and a decline of 18 percent in real wages if nominal payments to labor and capital both rise proportionately after a devaluation (that is, if λ is constant). Because of the increase in nominal factor payments allowed for in this scenario, the pass-through coefficient is 0.4 instead of the 0.3 that would result from the freeze in nominal wages and profits under scenario 1.a and 1.b.

Alternative Distributions of the Increase in Nominal Factor Payments between Wages and Profits. However, to strengthen incentives for expanding output and investment, it may be necessary for the *relative* return on capital to increase.[19] Hence, scenarios 2.b and 2.c retain the 100 percent nominal devaluation and the 15 percent increase in nominal factor payments but drop the assumption that nominal factor payments change proportionately (equation 13.10). These two scenarios are in effect a sensitivity test of postdevaluation variations in the coefficient λ, a parameter that may be difficult to estimate accurately in some countries because of lack of data, as explained in the appendix, or may vary considerably with changes in economic policies and conditions. Scenarios 2.b and 2.c illustrate the extreme possibilities. Scenario 2.b assumes that the nominal wage remains fixed at its initial level so that the real wage falls by 28 percent because of the price increases resulting from the devaluation. The entire increase in nominal factor payments is here assumed to accrue to capital, raising its nominal return by 50 percent and its real return by 7 percent. Scenario 2.c illustrates the much smaller decline in real wages (2 percent) that would occur if labor obtained the entire increase in nominal factor payments; but this is largely hypothetical since it would lead to an unrealistic decline of 28 percent in the real return to capital.

Greater Responsiveness of Wages to Prices. Scenario 3 assumes that postdevaluation nominal wages rise by 50 percent of the increase in

---

18. Scenario 2.a is effectively the same as using equation 13.13 to determine the change in nominal wages as a function of the nominal devaluation with the reaction coefficient, ρ_2, equal to 0.15.

19. See appendix B of Chapter 2 for a discussion of the relationship between profitability and the RER.

prices—that is, that wages respond to prices in accordance with equation 13.12, with the reaction coefficient, ρ_1, equal to 0.5. This scenario leads to a greater increase in nominal wages (24 percent instead of 15 percent), higher inflation (47 percent vs. 40 percent), a larger pass-through coefficient of 0.5, and a smaller real depreciation. It illustrates the inflationary effects of a large real depreciation when nominal wages are partially but significantly indexed to prices.

Sensitivity Analysis. Scenario 4 is a sensitivity analysis of the estimated size of the traded-goods sector as specified by the parameters τ (the share of imports of final goods in the general price index, 0.22) and α (the share of imported inputs in the cost of producing nontraded goods, 0.11). As explained in the appendix and Chapter 3 on the two-good internal RER, there are several ways of measuring the size of the tradable sector and considerable uncertainty is involved in doing so. The tradable sector, whose prices are effectively determined by foreign prices, may be significantly larger than the import sector, the size of which was used to estimate the parameters τ and α. Scenario 5 assumes that τ and α are, in fact, 50 percent larger than estimated (that is, 0.33 and 0.16, respectively) and calculates the effect of a 100 percent nominal devaluation with a 15 percent increase in nominal factor payments. In this case, because of the larger weight of traded goods in the price indexes, the effect of the devaluation on the price level is greater. Consequently, the pass-through coefficient rises from 0.40 in scenario 2.a to 0.56 even though the increases in nominal wages and profits are the same in the two scenarios. The magnitude of the price increases and pass-through coefficient in this scenario are similar to those that may be experienced during devaluations in very open small economies.

The Technical Approach: Determination of the Size of the Required Nominal Devaluation

In addition to computing the amount of inflation and real depreciation that would result from a given nominal devaluation, the consistency framework can also be used to determine the size of the nominal devaluation required to achieve a given real depreciation. Again, the central analytical problem is to establish the relationship between a nominal devaluation, the depreciation of the real exchange rate, and the change in the domestic price level. Essentially, there are two ways of addressing this problem: (a) by establishing a policy target for the inflation rate as in scenario 2.a above or (b) by specifying an assumed relationship between the increase in prices and domestic factor costs as in scenario 3.

Scenarios 5 and 6 in table 13.3 compute the nominal devaluation required to achieve a 40 percent real depreciation in *IRERT*$_G$ under two

Table 13.3 Determination of the Nominal Devaluation Required to Achieve a 40 Percent Depreciation in the Internal RER (IRERT$_g$)

Scenario	E_{dc}	$ERER_{dc}$	P_{Gd}	P_{Nd}	P_{Td}	W_d	π_d	$\dfrac{W_d}{P_{Gd}}$	$\dfrac{W_d}{P_{Nd}}$	p.t.c	e.i.
5. 15 Percent increase in nominal wages and profits with a reduction in trade taxes[a]	112.0	47.6	43.6	25.9	101.0	15.0	15.0	−19.9	−8.6	.39	.43
6. Nominal wages and profits both increase by one-half as much as the general price level with a reduction in trade taxes[a]	133.3	47.6	58.0	38.6	121.0	29.0	29.0	−18.4	−6.9	.44	.36

Variables:

E_{dc} = Nominal exchange rates in domestic currency terms

$ERER_{dc}$ = External RER in domestic-currency terms

P_{Gd} = Domestic general price index

P_{Nd} = Domestic price of nontraded goods

P_{Td} = Domestic price of traded goods

W_d = Nominal wage rate

p.t.c. = Pass-through coefficient

π_d = Nominal profit rate

$\dfrac{W_d}{P_{Gd}}$ = Real wage in terms of the general price level

$\dfrac{W_d}{P_{Nd}}$ = Real wages in terms of nontraded goods

e.i. = Effectiveness index

a. Assumed reduction in average trade taxes on final goods from 0.13 to 0.07 and in average trade taxes on imported inputs from 0.16 to 0.11.
Source: Computed using the equations given in the appendix.

such different assumptions about the postdevaluation behavior of wages. Scenario 5 assumes the same increase in nominal wages and profits of 15 percent as in the base-case scenario, 2.a. It indicates that if trade tax rates are reduced, a nominal devaluation of 112 percent rather than 100 percent would be needed to achieve the targeted real depreciation of 40 percent. Scenario 6 assumes, as in scenario 3, that nominal wages and profits rise by one-half of the increase in the general price level. In this case, a nominal devaluation of 133 percent would be needed because nominal wages and profits would increase by 29 percent rather than by the 15 percent assumed in scenario 2.a.

The Actual Outcome in Côte d'Ivoire

Since the devaluation of the CFA franc took place some time ago, it is possible to compare the ex ante estimated price changes from the framework with the actual outcome in Côte d'Ivoire. The programmed devaluation scenario, 2.a, involved two key assumptions, one of which proved to be reasonably accurate but the other of which was far off.

The first assumption concerned the size of the nominal devaluation and changes in foreign prices. While a nominal devaluation of 100 percent relative to the French franc was implemented as envisaged in scenario 2.a, Côte d'Ivoire's nominal effective exchange rate only depreciated by 49 percent in domestic-currency terms between 1993 and 1997 because of movements in exchange rates with third countries. However, the price level in competitor countries also rose by 30 percent rather than remaining constant as assumed in scenario 2.a. Together these changes in exchange rates and foreign prices raised the foreign price level by 94 percent in CFA franc terms, an outcome that was not greatly different from the 100 percent assumed in scenario 2.a.

The second key assumption was that since Côte d'Ivoire had been a relatively low-inflation country, tight demand management and wage policies would hold the increase in nominal wages between 10 percent and 15 percent. These policies, however, turned out to be considerably less restrictive than assumed. Only limited data are available on wages in Côte d'Ivoire, but average government wages appear to have risen by 38 percent between 1993 and 1997. National accounts data indicate that the prices of domestic (nontraded) goods rose by somewhat more. The estimated values of the parameters τ and α may also have been somewhat too low. Consequently the actual outcome after the devaluation was an increase of 56 percent in the price level and a pass-through coefficient of 60 percent, near the upper end of the range for successful devaluations, rather than the 40 percent increase in the price level and pass-through coefficient of 0.4 projected in scenario 2.a. As a result, the external RER depreciated by only 24 percent rather than the projected

43 percent, and the reductions in real wages were also correspondingly smaller.[20]

These results highlight two key features of the consistency framework. First, accurate assumptions about the postdevaluation behavior of factor costs are essential for making accurate projections. But second, given accurate assumptions, the consistency framework will calculate reasonably accurate estimates of the changes in key nominal and real variables.

Implications of a Real Depreciation

The figures in tables 13.2 and 13.3 illustrate both a number of standard patterns in the adjustments in relative prices accompanying a real depreciation and some of the policy implications of a real depreciation.

Standard Patterns in Relative Price Adjsutments

Four standard patterns in the adjustments in relative prices accompanying a real depreciation are worth noting. First, because of the assumption that the foreign price of traded goods changes by the same amount as the foreign price level, the percentage change in $IRERT_G$ always equals that in the external RER, $ERER_{dc}$, when trade taxes are not changed. If this assumption is relaxed and the foreign price of traded goods increases less rapidly than aggregate foreign price (for example, because of more rapid productivity increases in the traded goods), then $IRERT_G$, which has the domestic price of traded goods in its numerator, would depreciate by less than $ERER_{dc}$, which has the aggregate foreign price level in its numerator.

Second, when trade taxes are reduced, $IRERT_G$ also depreciates by less than $ERER_{dc}$ as the reduction in trade taxes offsets part of the effect of a devaluation on the domestic price of traded goods, somewhat paradoxically decreasing the depreciation of the internal RER but increasing the depreciation of the external RER.

Third, the price of nontraded goods, P_{Nd}, necessarily increases by less than the aggregate domestic price level, P_{Gd}, when the internal RER depreciates. Hence, other things being equal, the depreciation in the internal RER expressed relative to the price of nontraded goods, $IRERT_N$, which has P_{Nd} in its denominator, is always greater than the depreciation in $IRERT_G$ and $ERER_{dc}$, which have P_{Gd} in their denominators.

---

20. As Côte d'Ivoire's terms of trade improved in the mid-1990s, appreciating its equilibrium RER, the misalignment of its exchange rate was probably reduced by somewhat more than the depreciation in the actual RER.

Fourth, the size of the reduction in real wages depends upon the numeraire. The reduction is always the largest in terms of foreign exchange and traded goods and is always the smallest in terms of nontraded goods. The change in real wages in terms of the general domestic price level falls between these extremes.

Policy Implications of a Real Depreciation

In considering the policy implications of the accounting framework, it is worth reiterating in opening that the framework assumes that the targeted real depreciation is designed to correct an initial overvaluation of the RER and help guide the economy back to equilibrium. If a devaluation, in fact, reflects a movement away from equilibrium, it will create excess demand in the market for nontraded goods and other inflationary pressure that will fairly quickly undo the effects of the devaluation. Furthermore, even when an exchange rate is significantly overvalued, this misalignment may not be a policy problem; and, if it is a policy problem, a devaluation may not be the appropriate policy response. In some cases of misalignment—for example, when macroeconomic policies are appropriate and the misalignment is due to short-term cyclical factors—no policy response may be required. In other cases of real overvaluation, a policy response other than a devaluation may be appropriate—for example, reduction of an excessive fiscal deficit.[21]

Even when a devaluation represents a movement toward equilibrium and is the appropriate policy response to an overvaluation, a country still does not want to lose control of its general price level in the process of making the required realignment in relative domestic prices. Unfortunately, there are no simple nominal exchange rate rules that provide a reliable basis for postdevaluation monetary policy.[22] Increasing financial market integration and highly variable capital flows pose serious problems for macroeconomic management with a fixed exchange rate.[23] Hence, targets for inflation or monetary aggregates are increasingly replacing fixed exchange rates as nominal anchors for economic policy. Furthermore, estimates of both the required change in the real exchange rate and of the corresponding change in the nominal exchange rate may

---

21. See Isard and Faruqee (1998) for a further discussion of the interpretation of exchange rate misalignment.

22. Except for currency board or monetary union arrangements, which are applicable only in special circumstances. See Obstfeld and Rogoff (1995), pp. 92–94.

23. See, for example, World Bank (1997), p. 43. Goldfajn and Valdes (1996) also find that excessive real appreciations are more likely to occur under fixed rate regimes.

have significant margins of error, a situation that increases the operational advantages of a flexible postdevaluation exchange rate policy.

In order to depreciate the internal RER, a one-time structural increase in the relative prices of traded goods must take place. Without such a structural shift in relative prices, no real depreciation is possible.[24] If nominal wages and other nominal factor costs are rigid downward (or only decline very slowly), an upward shift in the aggregate price level must necessarily accompany the structural increase in the relative price of traded goods. Monetary and interest rate policy must be designed to accommodate this upward shift in the general price level, or it will provoke a lengthy recession with little ultimate impact on the downwardly rigid prices of nontraded goods. For designing the policy measures to accompany a devaluation and monitoring events afterwards, it is also desirable to have a consistent set of targets both for an acceptable increase in the general price level and for the necessary adjustments in relative prices and factor costs that are required to depreciate the internal RER.

On the one hand, demand management policy needs to minimize secondary inflationary pressures of a devaluation by keeping the fiscal deficit under control and constraining wage increases. Any increase in nominal wages and other domestic factor costs after a devaluation will only create additional inflation that will erode part of the initial real depreciation. A corresponding decline in real wages is an inevitable consequence of a real depreciation. On the other hand, some increase in the demand for nontradables and factor costs is often inevitable as production and income expand in the traded-goods sector. Hence, to limit the inflationary impact of a devaluation, demand management policies need to ensure that factor costs and nontraded-good prices increase no more than necessary while the prices of traded goods rise as needed to raise the relative prices of traded to nontraded goods and depreciate the internal RER. Keeping increases in nominal factor costs and the price of nontraded goods to the minimum necessary maximizes the gain in competitiveness from a given nominal devaluation. Thus, while monetary and interest rate policy must accommodate the necessary upward structural shift in the aggregate price level, it must still be tight enough to avoid wage and price increases driven by inflationary expectations and to ensure that there is not excessive demand for nontraded goods that would drive up their nominal prices beyond the minimum necessary.

In addition to the upward shift in the aggregate price level, a second likely consequence of the structural increase in the relative price of traded

---

24. Such a structural shift could occur gradually in a country with a crawling peg that depreciates steadily in real terms.

goods is that real wages will normally fall in terms of both foreign exchange and traded goods.[25] Real wages will usually also decline in terms of nontraded goods to the extent that imported inputs are used in producing them. The accompanying decline in real wages is one reason why devaluations are often resisted and why full indexation of wages (real wage rigidity) usually makes it impossible to achieve a real depreciation without structural reforms in the labor market. This aspect of a real depreciation may be problematic politically, but it is an economic reality. However, the structural reduction in real wages in terms of the average price level will be smaller; the smaller is τ, the share of traded goods in the general price index, and the more nontraded goods are substituted for traded goods in consumption after the depreciation of the RER. The decline is also just a one-time downward shift—if growth resumes after the depreciation of the RER, labor incomes should also grow.

In the aftermath of a major devaluation like that of the CFA franc, the price situation is often very confusing. The general price level is a weighted average of the prices of tradable and nontradable goods. Movements in it after a devaluation may reflect the desired increase in the prices of tradables or an undesired increase in the prices of nontradables. Hence, it is difficult to determine solely from the movement in the general price level to what extent the RER is depreciating as desired and to what extent the general price level is simply increasing without any change in domestic relative prices.

If the required data are available in the 12- to 24-month period after a large nominal devaluation, it may be easier to judge whether monetary policy is too tight or too loose by analyzing what is happening to wages—which are the largest and most easily monitorable component of domestic factor costs—and the prices of nontraded goods rather than by looking only at the aggregate price level. Although price indexes for traded goods can often be constructed from data on export and import prices, current price indexes for nontraded goods are usually not readily available. The availability of data on wages is also often spotty in low-income countries such as those of the CFA zone. Hence monthly data on these variables, if not available in a particular developing country, should

---

25. Strictly speaking, from equations 13.8 and 13.9, it is real factor payments (the total of wages and profits), rather than real wages per se, that must fall in terms of foreign exchange and traded goods. It is possible to imagine hypothetical situations similar to scenario 2.c above in which the entire reduction in real factor payments would be in profits. Empirically, however, in nearly all cases real wages are likely to have to fall since the profit rate will usually need to be maintained or increased to provide incentives for expanding output and investment.

be a priority for data collection efforts. In cases in which these data are not available, one is limited to analyzing the inflation in the CPI to assess (a) whether the initial inflationary bulge from the devaluation is fading away and (b) how much higher inflation is than would be expected on the basis of the increase in import costs alone.[26]

Conclusion: Advantage and Limitations of the Consistency Framework

This chapter has set out the stylized facts concerning devaluations and inflation and presented a simple consistency framework for examining the linkages between a nominal devaluation, a real depreciation, prices, and wages. In the absence of a more sophisticated methodology, the stylized facts and accounting framework provide starting points for analyzing the impact of a devaluation on prices and wages.

The accounting framework can be used to illuminate the implications of different policy choices and provides a means for ensuring consistency among them. It quantifies, in a fairly transparent way, the changes in the key relative prices that must take place in order to depreciate the RER. Some of this clarity may be politically awkward (for example, the likely reduction in real wages), but the quantitative relationships reflect the economic reality that a real depreciation entails. A major advantage of the framework is its limited data requirements and simple structure with only three parameters to be estimated. These make it a practical tool for policy analysis at times of balance-of-payments crises in developing countries when the availability of time and data are often limited.

---

26. Similarly, the upward structural shift in the aggregate price level will give a distorted picture of what is happening to real interest rates during the 12- to 24-month period of adjustment in relative prices. Like real wages, real interest rates can be expressed in terms of the prices of traded and nontraded goods or the aggregate price level. As in the case of real wages, these measures will change by different amounts when the internal RER depreciates and may give very different impressions of what is happening to real interest rates. A monetary policy that accommodates the upward structural shift is likely to lead to real interest rates that appear excessively negative unless the effects of the upward shift in the price level are excluded from the inflation measure. During this period, real interest rates should be computed using the rate of inflation in the price of nontraded goods rather than by using the rate of inflation in the aggregate domestic price level. If data on the price of nontraded goods are not available, a weighted average of the rate of inflation in foreign prices and of the inflation in nominal wages (and other domestic factor costs, if available) could be used as a proxy for the rate of inflation in the prices of nontraded goods.

However, the consistency framework's advantage—its simplicity—is also its limitation. First, the usefulness of the framework depends critically upon one's ability to make reasonable assumptions about the postdevaluation behavior of nominal wages and prices of nontraded goods—either on the basis of experience elsewhere or of the economic structure and likely postdevaluation policies of the country concerned. But the framework itself does not shed much light on the likely behavior of nominal wages and prices. In cases in which postdevaluation wage-price behavior is unpredictable or uncontrollable, so too will be the outcome of a devaluation. The data required for estimating the parameter λ, the share of labor in value added in the nontraded goods sector, may also be hard to come by in some cases.

Second, the accounting framework assumes that import shares in absorption and in the production of nontraded goods are constant and that these are reasonable measures of the size of the tradable-goods sector. Such assumptions may not be realistic in some cases. The tradable-goods sector, whose prices are effectively determined by foreign prices, may be significantly larger in very open economies. Moreover, there is usually some substitutability in consumption between imports and domestic goods. Similarly, a large increase in the price of imported inputs as a result of a substantial real depreciation will provide an impetus for domestic producers to look for domestic substitutes for suddenly expensive imported inputs. The uncertainty in measuring the size of the tradable-goods sector and the possibility of substitution of tradable and nontradable goods in consumption and production after a devaluation suggest that the model's calculations should be interpreted with caution. They should be considered as rough first approximations of what changes in prices to expect. A sensitivity analysis, as illustrated in scenario 4, is therefore desirable to explore the likely range of probable outcomes.

Third, a more elaborate framework with three goods is required in order to take into account the differences between exports and imports. Such a framework would permit examining the differential impact of changes in terms of trade and trade policy on exports and imports, and the links between wages in the export sector and those in the nontraded-goods sector.[27]

Finally, in countries in which monetary policy does not target the inflation rate, quantitative estimates are needed for the time path of both prices and output to determine appropriate monetary targets. The accounting framework, as noted above, can provide the estimates for prices.

---

27. A note outlining such a framework is available from the authors.

However, the accounting framework will determine neither the supply response to a devaluation nor the time path of real output. Variations in real output in the first two years after a devaluation are often small compared with the changes in prices and hence have less overall impact on the changes in the nominal value of output, which is usually used in determining monetary targets. Nevertheless, variations in real output may still differ considerably among countries, depending upon the situation in the country concerned, and they need to be taken into account in designing monetary, fiscal, and other accompanying policies.[28]

---

28. For a discussion of the supply response to changes in the RER, see Chapter 11 on the RER and trade flows.

Appendix

The Accounting Framework for the Two-Good Internal RER

This appendix discusses in detail the individual equations in the two-good accounting framework with traded and nontraded sectors that is summarized on pages 553–57 of the text.[29]

The Internal RER: Empirical Definition

The internal RER, typically defined theoretically as the domestic relative price of traded goods to nontraded goods, can alternatively be defined in terms of the general price level in the home country. Using the subscript "G" to indicate that the general price level is in the denominator, this concept of the internal RER, denoted $IRERT_G$, is defined as shown in equation 13.A.1:

$$(13.A.1) \qquad IRERT_G = \frac{P_{Td}}{P_{Gd}} = \frac{E_{dc} \cdot P_{Tf}}{P_{Gd}}$$

where P_{Td} is an index of the domestic price of traded goods, P_{Tf} is an index of foreign prices of traded goods, and P_{Gd} is the general domestic

---

29. The choice between a two-good and a three-good framework is quite important analytically. Both the level and the changes in the RERs for imports, exports, and traded goods can vary quite substantially as a result of terms-of-trade shocks. A three-good model is needed to fully incorporate the impact of such shocks on the RER as discussed in Chapter 4. The presentation in this appendix is, however, restricted to a two-good model, in which all goods are classified as traded or nontraded. The use of a two-good framework simplifies the analysis and focuses the discussion on the impact of a devaluation on prices and real wages. An outline of an extended three-good framework, which could be used to analyze the impact of terms-of-trade shocks occurring separately or in combination with a devaluation of the nominal exchange rate or of differences in trade policies affecting imports and exports, is available from the authors.

price index in domestic-currency terms. Traded goods are assumed to behave in accordance with the law of one price so that equation 13.A.2 holds:

$$(13.A.2) \qquad P_{Td} = E_{dc} \cdot P_{Tf}.$$

P_{Gd} is a weighted average of the prices of traded and nontraded goods and is discussed in more detail below. As long as the weights of traded and nontraded goods in the general price index remain constant, or new values can be calculated for them, then the standard version of the two-good internal RER (the ratio of the domestic prices of traded and nontraded goods) can be calculated from $IRERT_G$ and vice versa. For empirical reasons, $IRERT_G$ is used in the presentation that follows.[30]

Domestic Prices

The Aggregate Price Level

As noted above, the general price level in the home economy, P_{Gd}, is a weighted average of the prices of traded and nontraded goods and services. The general price level may be measured in terms of either production, in which case traded goods are exports, or expenditure (absorption), in which case traded goods are imports. Since nontraded goods are both produced and absorbed entirely within the home economy, their price index is the same whether measured on the production or the expenditure side. The simplest formulation of the domestic price level is given in equation 13.A.3:

$$(13.A.3) \qquad P_{Gd} = \tau P_{Td} + (1-\tau)P_{Nd} = \tau E_{dc} \cdot P_{Tf} + (1-\tau)P_{Nd}$$

where τ is the share of traded goods in total domestic output or expenditure (that is, the share of export value added in GDP or the share of imported *final* goods in total domestic absorption).[31]

---

30. $IRERT_G$ is more comparable with the common external real effective exchange rate (REER) indexes, which are expressed in terms of the general price level and are often used as empirical proxies for the internal RER. The use of $IRERT_G$ is also more consistent with most empirical work on trade elasticities, which utilizes elasticities expressed relative to the general domestic price level. As explained in appendix A of Chapter 7 on the trade-elasticities methodology, use of trade elasticities expressed relative to the general price level yields estimated changes in the RER that are also expressed relative to the general price level.

31. In principle, it is better to use a geometric average in calculating P_{Gd} since it treats increases and decreases symmetrically and rates of change in a geometric index are not affected by rebasing. However, an arithmetic average has been used here to simplify the presentation.

The implicit assumption in adopting a fixed value for τ is that there is no substitution between traded and nontraded goods in consumption. If the share of traded goods in consumption falls when the relative price of traded goods rises, the increase in the price level will be smaller than that given by equation 13.A.3, which assumes no change in the composition of consumption.[32]

In addition, there are at least two different empirical measures of τ, depending on whether the term "traded goods" refers to exports or imports. If the measure of τ is based on the concept of traded goods in output, τ should be computed as the share of value added in exporting in GDP excluding the imported inputs that are used directly in producing exports (and also excluding re-exports of imports). This measure is labeled τ_o.[33] Alternatively, if τ is based on the concept of traded goods in expenditure, it should be computed as the share of imports of final goods (excluding imported inputs and re-exports) in expenditure; this measure is called τ_a. There is no reason, a priori, that these two alternative measures of τ should be equal. In fact, such an outcome is unlikely, since a country's exports seldom equal its imports. An additional empirical complication is that when the terms of trade change, import and export prices, and the GDP and absorption deflators, can behave quite differently.[34]

In order to calculate τ, it is necessary to estimate the share of imports used directly in producing exports, the value of which should be subtracted from either exports or imports in calculating the alternative measures of τ. These measures of τ are lower bounds for either concept of τ because they are based on traded, rather than tradable, goods. Since the empirical measures of τ are most probably underestimates, the resulting estimated increases in the general price level and the reduction in the real wage needed to achieve a specified depreciation in the internal RER are probably somewhat underestimated as well. In view of the various difficulties in estimating τ, the sensitivity of the results to alternative estimates of τ is discussed further in scenario 4.

In a three-good framework with exports, imports, and nontraded goods, τ_o should be used for the production side of the economy and τ_a

---

32. The resulting decline in the real wage (in terms of domestic prices) may also be correspondingly smaller (see the text below).

33. Another way of measuring τ_o on the production side of the economy would be as the ratio of exports, including imported inputs to the total value of final output—in other words, to the sum of value added and imported inputs.

34. See Chapter 3 on the two-good internal RER for a further discussion of ways of measuring the size of the nontraded-goods sector and the uncertainties involved in doing so.

for the expenditure side. However, in a two-good framework with only one aggregate traded good, one is forced to chose between using one measure of τ or the other, or some average of them. For consistency, one should use the expenditure-side measure of τ (τ_a) when working with an expenditure price index and the production-side measure of τ (τ_o) when working with a production price index or value-added deflator. In the presentation below, the absorption measure for τ is used since expenditure price indexes are more commonly used in analyzing RERs than in production price indexes and imports, which tend to be more diversified and their prices more broadly representative of international price trends than exports, which are incorporated in expenditure price indexes. In instances in which export prices diverge significantly from import prices and changes in the terms of trade are important analytically, one should in any case switch to a three-good framework as explained in Chapter 4.

The Price of Nontraded Goods.

The domestic production of nontraded consumer and investment goods typically requires both imported inputs and domestic factors of production, and the imported content of domestically produced nontraded goods is included in their price. If the home country's economy is reasonably competitive and the prices of nontraded goods reflect their production costs, the price of nontraded goods is given by equation 13.A.4:

$$(13.A.4) \qquad P_{Nd} = \alpha E_{dc} \cdot P_{Tf} + (1-\alpha)F_N$$

where α is the share of imported goods (both imports of intermediate inputs and capital equipment) in the cost of producing nontraded goods and services.[35] P_{Tf} is the foreign-currency price of imports used as inputs in producing nontraded goods and services.[36] $(1-\alpha)$ is the share of domestic factors of production in the cost of producing nontraded goods,

---

35. The ratio of intermediate and capital goods imports to GDP is used below as an estimate for α on the assumption that imported inputs account for the same share of the production costs of both traded and nontraded goods.

36. The foreign price indexes for final imported goods and for imported intermediate and capital goods are all assumed here to be the same. That is, $P^F_{Tf} = P^I_{Tf} = P_{Tf}$ where P^F_{Tf} is the index of foreign prices of imported final goods and P^I_{Tf} is the index of foreign prices of imported intermediate and capital goods. This assumption is made to simplify the presentation since the analysis here is concerned with a change in the nominal exchange rate rather than with changes in the relative prices of different categories of imported goods.

and F_N is the cost per unit of output of domestic factors of production used in the nontraded sector.[37]

Fixed factor proportions in the production of nontraded goods are also assumed. If substitution between imported inputs and domestic factors is possible, an increase in the relative domestic price of imported inputs may result in a fall in their share, α. Such substitution, in turn, would imply a smaller increase in the price of nontraded goods after a nominal realignment than given by equation 13.A.4.[38]

Domestic Factor Costs

Factor Payments

The index of total payments to domestic factors of production (F_N) per unit of output in the nontraded-goods sector is in turn composed of payments to labor and capital, as shown in equation 13.A.5:

$$(13.A.5) \qquad F_N = \lambda \cdot W_d + (1 - \lambda) \cdot \pi$$

where λ is the share of labor in factor payments, W_d is the nominal wage index in domestic currency (and is an average of the formal and informal sector wages), $1 - \lambda$ is the share of capital, and π is an index of the average rental rate of a unit of capital employed in the nontraded sector.[39]

If nominal wages and prices are assumed to change proportionately in the nontraded sector after a devaluation so that the relative shares of labor and capital remain constant, then equation 13.A.6 will hold:

$$(13.A.6) \qquad \frac{\Delta W_d}{W_d} = \frac{\Delta \pi}{\pi}.$$

If the nominal returns to the labor and capital change proportionately, then the percentage change in the nominal wage is also equal to the percentage change in total factor payments, F_N.[40] The assumption of proportional changes is plausible for many low-income developing countries in which a large segment of the labor force is self-employed. In such cases, ownership of the factors of production is embodied in a single individual or household, and it is virtually impossible to determine

---

37. We assume here that producers of nontraded goods behave competitively.

38. Scenario 4 in the text gives a sensitivity analysis of assumptions about α.

39. Capital is defined here to include natural resources as well as the man-made capital stock.

40. Note, however, that, if equation 13.A.6 holds, the value of λ does not affect the results; and no estimate of λ is required.

returns to individual factors separately. Thus, the assumption that any change in factor returns is distributed proportionately is reasonable as an initial starting point for the analysis. If wages need to decline relative to profits to raise the domestic saving and investment rates, equation 13.A.6 can be modified to provide for a smaller relative increase in nominal wages.[41]

The real wage is simply the nominal wage divided by the price level. In this model, there are three possible price levels or numeraires: the aggregate price level, the price of traded goods, and the price of nontraded goods. Equation 13.A.7 gives the real wage (w_G) expressed in terms of aggregate price level, the most common numeraire:

$$(13.A.7) \qquad\qquad w_G = \frac{W_d}{P_{Gd}}.$$

The real wage may also be expressed in terms of the prices of traded goods (w_T), as shown in equation 13.A.8:

$$(13.A.8) \qquad\qquad w_T = \frac{W_d}{P_{Td}} = \frac{W_d}{E_{dc} \cdot P_{Tf}}$$

or nontraded goods (w_N), as shown in equation 13.A.9:

$$(13.A.9) \qquad\qquad w_N = \frac{W_d}{P_{Nd}}.$$

In analyzing external competitiveness, it is often common to measure nominal wages in foreign currency terms (W_F), as shown in equation 13.A.10:

$$(13.A.10) \qquad\qquad W_F = \frac{W_d}{E_{dc}}.$$

If a real depreciation is to take place, the real wage must fall in terms of traded goods and foreign exchange. However, since the prices of traded and nontraded goods and the aggregate price level will change by different amounts when the internal RER depreciates, the three measures of real wages will also change by different amounts and may give different impressions of the decline in real wages. Because the price of traded

---

41. Scenario 2 in the text considers the case of differential increases in the nominal payments to labor and capital.

goods will increase by more than the price of nontraded goods and the aggregate price level, the real wage will fall the most in terms of traded goods. The nominal wage expressed in foreign currency terms, which is often used as a measure of the international competitiveness of labor-intensive industries, will fall as the result of a devaluation unless domestic wages increase by the full amount of the devaluation. If the foreign price level does not change at the time of a devaluation,[42] the change in the real wage in terms of traded goods, equation 13.A.8, will equal the change in the nominal wage expressed in foreign currency, equation 13.A.10, and international competitiveness will improve accordingly. Because the price of nontraded goods will rise the least when the internal RER depreciates, the purchasing power of wages in terms of nontraded goods will fall the least. The reduction in the real wage in terms of aggregate price level, which is an average of the prices of traded and nontraded goods, will fall between these two extremes.

Wage Differentials

Any analysis of the impact of a nominal devaluation on real wages and wage differentials is considerably complicated by the imperfections in the labor market that typically exist in developing countries. The wage level in equation 13.A.6 is the average for the economy. However, labor markets tend to be segmented into formal and informal sectors, and the wage differentials between these sectors may be quite large. Formal sector wages are often influenced by the existence of labor unions, the presence of some large firms with market power in the import-substituting and nontraded sectors, and government regulations and wage-setting practices. Hence, the wage-setting process in the formal sector may be very different from that governing wages in the more competitive informal sector, and formal-sector wages need not be closely linked to either labor productivity in the formal sector or to prevailing demand and supply conditions in the labor market. Consequently, substantial wage differentials may exist between the formal and informal sectors. It is possible that these differentials could decrease after a devaluation if firms in the noncompetitive parts of the nontraded and import-substituting sector are not able to fully pass along increased labor costs. Alternatively, labor in the formal sector may be able to exert enough pressure to maintain the previous wage differentials. The ultimate result, with regard both to the average real wage and wage differentials across sectors, will depend in large part on the policies that accompany a devaluation.

---

42. If trade policy is also changed at the time of a devaluation, the domestic price of traded goods will not change by the same amount as the foreign price.

Unless nominal wages increase by the full amount of the devaluation, preventing any depreciation of the RER, wages expressed in foreign-currency terms will usually fall across the board as a result of a devaluation. However, the impact of a devaluation on relative wages in domestic-currency terms may vary between the export and nontraded-goods sectors. Returns to labor in domestic-currency terms in export sectors will increase initially after a devaluation because of higher export prices in domestic currency, particularly if much of export production is by households, not corporations. The real wage will fall in the nontraded-goods sector, as domestic prices rise, as long as the cumulative increase in nominal wages (if any) is less than the increase in the general price level. Hence, a devaluation is likely to result initially in a wage differential between the export and nontraded sectors. As labor moves to the export sector, in which returns are higher, downward pressure will be put on wages there. Labor movements could, in turn, result in increasing wages in the nontraded sector. Hence, there would be market pressure to reduce the initial wage differential and equalize wages in the export and nontraded sectors in the longer run. However, the eventual outcome is difficult to predict without detailed information about the nature of the labor market in the country concerned.

Trade Taxes, Subsidies, and Administered Prices

In order to simplify the presentation, the foregoing analysis has not taken into account the possibility of differential taxes being levied on traded goods. However, countries often levy taxes on traded goods—commonly on imports and sometimes on exports. Usually, the tax rates on exports and imports are different. Sometimes the prices of traded goods are subsidized (the taxes on them being, in effect, negative)—export subsidies are not uncommon, and imports of key consumer goods are sometimes subsidized for political or social reasons. Marketing board arrangements for exports, and occasionally for imports, and administered prices may also cause the domestic price of traded goods to differ from the domestic-currency equivalent of the border price. The differential taxation of traded goods through tariffs, subsidies, marketing arrangements, or administered pricing can have an impact on all prices, including the exchange rate. When these distortions are present, changes in border prices may no longer necessarily be fully, or even partially, passed through to domestic prices. This section modifies the formulation of the consistency framework to allow for the effects of differential taxation of traded goods. The analysis in the main text of this chapter uses the definitions of the RER and domestic price indexes including trade taxes set out below.

The definition of the internal RER can be revised to take into account differential taxation (net of subsidies) of traded goods. It will then have the form shown in equation 13.A.11:

$$(13.A.11) \qquad IRERT_G = \frac{E_{dc} \cdot P_{Tf}(1+t)}{P_{Gd}}$$

where τ is the average *ad valorem* tax on traded goods. The variable τ in this equation is a broad measure of the average net effect of taxes, subsidies, marketing board margins, and administered pricing policies on the prices of traded final goods.[43]

Exports are typically taxed at different rates from imports in developing countries. In order to analyze the effects of differential taxation of exports and imports, traded goods must be disaggregated into imports and exports. Such a disaggregation requires a three-good framework as explained in Chapter 4.

Even in the simpler two-good framework used here, the inclusion of trade taxes necessitates modifying the definitions of the domestic price indexes to reflect them. The tariff regimes in many developing countries tend to sharply differentiate between imports of final (consumer) goods and those of raw materials, intermediate inputs, and capital goods. Typically, tariffs on imported final goods are substantially higher than those on imported intermediate and capital goods. Thus, at least two import taxes need to be distinguished: those levied on final goods and those on intermediate goods.

The index for the general price level (equation 13.5) revised to reflect the inclusion of tariffs is given in equation 13.A.12:

$$(13.A.12) \qquad P_{Gd} = \tau \cdot E_{dc} \cdot P_{Tf}(1+t) + (1-\tau)P_{Nd}$$

---

43. Taxes and subsidies on traded goods have asymmetric effects on the domestic prices of imports and exports. The domestic-currency price of imports increases and that of exports decreases when import and export taxes are imposed. Similarly, a subsidy on imports lowers the consumer price inclusive of the subsidy, whereas an export subsidy raises the producer price inclusive of the subsidy. Hence, taxes and subsidies on imports and exports must be entered with opposite signs in equations 13.A.11 and 13.A.12. A value-added tax (VAT) or excise tax may also be levied on import or exports. If these taxes are levied at the same rates on domestic and imported products, they will affect the overall price level but not the relative prices of traded and nontraded goods. If a VAT or excise tax is levied at differential rates on domestic and imported products, the differential is, in effect, a tax on traded goods and should be taken into account in calculating it.

where t is the average tariff on final traded goods. If the absorption approach for measuring τ is used as earlier, the average tariff (net of subsidies) on imports, t_m, is the appropriate rate to use for t. Equation 13.A.4 will now have the revised form shown in shown in equation 13.A.13:

$$(13.A.13) \qquad P_{Nd} = \alpha \cdot E_{dc} \cdot P_{Tf}(1 + t_m) + (1 - \alpha)F_N$$

where t_m is the average tariff on imported inputs used to produce nontraded goods.[44]

Some countries that choose not to devalue an overvalued currency adjust trade taxes instead to attempt to mimic the effects of a devaluation. Such adjustments typically take the form of increased import tariffs and export subsidies. Increased tariffs make imports more expensive for consumers; subsidies make exports more profitable to domestic producers. These effects on the relative prices of exports and imports are like those of a devaluation. Similarly, a tariff cut reduces the domestic-currency price of imports, the opposite of the effect of a devaluation. Thus, a reduction in import tariffs and export subsidies that takes place simultaneously with a devaluation will effectively offset a part of the devaluation.

Countries often reform trade policies at the same time as they devalue in order to achieve a more neutral structure of incentives for producing different categories of traded goods. A tariff reform designed to reduce the dispersion in tariff rates and produce a more uniform structure of protection may result in an increase, a decrease, or no change in revenues and in the average effective tariff—depending upon how much of the revenue loss from cutting rates on high-tariff items is offset by increases from eliminating exemptions and raising rates on zero- and low-tariff items. In order to keep the fiscal deficit from widening and putting inflationary pressure on domestic prices, any decline in government revenues as a consequence of tariff cuts generally needs to be offset either by reducing expenditures or by finding alternative sources of revenue (for example, by raising direct taxes or by increasing indirect taxes on all goods, both traded and nontraded) in a way that does not distort the relative prices between traded and nontraded goods. To simplify the analysis, it is assumed here that any revenue loss from reductions in trade taxes is offset through other measures that do not affect

---

44. When the effects of taxes on traded goods are taken into account, the initial values of the indexes for the domestic prices of traded and nontraded goods, the average domestic price level, and the internal and external RERs are no longer 1.0.

the relative prices of traded and nontraded goods. The effects of such compensated changes in trade taxes are illustrated in scenario 1, in which the impact of a devaluation is estimated both with and without a reduction in trade taxes.[45]

The Complete Framework for Estimating Consistent Nominal and Relative Prices

This section summarizes the accounting framework for estimating consistent changes in nominal and relative prices after a currency realignment. In the summary of the formulas below, a subscript "0" indicates the prerealignment value and a subscript "1" indicates the postrealignment value of a variable.

To minimize the data required and simplify the presentation, indexes with an initial value of 1.0 are used for all variables. All changes are measured with respect to the initial values of each variable and are expressed as percentages. Hence, the initial (prerealignment) value of the nominal exchange rate (E_{dc0}), the foreign price of traded goods (P_{Tf0}), the aggregate foreign price level (P_{Gf0}), the return to capital (π_0), and the nominal wage (W_{d0}) indexes are assumed to be 1.0. That is, as shown in equation 13.A.14:

$$(13.A.14) \qquad E_{dc0} = P_{Tfo} = P_{Gfo} = W_0 = \pi_0 = 1.0.$$

In addition, we also assume that both the foreign price of traded goods and the aggregate foreign price level do not change. Hence, we obtain equations 13.A.15 and 13.A.16:

$$(13.A.15) \qquad P_{Tfo} = P_{Tf1} = 1.0$$

$$(13.A.16) \qquad P_{Gfo} = P_{Gf1} = 1.0$$

These assumptions are made only to simplify the presentation—both P_{Tf} and P_{Gf} can easily be treated as exogenous with assumed postrealignment

45. In addition, since the focus of this chapter is on the exchange rate and related taxes on international trade, for simplicity it is further assumed that there are no other changes in either indirect domestic taxes on nontraded goods or in direct taxes on factor payments that affect the relative prices of traded and nontraded goods. It is assumed also that the effects on the fiscal deficit of any other tax or expenditure changes are offset by other measures that do not change the relative prices of traded and nontraded goods. If such changes in taxes or expenditures affecting relative prices do occur, their effects should be taken into account in estimating t and t_m.

values. However, if there is a change in the relative foreign prices of the home country's imports and exports, the analytical problem is more complex. A three-good model is then needed to analyze the impact of the change in the home country's terms of trade.

The initial values of average trade taxes on imported inputs, t_m, and on final goods, t, were 0.16 and 0.13, respectively, in the Côte d'Ivoire example. Because of these trade taxes, the initial values of the domestic prices of traded and nontraded goods, the aggregate domestic price level, the internal and external RERs, and the real wage and profit rates are no longer 1.0 as in the case in which there are no trade taxes. These initial values can be readily calculated using the above equations.

The full system is composed of the eight equations, 13.A.17 through 13.A.24, summarized in the main text and reproduced below for reference:

(13.A.17)
$$ERER_{dc} = E_{dc} \cdot \frac{P_{Gf}}{P_{Gd}}$$

(13.A.18)
$$P_{Td} = E_{dc} \cdot (1+t) \cdot P_{Tf}$$

(13.A.19)
$$IRERT_{G} = \frac{E_{dc} \cdot P_{Tf}(1+t)}{P_{Gd}}$$

(13.A.20)
$$P_{Gd} = \tau \cdot E_{dc} \cdot P_{Tf}(1+t) + (1-\tau)P_{Nd}$$

(13.A.21)
$$P_{Nd} = \alpha \cdot E_{dc} \cdot P_{Tf}(1+t_m) + (1-\alpha)F_{N}$$

(13.A.22)
$$F_{N} = \lambda \cdot W_{d} + (1-\lambda) \cdot \pi$$

(13.A.23)
$$\frac{\Delta W_{d}}{W_{d}} = \frac{\Delta \pi}{\pi}$$

(13.A.24)
$$w_{G} = \frac{W_{d}}{P_{Gd}}.$$

Parameter Estimates

The above accounting framework requires estimates for three parameters:

t_a = the share of imports of final goods in total absorption;
a = the share of imported inputs in the cost of producing nontraded goods; and
l = the share of labor in value added in the nontraded-goods sector.

The following estimates of these parameters were used in the Côte d'Ivoire example in the text:

$$\tau = 0.22$$
$$\alpha = 0.11$$
$$\lambda = 0.70$$

The values of τ and λ can usually be estimated from a country's trade statistics. In the Côte d'Ivoire case, τ was calculated as the ratio of imports of final goods to absorption. In estimating α, we assumed that imported inputs were used in the same proportion in the production of traded and nontraded goods. α, then, was the ratio of imported intermediates to GDP. Both τ and α were estimated from balance of payments and national income statistics for 1993. Since imports were larger than exports in 1993, the absorption approach gives a larger estimate of the size of the tradable-goods sector than using the value-added approach and exports would.

Estimating the value of λ may be more problematic. For countries with complete national income and product accounts, λ can usually be estimated directly from these. However, a number of low-income countries have only partial national income accounts, with the breakdown of national income into wages, profits, and other factor returns often missing. In these cases, one may be forced to rely on parameter estimates for similar countries and adjust these in light of whatever fragmentary data may be available for the country concerned on the shares of labor and capital. In Côte d'Ivoire, the share of wages in total value added was estimated by World Bank staff at 70 percent and the share of capital at 30 percent. On the assumption that labor and capital are used in the same proportions in the production of both traded and nontraded goods, λ equals 0.7. Note that λ is only needed for those scenarios in which the nominal returns to labor and capital change by different amounts.

Because of the difficulties involved in obtaining accurate estimates for the parameters τ, α, and λ, it is important to carry out sensitivity analyses of these similar to those in scenarios 2 and 4 in the text.

References

The word *processed* describes informally reproduced works that may not be commonly available through libraries.

Abdelkhalek, Touhami, and Jean-Marie Dufour. 1997. "Statistical Inference for Computable General Equilibrium Models, with Application to a Model of the Moroccan Economy." Cahiers de CRDE, University of Montreal, 1997. Processed.

Agenor, Pierre-Richard. 1992. "Parallel Currency Markets in Developing Countries: Theory, Evidence, and Policy Implications." *Princeton Essays in International Finance* no. 188.

————. 1996. "Capital Inflows, External Shocks, and the Real Exchange Rate." International Monetary Fund, March. Processed.

————. 1997. "Capital-Market Imperfections and the Macroeconomic Dynamics of Small Open Economies." *Princeton Studies in International Finance* no. 82.

Agenor, Pierre-Richard, and Peter J. Montiel. 1999. *Development Macroeconomics*. Princeton, New Jersey: Princeton University Press.

Akiyama, Takamasa, and Donald Larson. 1994. "The Adding-Up Problem: Strategies for Primary Commodity Exports in Sub-Saharan Africa." Policy Research Working Paper 1245. World Bank, Washington, D.C.

Akiyama, Takamasa, and Panayotis Varangis. 1988. "Impact of the International Coffee Agreement's Export Quota System on the World's Coffee Market." PRE Working Paper 92, World Bank, Washington, D.C.

Alexander, Sidney. 1951. "Effects of Devaluation on a Trade Balance." *IMF Staff Papers* 2 (April): 263–78.

Allen, Polly Reynolds. 1995. "The Economic and Policy Implications of the NATREX Approach." In Jerome L. Stein, P. R. Allen, and Associates, *Fundamental Determinants of Exchange Rates*, 1–37. Oxford: Clarendon Press.

Amjadi, Azita, Ulrich Reinke, and Alexander Yeats. 1996. "Did External Barriers Cause the Marginalization of Sub-Saharan Africa in World Trade?" World Bank, International Economics Department, International Trade Division, Washington, D.C. Processed.

Arize, Augustine, and Rasoul Afifi. 1986. "A Simultaneous Model of Demand for Imports in Twenty-Seven African Countries: Evidence of Structural Change." *The Indian Economic Journal* 33(2): 93–105.

Armington, Paul S. 1970. "Adjustment of Trade Balances: Some Experiments with a Model of Trade Among Many Countries. *IMF Staff Papers* 17(3): 488–526.

Bacchetta, Phillipe, and Eric van Wincoop. 1998. "Capital Flows to Emerging Markets: Liberalization, Overshooting, and Volatility." Working Paper 6530. National Bureau of Economic Research, Cambridge, Mass.

Bacha, Edmar, and Lance Taylor. 1971. "Foreign Exchange Shadow Prices: A Critical Review of Current Theories." *Quarterly Journal of Economics* 85(2).

Bahami-Oskooee, Mohsen. 1986. "Determinants of International Trade Flows: The Case of Developing Countries." *Journal of Development Economics* 20(1): 107–123.

Balassa, Bela. 1964. "The Purchasing Power Parity Doctrine: A Reappraisal." *The Journal of Political Economy* 72: 584–96.

————. 1990. "Incentive Policies and Export Performance in Sub-Saharan Africa." *World Development* 18: 383–91.

Balassa, Bela, E. Voloudakis, P. Fylaktos, and Suk Tai Suh. 1989. "The Determinants of Export Supply and Export Demand in Two Developing Countries." *International Economic Journal* 3(1): 1–16.

Banerjee, Anindya, J. Dolado, John W. Galbraith, and David F. Hendry. 1993. *Co-Integration, Error-Correction, and the Econometric Analysis of Non-Stationary Data*. Oxford University Press.

Baumol, William J., and William G. Bowen. 1966. "Performing Arts: The Economic Dilemma." The Twentieth Century Fund, New York. Processed.

Bayoumi, Tamim, Peter Clark, Steve Symansky, and Mark Taylor. 1994. "The Robustness of Equilibrium Exchange Rate Calculations to Alternative Assumptions and Methodologies." In John Williamson, ed., *Estimating Equilibrium Exchange Rates*, 19-60. Washington, D.C.: Institute for International Economics.

Bayoumi, Tamim, and Hamid Faruqee. 1998. "A Calibrated Model of the Underlying Current Account." In Peter Isard and Hamid Faruqee, eds., "Exchange Rate Assessment: Extensions of the Macroeconomic Balance Approach." Occasional Paper 167. International Monetary Fund, Washington, D.C.

Beenstock, Michael, and Patrick Minford. 1976. "A Quarterly Econometric Model of Trade and Prices 1955–72." In Michael Parkin and

George Zis, eds., *Inflation in Open Economies*. Manchester: Manchester University Press.

Bennett, Adam. 1995. "Currency Boards: Issues and Experiences." *Finance and Development* 32(3): 39–42.

Bernanke, Ben S. 1986. "Alternative Explanations of the Money-Income Correlation."*Carnegie-Rochester Conference Series in Public Policy* 25: 49–99.

Beveridge, Stephen, and Charles R. Nelson. 1981. "A New Approach to Decomposition of Economic Time Series into Permanent and Transitory Components with Particular Attention to Measurement of the Business Cycle." *Journal of Monetary Economics* 7: 151–74.

Bhandari, Jagdeep S., Nadeem Ul Haque, and Steven Turnovsky. 1990. "Growth, External Debt, and Sovereign Risk in a Small Open Economy." *IMF Staff Papers* (June): 388–417.

Black, Stanley W. 1994. "On the Concept and Usefulness of the Equilibrium Rate of Exchange." In John Williamson, ed., *Estimating Equilibriumm Exchange Rates*, 279–92. Washington, D.C.: Institute for International Economics.

Blanchard, Oliver Jean, and Charles Kahn. 1980. "The Solution of Linear Difference Models Under Rational Expectations." *Econometrica* 48(5): 1305–11.

Bond, Marian. 1985. "Export Demand and Supply for Groups of Non-Oil Developing Countries." *International Monetary Fund Staff Papers* 32(1) (March) 1985: 56–77. IMF, Washington, D.C.

———. 1987. "An Econometric Study of Primary Commodity Exports from Developing Country Regions to the World." *IMF Staff Papers* 34(2) (June): 191–227. IMF, Washington, D.C.

Boswijk, H. Peter. 1995. "Efficient Inference on Cointegration Parameters in Structural Error Correction Models." *Journal of Econometrics* 69: 113–58.

Bosworth, Barry, Susan Collins, and Yu-Chin Chen. 1996. "Accounting for Differences in Economic Growth." In Akira Kohsaka and Kenichi Ohno, eds., *Structural Adjustment and Economic Reform: East Asia, Latin America, and Central and Eastern Europe*. Tokyo: Institute of Developing Economies.

Breuer, Janice Boucher. 1994. "An Assessment of the Evidence on Purchasing Power Parity." In John Williamson, ed., *Estimating Equilibrium Exchange Rates*, 245–77. Washington, D.C.: Institute for International Economics.

Brodsky, David A. 1982. "Arithmetic Versus Geometric Effective Exchange Rates." *Weltwirtschaftsliches Archiv (Review of World Economics)* Band 118, Heft 3: 546–62.

Bruno, Michael. 1976. "The Two-Sector Open Economy and the Real Exchange Rate." *American Economic Review* 66(4): 566–77.

Caballero, Ricardo J., and Vittorio Corbo. 1989. "How Does Uncertainty about the Real Exchange Rate Affect Exports?" Working Paper Series 221. World Bank, Country Economics Department, Washington, D.C.

Callier, Philippe. 1992. "Monetary Policies after a Devaluation." World Bank, Washington, D.C. Processed.

Calvo, Guillermo, C. Reinhart, and C. Vegh. 1995. "Targeting the Real Exchange Rate: Theory and Evidence." *Journal of Development Economics* 47: 97–133.

Calvo, Guillermo, Leonardo Leiderman, and Carmen Reinhart. 1993. "Capital Inflows to Latin America: The Role of External Factors." *IMF Staff Papers* 40 (March): 108–51.

———. 1994. "Capital Inflows to Latin America: the 1970s and 1990s." In E. Bacha, ed., *Development, Trade, and the Environment*, vol. 4 of *Economics in a Changing World*: London: Macmillan.

Canzoneri, Matthew B., Robert E. Cumby, and Behzad Diba. 1996. "Real Labor Productivity and the Real Exchange Rate in the Long Run: Evidence from a Panel of OECD Countries." Discussion Paper 1464. Centre for Economic Policy Research, London.

Caramazza, Francesco, and Jahangir Aziz. 1998. "Fixed or Flexible? Getting the Exchange Rate Right in the 1990s." *Economic Issues* 13 (April). IMF, Washington, D.C.

Cardenas, Mauricio. 1997. *La tasa de cambio en Colombia.* Bogotá: Cuadernos Fedesarrollo.

Chari, V., P. Kehoe, and E. McGrattan. 1997. "Monetary Shocks and Real Exchange Rates in Sticky Price Models of International Business Cycles." Working Paper 5876. National Bureau of Economic Research, Cambridge, Mass.

Cheung, Yin Wong, and Kon S. Lai. 1993. "Finite Sample Sizes of Johansen's Likelihood Ratio Tests for Cointegration." *Oxford Bulletin of Economics and Statistics* 55: 313–28.

Chhibber, Ajay. 1991. "Africa's Rising Inflation: Causes, Consequences and Cures." PRE Working Paper 577. World Bank, Washington, D.C.

Chhibber, Ajay, and N. Shaffik. 1991. "Exchange Reform, Parallel Markets and Inflation in Africa: The Case of Ghana." In Ajay Chhibber and S. Fischer, eds, *Economic Reform in Sub-Saharan Africa*. World Bank, Washington, D.C.

Chinn, Menzi, and Louis Johnston. 1997. "Real Exchange Rate Levels, Productivity, and Demand Shocks: Evidence from a Panel of 14 Countries." IMF Working Paper WP/97/66 (May), IMF, Washington, D.C.

Clark, Peter, Leonardo Bartolini, Tamim Bayoumi, and Steven Symansky. 1994. "Exchange Rates and Economic Fundamentals: A Framework for Analysis." IMF Occasional Paper 115 (December). IMF, Washington, D.C.

Clark, Peter, and R. MacDonald. 1998. "Exchange Rates and Economic Fundamentals: A Methodological Comparison of BEERs and FEERs." IMF Working Paper WP/98/67 (May). IMF, Washington, D.C.

Cochrane, John H. 1988. "How Big Is the Random Walk in GNP?" *Journal of Political Economy* 96: 893–920.

Corden, W. Max. 1989. "Macroeconomic Adjustment in Developing Countries." *World Bank Research Observer* 4: 51–64.

Cottani, Joaquin A., Dominique F. Cavallo and M. Shahbaz Khan. 1990. "Real Exchange Rate Behavior and Economic Performance in LDCs." *Economic Development and Cultural Change* 39: 61–76.

Cuddington, John T. 1997. "Analyzing the Sustainability of Fiscal Deficits in Developing Countries." Policy Research Working Paper 1784. World Bank, Policy Research Department, Washington, D.C.

Cumby, Robert E. 1996. "Forecasting Exchange Rates and Relative Prices with the Hamburger Standard: Is What You Want What You Get with McParity?" Working Paper 5675. National Bureau of Economic Research, Cambridge, Mass.

De Gregorio, Jose, Alberto Giovannini and Holger C. Wolf. 1994. "International Evidence on Tradables and Nontradables Inflation." *European Economic Review* 38(6): 1225–44.

De Gregorio, Jose, and Holger C. Wolf. 1994. "Terms of Trade, Productivity, and the Real Exchange Rate." Working Paper 4807. National Bureau of Economic Research, Cambridge, Mass.

Dell'Ariccia, Giovanni. 1998. "Exchange Rate Fluctuations and Trade Flows: Evidence from the European Union." IMF Working Paper WP/98/107, IMF, Washington, D.C.

De Masi, Paula. 1997. "IMF Estimates of Potential Output: Theory and Practice." IMF Working Paper WP/97/177. IMF, Washington, D.C.

De Melo, Jaime, and Shantayanan Devarajan. 1987. "Adjustment with a Fixed Exchange Rate: Cameroon, Côte d'Ivoire, and Senegal." *The World Bank Economic Review* 1(3): 447–87.

DeRosa, Dean. 1990. "Protection and Export Performance in Sub-Saharan Africa." IMF Working Paper WP/90/83. IMF, Washington, D.C.

Dervis, Kemal, Jaime De Melo, and Sherman Robinson. 1982. *General Equilibrium Models and Development Policy*. Cambridge: Cambridge University Press.

Devarajan, Shantayanan, Delfin S. Go, and Hong-yi-Li. 1998. "Import-Substitution and Export-Transformation Elasticities." World Bank, Development Research Group, Washington, D.C. Processed.

Devarajan, Shantayanan, Delfin S. Go, M. Schiff, and S. Suthiwart-Narueput. 1996. "The Whys and Why Not of Export Taxation." Policy Research Working Paper 1684. World Bank, Washington, D.C.

Devarajan, Shantayanan, Jeffrey D. Lewis, and Sherman Robinson. 1993. "External Shocks, Purchasing Power Parity, and the Equilibrium Real Exchange Rate." *World Bank Economic Review* 7 (January): 45–64.

Devarajan, Shantayanan, and Lawrence E. Hinkle. 1994. "The CFA Franc Parity Change: An Opportunity to Restore Growth and Reduce Poverty." *Afrika Spectrum* 29(2): 131–51.

Devereux, John, and Michael Connolly. 1996. "Commercial Policy, the Terms of Trade, and the Real Exchange Rate Revisited." *Journal of Development Economics* 50: 81–99.

Diaz-Alejandro, Carlos F. 1980. "Exchange Rates and Terms of Trade in the Argentine Republic." Discussion Paper No. 341. Yale University, Economic Growth Center, New Haven, Conn.

Dollar, David. 1992. "Outward-Oriented Developing Economies Really Do Grow More Rapidly: Evidence from 95 LDCs, 1976–85." *Economic Development and Cultural Change* 40(3): 545–66.

Dornbusch, Rudiger. 1976. "Expectations and Exchange Rate Dynamics." *Journal of Political Economy* 84: 1161–76.

———. 1980. *Open Economy Macroeconomics.* New York: Basic Books.

———. 1983. "Real Interest Rates, Home Goods, and Optimal External Borrowing." *Journal of Political Economy* 91(1): 141–153.

Dornbusch, Rudiger, D.V. Dantos, C. Pechman , R.R. Rocha and D. Simoes. 1983. "The Black Market for Dollars in Brazil." *Quarterly Journal of Economics* 98: 25–40.

Dupont, Dominique, and V. Hugo Juan-Ramon. 1996. "Real Exchange Rates and Commodity Prices." Working Paper WP/96/27, IMF, Washington, D.C.

Edison, Hali J. 1987. "Purchasing Power Parity in the Long Run: A Test of the Dollar-Pound Exchange Rate (1890-1978)." *Journal of Money, Credit, and Banking* 19(3): 376–87.

Edison, Hali J., Joseph E. Gagnon, and William R. Melick. 1994. "Understanding the Empirical Literature on Purchasing Power Parity: The Post-Bretton Woods Era." International Finance Discussion paper 465 (April). Board of Governors of the Federal Reserve System, Washington, D.C.

Edwards, Sebastian. 1988. "Real and Monetary Determinants of Real Exchange Rate Behavior, Theory and Evidence from Developing Countries." *Journal of Developing Economics* 29: 311–41.

———. 1989. *Real Exchange Rates, Devaluation, and Adjustment.* Cambridge, Mass.: MIT Press.

———. 1990. "Real Exchange Rates in Developing Countries: Concepts and Measurement." In T. J. Grennes, ed., *International Financial Markets and Agricultural Trade,* 56–108. Boulder, Colo.: Westview Press.

———. 1994. "Real and Monetary Determinants of Real Exchange Rate

Behavior: Theory and Evidence from Developing Countries." In John Williamson, ed., *Estimating Equilibrium Exchange Rates*. Washington, D.C.: Institute for International Economics.

Elbadawi, Ibrahim. 1994. "Estimating Long-Run Equilibrium Real Exchange Rates." In John Williamson, ed., *Estimating Equilibrium Exchange Rates*. Washington, D.C.: Institute for International Economics.

Elbadawi, Ibrahim, and Stephen A. O'Connell. 1990. "Real Exchange Rate and Macroeconomic Adjustment in the CFA Zone." World Bank, Macroeconomic Adjustment and Growth Division, Country Economics Department, Washington, D.C. Processed.

Elbadawi, Ibrahim, and Raimundo Soto. 1994. "Capital Flows and Equilibrium Real Exchange Rates in Chile." Policy Research Working Paper 1306. World Bank, Washington, D.C.

———. 1995. "Real Exchange Rates and Macroeconomic Adjustment in Sub-Saharan Africa and other Developing Countries." African Economic Research Consortium (November). Nairobi, Kenya. Processed.

———. Forthcoming. "Real Exchange Rates and Macroeconomic Adjustment in Sub-Saharan Africa and Other Developing Countries." In Elbadawi and Soto, eds., *Foreign Exchange Market and Exchange Rate Policies in Sub-Saharan Africa*, a special issue of *Journal of African Economies*.

Engel, Charles. 1996. "Long-Run PPP May Not Hold After All." Working Paper 5646 (July). National Bureau of Economic Research, Cambridge, Mass.

Engle, Robert F., and Clive Granger. 1987. "Co-Integration and Error-Correction: Representation, Estimation, and Testing." *Econometrica* 55: 251–76.

Engle, Robert F., David F. Hendry, and Jean-François Richard. 1983. "Exogeneity." *Econometrica* 51: 277.

Ericsson, Neil R. 1992. "Cointegration, Exogeneity, and Policy Analysis: An Overview." *Journal of Policy Modeling* 14: 251–80.

———. 1995. "Conditional and Structural Error Correction Models." *Journal of Econometrics* 69: 159–71.

Ericsson, Neil R., and John S. Irons, eds. 1995. "The Lucas Critique in Practice: Theory Without Measurement." In K. D. Hoover, ed., *Macroeconometrics: Developments, Tensions and Prospects*, 263–312. Boston: Kluwer Academic

Ericsson, Neil R., Julia Campos, and Hong-Anh Tran. 1991. "PC-Give and David Hendry's Econometric Methodology." International Finance Discussion Papers 406. Board of Governors of the Federal Reserve System, Washington, D.C.

Faruqee, Hamid. 1995a. "Long-Run Determinants of the Real Exchange Rate: A Stock-Flow Perspective." *IMF Staff Papers* 42(1): 80–107.

———. 1995b. "Pricing to Market and the Real Exchange Rate." IMF Working Paper WP/95/12. IMF, Washington, D.C.

Faruqee, Hamid, and G. Debelle. 1998. "Saving and Investment Balances in Industrial Countries: An Empirical Investigation." In Peter Isard and Hamid Faruqee, eds., "Exchange Rate Assessment: Extensions of the Macroeconomic Balance Approach," Occasional Paper 167. IMF, Washington, D.C.

Feinberg, Richard. 1997. "The Impact of Exchange Rate Movements on Domestic Prices in Developing Countries." PSD Occasional Paper 28. World Bank, Washington, D.C.

Fernandez-Arias, Eduardo, and Peter J. Montiel. 1996. "The Surge in Capital Inflows to Developing Countries: An Overview." *World Bank Economic Review* (January): 51–7.

Feyzioglu, Tarhan. 1997. "Estimating the Equilibrium Real Exchange Rate: An Application to Finland." IMF Working Paper WP/97/109. Washington, D.C.

Fleissig, Adrian, and Thomas J. Grennes. 1994. "The Real Exchange Rate Conundrum: the Case of Central America." *World Development* 22(1): 115–28.

Frankel, Jeffery, and Andrew Rose. 1995. "Empirical Research on Nominal Exchange Rates." In G. Grossman, and K. Rogoff, eds., *Handbook of International Economics*, Vol. 3, Chapter 33. Elsevier Science, B.V., North Holland.

Frenkel, Jacob A. 1981. "The Collapse of Purchasing Power Parities During the 1970s." *European Economic Review* 16: 145–65.

Froot, Kenneth A., and Kenneth Rogoff. 1994. "Perspectives on PPP and Long-Run Real Exchange Rates." Working Paper 4952 (December). National Bureau of Economic Research, Cambridge, Mass.

Geraci, Vincent J. and Wilfried Prewo. 1982. "An Empirical Demand and Supply Model of Multilateral Trade." *Review of Economics and Statistics* 64(3): 432–41.

Ghei, Nita, and Miguel A. Kiguel. 1992. "Dual and Multiple Exchange Rate Systems in Developing Countries: Some Empirical Evidence." Policy Research Working Paper 881. World Bank, Washington, D.C.

Ghei, Nita, Miguel A. Kiguel, and Stephen A. O'Connell. 1996. "Parallel Exchange Rates in Developing Countries: Lessons from Eight Case Studies." In M. A. Kiguel, J. S. Lizondo, and Stephen A. O'Connell, eds., *Parallel Exchange Rates in Developing Countries*. London: Macmillan; New York: St. Martin's Press.

Ghosh, Atish, Ann-Marie Gulde, Jonathan Ostry, and Holger C. Wolf.

1996. "Does the Exchange Rate Regime Matter for Inflation and Growth?" Economic Issues Series, International Monetary Fund, Washington, D.C.

Ghurra, Dhaneshwar, and Thomas Grennes. 1994. "Aggregate Trade Response to Economy-Wide Distortions in Sub-Saharan Africa." *Journal of African Economies* 3(3): 359–86.

Goldberg, Pinelopi K., and Michael M. Knetter. 1997. "Goods Prices and Exchange Rates: What Have We Learned?" *Journal of Economic Literature* 35 (September).

Goldfajn, Ilan, and Rodrigo Valdes. 1996. "The Aftermath of Appreciations." Working Paper 5650 (July). National Bureau of Economic Research, Cambridge, Mass.

———. 1997. "Are Currency Crises Predictable?" IMF Working Paper WP/97/159. IMF, Washington, D.C.

Goldstein, Morris, and Mohsin Khan. 1978. "The Supply and Demand for Exports: A Simultaneous Approach." *Review of Economics and Statistics* 62(2): 190–99.

———. 1985. "Income and Price Effects in Foreign Trade." In *Handbook of International Economics*.

Goldstein, Morris, and Lawrence H. Officer. 1979. "New Measures of Prices and Productivity for Tradable and Nontradable Goods." *Review of Income and Wealth* 25 (December): 413–27.

Gordon, Robert J. 1994. "Comments on International Evidence on Tradables and Nontradables Inflation by J. De Gregorio, A. Giovanni, and H.C. Wolf." *European Economic Review* 38: 1245–49.

Granger, Clive W. J. 1981. "Some Properties of Time Series Data and Their Use in Econometric Model Specification." *Journal of Econometrics* 16: 213–28.

Grobar, Lisa Morris. 1993. "The Effects of Real Exchange Rate Uncertainty on LDC Manufactured Exports." *Journal of Development Economics* 41: 367–76.

Guerguil, Martine, and Martin Kaufman. 1998. "Competitiveness and the Evolution of the Real Exchange Rate in Chile." IMF Working Paper WP/98/58 (April). IMF, Washington, D.C.

Guillaumont Jeanneney, S. 1993. "Les Difficutés de la mesure du taux de change réel: l'exemple du Sénégal." *Revue d'Economie du développement* 1993/1, Presses Universitaires de France, Paris.

Gylfason, T. 1978. "The Effect of Exchange Rate Changes on the Balance of Trade in Ten Industrial Countries." IMF, Washington, D.C. Processed.

Hakkio, Craig. 1984. "A Reexamination of Purchasing Power Parity: A Multi-Country and Multi-period Study." *Journal of International Economics* 17: 265–77.

Halpern, Laszlo, and Charles Wyplosz. 1997. "Equilibrium Exchange Rates in Transition Economics." *IMF Staff Papers* 44(4): 430–61. IMF, Washington, D.C.

Hamilton, James D. 1994. *Time Series Analysis*. Princeton, N.J.: Princeton University Press.

Haque, Nadeem Ul, Kajal Lahiri, and Peter J. Montiel. 1990. "A Rational-Expectations Macroeconometric Model for Developing Countries." *IMF Staff Papers*. IMF, Washington, D.C.

———. 1993. "Estimation of a Macroeconomic Model with Rational Expectations and Capital Controls for Developing Countries." *Journal of Development Economics* 42.

Haque, Nadeem Ul, and Peter J. Montiel. 1990. "How Mobile is Capital in Developing Countries?" *Economics Letters* 33: 359–62.

———. 1991. "Capital Mobility in Developing Countries—Some Empirical Tests." *World Development* 19(10): 1391–98.

Hargreaves, Colin. 1994. "A Review of Methods of Estimating Cointegrating Relationships." In Colin Hargreaves, ed., *Nonstationary Time Series Analysis and Cointegration*, Chapter 4. Oxford: Oxford University Press.

Hendry, David F. 1995. *Dynamic Econometrics*. Oxford: Oxford University Press.

Hendry, David F., Adrian R. Pagan and J. Denis Sargan. 1984. "Dynamic Specification." In Z. Griliches, and Michael D. Intriligator, eds., *Handbook of Econometrics* Vol. 2, 1023–92. Amsterdam: North-Holland.

Houthakker, Hendrik S., and Stephan P. Magee. 1969. "Income and Price Elasticities in World Trade." *Review of Economics and Statistics* 51(2): 111–25.

Imran, Mudassar, and Ron Duncan. 1988. "Optimal Export Taxes for Exporters of Perennial Crops." PRE Working Paper 10. World Bank, Washington, D.C.

Inter-American Development Bank. 1995. "Overcoming Volatility: A Special Report." In *Economic and Social Progress in Latin America: 1995 Report*. Washington, D.C.: Johns Hopkins University Press.

Isard, Peter. 1997. "How Far Can We Push the Law of One Price?" *The American Economic Review* 67(5).

Isard, Peter, and Hamid Faruqee. 1998. "Exchange Rate Assessment: Extensions of the Macroeconomic Balance Approach." Occasional Paper 167. IMF, Washington, D.C.

Johansen, Soren. 1988. "Statistical Analysis of Cointegration Vectors." *Journal of Economic Dynamics and Control* 12: 231–54.

———. 1992. "Cointegration in Partial Systems and Efficiency of Single-Equation Analysis." *Journal of Econometrics* 52: 389–402.

Johansen, Soren, and Katarina Juselius. 1994. "Identification of the Long-Run and the Short-Run Structure: An Application to the ISLM

Model." *Journal of Econometrics* 63: 7–36.

Jorgensen, Steen L., and Martin Paldam. 1988. "The Real Exchange Rate of Eight Latin American Countries 1946–1985: An Interpretation." *Geld und Wahrung/Monetary Affairs*.

Kamin, Steven B. 1988a. "Devaluation, External Balance and Macroeconomic Performance: A Look at the Numbers." Princeton Studies in International Finance 62.

————. 1988b. "Devaluation, Exchange Controls, and Black Markets for Foreign Exchange in Developing Countries." International Finance Discussion Papers 334. Board of Governors of the Federal Reserve, Washington, D.C.

————. 1993. "Devaluation, Exchange Controls and Black Markets for Foreign Exchange in Developing Countries." *Journal of Development Economics* 40: 151–169.

————. 1995. "Contractionary Devaluations with Black Markets for Foreign Exchange." *Journal of Policy Modeling* 17(1): 39–57

————. 1998. "A Multi-Country Comparison of the Linkages between Inflation and Exchange Rate Competitiveness." International Finance Discussion Paper 603. Board of Governors of the Federal Reserve, Washington, D.C.

Kaminsky, Graciela. 1988. "The Real Exchange Rate in the Short Run and the Long Run." Discussion Paper, University of California at San Diego, Department of Economics (August). Processed.

Kaminsky, Graciela, Saul Lizondo, and Carmen Reinhardt. 1997. "Leading Indicators of Currency Crises." Policy Research Working Paper 1852. World Bank, Washington, D.C.

Khan, Mohsin S. 1974. "Import and Export Demand in Developing Countries." *IMF Staff Papers* 21, 678–93. IMF, Washington, D.C.

Khan, Mohsin S., and Malcolm Knight. 1986. "Import Compression and Export Performance in Developing Countries." World Bank DRD Discussion Paper 197. Washington, D.C.

Khan, Mohsin S., and Saul Lizondo. 1987. "Devaluation, Fiscal Deficits, and the Real Exchange Rate." *World Bank Economic Review* 1 (January): 357–74.

Khan, Mohsin S., and Peter J. Montiel. 1987. "Real Exchange Rate Dynamics in a Small, Primary-Exporting Country." *IMF Staff Papers* (December). IMF, Washington, D.C.

Khan, Mohsin S., Nadeem Ul Haque, and Peter J. Montiel. 1990. "Adjustment with Growth: Relating the Analytical Approaches of the World Bank and the IMF." *Journal of Development Economics* (January).

Kiguel, Miguel A. 1992. "Exchange Rate Policy, the Real Exchange Rate, and Inflation: Lessons from Latin America." Policy Research Working Paper 880. World Bank, Washington, D.C.

Kiguel, Miguel A., J. Saul Lizondo, and Stephen A. O'Connell, eds. 1996.

Parallel Exchange Rates in Developing Countries. London: MacMillan; New York: St. Martin's Press.

Kiguel, Miguel A. and Nita Ghei. 1993. "Devaluations in Low-Income Countries." Policy Research Working Paper 1224. World Bank, Washington, D.C.

Kiguel, Miguel A., and Stephen A. O'Connell. 1995. "Parallel Exchange Rates in Developing Countries." *World Bank Research Observer* 10(1): 21–52.

Killick, Tony. 1993. *The Adaptive Economy: Adjustment Policies in Small, Low-Income Countries*. Washington, D.C.: World Bank; New York: Oxford University Press,

Knight, Malcom, and Fabio Scacciavillani. 1998. "Current Accounts: What is their Relevance for Economic Policy making?" IMF Working Paper WP/98/71. IMF, Washington, D.C.

Krajnyák, Kornelia, and Jeromin Zettelmeyer. 1997. "Competitiveness in Transition Economies: What Scope for Real Appreciations?" IMF Working Paper WP/97/149. IMF, Washington, D.C.

Kramer, Charles. 1996. "FEERs and Uncertainty: Confidence Intervals for the Fundamental Equilibrium Exchange Rate for the Canadian Dollar." IMF Working Paper WP/96/68. IMF, Washington, D.C.

Kravis, Irving B., Alan Heston, and Robert Summers. 1982. *World Product and Income: International Comparisons of Real Gross Domestic Product*. Baltimore: U.N. Statistical Office and the World Bank, Johns Hopkins University Press.

Kravis, Irving B., and Robert E. Lipsey. 1988. "National Price Levels and the Prices of Tradables and Nontradables." National Bureau of Economic Research Working Paper 2536 (March). Cambridge, Mass.

Kreuger, Anne O. 1978. *Liberalization Attempts and Consequences*. Published for the National Bureau of Economic Research. Cambridge, MA.: Ballinger Publishing Co.

Kreuger, Anne O., Maurice Schiff, and Alberto Valdes. 1988. "Agricultural Incentives in Developing Countries: Measuring the Effect of Sectoral and Economy-wide Policies." *World Bank Economic Review* 2(3).

Krugman, Paul. 1994. "Competitiveness: A Dangerous Obsession." *Foreign Affairs* 73(2): 28–44.

Lane, Philip. 1994. "Openness, Inflation, and Exchange Rate Regimes." Harvard University, Economics Department. Processed.

Lane, Philip, and Roberto Perotti. 1996. "Profitability, Fiscal Policy, and Exchange Rate Regimes." Discussion Paper 1449. Center for Economic Policy Research, London.

Larson, Donald F., Takamasa Akiyama and L. Lau. 1996. "Does the 'Adding-Up Problem' Add Up?" DEC Notes 13 (June). World Bank, Washington, D.C.

Lewis, Jeffrey D., and Shujiro Urata, 1984. "Anatomy of a Balance of Payments Crisis: Application of a Computable General Equilibrium Model to Turkey." *Economic Modeling* 1 (July): 281–303.

Lipschitz, Leslie, and Donogh McDonald. 1991. "Real Exchange Rates and Competitiveness: A Clarification of Concepts, and Some Measurements for Europe." IMF Working Paper WP/91/25. IMF, Washington, D.C.

Loayza, Norman, and J. Humberto Lopez. 1997. "Misalignment and Fundamentals: Equilibrium Exchange Rates in Seven Latin American Countries." World Bank, Washington, D.C. Processed.

MacDonald, Ronald. 1995. "Long-Run Exchange Rate Modeling: A Survey of the Recent Evidence." *IMF Staff Papers* 42(3) (September). IMF, Washington, D.C.

———. 1997. "What Determines Real Exchange Rates? The Long and the Short of It." IMF Working Paper WP/97/21 (January). IMF, Washington, D.C.

Maciejewski, Edouard B. 1983. "Real Effective Exchange Rate Indexes: a Re-examination of the Major Conceptual and Methodological Issues." *IMF Staff Papers* 30. IMF, Washington, D.C.

Mark, Nelson. 1990. "Real and Nominal Exchange Rates in the Long Run: An Empirical Investigation." *Journal of International Economics* 22: 115–32.

———. 1995. "Exchange Rates and Fundamentals: Evidence on Long-Horizon Predictability." *American Economic Review* 85(1): 201–18.

Marquez, Jaime. 1990. "Bilateral Trade Elasticities." *Review of Economics and Statistics* (February): 70–77.

Marsh, Ian W., and Stephan P. Tokarick. 1994. "Competitiveness Indicators: A Theoretical and Empirical Assessment." IMF Working Paper WP/94/29. IMF, Washington, D.C.

M'Bet, Allechi, and Niamkey Madeleine. 1994. "External Shocks, Macroeconomic Adjustment and Behavior of the CFA Economies Under a Flexible CFA Pegging Scenario: The Cases of Côte d'Ivoire and Burkina Faso." Revised Report Presented at the AERC Workshop, Nairobi, Kenya.

McGuirk, Anne Kenny. 1987. "Measuring Price Competitiveness for Industrial Country Trade in Manufactures." IMF Working Paper WP/87/34. IMF, Washington, D.C.

Meier, Gerald M. 1995. *Leading Issues in Economic Development*. Oxford University Press.

Milesi-Ferretti, Gian-Maria, and Assaf Razin. 1996. "Current Account Sustainablity: Selected East Asian and Latin American Experiences." Working Paper 5791, National Bureau of Economic Research, Cambridge, Mass.

———. 1998. "Current Account Reversals and Currency Crises: Empirical Regularities." IMF Working Paper WP/98/89. IMF, Washington, D.C.

Mills, Cadman Atta, and Raj Nallari. 1992. "Analytical Approaches to Stabilization and Adjustment Programs." EDI Seminar Paper 44. World Bank, Washington, D.C.

Monfort, Alain, and Roger Rabemanajara. 1990. "From a VAR Model to a Structural Model: With an Application to the Wage-Price Spiral." *Journal of Applied Econometrics* 5: 203–27.

Mongardini, Joannes. 1998. "Estimating Egypt's Equilibrium Real Exchange Rate." IMF WP/98/5 (January). IMF, Washington, D.C.

Monteil, Peter J. 1993. "Applied Macroeconomic Models for Developing Countries." Oberlin, Ohio, Oberlin College. Processed.

———. 1995. "Capital Mobility in Developing Countries: Some Measurement Issues and Empirical Estimates." *World Bank Economic Review* (September).

———. 1986. "Long-Run Equilibrium in a Keynesian Model of a Small Open Economy." *IMF Staff Papers* (March). IMF, Washington, D.C.

———. 1997. "Exchange Rate Policies and Macroeconomic Management in ASEAN Countries." In J. Hicklin, D. Robinson, and A. Singh, *Macroeconomic Issues Facing ASEAN Countries*. Washington, D.C.: International Monetary Fund.

———. 1998. "The Long-Run Equilibrum Real Exchange Rate: A Simple Analytical Model." Working Paper 30, Williams College, Department of Economics, Williamstown, Mass. Processed.

Montiel, Peter J., and Jonathan D. Ostry. 1994. "The Parallel Market Premium: Is it a Reliable Indicator of Real Exchange Rate Misalignment in Developing Countries?" *IMF Staff Papers* 41, 55–75. IMF, Washington, D.C.

Moran, Cristian. 1986. "Import Models for Developing Countries." EPDGL Working Paper 1986–7. World Bank , Washington, D.C.

Mussa, Michael. 1986. "The Effects of Commercial, Fiscal, Monetary, and Exchange Rate Policies on the Real Exchange Rate." In S. Edwards and L. Ahamed, eds., *Economic Adjustment and Exchange Rates in Developing Countries*, 43–88. Chicago: University of Chicago Press.

Neary, J. Peter, and K. W. S. Roberts. 1980. "The Theory of Household Behavior under Rationing." *European Economic Review*, 25–42.

Nowak, Michael. 1984. "Quantitative Controls and Unofficial Markets for Foreign Exchange." *IMF Staff Papers* 31, 404–31. IMF, Washington, D.C.

Nurkse, Ragnar. 1945. "Conditions of International Monetary Equilibrium." *Essays in International Finance* 4 (Spring). Princeton, New Jersey: Princeton University Press, International Finance Section.

Obstfeld, Maurice, and Kenneth Rogoff. 1995. "The Mirage of Fixed Exchange Rates." *Journal of Economic Perspectives* 9(4): 73–96.

Obstfeld, Maurice, and Kenneth Rogoff. 1996. *Foundations of International Macroeconomics*. Cambridge, Mass: MIT Press.

Officer, Lawrence H. 1982. *Purchasing Power Parity and Exchange Rates: Theory, Evidence and Relevance*. Greenwich, Conn: JAI Press.

Osterwald-Lenum, Michael. 1992. "A Note with Quantiles of the Asymptotic Distribution of the Maximum Likelihood Cointegration Rank Test Statistics." *Oxford Bulletin of Economics and Statistics* 54: 461–72.

Panagariya, Arvind, Shekhar Shah, and Deepak Mishra. 1996. "Demand Elasticities in International Trade: Are they Really Low?" Policy Research Working Paper 1712 (December). World Bank, Washington, D.C.

Pearson, Scott, J. Dirck Stryker, and Charles Humphreys. 1981. *Rice in West Africa: Policy and Economics*. Stanford, Calif: Stanford University Press.

Penati, Alessandro. 1987. "Government Spending and the Real Exchange Rate." *Journal of International Economics* 22: 237–56.

Phillips, Peter C. B. 1995. "Fully Modified Least Squares and Vector Autoregression." *Econometrica* 63: 1023–78.

Phillips, Peter C. B., and Yoosoon Chang. 1995. "Time Series Regression with Mixtures of Integrated Processes." *Econometric Theory* 11.

Pritchett, Lant. 1988a. "Import Demand Elasticities in Developing Countries: Estimates and Determinants." Unpublished Ph.D. dissertation, Massachusetts Institute of Technology, Cambridge, Mass.

———. 1988b. "Imports and Foreign Exchange Constraints: Estimation of Import Demand in LDCs." Unpublished Ph.D. dissertation, Massachusetts Institute of Technology, Cambridge, Mass.

———. 1991. "The Real Exchange Rate and the Trade Surplus: The Missing Correlation." World Bank, Washington, D.C. Processed (revised, November 1994).

———. 1993. "The Evolution of Import Restrictiveness in Sub-Saharan Africa in the 1980s." World Bank, Washington, D.C. Processed.

———. 1996. "Measuring Outward Orientation in LDCs: Can it be Done?" *Journal of Development Economics* 49: 307–35.

Razin, Ofair, and Susan M. Collins. 1997. "Real Exchange Rate Misalignments and Growth." Working Paper 6174, National Bureau of Economic Research, Cambridge, Mass.

Reinhart, Carmen M. 1995. "Devaluation, Relative Prices and International Trade: Evidence from Developing Countries." *IMF Staff Papers* 42(2): 290–312. IMF, Washington, D.C.

Rodriguez, Carlos Alfredo. 1994. "The External Effects of Public Sector Deficits." In William Easterly, Carlos Alfredo Rodriguez, and Klaus Schmidt-Hebbel, eds, *Public Sector Deficits and Macroeconomic Performance*, Chapter 2. Oxford: Oxford University Press.

Rodrik, Dani. 1993. "Trade Liberalization in Disinflation." Discussion Paper 832 (August). Centre for Economic Policy Research, London.

Rogoff, Kenneth. 1996. "The Purchasing Power Parity Puzzle." *Journal of Economic Literature* 34 (June): 647–68.

Rose, Andrew K. 1990. "Exchange Rates and the Trade Balance: Some Evidence From Developing Countries." *Economics Letters* 34: 271–75.

Rose, Andrew K. 1991. "The Role of Exchange Rates in a Popular Model of International Trade: Does the 'Marshall-Lerner' Condition Hold?" *Journal of International Economics* 30: 301–16.

Rose, Andrew K., and Janet L. Yellen. 1989. "Is There a J-Curve?" *Journal of Monetary Economics* 24: 53–68.

Salter, W. E. G. 1959. "Internal and External Balance: The Role of Price and Expenditure Effects." *Economic Record* 35: 226–38.

Samuelson, Paul A. 1964. "Theoretical Notes on Trade Problems." *Review of Economics and Statistics* 46: 145–64.

————. 1973. "Relative Shares and Elasticities Simplified: Comment." *American Economic Review* 63(4): 770-71.

Sekkat, Khalid, and Aristomene Varoudakis. 1998. "Exchange Rate Management and Manufactured Exports in Sub-Saharan Africa." Technical Paper 134, Organization for Economic Cooperation and Development, Development Centre, Paris.

Senhadji, Abdelhak. 1997. "Time-Series Estimation of Structural Import Demand Equations: A Cross-Country Analysis." IMF Working Paper WP/97/132. IMF, Washington, D.C.

Sheik, M. A. 1976. "Black Market for Foreign Exchange, Capital Flows and Smuggling." *Journal of Development Economics* 3: 9–26.

Sjaastad, Larry A. 1998. "Why PPP Real Exchange Rates Mislead." University of Chicago. Processed.

Stein, Jerome L. 1994. "The Natural Real Exchange Rate of the US Dollar and Determinants of Capital Flows." In John Williamson, ed., *Estimating Equilibrium Exchange Rates*, 133–176. Washington, D.C.: Institute for International Economics.

Stein Jerome L., P. R. Allen, and Associates. 1995. *Fundamental Determinants of Exchange Rates*. Oxford: Clarendon Press.

Stern, Robert. M., Jonathan Francis, and Bruce Schumacher. 1976. *Price Elasticities in International Trade—An Annotated Bibliography*. London: Macmillan.

Summers, Robert, and Alan Heston. 1991. "The Penn World Table (Mark 5): An Expanded Set of International Comparisons, 1950–1988." *Quarterly Journal of Economics* (May).

Swan, T., 1960. "Economic Control in a Dependent Economy." *Economic Record* 36: 51–66.

Taplin, Grant B. 1973. "A Model of World Trade." In R. J. Ball, ed., *The International Linkage of National Economic Models*. Amsterdam: North-Holland.

Taylor, Mark P. 1995. "The Economics of Exchange Rates." *Journal of Economic Literature* 33(1): 13–47.

The Economist. 1995, August 26. "Buy Hard: with a Vengeance," 66.

———. 1996, April 27. "McCurrencies: Where's the Beef?" 88.

Tokarick, Stephen. 1995. "External Shocks, the Real Exchange Rate and Tax Policy." *IMF Staff Papers* 42(1). IMF, Washington, D.C.

Urbain, Jean-Pierre. 1992. "On Weak Exogeneity in Error-Correction Models." *Oxford Bulletin of Economics and Statistics* 54: 187–207.

Wagner, Nancy L. 1995. "A Review of PPP-Adjusted GDP Estimation and its Potential Use for the Fund's Operational Purposes." IMF Working Paper WP/95/18 (February). IMF, Washington, D.C.

Wickham, Peter. 1987. "A Revised Weighting Scheme for Indicators of Effective Exchange Rates." IMF Working Paper WP/87/87. IMF, Washington, D.C.

Wickham, Peter. 1993. "A Cautionary Note on the Use of Exchange Rate Indicators." IMF Paper on Policy Analysis and Assessment PPAA/93/5. IMF, Washington, D.C.

Williamson, John. 1994. *Estimating Equilibrium Exchange Rates*. Washington, D.C.: Institute for International Economics.

Williamson, John, and Molly Mahar. 1998. "Current Account Targets." Appendix A in Simon Wren-Lewis and Rebecca Driver, eds., *Real Exchange Rates for the Year 2000*. Washington, D.C.: Institute for International Economics.

Wilson, John F., and Wendy E. Takacs. 1979. "Differential Responses to Price and Exchange Rate Influences in the Foreign Trade of Selected Industrial Countries." *Review of Economics and Statistics* 61(2): 267–79.

World Bank. 1989. *Sub-Saharan Africa: From Crisis to Sustainable Growth: A Long-Term Perspective Study*. Washington, D.C.

———. 1991. "External Adjustment in the CFA Zone: Issues and Options." Western and Central Africa Department, World Bank, Washington, D.C. Processed.

———. 1993a. *The East Asian Miracle: Economic Growth and Public Policy*. New York: Oxford University Press.

———. 1993b. "Purchasing Power of Currencies: Comparing National Incomes Using ICP Data." World Bank, International Economics Department, Washington, D.C.

———. 1997a. "RMSM-X Reference Guide." World Bank, Development Economics Department, Washington, D.C. Processed.

———. 1997b. *Private Capital Flows to Developing Countries: The Road to*

Financial Integration. World Bank Policy Research Report. New York: Oxford University Press.

Wren-Lewis, Simon. 1992. "On the Analytical Foundations of the Fundamental Equilibrium Exchange Rate" In C. P Hargreaves, ed., *Macroeconomic Modeling of the Long Run.* Aldershot, U.K.: Edward Elgar.

Wren-Lewis, Simon, and Rebecca Driver. 1998. *Real Exchange Rates for the Year 2000.* Washington, D.C.: Institute for International Economics.

Zanello, Alessandro, and Dominique Desruelle. 1997. "A Primer on the IMF's Information Notice System." IMF Working Paper WP/97/71. IMF, Washington, D.C.

Index